Marxism and Education

Series Editor
Richard Hall
Education and Technology
De Montfort University
Leicester, UK

This international series assumes the ongoing relevance of Marx's contributions to critical social analysis, and encourages the development of the full-range of engagement with Marxist traditions both in and for education. It celebrates scholarship and analysis across intersections, geographies, histories and sectors, with a focus upon how the dynamics of capitalism and developments in political economy impact formal and informal education. As a result, it aims for critique that can describe and analyse how education informs resistances to capitalist social relations, and how those might be abolished or transcended. The series proceeds in a spirit of openness and dialogue within and between various conceptions of Marxism and education. However, the series also brings those conceptions, and analyses that are informed by Marxist scholarship, into dialogue with their critics and other anti-capitalist traditions. The essential feature of the series is that Marxist modes of critique and Marxist frameworks provide living methodologies, which form inspirational resources for renewing both educational practices and research. In this way, the series develops socially-useful knowledge that can support action inside and against existing structures, policies and processes of education, by rethinking their relationship to society. The series is dedicated to the realization of positive human potentialities through education and with Marx.

Richard Hall • Inny Accioly
Krystian Szadkowski
Editors

The Palgrave International Handbook of Marxism and Education

palgrave
macmillan

Editors
Richard Hall
De Montfort University
Leicester, UK

Inny Accioly
Fluminense Federal University
Rio de Janeiro, Brazil

Krystian Szadkowski
Adam Mickiewicz University
Poznań, Poland

Marxism and Education
ISBN 978-3-031-37251-3   ISBN 978-3-031-37252-0   (eBook)
https://doi.org/10.1007/978-3-031-37252-0

© The Editor(s) (if applicable) and The Author(s), under exclusive licence to Springer Nature Switzerland AG 2023
This work is subject to copyright. All rights are solely and exclusively licensed by the Publisher, whether the whole or part of the material is concerned, specifically the rights of translation, reprinting, reuse of illustrations, recitation, broadcasting, reproduction on microfilms or in any other physical way, and transmission or information storage and retrieval, electronic adaptation, computer software, or by similar or dissimilar methodology now known or hereafter developed.
The use of general descriptive names, registered names, trademarks, service marks, etc. in this publication does not imply, even in the absence of a specific statement, that such names are exempt from the relevant protective laws and regulations and therefore free for general use.
The publisher, the authors, and the editors are safe to assume that the advice and information in this book are believed to be true and accurate at the date of publication. Neither the publisher nor the authors or the editors give a warranty, expressed or implied, with respect to the material contained herein or for any errors or omissions that may have been made. The publisher remains neutral with regard to jurisdictional claims in published maps and institutional affiliations.

Cover illustration © ManuelVelasco / Getty Images

This Palgrave Macmillan imprint is published by the registered company Springer Nature Switzerland AG.
The registered company address is: Gewerbestrasse 11, 6330 Cham, Switzerland

Paper in this product is recyclable.

This work is dedicated to all those who teach us to struggle for other worlds, inside, against and beyond education. They help us to weave the world otherwise.

Praise for *The Palgrave International Handbook of Marxism and Education*

"This handbook represents urgent and necessary work. The struggles of the workers and the oppressed for the socialization of knowledge, their commitment to the emancipation of humanity, and the recomposition of socio-metabolism, all pulsate in education, and are central to the arguments presented here. Such struggles through education are the constant target of the dominant classes, aiming to profit from selling education as a commodity, capturing public resources, and, sadly, relegating education to mere labor force training, and as a result, we need the critical and active orientations discussed in the handbook."

—Virgínia Fontes, *Professor at the Fluminense Federal University and at the Florestan Fernandes National School of the Landless Workers' Movement (MST), Brazil*

"This collection brings together an impressive array of intellectuals who adroitly demonstrate the enduring relevance of various Marxist modes of analysis for exploring and interrogating our contemporary world, the ongoing destruction wrought by capitalism across the globe and the ways in which extant educational structures, cultures and practices reinforce those destructive tendencies.

The editors' comprehensive introduction along with 29 newly commissioned pieces by leading education scholars working theoretically and practically with and through Marx and *in dialogue* with decolonial, indigenous, queer, feminist and antiracist perspectives offer fresh and unique insights that traverse arbitrarily established conceptual boundaries.

This handbook will be an invaluable resource for educators, students, activists and all those committed to envisioning a social horizon beyond the alienating and exploitative nature of capitalist social organization and radically rethinking the role that liberatory pedagogy may play in achieving that goal."

—Dr. Valerie Scatamburlo-D'Annibale (she/her), Associate Professor, *Department of Communication, Media and Film, University of Windsor, Canada*

"At a time when critical and creative thinking is under attack as never before—whether by neoliberalism, the far Right, and artificial "intelligence" devices that substitute for independent thought—this volume's emphasis on how capitalism's valorization process is undermining education could not be more timely. It is one of the most comprehensive, engaging, and in-depth analyses of the challenges facing critical pedagogy that have ever appeared."

—Peter Hudis, *Professor of Humanities and Philosophy at Oakton Community College, USA*

"This Handbook in Marxism and Education aims to 'recalibrate' the conversation between Marxism and Education by renewing as many dialogues as possible from multiple critical standpoints. Each of the entries of this remarkable volume, written by authors from all over the world, offers a theoretical, explanatory, or empirical angle to this conversation, be it class, race, gender, queer, ideology, theology, ecology, or labor. The 'dialogues in Marxism and education are increasingly relevant for describing alternative conceptualizations of life' write the handbook's editors. They gathered contributors who pushed concepts and methods beyond established demarcations to be part of the wave of radical grassroots experiments against and beyond capitalism. The vital question for Marxism and Education today is how to learn and educate hope radically. This Handbook provides a guide in this direction."

—Ana Cecilia Dinerstein, *Professor of Political Sociology and Critical Theory, University of Bath, UK*

Contents

Part I In: Marxist Modes and Characteristics of Analysis in Education — 1

1. Introduction: The Relevance of Marxism to Education — 3
   Richard Hall, Inny Accioly, and Krystian Szadkowski

2. Marx, Materialism and Education — 25
   Richard Hall

3. Value in Education: Its Web of Social Forms — 47
   Glenn Rikowski

4. Breaking Bonds: How Academic Capitalism Feeds Processes of Academic Alienation — 71
   Mikko Poutanen

5. The Class in Race, Gender, and Learning — 93
   Sara Carpenter and Shahrzad Mojab

6. Foundations and Challenges of Polytechnic Education — 111
   Marise Nogueira Ramos

7. Liberation Theology, Marxism and Education — 129
   Luis Martínez Andrade and Allan Coelho

8. Marxism and Adult Education — 147
   John D. Holst

9 In-Against-Beyond Metrics-Driven University: A Marxist Critique of the Capitalist Imposition of Measure on Academic Labor   163
Jakub Krzeski

10 Classroom as a Site of Class Struggle   183
Raju J. Das

11 Science Communication, Competitive Project-Based Funding and the Formal Subsumption of Academic Labor Under Capital   201
Luis Arboledas-Lérida

12 Commodification, the Violence of Abstraction, and Socially Necessary Labor Time: A Marxist Analysis of High-Stakes Testing and Capitalist Education in the United States   223
Wayne Au

13 The Reproduction of Capitalism in Education: Althusser and the Educational Ideological State Apparatus   243
Toni Ruuska

Part II Against: Emerging Currents in Marxism and Education   261

14 Critique of the Political Economy of Education: Methodological Notes for the Analysis of Global Educational Reforms   263
Inny Accioly

15 The Beginnings of Marxism and Workers' Education in the Spanish-Speaking Southern Cone: The Case of Chile   281
María Alicia Rueda

16 Commodification and Financialization of Education in Brazil: Trends and Particularities of Dependent Capitalism   299
Roberto Leher and Hellen Balbinotti Costa

17 Critical Environmental Education, Marxism and Environmental Conflicts: Some Contributions in the Light of Latin America   317
César Augusto Costa and Carlos Frederico Loureiro

18	Green Marxism, Ecocentric Pedagogies and De-capitalization/Decolonization Sayan Dey	333
19	Indian Problem to Indian Solution: Using a Racio-Marxist Lens to Expose the Invisible War in Education Linda Orie	355
20	Re-reading Socialist Art: The Potential of Queer Marxism in Education Bogdan Popa	381
21	Making Sense of Neoliberalism's New Nexus Between Work and Education, Teachers' Work, and Teachers' Labor Activism: Implications for Labor and the Left Lois Weiner	397
22	Contemporary Student Movements and Capitalism. A Marxist Debate Lorenzo Cini and Héctor Ríos-Jara	413

Part III Beyond: Marxism, Education and Alternatives — 429

23	Revisiting and Revitalizing Need as Non-dualist Foundation for a (R)evolutionary Pedagogy Joel Lazarus	431
24	Reproduction in Struggle David I. Backer	453
25	State and Public Policy in Education: From the Weakness of the Public to an Agenda for Social Development and Redistribution Felipe Ziotti Narita and Jeremiah Morelock	471
26	Marxism, (Higher) Education, and the Commons Krystian Szadkowski	489
27	Marx, Critique, and Abolition: Higher Education as Infrastructure Abigail Boggs, Eli Meyerhoff, Nick Mitchell, and Zach Schwartz-Weinstein	509

28 Toward a Decolonial Marxism: Considering the Dialectics and Analectics in the Counter-Geographies of Women of the Global South 537
Lilia D. Monzó and Nidžara Pečenković

29 The (Im)possibilities of Revolutionary Pedagogical-Political Kinship (M)otherwise: The Gifts of (Autonomous) Marxist Feminisms and Decolonial/Abolitionist Communitarian Feminisms to Pedagogical-Political Projects of Collective Liberation 559
Sara C. Motta

30 Marxism in an Activist Key: Educational Implications of an Activist-Transformative Philosophy 581
Anna Stetsenko

31 Series Editor's Afterword: Weaving Other Worlds with, Against, and Beyond Marx 601
Richard Hall

Index 611

Notes on Contributors

Inny Accioly is Professor of Education at the Fluminense Federal University in Brazil. She develops projects that connect university and grassroots movements in Latin America, relating environmental education, anti-racist education, unionism, and indigenous and traditional knowledge. She is a researcher at the "Collective of Studies in Marxism and Education" (Brazil). In 2022, she was elected director of the Association of Professors of the Fluminense Federal University, a union section of the National Association of Higher Education Teachers (Brazil). She was also elected chair of the Paulo Freire SIG of the American Educational Research Association (AERA).

Luis Martínez Andrade received his PhD in Sociology from *Ecole des Hautes études en Sciences Sociales* (EHESS) in Paris. His previous books include *Religion Without Redemption. Social Contradictions and Awakened Dreams in Latin America* (2015), *Feminismos a la Contra* (2019), *Ecología y Teología de la Liberación. Crítica de la modernidad/colonialidad* (2019) *Textos sin Disciplina. Claves para una Teoría Crítica Anticolonial* (2020), and *Teoría Crítica Anticolonial* (2023). He currently holds the position of scientific collaborator at *Université Catholique de Louvain*, Belgium.

Luis Arboledas-Lérida does research and teaches at the University of Seville (Spain). His research interests cover a wide range of areas, from the methodological grounds of Marxian thought to scholarly communication and science communication. His PhD thesis focuses on the determinants of the capitalist relations of production that assert themselves in the genesis and development of science communication as a social practice. Luis is currently working on a research initiative that addresses how the so-called third mission of universities has been publicly portrayed in the Spanish press and in outlets such as *The Conversation*.

Wayne Au is a professor in the School of Educational Studies at the University of Washington Bothell, and he has published widely on critical analyses of education policies and practices. His most recent books include the second, revised edition of *Unequal By Design: High-Stakes Testing and the Standardization of Inequality* and *A Marxist Education: Learning to Change the World*.

David I. Backer is Associate Professor of Education Policy at West Chester University, USA. His research currently focuses on applying Marxist and critical theories to school finance. He writes a newsletter called *Schooling in Social America* on this theme.

Abigail Boggs is a cultural studies scholar and teaches sociology, feminist and gender studies, and education studies at Wesleyan University. She is writing a critical genealogy of US higher education told through the figure of the racialized noncitizen student.

Sara Carpenter is Associate Professor of Adult, Community, and Higher Education, Faculty of Education, University of Alberta. She is author of *The Ideology of Civic Engagement* (2021) and co-author, with Shahrzad Mojab, of *Revolutionary Learning: Marxism, Feminism, and Knowledge* (2017).

Lorenzo Cini is a Marie Curie Skłodowska Research Fellow at the University College Dublin (UCD), working on a research project titled "COntesting GOvernance by NUmbers: The Mobilizations of Food Delivery Couriers across Europe in Time of the Pandemic (COGONU)." He investigates the causes, trajectories, and outcomes of mobilizations of these workers since 2016 in different European cities before and during the Covid crisis. Lorenzo's main research interests are social movements and conflicts in the current transformations of the world of work. On these topics, he has published several articles and monographs. The full list of publications can be viewed on his Google Scholar profile.

Allan Coelho received his PhD in Religious Studies from the Methodist University of São Paulo. He received an Honourable Mention for the Coordination for the Improvement of Higher Education Personnel-Capes Thesis Award in the area of Theology/Philosophy. He carried out postdoctoral research under the supervision of Michael Löwy at *Ecole des Hautes études en Sciences Sociales* (EHESS). He currently holds the position of Researcher at Universidade São Francisco-USF. Most recently, he published *Capitalismo como Religião: Walter Benjamin e os Teólogos da Libertação* (Recriar 2021).

César Augusto Costa is a sociologist; CNPq/Brazil researcher; professor and researcher at the Graduate Program in Social Policy and Human Rights/UCPEL; coordinator of the Center for Latin American Studies (NEL/UCPEL); and researcher at the Laboratory for Investigations in Education, Environment and Society (LIEAS/UFRJ).

Hellen Balbinotti Costa is a doctoral candidate at the Graduate Program at the Federal University of Rio de Janeiro (UFRJ), researcher at the Coletivo de Estudos em Marxismo e Educação (Colemarx).

Raju J. Das is a professor at York University, Toronto. He is associated with Graduate Programs in Social and Political Thought, Geography, Environmental Studies, and Development Studies. His teaching and research interests are political economy, state, uneven development, and the politics of the Right and the Left. His recent books include *Marxist Class Theory for a Skeptical World* (2017), *Marx's Capital, Capitalism, and Limits to the State* (2022), *Contradictions of Capitalist Society and Culture* (2023), and *The Challenges of the New Social Democracy* (2023). He has editorial affiliations with *Science & Society, Class, Race and Corporate Power, Critical Sociology, Dialectical Anthropology* and *Human Geography*.

Sayan Dey grew up in Kolkata, West Bengal, and is currently working as a Postdoctoral Fellow at Wits Centre for Diversity Studies, University of Witwatersrand. He is also a Faculty Fellow at The Harriet Tubman Institute, York University, Canada; and Critical Cultural Studies Faculty, at NYI Global Cultural, Cognitive and Linguistic Studies, New York. Some of his published books are *Myths, Histories and Decolonial Interventions: A Planetary Resistance* (2022), and *Green Academia: Towards Eco-friendly Education Systems* (2022). His areas of research interests are postcolonial studies, decolonial studies, critical race studies, food humanities, and critical diversity literacy. He can be reached at: www.sayandey.com.

Richard Hall is Professor of Education and Technology at De Montfort University, and the research and evaluation lead for Decolonising DMU. A UK National Teaching Fellow, Richard writes about the political economy of higher education. He is the author of *The Hopeless University: Intellectual Work at the End of the End of History* (2021), and *The Alienated Academic: The Struggle for Autonomy Inside the University* (Palgrave Macmillan, 2018). Richard is an independent visitor for a looked-after child, and a governor of the Leicester Primary Pupil Referral Unit. He writes about life in higher education at http://richard-hall.org.

John D. Holst is Associate Professor of Lifelong Learning and Adult Education at the Pennsylvania State University-University Park Campus, USA. He is the author of *Social Movements, Civil Society, and Radical Adult Education* (2002), co-author with Stephen Brookfield of *Radicalizing Learning: Adult Education for a Just World* (2010), and co-editor with Nico Pizzolato of *Antonio Gramsci: A Pedagogy to Change the World* (2017).

Jakub Krzeski, PhD, is an assistant professor at the Department of Philosophy and Social Sciences of Nicolaus Copernicus University and researcher at the Scholarly Communication Research Group. He received his degree in 2021 defending his dissertation "A Philosophical Account of Metrological Conflict in the Field of Science Evaluation" at the Faculty of Philosophy, Adam Mickiewicz University. His research interests focus on the social theory of quantification, critical theory, and political ontology.

Joel Lazarus works as a postdoctoral researcher and lecturer in the Department of Social and Policy Studies, University of Bath. Joel works as qualitative lead researcher on WorkFREE, a project bringing together an alliance of UK and Indian researchers, Montfort Social Institute NGO, and over 1200 people living in slum communities in Hyderabad to explore the emancipatory potential of combining unconditional cash transfers and needs-oriented participatory action research. Joel's research focuses on relational approaches to development work and work on a new theory and praxis of needs.

Roberto Leher is a professor at the Faculty of Education, and the Graduate Program in Education at the Federal University of Rio de Janeiro (UFRJ) and researcher at CNPq and Scientist of Our State (FAPERJ). He works for the Collective for Studies in Marxism and Education—COLEMARX. He is collaborator of the Florestan Fernandes National School and a former dean of the Federal University of Rio de Janeiro (July 2015 to July 2019).

Carlos Frederico Loureiro holds PhD in Social Service (UFRJ). Loureiro is full professor at the Federal University of Rio de Janeiro/UFRJ, professor in the Graduate Program in Education (UFRJ), and coordinator of the Laboratory of Investigations in Education, Environment and Society (LIEAS/UFRJ).

Eli Meyerhoff wrote a book, *Beyond Education: Radical Studying for Another World* (2019), and works in the John Hope Franklin Humanities Institute at Duke University.

Nick Mitchell teaches about race, gender, power, and knowledge at the University of California, Santa Cruz.

Shahrzad Mojab is Professor in the Department of Leadership, Higher, and Adult Education, OISE/University of Toronto, and the Women & Gender Studies Institute, University of Toronto. She is co-editor, with Genevieve Ritchie and Sara Carpenter, of *Marxism and Migration* (Palgrave, 2023) and editor of Women of Kurdistan: A Historical and Biographical Study (2021).

Lilia D. Monzó is Professor of Education in the College of Educational Studies at Chapman University. She engages a Marxist-humanist, revolutionary critical pedagogy to develop a praxis against sexism, racism, and all forms of oppression and to develop an alternative to capitalism. She is the author of *A Revolutionary Subject: Pedagogy of Women of Color and Indigeneity* and has published extensively in academic journals, edited books, and online public sources. She teaches courses on critical pedagogy, educational philosophy, and social movements.

Jeremiah Morelock is an instructor of sociology at Boston College's Woods College of Advancing Studies. He is the author of *The Society of the Selfie: Social Media and the Crisis of Liberal Democracy* (2021), *O problema do populismo* (2019), and *Pandemics, Authoritarian Populism, and Science Fiction* (2021).

He is editor of *Critical Theory and Authoritarian Populism* (2018), *How to Critique Authoritarian Populism* (2021), and *The Return of History* (2022).

Sara C. Motta is a proud Indigenous-Mestiza of Colombia Chibcha/Muisca, Eastern European Jewish and Celtic lineages living, loving, resisting, and re-existiendo on the unceded lands of the Awabakal and Worimi peoples, NSW, so-called Australia. She is mother curandera, popular educator, and award-winning poet and political philosopher who is currently A/Professor in Politics at the University of Newcastle, NSW. Her latest book *Liminal Subjects: Weaving (Our) Liberation* (Rowman and Littlefield) was winner of the 2020 best Feminist Book, International Studies Associate (ISA). She has co-created numerous projects of decolonizing education as healing sovereignties in Abya Yala, UK and Australia, is a founding member of the women's/feminized survivors sanctuary project in Mulubimba-Newcastle and is currently dreaming into being her next book (M)otherwise: a politics of the wilds.

Felipe Ziotti Narita received a postdoctoral training at the University of São Paulo (USP) and Federal University of São Carlos (UFSCar) and all four of his degrees from the São Paulo State University (UNESP), Brazil. He is Lecturer in Public Policy and researcher at UNESP and pro-rector of research at Baron of Mauá University. He was commended with the Medal of the Order of Books of the National Library of Brazil. He is the author of *The Society of the Selfie* (2021) and the editor of *Latency of the Crisis* (2021), *The Return of History* (2022), and *Critique, Education and Emancipation: From Popular Education to Social Struggles* (2022).

Linda Orie is an enrolled member of the Oneida Nation of Wisconsin and Doctoral student in the Department of Curriculum & Instruction at the University of Wisconsin-Madison. Her research interests include facilitating and studying systemic change in public schools in efforts to decrease racial disproportionality of behavioral and academic outcomes and culturally responsive curricula creation. Prior to joining UW, Linda taught middle school science and served as summer school principal at Menominee Tribal School. Linda also obtained degrees from Stanford University (BA Psychology) and UW-Oshkosh (BS Education) prior to completing her MS in Curriculum & Instruction at UW-Madison.

Nidžara Pečenković is Associate Professor of English at Santiago Canyon College and a doctoral student in the College of Educational Studies at Chapman University. She is interested in engaging with intersectional Marxism as a framework to develop a pedagogy of anti-capitalism and of challenging white supremacist patriarchy as well as other systems of oppression but also one of co-constructing a more humanizing future.

Bogdan Popa (Transilvania University, Brașov) is an intellectual and cultural historian. His first book, *Shame: A Genealogy of Queer Practices in the Nineteenth Century* (2017), offers an analysis of shame in political thought and queer theory. His second book is titled *De-centering Queer Theory: Communist Sexuality in the Flow During and After the Cold War* (2022). The book analyzes competitive models of Cold War sexuality and inserts a Marxist epistemology in queer theory.

Mikko Poutanen is a postdoctoral researcher at Tampere University and a senior researcher at the University of Turku, Finland. His current research interests lie in the political economy of Nordic higher education policy and university democracy. He also actively works with science communication in the form of popularizing social science research to wider audiences.

Marise Nogueira Ramos graduated in Chemistry from the State University of Rio de Janeiro (UERJ). She completed her Master's and PhD in Education from the Fluminense Federal University (UFF), with postdoctoral studies in Ethnosociology of Professional Knowledge at the University of Trás-os-Montes e Alto Douro (UTAD), Portugal. She carried out her research at the Joaquim Venâncio Polytechnic School of Health, Oswaldo Cruz Foundation (EPSJV/Fiocruz). She is an associate professor at School of Education, UERJ, and permanent professor of the Post-Graduation Programs in Public Policies and Human Formation at UERJ and in Professional Education in Health at ESPJV/Fiocruz. She is one of the coordinators of the Group These—Integrated Research Projects in Work, History, Education and Health at UFF/UERJ/EPSJV-Fiocruz.

Glenn Rikowski is an independent scholar, based in Forest Gate, east London. He was previously a visiting fellow in the College of Social Science, University of Lincoln (2016–2022), a senior lecturer in the School of Education, University of Northampton (2002–2013), a senior research fellow in Lifelong Learning at Birmingham City University (1999–2001), and a research fellow in the School of Education, University of Birmingham (1994–1999). Prior to that Rikowski taught in further education colleges, adult education, and schools in London and Essex. He was a member of the Hillcole Group of Radical Left Educators (1994–2001).

Héctor Ríos-Jara is a researcher and writer from Chile. He received his PhD in Social Sciences from the University College of London and an MA in Methodology of Social Research from the University of Bristol. He is currently Lecturer in Social Sciences at the Faculty of Government and Public Policy of Universidad Alberto Hurtado, Chile. He also has been appointed as a special advisor for higher education funding policy for the Ministry of Education for the Government of Chile. His research specializes in neoliberalism, social and higher education policy, and social movements.

María Alicia Rueda is an independent researcher and adult education scholar based in the United States. Originally from Northern Chile, her research focuses on the working-class history of the area. María Alicia obtained a doctorate in Adult Education (EdD) from Northern Illinois University, and she has taught at different colleges and universities in the North American Midwest. She is the author of *The Educational Philosophy of Luis Emilio Recabarren: Pioneering Working-Class Education in Latin America* (2020).

Toni Ruuska (DSc) is University Researcher and Adjunct Professor of Sustainable Economy at the University of Helsinki. He is the co-editor of *Sustainability Beyond Technology* (2021) and the author of *Reproduction Revisited: Capitalism, Higher Education and Ecological Crisis* (2019). In his research, Ruuska seeks to find avenues for alternative agrarian political economy. Theoretically he is involved in critical theory, ecological Marxism, and (eco)phenomenology.

Zach Schwartz-Weinstein is a historian of university labor. He is writing a book about the history of university food service, custodial, and maintenance workers.

Anna Stetsenko is full Professor in Psychology and in Urban Education PhD Programs and chair of Developmental Psychology PhD training area, at the Graduate Center of the City University of New York (since 1999), with previous work experiences in Europe (Germany, Switzerland, Austria, and Russia). Her research is situated at the intersection of human development, philosophy, and education with particular interest in agency and social transformation. Rooted in Marxism and its extensions in Vygotsky's project, she advances this project and brings out its political-critical edge and activist agenda, while drawing connections to the scholarship of resistance. She has proposed the *transformative activist stance* approach that captures politically non-neutral nature of knowing-being-doing including research in psychology and education, culminating in a proposal for a *pedagogy of daring* (summarized in her book *The Transformative Mind: Expanding Vygotsky's Approach to Development and Education*, 2017). This research brings together and critically examines a wide spectrum of approaches to situate and further develop activist agendas of social justice and equity. The gist of this framework has to do with moving beyond the canons of "neutral objectivity," adaptation, and political quietism—to instead radically challenge the status quo and its dogmas in both research and wider social practices.

Krystian Szadkowski, PhD, researcher at Scholarly Communication Research Group, Adam Mickiewicz University, Poznań, Poland. His interests cover Marxist political economy and transformations of higher education systems in Central Eastern Europe. Currently he leads a research project "The Origins and Development of the Peripheral Academic Capitalism in Poland (1990–2021)" funded by National Science Centre (Poland). His upcoming book *Capital in Higher Education: A Critique of the Political Economy of the Sector* will be published by Palgrave in 2023.

Lois Weiner is a former career teacher, teacher educator, education researcher, and union activist who writes widely about politics and education, specializing in teachers' unions. She is a professor emerita at New Jersey City University.

List of Figures

Fig. 24.1 Ontological pedagogics of the schoolteacher's ego and orphanic entity (special thanks to Vincent W.J. van Gerven Oei at punctum books for the permissions to reproduce this image, cited from Dussel (2019), where it was Figure 3)   465

Fig. 24.2 Dussel's contrast between a dominating dialectic and a liberatory analectic (special thanks to Vincent W.J. van Gerven Oei at punctum books for the permissions to reproduce this image, cited from Dussel (2019))   466

PART I

In: Marxist Modes and Characteristics of Analysis in Education

CHAPTER 1

Introduction: The Relevance of Marxism to Education

Richard Hall, Inny Accioly, and Krystian Szadkowski

1.1 The Problem of Education

What is the role of education in the reproduction of the world? What is its role in capitalism's valorization process? How do educational structures, cultures and practices reproduce the ways in which capitalism mediates everyday life for-value, through private property, commodity exchange, the division of labor and the market? In response to the alienating realities of twenty-first-century life, how might we reimagine education for another world? These questions have gestated inside a space and time of polycrisis, or interconnecting crises of capitalist reproduction, ecosystem collapse and climate forcing, and systemic misrepresentation and marginalization for some communities. In response, there is a renewed need for critiques that can unfold authentic and humane educational possibilities beyond the commodity form.

This is not a new claim for education, its institutions and its laborers, be they support staff, students, teachers or academics. There has been long-standing

---

R. Hall (✉)
De Montfort University, Leicester, UK
e-mail: rhall1@dmu.ac.uk

I. Accioly
Fluminense Federal University, Rio de Janeiro, Brazil
e-mail: innyaccioly@gmail.com

K. Szadkowski
Adam Mickiewicz University, Poznań, Poland
e-mail: krysszad@amu.edu.pl

© The Editor(s) (if applicable) and The Author(s), under exclusive license to Springer Nature Switzerland AG 2023
R. Hall et al. (eds.), *The Palgrave International Handbook of Marxism and Education*, Marxism and Education,
https://doi.org/10.1007/978-3-031-37252-0_1

critique of what educational institutions have become under the intensification of capitalist social relations. In 1968, the Movimento studentesco (1968/2008) documented revolt inside-and-against the university in Italy, designed to prefigure a new type of society with a radically transformed school structure. At the heart of this lay concrete disenchantment with the university as a site of productive capability, within commodity capitalism. In these institutions, humans were produced as commodities, with labor-power that can be sold and then consumed within the cycle of social reproduction. This was a common thread in analyzing the university. In May 1968, Camarades (quoted in Feenberg, 1999, p. 24) noted that in France:

> the University has become more and more an essential terrain: the intensification of the repressive reality of the University, its increasing role in the process of social reproduction, its active participation in maintaining the established order (cf. the social sciences in particular), the role of science and research in economic development, all require the institution of a right to permanent contestation in the University, its goals, its ideology, the content of its 'products'.

Shortly after this, the Canadian academic Le Baron (1971, p. 567) emphasized how essentialism within educational institutions, and especially the university, was reproduced by academics whose egoism, competition and desire to possess deny the potential for a new consciousness of society and education-in-society. The idealism and utopian or positivist methods of academics in reproducing higher education (HE) and its disciplinary specificities are barriers to revolutionary change. However, these are not the only barriers the revolutionary movement encounters within educational domains.

Idealism and belief in the separateness of education has the effect of portraying teachers and academics as being situated outside the actual working class, in terms of interests and privileges. At times, this is fostered because some Marxists highlight the idea of productive labor and find it difficult to situate the revolutionary potential of educators against this idea. Delegating education (including HE) exclusively to the sphere of capitalist reproduction, they see educational labor as merely unproductive labor. Yet, we continue to witness the most profound transformations of education into capitalist sectors of production in the proper sense (Leher & Accioly, 2016; Szadkowski, 2023).

However, this perspective is also challenged by working-class movements fighting for liberation. The denial of access to schooling for the working class and the suppression of struggles and revolts have been key mechanisms for maintaining inequalities. Thus, in colonized societies, the educational ideals necessary for capitalist reproduction were implanted in scarce and limited ways, and only through the simple tasks of reading, writing and counting. In the 1960s, the number of native Africans who had access to education was so low that anyone who attended school was considered privileged and belonging to an elite (Rodney, 1973).

Yet, it is important to recognize how struggles are materially and historically nurtured, pedagogically. This requires that we do not fetishize ideas or practices from the North. For instance, while it was in northern universities that African leaders established articulations for decolonization struggles, this was developed on the ground, in-country. During his study period in Portugal, Eduardo Mondlane, one of the founders of the Liberation Front of Mozambique, had contact with Amilcar Cabral and Agostinho Neto, who led the independence struggles of Guinea-Bissau and Angola in the 1960s. Mutuality and revolutionary optimism fed into this process.

It was also in a university extension project that Paulo Freire developed his world-famous, adult literacy initiative in Angicos, Northeast Brazil, in 1962 (Accioly, 2020). In the late 1950s and early 1960s, the Cuban revolution inspired the emergence of grassroots movements to develop popular literacy projects in rural zones, as part of the political struggle for land and rights. It was a time of fruitful dialogue between students and grassroots movements, which was interrupted by military coups that tortured and murdered university leaders. The censorship of critical thinking had a long-term impact on educational institutions, especially in the depoliticization of teaching and research.

Witnessing and remembering how authoritarian regimes control education with violence is crucial in challenging hegemonic political economic norms. This matters because, over fifty years later, the restructuring of educational institutions and infrastructures as networks for the production, circulation, and valorization of capital has continued to accelerate. Alongside this, performative and toxic cultures, predicated upon particular modes of performance, and methodological practices, pivoting around value-production, have catalyzed reports of non-being, ill-being, overwork, illness, quitting and so on, from inside schools, colleges and universities (Hall, 2021). They have also led to analyses of symptomatic coping behaviors, like cynicism among educators (Allen, 2017).

Globally, these symptoms are analyzed for teachers in terms of a lack of autonomy, assaults on professional identity and professionalism, job dissatisfaction, absenteeism, worsening mental health, burnout and stress, alongside insufficient resources and high demands (see, e.g., Maingard, 2019; Nguyen et al., 2022). For students, symptoms analyzed include crises of mental health, burnout, the need to work while studying, neglecting caring responsibilities and increasing pressures around outcomes and employment (see, e.g., Ma & Bennett, 2021). Such symptomatic analyses are then refracted against deeper issues of representation, like race and ethnicity, gender, sexuality and disability. As will be seen below when we discuss the positionality of this volume, issues of systemic misrepresentation and marginalization connect to crises of distribution. These leave many without basic means of subsistence, let alone the possibility for a self-actualized life (hooks, 1994).

Holloway (2010) deepens our pedagogical engagement with these lived experiences of being without and being made Other, by linking them to the crises generated by the contradictions of capitalism. He (ibid., p. 919) identifies the importance of situating many-sided, scientific work 'against the suicidal rush towards human self-annihilation'. Holloway (ibid.) goes on to challenge the questions of reimagination at the head of this Introduction, by emphasizing that:

> the only scientific question that remains to us is: how the fuck do we get out of this mess? This includes the question: how do we stop the reproduction of this self-destructive society, capitalism? This is a question that it is becoming more and more difficult to pose within a university framework.

It is also one that is difficult to pose within wider frameworks of formal schooling that are governed, regulated and funded from inside states working with transnational activist networks and organizations, for-value (Ball, 2012; Zajda, 2021).

Yet, our epistemological and ontological assumptions about Holloway's question and our methodological response to it are crucial. As will be argued in the chapter, Marx's dialectical method, grounded in history and materialism, moves us away from evidence-based, positivist and idealist solutions that are one-sided. Such one-sidedness reflects the reality that inside capitalist social relations, humans are reproduced in specific ways, for instance as laborers, for-value. It was inherent in the Marxian project from the outset to seek an alternative, scientific expression of the relationship—one favorable to the development of the working class and its unlimited needs (Hudis, 2012; Lebowitz, 2003)—through a method that might bring the process of liberation to a conclusion. Thus, Marx's dialectical method builds from a foundation in which:

> All is encircled by capitalist accumulation—the red dust of living death—and all who attempt to flee are returned to it, in the end. Future communist prospects, then, will find no hope in reclusion. The only emancipatory politics is one that grows within and against the red dust of the material community of capital. (Chuǎng, n.d.)

Our educational futures are situated against our movement, or the steps that we take, through our methodological critique of the world as-is. Our critique of this world seeks to understand burnout, ill-being, non-being, as symptoms that emerge against the red dust of the material community of capital. This materialist critique is a pedagogical starting point for pushing beyond an understanding of those symptoms, to reach their root in the estrangement between Self and Other, and Self and the World. In reaching toward an analysis of the rational kernel of capitalist life, grounded in alienated labor, this is a methodology that desires the negation and sublation of that life.

Above all, there is an ethical duty in the critique of capitalism (Dussel, 2012), which is expressed in an active stance before the world. This is a stance claimed by Marx when he states: 'The philosophers have only interpreted the world in various ways; the point, however, is to change it' (Marx, 1845).

Having understood that capitalism relentlessly produces misery, hunger and death, there is a responsibility to transform this toxic reality.

> If I do not assume responsibility, I do not cease to be responsible for the death of the other, who is my/our victim, and of whose victimization I am/we are an accomplice, at least for being a human being, destined to the communal responsibility of the shared vulnerability of all living people. I am/we are responsible for the other by the fact of being human, 'sensitivity' open to the face of the other. Moreover, it is not responsibility for one's own life; it is now responsibility for the denied life of the other. (Dussel, 2012, p. 378, our translation)

Responsibility for human life in general achieves concreteness. This cannot remain a mere abstract conception, as we advance in critical analysis of the capitalist system, and recognize its real victims, in whose faces we also recognize ourselves. Here emerges a challenge for critical educators: to overcome the utopianism that reduces their function to the mere transformation of individual subjects. The dissociation between educators and learners, and also the hierarchization between enlightened educators who guide learners, needs to be overcome, since 'educators need to be educated' (Marx, 1845). Changing circumstances and changing oneself is a unitary and continuous process carried out in praxis (Accioly, 2021).

As we shall see, sublation is crucial in abolishing the educational world that is (its structures, cultures and practices) and preserving the world as it unfolds into a new, transformed educational reality. This defines a new ground, or identity, for educational life and struggle, which itself can be brought into relation with ideas and objects with a different, or non-, identity. As the recognition enabled through the dialectical relation of Subject and Object, or Self and Other, it forms a way of opening-up 'the wrongness of the world' (Holloway et al., 2009, p. 8), through the negative identity between the Subject and the Object. In recognizing and working through this negative relation, the internal relations that structure our alienating existence inside capitalism are revealed, with the possibility for 'negation-creation' (ibid.) of existing material/concrete histories and the concepts that dominate our lived experiences.

Crucially for moving beyond the symptoms of educational distress, amplifying the negative moment of dialectical materialism enables those internal relations that constitute the Subject or Object (in their relation) to be understood (Adorno, 1966). This negative moment reveals that which is left behind when the Subject is unable to integrate the Object, and this materializes as 'the constituted untruth of the world' (Bonefeld, 2014, p. 40). It is a critique of the one-sidedness of the Subject, as productive worker, or teacher, technician, librarian, student, rather than as many-sided human being. It is a critique of the reification of social relations between Objects that have been commodified. Inside schools and universities, revealing one-sidedness makes it possible to critique: the political economic basis for performance management and competition; the desire to generate surpluses, through student recruitment or knowledge spillover and commercialization; the domination of clock-time over the working lives of teachers and students; and so on.

Moreover, this process also reveals how capitalist education sublates the human, as it imposes particular, reductive constraints on teaching, learning, supporting or researching. It negates or abolishes many-sided, sensuous human activity based upon autonomy and agency, instead reducing it to the enrichment of labor-power or the capacity for knowledge exchange, commercialization, impact, and so on. Yet, at the same time it preserves the humane, sensuous core of this activity, for instance, in reproducing teaching as a labor of love, or the value of higher education accreditation for personal growth. Systemically, this is then used to transform practices such that they enable new levels of self-exploitation, for example, through lifelong learning aimed at entrepreneurship and commodification.

This unfolding sublation of education is accelerating in an era of intersecting crises, dubbed the Capitalocene (Moore, 2015), the Anthropocene (Malm, 2016) or the Metabolic Rift (Foster, 2017). Others argue that these modes of analysis are contained within a deeper crisis of value, and of the production of surplus-value, which is generating superfluous human beings (Jappe, 2014). Yet others argue that they are a conceit from the North that neglects centuries of expropriation in the South (Andreotti, 2021). These abstractions shape differential modes of dialectical analysis. They also open-up the need to analyze how and why education is repurposed to establish a foothold for capitalist reproduction, and through them to build alternative forms of social reproduction. Our starting point for this is to renew the connections between Marx, Marxism and education.

1.2 Renewing Dialogues in Marxism and Education

We have sketched some outlines of the relationship between education and capitalist reproduction. These point toward Marxist modes of analysis as socially useful in drawing upon and elaborating analytical and organizing concepts, including those highlighted above like competition, dialectical materialism, labor and labor-power, and abolition or sublation. These concepts help us to relate education to the emerging and unfolding, dominant political economy and its relationship with philosophy. They can be used fruitfully, in order to understand how the structures, cultures and practices of education are mediated for-value, and how this relates to those who labor in its sectors. For example, this highlights how educational development impacts and is impacted by modes of exploitation, expropriation and extraction inside the classroom, school, college and university; competition, markets and the generation of surplus labor, value and time through research and teaching excellence; and the division of labor, private property and commodity exchange in shaping the socially useful nature of educational labor.

Such deeper, conceptual analyses emerge from the material histories of estrangement as laborers work to valorize capital. Here, it is important to recognize that the alpha and omega of Marx's analysis, and a range of Marxist analyses from different traditions, are potentially revolutionary. This reflects Césaire's (1956/1969, p. 39) invocation that: 'I must begin. Begin what? The only thing in the world that is worth beginning: The End of the World, no less'. This is one of the core strands of this collection, namely that renewing dialogues between Marxist traditions and educational contexts and actors works to reveal the truth of the world as immanent causation, rather than as reified objectivity, and as a result offering the possibility to reframe marginalization and to generate agency.

This builds upon the work of Green (2008), who argued the importance of mapping educational concepts, like the curriculum, performance, assessment, impact and so on, to *both* the social world *and* the relations that construct subject and object in that world. Green (ibid., p. 15) stressed the importance of theorizing and articulating dialectically and dialogically, and avoiding reductionism in relation to, for instance, race, gender and class. Here, it is important to understand the complexities of the social relations of differentiation, as they are revealed inside the classroom, pedagogic practice, assessment regimes and so on. It is also crucial that they are revealed in our opposition to educational engagement as the production and engagement of labor-power. Dowling (2011, p. 207) notes that this means developing an understanding of how social individuals are 'situated within a global wage hierarchy that begins in the classroom'.

For Malott and Ford (2015), this is a dialectical process of becoming, with education predicated upon a subject's self-reflection, in relation to the objects of their existence. This draws out a range of contradictions, or the wrongness of the world, which itself is shaped by the dominant epistemological and ontological realities of capitalism. These are deeply positivist, grounded in ideas of universal reason and enlightenment that emerged from settler-colonial and racial-patriarchal societies. Such self-reflection demands forms of radical pedagogy that challenge students and teachers to become conscious of their own consciousness, and in this way to become self-mediating, rather than mediated, for instance, by the commodity-form or divisions of labor. Through self-reflection, one should seek to negate consciousness as defined through estranged or alienated labor inside capitalism.

Mészáros (2005) argues that teaching is central to this project of becoming self-mediating. This connects to Neary's (2020) reimagination of student-as-producer, and the idea that revolutionary teaching is the attempt to transgress beyond bourgeois, universal reason, as an approach that seeks to abolish the didactic, representative power of the teacher. It celebrates cooperative production in the classroom, as an attempt to uncover the rational kernel of life, through an understanding of how that concrete and material production is constructed socially, or for social ends. Here, revolutionary teaching is the revelation of capital's unwitting production of the material conditions for communism (Marx, 1894/1991), and how we might set that free through a new political and cultural apparatus that is not dependent upon capitalist institutions, like schools, colleges and universities.

Thus, Marxist analyses have sought to apply Marx's categorical critique in order to develop education in a new sense or as a new form of common sense. This takes education beyond the institution, in reintegrating Subject and Object, Self and Other, mind and body, affect and cognition, at the level of the individual-in-society. One outcome of this might be the subsumption of the general intellect (the ways of knowing, doing and being in society that have been commodified by capital for-value) back inside ourselves as social beings. The general intellect is the proletariat's ability to subsume the forces of production inside a new mode of production and a new set of relations of production.

For Marx and Engels (1846/1998, p. 57), this pointed toward communism as 'the real movement which abolishes the present state of things'. In relation to education, Carpenter and Mojab (2011) have highlighted the need for such a movement to embody living, learning and teaching revolution, as an immanent, material practice. They (ibid., p. 215) describe the need for 'dialectical moments of revolutionary learning', and the need to use such learning to overcome our timidity in the face of capital's power. For Carpenter and Mojab (ibid., p. 223), as practical beings, 'We must learn to overcome our adherence to their power'. Our revolutionary potential emerges through material, social activity that breaks the bonds of capitalist education, in order to liberate the general intellect (our knowing, doing and being) for other worlds (Marx, 1857/1993).

It is crucial here to note that for each of these authors, working theoretically and practically with and through Marx, there is no separation of educational theorizations from critical social theory. This would be to essentialize education or thinking about education in a way that reduces and commodifies human experience just as capitalism does. In addressing this, Allman (2007, pp. 51–52) argued:

> I contend that Marx would have scorned the idea of a separate Marxist educational theory because it implies that education belongs to some separate aspect of human life rather than being an integral part of the process of 'becoming', i.e. the lifelong process of developing all of our human potentials and powers. It also implies that our current existence can be understood as the sum of many separate and distinct parts rather than as a totality of inner-connected relations.

This reemphasizes the need to unfold the relations between education, political economy, philosophy and the lived experience of those who labor inside schools, colleges and universities, as well as those who work in alternative educational projects.

Here, our renewal of dialogue between Marxism and education situates the latter against social domination, containing the potential for social liberation. This is situated not simply in terms of place and space, for instance, in the fabric of the classroom. It is crucially a function of time, including the ways in which education accrues and commodifies past forms of knowing, doing and being, so that they can be valorized in the present. It is also a function of how capitalist education focuses upon acceleration and speed-up, as well as foreclosing upon the possibility that future time will be free, for the all-round development of human beings.

Wendling (2009) is clear that time and the control of human activity become encoded within the monstrousness of infrastructures and machinery. In this way, both concrete time of actual activity and abstract measures of time that standardize activity across a social field (as socially necessary time) are conditioned externally in ways that deny agency. This brings us back to symptoms of distress reported by educational laborers, in the form of overwork, a lack of autonomy, the attrition of professionalism, casualization, the modularization of learning and teaching, and so on.

Following Postone (1993), these are the symptoms of alienated social relations, with a tempo and depth that are set by socially necessary labor time. The latter confronts all educational workers with demands that the development and circulation of their labor-power consumes more of their lives. As Wendling (2009, p. 197) argues:

> In terms of alienated projections of the human being's activities and potentialities, time becomes the new god. We save it; we obey it; we do not question its existence or its history; and its sociality remains unseen.

Understanding this sociality, and its formation in space and time, is at the heart of Marx's dialectical method and of this volume. It is at the heart of how he brings our attention to a range of entanglements, including the social usefulness of education, and its relationship to the exchange of commodities; the wealth embedded within different ways of knowing, doing and being in the world, commodified in the search for value that drives knowledge production; and education as a humane process of self-actualization, self-knowledge and self-love, and schooling that is reduced to the abstract discipline of academic disciplines. Within this, there is the desire for free time (Marx, 1894/1991; Thompson, 1967), or for 'modern life freed from time's abstract and alienating dominations' (Wendling, 2009, p. 199).

This points to our liberation from the clock-time of the classroom, laboratory, studio, school and university, and to open-up new historical possibilities beyond those spaces and the times they produce (Meyerhoff et al., 2011). These impose artificial forms of scarcity, whereby control of time gives control over the labor process, the objects of labor, the laboring Self and the essence of what it means to be human. For students, time is also controlled, both in the present and in future, through the imposition of debt, and in how their lives are reproduced inside expanding regimes of financialization.

How then does Marx's method enable us to reveal capitalist education as 'a form of unfreedom' (Postone, 2007, p. 70)? How does his method enable us to analyze the historical dynamics of educational structures, cultures and practices in specific communal and social contexts? How does it offer us the potential for developing new horizons of possibility beyond capitalist foreclosure? These questions shape our engagement with Marx's writing, alongside the many Marxist traditions that seek to make sense of his work, in the contexts of formal and alternative education, and in knowing, doing and being in the world.

1.3   Marx and Education

Marx's writing, journalism and activism with and for working people centered the deep interconnections between political economy and philosophy as always-already unified science. It enables the richness of human essence—understood as the dynamic 'ensemble of social relations' (Marx & Engels, 1846/1998)—and the ways in which capitalist social relations feed off that richness, to be described and analyzed. This analysis is historical and immanent, shaped as a dialectical process, which refuses the reductionism of knowledge production and instead attempts to unfold ways of knowing oneself in the world. By cracking bourgeois political economy through a richer, philosophical analysis, Marx enables us to take a deeply ethnographic approach to our understanding of education, rather than one predicated upon economism (Krader, 1974).

Thus, in *The Communist Manifesto*, Marx and Engels (1848/2002, p. 13) remind us that the capitalist impulse is for 'constantly revolutionizing the instruments of production, and thereby the relations of production, and with them the whole relations of society'. The constant revolutionizing of production is social and relational, and transforms all of life into a constant, competitive terrain of uncertainty. Marx and Engels (ibid.) drive this home in relation to the recalibration of the Self by unholy power: 'All that is solid melts into air, all that is holy is profaned, and man is at last compelled to face with sober senses his real condition of life and his relations with his kind'. The humane and the human must be subsumed by new conditions and new relations.

In *The German Ideology*, Marx and Engels (1846/1998) begin to demonstrate clearly how these new conditions and new relations are imposed through the mediation of life by the division of labor, private property and commodity exchange. They also begin to articulate how capital, as value-in-motion, structures sociability, and how it seeks to separate and divide individuals from their labor process and its products, their whole self (corporeal, emotional, historical, social) and their very essence as human beings. Instead, Marx and Engels (ibid., p. 86) are clear that new forms of sociability are required and that 'only within the community has each individual the means of cultivating his gifts in all directions; hence personal freedom becomes possible only within the community'. Marx and Engels are clear that capitalism substitutes or other forms for the community, including in its infrastructures like schools and colleges.

Incarcerated inside these infrastructures, there is only the illusion of freedom and independence, and new modes of association are required in order that self-activity might reconnect material life with human becoming. This cracks the one-sided existence of humans inside capitalism, as labor-power, as means of enabling the social reproduction of that labor-power or as a surplus population, presents the possibility for a many-sided, sensuous life. Marx and Engels (ibid., pp. 438–439) also highlight that this possibility must erupt from 'individuals that are developing in an all-round fashion', in order to confront the totalizing mediations that reproduce capital as private property. The education of a revolutionary sensibility lies at the heart of such practice.

For Marx (1844/1974), this sensibility posits the individual as a social being, working communally and in association, such that the individual and their species-being are in relation. The particular mode of existence of an individual relates to the general mode of existence of their species, in *The Economic and Philosophical Manuscripts*. In this approach, the reduction of life inside capitalism to one's condemnation as a productive worker or as nothing is revealed alongside the potential for learning about and knowing oneself differently, as a social being. Self-education in community is central to this development of a positive self-consciousness, which itself emerges from the negation of the Self inside capitalist social relations.

Of course, Marx's work is itself historically grounded in the dialectical relation between idealism and materialism, such that he could integrate thinking about the philosophy of Feuerbach and Hegel, the political economy of Ricardo, Saint-Simon and Smith, and the realities of accelerating industrial and colonial development. At all times, this points back to human being and becoming in the world, even in the later work that is often described as more focused upon political economy than philosophy. Thus, in *The Grundrisse* (Marx, 1857/1993, p. 594), he is clear about how the development of fixed capital shows how social knowing and doing, and the skills, capacities and capabilities, and knowledges of the community have been subsumed as the general intellect inside capitalist infrastructures. He shows how this impacts social practices and real-life processes.

This matters in our analysis of education, precisely because Marx highlights how human creativity is being unfolded historically and materially in ways that are immanent to our social relations with the world. He highlights how this is co-opted and turned against us and then colonizes nonhuman animals and our ecosystems. This enables us to see the one-sided and alien power of capital inside educational space-times that claim to be open and creative, and yet which are conditioned by value production. Crucially, Marx (ibid., p. 308) points as to how academic disciplines contribute to this conditioning:

> all the progress of civilisation, or in other words every increase in the *powers of social production*... in the *productive powers of labour itself*—such as results from science, inventions, divisions and combinations of labour, improved means of communication, creation of the world market, machinery etc., enriches not the worker, but rather *capital*; hence only magnifies again the power dominating over labour.

This leads us to question the role of education in magnifying this power and in reducing the capacities of humans to abstract measures and modes of accreditation. How does education develop the productive force of labor in order to satisfy the demands of capital for value? How does education reproduce 'the *relation of capital and labour itself*, of *capitalist and worker*' (ibid., p. 458, *emphasis* in original)? Moreover, how does education reproduce an uncritical acceptance of the dehumanizing, historical and material realities of capitalist life, through which populations are rendered disposable or irrelevant?

Marx (1867/2004) helps us to think through these issues in *Capital: A Critique of Political Economy, Volume 1*. His critique enables us to center the relationships between the individual and the value of their social labor and function. Here, he analyzes the historical and material forms of production, which contain contradictions that capital is always seeking to overcome, in part through the development of labor-power through education. This shows us a degraded and foreclosed means of knowing the world, through which machinery, organization and infrastructure come to dominate both work and life, in ways that are expanded through performance management and competition, in order to impose control.

For Marx (ibid., p. 548), the example of machinery and the development of the factory are examples for how learning, knowing, becoming are separated out, commodified, instantiated inside alien things and then turned against the human. Moreover, he is clear that this appears to be transhistorical and that this is a fetishized view of capitalism. This shows us that our obsessive focus upon education as a positional good, and a means of self-enrichment, is an illusion. This illusion diverts us from a recognition of capitalism's revolutionary basis, which is constantly separating human existence, as labor-power, from the conditions of labor. It is constantly separating human learning, knowing and becoming from the conditions of life.

Moreover, through education, it normalizes the ways in which privilege and power can be reproduced as acceptable, and the ways in which divisions of labor, private property and the commodity shape everyday relations. In *Capital*, Marx (ibid., p. 784) lays out a mode of analysis that helps us to understand the precarious nature of work inside schools, colleges and universities, and the ways in which humans must be 'always ready for exploitation by capital in the interests of capital's own changing valorization requirements'. As a result, people become fragments of themselves, conditioned by their engagement with a fragmentary, formal education system.

Yet, Marx also helps us to realize that there are horizons beyond, which might constitute alternative modes of becoming beyond the one-sided fragmentation of capitalism. He also helps us to think this through in relation to our own agency-in-community, as we might decompose and reproduce our species-being beyond the universe of valorization. Rather than our human essence being negated in the search for value, this is the unfolding revelation of our many-sided, sensuous humanity. At present, the form of the educational institution, mirroring the demands of the capitalist state, frames ongoing exploitation that seeks to erase historical modes of social intercourse and the possibility for knowing the world otherwise.

Toward the end of his life in the *Ethnographic Notebooks* (Krader, 1974), Marx explored this in relation to indigenous communities and communes, and the potential for communal shares that might enable the material flourishing of the community. Thus later, Marx begins to look for paths away from a society predicated upon 'the enslaving subordination of the individual' (Marx, 1875/1970) toward a world where the recombination of intellectual and physical work enables the all-sided individual development of the social being.

Marx's (1875/1970) *Critique of the Gotha Programme* also articulates dynamic and dialectical principles with ramifications for the labor of education. First, he identifies the common ownership principles of cooperative society as a transitional movement of direct, social production. This negates the essentializing of labor-power and its circulation as alienated labor, built on formal schooling. Second, his *Critique* refuses ownership beyond the rights to individual means of consumption. As such, it refuses the abstract mediation of the market, as reflected in the principles underpinning experiments for cooperative, educational production or educational commons. Third, he rejects liberal rights rooted in 'the application of an equal standard', as realized in the abstraction of the productive laborer. This recognizes that the imposition of hegemonic performance measures inside schools reproduces differential levels of exploitation and domination.

These are a very few traces of Marx's work, which remained always in a process of becoming. We might state that his overall project of capital, incorporating volumes that he planned but would never have the time or energy to produce, was unfinished. However, his dialectical, historical, material methodology allows us to see that our knowing the world is always unfinished and in motion. As such, our relationships to our sensuous practice and its conditions, ourselves and our essence in community and in the world are always unfolding. By reflecting on the potential for applying his methodology to our educational world, we develop the potential to negate, abolish and transcend our dehumanization inside capitalism.

1.4   Marx, In, Against and Beyond Education

One intriguing way of thinking about the relationship between education and capitalism, and for enriching the potential for liberation through self-education, is to center the negation of our existing educational institutions and infrastructures, and the cultures and practices that flow through them. This consideration is grounded historically and materially against global flows of value that recalibrate education across a transnational terrain. Thus, we must analyze being, doing and knowing inside education in order to understand the contradictions and tensions that are against education and to strive for a life beyond the toxicity of education as it is reproduced inside capitalist social relations.

This idea of being in, against and beyond, at one-and-the-same time, reflects the development of autonomist Marxism as a conglomerate of different perspectives from a European sensibility (for a list of resources, see Hall, 2015). This mode of analysis enabled a focus on why and how capital has been transformed into a globalized, transnational apparatus for accumulating wealth. Entangled with this is the changing nature of the structure and agency of the working class, and the role of education in generating oppositional spaces or cracks through which to resist and push-back. *In-against-beyond* then questions 'the structures that reproduce capitalism's domination, like the State and its educational institutions. These questions emerge from *inside* those structures and from perspectives that are *against* them, so that alternatives that lie *beyond* might be opened up' (ibid., 4).

In Marx's writing, moving beyond is not simply the negation or abolition of the world as-is. Rather, it is a more complex and entangled process of sublation, through which objects are canceled or negated, preserved and lifted up or transformed. In the historical and material working out of their contradictions, the characteristics of specific objects are manifested in relation to each other, internally. As these characteristics are negated, the particular set of social relations and conditions with other objects that they define is also abolished. Yet, the object and its characteristics are also preserved inside new sets of social relations and conditions, which finally transform the subject and the objective world that they construct through a set of internal relations with these objects-in-motion.

Thus, what it means to teach or study unfolds as society unfolds historically and materially. As new legal and administrative forms, mental conceptions of the world and of nature, relations to the world, organization of work and so on emerge, old characteristics of learning, teaching, education and so on are negated and abolished. However, they are also preserved and carried forward inside new discourses. This affects classroom relationships, curricula, governance and regulation of educational sectors, the role of educational technology, the place of debt and funding regimes inside national education systems.

For Marcuse (1941), sublation or *Aufhebung* offers the possibility for a restoration of the contents of an object to its true form, rather than one fetishized and distorted inside capitalism. *In-against-beyond* therefore signals a transformation in self-identity, constructed historically and materially as internal relations—they are the transformed reflection of the self in relation to the object. This is the pivot for a renewal of ways of knowing and becoming in the world, actualized through doing and being. It is a constant movement of becoming, which resonates with the words of Marcos (2002, p. 321), 'The moral of the story, I repeat, is that all final options are a trap'. The centrality of this to Marx's own working methodology is in realizing the connection between self-knowing and a dialectical opening of the Self in relation to the world.

Of course, those who write so powerfully about abolition, for instance, of the police or prisons, situate this work in time and place, asking *around what do we organize* (Davis, 2016). Is this the school or college, the curriculum, the lived experiences of communities made marginal? How do we relate this, through our engagement with core Marxist concepts like alienated labor and estrangement, which structure our schools and colleges, curricula and lived experiences, against the demands of the commodity, private property and the division of labor? Moreover, how do we relate this engagement to the possibilities for self-knowing, rather than collapsing it simply into an analysis of symptoms or economic concepts (Marcuse, 1932)? Such engagement pushes beyond simply abolishing what-is, like schools or national curricula, and instead works as sublation or the positive abolition of the abstractions that structure human and nonhuman existence.

As a result, it is important to see this work of moving beyond, as a revelation of an ontological essence that refuses to be shaped by private property, commodity exchange and divisions of labor (Marx, 1844/1974). This is the detonation of the limitations of knowing, doing and being as they are defined by the compulsion to labor inside capital. Instead, it is a revelation that there exists the possibility for humans to relate freely to each other, rather than being condemned as one-sided labor-power. As a social and sensuous process, this carries the potential for self-actualization of the essence of what it means to be human, inscribed inside particular individuals as they relate to their rich differences with others, and the reality that these rich differences are universal.

As a process of self-education, this enables a richer contemplation of Self and Other, subject and object, and the world (rather than value) in motion, than that foreclosed upon in our stunted, individualized existences inside capitalism. Self-consciousness and self-actualization, as reflections of self-education, enable the particular to move beyond the preexisting conditions with which its existence is confronted and that shape its essence. This is a historical and material process of liberation, as a practical, dialectical working out. In Marx's (1844/1974) terms, it is a dialectic of negativity as a moving and generating principle, in which self-creation as an ongoing process is pivotal.

Following Marcuse (1941), education-as-praxis enables self-consciousness and self-actualization through continuous confrontation of the Self with its contradictions in the world, which can be taken up, superseded and transformed. Such continuous confrontation offers the potential for rupturing the abstract world imposed by capital, through realizing the particular, concrete and material experiences of those made marginal. There are constant possibilities here for alternative modes of world-making, which challenge the ontological and epistemological foreclosure of capitalist education (Meyerhoff, 2019).

Such challenges, enriched through the application of Marx's writing and methodology, and Marxist analyses to education, sit at the heart of this volume and generate its motive energy. They enable us to question the place of education in the liberation of the social individual from alienating wage labor, and from a world of social reproduction inside which alienation and estrangement normalize exploitation, expropriation and extraction. In this, it is important to push beyond the reduction of Marx's work to historical laws, and to point toward the potential for the autonomous creation of other futures through self-education, as knowing, doing and being in the world.

1.5 Overview of the *Handbook*

In *The Palgrave International Handbook of Marxism and Education*, we encourage readers to engage with Marx's work and Marxist traditions, by offering relevant, theoretically situated case studies from a range of international and interdisciplinary contexts. In this, we see our contributions connected to other writings on Marx and education in a range of series (see, for instance, Maisuria, 2022; Rasinski et al., 2017). In this *Handbook*, we demonstrate the relevance of thorough and precise engagements with emergent developments in Marxist theory from extant traditions and scholars, in both the Global South and North.

The intention of the *Handbook* is to develop a dialectical understanding of the interactions between the following.

- Marx's method for the critique of political economy and its abstract, organizing categories.
- Formal/informal educational structures, cultures and practices.
- Transnational and national governance, regulation and funding of education.
- Histories and geographies of educational development and change, for instance, in relation to corporate forms, the binaries of public/private education and issues of marketization and commodification.
- The lived experiences of education and the rich range of intersectional analyses continually rupturing critiques of education. These include the educational role of movements that center abolition, decolonizing, indigenous rights, critical feminism, queer studies, Black Lives Matter and Rhodes Must Fall.
- Established and practical work on alternative, ecological perspectives, including *buen vivir*, critical environmental education, environmental justice and the web of life.

This work proceeds in a spirit of openness and dialogue within and between various conceptions and traditions of Marxism from the South and North, and the ways in which explanatory categories and lived experiences can be brought into conversation. In this, the intention is for the *Handbook* to contribute to the development of Marxist analyses that push beyond established limits by engaging with fresh perspectives and views.

Thus, the studies collected here make three points. First, Marxist modes and characteristics of analysis need to be situated against the broad conceptual and historical contexts for educational critique. Second, tracking emerging currents in Marxism and education enables us to concretize the trajectories of issues that are rupturing education as a social good. Third, dialogues in Marxism and education are increasingly relevant for describing alternative conceptualizations of life. In interpreting Marx from a range of concrete, specified positions, we intend to model how others might generate analytical tools for themselves in their own contexts.

It is important to emphasize the focus here on a set of emergent issues in context, rather than on developing a standard genealogy or archaeology of Marxist categories as they apply to education. Thus, there is a deep engagement with issues of social justice, which brings Marx's categories into conversation with identity, environment, social reproduction and so on. The shape of our conversations around Marxism and education matters in a time that is itself shaped against crises and fragmentation, especially for those made marginal inside-and-against an alienating system of production.

Thus, we are reminded by Bannerji (2011, p. 56) that:

> Theorists of the left or Marxists have no reason to fear 'identity,' because there is enough ground in the works of Marx himself to create social movements that do not have to choose between culture, economy, and society or 'race,' class, and gender in order to organize politics of social revolution. Going beyond gestures of intersectionality, coalition, and social cohesion, Marxists have recourse to a non-fragmentary understanding of the social, which could change the world as we know it.

Critiquing universal ideas and concrete experiences of the social, and the abilities we have to remake the world as a movement of dignity that recognizes our unity-in-difference, uncovers a complex ecosystem of knowing, doing and being. Carpenter and Mojab (2011, p. 213) remind us of the challenges in working pedagogically through this, in terms of the reductionist 'rejection of Marxism as an economic determinism devoid of human agency and consciousness', 'the complex history of Marxist scholarship and activism and its relationship to questions of race, gender, sexuality, and identity' and the constant questioning of ways of knowing generated from subject positions made marginal. Fraser (2013) situates this against the distinction between 'injustices of distribution and injustices of recognition', as 'equally primary, serious, and real', and which demand eradication.

The point here is to elevate the deep, social and ecological fractures that are reproducing a disfigured world, inside which education is formalized or ruptured informally. The white, male factory worker of the North cannot stand-in for the hegemonic social subject, even while the self-exploiting, white, male entrepreneur of the North is used to define the characteristics of a productive life. Yet, there is a need to overcome internal divisions within those differentially exploited and expropriated by the capital-relation. How might struggles in/for education or over the general intellect/mass intellectuality draw us together inside-and-against injustices of distribution and recognition? How might we do this work with an open pedagogy, which, first, accepts that in a world of class fractions the development of hegemonic counter-positions is impossible and, second, enables mutuality and dignity as the revolutionary opportunity?

This draws us toward Mbembe's (2017, pp. 182, 183) critique of black reason, and the liberatory potential of working for restitution and reparation of 'the humanity stolen from those who have historically been subjected to processes of abstraction and objectification', 'based on the idea that each person is a repository of a portion of intrinsic humanity. This irreducible share belongs to each of us'. Mutuality and dignity refuse Western ontological idealism (Mignolo & Walsh, 2018), projected onto the world through settler colonialism and racial patriarchy.

Thus, the inflection and recalibration of our dialogues is manifold and moves us away from a one-sided critique, toward a many-sided critique, driven from, first, subaltern positions; second, the experiences of those in struggle over social reproduction; and, third, those fighting for a livable planetary web of life. In this historical moment, the relations between Marxism and education ask us to consider whether we can sublate the structuring alienations of whiteness, and instead 'live a true humanism—the humanism made to the measure of the world' (Césaire, 1972/2000).

Our intention is to respect and reflect this humanism, through the rich diversity of interpretation and applications of Marx in differing contexts. As a result, the chapters presented here weave the following.

1. Core organizing and explanatory categories used by Marxists, including abolition; abstract labor; abstraction; accumulation; alienation, class struggle; commodification; competition; dialectics; exploitation; expropriation; general intellect; historical materialism; human capital; labor-power; reproduction schemas; social reproduction; socially necessary labor time; struggle; and valorization.
2. Theoretical and conceptual discussions of the abolition of higher education; adult education; alienation and education; academic labor; the classroom; critical pedagogy; decolonizing the school; dialectical materialism; the educational commons; educational reforms; feminist pedagogies; financialization of education; fixed capital and infrastructures; green Marxism, eco-socialism and pedagogy; liberation theology and education; Marxist humanism and women of color; measurement in education; needs in the Capitalocene; onto-epistemologies and world changing; polytechnic education; queer Marxism as pedagogy; redistribution and public policy; research and commercialization in education; student movements; subsumption of education; workers' education; and value in education.
3. Contextual discussions from Australia, Bhutan, Brazil, Chile, Columbia, England, the European Union, Finland, India, Latin America, Mozambique, Poland, Romania, South America, Spain and the United States.

Thus, the *Handbook* has a rich set of chapters with coverage from authors based in, or writing about, Africa, Asia, Australasia, Europe, South America and North America.

In our structure, we have sought to group chapters loosely in three sections. Of course, all such divisions or separations are false, and many of the chapters have cross-cutting themes, or focus theoretically, or in-country or regional contexts, in ways that create links across sections. However, we have grouped them to give some conceptual organization, around the idea of being *in-against-beyond*, in order to develop a practical critique of capital's competitive dynamics and to imagine the world otherwise.

As a result, we have a set of 12 chapters that develop thinking around core terms like dialectical materialism, value, subsumption and alienation, and which set those up theoretically, or in relation either to specific areas of practice, like liberation theology and adult education, or to Marxist authors, like Althusser. These chapters are described as 'In: Marxist Modes and Characteristics of Analysis in Education'. They are followed by nine chapters that place critique in context, as being 'Against: Emerging Currents in Marxism and Education'. These chapters develop their analyses globally or regionally, in relation to key themes like financialization, decoloniality and green Marxism or environmentalism, and also by queering our engagement with Marxism or focusing on student movements. Finally, a set of eight chapters focus our attention 'Beyond: Marxism, Education and Alternatives'. These chapters lead us into dialogue with human needs and the idea of social reproduction, and thinking about these issues in public policy and HE. We deliberately end by discussing the world otherwise, in relation to feminist counter-geographies from the South, decolonial feminisms and a deep, relational activism.

This is important because, while the *Handbook* criticizes capitalist education and attempts to present the reader with perspectives for overcoming its alienating realities, it is also subject to its effects. In inviting authors and curating the chapters, sickness and work overload have disproportionately affected women and groups systemically made marginal. It grieves us that these invited voices are not present, because of the everyday realities of survival inside capitalism. This reiterates the importance of the work that we must undertake, of liberation through mutuality and dignity in action. It reiterates the importance of material and historical solidarity as a pedagogical process emanating from within and across society.

As such, a more diverse spread of chapters was commissioned but proved impossible to deliver. This would have included more work: from national liberation struggles in the Middle East and North Africa; in theory generated from sub-Saharan Africa; in the praxis of community struggles in alternative cultural systems, like that of India; and from the development of Marxism in China. Such analyses would also have drawn in thinkers not represented here in detail. However, we encourage readers to engage with our *Handbook* as a contribution to the rich archive detailing how Marx's work has been infused with concrete, material struggles. In so doing, we ask readers to reflect upon their own work in relation to what Marx and Engels (1846/1998, p. 57) called communism, which, as the infinite process of critique, is 'the real movement which abolishes the present state of things'.

Disclosure Statement The authors have no financial interest or benefit that has arisen from the direct applications of this research.

References

Accioly, I. (2020). The Attacks on the Legacy of Paulo Freire in Brazil: Why He Still Disturbs So Many? In S. Macrine (Ed.), *Critical Pedagogy in Uncertain Times: Hope and Possibilities* (2nd ed., pp. 117–138). Palgrave Macmillan.

Accioly, I. (2021). Reinventing Freire's Praxis in The Fight for Life with Dignity: Theoretical and Methodological Paths for Critical Educators. *Postcolonial Directions in Education*, *10*(2), 327–352.

Adorno, T. W. (1966). *Negative Dialectics* (E. B. Ashton, Trans.). Seabury Press.

Allen, A. (2017). *The Cynical Educator*. Mayfly Books.

Allman, P. (2007). *On Marx: An Introduction to the Revolutionary Intellect of Karl Marx*. Sense Publishers.

Andreotti, V. (2021). *Hospicing Modernity: Facing Humanity's Wrongs and the Implications for Social Activism*. North Atlantic Books.

Ball, S. (2012). *Global Education Inc.: New Policy Networks and the Neoliberal Imaginary*. Routledge.

Bannerji, H. (2011). Building from Marx: Reflections on 'Race,' Gender, and Class. In S. Carpenter & S. Mojab (Eds.), *Educating from Marx: Race, Gender, and Learning* (pp. 41–60). Palgrave Macmillan.

Bonefeld, W. (2014). Antisemitism and the Power of Abstraction: From Political Economy to Critical Theory. In M. Stoetzler (Ed.), *Antisemitism and the Constitution of Sociology* (pp. 314–332). University of Nebraska Press.

Carpenter, S., & Mojab, S. (2011). Epilogue: Living Revolution, Learning Revolution, Teaching Revolution. In S. Carpenter & S. Mojab (Eds.), *Educating from Marx: Race, Gender, and Learning* (pp. 211–225). Palgrave Macmillan.

Césaire, A. (1956/1969). *Return to My Native Land*. Archipelago Books.

Césaire, A. (1972/2000). *Discourse on Colonialism*. Monthly Review Press.

Chuǎng (n.d.). Red Dust: The Transition to Capitalism in China. Chuǎng, 2. Retrieved 27 March 2023, from http://chuangcn.org/journal/two/red-dust/

Davis, A. Y. (2016). *Freedom Is a Constant Struggle: Ferguson, Palestine and the Foundations of a Movement*. Haymarket Books.

Dowling, E. (2011). Pedagogies of Cognitive Capitalism – Challenging the Critical Subject. In M. A. Peters & E. Bulut (Eds.), *Cognitive Capitalism, Education and Digital Labour* (pp. 195–210). Peter Lang.

Dussel, E. (2012). *Ética da Libertação na idade da Globalização e da exclusão*. Vozes.

Camarades, *Action*, no. 1, 7 Mai 1968. In A. Feenberg (1999). *Questioning Technology*. Routledge.

Foster, J. B. (2017). The Long Ecological Revolution. *Monthly Review*, *69*(6). Retrieved March 27, 2023, from https://monthlyreview.org/2017/11/01/the-long-ecological-revolution/

Fraser, N. (2013). *Fortunes of Feminism: From State-Managed Capitalism to Neoliberal Crisis*. Verso.
Green, A. (2008). Marxism, Education and Dialogue. In A. Green, G. Rikwoski, & H. Raduntz (Eds.), *Renewing Dialogues in Marxism and Education: Openings* (pp. 11–31). Palgrave Macmillan.
Hall, R. (2015). The Implications of Autonomist Marxism for Research and Practice in Education and Technology. *Learning, Media and Technology, 40*(1), 106–122. https://doi.org/10.1080/17439884.2014.911189
Hall, R. (2021). *The Hopeless University: Intellectual Work at The End of The End of History*. Mayfly Books.
Holloway, J. (2010). Cracks and the Crisis of Abstract Labour. *Antipode, 42*(4), 909–923.
Holloway, J., Matamoros, F., & Tischler, S. (2009). Introduction. In J. Holloway, F. Matamoros, & S. Tischler (Eds.), *Negativity and Revolution: Adorno and Political Activism* (pp. 3–11). Pluto Press.
hooks, b. (1994). *Teaching to Transgress: Education as the Practice of Freedom*. Routledge.
Hudis, P. (2012). *Marx's Concept of the Alternative to Capitalism*. Brill.
Jappe, A. (2014). Towards a History of the Critique of Value. *Capitalism Nature Socialism, 25*(2), 25–37. https://doi.org/10.1080/10455752.2014.906820
Krader, L. (1974). *The Ethnographical Notebooks of Karl Marx. (Studies of Morgan, Phear, Maine, Lubbock)* (Transcr. and Ed., with an Introduction by L. Krader). Van Gorcum & Co.
Le Baron, B. (1971). Marx on Human Emancipation. *Canadian Journal of Political Science, iv*(4), 559–570.
Lebowitz, M. A. (2003). *Beyond Capital. Marx's Political Economy of the Working Class*. Palgrave.
Leher, R., & Accioly, I. (Eds.). (2016). *Commodifying Education: Theoretical and Methodological Aspects of Financialization of Education Policies in Brazil*. Sense Publishers.
Ma, Y., & Bennett, D. (2021). The Relationship Between Higher Education Students' Perceived Employability, Academic Engagement and Stress Among Students in China. *Education + Training, 63*(5), 744–762. https://doi.org/10.1108/ET-07-2020-0219
Maingard, J. L. (2019). Development and Empirical Evaluation of an Intention to Quit Structural Model for Teachers in South Africa. Unpub. M.Comm. Stellenbosch University. Retrieved March 27, 2023, from http://scholar.sun.ac.za/handle/10019.1/105934
Maisuria, A. (Ed.). (2022). *Encyclopaedia of Marxism and Education*. Brill.
Malm, A. (2016). *Fossil Capital: The Rise of Steam Power and the Roots of Global Warming*. Verso.
Malott, C. S., & Ford, D. R. (2015). *Marx, Capital, and Education: Towards a Critical Pedagogy of Becoming*. Peter Lang.
Marcos, S. (2002). *Our Word Is Our Weapon: Selected Writings*. Serpent's Tail.
Marcuse, H. (1932). The Foundation of Historical Materialism. Marxists.org. Retrieved March 27, 2023, from https://www.marxists.org/reference/archive/marcuse/works/historical-materialism/index.htm
Marcuse, H. (1941). *Reason and Revolution: Hegel and the Rise of Social Theory*. Routledge and Kegan Paul.
Marx, K. (1844/1974). *Economic and Philosophical Manuscripts*. Progress Publishers.

Marx, K. (1845). *Theses on Feuerbach*. Marxists.org. Retrieved March 27, 2023, from https://www.marxists.org/archive/marx/works/1845/theses/theses.htm
Marx, K. (1857/1993). *Grundrisse: Outline of the Critique of Political Economy*. Penguin.
Marx, K. (1867/2004). *Capital, Volume 1: A Critique of Political Economy*. Penguin.
Marx, K. (1875/1970). Critique of the Gotha Programme, in *Marx and Engels Selected Works*, 3, 13–30. Moscow: Progress Publishers.
Marx, K. (1894/1991). *Capital, Volume 3: A Critique of Political Economy*. Penguin.
Marx, K., & Engels, F. (1846/1998). *The German Ideology: Including Theses on Feuerbach and Introduction to the Critique of Political Economy*. Prometheus.
Marx, K., & Engels, F. (1848/2002). *The Communist Manifesto*. Penguin.
Mbembe, A. (2017). *Critique of Black Reason*. Wits University Press.
Mészáros, I. (2005). *Marx's Theory of Alienation*. Merlin Press.
Meyerhoff, E. (2019). *Beyond Education: Radical Studying for Another World*. University of Minnesota Press.
Meyerhoff, E., Johnson, E., & Braun, B. (2011). Time and the University, *ACME. An International E-Journal for Critical Geographies*, 10(3), 483–507.
Mignolo, W. D., & Walsh, C. E. (2018). *On Decoloniality: Concepts, Analytics, Praxis*. Duke University Press.
Moore, J. (2015). *Capitalism in the Web of Life: Ecology and the Accumulation of Capital*. Verso.
Movimento Studentesco (Ed.). (1968/2008). *Documenti della rivolta Universitaria*. Laterza.
Neary, M. (2020). *Student as Producer: How Do Revolutionary Teachers Teach?* Zero Books.
Nguyen, L. T., Dang, V. H., & Pham, H. T. (2022). The Effects of School Climate on High School Teacher Stress and Self-efficacy in Ho Chi Minh City. *Educational Psychology*. https://doi.org/10.1080/01443410.2022.2128054
Postone, M. (1993). *Time, Labor and Social Domination: A Reinterpretation of Marx's Critical Theory*. Cambridge University Press.
Postone, M. (2007). Critical Social Theory and the Contemporary World. *International Journal of Politics, Culture and Society*, 19, 69–79.
Rasinski, L., Hill, D., & Skordoulis, K. (Eds.). (2017). *Marxism and Education: International Perspectives on Theory and Action*. Routledge.
Rodney, W. (1973). *How Europe Underdeveloped Africa*. Tanzanian Publishing House.
Szadkowski, K. (2023). *Capital in Higher Education: A Critique of Political Economy of the Sector*. Palgrave Macmillan.
Thompson, E. P. (1967). Time, Work-Discipline and Industrial Capitalism. *Past and Present*, 38(1), 56–97. Retrieved March 27, 2023, from http://past.oxfordjournals.org/content/38/1/56.full.pdf
Wendling, A. E. (2009). *Karl Marx on Technology and Alienation*. Palgrave Macmillan.
Zajda, J. (2021). *Globalisation and Education Reforms: Creating Effective Learning Environments*. Springer.

CHAPTER 2

Marx, Materialism and Education

Richard Hall

2.1 Introduction: The Importance of Material History

How might we understand the essence of our existence in the world? How might we understand what capitalism does to that essence? This lies at the heart of Marx's attempts to relate: first, the philosophical to the political economic; and second, conceptions of the ideal/universal to the material/concrete. In so doing, his methodological process reveals a humane critique of labor inside capital, as a relation of exploitation, expropriation and extraction. For Marx, such relationality unfolds through concrete, material, historical practices, and connects us with ourselves, other humans and non-human animals, and the ecosystems and environments that enable us. These material practices bring us into relation with objects upon which we work, and that, inside capitalism, we seek to animate in very particular ways, to generate value.

This animation is a flow or a movement of our labor, as an activity that brings *both* our knowledges and ways of knowing the world, *and* our skills and expertise, to life. The ways in which we conceptualize and realize education lie at the heart of this laboring activity, enabling particular modes of educational production that have value, and foreclosing on others. Yet for Marx (1867/2004), it was empirically important for us to analyze our material practices, or labor, historically, and to resist the view that any one mode of production, like capitalism, might be definitive.

R. Hall (✉)
De Montfort University, Leicester, UK
e-mail: rhall1@dmu.ac.uk

© The Editor(s) (if applicable) and The Author(s), under exclusive license to Springer Nature Switzerland AG 2023
R. Hall et al. (eds.), *The Palgrave International Handbook of Marxism and Education*, Marxism and Education,
https://doi.org/10.1007/978-3-031-37252-0_2

Material practice cannot be analyzed 'independently of the particular form it assumes under given social conditions' (*ibid.*, p. 177), and this applies to schooling, teaching, learning and researching. By analyzing the resulting social formations in their historical entirety, their alienating realities might be overcome. Otherwise, we risk focusing our analysis on: first, finding solutions to the symptoms of those realities, like the mental health crisis amongst school children in the global North, and the chronic overwork reported by teachers; second, utopian thinking, for instance in fetishizing an idealized, former, golden age of schooling; and third, wishful thinking about educational utopias beyond capitalism.

In his material, historical analyses, Marx used specific moments pedagogically, for instance, the 1848 revolutions in Europe (in *The Communist Manifesto* (Marx & Engels, 1848/2002)), or the 1851 coup in France of Louis-Napoléon Bonaparte (*The Eighteenth Brumaire of Louis Napoleon* (Marx 1852)). They situate the energy of particular events against the deep, historical relations between: humans and nature in the direct process of the production of life; the process of the production of the social relations of life; and, the mental conceptions that flow from those relations (Marx, 1867/2004). He used this as an activist, journalist, and philosopher, to help working people reveal the logic of their existences.

Yet, Marx was clear about the limits to agency. The unfolding process of history is so deeply entwined in our ways of knowing, doing and being in the world, that people may:

> make their own history, but they do not make it as they please; they do not make it under self-selected circumstances, but under circumstances existing already, given and transmitted from the past. The tradition of all dead generations weighs like a nightmare on the brains of the living. (Marx, 1852)

Here, the role of ideas is crucial, but only in relation to material activity, or *doing* in the world. However, a broader examination of circumstances is fundamental in understanding how Marx conceptualizes human existence inside capitalism, and the ways in which it relates to an alienated human essence (Hall, 2018). This is in terms of: first, the concrete, material activities that humans undertake in the world and that reflect their existence (like classroom practices and relationships); and second, our more abstract conceptualizations of what that activity represents (like socially-defined ideals of good/bad teaching and learning). The flow between the concrete and the abstract is at the heart of the methodological movement of Marx's materialist critique.

In this flow, Postone's (1993) analysis of Marx's materialism as a critique of labor inside capital, which itself constructs deeply alienating-yet-entangled social relations, is important. Analyses of the movement of labor or capitalist work, through the control of labor-power as the key commodity that humans have to trade (Marx, 1867/2004), enable us to trace access to surplus-value, profit, and ultimately money (as commodity or capital), and the expansion of power and privilege. This is catalyzed in the alchemy between labor-power and: first, social skills/being, knowledge/knowing and expertise/doing (congealed inside the individual worker); and second, other means of production organized in specific ways (such as through the division of labor in research laboratories).

As a result, this particular, alchemical process of production, distils a surplus, for instance increased research income generated from knowledge exchange or commercialization. Yet, it also reveals entangled contradictions in our social relations, like great wealth co-existing with great misery, or opportunity for some with precarious prospects for others. Dialectical materialism is the methodological movement that promises an understanding of these processes and their imminent, entangled contradictions.

It is important to note that Marx did not use the term dialectical materialism, and that Engels (1886) engaged with the term materialist dialectics, stating:

> For dialectical philosophy nothing is final, absolute, sacred. It reveals the transitory character of everything and in everything; nothing can endure before it except the uninterrupted process of becoming and of passing away, of endless ascendancy from the lower to the higher.

Whilst, Kautsky, Plekhanov and Dietzgen later foregrounded an expanding analysis of Marx's methodological approach (Gorman, n.d.; Skordoulis, 2022), under Stalinist conceptions of dialectical and historical materialism, a positivist description of, and prescription for, the success of the proletarian revolution was to be enacted (Stalin, 1938). Education was central to this approach, through which a vanguard/Party could direct Marx's active subject in Nature (the proletariat), through its control of universal cognition (the ontological, revolutionary meaning of socialism). Working people could then have their concrete existences directed, as a form of predefined, revolutionary curriculum.

Others held to a less positivist and metaphysical view of dialectics and dialectical materialism. Following Lenin, Ilyenkov (1979/1982, p. 12) argued that dialectics emerges historically, in relation to its social context, and was 'the "soul of Marxism"… The logic of cognition of Marx and Engels'. It is crucial to recognize that this logic was not of dialectics in general, but the dialectics of capital. This recognizes Marx's (1894/1991, p. 205) position that humans must understand the historical and situated 'Relationship between the surface, finished pattern of economic relations, and the ways in which these are understood, in relation to the inner, essential and concealed core concepts.' For instance, we might situate the practices of educators in the context of the historical, contextual construction of teaching for specific social ends.

The flow between concrete and abstract centers dialectics as an immanent process, and one of transcendence (*aufhebung* or sublation). As concrete, educational experiences are constructed and revealed, they are brought into relation, including conceptually, and qualitative movements or shifts in social ideas or constructions can be enacted, as universal concepts are ruptured. For Hegel (2018), this was the negation of what-was by what-is, as a process that abolishes the former, whilst also preserving and transcending it within a new consciousness. It is a qualitative shift, revealed, for example, in how to fund higher education, or in changes to the social purpose of national curricula.

However, Marx's analysis reveals the limited capacity for sublation emerging from the one-sidedness of concrete experiences inside capitalism, for instance, as humans are compelled to perform as students, teachers or workers. Understanding one's material activity as representative of this one-sidedness gives the possibility for transcending the alienating abstraction of humans, who are only fit to labor (as an activity) or to develop their labor-power (as a commodity that can generate surplus). Thus, transcendence demands a reconnection with Lenin's focus upon 'the organic unity' of life, which:

> Arms the cognition of [humans] with the means and ability to construct an objectively-true image of the surrounding world, the means and ability to reconstruct this world in accordance with the objective tendencies and lawful nature of its own development. (Ilyenkov, 1979/1982, p. 1)

Here, the work of Hegel (2018), and in particular his *Phenomenology*, is central the understanding of Marx, Lenin, Luxemburg, Mao, and others (Dunayevskaya, 1991, 2002). For Hegel, consciousness, self-consciousness, and reason could be understood as positive, deterministic, and objective. Moving beyond this, Marx claims to stand Hegel's methodological approach the right way up, by beginning from and working towards analyzing the individual and their particular experience on its own terms, rather than from universal or ideal constructions. In the 1873 postface to *Capital*, Marx (1867/2004, p. 103) is clear about the importance of moving beyond Hegel's mystification of the idea or ideal of Absolute Reason and Spirit, and re-centering the 'rational kernel [of life from] within its mystical shell'.

This chapter will wrestle with Marx's re-centering of the rational kernel, in order to understand how dialectical materialism helps us to analyses the social, historical unfolding of knowing, doing and being. It will highlight the tensions and contradictions between identity and non-identity, and how this is reproduced educationally and pedagogically in historically-contingent ways. Such contingency connects to the lived experiences of individuals, communities and ecosystems, suffering at the intersection of political economic, socio-cultural, and ecological catastrophes. Here, we must be mindful of Adorno's (1966, p. 197) adage that 'You have to work out the dialectic for your age; you can't just "apply" it'.

2.2 Social and Sensuous

As a process, dialectical materialism integrates multiple positions in relation to materiality, idealism and storytelling or lived experiences. It refuses to view human activity as innately governed by a universal view of reason, governed by an idealized and objective truth. For instance, it helps to critique policy that situates educational activity against an abstract, universal ideal of the entrepreneurial teacher or student, responsible to society for their ability to generate value. It is important to consider dialectical materialism in opposition to universal abstractions, as a deeply relational, ontological, process of *social* formation. This enables humans to constitute themselves: first, as socially and historically 'objective', able to take a standpoint on objects like the school or curriculum; and, second, as practical beings, able to analyses their subjectivity against that of the Other, or in the world where their being, doing and knowing materialize.

Dialectical materialism is a revolutionary methodology (Neary, 2020), able to uncover the reproductive heart of the social formation of capital, and illuminate the potential for agency, praxis and liberation. In *Capital*, Marx (1867/2004, p. 409) describes this formation as a process of constant revolution, driving production 'beyond natural barriers and prejudices... [for] the development of the forces of production, the expansion of needs, the all-sided development of production, and the exploitation and exchange of natural and mental forces.' It is 'a total, connected process... [that] also produces and reproduces the capital-relation itself: on the one hand the capitalist, on the other the wage-labourer' (*ibid.*, p. 724). Education is a crucial moment inside this expansive process of production, in relation to: technological and organizational forces; consumption and needs; all-sided developments in the division of labor and property rights; and, the place of Nature and culture.

Marx's materialist dialectics reveals capital's energy, emerging from social, historical and material processes that shine a light upon the systemic reification 'of production relations among people' (Rubin, 1972, p. 24). Such reification gives primacy to the abstract/ideal, rather than to concrete experiences, and enshrines capitalist social relations as natural and transhistorical. Thus, hegemonic schooling helps it to operate as a mysterious, totalizing system, which can be made more efficient but never abolished, with an internal logic that appears to be its own beginning and end, and where the production of commodities for surplus (or value) is the defining characteristic.

For Clarke (1991, p. 54), reification is represented by the abstract individual, whose specific, 'social qualities are concealed behind a property relation between the individual and a thing'. So, particular teachers are measured against this abstract individual, in terms of their performance or the social utility of their educational labor-power. Marx (1867/2004, p. 166) reiterates this objectification and dehumanization, in relation to fetishism:

> To the producers, therefore, the social relations between their private labours appear as what they are, i.e. they do not appear as direct social relations between persons in their work, but rather as material relations between persons and social relations between things.

So, the teacher's relation to their students is realized as the fetish of accreditation or learning gain, which can be exchanged, socially, as a commodity in the labor market, or to gain access to new educational opportunities. Social, classroom relations are value-driven and anti-human, as opposed to values-driven and humane. At issue is deconstructing these historically-developed, social relations, in order to understand the forces behind the social reproduction of the classroom, rather than the narrow, economic interests that appear to do so (Lukács, 1968).

This understanding is important in the development of dialectical materialism as a revolutionary and pedagogical methodology, which pushes beyond any determinism of an economic base supporting a superstructure of political and civil society (Engels, 1890). Capitalism seeks to define particular economic relations as the totality of social relations, and mobilize the potential energy of humans around its kinetic needs. Yet, in revealing the production of life as social, historical and material, it also becomes possible to respect difference and define a new moment of sociability. This applies to the expressions of the many-sided nature of the human essence across social contexts, the uneven colonization of this essence by the capital-relation, and the range of contradictions and struggles that ensue.

Such contextual and historical unevenness means that we must think about dialectical materialism in relation to the motion of tendencies and their relations, rather than the idealism of abstract laws. Thus, sensuous, social motion, as the movement of knowing, doing and being in the world, might be framed in relation to matter, the worker, or value in society (Nail, 2020), but it might also enable alternative, indigenous stories to shine (Andreotti, 2021; Smith, 2018). As a result, the dialectics of movement between objects and subjective action, framed individually and collectively, shapes a social formation that could, potentially, be repurposed. This is the revolutionary potential of dialectical materialism—as the revelation of social contingency and other worlds.

In the movement of such revelation, Marx's dialectics can be framed against his earlier works, in *The Economic and Philosophical Manuscripts* (Marx, 1844/1974), the *Theses on Feuerbach* (Marx, 1845/1998), and *The German Ideology* (Marx & Engels, 1846/1998), to focus upon *sensuous* human practice and sense-experience. This is an all-round, multi-sensory appreciation of the objects of need or desire, which include: Self in the world; Other(s); objects of labor; Nature and non-human animals; and, ecosystems. It enables an opening-out of understanding, beyond an empirical, systematizing and transhistorical view of existence. Enabling an engagement with past, present and future, as well as with people, place, philosophy, values, communities, axiologies, cosmologies, this offers 'relational accountability' (Wilson, 2008, p. 77). Such revolutionary practice, as knowing, doing and being, pushes beyond the economism of orthodox interpretations of human existence, towards a personal and collective re-engagement with the entanglements of appearance and essence, Self and Other, and subject and object. This is the challenge that storytelling as a living critique brings to the domination of value over human and non-human life.

Moreover, sensuous human practice points towards the integration of materialism and idealism, and analyses that refuse settler-colonial and racial-patriarchal narratives. This includes the ways in which social reproduction, reimagined through feminist critique, sits in dialectical relation with production, and how they are mutually constitutive (Federici, 2019; Fraser, 2013, 2016; Katz, 2001). In negating economic determinism, and the idea that the economy stands-in for all existence, this describes the qualities of non-labor as the reality for most of human and non-human life. Thus, understanding how human practice is historically- and socially-emergent, with an evolutionary metabolism (Skordoulis, 2022, p. 197), requires an unfolding, pedagogical analysis denied within commodified, capitalist schooling. This is in line with Marx's later, ethnographic work, which centered the transcendent potential of personal and collective, sense-experience of the world (Krader, 1974), as the non-identity of capitalism's colonization of the human.

2.3 Negativity: Identity and Non-identity

The Unity of Opposites

Dunayevskaya (1991) noted that at the core of dialectical practice lay the unity of opposites, and the relationship between the subject and the object. For any human subject, that object, for instance, as a classroom relationship with another, a curriculum artefact, or one's own workload, reveals oppositions within the Self. In understanding the relationship between subjects and objects, tensions, contradictions and alignments are revealed as internal relations, either visible to or hidden from the subject. Here, Adorno (1966, p. 31) saw dialectics as the ongoing, failed attempt to integrate the object: effectively, the non-identity of the subject and object, or the non-identity of the subject's internal relations with the object.

This negative dialectics articulates how capitalism constantly seeks the abolition of the individual through their integration, as objectified labor, with *it* as the self-actualizing subject. Thus, for Adorno (*ibid.*, p. 393) it is crucial to move beyond a positive critique of what-is, as an attempt to overcome/negate the insufficiency of the object in relation to the subject. Trying to address insufficiency through idealized blueprints, recommendations or utopias that lie beyond capitalism is delusional thinking, which cannot escape its context as work, for-value. Instead, we require a relentless restating of the insufficiency of the objective world in providing for human needs, as the non-identity of our (one-sided) material existence with our (many-sided) humane essence. This restating demands that humans and their practices are able to critique their lack of freedom, in relation to all of the objects of capitalist society, and the relations with the Self that flow from them.

Here, it is useful to reiterate that Marx regarded activity and phenomena in capitalist society as both concrete/material and abstract/social. So, the production of an essay, *both* creates a concrete, material artefact, *and* reproduces an abstract, social relation between: the student and their tutor; the student and their awarding institution; the student and society; and, the student and their idealization of their Self. Thus, the relationship between the student and their essay contains a range of internal relations, and reveals the estranged nature of human subjectivity/identity. Estrangement is an outcome of the non-identity between the individual (who appears one-sidedly as a student) and the thing (their objectified grade, teacher or institution), and the ways in which the latter comes to dominate the former. This opposition is framed negatively because the concrete abilities of individuals (for instance, in generating impact from research) can never completely match the abstract, socially-necessary labor-time against which they are compelled to produce (Dunayevskaya, 1991). Moreover, it is a one-sided estrangement of the Self-in-society, which denies self-actualization.

At the core of this lies Marx's focus on alienated labor, in relation to labor-power, the objects of labor, the Self, and species-being (the essence of what it means to be human) (Hall, 2018). This analysis is predicated upon a complex network of internal relations, within which particular elements of the world congeal or become, in relationship to other elements (Sayer, 1987). Each subject comes to itself in any one instance (for example, as student, tutor, librarian, technician), in direct relation to an object (for example, an assessment, research impact, catalogue, new technology) that is itself constituted out of a set of internal relations, including particular skills, capabilities and knowledges. Through the alchemical reaction of these shifting relations, subjects are in constant transformation, and 'are developed in their historical or logical process of formation' (Engels, 1894/1991, p. 103). Whilst this is fixed inside capitalism through ideals of productivity, entrepreneurship, and so on, a negative critique highlights that human subjectivity is, in reality, epistemologically and ontologically open-ended (Engels, 1883/1987).

In his reflections on Lenin's dialectics, Ilyenkov (1979/1982) emphasized the (non-)identity of concrete/material practices in relation with abstract/social forms, in order to analyze the (congruent or tense) relationship between individual/particular experiences and universal conceptions. So, one might elevate the contradictions and tensions between the experiences of those made marginal in education (queer, Black, indigenous, feminist, intersectional) and curricula imposed by those in power, which represent universal determinations (of universal, subject positions like student, tutor, worker). Understanding these particular/universal positions in opposition enables social and historical contradictions to be voiced and worked through in practice, as an attempt to sublate the negative relation and non-identity between subject and object. In opening-up the internal relations between identity and non-identity of subject and object lies the possibility for recovering the characteristics of a shared, common humanity *with* the world and its ecosystems. Here, Ilyenkov (*ibid.*) stressed Lenin's focus upon quantitative, concrete experiences expressed in abstract, qualitative terms, and that those experiences might coalesce into a new qualitative understanding. This new understanding, whilst categorical, is also deeply relational. Such relationality opens-up the potential for a politics centered on unity-in-difference.

One outcome is a refusal to deduce or induce fixed characteristics of things or concepts, for instance, of effective classroom practices or pedagogic theories. These have to be seen dialectically in relation, against the internal relations that construct the Self in the classroom, in order to prescribe another world beyond the Self. *Pace* Ilyenkov (*ibid.*), a subject (student/teacher) cannot be understood in relation to an object (essay), rather in relation to themselves reflected through the negative relation they have to that object. The logic of an individual's experience, as a student, technician or professor, is the aggregation of objects and their internal relations, expressed historically and concretely against universal, social definitions of those roles.

A Movement of Contradictions

For Lenin, this was a process of scientific abstraction, which unfolded socially through new conceptual understandings, grounded historically and logically. Thus, the revelation of marginalized experiences inside universities in the global North uncovers negative relations with those institutions in their reproduction of coloniality (Andreotti, 2021). These experiences reveal the aggregation of characteristics and objects, described and experienced: first, negatively in relation to universalized norms and ideals; and second, positively in relation to alternative conceptualizations of the world.

Ilyenkov (1979/1982) defines this in terms of logical development of critique, grounded in concrete historicism. Here, universal concepts are in movement, tension and contradiction with direct, material and sensuous observation, rather than emerging from events or ideas that preceded it. This also enables the revelation of contradictions between how things appear in the world and their essence. Contradictions describe things in-capitalism/for-value with the potential to be things for-themselves. The process of sublation offers a way of overcoming these contradictions, and for generating ways of knowing that are more socially appropriate. This is a movement of reality, which resolves in a new form of expression:

> Expressed objectively, the goal lies in tracing, through analysis of new empirical materials, the emergence of reality in which an earlier established contradiction finds its relative resolution in a new objective form of its realisation. (Ilyenkov *ibid.*)

Whilst Capital puts this motion to use to drive the expansion of the universe of value, Lenin (1894, pp. 141–42) demonstrated that through a dialectical method, Marx 'showed the whole capitalist social formation to the reader as a living thing'. This opens-up the potential to refuse its metabolism, once we uncover how forms of capitalist education emerge inside-and-against the ideological, political, legal, and scientific relations and contradictions that are immanent within them. For example, we might trace the construction of student fee regimes, not in terms of their colonization by a rentier economy, but in their immanent relation to debt, deduced from the contradictions of concrete life as they relate to the wider, social reproduction/expansion of capital and the universe of value. Such a deeper analysis offers space and time to refuse to feed the political economy of capitalism rather than its symptoms.

Dunayevskaya (1991, p. 93) was clear that Marx's dialectical method points away from describing absolutes that are syntheses of history and philosophy, theory and practice, subject and object (*pace* Hegel), towards analyzing concrete crises grounded in contradiction. It refuses scientific essentialism and the triumph of reason, in the face of crises of political economy, climate forcing, ocean acidification, and so on. Such reason denies the 'need to let suffering speak [as] a condition of all truth' (Adorno, 1966, p. 17). Instead, Marx's method focuses upon total diremptions, or 'absolute, irreconcilable contradictions of technical base and social character, of accumulation and misery, of dead labour and living labour' (Dunayevskaya, 1991, p. 93).

Thus, for Marx (1844/1974) it was vital to see this moving dynamic as the unfolding self-production of human beings, incorporating the internalized relation of opposites that brings the particular into relation with the universal. In this relation, emancipation and many-sided self-production is the potentiality imminent in the contradiction between identity and non-identity. Emerging as a deliberate act of sublation, this pushes beyond the false consciousness of attempts to identify with an abstract Universal identity that appears to have power (Lenin, 1981).

Storytelling as Emancipation

Instead, emancipatory self-production is generated dialectically, through 'the consistent consciousness of nonidentity' (Adorno, 1966, p. 5), which brings material suffering and disenchantment into relation with their estrangement from the objects of their needs. This is crucial in thinking dialectically about intersectional experiences in education, for instance the construction of structures, cultures and practices against particular identities, which reduce some to passive subjects. Here, there have been critiques of Marxist, dialectical orthodoxy, which themselves center the agency and subjectivity of a white, revolutionary proletariat, standing in opposition to a bourgeoisie constructed conceptually and historically as a thing of whiteness (Robinson, 2001; Thompson, 2022). Bringing determinations of race into an understanding of identity and non-identity brings current struggles into relation with contexts of coloniality, which themselves shape the materiality of schools and universities (Césaire, 1972/2000).

Here, storytelling has been articulated as a rich methodological approach for relating particular, Black, feminist subjectivities to historical consciousness, in order to overcome the abstractions of class-based identities and communities. This points towards new modes of agency beyond the contradictions imposed by these intersections (Ahmed, 2017; Hull, 1982). For Hull and Smith (1982, p. xxiv) this is revealed dialectically inside universities:

> it is important for Black women teaching in the white-male Academy always to realize the inherently contradictory and antagonistic nature of the conditions under which we do our work. These working conditions exist in a structure not only elitist and racist, but deeply misogynist.

There is no struggle to integrate Black, feminist identities into a universal identity. Rather the struggle is the contradiction between the identity of Black, female, working class academics into contradiction and universal, white, male, bourgeois ideals of academic production. This is the struggle for universal liberation and autonomy, as the outcome of an imminent process that sublates 'our specific economic situation as Black women' (The Combahee River Collective, 1977). The work is to negate, abolish and transcend that situation, as a generative, unfolding process.

Mbembe (2017) echoes this, arguing that identity and non-identity bring Blackness into relation with a non-Black universal, not in order to reify the signifier 'Black' but to move through and beyond it. Through the movement of identity and non-identity, we might know the world otherwise (Andreotti, 2021), or use this practical, methodological and negative dialectics to constitute 'a radical structural hate for what the world has become' (Neary, 2017). Either way, negative dialectics, as a representation of the suffering of identity in its relationship to non-identity, presents the potential for the deepening of sensuous, subjective practice with the object and the other, as a process of reaching towards many-sided humanity.

2.4 A Practical Methodology Grounded Epistemologically and Ontologically

The Relationship Between Consciousness and Practical Experience

In his *Theses on Feuerbach*, Marx (1845/1998) reflected upon the movement of objectivity as a practical, rather than a theoretical question. What is perceived by bourgeois society as the truth is simply 'the this-sidedness of [ ] thinking in practice', because comprehension of practice is historically-constructed by the individual, situated socially. In working with this social reality, dialectics forms a practical methodology, through which critique analyses of the movements of interconnected, individual objects that define and are defined against a specific historical moment (Marx, 1885/1992).

In generating agency, reflexivity is crucial in understanding the this-sidedness of thinking in practice. This enables self-reflection upon one's actual, life-process as a social activity, and how the individual makes themself for society, whilst being conscious that they are social beings (Marx, 1844/1974). In capitalism, the general consciousness of being a productive, responsible, social being dominates and restricts the educational activity of humans against discourses of value-for-money, efficiency, entrepreneurship, impact, and so on. These are then reinforced through governance, regulation and funding that set a historical tempo for classroom labor, but which are also reproduced by that labor. As Marx (1867/2004, p. 361) notes 'Labour is the living, form-giving fire; it is the transitoriness of things, their temporality, as their formation by living time.'

This focus upon practical activity embeds materialism within the dialectic, and anchors Marx's (1845/1998, pp. 569–70) thesis 'that circumstances are changed by [humans]', and that 'the educator [themself] must be educated.' In the *Economic and Philosophical Manuscripts* (Marx, 1844/1974), he argues that to be meaningful, education must be reflexive, focused upon human activity that is socially-useful, rather than being one-sided and destructive of life. Practical activity enables a more humane, epistemological and ontological engagement with the world, such that knowing the world and organizing oneself within it can move beyond idealization or rationalization. Marx's methodological approach pushes beyond the fragmentary analysis enabled by subject specialisms, as enabled inside universities or national curricula. Instead, his scientific method is grounded in concrete, many-sided, self-education.

In this method, there is no ahistorical, ontological reality, or universal set of disciplinary concepts waiting to be discovered. There is simply an emergent, methodological, epistemological and ontological dialectics, predicated upon dynamic interactions and sense-making. The epistemological and ontological underpinnings of this dialectics shape the critique of the production of one-sided thinking and feeling, and offer the potential to know the world otherwise. As a result, it cannot be stated that Marx and Engels were economistic in their analyses of social totality (Engels, 1890). Instead, they shaped ways of knowing the world through which 'It is not the consciousness of [humans] that determines their being, but, on the contrary, their social being that determines their consciousness' (Marx, 1859).

Ilyenkov (1979/1982, p. 15) developed this in relation to Lenin's thinking, noting that we must move beyond simply acknowledging the existence of an external world that can be recognized and categorized, towards a materialist, objective reality that is given to us in sensation. This is the basis of a dialectical, materialist theory of knowledge, which seeks to overcome the contradictions between matter/object and consciousness/subject. Here, the roles of teachers, mentors, peers and friends, connected to ancestors, form a social consciousness that is in relation with individual consciousness. This is social consciousness forged from social being, doing and knowing, and it shapes an epistemology grounded in the activity of thought, and at the same time, the thought of activity. Ontologically, individual consciousness is organized in relation to itself as it is reflected in its negative relation to social consciousness. Yet. it is always integrating itself socially, materially and historically, through movement.

This practical methodology is in opposition to post-structural analyses of linguistics and signs, through which language might be taken as the starting point for a theory of knowledge. For Ilyenkov (*ibid.*, p. 16) this avoids an illusory idealism, based upon sign-symbolic variation. Instead, dialectical materialism brings individual consciousness and being into a dependent and mutually-constitutive relationship with social consciousness and being, and to perceptions of objective reality in the external world, given to humans through sensuous, practical activity.

The Practicality of Social Entanglements

Again, Marx (1857/1993) argues that his scientific method for knowing and organizing the world takes concrete activity by the subject as the concentration of relations with the object. As such, it enables the unity of diverse determinations, as *both* the result of *and* the departure point for knowing, doing and being in the world. Here, concrete activity yields universal understandings about human practice (abstract determinations based upon internal relations), alongside further concrete practices, as ways of knowing the world are sublated. For instance, the production of alternative education projects inside social movements yields abstract understandings about the structural conditioning of formal schooling. They are produced against that structural conditioning as a form of social consciousness and being. Yet this is also a departure point for the practical relations that emerge between such projects and the State/transnational organizations seeking to regulate education for profit/surplus.

Thus, we might situate an authentic understanding of academic or educational labor, against concrete relations and activities, defined historically. This is in terms of that labor as an abstract, organizing category, and in its manifold, concrete forms (as student, professional services, casualized academic, tenured professor, and so on). Yet again, this critique needs to center those identities and communities made marginal inside capitalism, in order to generate validity in our understanding of the (negative) relations that constitute consciousness and being, both individually and socially. Here, Motta (2018) argues that the white, masculine, bourgeois subject has become the pinnacle of knowing-subjectivity, able to label the world. As a result, those whose identities are forged against this abstract determination, but whose appearance does not reflect its core characteristics, are expected to remove elements of their essence, and to become non-beings.

Non-being is ontologically and epistemologically crucial in reproducing capitalist social relations. However, its revelation also offers potential to decenter and dismantle whiteness, and its desire/need to objectify and mark other humans as Other. Revealing the lived experiences of non-being is pedagogically crucial in illuminating the historical, material violence of the relations of domination and exploitation that flow through whiteness as a universal, organizing concept (Mbembe, 2017). Here, we might analyze decolonizing schooling or the University against non-being. Is decolonizing a concrete, practical attempt to dismantle whiteness, and to create a universal humanity, grounded in a storied epistemology that helps us to know the world beyond capital? How does non-being or non-identity work negatively to sublate abstracted and epistemically-foreclosed modes of knowledge production? Can the internal relations of non-being help us to define an ontology beyond the fetishized reproduction of identities for-value?

Such questions contains a radical openness to the entanglements of knowing, doing and being, between humans and the World. They are predicated upon the epistemological authenticity of counter-narratives, and the ontological validity of others as sensuous humans. This also digs deeper into the social consciousness of the land in its fullness or full flourishing, witnessed as *abya yala*, and the relationality between place, ancestors, stories, and responsibilities (Carola, 2017). It refuses to categorize the Other (including non-human animals and the environment) as an object that is less-than (Mignolo & Walsh, 2018), and instead builds relations from the 'pluriversality of nonlinear co-existences' (Amawtay Wasi Pluriversity, 2023).

Marx demonstrated in his *Ethnographic Notebooks* (Krader, 1974) how the historical realities of communities and societies defined non-capitalistically, or struggling against their formal subsumption inside capitalist social relations, might enable us to imagine other worlds. This sits in contradiction with the ontological and violent denial of humanity of the University, and its disciplinary desires for objective knowledge production, and epistemic foreclosure.

2.5 AGAINST THE VIOLENCE OF EPISTEMIC FORECLOSURE

Dialectical materialism is situated against what Marx (1867/2004, p. 406) called 'the abstract materialism of natural science that excludes history and its process.' Instead, his method was open, infusing idealism with materialism, and enabling us to see openings with indigenous, anti-racist, gendered, queer struggles and storytelling (Robinson, 2001). Yet, the unfolding of capitalist social relations tends to reduce our manifold or many-sided ways of knowing the world towards dominant forms of knowledge production. The power of these forms then tends to essentialize the idea of objective knowledge or the truth.

Lukács (1968) argued that such essentialized, objective knowledge, and the belief in the disciplinary methodologies that enable its birth, are fundamental to the survival of the bourgeoisie. He argues that they project their existence onto one-sided, scientific rationality, born inside atomized disciplines. Such disciplines and their methodologies foreclose upon a dialectical analysis of the internal, object relations of bourgeois society. Instead, they connect to a fetishism of data-driven policy, evidenced-based practice, the primacy of science, and a rarefied scientific method. This negates both the historical grounding from where subjects emerge, and 'a self-knowledge which would inevitably make that society appear problematic to itself' (Lukács, 1968, p. 228).

For Adorno (1966, pp. 20–1), we must address this negatively, in that the development of enclosed, academic disciplines represent bourgeois attempts to produce order from the objects that they could not integrate inside themselves. The reduction of human practice and existence to disciplinary methods or norms inside schools, colleges and universities, enables very particular constructions of who is Subject and who is Other. For Thompson (2022, p. 31) this represents the oppressive grammar of the West, and shapes an antidialectical or non-dialectical approach.

In developing resistances, some analyses situate hegemonic, disciplinary narratives against material and historical realities of slavery and capital, for instance, in terms of: ecology (Ferdinand, 2022); geology (Yusoff, 2018); medicine (Downs, 2021); and physics (Prescod-Weinstein, 2021). This also resonates inside critiques of ideas like decolonizing the University, which are enclosed within institutionalized language of anti-racism and can become stuck (for instance in arguing about cancel culture, woke agendas and academic freedom), as ideas divorced from the material history of social struggle.

Against such positions, Marx (1856) argued that scientific disciplines emerge alongside and contribute to particular social relations, technologies and modes of organizational development, mental conceptions of the world, legal and administrative forms, and so on. As a result:

> [a]t the same pace that [hu]mankind masters nature, [the individual] seems to become enslaved to other [humans] or to [their] own infamy. Even the pure light of science seems unable to shine but on the dark background of ignorance. All our invention and progress seem to result in endowing material forces with intellectual life, and in stultifying human life into a material force.

As human life is stultified into a material force lacking intellectual, creative capacity, capitalism comes to reify empiricism or the process of valorization of empirical evidence or data. This negates the process of producing life materially and historically, and fetishizes objective truth as an idealized end-state. As a result, intellectual labor seeks to fix objects through classification, and for universal, utilitarian use, independent of consciousness (Ilyenkov, 1979/1982).

Thus, as Yazzie Burkhart (2004, p. 26) argues, 'Western intellectual activity places in our heads in the clouds, and forgets where our feet are placed', *both* in the land and in historically-constituted relations. Instead, dialectical materialism enables concrete movements, for instance of Black feminism and queer ecology, to become entangled with critiques of political economy. Entanglements bring together and grounds identity and non-identity, and the universal and the material, thereby generating a recognition of the many-sided, epistemically-open, realities of sensuous, social production.

An open recognition follows Lenin in situating dialectical materialism as a means of remembering and understanding the world beyond the forms given by specific disciplines (Ilyenkov, 1979/1982, pp. 61–2). What is required is a deepening of our collective understanding of the interconnections between: first, the form of materialism, as concrete, scientific ideas about the physical world, entangled with natural-philosophical generalizations about those ideas (defined historically and in practice); and second, the essence of materialism, as the recognition that objective reality exists independent of human cognition and is reflected against that cognition (and that this cognition is developed sensuously and historically). As a result, dialectical practice deepens human understanding about Self and Other, subject and object, cognition and the world.

This deepening is the moving spirit of dialectical materialism, defined as anti-essentialist, precisely because it demonstrates how the universal/abstract and the particular/concrete presuppose each other. Opening-out difference and contradiction, as the entangled threads of common, material existence, refuses to dissolve them inside universal abstractions. Opening-out is a process of accepting the many-sided, concrete experience of the material world, so that the object (as Other) cannot be excluded, willed-away, reified or controlled through scientific endeavor that reflects capitalist rationality. Storytelling or revelation about these concrete experiences enables a heterogeneous formation of humankind, inclusive of difference (Ciccariello-Maher, 2016).

For Marcuse (1967), this opening-out is a function of an embodied dialectic, through which antagonism, contradiction, struggle, sublation or transformation occur organically and biologically inside individuals. It is immanent, within us and our relations, and storytelling and witnessing enable both an understanding of dialectical unfolding, and connections between philosophy and political economy that challenge foreclosed and arrogant, disciplinary methods for uncovering objective truth (Andreotti, 2021; Rizvi, 2022). As Evans-Winters (2019, p. 23) notes, 'our "truths" must be validated from within, with less concern for how outsiders legitimate (or receive and perceive) our assertions'. This is shaped through the revolutionary unfolding of the world.

2.6 Conclusion: Dialectical Materialism as an Unfolding Movement

Marx, like Hegel, looks at an object in its movement, and seeks to understand the relationship between its appearance and its essence, or its becoming, through the full range of its internal relations with the world. Objects are never static, and can never be explained simply in relation to a physical cause. This is why the reduction of the educational world to ideals of student, teacher, manager, consultant, policy adviser, expected to embody impact, excellence, entrepreneurialism, exchange, are so deeply problematic. It is also why the expansion of the conception of the student through a process of becoming, like student-as-producer (Neary, 2020), is so important.

Dialectical materialism as the analysis of relations at the level of the individual, concrete object, contains revolutionary potential. As it defines the characteristics of those individual objects operating as a unity (Sayers, 2015), this is a deeply revelatory and pedagogical process, where subjects become open to deep self-reflection. The student or teacher is a unity that congeals an assemblage of internal relations in a particular historical moment, from a particular historical perspective. This means that it is possible to see new phenomena or characteristics emerging from new assemblages or from different perspectives, in the aggregate of objects interacting essentially (i.e. internally) (*ibid.*, p. 26). One result of this is that characteristics that congeal as student employability or teacher entrepreneurialism, might be actualized through a range of other social relations. They might be negated, abolished and transformed (sublated) for other worlds.

This process of sublation is, as Hegel (2010, p. 259) articulated, changeable and transient, as such constructions and associations are neither eternal nor inseparable. As such, dialectical materialism, as a method, teaches us that our critique is also neither eternal nor inseparable. Rather, the unfolding or movement of that critique in its essential relations to the world is the heart of the matter of knowing, doing and being (Hegel, 1942). This aligns with Mao's unity of materialist dialectics with epistemology, in studying the movement of nature and society, and the tendencies (Mao says laws) of this motion, as it is reflected more profoundly and more extensively in the mind of humanity (Dunayevskaya, 1991).

As an unfolding, epistemological process, Nail (2020, pp. 13–15) refers to kinetic dialectics and a new materialism, which reflects that matter is active and creative, and that what we reduce to laws are essentially emergent tendencies. Here, there is a need to read the motion of object relations transformed socially through sensuous activity. In this, individual activity takes on new characteristics and phenomena at the collective level, under specific historical and material circumstances. This shapes a kinetic transformation and redistribution of the whole historical situation, beyond isolated phenomena, to address the abolition or sublation of the order of social production. It moves us away from idealizing and glorifying: education as commodity; certification as positional good; league tables as quantifying social use; competition between teachers, subject areas and institutions, as the natural order; and so on.

Marx (1867/2004) also argues that his methodological approach seeks to negate, sublate, and transform what-is, through its critical and revolutionary essence. Yet, one of the crucial contradictions at the heart of capitalist education is that those who suffer inside it, as precarious or overworked, also reproduce the mediations (commodity exchange, divisions of labor, private property, the market), which continually estrange them from a many-sided, human essence (Hall, 2018). Following Lenin (1981), it is more useful to excavate such contradictions beyond addressing their symptoms. Uncovering the relation between the individual and the conditions of their one-sided existence as educational labor-power, is more generative in identifying the initial negativity of that relation, and seeking to negate it. This takes at its heart human agency as the absolute movement of becoming (Marx, 1857/1993, p. 85).

This dialectical and material movement is inflected through the richness of storytelling from the margins. As Ahmed (2017, p. 4) argues 'patriarchal reasoning goes all the way down, to the letter, to the bone.' She (*ibid.*, 10) is clear that 'theory can do more the closer it gets to the skin'. However, enacting this relationship between, first, the skin/concrete experience and activity, and second, universal/theoretical idealizations, takes courage and faith, in order to realize forms of (in)justice. Such relations of courage and faith, enacted inside sensuous, material practices that have been made marginal inside capitalist social relations, bring our conceptualizations, and our ways of knowing and being, forward as contradictions that challenge the existing foreclosure of our horizons of possibility. It is here that the movement of negativity aligns with Andreotti's (2012, 2021) metaphor of digesting the lessons and stories of what-is, and composting its waste.

This process of pedagogical and educational renewal is discomforting, and requires strength in refusing the monstrous power of the commodity-form, which reproduces particular, settler-colonial and racial-patriarchal, power and privilege. Refusing this, pushes against disciplinary boundaries with tight methodological frames, and against the obsessive requirement to generate positionality based upon quantifiable excellence, impact, knowledge exchange, and so on. The reproduction of people as revolutionary subjects in struggle might take the form of students-as-producers, happen inside co-operative or free universities, or be revealed in movements for the abolition of the school-prison pipeline. These are struggles-in-motion, and they reproduce different, internal qualities and characteristics, which offer the potential to reshape horizons of possibility.

Thus, in his inversion of the dominant, idealistic interpretation of the dialectic, and in fusing its moving, negative essence with sensuous, social, practical activity in the world, Marx offers us the opportunity to realize contradictions and struggles as deeply pedagogical moments, which release kinetic energy. They offer us the ability to think about practical activity and its impact upon our lived experiences and identities, and to envisage an essence beyond capitalist space and time. Marxist dialectical materialism offers us the possibility that we might 'imagine a modern life freed from time, or at least modern life freed from time's abstract and alienating dominations' (Wendling, 2009, p. 199). It is in teaching this that a many-sided, human essence as a movement of knowing, doing and being might be realized. In a world increasingly shaped against crises of objectification and dehumanization, this is the alternative.

Disclosure Statement The author has no financial interest or benefit that has arisen from the direct applications of this research.

REFERENCES

Adorno, T. W. (1966). *Negative Dialectics* (E. B. Ashton, Trans.). Seabury Press.
Ahmed, S. (2017). *Living a Feminist Life*. Duke University Press.
Amawtay Wasi Pluriversity. (2023). Retrieved 27 March 2023, from https://amawtay-wasi.org/nosotros/
Andreotti, V. (2012). Editor's Preface: HEADS UP. *Critical Literacy: Theories and Practices, 6*(1), 1–3.
Andreotti, V. (2021). *Hospicing Modernity: Facing Humanity's Wrongs and the Implications for Social Activism*. North Atlantic Books.
Carola, C. R. (2017). Precursors of Decolonial Pedagogical Thinking in Latin America and Abya Yala. In O. Bernad-Cavero, & N. Llevot-Calvet (Eds.), *New Pedagogical Challenges in the 21st Century: Contributions of Research in Education*. InTechOpen. Retrieved 27 March 2023, from https://tinyurl.com/y939b5eb
Césaire, A. (1972/2000). *Discourse on Colonialism* (J. Pinkham, Trans.). Monthly Review Press.
Ciccariello-Maher, G. (2016). *Building the Commune: Radical Democracy in Venezuela*. Verso.
Clarke, S. (1991). *Marx, Marginalism and Modern Sociology: From Adam Smith to Max Weber*. Palgrave.FH.
Downs, J. (2021). *Maladies of Empire: How Colonialism, Slavery, and War Transformed Medicine*. Havard University Press.
Dunayevskaya, R. (1991). *Philosophy and Revolution: From Hegel to Sartre, and from Marx to Mao*. Aakar Books.
Dunayevskaya, R. (2002). *The Power of Negativity: Selected Writings on the Dialectic in Hegel and Marx*. Lexington Books.
Engels, F. (1883/1987). *Dialectics of Nature*. In K. Marx & F. Engels, *Collected Works*, 25. Moscow: Progress Publishers.
Engels, F. (1886). Ludwig Feuerbach and the End of Classical German Philosophy. Retrieved 27 March 2023, from https://www.marxists.org/archive/marx/works/1886/ludwig-feuerbach/index.htm
Engels, F. (1890). Letter to J. Bloch, 21/22 September 1890. Retrieved 27 March 2023, from https://www.marxists.org/archive/marx/works/1890/letters/90_09_21.htm
Engels, F. (1894/1991). Preface. In K. Marx (Ed.), *Capital, Volume 3: A Critique of Political Economy*. Penguin.
Evans-Winters, V. E. (2019). *Black Feminism in Qualitative Inquiry: A Mosaic for Writing Our Daughter's Body*. Routledge.
Federici, S. (2019). Social Reproduction Theory: History, Issues and Present Challenges. *Radical Philosophy, 204*, 55–57. Retrieved 27 March 2023, from https://www.radicalphilosophy.com/article/social-reproduction-theory-2
Ferdinand, M. (2022). *Decolonial Ecology: Thinking from the Caribbean World*. Polity Press.
Fraser, N. (2013). *Fortunes of Feminism: From State-Managed Capitalism to Neoliberal Crisis*. Verso.
Fraser, N. (2016). Expropriation and Exploitation in Racialized Capitalisms: A Reply to Michael Dawson. *Critical History Studies, 3*(1), 163–178.
Gorman, D. (n.d.). Joseph Dietzgen—Radical Chains. *Libcom.org*. Retrieved 27 March 2023, from https://libcom.org/article/joseph-dietzgen-radical-chains

Hall, R. (2018). *The Alienated Academic: The Struggle for Autonomy Inside the University*. Palgrave Macmillan.

Hegel, G. W. F. (1942). *Philosophy of Right* (T. M. Knox, Ed. & Trans.). Clarendon Press.

Hegel, G. W. F. (2010). *The Science of Logic* (G. di Giovanni, Ed. & Trans.). Cambridge University Press.

Hegel, G. W. F. (2018). *The Phenomenology of Spirit* (T. Pinkard, Ed. & Trans.). Cambridge University Press.

Hull, G. T. (1982). Researching Alice Dunbar-Nelson: A Personal and Literary Perspective. In G. T. Hull, P. Bell Scott, & B. Smith (Eds.), *All the Women Are White, All the Blacks Are Men, But Some of Us Are Brave: Black Women's Studies* (pp. 189–195). The Feminist Press.

Hull, G. T., & Smith, B. (1982). Introduction: The Politics of Black Women's Studies. In G. T. Hull, P. Bell Scott, & B. Smith (Eds.), *All the Women Are White, All the Blacks Are Men, But Some of Us Are Brave: Black Women's Studies* (pp. xvii–xxxiv). The Feminist Press.

Ilyenkov, E. (1979/1982). *Leninist Dialectics and the Metaphysics of Positivism. Reflections on Lenin's book: 'Materialism and Empirio-Criticism*. New Park Publications. Retrieved 27 March 2023, from https://www.marxists.org/archive/ilyenkov/works/positive/positivism.pdf

Katz, C. (2001). Vagabond Capitalism and the Necessity of Social Reproduction. *Antipode, 33*, 709–728. https://doi.org/10.1111/1467-8330.00207

Krader, L. (1974). *The Ethnographical Notebooks of Karl Marx. (Studies of Morgan, Phear, Maine, Lubbock)* (Transcr. and Ed., with an Introduction by L. Krader). Van Gorcum & Co.

Lenin, V. I. (1894). What the 'Friends of the People Are' and How They Fight the Social-Democrats. In V. I. Lenin (Ed.), *Collected Works* (p. 1). Progress Press.

Lenin, V. I. (1981). Philosophical Notebooks. In V. I. Lenin (Ed.), *Collected Works* (p. 38). Progress Press.

Lukács, G. (1968). *History and Class Consciousness*. Merlin Press.

Marcuse, H. (1967). Liberation from the Affluent Society, (1967 lecture in London). *Herbert Marcuse Official Homepage*. Retrieved 27 March 2023, from https://tinyurl.com/2uxy5nk3

Marx, K. (1844/1974). *Economic and Philosophical Manuscripts*. Progress Publishers.

Marx, K. (1845/1998). Theses on Feuerbach. In K. Marx & F. Engels (Eds.), (1846/1998), *The German Ideology: Including Theses on Feuerbach and Introduction to the Critique of Political Economy* (pp. 569–574). Prometheus.

Marx, K. (1852). The Eighteenth Brumaire of Louis Bonaparte. *Marxists Internet Archive*. Retrieved 27 March 2023, from https://www.marxists.org/archive/marx/works/1852/18th-brumaire/ch01.htm

Marx, K. (1856). Speech at Anniversary of the *People's Paper*. *Marxists Internet Archive*. Retrieved 27 March 2023, from https://www.marxists.org/archive/marx/works/1856/04/14.htm

Marx, K. (1857/1993). *Grundrisse: Outline of the Critique of Political Economy*. Penguin.

Marx, K. (1859). A Contribution to the Critique of Political Economy: Preface. *Marxists Internet Archive*. Retrieved 27 March 2023, from https://www.marxists.org/archive/marx/works/1859/critique-pol-economy/preface.htm

Marx, K. (1867/2004). *Capital, Volume 1: A Critique of Political Economy*. Penguin.

Marx, K. (1885/1992). *Capital, Volume 2: A Critique of Political Economy*. Penguin.

Marx, K. (1894/1991). *Capital, Volume 3: A Critique of Political Economy*. Penguin.

Marx, K., & Engels, F. (1846/1998). *The German Ideology: including Theses on Feuerbach and Introduction to the Critique of Political Economy*. Prometheus.
Marx, K., & Engels, F. (1848/2002). *The Communist Manifesto*. Penguin.
Mbembe, A. (2017). *Critique of Black Reason* (L. Dubois, Trans.). Duke University Press.
Mignolo, W. D., & Walsh, C. E. (2018). *On Decoloniality: Concepts, Analytics, Praxis*. Duke University Press.
Motta, S. (2018). *Liminal Subjects: Weaving (Our) Liberation*. Rowman & Littlefield International.
Nail, T. (2020). *Marx in Motion: A New Materialist Marxism*. Oxford University Press.
Neary, M. (2017). Pedagogy of Hate. *Policy Futures in Education, 15*(5), 555–563.
Neary, M. (2020). *Student as Producer: How Do Revolutionary Teachers Teach?* Zero Books.
Postone, M. (1993). *Time, Labor and Social Domination: A Reinterpretation of Marx's Critical Theory*. Cambridge University Press.
Prescod-Weinstein, C. (2021). *The Disordered Cosmos: A Journey into Dark Matter, Spacetime, and Dreams Deferred*. Bold Type Books.
Rizvi, S. (2022). Racially-just Epistemologies and Methodologies That Disrupt Whiteness (Part II). *International Journal of Research & Method in Education, 45*(4), 323–329. https://doi.org/10.1080/1743727X.2022.2117519
Robinson, C. (2001). *An Anthropology of Marxism*. Pluto Press.
Rubin, I. I. (1972). *Essays on Marx's Theory of Value*. Black and Red.
Sayer, D. (1987). *The Violence of Abstraction*. Basil Blackwell.
Sayers, S. (2015). Marxism and the Doctrine of Internal Relations. *Capital and Class, 39*(1), 25–31. https://doi.org/10.1177/0309816814564129
Skordoulis, C. (2022). Dialectical Materialism (Materialist Dialectics). In A. Maisuria (Ed.), *Encyclopaedia of Marxism and Education* (pp. 186–202). BRILL.
Smith, L. T. (2018). In L. E. Tuck & K. W. Yang (Eds.), *Indigenous and Decolonizing Studies in Education: Mapping the Long View*. Routledge.
Stalin, J. V. (1938). Dialectical and Historical Materialism. *Marxists Internet Archive*. Retrieved 27 March 2023, from https://www.marxists.org/reference/archive/stalin/works/1938/09.htm
The Combahee River Collective. (1977). The Combahee River Collective Statement. *Black Past*. Retrieved 27 March 2023, from https://www.blackpast.org/african-american-history/combahee-river-collective-statement-1977/
Thompson, M. C. (2022). *Phenomenal Blackness Black Power, Philosophy, and Theory*. University of Chicago Press.
Wendling, A. E. (2009). *Karl Marx on Technology and Alienation*. Palgrave Macmillan.
Wilson, S. (2008). *Research Is Ceremony: Indigenous Research Methods*. Fernwood Publishing.
Yazzie Burkhart, D. (2004). What Coyote and Thales Can Teach Us: An Outline of American Indian Epistemology. In A. Waters (Ed.), *American Indian Thought: Philosophical Essays* (pp. 15–26). Blackwell Publishing.
Yusoff, K. (2018). *A Billion Black Anthropocenes or None*. University of Minnesota Press.

CHAPTER 3

Value in Education: Its Web of Social Forms

Glenn Rikowski

3.1 Introduction

For Marx, 'education produces labour-power' (1975, p. 210). Additionally, in the first volume of *Capital,* in his well-known 'sausage factory' example, Marx argues that capitalist production is 'essentially the production of surplus-value', and teachers working for a privately-owned school produce surplus-value for the school proprietor (1977a, p. 477). As Marx notes, commodities that incorporate surplus-value do not always take the physical form of hard, visible commodities, like bricks; the social mode of existence of the commodity 'has nothing to do with its corporeal reality' (1975, p. 171). Transport and theatrical performances are examples of incorporeal commodities for Marx, as education can be too. In capitalism, commodities incorporate value, and, for Marx, there are two kinds of commodities, 'two great categories': the general class and labor-power (*ibid.*).

In past works, I have explored commodity-forms and value in education starting out from these considerations (e.g. Rikowski, 2000, 2019a, pp. 146–72). Although the 'two great categories' of commodities referred to above will play a significant role in this article, it is *social form* that takes center stage. A web of capital's forms grounds and facilitates value production in education.[1] These social forms are given institutional life and maintain existence through our labor. But before uncovering capital's social forms that plague education in contemporary societies, understanding of *abstract labor* is crucial, for abstract labor is the substance of value (see Cleaver, 2000, pp. 110–17).

G. Rikowski (✉)
London, UK
e-mail: Rikowskigr@aol.com

For Marx, labor in capitalism is two-fold in nature: on the one hand it is concrete, useful labor that produces use-value (useful things); on the other, it is abstract labor that produces value, and it is this aspect of labor that attains specific social existence in capitalism. Marx notes that 'so far as it [labor] finds expression in value, it does not possess the same characteristics that belong to it as a creator of use-value', and adds that he 'was the first to point out and to examine critically this two-fold nature of labour contained in commodities' (Marx, 1977a, pp. 48–9).

There are not two types of labor in capitalist commodity production; but one form of labor that has these *two aspects*. Regarding the use-value aspect of capitalist labor, it can be viewed directly (e.g. workers in factories, computer programmers at the keyboard), and the use-value aspect of commodities can be observed directly (e.g. bricks, coats, wheat) or *experienced* directly (e.g. transport, drama performances—the sorts of examples Marx explores: in Marx, 1975). On the other hand, abstract labor is not perceptible to the senses; as anything 'abstract' would not be. Indeed, Marx notes that: '…in the analysis of economic forms … neither microscopes nor chemical reagents are of use. The force of abstraction must replace both' (Marx, 1977b, p. 19). Abstract labor, like value itself, 'has a purely social reality' (Marx, 1977a, p. 34). Value, as abstract labor, 'is a *social* rather than a natural phenomenon' (MacNeill, 2021, p. 1—emphasis added). We are ruled by such abstractions, abstractions that we create, maintain, and which oppress us, and haunt our lives in myriad ways.[2]

For Marx, 'a commodity has value only because of the abstract labour that has materialized in it', and, 'This is measured by the quantity of the value forming substance that the object contains' (Neary & Rikowski, 2002, p. 56): that is, *labor-time*. However, Marx realized that:

> …this time could not be based on direct, concrete time, as this would clearly cause insurmountable problems due to reconciling the different speeds at which people work. For example, one consequence of focusing on concrete time was that the lazier the worker, the more labour time it would take to produce a commodity, hence the greater that commodity's value, with the opposite result for the speedy and diligent worker. … Rather, Marx posited the quantity of time involved in producing a commodity as a … social *average* of the total amount of time that labour power was expended in society. (*ibid.*,—original emphasis)

Thus, for Marx:

> Socially necessary labour time is then the labour time required to produce any use value under the condition of production normal for a given society and with the average degree of skill and intensity prevalent in that society. (Marx, 1979a, p. 129)

Socially necessary labor-time is, therefore, the *socially average* time it takes to produce a use-value of any description. Hence, the degree of skill, education, and physical condition of the worker is taken as a social average for producing a specific commodity. Means of production—including the prevailing technology—are also taken as social averages. These social averages are, therefore, *abstractions* that ground the existence of abstract labor. If they vary, if there is an increase in the *average* skill of the worker, then socially necessary labor-time is reduced, worker productivity increases, and more value is produced within a given time-frame.

While socially necessary labor-time is a measure of abstract labor, it is also capital's time, the *real time* of capitalist society. It is Karl Marx's *social time*: the form of time that has social validity on the basis of capital, and Rikowski (2016) indicates conditions under which the flow of time in capitalist society either speeds up, or slows down. For education, the existence and strength of value production within, schools, colleges and universities, rests on the extent to which educational institutions and processes incorporate abstract labor in their operations and everyday life. But abstract labor does not penetrate educational institutions without concomitant development of related *social forms*. The flowering of abstract labor—and thence value production—in education institutions in contemporary society requires the development of a supporting *web of social forms*. Prior to examining this enchanting web, the following section explores the category of social form.

3.2 Social Form

The notion of social form does not point specifically to the mere existence of phenomena but to the *way* they exist; their *mode of existence* (Bonefeld et al., 1992, pp. xv–xvi). Mainstream social science is 'blind to the question of form: commodities and money (and so on) are not even thought of as being forms, or modes of existence, of social relations', argues Holloway (2002, p. 28). Capitalism changes everything. Capital is the 'general illumination which bathes all the other colours and modifies their particularity' (Marx, 1973a, p. 107, in Bonefeld, 1987a, p. 35).

In capitalist society, social forms incorporate antagonistic social relations. Specifically, social forms in capitalism incorporate the capital-labor relation; that is, the *class* relation. As John Holloway indicates: 'Value, money, rent, state are forms of social relations … [and therefore] … specifically capitalist forms of struggle' (Holloway, 1991a, p. 172). Of these—indeed of *all*—social forms in capitalism, value is 'the *dominant* form through which our need for the useful products of other people's work is satisfied' (*ibid.*, emphasis added). We want, we need, food, bricks, coats, wheat etc., but in capitalist society we only get them to buy and consume through simultaneously creating value through acts of collective labor in capitalist labor processes. The value-form presents itself, is manifested, as exchange-value—which Marx takes great care to uncover in *Capital*, a process oiled by capital's money-form and price-form (Marx, 1977a, pp. 54–75), a process explained expertly by Harry Cleaver (2019, pp. 98–167).

Social relations 'are not easily detained in forms' (Holloway, 1991a, p. 172). In capitalism, these forms *mediate*, though never synthesise, antagonistic social relations, which may erupt as crises when capital's forms fail to contain them. For Marx, notes Bonefeld (1987b, p. 68) 'antagonistic relations express themselves always in forms (value-form, state form)'. Referring to commodity and money forms, Marx (1977a, p. 106) argues that although these contain 'contradictory and mutually exclusive conditions', nevertheless commodities and money do 'not sweep away these inconsistencies, but develop a *modus vivendi* [allowing conflicting parties to co-exist], a form in which they can exist side by side'. Therefore, as Bonefeld (1987b, p. 68) argues:

> … it is within 'form' that antagonistic relations can articulate themselves …[and] … Form mediates the existence of antagonisms as a condition of their own existence. As such, the existence of antagonism is a mediated existence …

As Holloway (2022) argues, mainstream social science—bourgeois thought—does not work through a concept of social form(s), and therefore fails to uncover the antagonisms and hence *fragilities* in these structuring phenomena in capital's social universe. For Holloway, we overflow these forms; they cannot contain our richness and variability, and hence crisis is latent and immanent within them.

The existence of capital's social forms is dependent on our labor. We create, maintain, challenge, and at times break out of them. It is not a case of filling 'abstract' forms with the content of our labor; form and content develop together, though they can move radically out of synch. These points can be viewed most clearly when it is recognized that capital's social forms *materialize* as institutional forms: 'the form must have some institutional embodiment' (Holloway, 1991b, p. 254). Institutions appear as 'crystalized social relationships' and 'relationships between active people' (Holloway & Cecchetto, 2007, p. 7). They give some measure of stability and organization to capital's social forms, thereby to some extent screening their instability and fragile nature. In capitalism, we are pushed, or forced, or resigned to fitting into *roles* within these institutional forms (Holloway, 2022, p. 93). We may even welcome them with open arms. Within them we wear character masks, playing parts in dramas not of our own making. These social roles in capitalism are 'mediations of class struggle, i.e. they are modes of existence of class struggle' and therefore 'as mediated in terms of roles, class struggle exists in the mode of being denied' (Gunn, 1987, p. 20).

That is, manifestations of social forms in capitalist institutions and their related roles deny the fullness of our being, and our becoming: of what we are, and what we might, developmentally, *become*. Flows of our richness, our capacities, desires and yearnings are blocked, stunted and perverted by the institutionalization of capital's social forms.[3] Institutionalization 'means trying to set life on railway tracks or highways, whereas rebellion is the constant attempt to break from that, to invent new ways of doing things' (Hardt & Holloway, 2012, p. 4). These social forms and their materialization as and through institutionalization are a 'forced socialization' (Micocci, 2012, p. 2); forced because we have to set our labor-power in motion in commodity production for human representatives of capital for our wages, or rely on paltry state payments where they exist.

We kick against these social forms and their rigid institutional manifestations in three main ways. This is where social forms and their contents become out of synch, or labor-capital antagonisms rise to the surface *within* capital's structured forms. First, we exceed the given social forms and their institutional manifestations: we subvert, and *overflow* their institutional and role structuring prerogatives. We aim to recast them as *something else*; a mode of existence that more closely matches our mode of being which has been denied by capitalist institutionalized containments. On the other hand, there may be an *underflowing*, a failure to fill adequately capital's social forms as given by their institutional manifestations as sets of related roles. This underflowing, a lack of pressure and intensity within capitalist forms resulting from our recalcitrance may be accompanied by our overflowing from these social cages. The third aspect is class struggle *within* capital's institutional structures, which traditional Marxism focuses on to the detriment of the other two crisis-inducing scenarios. That is, to seek to gain advantages within the confines of capital's life-world, within and through the class relation, but falling short of seeking to abolish it.[4]

These challenges to capital's social forms invoke the power of the state-form of capital to *restructure* social forms through revamping their institutional underpinnings. Social forms in capitalist society are never stable. On the one hand, they are susceptible to the three cases of undermining and overcoming noted previously. On the other hand, they are subject to restructuring as a capitalist state *attack* which seeks to confine our labors, our *selves*, within capitalized institutions and roles. The capitalist state constantly restructures institutions (and related roles) in favor of capital accumulation, especially in response to crises. Thus, there is a constant *re-forming* of capital's social forms, as 'The power of labour is not contained within the forms of capital, it constantly overflows and forces these forms to reconstitute themselves, to reform' (Holloway, 1991c, p. 75). The capitalist state can step in to *re-formulate* social forms through altering their institutional organization in favor of capital accumulation, and to knock back our efforts to overcome the confines of these rigidifying forms to further our own needs and desires. This is in addition to any restructurings that representatives of capital might pursue themselves.

Thus, social forms in capitalism are always in the process of *re-*formulation or *de-*formulation, either because of our struggles against and through them, or in relation to crises, or as part of projects for enhancing and developing the intensity of capital in societal spaces (as in education policy initiatives, with examples explored later). These restructuring efforts constitute an *attack* on us: 'Capital is an unceasing attack, a constant drive to create more and more value' (Holloway, 2022, p. 136), to create surplus-value over-and-above money shelled out for means of production and labor-power.

Capital's social forms are never static and depend on our labor regarding the institutions and roles that give them substance. Value, money, rent, state and other social forms in capitalism are:

> ...forms of social relations... [and] ...specifically capitalist forms of struggle. They are *form-processes*: processes of *forming* social relations into a pattern compatible with the reproduction of the capitalist relations of production. (Holloway, 1991a, pp. 172–73, emphases added)

Capital's social forms impose a restless, disruptive mode of life on the inhabitants of its society.

Marxist science deciphers these forms. This involves a critique indicating the human content of these aggressive forms (Bonefeld, 2005, p. 3). Indeed, argues Holloway, Marx's *Capital* can be viewed as a 'science of forms', and they should be critiqued by 'revealing their content', but also 'tracing the genesis and internal connections between those forms' (1991b, p. 233). This chapter lacks the space to pursue these tasks. All that can be done here is to alert the reader to how some of these myriad social forms nurture the production of value and surplus-value in contemporary educational institutions.

In the following two sections, a radical interpretation of social form is adopted. Most discussions of social form focus on 'economic' examples—value, money, commodity, and so on. The view taken here is that capital's social forms are present throughout contemporary society, and they cannot be designated as being strictly 'economic', or basically 'political' or 'educational', or pedagogic in nature. These forms cut across any structuralist and exclusivist borders in capitalist social reality. This is an aspect of the One Science, the unity of sciences that Marx and Engels alluded to in *The German Ideology* (Marx & Engels, 1976, p. 34), and Marx mentions more decisively in his *Economic and Philosophic Manuscripts of 1844* (Marx, 1977c, p. 105).

3.3 Social Forms, Education and the General Class of Commodities

Before proceeding a few methodological points are necessary. First, empirical and historical examples referred to hereafter focus on schools in England and higher education institutions (HEIs) in the United Kingdom. There is insufficient space for exploring schools and HEIs for each of the social forms analysed. Secondly, this section, and the next, builds upon Marx's view that there are two categories of commodities in capitalist society: the general category and the 'category of one' (labor-power). Thirdly, these two commodity categories are not conceptually closed to each other, and empirically in capitalism they are internally related, and these interrelations are open to each other too. As Bonefeld (1987b, p. 67) notes:

The marxist categories contain the reciprocal recognition of labour and capital as an intrinsic relation of struggle. This applies for all the marxist categories. The marxist concepts have to be open to the changes in the composition of the social relations which occur during the process of transformation.

The significance of Bonefeld's characterisation of Marxist categories, as incorporating reciprocal openness, gains force as we move through this section and the next.

What is a matter of social logic is that *whatever* the institutional arrangements of education (e.g. curriculum, grading conventions) in capitalism, and whatever the strength of their penetration by capital's social forms, labor-power is *necessarily* socially produced, enhanced, reconfigured, or even destroyed in terms of its aspects and attributes in capitalist educational settings.[5] Indeed, our labor-power is constantly changing wherever we are; even when sleeping, our bodies, which incorporate our labor-powers, continually change. Furthermore, changes in the quality of labor-power affects the 'average degree of skill' (Marx) of laborers, which in turns affects (negatively or positively) the socially necessary labor-time it takes to produce a commodity, and hence value and surplus-value-production. Conversely, changes in the means of production—especially technology—call forth new sets of labor-power attributes within workers, that education and training institutions are charged with responding to. This is reflected in the 'long moan of history' from employers, that 'education does not meet the needs of industry' in general, or falls short on specific labor-power attributes or for specific sectors of capital (see Rikowski, 2006a).[6] Thus, in these various ways, the two categories of commodity—general and labor-power—can be seen to be open categories.

Four social forms in relation to the general category of commodities have been chosen for detailed study in this section: competition (competitionalization), commodity (commodification), market (marketization), and money (monetization). These have been chosen as they illustrate how value production in educational institutions relies on a web of social forms most intensely.

Competition (Competitionalization)

We begin with competition, as capitalist education has developed competition as a social form to a greater extent than commodification. 'Competitionalization' is the insertion and development of competition in educational institutions in contemporary society, a process continually under review by capitalist states. Competitive practices and institutions are rife in contemporary education.

For Marx, '*competition* is nothing other than the inner *nature of capital*' (Marx, 1973b, p. 414—original emphases), and:

> Competition merely *expresses* as real, posits as an external necessity, that which lies within the nature of capital; competition is nothing more than the way in which

the many capitals force the inherent determinations of capital upon one another and upon themselves. (*ibid*., p. 651—original emphasis)

Thus, competition is incorporated within capital and it is one of its 'inherent determinations' which is expressed in relations between many capitals, and now we have to show how this pans out for education. This is not so easy, as the existence of value production in educational institutions is not as developed as compared with the production of bricks. The state form of capital, under which educational institutions are organized to a substantial degree in many advanced capitalist countries, muddies the waters, as we shall see.

We begin with a repetition of Marx's concept of socially necessary labor-time. This is:

> The labour-time socially necessary is that required to produce an article under the normal conditions of production, and with the average degree of skill and intensity prevalent at the time. (Marx, 1977a, p. 47)

If labor-time, as opposed to socially necessary labor-time, was at the basis of the constitution of value and its measure, then the lazier the workers employed, the less reliable and antiquated the technology used, and the poverty of raw materials brought in, then the greater would be the value produced (*ibid*., p. 46). However, in the search for higher productivity in order to beat off rivals and gain bigger market shares in the commodities they produce, the effect is that individual capitals are engaged in reducing socially necessary labor-time. Thus, says Marx, on this basis: 'what determines the magnitude of the value of any article is the amount of labour socially necessary … for its production', and therefore each 'commodity in this connexion, is to be considered as an *average* of its class' (*ibid*., p. 47—emphasis added). Marx lists a bunch of factors making for increased productivity (*ibid*.), one of which is the 'average amount of skill of the workmen' (*ibid*.).

Hence, we are dealing with *social averages* regarding socially necessary labor-time. These change constantly 'with every variation in the productiveness of labour' (*ibid*.), which is powered by competition. Even when we sleep, in another part of the world changes in productivity affects these social averages, and hence socially necessary labor-time.

These *social* averages include all relevant players: that is what an average involves. Thus, when a particular commodity is produced in capitalist society, all units of capital (particular enterprises) are in competition—from the most feeble outfit with poorly skilled, de- un-motivated workers with low quality raw materials and antiquated technology, to the most whiz-bang producer with top notch, highly skilled and motived workers using state-of the-art technology and the finest raw materials. In this way, abstract labor becomes the flipside of concrete labor: in the competitive struggle over producing a particular commodity concrete labor spawns abstract, value-creating labor; labor takes the *form* of value in capitalist labor processes. The value-form of labor is expressed through the social form of time in capitalist society, which is socially necessary labor-time, Karl Marx's social time, capital's time.

From this, regarding the presence of value production in education, several points flow. First, Marx's characterization of socially necessary labor-time incorporates 'the average degree of skill of the worker', and this invokes the quality and quantity of education, training and other forms of labor-power development workers receive. When these are enhanced, then, all else being equal, socially necessary labor-time is reduced through rises in productivity, and more value is produced in a given time period.

Secondly, on this basis, capitalist enterprises compete in terms of employing the highest quality labor-power they can purchase. In contemporary society, they rely, to some extent, on the quality of labor-power produced by educational institutions. From the perspective of capitalist states, these are involved in 'skill wars' through the educational institutions that they control and finance, and which are vital elements in labor-power production (Gordon, 2000). This separation of *part* of the social production of labor-power in capitalism—where the capitalist state takes charge—grounds the 'long moan of history' (Rikowski, 2006a) and the constant employer groans that schools, colleges and universities are 'not meeting the needs of industry'. As Rikowski (2001) indicates, they *never can*.

But, thirdly, what does this mean in relation to education institutions competing on the basis of the *general category* of commodities (as opposed to competing on labor-power quality)? Schools in England are relatively underdeveloped in terms of value production to date. Although they 'compete' through a range of state-enforced measures (e.g. examination league tables, inspection grades), thus far the strength of capital, specifically the existence of abstract labor, and hence value production, is weak. This is so despite the complex interventions of profit-seeking enterprises in schools detailed by Ball (2007) and Rikowski (2003), and for a number of reasons.[7]

Competition as a social form expressing value production in state-financed schools is weak in England. There is some small-scale production of education revision materials in a few schools, but the key point is that state schools are not profit-making enterprises: any surpluses made from such activities do not become *owned* by the schools, or head teachers, or shareholders. They are not *profits*, as such. Furthermore, the state in England can always claw back any surpluses made from these activities. As profit-making is a missing vital ingredient for value and surplus-value production in England's state schools, then capital's dynamic for increasing productivity, and thereby cutting socially necessary labor-time, is correspondingly weak. That is, apart from the IES Breckland free school that was set up in Brandon, Suffolk, and approved by the then Education Secretary Michal Gove in 2012 (BBC, 2012). However, the Swedish-run IES Breckland free school failed to make profits from 2016–2018, and indeed made significant operating losses in those years, even with a 10-year £21 million management contract to run the school (Warrell, 2014). Only in 2014 and 2015 were profits made (Whittaker, 2018). Of course, there are private schools in England, which take up around 6% of schoolchildren (Green & Kynaston, 2019). These schools can make profits, but as Martin and Dunlop (2019) note, those claiming charitable status must show benefits to their local communities (e.g. by sharing facilities with local schools). The other, for-profit schools, those not claiming charitable status, comprised a total of 977 schools out of the 2640 private schools, though Martin and Dunlop found that 34 of these provided no online or paper data, leaving 943 for-profit schools operating in England (2019, p. 4). Thus, these are the schools most clearly approximating Marx's sausage factory as outlined in *Capital* (Marx, 1977a, p. 477), where the exigencies of competition allied to value production apply. Ironically, the Labour Party's proposals to end the charitable status of private schools would send some to the wall but the rest would be forced to join the 943 schools in the for-profit sector, thereby increasing the grip of value production in education.

The other possibility for profit-making in schools in England is through outsourcing (see Rikowski, 2003, pp. 94–6). Basically, this is where a school or schools are run by a private sector operator on a contract. The profit is made by running them for less money than the contract price. There is competition to attain the contracts, and therefore, importantly, a dynamic for driving down wage and other costs, thereby attaining some features of capitalist value production. However there are also targets set by local education authorities that, if not attained, result in financial claw backs. This is a precarious form of profit-making that depends on private operators transforming state revenue gained through taxation into private profit. When the UK capitalist state reduces spending on schools, then the house of cards collapses, as in the current crisis of school funding, where 90% of schools will 'run out of money next year' according to National Association of Head Teachers data (Fazackerley, 2022).

Commodity (Commodification)[8]

Our attention shifts now to the commodity form, commodification and higher education institutions. In this section, it is easier to see what the 'general category' of commodities actually means in relation to education. Think of a car as a commodity: the average car is made up of around 30,000 parts—each of these being a commodity in its own right (Compass VSC, 2022). There are similarities here between the car and a university (although some important differences, not explored here). A university is composed of many education *services*[9]—e.g. pedagogic, counselling, English teaching for foreign students, student welfare, and tutoring. These, in turn, can be broken down. For example, pedagogic services could be spliced into degree programs, modules, or even a series of digital lectures.

A university could be bought as a *bundle* of variegated services, a related set of educational services, initiating a process of *commodification*, the 'becoming of capital' (Marx, 1973b, pp. 459–60) in education, or educational *capitalization* (Rikowski, 2019a). This has rarely happened in UK higher education.

McGettigan (2013, pp. 130–31) notes the example of the College of Law being sold to Montagu Private Equity in 2012, but argues that 'Hostile takeovers are not possible given the absence of shareholders' in UK HEIs (*ibid.*, p. 133).

What has been taking place for many years in UK higher education is 'unbundling'. This is where some university services—including teaching services—are run by profit-making operators. As McCowan (2017, p. 733) indicates: 'Unbundling is occurring in the context of increasing difficulties for nation-states to finance the expanding enrolments of higher education through taxpayer funds', and can be witnessed in the establishment of massive open online courses (MOOCs), and the insertion of outside IT specialists for digital course provision, for example.[10] For-profit providers were moving into English as a foreign language (EFL) provision in UK HEIs at least as early as 2005 (see Rikowski, 2006b).

Another feature making for commodification in UK HEIs is the incorporation of new for-profit providers. The Conservative / Liberal Democrat Coalition and then Conservative government post-2015 made it easier for these to enter UK higher education after 2010. The key sticking point was whether students at these institutions should get loans for fees and living costs. The outcome was that private providers were to have some of their 'freedoms' curtailed through regulation (e.g. student numbers, information provision) so as to enable their students to get financial support (McGettigan, 2013, p. 99).[11]

Market (Marketization)

Value *appears* as exchange-value. In turn, exchange-value reveals itself through *market* institutions—the buying and selling of commodities. Marketization is the creation, development, and maintenance of institutions involved in buying and selling commodities: that is, 'the concrete processes through which market competition is created, intensified, extended and maintained' (Greer & Umney, 2022, p. 3).

In relation to schools in England a massive literature emerged in the late-1980s and early-1990s focusing on the 'marketization' of schools after the 1988 Education Reform Act. In terms of marketization, this Act brought in a National Curriculum, with funding following pupils (thereby framing competition between schools), parental choice of schools, and examination and inspection league tables informing parents on school quality. Thus, schools competed with each other for students and therefore money in the form of state revenue. With a few exceptions, this stunted literature attempted 'to theorise education markets without any sustained exploration which links these marketised forms with education as production' and so 'we have … 'Education Markets and Missing Products' (Rikowski, 1996, pp. 1–2). However, it was not the case that parents 'bought' a set of educational services for their children; schools in England were still funded by state revenue. Thus, researchers have designated this arrangement as a form of 'quasi-market' (e.g. Allen & Higham, 2018).

Further marketization occurred as types of schools proliferated, on the basis that this enhanced choice in the schools market (Exley, 2015, p. 2). Thus, Academies (originally brought in by Blair's New Labour government in 1998), free-standing schools outside local education authority control, were championed by the Conservative & Liberal Democrat Coalition and Conservative governments post-2010. Free Schools were established after 2010 where parents were dissatisfied with choices offered by their local schools.[12]

From 2003–2007, Tony Blair's New Labour government advocated co-payment or co-funding. This is where users of a public service pay 'a contribution towards the costs of services that were previously wholly paid for by the state out of revenue deriving from taxation' (Rikowski, 2005, p. 24). Co-payment was advocated by Blair as part of New Labour's discussions on injecting for-profit schools into the schools system (see Paveley, 2003; Oliver, 2004; Rikowski, 2007). It didn't happen. If it had, it would have meant parents of schoolchildren paying schools money as capital if schools were run by one of the business operators. It would have meant further significant capitalization of schooling in relation to marketization: parents would pay (partially) for school education services (as commodities) within a market where individual schools touted for pupils with money perched over their heads.

But in higher education co-payment *did* happen. From 1998, under Blair's New Labour government, university fees were brought in—rising to £9000 later under the Conservative & Liberal Democrat Coalition government. This meant that, in a roundabout way, students bought education services in a developing education market. With student loans paying for tuition fees and living expenses, these were subject to repayments when postgraduates earned above a threshold (with interest payments added). What transpired was that students were paying, retrospectively, for educational services to develop their labor-powers (to enhance their labor-power *values*) as HEIs competed for students in this emerging market in an environment of cutthroat competition. In the process, HEIs' educational services are more decisively formed as *capital*, as value-producing enterprises. It is also clear from this example that the two categories of commodities—the general class and labor-power—are entangled and interwoven, thus validating the point that Marx's concepts are not closed to each other. Finally, the UK HEI student loans system highlights an important point regarding capital: when wage laborers in capitalism stand in a relation of '*capital as capital*', rather than as capital to state revenue, then capital reaches its 'highest development' (Marx, 1973b, p. 532—original emphasis). Thus, the current student loans / payback arrangements deepen the development of value-creation (and the value-form of labor for university teachers), marketization and commodification, as capital in its money-form strengthens these social forms.

Money (Monetization)

Indicating how the money-form of capital infects and degrades education, by bringing in examples, would require a text of prodigious proportions. Here, via the work of John Holloway (1991c, 2022), is a brief look at money as a social form and its adventures in UK HEIs.

Money, for Holloway, is 'a process of monetising life, of subjecting human existence to the command of money, which implies a constant and violent struggle.'(1991c, p. 76). Money 'increasingly invades all our relationships, monetising all social relations' (Holloway, 2022, p. 85). We see this in UK HEIs with the loans / fees system. Students sell their personhoods to university degree programs as *raw materials* to be enhanced as labor-power, with expectations they can then sell their labor-powers to representatives of capital for a wage higher than if they had not so developed their labor-power. In this, through purchasing education services from universities, the flow of capital, M-C-M' (Money-Commodity-Money+) is strengthened. The commodities (C) being the students' own labor-powers, and the services being the various courses, modules, seminars, lab work etc., provided by the university. The university aims to make a surplus (surplus-value) (M' or Money+) out of this arrangement. Again, the two categories of commodities are *open* to each other. A significant example of the 'violent struggle' over monetization of student life occurred in the protests and demonstrations against raising student course fees (and thereby the loan debt needed to finance courses) in November and December 2010.[13]

Value is not only incorporated in commodities. It also inheres within money. As Holloway notes, there is also the social flow of M—M', advancing money to make more money, and 'commodity and money are distinct forms of value, the product of abstract labour' but it is the 'money form that reveals the self-expansion of value is the driving force of social development. The self-expansion of money is capital' (*ibid.*, pp. 91–2). Student finance regimes establish huge piles of student debt, attracting investment. In March 2012, student debt in the USA was $904 billion (Lazzarato, 2013, p. 65). In the UK, current outstanding student debt totals £200.1 billion (Statista, 2022). This debt can be 'securitized'. That is, thousands of these student loans can be bundled together and sold as derivative products to investors, who reap payoffs from the loans. In the USA, over a third of student debt was securitized by 2013 (Lazzarato, 2013, p. 67), and in 2017 in the UK government raised £1.7 billion through selling student loan-backed securities (Hale, 2017).

These examples from higher education point to money being a totalizing force 'which draws us all deeper into a totality' of capital's social relations (Holloway, 2022, p. 85). It binds us to capital's social forms—commodity, competition, and so on. Money is the 'most public face of a complex of social forms' (*ibid.*) in contemporary society.

3.4 Social Forms, Education and Labor-power

Labor-power is that other great category of commodities. It is the unique, special commodity; the only commodity that enables the expansion of surplus-value (value over-and-above what it costs to produce itself through wages, and value higher than payments shelled out on means of production plus the laborers' wages). Value is produced in capitalist labor processes when labor-power of the laborer is transformed into actual labor for the production of commodities (Rikowski, 2002b). The sale (by the laborer) and purchase (by the capitalist) of labor-power in the labor-market 'forms the *absolute foundation* of capitalist production' (Marx, 1979b, p. 1005—original emphasis). Labor-power is that commodity 'whose *use-value* possesses the peculiar property of being a *source of value*,' and being a source of 'more value than it has itself,' surplus-value (Marx, 1977a, pp. 164, 188—original emphases). Raising labor-power quality through education and training therefore increases surplus-value (Rikowski, 2002a, p. 196). For Marx:

> By labour-power or capacity for labour is to be understood the aggregate of those mental and physical capabilities existing in a human being, which he exercises whenever he produces a use-value of any description. (Marx, 1977a, p. 164)

In *Capital* volume 1, Marx assumed that labor-power 'is always on hand' (Marx, 1978, p. 577), hence there was 'no need to provide an account of how labor-power was socially produced through education and training' (Rikowski, 2002b, pp. 119–20). Yet Marx also knew that 'education produces labor-power', and this points towards various *social forms* of labor-power production. Of course, labor-power itself is a social form (Ciccarelli, 2021; Jaffe, 2020, pp. 46–57). But it is to forms of labor-power production we now turn.

The social production of labor-power is at the 'heart of contemporary education and training policy' (Rikowski, 2002a, p. 193). It is a social form that manifests itself in a plethora of educational institutions. Institutionally, the social production of labor-power is highly fragmented in contemporary society. Today, 'it typically includes compulsory education' and nursery education and can include:

> …training (on-and-off-the job), various forms of personal development programmes, further and higher education, computer-based education/training and many other elements. (*ibid.*, p. 195)

It also includes laboring in capitalist labor processes, where the laborer's skills are enhanced through practice, and learning from other laborers. In education institutions in particular, there are constant struggles by capitalist states, employers' organizations and individual capitalists to ensure that curricula and study programs are aimed at preparing young people for laboring in capitalist enterprises. Educational programs for 'employability' are at the forefront of contemporary capitalist strategies for reducing education to labor-power production.

The social production of labor-power as described above is just *one* form in which labor-power is socially produced. For individual students and laborers, there is a *confluence* of labor-powers' productive social forms within their bodies and consciousnesses.[14] These forms flow together within individuals, they become entangled, causing turbulence, and in some cases social contradictions in our lives. The following brings together some of the other social forms of labor-power production at work in our bodies and intellects. To describe relations between these forms of labor-power production would involve another writing project. Thus, what follows can best be described as programmatic, a future program of intellectual work.

Social *re*-production refers first of all to the ways in which labor-power is developed within family institutions. This social form of labor-power development is at the heart of much Marxist-Feminist theory (e.g. Bhattacharya, 2017; Jaffe, 2020). This form of labor-power production is *open* to the social production of labor-power production in education, as the contemporary debates around schoolchildren being sent to school hungry indicate. They are not separate social forms. If this is Social Reproduction 1, then Social Reproduction 2 refers to the state-form of capital supporting non-laborers. Institutions such as state pensions for senior retirees and unemployment benefits, for what Marx called the Industrial Reserve Army, are pertinent here.

In the *Grundrisse* in particular, Marx refers to the *maintenance* of laborers, and indeed the working-class. That is, 'their own consumption' (Marx, 1973b, p. 772). For: 'as regards the worker's consumption, this reproduces one thing—namely himself, as living labour capacity' (*ibid.*, p. 676). On this basis, 'Capital therefore calls this consumption productive consumption … [as it reproduces] …individuals as labour capacities' (*ibid.*). This social form is related to another: the *value of labor-power* itself; the cost of the 'bundle of necessities' that Marx refers to in the first volume of *Capital* (see Marx, 1977a, pp. 167–72). In turn, the value of labor-power is transformed into the wage-form (the appearance of the value of labor-power), which takes many concrete forms (*ibid.*, pp. 501–28). These social forms could be referred to as Maintenance 1. But there is another form of labor-power maintenance that Marx makes less direct reference to in terms of maintaining labor-power quality: the health of workers. This could be referred to as Maintenance 2. There are brief references to the 'health' of workers (e.g. Marx, 1979b, p. 1067), descriptions of terrible working conditions in *Capital*, and the importance of 'the doctor's services, in so far as he maintains health and so conserves the source of all values, labour-power itself' (Marx, 1975, p. 172), but Marx gives more attention to Maintenance 1.

It might be thought that social forms of labor-power reproduction and maintenance have little to do with the social production of labor-power and its education elements and institutions. This would be wrong. There is much research to show that, empirically, these forms are related at the institutional level, but I would also maintain that these social forms of labor-power are *open* to each other. They are not closed social forms. An example: school homework. The schoolchild's home conditions (consumption of food, heating, a quiet room to study) do not just affect educational performance, but indicate *relations* between the social production of labor-power and Reproduction of labor-power 1.

Finally, little has been said of the state-form of capital directly, but the capitalist state attempts to *regulate*, develop and maintain relations between the various social forms referred to above—the general category and labor-power—in their concrete manifestations through institutions. The state also seeks to contain antagonisms and contradictions within and between these forms. State-centred education policy can be seen in this light.

3.5   Conclusion: A Web of Social Forms

This chapter carries significant shortcomings. First, it does not offer historical accounts of the rise and development of the social forms examined within the context of education and its institutions. Secondly, there is no overall *recasting* of education in terms of value; that is, how the growth of value and its web of social forms necessitates *reinterpretation* of the nature of education when under the growing strength of the rule of capital. Thirdly, the interconnections between the social forms explored are established only in fragmentary and partial ways. Fourthly, there is insufficient attention to our struggles against these forms, and *within* them. Fifthly, although hinted at, there is no actual account of any 'educational' forms (e.g. curriculum, examination, qualification, tests etc.), as opposed to the usual suspects, that is, 'economic' social forms (e.g. money, commodity etc.), though of course there is no actual separation between 'economic' and 'educational' forms. Finally, following Thomas Nail (2020, pp. 77–99), the question of *devalorisation* through exclusion of particular social forms within capitalist education has not been addressed. Regarding my views on the merits of the chapter, these are delivered at the end.

My previous work has largely focused on two of capital's social forms as they are developing in schools (England) and HEIs (UK): commodity forms (e.g. Rikowski, 2017a, 2017b, 2019b), and the social production of labor-power (e.g. Rikowski, 1990, 2002c). What these studies show is that capital's invasive social forms in contemporary education constitute a 'binding' of education to capital. For Holloway (2022), this is an aspect of what capital *is*: 'The binding that holds us in place … is a logical weaving, a *web* that we can call 'capital' (*ibid.*, p. 97—emphasis added). Our enemy is this binding, which is *capital* (*ibid.*, pp. 83–5). Capital *is* the web of social forms that binds us, contains us, as limiting force, for the ends of value and surplus-value creation. There is a logical weaving, argues Holloway: a 'binding of our relatings to one another within a certain logic. The logic of money…' (*ibid.*, p. 84). Money is capital's binding agent *par excellence*. The logical weaving can be viewed as a series of derivations: 'if commodity, then value; value, then labour; if value and labour, then money; if money then capital; if capital, then exploitation; if exploitation, then the constant, uncontrolled, uncontrollable drive towards accumulation' (*ibid.*, p. 86).

Thus, insofar as capital's social forms are developed within education, then education becomes *bound* and glued to this logical weaving. The forms move and change constantly as their institutional patterns shift (e.g. restructuring through state education policy development). The binding is also *uneven*: the threads of the bindings that constitute the web of social forms are of different strengths and widths. The capitalist state tends to focus more on some forms than others in relation to education. For state schools in England, marketization has been developed more than commodification or monetization, for example.

To *unbind* and destitute (Tari, 2021) these social forms would be central to their dissolution, along with unearthing new education forms that seek to leave capital behind (e.g. through the kinds of co-operative educational movements advanced by Neary 2020). As Holloway (2022, p. 83) puts it: 'Hope lies in the breaking of the binding'.

It could be argued that the merits and advances of this chapter consist in the following. First, some social forms from the perspective of labor-power (as opposed to the general category of commodities) have been uncovered in relation to education. Secondly, there is the hint that 'educational' forms (as opposed to 'economic' ones) can be foci of anti-capitalist analysis and struggle. Thirdly, it indicates how capital's social forms comprise a *web* binding us to value production in the context of education and its institutions. Each of these nodes invokes fragilities for capital.

Yet we are not mere flies in a spider's web. We are also the spider, as *our labor* constructs the web. We appear to be victims in traps of our own making. We need to stop making the web of social forms, in education and elsewhere, and to build new webs of social connection unmediated by capital's social forms. Individually and collectively, we must stop acting like mummies in a Hammer horror film, struggling but failing to cast off our bindings, but act more like grave robbers stripping them off before forming new socialities adrift from capital's social forms through communizing practice and intellect.

Our unbinding of capital's web of social forms involves dissolving the institutions and related roles through which they manifest themselves. This involves us in adventures. Adventure 'only exists as a "time of now"' (Campagna, 2013, p. 67). Thus, we cannot predict how we will feel about this unbinding, but in destroying the web of capital's social forms in education and throughout capital's social universe, then new, alternative institutional forms must be created *simultaneously*. There must be new forms of security for post-capitalist human life. This can only be a co-operative effort, in comradeship, for 'Cooperative action within the dreamscape of reality opens a range of possibilities that would be unobtainable by solitary action' (Campagna, 2013, p. 71).

Disclosure Statement The author has no financial interest or benefit that has arisen from the direct applications of this research.

Notes

1. In capitalist production, value is incorporated within commodities that are produced in labor processes. However, it is not sufficient just to produce value as an aspect of commodities. Value produced equivalent to, or less than, money capital invested in means of production, raw materials and labor-power falls short of what is required: *surplus value*. Capitalist enterprises require value over-and-above that invested in the means of production, raw materials and labor-power, for a number of reasons. They will need to invest in the next production cycle (and may have to borrow from banks for this, therefore paying interest), and may seek to expand their production (needing more resources than for the previous production cycle). They have taxes to pay, perhaps rents (e.g. for premises, machinery), insurance, maybe interest on business loans, but most of all they seek to produce *profits*. Profits for themselves as owners, or for shareholders, or for private equity investors. The fear of making zero profits drives on human representatives of capital (e.g. company owners, managers) to squeeze as much work out of laborers' labor-power as possible; labor-power being the living commodity, the only commodity that can create new, additional, value: *surplus value*. The nature and uniqueness of labor-power as a value-creating social force is explained in more depth later on.
2. In the *Grundrisse*, Marx points out that 'individuals are now ruled by *abstractions* …The abstraction, or idea, however, is nothing more than the theoretical expression of those material relations which are their lord and master' (1973b, p. 164—original emphasis). Marx's second point grounds these abstractions as *realities* in contemporary society. It has already been noted that labor has an abstract aspect in capitalism (abstract labor). We are ruled and oppressed by many other phenomena that have the dual character of being at once concrete (expressing materiality), yet are also abstract and social in capitalism. In capitalism, people are 'ruled by economic abstractions over which she has no control … [and] … the economic categories manifest social *compulsion* by real abstractions as natural necessity' (Bonefeld, 2019, p. 2—emphasis added). Kurz (2016, pp. 8–22) expands on real abstraction and the abstract aspect of labor (abstract labor) in capitalist society. In capitalism, money is a key example of real abstraction. For Neary and Taylor, 'money is simultaneously both the most concrete and the most abstract expression of the contradictory relations of capitalist production' (1998, p. 5). Our everyday lives are shaped by money, both in terms of its concrete materiality (we don't have enough of the stuff to pay bills, or positively when buying a new pair of shoes), but also as an abstract force hanging over us (fear of debt, bankruptcy etc.). For Simon Clarke, money exists 'as the supreme social power through which social reproduction is subordinated to the reproduction of capital' (1988, p. 14, in Neary & Taylor, 1998, p. 5). Money socially glues us to the reproduction of capital and its society; it makes the capitalist world go round, and we are key players in the drama given our social addictions to money. Interestingly, the concrete materiality of money has become ever more 'abstract' historically, with the development of capitalism.

Transitions from pure gold and silver to gold and silver coins (which began well before capitalism), to 'debased' coinage (including copper and nickel additions), and then paper money, indicates this. The movement from paper money to debit and credit card payment, with 'contactless' payment in recent years, eviscerates the materiality of money further still. In the sphere of education, 'qualification' in its relation to labor-power production, could be viewed as a real abstraction. To demonstrate this would require another chapter.

3. A *flow* 'is continuous movement' and 'Being flows *if and only if* the twin conditions of *continuity* and *motion* are satisfied' (Nail, 2019, p. 68—original emphases). Value is 'not separate from the flows that support it' (Nail, 2020, p. 75). That is, it is not separate from its web of social forms. Capital *moves* says John Holloway; 'capital is inherently mobile' (1995, p. 141). Yet capital's social forms have the effect of congealing or blocking some of these life-flows, but they are not always successful; in one way or another they mostly fail as our richness and variability exceeds these social forms and their manifestation in institutions and constraining roles. Many years ago, I was a production worker in an engineering factory, grinding rough edges off metal blocks. Yet, given the monotony of the work, my mind was relatively free to roam; the *flow of ideas*. An example from education: primitive socialisation. As education is involved in the social production of labor-power, then each cohort of youth *flows* through the education system and is subject to this process. In this productive process, 'Each new generation has to be socialised into capitalist life in general and capitalist work in particular' (Rikowski, 2015, p. 37). For more on the notion of primitive socialisation, see Rikowski (2015, pp. 36–8). Thomas Nail explores the concept of flow in depth (2019, pp. 67–96).

4. Contemporary examples in education would include the current strikes by teachers in schools and university lecturers in the UK. These are about gaining advantages, or at least not suffering material loses regarding pay (when set against inflation), and pensions (for university lecturers). They are not primarily about ending the wage form or wage system, state pensions, or much less capitalism as a whole. In capitalism, workers, including education workers are *driven* to defend their pay and working conditions in the face of attacks by human representative of capital.

5. The difference between labor-power *aspects* and labor-power *attributes* is explained in Rikowski (2002a).

6. Simon Frith (1980) indicates employer criticisms of school leavers' employability can be traced back to at least the late nineteenth century in England.

7. The main reasons for value production being weak in schools in England are, firstly, the capitalist state has not created conditions conducive for significant profit-making. For example, the claw-back clauses in contracts linked to targets (e.g. for examination results) need to be weakened (or abolished), and selling off assets (e.g. school playing fields) needs to be made easier, and so on. Secondly, private operators in schools in England need control of significant numbers of schools so economies of scale can be made (e.g. with joint services such as payroll, recruitment and estate management established). This point is being addressed by policymakers through the forced academization process, where schools are taken out of local authority control on the one hand, and the processes of combining schools into Federations and Trusts is encouraged on

the other. School 'brands' and companies are in *formation* through these policies.
8. This section draws material from Rikowski (2019a, pp. 160–65).
9. Remembering that, for Marx, commodities do not have to be 'hard', directly tangible and occupying specific space time (e.g. coats and linen—examples that Marx uses in *Capital* 1977a, pp. 54–75, when pinning down exchange-value and the money form). Theatres, brothels, and musical performances provide services that 'in the strict sense … assume no objective form … [and] … do not receive an existence as things separate from those performing the services … can be in part subsumed under capital' and therefore 'the commodity … has nothing to do with its corporeal reality' (Marx, 1975, pp. 166–67, and 171). Services here refers to certain *experiences* that take a commodity form, and labor that performs these services creates value for owners of brothels, schools, transport services, theatres and so on. It is not easy to find worthwhile characterizations of *educational services*. As Ng and Forbes note, in relation to HEIs: 'Service literature tends to view services generally whilst education literature tends to focus on the learning aspect of higher education' (2008, p. 8). They tend to focus on service quality and the marketization of these services in HEIs, while ignoring them as commodities and their commodification.
10. For a detailed portrayal of unbundling see McCowan (2017, pp. 735–39).
11. For more on the insertion of for-profit providers in UK HEIs, see McGettigan (2013, pp. 96–109).
12. 'Free schools are part of an ongoing policy agenda to liberalize the 'supply side' of the school quasi-market system in England' (Allen & Higham, 2018, p. 191).
13. See McGettigan for an excellent account on the UK HEIs fees/loans system (2013, pp. 37–51). For a detailed and participatory account of these students protests, see Neary (2020, pp. 68–80).
14. As Thomas Nail notes regarding flows of being, it is possible for flows to 'flow together in a confluence, which is an intersection of two or more flows that intersect' (2019, p. 86). What is being advanced here is that the various forms of labor-power production described in this section *intersect* and affect each other's development and direction. This occurs in the lives of individuals, within their bodies, modes of thought and ideas, and relations with others. These points require development in further work. For more on the confluence of flows, see Nail (2019, pp. 86–96).

References

Allen, R., & Higham, R. (2018). Quasi-markets, School Diversity and Social Selection: Analysing the Case of a Free School in England, Five Years On. *London Review of Education, 16*(2), 191–213.

Ball, S. (2007). *Education Plc: Understanding Private Sector Participation in Public Sector Education*. Routledge.

BBC. (2012, January 25). Breckland Free School in Suffolk Approved by Government. *BBC News*. Retrieved November 9, 2022, from https://www.bbc.co.uk/news/uk-england-suffolk-16721264

Bhattacharya, T. (Ed.). (2017). *Social Reproduction Theory: Remapping Class, Recentering Oppression*. Pluto Press.

Bonefeld, W. (1987a, May). Open Marxism. *Commons Sense: Journal of the Edinburgh Conference of Socialist Economists*, (1), 34–37.

Bonefeld, W. (1987b, July). Marxism and the Concept of Mediation. *Common Sense: Journal of the Edinburgh Conference of Socialist Economists*, (2), 67–72.

Bonefeld, W. (2005, July 31). *Social Form, Critique and Human Dignity*. Posted to libcom.org. Retrieved May 24, 2014, from https://libcom.org/library/social-form-critique-and-human-dignity

Bonefeld, W. (2019). On Capital and Real Abstraction. Preprint retrieved from https://www.researchgate.net/publication/334132183_On_Capital_as_Real_Abstraction

Bonefeld, W., Gunn, R., & Psychopedis, K. (1992). Introduction. In W. Bonefeld, R. Gunn, & K. Psychopedis (Eds.), *Open Marxism: Volume I—Dialectics and History* (pp. ix–xx). Pluto Press.

Campagna, F. (2013). *The Last Night: Anti-work, Atheism, Adventure*. Zero Books.

Ciccarelli, R. (2021). *Labour Power: Virtual and Actual in Digital Production* (E. M. Gainsworth, Trans.). Springer. (Original work published 2018).

Clarke, S. (1988, October). *Money, the State and the Illusory Community*. Unpublished paper presented at the International Conference 'Socialism and the Spiritual Situation of the Age', Cavtat, Yugoslavia.

Cleaver, H. (2000). *Reading 'Capital' Politically*. Anti-Theses & AK Press.

Cleaver, H. (2019). *33 Lessons on 'Capital': Reading Marx Politically*. Pluto Press.

Compass VSC (2022, January 22). *How Many Parts Are in a Car?* Compass Vehicle Servicing Coverage. Retrieved November 10, 2022, from https://www.compassvsc.com/post/how-many-parts-are-in-a-car

Exley, S. (2015, May). Are Quasi-markets in Education What the British Public Want? *LSE Research Online*. Retrieved November 16, 2022, from http://eprints.lse.ac.uk/47472/

Fazackerley, A. (2022, October 22). 90% of Schools in England Will Run Out of Money Next Year, Heads Warn. *The Observer*. Retrieved November 9, 2022, from https://www.theguardian.com/education/2022/oct/22/exclusive-90-of-uk-schools-will-go-bust-next-year-heads-warn

Frith, S. (1980). Education, Training and the Labour Process. In M. Cole & B. Skelton (Eds.), *Blind Alley: Youth in a Crisis of Capital* (pp. 25–44). G W. & A. Hesketh.

Gordon, E. (2000). *Skill Wars: Winning the Battle for Productivity and Profit*. Butterworth-Heinemann.

Green, F., & Kynaston, D. (2019, January 13). Britain's Private School Problem: It's Time to Talk. *The Guardian*. Retrieved November 9, 2022, from https://www.theguardian.com/education/2019/jan/13/public-schools-david-kynaston-francis-green-engines-of-privilege

Greer, I., & Umney, C. (2022). *Marketization: How Capitalist Exchange Disciplines Workers and Subverts Democracy*. Bloomsbury Academic.

Gunn, R. (1987, July). Notes on 'Class'. *Common Sense: Journal of Edinburgh Conference of Socialist Economists*, (2), 15–25.

Hale, T. (2017, December 6). UK Raises 1.7bn Via Student Loan-Backed Securitisation. *Financial Times*. Retrieved November 21, 2022, from https://www.ft.com/content/5f45d363-440a-3fc6-9403-23407b230a0e

Hardt, M., & Holloway, J. (2012, December 11). Creating Common Wealth and Cracking Capitalism: A Cross-reading (Part 1). *Shift Magazine*, issue 14, posted to libcom.org. Retrieved July 2, 2014, from https://libcom.org/library/creating-common-wealth-cracking-capitalism-cross-reading-part-i

Holloway, J. (1991a). Capital *is* Class Struggle (And Bears are not Cuddly). In W. Bonefeld & J. Holloway (Eds.), *Post-Fordism & Social Form* (pp. 170–175) Macmillan.

Holloway, J. (1991b). The State and Everyday Struggle. In S. Clarke (Ed.), *The State Debate* (pp. 225–259). Macmillan Academic and Professional Ltd..

Holloway, J. (1991c, Winter). In the Beginning was the Scream. *Common Sense: Journal of the Edinburgh Conference of Socialist Economists*, (11), 69–77.

Holloway, J. (1995, Autumn). Capital Moves. *Capital & Class, 57*, 134–144.

Holloway, J. (2002). Class and Classification: Against, in and Beyond Labour. In A. Dinerstein & M. Neary (Eds.), *The Labour Debate: An Investigation into the Theory and Reality of Capitalist Work* (pp. 27–40). Ashgate.

Holloway, J. (2022). *Hope in Hopeless Times*. Pluto Press.

Holloway, J., & Cecchetto, S. (2007, October). Fight against Capital Always Means Fighting Abstract Labor. Interview with John Holloway by Sergio Cecchetto. *Herramienta*, (36). Retrieved April 9, 2019, from http://www.herramienta.com.ar/articulo.php?id=523

Jaffe, A. (2020). *Social Reproduction Theory and the Socialist Horizon: Work, Power and Political Strategy*. Pluto Press.

Kurz, R. (2016). *The Substance of Capital*. Chronos Publications.

Lazzarato, M. (2013). *Governing by Debt*. Semiotext(e).

MacNeill, D. (2021, January 28). What Is Value? A Marxist Perspective. *Progress in Political Economy*. Retrieved May 12, 2021, from https://www.ppesydney.net/what-is-value-a-marxist-perspective/

Martin, J., & Dunlop, L. (2019). For-profit Schools in England: The State of a Nation. *Preprint for Journal of Education Policy, 34*(5), 726–741. Retrieved November 9, 2022, from https://eprints.whiterose.ac.uk/130803/1/forprofit.pdf

Marx, K. (1973a). Introduction. In *Grundrisse: Foundations of the Critique of Political Economy (Rough Draft)*. Penguin Books

Marx, K. (1973b). *Grundrisse: Foundations of the Critique of Political Economy (Rough Draft)*. Penguin Books.

Marx, K. (1975). *Theories of Surplus Value—Part 1*. Lawrence & Wishart.

Marx, K. (1977a). *Capital: A Critique of Political Economy—Volume I*. Lawrence & Wishart.

Marx, K. (1977b). Preface to the First German Edition. In K. Marx (Ed.), *Capital: A Critique of Political Economy—Volume I* (pp. 18–21). Lawrence & Wishart.

Marx, K. (1977c). *Economic and Philosophic Manuscripts of 1844*. Progress Publishers.

Marx, K. (1978). *Capital: A Critique of Political Economy—Volume Two*. Penguin Books.

Marx, K. (1979a). *Capital: A Critique of Political Economy—Volume One*. Penguin Books.

Marx, K. (1979b). Appendix: Results of the Immediate Process of Production. In K. Marx (Ed.), *Capital: A Critique of Political Economy—Volume One* (pp. 948–1084). Penguin Books.

Marx, K., & Engels, F. (1976). *The German Ideology*. Progress Publishers.

McCowan, T. (2017). Higher Education, and the End of the University as We Know It. *Oxford Review of Education, 43*(6), 733–748.

McGettigan, A. (2013). *The Great University Gamble: Money, Markets and the Future of Higher Education*. Pluto Press.

Micocci, A. (2012). *Moderation and Revolution*. Lexington Books.

Nail, T. (2019). *Being and Motion*. Oxford University Press.

Nail, T. (2020). *Marx in Motion: A New Materialist Marxism*. Oxford University Press.

Neary, M. (2020). *The Student as Producer: How do Revolutionary Teachers Teach?* Zero Books.

Neary, M., & Rikowski, G. (2002). Time and Speed in the Social Universe of Capital. In G. Crow & S. Heath (Eds.), *Social Conceptions of Time: Structure and Process in Work and Everyday Life* (pp. 53–65). Palgrave Macmillan.

Neary, M., & Taylor, G. (1998). *Money and the Human Condition.* Macmillan Press Ltd..

Ng, I. & Forbes, J. (2008). Education as Service: The Understanding of University Experience through the Service Logic (Draft). *Journal of Marketing of Higher Education*, 19(1), 38–64. Retrieved November 13, 2022, from https://ore.exeter.ac.uk/repository/bitstream/handle/10036/33054/ng12.pdf;jsessionid=A759AFD974BEF10F6141519B243D8F53?sequence=2

Oliver, J. (2004, March 14). Fury over Labour's Schools for Profit. *The Mail on Sunday*, pp. 1 & 8.

Paveley, R. (2003, February 21). Co-payment: Blair's Buzzword That Means You May Be Charged for Roads, Schools and NHS. *Daily Mail*, p. 15

Rikowski, G. (1990, July 25). *The Recruitment Process and Labour Power.* Unpublished paper, Division of Humanities & Modern Languages, Epping Forest College, Loughton, Essex. Retrieved November 25, 2022, from https://www.researchgate.net/publication/349482929_The_Recruitment_Process_and_Labour_Power

Rikowski, G. (1996). *Education Markets and Missing Products.* A paper first presented at the Conference of Socialist Economists, University of Northumbria, Newcastle, July 7–9, 1995. Revised and extended, December 18, 1996. Retrieved November 15, 2022, from https://www.researchgate.net/publication/318380079_Education_Markets_and_Missing_Products

Rikowski, G. (2000). *That Other Great Class of Commodities: Repositioning Marxist Educational Theory.* A Paper presented at the British Educational Research Association Conference, Cardiff University, September 7–10. Retrieved November 13, 2022, from https://www.researchgate.net/publication/277068478_That_other_great_class_of_commodities_Repositioning_Marxist_educational_theory

Rikowski, G. (2001). Education for Industry: A Complex Technicism. *Journal of Education and Work*, 14(1), 27–49.

Rikowski, G. (2002a). Fuel for the Living Fire: Labour-Power! In A. Dinerstein & M. Neary (Eds.), *The Labour Debate: An Investigation into the Theory and Reality of Capitalist Work* (pp. 179–202). Ashgate.

Rikowski, G. (2002b). Education, Capital and the Transhuman. In D. Hill, P. McLaren, M. Cole, & G. Rikowski (Eds.), *Marxism Against Postmodernism in Educational Theory*. Lexington Books.

Rikowski, G. (2002c). *Methods for Researching the Social Production of Labour Power in Capitalism.* Presentation, School of Education, Research Seminar, University College Northampton, March 7. Retrieved November 25, 2022, from https://www.researchgate.net/publication/253074133_METHODS_FOR_RESEARCHING_THE_SOCIAL_PRODUCTION_OF_LABOUR_POWER_IN_CAPITALISM

Rikowski, G. (2003). The Business Takeover of Schools. *Mediactive*, (1), 91–110.

Rikowski, G. (2005). *Silence on the Wolves: What is Absent in New Labour's Five Year Strategy for Education.* Education Research Centre, University of Brighton, Occasional Paper, May. University of Brighton.

Rikowski, G. (2006a, August 28). *The Long Moan of History: Employers on School-Leavers.* Unpublished paper, London. Retrieved November 2, 2022, from https://www.academia.edu/6623898/The_Long_Moan_of_History_Employers_on_School_Leavers

Rikowski, G. (2006b, April 4). *Creeping Privatisation in Higher Education?* Unpublished paper, London. Retrieved November 14, 2022, from https://www.academia.edu/6605112/Creeping_Privatisation_in_Higher_Education

Rikowski, G. (2007, February 15). *Ultra-Blairite, Contra Progress: Co-payment in Hospitals and Schools.* Unpublished paper, London. Retrieved November 17, 2022, from https://www.academia.edu/11770442/Ultra_Blairite_Contra_Progress_Co_payment_in_Hospitals_and_Schools

Rikowski, G. (2015). *Crises, Commodities and Education: Disruptions, Eruption, Interruptions and Ruptions.* A Paper prepared for the Research in Critical Education Studies (RiCES) Seminar, School of Education, University of Lincoln, November 19. Retrieved December 18, 2022, from https://www.researchgate.net/publication/309431122_Crises_Commodities_and_Education_Disruptions_Eruptions_Interruptions_and_Ruptions

Rikowski, G. (2016, June 20). *Karl Marx's Social Time.* Unpublished paper, Forest Gate, London. Retrieved October 10, 2022, from https://www.researchgate.net/publication/364102971_Karl_Marx's_Social_Time

Rikowski, G. (2017a). Privatisation in Education and Commodity Forms. *Journal for Critical Education Policy Studies, 15*(3), 29–56.

Rikowski, G. (2017b, October 3). *Misrepresentations: Critical Notes on Commodification and Education.* Unpublished paper, Forest Gate, London. Retrieved November 25, 2022, from https://www.researchgate.net/publication/343046724_Misrepresentations_Critical_Notes_on_Commodities_and_Education

Rikowski, G. (2019a). Education Crises as Crises for Capital. *Theory in Action, 12*(3), 146–165.

Rikowski, G. (2019b). *Notes on Commodity Forms and the Business Takeover of Schools.* A presentation at a seminar with second year Education Studies students at the University of East London, Stratford Campus, November 20. Retrieved November 25, 2022, from https://www.researchgate.net/publication/338633924_Notes_on_Commodity_Forms_and_the_Business_Takeover_of_Schools

Statista. (2022, October 28). *Amount Outstanding in Student Loans in England, Scotland, Wales, and Northern Ireland from Financial Year 2010/11 to 2021/22.* Statista Research Department. Retrieved November 21, 2022, from https://www.statista.com/statistics/750679/outstanding-amount-in-student-loans-uk/

Tari, M. (2021). *There Is No Unhappy Revolution: The Communism of Destitution* (R. Braude, Trans.). Common Notions. (Original work published 2017).

Warrell, H. (2014, August 17). Swedish-run UK School Seeks to Improve Performance. *Financial Times.* Retrieved from November 9. 2022, from https://www.ft.com/content/98d89788-2de7-11e4-b330-00144feabdc0

Whittaker, F. (2018, November 4). Firm Behind First For-Profit Free School Is Still Losing Money. *Schools Week.* Retrieved November 9, 2022, from https://schoolsweek.co.uk/firm-behind-first-for-profit-free-school-is-still-losing-money/

CHAPTER 4

Breaking Bonds: How Academic Capitalism Feeds Processes of Academic Alienation

Mikko Poutanen

4.1 Introduction

Marxist critique stipulates that as capital seeks new areas to incorporate into its accumulation processes, it expands its logic and practice into domains previously excluded from the profit-motive. According to Harvey (2018), this process often proceeds as dispossession: public goods are moved into the reproductive sphere of (private) capital. This typically includes an expansion from private to public economies: as states have embraced the hegemonic idea of knowledge economies in global competition (Olssen & Peters, 2005; Poutanen, 2022; Sum, 2009), they are looking to leverage public institutions to support their economic interests (Wright & Shore, 2017). This expansion reinforces competitive tendencies that filter down from the global competition of nation-states down to the (global and national) competition of higher education institutions (HEIs) (e.g. through rankings: Marginson, 2014) all the way to the level of individual academics working under conditions of scarcity and precarity (Fleming, 2021; Loveday, 2018). The encroachment of capital into the field of higher education can be characterized as academic capitalism (Cantwell & Kauppinen, 2014; Münch, 2020; Slaughter & Rhoades, 2004). Academic capitalism entails a reordering of priorities in higher education institutions (HEIs), emphasizing productivity and competitive logic, which reframe the realities of academic labor.

M. Poutanen (✉)
Tampere University, Tampere, Finland
e-mail: mikko.poutanen@tuni.fi

As academic capitalism expands, Marxist critique of capitalist logic becomes an increasingly relevant frame of analysis (Szadkowski, 2019; Szadkowski & Krzeski, 2019; Szadkowski & Krzeski, 2021). The material conditions dictating academic work become more visible, as new subjectivities are imposed by the encroachment of capital: academics are in material terms cast more as regular employees rather than autonomous, self-guided academic professionals (Hall, 2021). The relative distinction of academics from the modern working class of the knowledge economy is reduced. Social relations of academic work become increasingly characterized as relations of exchange for various forms of capital. Laboring under conditions of (academic) capitalism has led to widespread disassociation and disaffection among academics—alienation (Hall, 2018b; Harvie, 2000; Oleksiyenko, 2018).

Alienation as a concept is derived from Marx's early writings as an amalgamation of political economic and philosophical critique of capitalism (Marx 1961/2007; see also Musto, 2021; Sayers, 2011a). The argument is that the capitalist mode of production commodifies all labor into simple, measurable and exchangeable things. Commodity fetishism is the process by which products of academic labor as much as the academics themselves are alienated: they are reduced in relation to the labor process, the products of their labor, their colleagues, and, finally, within themselves (Marx 1961/2007, pp. 72–74). Among commodities, instrumental value rules supreme, rendering human relations essentially inhuman. This rendition of inhumanity enables exploitation, which is not limited to labor (or class) but includes also gender and ethnicity—alienation intensifies marginalization and human vulnerability.

In this chapter, alienation is seen as a process of academic capitalism, often subjectively experienced in ruptures of academic labor that emphasize how little control academics retain over their work. As the effect of the encroachment of capital onto higher education has progressed further in the Anglophone world (US, UK, Australia and New Zealand), this is the context where most theorizations of academic alienation have taken place (most notably Hall, 2018a, 2018b). This chapter expands the scope to Finland, where public universities have previously been relatively sheltered by the Nordic welfare state, but which is now building its own strain of academic capitalism (Poutanen, 2023b). There are signs of increasing experiences of alienation among Finnish academics, who experience a narrowing of their professional autonomy (Poutanen, 2023a; Rinne et al., 2014). Operationalizing alienation as a concept allows for a critical inquiry of structural problems, which all too often are relegated to questions of individual job satisfaction or well-being.

This chapter proceeds first to outline Marx's idea of alienation in general and then specifically applied into higher education and how the concept has since developed. Thereafter, we discuss academic capitalism and how it shapes the conditions in the field of higher education. Struggles against (academic) capitalism are at once uniform but locally determined, and as such processes of alienation also vary. Different positions of power or vulnerability relating to gender and ethnicity should be considered in all Marxist analysis (Rodney,

2022; Roediger, 2019). Subjective experiences of alienation are tempered with one's position in the competitive structure of academic capitalism. Finally, the chapter discusses possible paths of disalienation going forward.

4.2 What Does Marx Say About Alienation?

The Marxist concept of alienation stems from Marx's early treatment of Hegelian ideas in his *Economic and Philosophic Manuscripts of 1844* (Marx 1961/2007), where he reconceptualizes alienation from an essentialist-naturalist term to a concept for explaining fundamental lack of human self-realization through labor under the political economy of capitalism. Marx's alienation breaks with Hegel to focus on the material constraints to self-realization under capitalism. Though capitalism is often represented as a social system of self-realization, it acts as such only for the very few. While alienation for Hegel meant an ontological state, for Marx it was a process of dispossession of public goods into private property: for Marx all social relations under capitalism are subjected to the political economy of capitalism, which reduces labor as a fundamentally human activity into an act of production for the sole purpose of exchange. Workers themselves become commodities within the production process, much like the commodities they produce; workers are alienated from the fruits of their labor, their own part in the labor process and other workers and finally alienated from and within themselves (Marx 1961/2007, pp. 72–74; see also: Musto, 2021, pp. 6–7; Hall, 2018a, p. 98).

To elaborate, anything that the worker produces is turned into a commodity and entered into the circulation of capital; as an element of capital, the produced commodity becomes alien to them. Moreover, they exert little to no control over the labor process, which is organized according to the interests of capital. In a competitive capitalist working environment, others are easily seen as threats to one's own survival: competition over scarce resource alienates workers from collective interests. Finally, as the worker, like those around him, is recast as human capital—human commodity—they themselves become less than human, mere extensions of capital (Swain, 2012, pp. 54, 69; see also Mészáros 1970/2005). Human capital is engaged in a 'war of competition' (Marx 1961/2007, p. 68), which makes workers responsible also for the competitive capacity of their employer—in the case of academics, their institutions—but also for their own competitiveness as personifications of human capital.

In formulating alienation, Marx challenges the capitalist idea that 'every man is a merchant, and society is a commercial society' (ibid., pp. 126, 133): because capitalist labor processes are not equal processes of exchange. Wage labor as mere necessity for survival becomes a vehicle of alienation (ibid., p. 74). The more society is based on exchange, of private property relations, the more emphasized egoistic and asocial actions that are deleterious to common or communitarian impulses—like building knowledge through educational endeavors—become. Considering how significant labor is to humanity—in

Marx's terms it is an activity that is natural to the species and the method of seeking fulfillment and self-realization (McLellan, 2000, p. 89)—lacking control over their working conditions, the products they make, their working community and, ultimately, over themselves, is expressed as lost agency, meaning, sense or purpose in labor.[1]

Marx thought the abolition of (the accumulation of) private property and the collective ownership of the means of production could overcome the alienation of labor, because it would no longer dispossess labor or the public good from the production process. Similarly, the privatization of knowledge runs counter to Marx's idea of social emancipation: in the *Grundrisse* (Marx, 1993), he develops the idea of social intellect—societally formed general and common knowledge—as a necessary force of production, which capitalism seeks to commodify and privatize, thus eliminating knowledge as a public, social good (see also: Zoubir, 2018). Marx stresses that

> the essential connection of private property, selfishness, the separation of labor, capital, and landed property, of exchange and competition, of the value and degradation of man, of monopoly and compensation, etc.—the connection of all this alienation with the money system. (McLellan, 2000, p. 86)

Furthermore, the money system of capitalism supplants the human world with a world of commodities—a world of things with only instrumental value in competition:

> The worker becomes a commodity that is all the cheaper the more commodities he creates. The depreciation of the human world progresses in direct proportion to the increase in value of the world of things. ... The product of labor is labor that has solidified itself into an object, made itself into a thing, the objectification of labor. (Ibid.)

In an educational context, students and their teachers become things in equal measure, simply at different stages of the societal production process. Academics are things from the perspective of higher education policy, creating educational outputs, whereas students become things produced through the university under the supervision of the staff, destined to become instrumental cogs in the productive machinery of capitalism. They never become private property per se, but the logic of their actions serves a purpose with assigned monetary value. The alienation of social relations is a mechanism mediated by money: money-fetishism means people place more faith in a thing—money—than they place in each other (Marx, 1993, p. 160 (cf. Harvey, 2023, p. 63)).

The commodified object becomes externalized from its producer and/or self, and is appropriated into capitalist accumulation, thus placing dispossession at the heart of alienation (Marx 1961/2007, p. 83). Laborers as producers and products of labor belong to capital:

Estrangement[2] is manifested not only in the fact that my means of life belongs to someone else, that my desire is the inaccessible possession of another, but also in the fact that everything is in itself something different from itself—that my activity is something else and that, finally [...] all is under the sway of inhuman power. (Ibid., p. 126)

Alienation takes on existential meaning for the workers—including academics—since the more one takes out of themselves and places into objects, the less they retain in themselves beyond simple reproduction of their being: '[a]lienated labor reverses the relationship [of labor as man's species-being] so that, just because he is a conscious being, man makes his vital activity and essence a mere means to his existence' (McLellan, 2000, p. 90). Labor itself is meaningful only in exchange for private property (wages):

for wages, in which the product, the object of the labor, renumerates the labor itself, are just a necessary consequence of the alienation of labor. In the wage system the labor does not appear as the final aim but only as the servant of the wages. (Ibid., p. 93)

The object the worker has created is alien to them, valueless beyond exchange and as such yet another element in value aggregation and a proxy for competition. There is no space for labor being personally fulfilling or meaningful—unless by lucky coincidence.

Capitalism and alienation are linked for Marx as a historical, not a natural, process. Since capitalism is more than a mere economic system, shaping all social relations, in similar fashion alienation is more than a subjective experience of dissatisfaction—it is 'an objective, social condition, which can be overcome only through historical changes' (Sayers, 2011b, p. 288). The commodifying and dispossessive processes of capitalism that produced alienation had to be surpassed through a different political economy, which wouldn't set capital up as the alien opposite to labor. From Marx's perspective of historical progression, only moving past capitalism and its associate alienation can there be enough momentum for disalienation (Harvey, 2018, p. 140). For Marx, the solution was a material shift in political economy and social relations in the form of communism—the abolishment of private property—as a necessary dimension for any disalienating social progress (McLellan, 2000, pp. 97, 266). However, Marx acknowledged, against determinism projected onto him, that historical processes are complex and unpredictable (Sayers, 2011b, p. 298).

4.3 Conceptualizations of Alienation After Marx

Marx's *Economic and Philosophic Manuscripts of 1844* includes his best-known passages on alienation, but the concept does come across in (fragments of) his other works, too. Since the manuscripts dealing with alienation were only discovered and furthermore translated in the 1900s, Marx's conceptualization is mediated by post-Marxist interpretations of alienation—including detours from the original idea. Marcello Musto (2021) points out that since the manuscripts that discuss alienation were discovered much later compared to Marx's published works, it is easy to dismiss alienation as something Marx toyed with, but then ultimately abandoned, as the concept no longer appears in *Capital*. Musto (ibid., p. 31) points out, however, that in draft versions and unpublished sections of the first volume of *Capital* and the *Grundrisse* (1993) (see also: Harvey, 2023; Harvey, 2018, p. 137), Marx keeps alienation close to his analyses on political economy.

David Harvey admits that while alienation as a concept fades into the background in *Capital* and in subsequent works, it is prominently present in the *Grundrisse*, but in a different form than in the *Economic and Philosophical Manuscripts of 1844*. The more humanist and idealist conception of alienation is reintroduced directly linked to historical materialism and the ruling power of capital over labor under the coercive laws of competition (Harvey, 2023, pp. 59–60). For Harvey, the crux of alienation in the *Grundrisse* is that while we like to believe ourselves free individuals, 'we are, in practice, ruled by the abstractions of capital', which serves the interests of the ruling class (ibid., p. 60).

Thus, arguing that alienation disappearing from Marx's later works is proof of the concept's 'immaturity' is incorrect (Sayers, 2011b): rather it was assumed under commodity fetishism[3] (Musto, 2010), and in some post-Marxist theorizations, under reification (Adorno & Horkheimer, 1947/1997; Lukács, 1971),[4] which captures Marx's essential idea of social relations between humans being reduced to social relations between things. The Frankfurt School was divided on how to approach alienation: for Adorno and Horkheimer, the technological rationale of modern society was the rationale of domination, and thus the rationale of a society alienated from itself (Musto, 2021, p. 11), while Erich Fromm rather sought to bridge Marxist thought and psychoanalysis and, as such, emphasized the role of subjectivity in alienation (ibid., pp. 11–12).[5]

The latter approach, but with decreasing emphasis on Marx, was utilized also by American sociologists (e.g. Seeman, 1959, 1975), who sought to operationalize a quantitative analytical framework for alienation, but in so doing started to veer alienation away from its core idea as a critique of capitalism (Musto, 2010, pp. 93–95). Abandoning Marx's critique of capitalist political economy, social psychologists also analyzed alienation as a subjective problem that could be remedied or mitigated by professional well-being interventions at the workplace (Kalekin-Fishman & Langman, 2015; Musto, 2021, p. 25). Alienation was further recast as citizen dissatisfaction with traditional social values, or industrial production in general, so as to distance it from its Marxist political baggage (Musto, 2021, pp. 26–17).

In these disparate contexts, alienation as a term became used notoriously vague in social science research and emphatically subjective, with little to do with structural critique of capitalism.[6] Alienation was devalued notably by Louis Althusser (Althusser, 1965/2005), who argued that as concept or theory, alienation was too fungible for strict, Marxist scientific analysis (see similar evaluations also by e.g. Geyer & Schweitzer, 1976; Schacht, 1970; see also Musto, 2021, pp. 15–17).[7] And yet, alienation has remained salient in critical social analysis of modern capitalism even very recently (Øversveen, 2021; Skotnicki & Nielsen, 2021; Westin, 2021). Archibald (2009a, 2009b) has argued that the global, competitive labor market has created powerlessness and insecurity, which calls for updating the conceptualization of Marxist alienation.

There are insights from post-Marxist theorizations that also still apply. For example, Ernest Mandel's characterization of how bureaucratization and technocratization alienate people from the very institutions that are expected to serve them (Mandel, 1970/2009, p. 45) readily calls to mind the overgrowth of university administrations in relation to teaching and research in neoliberal universities. If anything, alienation persists as a social dynamic under capitalism, not as a state that can be definitely measured, or a set of variables in a quantitative analysis akin to satisfaction at work. Alienation undergirds capitalist social relations immiserating modern working life. As capitalist accumulation expands, alienating processes expand with it.

This manifests most clearly as subjective experiences of meaninglessness and powerlessness explored by Seeman (1959), but which should be placed in the context of structural disempowerment driven by top-down managerialism, the reframing of universities as post-industrial knowledge factories and higher education policy that seeks to instrumentalize higher education as a competitive edge for the national economy (Poutanen, 2022). Williamson and Cullingford (1997) argue that with suitable rigor, Marx's conceptualization of alienation still has untapped explanatory and exploratory potential for modern academic work. Indeed, important perspectives emphasizing the significance of gender, race and colonialism that have supplemented Marxist theory (Coontz & Henderson, 1986; Rodney, 2022; Roediger, 2019) would give alienation more conceptual depth, also in academia.

4.4 A Review of Academic Capitalism

As a concept, academic capitalism is typically defined as the application of knowledge primarily for commercial purposes: it is a departure from academic work as a public good (Slaughter & Rhoades, 2004: 132; see also Cantwell & Kauppinen, 2014). Although literature on academic capitalism stops shy of an openly materialist analysis (Szadkowski & Krzeski, 2021), it is useful for recognizing how deeply the economic impact of HEIs—and of knowledge in general—is prioritized higher than its scientific or social impact (Münch, 2020, p. 101). The expansion of academic capitalism is part and parcel of the neoliberalization of academia (Olssen & Peters, 2005): state action reforms public higher education to be more conducive to the interests and expansion of capital. Expanding academic capitalism has been predicated by the paradigm of the knowledge economy, where the state reorients policy to drive competitiveness in a global capitalist political economy (Sum, 2009; Sum & Jessop, 2013), which also impacts particularly public HEIs directly (Wright & Shore, 2017).

The post-industrial competitive state takes ownership of the relatively autonomous field of higher education, as the knowledge economy represents 'not only the highest form of social organization but also the most effective system of wealth accumulation' (Moisio & Kangas, 2016, p. 272). Academic capitalism explains the ideological framework within which capital accumulation in higher education, in its various forms, is introduced to different national contexts. Education policy within the EU is informed by EU-level policy (the Bologna process more specifically: Fairclough & Wodak, 2008), and the goal of said policy is to make Europe 'the most competitive knowledge-based economy in the world' (Kauppinen & Kaidesoja, 2014, p. 32; Slaughter & Cantwell, 2012, p. 590). The OECD is also driving reforms into HE systems in this same vein (Hunter, 2013; Sellar & Lingard, 2012).

The discourse of competitiveness is realized under ideological praxis: competitiveness becomes the core concept around which academic activities are to be organized on policy and institutional levels. Different measurements and metrics, such as university rankings, which serve as the markings of the global competition of HEIs (Brankovic et al., 2018; Hazelkorn, 2015; Marginson, 2014), give the discourse of competitiveness seemingly objective, material dimensions and can also be used nationally to determine performance-based funding of 'excellence' (Münch, 2020). These objectified measurements are a feature of the commodification of academia, supported further by managerial technologies, such as auditing culture (Shore, 2008). Auditing serves a role in capitalist political economy by rendering 'commensurable and controllable all kinds of disparate individuals, institutions and objects with diverse and incommensurate features' (Shore & Wright, 2015, p. 430). This neoliberal style of governance de-democratizes institutions by marginalizing professionals from direct involvement in managing themselves. Marx himself had acknowledged the possibility of making scientific and academic activities 'mere objects of the capitalists' rationalization of the process of production' (Zoubir, 2018, p. 727).

In Europe, the higher education system in the UK—more accurately in England—has been at the leading edge of this development, with universities pressured to meet their performance metrics and strive for reputation, which determine their economic prospects as proxies for their public legitimacy (Watermeyer, 2019). This is typically expressed as a competing framework that takes on connotations of outright survival (Docherty, 2015). Experience from the UK has already shown that managerial governance, regardless of its dynamic discourse, leads to centralized, administrative control of HEIs (Lorenz, 2012; McCann et al., 2020), and anxiety-ridden precarity and casualization for academics (Loveday, 2018). These intensify the social construction of competition between academics and institutions (Szadkowski, 2019) and an atomized academic individuality (Brandist, 2017; Guillem & Briziarelli, 2020, p. 358).

Competitive pressures are not divided equally: the optimally commodified competitive academic archetype is often white, male and able. Women, ethnic or sexual minorities, but also younger academics in general, are disproportionately impacted. As a consequence, a sense of community and collegiality erodes under conditions of competition, encouraging bureaucratic conformity (Fleming, 2021, pp. 42–43). According to Erickson et al. (2021), UK academics are reacting very negatively to managerialist governance. The growing dissatisfaction of academics in the UK is exemplified by an increasing number of books outlining the degeneration of the academic working environment, which range from the mid-1990s (e.g. Readings, 1996) to the 2020s (e.g. Fleming, 2021; Hall, 2021).

The transnational pressure of expanding academic capitalism has also been noted in research on the demands to reform Nordic HE systems (Krejsler, 2006; Nokkala, 2008; Pettersson et al., 2017). As the welfare state, which was the foundation of the Finnish public university system (Jalava, 2012), gives way to a competitive state policy framework, Finnish academics also experience less control over their own institutions and their work (Jauhiainen et al., 2014; Nikkola & Tervasmäki, 2020). Academic capitalism has spread under the discourse of securing Finnish competitiveness, which has become a dominating discourse in HE governmental memos and reports (Rinne et al., 2014; Välimaa & Hoffman, 2008), realized in practice through administrative policy reforms (Poutanen et al., 2022). While Finnish public universities are not market actors per se, but when encouraged by state policy—particularly through public funding mechanisms (Poutanen, 2023b)—they increasingly engage in market-like behavior under academic capitalism and favor corporate management models (Välimaa, 2011).[8]

Finnish academics are noticing the same trends seen in the UK in their own work: academics find it increasingly hard to adapt to the decisions that concern their work and report a disconnect between the university leadership and the academic community (Kuusela, 2020). Over 60% of surveyed respondents stated that their opinions directed at university decision-makers do not matter (Tapanila et al., 2020). Piironen (2013, p. 138) comments that the discourse of autonomy is used prolifically in managerialist reforms, which, in fact, relocate professional academic autonomy to institutional management.[9] From the Finnish perspective, the development of the UK HE sector toward precarity, anxiety and marketization of HE seems, at worst, like a foreseeable yet inevitable future under academic capitalism.

4.5 Academic Alienation

Under capitalism, universities appropriate education under economic priorities which amplify processes of commodity fetishism and objectification, leading to endemic ill-being, overwork and precarity (Hall, 2018b, p. 12; see also Fleming, 2021, p. 27). This competition has a deleterious effect on collaboration and cooperation and producing knowledge as a public good: capitalist academic publishing industry is an example of foreclosing on knowledge as a public good—the appropriation of knowledge through dispossession (Peekhaus, 2012). The dispossession on a single academic takes place in the tapestry of universal capitalist dispossession. The more an academic works for the appropriating university—as opposed to science as a public good—whose metrics determine the value and efficacy of his labor, the more alienated they become not only from their work in general, but from the community of academics, the results of their research (outputs as 'deliverables' in a CV) and those who appropriate their work (university management or the state by proxy of HE funding mechanisms). As a result, academics are finding it increasingly difficult to reconcile their intrinsic motivations with extrinsic and imposed ones (Cannizzo, 2018; Hall, 2018b, p. 49; Lorenz, 2012). Academics are increasingly dispossessed of their intrinsic motivation.

Alienation is further intensified by processes of proletarianization and deprofessionalization of academic labor (Faucher, 2014; McCarthy et al., 2017), administrative models emphasizing centralized, managerial power over collegial and communal decision-making and autonomy (Brandist, 2017; Grönblom & Willner, 2013; Oleksiyenko, 2018), the closure of academic public commons (Harvie, 2000) and imposed, performative neoliberal academic subjectivities (Ball, 2012; Brankovic, 2018; Silva, 2017). Hierarchically organized academia is nonantagonistic toward capital and the managerial power that operationalizes it (Szadkowski, 2016). Capital seeks to remove barriers to consumption and production and increase the rate of extraction of surplus value through breeding anxiety among academics (Hall, 2021, p. 44; Hall & Bowles, 2016).

The blurring lines of labor and leisure increase 'the compulsion for academics to overwork as a defensive action against proletarianization, casualization and precarity, alongside institutional or national strategies focused upon productivity' (Hall, 2018b, p. 49). Just as in Marx's original conceptualization, academic alienation arises from (1) the selling of labor power for instrumental purposes; (2) being alienated from one's labor outputs, as knowledge is treated more as a market commodity than a social good; (3) being alienated from self as a self-exploiting entrepreneur; (4) being alienated from other humans through global competition, with social relations becoming marked by instrumentalism.

Alienation is visible in the loss of control over academic time: assessment tools and metrics institutionalize competition, and academics are pressed to find time to realize their intrinsic motivation between externally imposed tasks: 'academics have increasingly little control over the surplus time that the University demands from them' (Hall, 2018b, p. 99; see also Hall, 2021, p. 172). The university requires ever more outputs in ever more fragmented time, restricting meaningful autonomy. As capital demands more efficiency and appropriates academic capital, academic work is accelerated to create new labor structures and subjectivities (Vostal, 2015).[10] In addition to managerial technologies intervening in academic time, educational technology also increases alienation by mediating human contact and casualizing staff (Guillem & Briziarelli, 2020; Wendling, 2009).

Academic employees feel that they are called to offer unreciprocated commitment to the university: academic staff has been loyal and dedicated to the idea of the university (as a public good) *despite of*, rather than *because of*, policy and administrative reforms. Compared to the UK, reforms of academic capitalism are still relatively new in Finland, which can explain a difference in tenor when academics describe their respective working conditions (cf. e.g. Fleming, 2021; Rinne et al., 2014), though also in Finland, academic protests to reforms have been largely ineffectual (see e.g. Poutanen et al., 2022), with Finnish academics feeling increasingly replaceable (Brunila & Hannukainen, 2017; Jauhiainen et al., 2014). Alienation forces academics to renegotiate their identities and their relationship to their institutions, their community and themselves. Focusing on one's own work means focusing on productivity and trying to leverage personal performance in a competitive environment of persistent precarity demanding more output with less resources (Tapanila et al., 2020).

A materialist analysis of alienating structures within academic capitalism may clash with a subjective rationalizing of the circumstances: while Mészáros (1970/2005) argues that revealing social relations prone to exploitation is necessary for identifying processes of alienation, academics also engage in cognitive dissonance about selling their time and labor power, trying to convince themselves that economic value isn't the determining factor of doing what they love (Hall, 2018a, p. 102; see also: Federici, 2012). Assuming a neoliberal subjectivity, despite the negative impact of alienation, offers false security under high-performance academic capitalism. Many academics simply wish to be left alone to do their jobs—to focus on the one dimension of their academic labor of love still accessible to them (cf. Poutanen, 2023a).

It should thus be stressed that alienation shouldn't be approached as a singular, universal experience (Sayers, 2011b), even if alienation is universal under capitalism (Harvey, 2018). There is a degree of subjective difference, as some welcome capitalist competition and seek the prestige or success that comes with it. For the 'winners' of academic capitalism, the negative effects of alienation are mitigated by the meritocratic culture within academia, where the individual success or failure of each academic is attributed to their own capabilities, rather than structural causes. Similarly, commenting on the *Grundrisse*, David Harvey notes that 'workers may accept the objective alienation of wage labor in return for sufficient access to commodities to fulfil their personal wants, needs and desires. Alienated wage labor may in this way be offset by compensatory consumerism' (Harvey, 2023, p. 61). As such, these 'winning' academics are nonetheless alienated—from academic work and the academic community—but may experience it subjectively less negatively than those more forcefully proletarianized by academic capitalism.[11]

Furthermore, from the perspective of alienation, being left to focus on one's own tasks, detached from organizational or collegial responsibilities (Rhodes, 2017), intensifies alienation processes. In HE systems such as the Finnish one, where collegial decision-making and university democracy still exist, being absolved from organizational responsibilities entails signing away the burden but also the right of determining one's own working conditions. The promise of being left 'alone' to focus on your work is an inviting, but ultimately self-defeating, coping mechanism. Dissatisfaction in academia is typically connected only to the symptoms, rather than the root cause of alienation, which is the competitive hierarchy of exploitation: in the end, we are faced with 'the inability to escape from capital's domination' (Hall, 2018a, p. 104). Under competition, we struggle for position, rather than from being liberated from this struggle (Hall, 2021, p. 134; see also Reitz, 2017). The system is by default an ever-accelerating mechanism of appropriation and control while maintaining the appearance of autonomy.

4.6 Disalienating Openings

In Marx's thinking, alienation is a transitory but necessary element in a human process of becoming (Sayers, 2011b, p. 292). As a part of Marx's emancipatory social critique, alienation encompasses a normative theory of social movement toward a disalienating society (Byron, 2013). In locating disalienating openings, given the resilience of the neoliberal university to reforms outside of its own logic, Hall (2021) rejects the liberal idea of progress through reform, which symbolizes the separation of the political economy of academia and intellectual or political activity. Rather than engaging in the hopeless task of trying to reform the neoliberal university, we should look to new forms and opportunities of higher learning and intellectual work—as only through acknowledging alienation can we arrive at attempts of disalienation. In other words, the potential for new hope of an intellectuality formed around care and solidarity can only rise out of acknowledged hopelessness within the current system.

On the level of academic labor, it is necessary for academics to welcome—even embrace—political struggle: '[o]vercoming alienation is a key element in the work of abolishing the system of capital and in transforming social metabolic control so that it values the human' (Hall, 2018b, p. 11). In this regard, we should recognize, as Harvey does in his reading of the *Grundrisse* (Harvey, 2023), that also capitalists are alienated by the coercive laws of capital. Recognizing and leveraging university administrators' alienation as mid-level proxies of academic capitalism should also be considered as a potential strategy. Swain (2012, p. 96) similarly argues that Marx was extremely skeptical of mechanisms of giving back control, rather than taking control; alienation can be only countered from the bottom-up, not top-down. Hence, Marxist theory involves the revolution—a political transformation.

Strategies of resistance would require introducing a new concept of mass intellectuality, which would require breaking down much of the institution of the university as it now stands and reopening the academic and intellectual commons. The modern university is buttressed by capital, exudes caustic exclusivity and refuses to acknowledge work that does not contribute to capital accumulation as valuable. This would require introducing alternative educational practices to develop deliberately collective/cooperative socialized knowledge, which could also reclaim capitalist time to the individual and for society

(Hall, 2018a, p. 105). Pursuing this goal would require active social reimagining and democratic and participatory praxis, which reemphasize the autonomy of academic labor—disalienating social practices predicate employee ownership of 'their workplace and the relationships within it' (Kociatkiewicz et al., 2021, p. 19). This is why universities need intersectional democratic praxis, which can seem radical under the current common sense of competitive academic capitalism. Overcoming alienation means regaining control over 'our own productive activity and social and economic lives' (Sayers, 2011b, p. 302). In this, academic labor is increasingly—despite existing and particularly past privileges—under the same effect of capitalist dispossession, as most other workers. Modern academics are drawn into the ranks of the working class and into the class struggle.

Marx stated in the *Grundrisse* (1993) that the material conditions for a classless and disalienated society are concealed in a capitalist society. The 'money system' of capitalism (McLellan, 2000, p. 86) can and should be overcome. Academics arguably have a special duty in this: the university's social and civic missions should be prioritized over marketizing or commodifying interests. But, and notably, this cannot take the form of nostalgic longing for days past, but an exploration of alternate academic identities and forms of intellectuality to those imposed by academic capitalism. Nostalgic reveries can, at worst, lead to compromises, which don't address other structural inequalities within the university. Materialist critique should be supplemented by insights from other disciplines, which have had (unfortunate) experience with trying to argue against hegemonic societal constructs, such as postcolonial and feminist theory (Federici, 2012; Rodney, 2022). For example, Jarrett (2017) discusses a feminist political approach toward gender, alienation and reproductive work under capitalism, and Veijola and Jokinen (2018) expand this framework to academic work specifically. As a term, 'academic housework', which reproduces communitarian academic labor, is explored by Macfarlane and Burg (2019) and Heijstra et al. (2017). Recognizing academic housework as legitimate and necessary offers countering readings to the prevalent atomization and individualization of academic work. These insights offer tools to deconstruct the competitive archetype, who is often white, male and able and without significant caring responsibilities.[12]

UK universities have also been subjected to postcolonial theory and decolonial social movements, which emphasize the problematic role of universities as elite institutions (Bhambra et al., 2018). While some universities may be more elite than others, they still are exclusive communities by default. Given the colonial history of the UK, these considerations make sense: material inequalities are not propagated by class alone. While Finland has less of a colonial history—though it exists particularly in relation to the Sámi—gender disparities in academia persist, and the welfare state has given way to self-serving and excluding welfare chauvinism. As such, decolonial arguments are resisted by academic capitalism, which has intertwined knowledge-economy supremacy with an existential economic struggle. Social imaginaries, even in receding welfare states, are less open to radical change that would hurt competitiveness. But where else would new social imaginaries be forged if not through radically free mass intellectuality, that includes the voices of those who are excluded by capitalist realism?

4.7 Conclusion

While alienation can have many meanings, and its negative effect on self-fulfillment is not limited to a Marxist analysis (see Jaeggi, 2014), a Marxist approach to alienation specifically deals with alienation as an outcome of capitalist social relations breaking bonds between people, turning them into things—commodity-producers but also commodities in themselves, cogs in the all-appropriating capitalist machine. Although that was the social context he was writing in, Marx never stipulated that alienation applied only to heavy industry. While it would be inviting to dismiss academic alienation as relatively privileged whining, it rather articulates the appropriation of yet another field of social activity into capital accumulation. Far from being intellectual free agents, academics are intertwined with their universities: university affiliation grants institutional legitimacy and, above all, access to necessary academic resources. In a capitalist system, profit-motive and capital accumulation define labor conditions and what labor can offer to a person as essential human activity. Labor that could be fulfilling is instrumentalized, appropriating both labor and laborer under capital accumulation processes. This means that labor as the source of human inspiration, a calling or a vocation, that is intrinsically motivated, is at the end reduced to little less than a simple exchange of labor time for sustenance. This is at the heart of the failure of self-fulfillment, made all the more tragic by the false promise of self-actualization through individualism and competition, through which competitive reforms are legitimized. Failure of self-fulfillment fuels processes of alienation, which academics experience and react to in different, but typically negative, ways. Their take on alienation may depend largely where one is positioned under academic capitalism.

The appropriation of academic labor under capital accumulation is described by Hall (2021, p. 102) as 'weaponizing' a 'labor of love'. Vital reproductive academic housework is left unappreciated. Intrinsic motivation is exploited ravenously to extract surplus value, with little regard for the damage inflicted, first, to vulnerable groups and then to the university community as a whole. The institution itself becomes alien to its members. From the perspective of disalienation, capitalist violence done against a labor of love legitimizes resistance—or at least it should. As stated earlier, Marx saw capitalist exchange relations as inherently unequal, which suggests that even a subjectively fulfilling job develops exploitative characteristics: the willingness of academics, for example, to sacrifice their own well-being for the sake of their labor. Academics are—like all workers under capitalism—appropriated and dispossessed.

As capital accumulation has expanded into higher education, it has introduced the logic of capital, often articulated in national higher education policy to drive national competitiveness, to institutions of higher education, and further to academics. The appropriation of science as a public good by capital had led to 'immense dissatisfaction and internal conflict between academics and higher education policy, academics and their institutions, and within academics themselves' (Poutanen, 2023a, p. 632). Alienation exists in an objective and universal sense under capitalism, but when laying out the experiences of academics from the UK to Finland, we must remind ourselves that on a subjective level, alienation is experienced in various ways. Some academics identify the problem too superficially in increased managerial control, excessive bureaucracy and imposed performative identities. As such, their response is to shirk all communal and collegial responsibilities that would distract them from focusing on their own (competitive) career success. In so doing, they are feeding their own alienation, and becoming merely a thing in the system, the purpose of which is to make more things. Their retreat weakens any collective power academic labor might have against capital. On the other hand, purposefully disempowering and irresponsive management systems invite disengagement: the managerial and neoliberal university feeds into alienation processes. This is then worsened by making alienated and disempowered academics responsible for their own emotional and intellectual well-being.

Arguably the tradition of active collegiality in institutional decision-making has shielded Finnish academics until structural changes have made academics acutely aware of what they have lost. On the other hand, UK, or rather English, academics have less of a tradition of administrative self-governance but are more sensitive to racial questions and exclusionary practices in universities. Within these differences there are also opportunities for more multifaceted and nuanced resistance and new interpretations of the university, and the role and purpose of emancipatory mass intellectuality. Unfortunately, there is no ready blueprint at hand for combating alienation inflicted by academic capitalism. We need time and space for communal and inclusive intersectional horizontal dialogue on how the conditions for not only academic work, but meaningful life, should be shaped (Hall, 2021, p. 227). Contesting alienation is not only a question of labor, but also a question of self-governance and democracy. Just as alienation is a process of capital—accumulation, appropriation, dispossession—disalienation is an ongoing process of democratic praxis, which appears radical under capitalism. The material foundations for a classless and disalienated society are attainable: they are simply concealed underneath the overwhelming competitive pressures of a capitalist society. Laying them out openly is conflicted, it is political and it is messy. But it is the more humane option for a sustainable future.

Acknowledgments This book chapter is made possible through funding from the Academy of Finland (325976).

Disclosure Statement No potential conflict of interest was reported by the author.

NOTES

1. For Marx, self-alienation often takes the form of putting yourself under the authority of others: under religion, the example he uses is the relationship between a layman and a priest (McLellan, 2000, p. 92). Under conditions of capitalist wage-labor, this would mean managers and bosses as proxies of capital.
2. Marx differentiates between *Entäusserung* and *Entfremdung* in his works, which in Marx (2007[1961], pp. 10–12) have been translated as alienation and estrangement, respectively. For space, this chapter does not engage in deeper separation between the two concepts.
3. This is why commodity fetishism was also discussed already in the previous section, although that term is used in *Capital* and not in *Economic and Philosophic Manuscripts of 1844*.
4. 'Technical rationality today is the rationality of domination. It is the compulsive character of a society alienated from itself' (Adorno and Horkheimer 1947/1997, p. 123).
5. Fromm assumed that the lower you are in the social division of labor, the more alienated one would be. However, Marx made no subjective differentiation between degrees of alienation, because the problem is objective-structural.
6. For Jaeggi (2014), alienation is relationlessness, meaning our relations to others and to ourselves have been broken: we no longer feel like active individual subjects of the neoliberal promise, but rather objects being squeezed by merciless outside forces. While Jaeggi's work on alienation is insightful and largely supports the connection of capitalism and alienation on the neoliberal subject, her work departs from a materialist reading.
7. Kalekin-Fishman and Langman (2015) offer an insightful review of how alienation has persisted as a critical approach, developed in different directions despite falling somewhat out of academic fashion (see also: Musto, 2010).
8. This applies particularly to the new type of administrative model, the foundation university, which centralizes power and breaks with the previous tradition of self-governance (Poutanen et al., 2022).
9. Though Finnish universities do not, in 2022, charge tuition from Finnish or EU students, there is strong push for tuition fees.
10. By extending Marx's critique of ground rent into alienation means that labor is also alienated from that commodified land and nature (Harvey, 2023, pp. 108–109). This is, once more, appropriation through dispossession (Marx, 2007[1961], p. 83). The same logic can be applied to alienation relating to closing of the academic commons (Harvie, 2000) and foreclosing on autonomous academic time. Hartmut Rosa (2010) has made a convincing connection between alienation and the acceleration of modern work, visible also at universities.
11. Kalekin-Fishman and Langman (2015, p. 925) note that not all, who experience alienation, are aware of it. Thus, it is difficult to capture alienation reliably in surveys. Prominent and established senior academics in relatively secure positions may feel that claims of alienation are overblown, until they experience the negative implications firsthand: in Nordbäck et al. (2022, p. 10), one senior researcher describes their own realization of disempowerment: 'What I knew from research I now experienced myself'.
12. Caring responsibilities are an often-neglected consideration that challenges the idealized, commodified efficient worker. Again, feminist theory offers opportunities for reimagining more inclusive academic work (Amsler & Motta, 2017; Tronto, 2018).

References

Adorno, T., & Horkheimer, M. (1997 [1947]). *Dialectic of Enlightenment*. Verso.
Althusser, L. (2005 [1965]). *For Marx* (B. Brewster, Trans.). Verso.
Amsler, S., & Motta, S. (2017). The marketised university and the politics of motherhood. *Gender and Education, 31*(1), 82–99. https://doi.org/10.1080/09540253.2017.1296116
Archibald, W. P. (2009a). Marx, Globalization and Alienation: Received and Underappreciated Wisdoms. *Critical Sociology, 35*(2), 151–174.
Archibald, W. P. (2009b). Globalization, Downsizing and Insecurity: Do We Need to Upgrade Marx's Theory of Alienation? *Critical Sociology, 35*(3), 319–342.
Ball, S. (2012). *Global Education Inc. New Policy Networks and the Neoliberal Imaginary*. Routledge.
Bhambra, G. K., Gebrial, D., & Nisancioglu, K. (Eds.). (2018). *Decolonising the University*. Pluto Press.
Brandist, C. (2017). The Perestroika of Academic Labour: The Neoliberal Transformation of Higher Education and the Resurrection of the 'command economy'. *Ephemera: Theory & Politics in Organization, 17*(3), 563–608.
Brankovic, J. (2018). The Status Games They Play: Unpacking the Dynamics of Organisational Status Competition in Higher Education. *Higher Education, 75*, 695–709.
Brankovic, J., Ringel, L., & Werron, T. (2018). How Rankings Produce Competition: The Case of Global University Rankings. *Zeitschrift für Soziologie, 47*, 270–288. https://doi.org/10.1515/zfsoz-2018-0118
Brunila, K., & Hannukainen, K. (2017). Academic Researchers on the Project Market in the Ethos of Knowledge Capitalism. *European Educational Research Journal, 16*(6), 907–920. https://doi.org/10.1177/1474904116685100
Byron, C. (2013). The Normative Force Behind Marx's Theory of Alienation. *Critique, 41*(3), 427–435. https://doi.org/10.1080/03017605.2013.851935
Cannizzo, F. (2018). 'You've got to love what you do': Academic Labour in a Culture of Authenticity. *The Sociological Review, 66*(1), 91–106. https://doi.org/10.1177/0038026116681439
Cantwell, B., & Kauppinen, I. (Eds.). (2014). *Academic Capitalism in the Age of Globalization*. John Hopkins University Press.
Coontz, S., & Henderson, P. (1986). *Women's Work, Men's Property: The Origins of Gender and Class*. Verso.
Docherty, T. (2015). *Universities at War*. Sage.
Erickson, M., Hanna, P., & Walker, C. (2021). The UK Higher Education Senior Management Survey: A Statactivist Response to Managerialist Governance. *Studies in Higher Education, 46*(11), 2134–2151. https://doi.org/10.1080/03075079.2020.1712693
Fairclough, N., & Wodak, R. (2008). The Bologna Process and the Knowledge-Based Economy: A Critical Discourse Analysis Approach. In B. Jessop, N. Fairclough, & R. Wodak (Eds.), *Higher Education and the Knowledge-Based Economy in Europe* (pp. 109–127). Sense Publishers.
Faucher, K. X. (2014). Alienation and Precarious Contract Academic Staff in the Age of Neoliberalism. *Confero, 2*(1), 35–71. https://doi.org/10.3384/confero.2001-4562.141007a
Federici, S. (2012). *Revolution at Point Zero: Housework, Reproduction and Feminist Struggle*. PM Press.

Fleming, P. (2021). *Dark Academia: How Universities Die*. Pluto Books.
Geyer, R. F., & Schweitzer, D. R. (Eds.). (1976). *Theories of Alienation*. Martinus Nijhoff.
Grönblom, S., & Willner, J. (2013). Marketization and Alienation in Academic Activity. In R. Sudgen, M. Valania, & J. R. Wilson (Eds.), *Leadership and Cooperation in Academia: Reflecting on the roles and responsibilities of University Faculty and management* (pp. 88–106). Edward Elgar.
Guillem, S. M., & Briziarelli, M. (2020). Against Gig Academia: Connectivity, Disembodiment, and Struggle in Online Education. *Communication Education, 69*(3), 356–372.
Hall, R. (2018a). On the Alienation of Academic Labour and the Possibilities for Mass Intellectuality. *triple, 16*(1), 97–113. https://doi.org/10.31269/triplec.v16i1.873
Hall, R. (2018b). *The Alienated Academic – The Struggle for Autonomy Inside the University*. Palgrave Macmillan.
Hall, R. (2021). *The Hopeless University: Intellectual Work at the End of the End of History*. Mayfly Books.
Hall, R., & Bowles, K. (2016). Re-engineering Higher Education: The Subsumption of Academic Labour and the Exploitation of Anxiety. *Workplace: A Journal for Academic Labor, 28*, 30–47. https://doi.org/10.14288/workplace.v0i28.186211
Harvey, D. (2018). Universal Alienation. *Journal for Cultural Research, 22*(2), 137–150.
Harvey, D. (2023). *A Companion to Marx's Grundrisse*. Verso.
Harvie, D. (2000). Alienation, Class and Enclosure in UK Universities. *Capital & Class, 71*, 103–132. https://doi.org/10.1177/030981680007100105
Hazelkorn, E. (2015). *Rankings and the Reshaping of Higher Education*. Palgrave Macmillan.
Heijstra, T. M., Steinthorsdóttir, F. S., & Einarsdóttir, T. (2017). Academic Career Making and the Double-Edged Role of Academic Housework. *Gender and Education, 29*(6), 764–780. https://doi.org/10.1080/09540253.2016.1171825
Hunter, C. (2013). Shifting Themes in OECD Country Reviews of Higher Education. *Higher Education, 66*, 707–723. https://doi.org/10.1007/s10734-013-9630-z
Jaeggi, R. (2014). *Alienation* (F. Neuhouser, Ed. and Trans. & A. E. Smith, Trans.). Columbia University Press.
Jalava, M. (2012). *The University in the Making of the Welfare State: The 1970s Degree Reform in Finland*. Peter Lang.
Jarrett, K. (2017). *Feminism, Labour and Digital Media: The Digital Housewife*. Routledge.
Jauhiainen, A., Jauhiainen, A., Laiho, A., & Laiho, R. (2014). Fabrications, Time-Consuming Bureaucracy and Moral Dilemmas – Finnish University Employees' Experiences on the Governance of University Work. *Higher Education Policy, 28*(3), 393–410. https://doi.org/10.1057/hep.2014.18
Kalekin-Fishman, D., & Langman, L. (2015). Alienation: The Critique That Refuses to Disappear. *Current Sociology Review, 63*(6), 916–933. https://doi.org/10.1177/0011392115591612
Kauppinen, I., & Kaidesoja, T. (2014). A Shift Towards Academic Capitalism in Finland. *Higher Education Policy, 27*(1), 23–41.
Kociatkiewicz, J., Kostera, M., & Parker, M. (2021). The Possibility of Disalienated Work: Being at Home in Alternative Organizations. *Human Relations, 74*(7), 933–957. https://doi.org/10.1177/0018726720916762

Krejsler, J. (2006). Discursive Battles About the Meaning of University: The Case of Danish University Reform and Its Academics. *European Educational Research Journal, 5*(3–4), 210–220. https://doi.org/10.2304/eerj.2006.5.3.210

Kuusela, H. (2020). Kuuleeko strateginen johto? Katsaus yliopistojen työhyvinvointikyselyjen tuloksiin. *Tiedepolitiikka, 2*(2020), 30–35.

Lorenz, C. (2012). If You're So Smart, Why Are You Under Surveillance? Universities, Neoliberalism, and New Public Management. *Critical Inquiry, 38*, 599–629. https://doi.org/10.1086/664553

Loveday, V. (2018). The Neurotic Academic: Anxiety, Casualization, and Governance in the Neoliberal University. *Journal of Cultural Economy, 11*(2), 154–166. https://doi.org/10.1080/17530350.2018.1426032

Lukács, G. (1971). *History and Class Consciousness*. Merlin Press.

Macfarlane, B., & Burg, D. (2019). Women Professors and the Academic Housework Trap. *Journal of Higher Education Policy and Management, 41*(3), 262–274. https://doi.org/10.1080/1360080X.2019.1589682

Mandel, E. (2009 [1970]). Progressive Disalienation Through Building a Socialist Society, Or the Inevitable Alienation in Industrial Society. In E. Mandel & G. Novack (Eds.), *The Marxist Theory of Alienation* (pp. 35–57). Pathfinder Press.

Marginson, S. (2014). University Rankings and Social Science. *European Journal of Education, 49*(1), 45–59.

Marx, K. (1993). *Grundrisse: Outline of the Critique of Political Economy*. Penguin.

Marx, K. (2007 [1961]). *Economic and Philosophic Manuscripts of 1844*. Dover Publications.

McCann, L., Granter, E., Hyde, P., & Aroles, J. (2020). 'Upon the gears and upon the wheels': Terror Convergence and Total Administration in the Neoliberal University. *Management Learning, 51*(4), 431–451.

McCarthy, G., Song, X., & Jayasuriya, K. (2017). The Proletarianisation of Academic Labour in Australia. *Higher Education Research & Development, 36*(5), 1017–1030. https://doi.org/10.1080/07294360.2016.1263936

McLellan, D. (Ed.). (2000). *Karl Marx: Selected Writings* (2nd ed.). Oxford University Press.

Mészáros, I. (2005 [1970]). *Marx's Theory of Alienation*. Merlin Press.

Moisio, S., & Kangas, A. (2016). Reterritorializing the Global Knowledge Economy: An Analysis of Geopolitical Assemblages of Higher Education. *Global Networks, 16*(3), 268–287. https://doi.org/10.1111/glob.12103

Münch, R. (2020). *Academic Capitalism. Universities in the Global Struggle for Excellence*. Routledge.

Musto, M. (2010). Revisiting Marx's Concept of Alienation. *Socialism and Democracy, 24*(3), 79–101. https://doi.org/10.1080/08854300.2010.544075

Musto, M. (Ed.). (2021). *Karl Marx's Writings on Alienation*. Palgrave Macmillan.

Nikkola, T., & Tervasmäki, T. (2020). Experiences of Arbitrary Management Among Finnish Academics in an Era of Academic Capitalism. *Journal of Education Policy, 37*(4), 548–568. https://doi.org/10.1080/02680939.2020.1854350

Nokkala, T. (2008). 'Finland is a small country' Narrative Construction of the Internationalisation of Higher Education. In B. Jessop, N. Fairclough, & R. Wodak (Eds.), *Higher Education and the Knowledge-Based Economy in Europe* (pp. 171–192). Sense Publishers.

Nordbäck, E., Hakonen, M., & Tienari, J. (2022). Academic identities and sense of place: A collaborative autoethnography in the neoliberal university. *Management Learning*, 53(2), 331–349. https://doi.org/10.1177/13505076211006543

Oleksiyenko, A. (2018). Zones of Alienation in Global Higher Education: Corporate Abuse and Leadership Failures. *Tertiary Education and Management*, 24(3), 193–205. https://doi.org/10.1080/13583883.2018.1439095

Olssen, M., & Peters, M. A. (2005). Neoliberalism, Higher Education and the Knowledge Economy: From the Free Market to Knowledge Capitalism. *Journal of Education Policy*, 20(3), 313–345. https://doi.org/10.1080/02680930500108718

Øversveen, E. (2021). Capitalism and Alienation: Towards a Marxist Theory of Alienation for the 21st Century. *European Journal of Social Theory*, 25(3), 440–457. https://doi.org/10.1177/13684310211021579

Peekhaus, W. (2012). The Enclosure and Alienation of Academic Publishing: Lessons for the Professoriate. *Triple*, 10(2), 577–599. https://doi.org/10.31269/triplec.v10i2.395

Pettersson, D., Prøitz, T. S., & Forsberg, E. (2017). From Role Models to Nations in Need of Advice: Norway and Sweden Under the OECD's Magnifying Glass. *Journal of Education Policy*, 32(6), 721–744. https://doi.org/10.1080/02680939.2017.1301557

Piironen, O. (2013). The Transnational Idea of University Autonomy and the Reform of the Finnish Universities Act. *Higher Education Policy*, 26(1), 127–146. https://doi.org/10.1057/hep.2012.22

Poutanen, M. (2022). Competitive Knowledge-Economies Driving New Logics in Higher Education – Reflections from a Finnish University Merger. *Critical Policy Studies*. Advance Online Publication. https://doi.org/10.1080/19460171.2022.2124429

Poutanen, M. (2023a). 'I am done with that now.' Sense of Alienations in Finnish Academia. *Journal of Education Policy*. Advance Online Publication. https://doi.org/10.1080/02680939.2022.2067594

Poutanen, M. (2023b). From R&D Innovation to Academic Capitalism in Finland. *Scandinavian Journal of Public Administration*, 27(1), 29–52. https://doi.org/10.58235/sjpa.v27i1.10969

Poutanen, M., Tomperi, T., Kuusela, H., Kaleva, V., & Tervasmäki, T. (2022). From Democracy to Managerialism: Foundation Universities as the Embodiment of Finnish University Policies. *Journal of Education Policy*, 37(3), 419–442. https://doi.org/10.1080/02680939.2020.1846080

Readings, B. (1996). *The University in Ruins*. Harvard University Press.

Reitz, T. (2017). Academic Hierarchies in Neo-feudal Capitalism: How Status Competition Processes Trust and Facilitates the Appropriation of Knowledge. *Higher Education*, 73, 871–886.

Rhodes, C. (2017). Academic Freedom in the Corporate University: Squandering Our Inheritance? In M. Izak, M. Kostera, & M. Zawadzki (Eds.), *The Future of University Education* (pp. 19–38). Palgrave Macmillan.

Rinne, R., Jauhiainen, A., & Kankaanpää, J. (2014). Surviving in the Ruins of the University? Lost Autonomy and Collapsed Dreams in the Finnish Transition of University Policies. *Nordic Studies in Education*, 34(3), 213–232.

Rodney, W. (2022). *Decolonial Marxism: Essays from the Pan-African Revolution*. Verso.

Roediger, D. R. (2019). *Class, Race, and Marxism*. Verso.

Rosa, H. (2010). *Alienation and Acceleration: Towards a Critical Theory of Late-Modern Temporality. Summertalk Vol. 3.* NSU Press & Nordiskt Sommaruniversitet.
Sayers, S. (2011a). Alienation as a Critical Concept. *International Critical Thought*, 1(3), 287–304. https://doi.org/10.1080/21598282.2011.609265
Sayers, S. (2011b). *Marx and Alienation: Essays on Hegelian Themes.* Palgrave Macmillan.
Schacht, R. (1970). *Alienation.* Doubleday.
Seeman, M. (1959). On the Meaning of Alienation. *American Sociological Review*, 24, 783–791.
Seeman, M. (1975). Alienation Studies. *Annual Review of Sociology*, 1, 91–123.
Sellar, S., & Lingard, B. (2012). The OECD and Global Governance in Education. *Journal of Education Policy*, 28(5), 710–725. https://doi.org/10.1080/02680939.2013.779791
Shore, C. (2008). Audit Culture and Illiberal Governance: University and the Politics of Accountability. *Anthropological Theory*, 8(83), 278–298. https://doi.org/10.1177/1463499608093815
Shore, C., & Wright, S. (2015). Audit Culture Revisited: Rankings, Ratings, and the Reassembling of Society. *Current Anthropology*, 56(3), 421–444. https://doi.org/10.1086/681534
Silva, N. R. (2017). Alienation Theory and Ideology in Dialogue. *Rethinking Marxism*, 29(3), 370–383. https://doi.org/10.1080/08935696.2017.1368623
Skotnicki, T., & Nielsen, K. (2021). Toward a Theory of Alienation: Futurelessness in Financial Capitalism. *Theory and Society*, 50, 837–865.
Slaughter, S., & Cantwell, B. (2012). Transatlantic Moves to the Market: The United States and the European Union. *Higher Education*, 63, 583–606. https://doi.org/10.1007/s10734-011-9460-9
Slaughter, S., & Rhoades, G. (2004). *Academic Capitalism and the New Economy: Markets, State, and Higher Education.* The Johns Hopkins University Press.
Sum, N.-L. (2009). The Production of Hegemonic Policy Discourses: 'Competitiveness' as a Knowledge Brand and its (Re-)contextualizations. *Critical Policy Studies*, 3(2), 184–203. https://doi.org/10.1080/19460170903385668
Sum, N.-L., & Jessop, B. (2013). Competitiveness, the Knowledge-Based Economy and Higher Education. *Journal of the Knowledge Economy*, 4(1), 24–44. https://doi.org/10.1007/s13132-012-0121-8
Swain, D. (2012). *Alienation: An Introduction Marx's Theory.* Bookmarks Publications.
Szadkowski, K. (2016). Towards an Orthodox Marxian Reading of Subsumption(s) of Academic Labour Under Capital. *Workplace: A Journal for Academic Labor*, 28, 9–29. https://doi.org/10.14288/workplace.v0i28.186210
Szadkowski, K. (2019). An Autonomist Marxist Perspective on Productive and Unproductive Academic Labour. *tripleC*, 17(1), 111–131. https://doi.org/10.31269/triplec.v17i1.1076
Szadkowski, K., & Krzeski, J. (2019). In, Against and Beyond: A Marxist Critique of Higher Education in Crisis. *Social Epistemology*, 33(6), 463–476. https://doi.org/10.1080/02691728.2019.1638465
Szadkowski, K., & Krzeski, J. (2021). Conceptualizing Capitalist Transformations: Marx's Relevance for Higher Education Research. *European Journal of Higher Education.* Retrieved March 17, 2023, from SocArXiv https://doi.org/10.31235/osf.io/78gaj

Tapanila, K., Siivonen, P., & Filander, K. (2020). Academics' Social Positioning Towards the Restructured Management System in Finnish Universities. *Studies in Higher Education, 45*(1), 117–128. https://doi.org/10.1080/03075079.2018.1539957

Tronto, J. C. (2018). Higher education for citizens of caring democracies. *South African Journal of Higher Education, 32*(6), 6–18. https://doi.org/10.20853/32-6-2710

Välimaa, J. (2011). The Corporatization of National Universities in Finland. In B. Pusser, K. Kempner, S. Marginson, & I. Odorika (Eds.), *Universities and the Public Sphere: Knowledge Creation and State Building in the Era of Globalization* (pp. 101–119). Routledge.

Välimaa, J., & Hoffman, D. (2008). Knowledge Society Discourse and Higher Education. *Higher Education, 56*, 265–285. https://doi.org/10.1007/s10734-008-9123-7

Veijola, S., & Jokinen, E. (2018). Coding Gender in Academic Capitalism: Landscapes of Political Action. *Ephemera, 18*(3), 527–549.

Vostal, F. (2015). Academic Life in the Fast Lane: The Experience of Time and Speed in British Academia. *Time & Society, 24*(1), 71–95. https://doi.org/10.1177/0961463X13517537

Watermeyer, R. (2019). *Competitive Accountability in Academic Life: Struggle for Social Impact and Public Legitimacy*. Edward Elgar.

Wendling, A. (2009). *Karl Marx on Technology and Alienation*. Palgrave Macmillan.

Westin, S. (2021). Un-homing with Words: Economic Discourse and Displacement as Alienation. *Cultural Geographies, 28*(2), 239–254.

Williamson, I., & Cullingford, C. (1997). The Uses and Misuses of 'Alienation' in the Social Sciences and Education. *British Journal of Education Studies, 45*(3), 263–275. https://doi.org/10.1111/1467-8527.00051

Wright, S., & Shore, C. (Eds.). (2017). *Death of the Public University? Uncertain Futures for Higher Education in the Knowledge Economy*. Berghahn Books.

Zoubir, Z. (2018). 'Alienation' and Critique in Marx's Manuscripts of 1857–1858 ('Grundrisse'). *The European Journal of the History of Economic Thought, 25*(5), 710–737.

CHAPTER 5

The Class in Race, Gender, and Learning

Sara Carpenter and Shahrzad Mojab

5.1 Introduction

In 2011, we published the first iteration of our scholarly work to produce a Marxist feminist reading of educational scholarship, research, and teaching. Located specifically within the field of critical adult education, and drawing from personal, intellectual, and scholarly histories of activism and community organizing, the collection titled *Educating from Marx: Race, Gender, and Learning* ambitiously sets out to address the contradiction between critical aspirations of educators and the reproductive function of education within capitalism by developing 'theoretical frameworks that expose and explain the underlying social relations that consolidate the social and material inequalities characterizing our communities' (Carpenter & Mojab, 2011, p. 4). We intended the text as a theoretical, empirical, and political intervention in both the Marxist and feminist theorizations of education.

Over the fifteen years prior to the publication of our text, Marxist education scholars Paula Allman (1999, 2007, 2010) and Glenn Rikowski (1996, 1997) completed detailed analysis to demonstrate the fault lines of a positivist reading of Marx's critique of capital and, particularly, the influence of that reading within the field of education. Rikowski went so far as to argue that it was time to set fire to a reliance on deterministic interpretations of the base/

S. Carpenter (✉)
University of Alberta, Edmonton, AB, Canada
e-mail: sara3@ualberta.ca

S. Mojab
University of Toronto, Toronto, ON, Canada
e-mail: shahrzad.mojab@utoronto.ca

© The Editor(s) (if applicable) and The Author(s), under exclusive license to Springer Nature Switzerland AG 2023
R. Hall et al. (eds.), *The Palgrave International Handbook of Marxism and Education*, Marxism and Education,
https://doi.org/10.1007/978-3-031-37252-0_5

superstructure model and the mechanistic reading of education that led to intractable debates about the relative autonomy of education systems and teacher agency. Rather, the renewed purpose of Marxist educational theory should be directed at 'class as an element of the constitution of a world of struggle in practice' (Allman et al., 2005, p. 135). Beginning from this position, we also felt as though Marxist and Marxian analysis in education struggled with the same problems of Marxist thought more broadly: the thorough and thoughtful centering of women, people of color, trans and queer people, Indigenous people, and non-European modes of non/capitalist social relations in their analysis. While deeming capitalism to be a world system, the way much of the world experienced capitalism seemed to be less relevant within the Marxist tradition and produced an analysis over-reliant on the false universalism of a cisgender, heterosexual white male worker in the historical center of capitalist development. This kind of analysis limited the world of capitalism to the manufacturing floor and paid less attention to the fields, the home, the school, the welfare office, the back alleys, the bordellos, and all the other domains in which labor not easily visible within the valorization process takes place.

We also argued that feminist analyses of education struggle with the same challenges that the 'cultural turn' and the liberal bourgeois-ification of feminism wrestle with more broadly. Following particular academic interventions in the 1980s and 1990s, feminist theory quite simply absented class from its analysis and continued to leave an analysis of race to a marginal position, while embracing discussions of race that left intact the essence of liberal and capitalist social relations (Bannerji, 2000). Through this 'turn', feminist theory disconnected itself from feminist movement-making, while feminist mobilization, particularly in parts of the world deeply living within relations of colonialism and continuing aggressions and intensification of imperialism, did not undergo a similar turn (Fraser, 2009). Instead, they struggled with a slow take over by the nongovernmental and nonprofit industrial complex (INCITE!, 2017; Jad, 2008; Korolczuk, 2016). Part of the fall out of this tremendous shift was that feminist educational theorists were educated within a body of theory that fragmented race, class, and capital from patriarchy, both conceptually and within their analysis of educational systems specifically.

Into this landscape, we endeavored to collectively build a framework that would direct our inquiry to an explicitly feminist, anti-racist, and dialectical historical materialist analysis of education. Our aim was to return to the labor-capital relation as a dialectical contradiction; as not only a unity of two opposites, but as an internal relation concretized in social relations of gender, race, sexuality, language, ability, and nation. The social universe of capital recreates and expands itself through, paradoxically, the labor of people. We followed Marx's assertion that this laboring life was a conscious life to a particular conclusion: the social universe of capital is learned, and it can be unlearned. Through the use of particular analytical tools, we can understand its complex ideological processes, its morphology, and its points of crisis, contradiction, and collapse. In the years since we first published our thinking, much has changed in the world and in the growing areas of scholarship that address lacunas in Marxist and feminist theorizing, including underdeveloped areas of our work.

In this chapter, we want to provide some discussion about how our thinking about Marxist feminism and education has developed and what are areas of growth and change within what should be constantly iterative and evolving theoretical debates. To accomplish this, we proceed as follows. First, we will revisit and situate our thinking within broader discussions of Marxist feminism and education. Second, we will revisit in more depth our discussion around 'social relations of difference' within capitalism and discuss how we might think of these relations as constitutive of capitalism as a whole. We do this through a comparative example of the recent critiques of the theorization of oppression that inform ongoing efforts at Equity, Diversity, and Inclusion (EDI) work in educational institutions. Third, we will consider the implications of expanding our feminist and anti-racist reading of historical materialist dialectics for ongoing analysis within educational research and theory.

5.2 Reading Marxist Feminism in Education

Our goal in this section is both to review our framing of Marxist feminism and education and to situate our reading of Marx. We recognize Marx's deficits in bringing his sharp analytical frame to questions of gender, sexuality, race, and nation, although he, and later Engels, developed some crucial insights. But we also recognize the work of extraordinary people like Dorothy Smith, Paula Allman, and Himani Bannerji who emphasized understanding the method of Marx rather than reading his texts in a prescriptive manner. In the work of these scholars, we find, as Dorothy Smith argued (2011, p. 20), a way to 'learn from a Marx who has seemed to me to have something different to teach than I have found in most of his interpreters'.

Thus, we read Marx and Marxian scholarship with an eye toward those who emphasize the ontological and, specifically, try to understand Marx's dialectics and take seriously his and Engels' guidance to

> not set out from what men [sic] say, imagine, conceive, nor from men as narrated, thought of, imagined, conceived, in order to arrive at men in the flesh. We set out from real, active men, and on the basis of their real life-process we demonstrate the development of the ideological reflexes and echoes of this life process. (Marx & Engels, 1968, pp. 37–38)

We also take guidance from those who take seriously his emphasis on history and the importance of historical processes and forces in understanding our reality. To this end, we find reading Marxist historical analysis to be crucial to the development of contemporary social analysis. And we try to stay grounded in his articulation of materialism, that is *historical* materialism, which helps us to address what Paula Allman (2007, p. 35) calls 'inversions and separations in thought and practice'. This mode of analysis helps us to constantly interrogate and recognize problems of abstraction, fragmentation, dichotomization, reification, and fetishism in social analysis. We do this through constant commitment to dialectical analysis as 'a way of thinking that brings into focus the full range of changes and interactions that occur in the world' (Ollman, 1993, p. 10).

In the introduction to *Educating from Marx*, we argued that a Marxist feminist framework for education, one that would be explicitly anti-racist, required five theoretical considerations. We called them 'considerations' instead of theories, because we wanted to encourage ongoing theoretical iteration, rather than suggest a rigid or dogmatic analysis, which has been a problematic tendency within positivist readings of Marxism more broadly. Further, we see theory-making as a form of praxis. As praxis, theory-making is constantly in motion, undergoing change, and in need of critical interrogation.

These considerations, however, were developed as a way to point Marxist feminist inquirers toward key questions for self and social, critical reflection. These theoretical considerations include a theory of the social (ontology), a theory of capitalist social relations and difference (an expansion of ontology), a theory of knowledge (epistemology), a theory of consciousness and learning (a dialectic of ontology and epistemology), and a theory of social change (teaching/learning for revolution). These five considerations were not conceived in a causal or linear manner, but rather as internally related. We believe they have heuristic value for Marxist feminist thinkers, and they help us not only to situate ourselves within the bodies of Marxist and feminist thought more broadly, but also to refine the analytical tools we use to interrogate and analyze the world we reproduce every day. And of course the purpose of these analytical tools is not simply to describe and explain, but to push for revolutionary social transformation.

The first of these considerations, that of ontology or a theory of the social, remains grounded in a feminist and anti-racist reading of dialectical historical materialism. We recognize that not all aspects of the Marxist tradition are particularly concerned with Marx's struggles with ontology, but we take seriously his critique laid out in the *Theses on Feuerbach*. For example, in the very first thesis, he refers to reality as 'not an object of contemplation', that is not an external 'thing', but as 'human sensuous activity' (Marx, 1968, p. 659). By turning his attention to the activity of being human, to the modes through which humans make and remake their material and social lives, Marx shifts the perspective of inquiry to the social and relational constitution of our lived reality. Beginning here, Marx emphasizes continually throughout his work, particularly on political economy, the active and conscious way in which humans construct their world socially and relationally and, in turn, then objectify and reify that world through specific acts of consciousness and forms of ideology, which he also understands as 'practical, human-sensuous activity' (ibid., p. 660). Through this reification of society as structures and systems, or what Dorothy Smith (2001, p. 166) calls 'blob-ontology', we arrive at 'violent abstractions' that reinforce, normalize, and naturalize our social reality. We use the term reification to refer to particular acts of consciousness that turn process and relations into static 'things'. Reification, as a mode of thinking, removes time, and thus history and motion, from our understanding of our social reality. It also removes human agency, labor, and consciousness, turning social phenomena into 'things' that come from who knows where. Sayer (1987, p. 19) summarizes this ontological position within Marx's method when he argues that

> Marx did not conceive social reality atomistically, as made up of clearly bounded, separate, interacting entities: the kind of analytic particulars which can be grasped in clear, consistent and exclusive definitions. He saw the world, rather, as a complex network of internal relations, within which any single element is what it is only by virtue of its relationship to others.

It is important that Sayer (ibid.) emphasizes Marx's ontology as conceptual. This is because, as Mao Tse-Tung (2007) argued in his interpretation of Marx, it is not possible, on the terrain of ontology, to differentiate between knowing and being. Marx and Engels (1968) emphasized this point when they repeatedly referred to life as 'conscious life'. Rather, Mao argued, it is on the terrain of epistemology where we develop modes of conceptualization to grasp our lived reality. In other words, all knowing is, in some way, an act of abstraction and is 'the mechanism by which thought can have access to and come to know objectively the realm of reality' (Knight, 2005, p. 175). It is for this reason that the method of abstraction, the epistemology of historical materialism, is crucial.

Marx's emphasis on concepts is replete throughout his writing, and his constantly shifting usage of them has been the subject of much objection and debate. It is his particular usage of concepts to name and ground his ontological position that is the root cause of so much misreading and ill-usage of his work. This is, in part, because Marx's method of critique often involved taking an already existing concept, for example, civil society, and reconceptualizing it in a relational way that is dialectical, historical, and materialist. As Bertell Ollman (2004, p. 25) argued, '[t]he relational is the irreducible minimum for all units in Marx's conception of social reality'. To produce knowledge in a way that is committed to the ontology of historical materialism and to a dialectical and empirical method of rigor is the basis of Marx's epistemology (Smith, 2011).

The inseparability of knowing and being, ontology and epistemology, is the basis for Marx's articulation of consciousness. We have written extensively about Marx's theorization of consciousness elsewhere (Carpenter & Mojab, 2017), but it is perhaps best summarized by Paula Allman (2007, p. 32) when she argues that

> Marx conceptualizes consciousness and reality as an internally related unity of opposites. Additionally, reality is conceptualized dynamically, as the sensuous, active experience of human beings in the material world. Therefore, at any one moment in time, consciousness is comprised of thoughts that arise from each human being's sensuous activity. Moreover, the consciousness of any human

being will also include thoughts that have arisen external to the individual's own sensuous activity, i.e., from other people's sensuous activity both historically and contemporaneously.

Allman directs our attention here to both the ontological core of Marx's theorization of consciousness, but also to the idea that consciousness is, even in an individual, fundamentally a social phenomenon. Thus, human beings are constantly mediating not only their own everyday reality and experience, but knowledge and ideology inherited from the past and circulating in the present.

Consciousness occupies a particular place of interest in Marx's work in part because of the necessity of his critique of philosophical idealism. But it is also important because of the final point made in the *Thesis on Feuerbach*, which famously reminds scholars that the point of our work is not just to interpret the world, but to help change it. In this way, how we theorize consciousness and praxis, and thus learning and education, is fundamental to a project of social change, as are the ways in which we learn to analyze our society and formulate proposals for transformation. For this reason, we assert that all social change is pedagogical; in order to change the world, we must develop a critical understanding of it and learn to formulate a vision of our shared future. This kind of learning, however, is only possible when we engage in critical and self-reflective praxis embedded within and for purposes of class struggle, which is within a collective effort to transform our world. Social change is not only a process of forms of power confronting one another, but also a process of building knowledge and engaging in forms of praxis and struggle. Thus, our commitments to our own ongoing reflection, engagement, study, and praxis are indispensable. Paula Allman (2007) says this differently when she asserts that Marx's theory of consciousness is in actuality a theory of praxis, of the unity of thought and action. Rather than understanding praxis in a linear or causal manner, this notion of critical revolutionary praxis emphasizes the emergence of critical knowledge within class struggle.

Evidently, this reading of ontology, epistemology, and consciousness is deeply grounded in Marx and Engel's elaborations in *The German Ideology*. We read Marx to understand his analysis of the logic of capitalism and to go beyond what he was able to articulate. Further, we read Marx to understand his method of social analysis, and to be able to use it to read other critical bodies of literature, including feminist, anti-racist, anti-colonial, and anti-imperialist writing. This transdisciplinary and emancipatory reading of social theory is necessary in the field of education, which is knee-capped by its devotion to staying in the realm of the 'visible'. Understanding the world in terms of what is immediately visible does not require historical materialist analysis or any other form of scientific inquiry beyond systematic observation. It also does not require us to ask any questions beyond 'what' we are seeing that move us toward 'why' or 'how'. When we stay in the realm of the visible, and the fetishized realm of experience, we keep our inquiry in step with the outward appearance of social phenomena. In doing this, we direct our attention toward the effects of social relations and thus confuse appearance with essence. The move from the individual to the social, from the fetishized to the relational, from the spontaneous to the critical, requires acts of inquiry that push further and further into the intricate processes and relations that constitute our social world. The goal is to understand what cannot be easily seen. Searching for the invisible is the ultimate goal of inquiry.

Reviewing recent debates on questions of race, gender, class, and sexuality has allowed us to think more deeply about the relationality of this explicitly dialectical, historical, materialist ontology and the phenomenon of social difference, by which we refer to processes of racialization and racial formation, gender, sexuality, ability, language, and nation. The existence of the diversity of the human species is not the crucial point of reflection, but rather the construction of certain forms of difference as significant, particularly within ongoing capitalist accumulation and, historically, for the development of capitalism. In the following section, we will continue our discussion of what we are referring to as 'capitalist social relations' and relations of difference. We want to emphasize the cruciality of this discussion within and among Marxist thinkers, readers, writers, and activists because of two key considerations. First, we believe that a social ontology articulated through concepts like social relations provides the best way to understand individuals and individual experiences and thus to resolve this inherent tension of what is 'individual' and what is 'social' and thus what constitutes social relations. Second, we contend that understanding the intricacies of social relations of difference within capitalism is the best, and perhaps only, way to actually approach an understanding of the 'universe' of capitalism.

5.3 Thinking Through Social Relations of Difference

In order to unpack our thinking about capitalist social relations and difference in a grounded way, we want to use the problem of Equity, Diversity, and Inclusion (EDI) work as an instructive and productive case. In following the previous discussion of our five considerations, our aim is not to look at EDI through these five considerations, but to use the complexity of EDI to elaborate one of these considerations. It is our hope that this will allow us to point out some of the difficulties of why the social relations of race, gender, sexuality, ability, and nation (among others) must be thought out as the *constitutive* relations of capitalism. In doing so, we reject a theorization of these social relations as mere 'effects' or epiphenomenal appearances of capitalist exploitation. But we also must contend with theorizations of forms of oppression that obscure the historical ontologies through which these relations come into being and what their continued, and persistent, organization has to do with the mode of production in which we live. In doing this work, we must all interrogate the forms of consciousness, praxis, teaching/learning, and activism that emerge from different ways of thinking through social relations of difference.

We have chosen EDI work as an instructive case in part because of its ubiquity, but also its specificity. Resulting from ongoing demands from historically oppressed and marginalized communities, EDI work can be found in many organizational spaces, but most certainly in educational institutions, from early childhood to postsecondary education and adult, workplace, and community education. EDI work, particularly in our context in Canada, includes an array of institutional practices and responses to persistent problems of discrimination, harassment, bias, exclusion, violence, and marginalization on the basis of race, sex and sexuality, gender, ability, language, ethnicity, age, and a host of other social positions related to civil and human rights. In other words, EDI work is the attempt by educational institutions to mitigate the racism, sexism, homophobia, ageism, ableism, and, very rarely, classism that infuse all aspects of schools and universities.

Typically, in its most visible iteration, EDI work refers to institutional practices related to hiring and supervision, that is, the labor of people working within these institutions. But there are also efforts to infuse EDI in curriculum revision, asking disciplines to account for their roles in histories of social injustice and to teach content that helps to address the ongoing power relations between education institutions and particular communities, histories, and bodies of knowledge. So, for example, we are currently involved in 'EDI' efforts related to changing tenure and promotion practices in universities, revising undergraduate and graduate curricula, supporting secondary schools principals to respond to incidents of racism in their schools, and supporting teachers to 'Indigenize' provincial curricula. The weeding out of white supremacist and colonial content from primary and secondary curricula and the retraining of teachers to address nationalist mythologies is only one part of the many EDI initiatives moving through educational institutions today. Universal design, building school climates that embrace gender and neurodiversity, addressing racial bias, supporting immigrant students through more robust language learning, and addressing the legacies of colonialism for Indigenous students are all activities that, depending on the politics of those advocating these positions, might be brought under an EDI banner.

EDI, which in our Canadian context is sometimes augmented to EDID (Equity, Diversity, Inclusion, and Decolonization), should also be of special interest to educational scholars and practitioners because it posits a theory of change which is pedagogical in form. The vast majority of EDI work is focused on trainings and workshops (compulsory or otherwise), with attention as well to policies around hiring, safety, and the rooting out of discriminatory and biased institutional practices. For the last thirty or forty years, there has been a growing industry of workplace training and human resource management that pays special attention to addressing issues of race, gender, sexuality, ability, and language in many different kinds of workplaces, including schools, through language such as unconscious bias, cultural competency, multiculturalism, and even sometimes anti-racism. How to make educational institutions more diverse, accessible, inclusive, and equitable has been reinvigorated as a major issue of public concern in North America, following prominent police murders of Black people in the United States and the huge uptick on a global scale to attention to issues of anti-Black racism.

Almost as soon as EDI policies emerged, they were critiqued from all sides. Conservative voices who believe in concepts such as 'meritocracy' and who purport to be 'color blind' rejected the need for these interventions. Similar calls named these problems as exclusively individual and not institutional in nature, for example, the bad apple argument. There may be one male teacher who sexually violates his students, but the problem begins and ends with that individual. There is also a raging debate in centers of empire, including North America and Europe, about how to teach the history of colonization and imperialism, with many detractors insisting these issues are best acknowledged and then left in the past. These critiques of EDI set out to disprove that there is anything social or institutional at work in the continued impunity around acts of discrimination and harassment, but also to forestall the critique that there is anything fundamentally oppressive about how educational institutions do their work. For more progressive and even some radical voices, EDI work is often met with suspicion, if not disdain. The hegemonic reality of EDI as a means to create the appearance of reform without any real substantive shifts in power became quickly apparent.

And yet, as a strategy for social change, it not only persists, but expands. EDI work cannot be seen as solely the brick wall described by Sara Ahmed (2012), despite the particularly apt and accurate description of the bureaucratic gaslighting that constitutes this kind of institutional practice. Critics of EDI must also recognize that the problem exists not just in how the institution responds to demands for change, but also in the demands themselves. To be clear, there is a continuum of demands made, but the ones that gain the most traction with institutions and protesters alike are those that ask for recognition of difference and forms of oppression, the inclusion of (some of) the people, and (some of) the ways of knowing historically excluded from the university and school curricula, and thus increased representation. The politics of recognition, representation, inclusion, and accommodation require that those within the institution learn to think about difference differently and, on a conflated and misunderstood continuum, acknowledge their bias, privilege, and, sometimes, structures/systems of oppression. Thus, the pedagogical component of this theory of change.

A problem emerges. EDI work, while pushing for greater recognition of the problems of racism, heterosexism, misogyny, and ableism, is positioned as performing a dual, and contradictory, act. On the one hand, it can recognize oppressive social relations and at the same time posit the institutions constituted through these relations and charged for decades with their reproduction, as the solution to this problem. In other words, as African American history scholar Robin D.G. Kelley (2016, para. 10) argued, 'core demands for greater diversity, inclusion, and cultural-competency training converge with their critics' fundamental belief that the university possesses a unique teleology: it is supposed to be an enlightened space free of bias and prejudice, but the pursuit of this promise is hindered by structural racism and patriarchy'.

There is a particular conundrum here: how did we get ourselves into a situation where we can acknowledge oppression and try to address it, but through our acknowledgment participate in concretizing a different form of the same social force? Without an understanding of class relations on an international scale, including their historical and contemporary forms within settler and colonial contexts, it is impossible to see from whence these educational institutions came, in what interests they continue to do their work, or how their appearance can shift without a fundamental revolution in the essence of their form or purpose. The contradictions within EDI work allow us to think deeper about the constitutive relations of capitalism and the limits of a conceptualization of social difference that does not allow us to ask questions about class, class formation, and class struggle. Through this lens of interrogation, we hope to be able to throw into sharper relief what differentiates a Marxist feminist analysis of capitalist social relations from other feminist and anti-racist approaches that naturalize existing class relations and their concretization in institutions such as schools and universities. In order to pursue this analysis, we must go beyond the dominant Marxist understanding of class as well as the dominant feminist understanding of gender and race.

Buried deep in notebook four of *Grundrisse*, Marx (1973) has an extended discussion of how limits are dealt with in the circulation of capital. In summating his analysis of this dynamic of capitalist accumulation, he argues, 'but from the fact that capital posits every such limit as a barrier and hence gets *ideally* beyond it, it does not by any means follow that it has *really* overcome it' (ibid., p. 410, emphasis in original). In discussing the universe of capital in this way, he points us toward a crucial aspect of this dynamic when he uses the concepts of *ideally* and *really* in his description. By *ideally*, he is of course referring to the realm of the ideal, of consciousness, and of ideology, and with *really*, he signals another, different, material reality. In other words, it is through human consciousness that limits to capital are transformed into mere barriers and are then overcome. In the passage immediately preceding this quote, Marx is discussing how humans, in the development of capitalism, shifted their consciousness around nature and engaged in 'nature idolatry' where nature 'becomes purely an object for humankind, purely a matter of utility; ceases to be recognized as a power for itself' (ibid.). In other words, through ideological praxis, capitalism absorbs its own limits and contradictions. We have many, many examples of the ways in which a politics of representation functions in this regard. The entire episode of American history in which the election of Barack Obama and the establishment of a 'post-racial' society was immediately followed by the election of a proto-fascist, white supremacist is sufficient to make this point.

One of the great ideological tricks has been our own production of explanations of capitalism that fragment the ontology of this mode of production and allow the constitutive relations of capitalism to be obscured in favor of abstract 'bodies', or falsely universal, white male bodies, that act and are acted upon in particular ways. In other words, this involves taking apart the entirety of the ontology of capitalism and breaking into different forms of oppression, different identities, that somehow must be philosophically reconstituted on the terrain of epistemology when they are in fact ontologically inseparable and historically co-constitutive. The current punching bag for this form of analysis, although liberalism and positivism are the culprits, is intersectionality, a feminist framework emerging from the theorization of a diverse range of Black, feminist scholars (Collins & Bilge, 2020; Taylor, 2018).

A great deal has already been written, either to dismiss intersectionality as ontologically incompatible with a dialectical and historical materialist approach, or to try and reconcile these two 'traditions' (Bohrer, 2019). It is not our intent to rehash that discussion here as we have done it somewhere else, but we read intersectionality as a concept that fragments the social totality of capitalism and cannot articulate modes of oppression through their constitution in class relations. Paradoxically, it emerged out of an attempt to do just this, but its refinement into a fetishized theory has relied upon an absenting of capitalism from its analysis. Its current popularity, in part, stems from the extent and ease of its co-optability. In this way, intersectionality, no matter how radical the intent of its user, requires the stitching back together of a social universe that cannot be ruptured in such ways (Mojab & Carpenter, 2019).

Regardless of the reasons why Marxists are either uncomfortable with, or perhaps too easily accept, the premises of intersectionality, this framework is not the only approach to theorizing oppression that struggles to overcome a fragmentation of social relations. Attention to this work is sorely needed as much Marxian scholarship continues to struggle with the same problems of reification and fragmentation of social relations. We would include a host of critical scholars, including Marxist scholars and ourselves, in this complaint. One important lesson of Marx's work is that dialectical analysis is always changing and never ending. And so, we carry on. In this section, we want to weave together some recent analyses that challenge dominant theorizations of oppression, and which highlight the corrosive and insidious ways in which neoliberal ideology has infused our thinking about capitalist social relations and shaped our demands within its universe.

We bring neoliberalism as a concept to the discussion here to help make visible the ways in which class warfare has operated at the level of public policy, discourse, and institutional reorganization over the last forty years, resulting in the extension, differentiation, and intensification of capitalism into all domains of human life, including our own subjectivities. Neoliberal policy and ideology, enacted and circulated by *people*, has so effectively riddled the domain of social reproduction with crisis that more and more aspects of life have been subsumed within the labor-capital relation, or simply disappeared entirely. At the same time, the normalization, naturalization, and, thus, neutralization of these processes and relations have left many of us grasping for moments when these ideologies crack open. These theorizations of capitalist social relations determine our political demands and proposals for social change, and thus critical engagement with them is important, but also generative, for developing our thinking as Marxist feminist educators.

Difference, Identity, and the Pain of Oppression

Following the 2014 murder of Michael Brown by police in Ferguson, Missouri, a new era of activism against police violence and anti-Black racism began in the United States. Characterized by Black Lives Matter and the Movement for Black Lives, these political movements have crossed borders and circulate widely on the global scale. They also contain multitudes and fractious debates across a political spectrum. In 2016, Robin D.G. Kelley contributed a critique of the shape of some of this movement building, particularly on university campuses, to a forum in *Boston Review*. This critique emerged again, recently, when it was censored from an Advanced Placement curriculum in African America History by the actions of the Florida State Legislature.

His critique, however, concerns not only activism against anti-Black racism, but the question of political resistance and struggle within the academy at all, and perhaps even educational institutions more broadly. He begins with a critique of what he calls the 'more modest' politics of inclusion, accommodation, and recognition; in other words, the project of EDI. These demands, he argues, express a felt and lived reality of the trauma of anti-Black racism and its constant, unrelenting, and trans-local visibility given the advent of digital communication technologies. However, embodied in these 'modest' demands, Kelley sees a theorization of oppression that reduces Blackness to suffering, psychologizes and individualizes that suffering, and engages in a historical forgetting of the myriad and creative forms of Black resistance that have charted the freedom dreams of not only Black diasporic communities, but many other racialized and oppressed peoples as well.

Kelley is not, by far, the only scholar who has raised concerns over the individualizing of oppressive social relations through the language of trauma, despite demands for trauma to be recognized as part of the history of particular social groups. Chi Chi Shi (2018, para. 6) has gone as far as to argue that 'the psychic dimension of recognition permeates the language of the left' and that demands for inclusion are increasingly based in 'affective recognition from institutions and those in positions of power'. Shi (ibid., para 7) argues that underneath the discursive demand for recognition, particularly of trauma, lies 'pressures of individualisation produced by neoliberalism' that 'have created a political climate where the demand for emancipation sounds as a demand to de-stigmatize and make visible oppressed identities' (ibid.). For Shi, this turn in left politics, and the theorization of oppression that underpins it, is inseparable from 'neoliberalism as a rationality that structures subject-formation' (ibid., para 13). Neoliberal rationality not only seeks to reorient our understanding of ourselves as rational, self-interested, and competitive individuals, it seeks to promote politics that undermine any sense of public or common good, social solidarity, or collective identity. In this way, Shi (ibid., para 14) argues that

> Neoliberalism, in its attempts to destroy the basis for collectivity, provides the basis on which movements privilege individuality. Reflected in the theory and

practice of contemporary identity-politics is a depoliticisation of struggle which frames oppression as subjective and individual. The discursive shifts enacted in the language of identity politics evince the shifting assumptions concerning the boundaries of possibility. In general terms, the primary shift has been from language that signals collective and structural issues to language which privileges individual behaviors and emphasizes difference. Even though it is stressed that oppression is 'systemic,' it is the effects of oppression that are focused upon ... The problem with this reading is that focusing on the victims of misrecognition often overshadows analysis of the causes of misrecognition.

Shi takes pains to recognize that the concept of 'identity politics' is now largely divorced from the anti-capitalist and anti-imperialist usage first articulated by the Combahee River Collective. While there are many insights to her analysis, we want to focus on her insistence that the current recalibration of oppression through its affective dimensions not only colludes with neoliberalism, it does so by reducing our focus to the effects of oppression. Our gaze, directed in this manner, remains out of focus of the causes, or roots, of these social relations. We have argued many times that the purpose of Marxist feminist analysis is to overcome exactly this problem; our aim is not only the effect of social relations, but the constitution of them. We must investigate not only the appearance of these social relations, but their essence.

Kelley (2016) makes a similar point in his piece. The forum in *Boston Review* offered several affirmative and dissenting opinions on Kelley's argument, but as a whole the forum raised the question of the difference between political strategy and political analysis. As a strategy, some may see efficacy to demands for institutional reform via the politicization of suffering, particularly if they build to bigger demands for change. However, Kelley's critique is not only leveled at the strategies of EDI. It is directed at the theorization of oppression that underpins these demands and which articulates oppression as policies and practices within institutions, and sometimes bias within people, as forces that truncate the life chances of *individuals*. He addresses the individualizing tendencies of these discourses and theories of trauma through attention to 'bodies'. He argues that

> to identify anti-Black violence as heritage may be true in a general sense, but it obscures the dialectic that produced and reproduced the violence of a regime dependent on Black *life* for its profitability. It was, after all, the resisting Black body that needed 'correction.' Violence was used not only to break bodies but to discipline *people* who refused enslavement. And the impulse to resist is neither involuntary nor solitary. It is a choice made in community, made possible by community, and informed by memory, tradition, and witness. (*ibid.*, para 25, emphasis in original)

Kelley identifies here a problem of social fragmentation, specifically of 'the dialectic' of white supremacy and capitalism. It is not the only fragmentation he cogently and concisely identifies within this passage and to which we will return. But for now, we turn our attention to a re-constitutive approach to conceptualizing capitalist social relations and difference.

The Struggle to Overcome Fragmentation and False Universalisms

Through the struggle to reorient our thinking toward social relations, or as Ollman (2004) posits to see 'social relations as subject matter' (p. 23), we must fully move our ontological grounding to the relational, dialectical, historical, and materialist approach Marx and Engels (1968) repeatedly articulate throughout *The German Ideology*. We then struggle to reformulate and use concepts that signal, as Dorothy Smith (2005) was fond of saying, the 'ontological shift' (p. 4). *Social relations* is one such concept, and to use it signals a different ontology and epistemology than systems, structures, discourses, or any similar conceptualization that accomplishes the taken-for-granted task of reifying and fragmenting social totality. In *Educating from Marx*, we described social relations as 'both forms of consciousness and practical, sensuous, human activity (not just what we think, but also what we do)' (Mojab & Carpenter, 2019, p. 5). We then argued that the concept of social relations becomes a useful tool for contemporary social analysis when we understand that we are consciously living *capitalist* social relations.

Capitalist social relations, or the capitalist mode of production as a 'mode of life' (Marx & Engels, 1968, p. 32), is then taken beyond an economistic or determinist emphasis on the economy or even simple production, consumption, and circulation. To understand the mode of life of capitalism, it is necessary to understand all its particulars and how, within those particulars, the totality of capitalism might be found. To this end, every form of 'social difference' or 'othering' is an opportunity to better understand the universe of capitalism. To be clear, we are speaking specifically of social relations of race, gender, sexuality, nation, and ability, which are the forms through which class relations have emerged and are continually concretized within capitalism.

But the way we go about inquiry into 'the social' is key, and it begins with conceptualization. Hopefully, at this point we have put to rest the theorizations of race or gender or sexuality as purely cultural or epiphenomenal. It should be obvious after so much careful scholarship of race, gender, and sexuality that these are the relations that constitute the most intimate aspects of our material reality (see, among many others, Anievas & Nişancioğlu, 2015; Federici, 2004; Horne, 2020). As Nancy Fraser (2014, p. 55) argued, they are 'behind Marx's hidden abode'. If Marx sought to go from the appearance of the market to the 'hidden abode' of production, then Marxist scholarship must move beyond into the hidden abodes of reproduction in order to understand how the abode of production is constituted. Education is one of these crucial abodes. As Bannerji argued, to work in the realm of these sorts of abstractions presupposes false universalisms of male-ness, white-ness, cis-ness, hetero-ness, and able-bodied-ness. This is a significant blind spot in some Marxian scholarship since 'the actual realization process of capital cannot be outside a given social and cultural form or mode. There is no capital that is a universal abstraction. Capital is always a practice, a determinate set of social relations- and a cultural one at that' (Bannerji, 2011, p. 47).

But the authors discussed in the previous section are also pointing toward other problems in our conceptualizations and articulations of difference and 'otherness'. To the extent that we rely upon fragmented ontologies that divvy-up social relations into ossified identity categories with essentialist characteristics, we are then left with only the option of conceiving of these identities as *externally* related. This puts us back into the realm of reified ontology. It also opens us up to problems of equating identity with consciousness, which can obscure very real class interests as well as complex collusion with white supremacy, patriarchy, and so forth, not to mention paternalistic forms of racism, sexism, classism, and ableism. Kelley and Shi also caution against equating the appearance of oppressive social relations with their essence. They explicitly argue that placing a determining primacy on affect renders invisible the actual constitution of capitalist social relations and, importantly, substitutes collective, revolutionary struggle for individual well-being.

But again, the question of how we theorize capitalist social relations is not just key for the development of political strategy, but it is crucial for political analysis and thus pedagogical processes of politicization and conscientization. As educational researchers and activists, we must direct our attention to constitutive questions, such as how does schooling and education, more broadly, produce and reproduce not only classed relations, but racialized and gendered class relations? How can we move beyond inclusion, accommodation, and equity politics that leave these class relations untroubled and simply seek to propagate mythologies of mobility? To answer such questions requires shifting the starting point and standpoint of analysis away from how individuals experience the effects of social relations as well as refusing a posited duality of the self and the social. Overcoming such fragmentation of the self and the social is the same ontological struggle to overcome the reification of capitalism in undialectical readings of Marxist analysis. This ontological struggle leads to an epistemological one and, hopefully, a changed pedagogical praxis and the taking up of education as a domain of class struggle.

5.4 Returning to Living, Learning, and Teaching Revolution

In the epilogue to *Educating from Marx: Race, Gender, and Learning*, we proposed that there were three important dialectical 'moments' at the core of revolutionary pedagogy. These were the dialectics of matter/consciousness, necessity/freedom, and essence/appearance. We proposed these moments to guide the critical and reflective praxis of educators; we argued that these moments should guide the choices we make regarding content and pedagogy as well as the myriad of other choices, decisions, and processes that critical educators encounter in their teaching/learning work. We chose the dialectic of matter and consciousness to remind educators of the necessity of working from an ontology that understands human activity, social relations, and forms of consciousness as conscious, sensuous, active relations.

In other words, as Freire (1973, p. 60) argued, 'consciousness as consciousness of consciousness'. We chose the dialectic of freedom and necessity to remind ourselves that the actually existing world and its complex forms of exploitation and oppression are the conditions in which we live and the relations we must revolutionize. We must work with the world as we find it, and, in this struggle, we must constantly remind ourselves that our freedom dreams, as Robin D.G. Kelley calls them, must be radical and 'go to the root'. Finally, we chose the dialectic of appearance and essence to remind ourselves of the purpose of critical science. As Marx (1959, p. 817) famously cautioned in the third volume of capital, 'all science would be superfluous if the outward appearance and the essence of things directly coincided'. The way things appear in the everyday conceals the social relations, ideologies, and contradictions that actually constitute the concretized relations of capital. Looking beyond the appearance of a social problem and into its essence is the epistemological mandate of critical, educational praxis.

The discussion we have provided earlier offers divergent ways of understanding and analyzing the oppressive social relations of capitalism. These divergent theoretical positions also offer different ways forward in terms of a collective pursuit of freedom. What Kelley and Shi are pointing toward are the many problems, both philosophically and politically, that arise when our theorization of various forms of oppressive social relations is focused on the appearance of these forms rather than their essence. Another reason why we want to expand on our theorization of 'difference' and capitalist social relations, within our own work and Marxism and education scholarship more broadly, is because of the enormous implications this conceptualization has for social change broadly and education specifically. How we work to conceptualize oppression and its constitution and function within capitalism is clearly crucial to understanding problems of white supremacy, patriarchy, heteronormativity, ableism, and other forms of oppressive social relations.

Articulating these forms of oppression as class struggle is the next challenge to Marxist feminist thinkers. Exploring the dialectics of reform and revolution in educational spaces, particularly as articulated through the social relations of difference, is a necessary turn. In the dialectical contradiction between the human vocation of becoming and the social universe of capitalism, education workers are uniquely positioned to revolutionize at the point of reproduction. Such a collective undertaking would certainly be a sight to behold. But for this struggle to emerge, exploring these formations is crucial to an understanding of what capitalism is, how it emerged, how it functions, how it reproduces itself, and how we have failed to make a revolution against it. The story of capitalism is not exclusively a European story, it is not a white story, it is not a male story, and it is not an able-bodied story. If we take seriously Marx's assertion that capital is a *relation*, then what and who constitutes that relation should be the focus of our inquiry.

Acknowledgments We would like to thank the editors of the volume for their careful reading and support of this chapter. We also thank the Social Sciences and Humanities Research Council (SSHRC) Canada for their support.

Disclosure Statement None of the co-authors has any financial interest or benefit that has arisen from the direct applications of this research.

References

Ahmed, S. (2012). *On Being Included: Racism and Diversity in Institutional Life*. Duke University Press.
Allman, P. (1999). *Revolutionary Social Transformation: Democratic Hopes, Political Possibilities, and Critical Education*. Bergin and Garvey.
Allman, P. (2007). *On Marx: An Introduction to the Revolutionary Intellect of Karl Marx*. Sense.
Allman, P. (2010). *Critical Education Against Global Capitalism: Karl Marx and Revolutionary Critical Education* (2nd ed.) Sense.
Allman, P., McLaren, P., & Riskowski, G. (2005). After the Box People: The Labour-Capital Relation as Class Constitution- and Its Consequence for Marxist Education Theory and Human Resistance. In P. McLaren (Ed.), *Capitalists and Conquerors: A Critical Pedagogy Against Empire* (pp. 135–165). Rowman & Littlefield.
Anievas, A., & Nişancioğlu, K. (2015). *How the West Came to Rule: The Geopolitical Origins of Capitalism*. Pluto.
Bannerji, H. (2000). *The Dark Side of the Nation: Essays on Multiculturalism, Nation, and Gender*. Canadian Scholars' Press.
Bannerji, H. (2011). Building from Marx: Reflections on "Race," Gender and class. In S. Carpenter & S. Mojab (Eds.), *Educating from Marx: Race, Gender, and Learning* (pp. 41–60). Palgrave.
Bohrer, A. (2019). *Marxism and Intersectionality: Race, Gender, Class, and Sexuality Under Contemporary Capitalism*. Transcript Publishing.
Carpenter, S., & Mojab, S. (2011). A Specter Haunts Adult Education: Crafting a Marxist Feminist Framework for Adult Education and Learning. In S. Carpenter & S. Mojab (Eds.), *Educating from Marx: Race, gender, and learning* (pp. 3–18). Palgrave.
Carpenter, S., & Mojab, S. (2017). *Revolutionary learning: Marxism, feminism, and knowledge*. Pluto Press.
Collins, P. H., & Bilge, S. (2020). *Intersectionality* (2nd ed.). Polity.
Federici, S. (2004). *Caliban and the Witch: Women, the Body, and Primitive Accumulation*. Autonomedia.
Fraser, N. (2009). Feminism, Capitalism, and the Cunning of History. *New Left Review, 56*(Mar-April), 97–117.
Fraser, N. (2014). Behind Marx's Hidden Abode: For an Expanded Conception of Capitalism. *New Left Review, 86*, 55–72.
Freire, P. (1973). *Pedagogy of the Oppressed*. Continuum.
Horne, G. (2020). *The Dawning of the Apocalypse: The Roots of Slavery, White Supremacy, Settler Colonialism, and Capitalism in the Long Sixteenth Century*. Monthly Review Press.

Incite! (2017). *The Revolution Will Not be Funded: Beyond the Non-profit Industrial Complex*. Duke University Press.

Jad, I. (2008). The Demobilisation of Women's Movements: The Case of Palestine. In S. Batliwala (Ed.), *Changing Their World* (1st ed.). Association for Women's Rights in Development. www.awid.org

Kelley, R. D. G. (2016, March 1). Black Study, Black Struggle. *Boston Review*. https://www.bostonreview.net/forum/robin-kelley-black-struggle-campus-protest/

Knight, N. (2005). *Marxist Philosophy in China: From Qui Qiubai to Mao Zedong, 1923–1945*. Springer.

Korolczuk, E. (2016). Neoliberalism and Feminist Organizing: From "NGO-ization of Resistance" to Resistance Against Neoliberalism. In E. Kováts (Ed.), *Solidarity in Struggle: Feminist Perspectives on Neoliberalism in East-Central Europe* (pp. 32–41). Friedrich-Ebert-Stiftung Budapest.

Marx, K. (1959). *Capital*. Volume 3. Lawrence Wishart.

Marx, K. (1968). Theses on Feuerbach. In in K. Marx and F. (Ed.), *Engels The German Ideology* (pp. 659–662). Progress Publishers.

Marx, K. (1973). *Grundrisse*. Penguin.

Marx, K., & Engels, F. (1968). *The German Ideology*. Progress Publishers.

Mojab, S., & Carpenter, S. (2019). Marxism, Feminism, and Intersectionality. *Journal of Labor and Society*, 22(2), 275–282.

Ollman, B. (1993). *Dialectical Investigations*. Routledge.

Ollman, B. (2004). *Dance of the dialectic: Steps in Marx's method*. University of Illinois Press.

Rikowski, G. (1996). Left Alone: End Time for Marxist Educational Theory? *British Journal of Sociology of Education*, 17(4), 415–451.

Rikowski, G. (1997). Scorched Earth: Prelude to Rebuilding Marxist Educational Theory. *British Journal of Sociology of Education*, 18(4), 551–574.

Sayer, D. (1987). *The Violence of Abstraction: The Analytic Foundations of Historical Materialism*. Basil Blackwell.

Shi, C. C. (2018). Defining My Own Oppression: Neoliberalism and the Demands of Victimhood, *Historical Materialism*, 26(2). https://www.historicalmaterialism.org/articles/defining-my-own-oppression

Smith, D. (2001). Texts and the Ontology of Organizations and Institutions. *Studies in Cultures, Organizations, and Societies*, 7(2), 159–198.

Smith, D. (2005). *Institutional Ethnography: A Sociology for People*. AltaMira.

Smith, D. (2011). Ideology, Science, and Social Relations: A Reinterpretation of Marx's Epistemology. In S. Carpenter & S. Mojab (Eds.), *Educating from Marx: Race, Gender, and Learning* (pp. 19–40). Palgrave.

Taylor, K. Y. (Ed.). (2018). *How We Get Free: Black Feminism and the Combahee River Collective*. Haymarket.

Tse-Tung, M. (2007). On Practice: On the Relation Between Knowledge and Practice, Between Knowing and Doing. In S. Žižek (Ed.), *On Practice and Contradiction* (pp. 52–67). Verso.

CHAPTER 6

Foundations and Challenges of Polytechnic Education

Marise Nogueira Ramos

> *The human essence is not an abstraction inherent in the singular individual. In its reality, it is the ensemble of social relations.*
> —Marx (1991, p. 13)

6.1 Introduction

This chapter discusses the concept of polytechnic education in the context of historical materialism, starting from the ontological assumptions of the thought of Marx and Engels, and the centrality of the category labor in the formation of man. The analysis goes in the direction of understanding the principle of the union between instruction and production in working-class education. It does so in political and programmatic terms, through the intellectual elaboration of these philosophers, as well as their appropriations and respective debates in concrete experiences. It seeks to contemplate synthetic approaches about theoretical assumptions of historical materialism, specifically on the conception of the human being and of labor,[1] the division of work and production of human existence, labor-education unity, the union between instruction and work, issues and contradictions of the Soviet educational experience, and contradictions in Brazil of crossing over to polytechnic education.

M. N. Ramos (✉)
State University of Rio de Janeiro, Rio de Janeiro, Brazil

© The Editor(s) (if applicable) and The Author(s), under exclusive license to Springer Nature Switzerland AG 2023
R. Hall et al. (eds.), *The Palgrave International Handbook of Marxism and Education*, Marxism and Education,
https://doi.org/10.1007/978-3-031-37252-0_6

Through this analysis, the educational thought of Lenin and the socialist educators and the Italian philosopher Antonio Gramsci acquire emphasis as a legacy of the elaborations of Marx and Engels. An attempt is made to grasp their historical elaboration, considering the political and pedagogical issues of each time and context, such as debates on the construction of socialist pedagogy, the counterpoint to new pedagogy, and the proposals of the Italian government that kept Gramsci in prison.

Theoretical and political contradictions produced in the disputes of educational projects of the working class in Brazil are exposed, especially since 2003, when attempts were made to rescue the conception of polytechnic education as a reference for basic education. This was a movement that began in Brazil in the 1980s, but weakened under the hegemony of neoliberalism around the world. In particular, the proposal of the Integrated High School is problematized, understood as a historical form of 'crossing over' toward the construction of polytechnismin Brazilian society, given its specificity as a concrete social formation of 'dependent capitalism' (Fernandes, 2009).

6.2 Theoretical Assumptions of Historical Materialism for the Formation of Man

Marx (2001) tells us about the general meaning of labor as human production in his *Economic and Philosophical Manuscripts of 1844*. Labor as vital activity or productive life is the only means that satisfies a primary need, that of maintaining physical existence. The productive life of the human being then is initially the very creation of life. 'In the type of vital activity lies the whole character of a species, its generic character; and free, conscious activity constitutes the generic character of man' (Marx, 2001, p. 116). Thus, labor in general and its product—as past, objectified labor—are creators of wealth and producers of human life in any time or place, which is to say that human labor has an ontological or ontocreative determination.

Lukács (1981) explains that, for Marx, labor is the only place where one can ontologically demonstrate the presence of a true teleological position as an effective moment of material reality. The author says that the first impulse toward satisfying a need is a common feature of both human and animal life. The paths begin to diverge when labor, the teleological position, is inserted between necessity and satisfaction. The teleological position is aborded by Lukács also as the previous ideation—the rational plane that only human beings are capable of devising to achieve a goal, in this case, satisfying a need by itself. Marx has a phrase that illustrates this human specificity compared to other animals, which, in turn, defines a generality of the species: 'what distinguishes the worst architect from the best bee is that he figures his construction in his mind before he turns it into reality. At the end of the labor process there appears a result which already existed before ideally in the worker's imagination' (Marx, 1999, p. 211).

Thus, the relationship between the 'teleological position' and the cognitive nature of work is understood:

> In this same fact [the teleological position], which implies the first impulse to labor, its cognitive nature becomes evident, since it is undoubtedly a victory of conscious behavior over the mere spontaneity of biological instinct that between necessity and immediate satisfaction labor is introduced as a mediating element. (Lukács, 1981, p. 23)

This characteristic of labor, considered in its ontologically original form, that is as an organ of organic exchange between man and nature, constitutes it as the model of social praxis in general, of any active social conduct. This is so for some fundamental reasons: first, because praxis is only possible from the teleological position of the subject; second, because labor is the only complex of being in which the teleological position has an authentic, real role in modifying reality; and, finally, because,

> from the ontological coexistence between teleology and causality in the labor (practice) of man derives the fact that, on the plane of being, theory and praxis, given their social essence, are moments of a single and identical complex of being, the social being, which means that they can only be adequately understood by taking this reciprocal relationship as a starting point. And precisely here labor can serve as a fully enlightening model. This may seem a little strange at first glance, since labor is clearly oriented in a teleological sense, and therefore interest in the realization of the end in view appears in the foreground. (Lukács, 1981, p. 30)

Marx insists on the historical determination of the nature of labor. We will, then, find in his texts the reference to labor as 'vital activity', and 'productive life', following the example extracted from the *Economic and Philosophical Manuscripts of 1844*.

> Certainly labor, vital activity, productive life, now appears to man as the only means that satisfies a need, that of maintaining physical existence. Productive life, however, is generic life. It is life creating life. In the type of vital activity lies the whole character of a species, its generic character; and free, conscious activity constitutes the generic character of man. Life reveals itself simply as a means of life. (Marx, 2001, p. 116)

So, for Marx, the human praxis—the action of satisfying needs by articulating intellectual and manual work—corresponds to the conversion of the 'teleological position' (Lukács, 1981) into the concrete object that operates the required satisfaction. The human existence production is not only a natural relation—the production of life in procreation—but also a social relation, because in labor, cooperation between individuals extends to produce conditions of life for itself and for others.

Originally, thus, the 'natural' division of labor develops due to natural dispositions (e.g. physical vigor), needs, accidents, and so forth. Later, when intellectual and material activity pass to different individuals, there is a real division of labor (between manual and intellectual work) (Marx & Engels, 1991, p. 42). Under these conditions, consciousness is detached from the real world and enters into contradiction with the objective determinations of production relations centered on private property.

In the *Economic and Philosophical Manuscripts*, the philosopher explains this phenomenon as the alienation of the worker in relation to the means of production, the process and the product of his work, and in relation to himself, forming a dialectical unit of this with the private property of the means of production: 'it is only at the last culminating point in the development of private property that its secret is unveiled, to know, on the one hand, that it is the *product* of alienated labor and, on the other, that it is the *means* by which labor becomes alienated, *the realization of alienation*' (Marx, 2001, p. 120, *emphasis* in original).

'Property is the power to dispose of the workforce', say Marx and Engels (1991, p. 46), recognizing the definition of the classical economists. Moreover, whoever disposes of this power becomes the 'master of work' (Marx, 2001, p. 120), such that 'capitalism' is the mode of production based on the private property, and in which the workforce is transformed into merchandise.

Understanding alienated labor as the historical form of work in capitalism is fundamental to apprehend the disputes related to the education of this class. This is because, under the logic of subsumption to capital, the qualification of the workforce cannot be a threat either to the increase in profits, or to the passivation of the class resulting from the alienated conscience. But in the contradiction, capital cannot absolutely do without some qualification of the worker—already recognized by Adam Smith, in the eighteenth century—to avoid the 'complete degeneration of the mass of the people' (Marx, 2001, p. 417).

6.3 Labor and Education in Capitalism

Capitalism will split the relationship between labor and knowledge with the introduction of machinery into production and especially the manufacturing division of labor. In capitalist production, this knowledge is required only by the combined production as a whole, separated from the individual worker, just as the product itself and its use value are separated from him. The division then occurs between the spheres: of knowledge and production, of science and technique, and of theory and practice. Labor is divided into intellectual labor and manual labor. The worker, instead of being the subject of knowledge, reflection, and imagination, is now considered part of the machines:

> The intellectual forces of production develop only in one direction, because they are inhibited in relation to everything that does not fit into their one-sidedness.

What partial workers lose, is concentrated in the capital that confronts them. The manufacturing division of labor opposes them to the intellectual forces of the material process of production as the property of others and as a power that dominates them. This process of dissociation begins with simple cooperation, in which the capitalist represents, before the isolated worker, the unity and will of the collective worker. This process develops in manufacturing, which mutilates the worker, reducing him to a fraction of himself, and is completed in modern industry, which makes science a productive force independent of labor, recruiting it to serve capital. (Marx, 2001, p. 416)

Considered exclusively from the point of view of the parceling and simplification of work, the worker's school education would not be immediately necessary, since tasks could be quickly learned at the workstation itself. Nevertheless, as Saviani (2007, p. 159) states,

If the machine made possible the materialization of intellectual functions in the productive process, the way to objectify the generalization of intellectual functions in society was the school. With the impact of the Industrial Revolution, the main countries took on the task of organizing national education systems, seeking to generalize basic schooling. Thus, to the Industrial Revolution corresponded an Educational Revolution: the former put the machine at the center of the production process; the latter erected the school as the main and dominant form of education.

It was also with the perspective of training the sons of workers, their future substitutes, that the installation of schools was undertaken, aimed less at teaching work techniques and more at adapting these children to the routine and rhythm of work with discipline and docility. It was the workhouses, which became Schools of Industry or Colleges for Labor, which appeared primarily in England in the eighteenth century, that introduced the practice of training for work in Western culture.

Reflecting this, the employment of child labor in the factories of England was a topic considered by Marx and Engels to be important for understanding the question of the union between production and instruction. Engels (2010), in *The Situation of the Working Class in England*, describes the reasons and ways in which children were employed in factories. The small size of the machines, which would later become larger, was suitable for operation by children. They were recruited from the workhouses and placed at the service of the industrialists, from whom they became 'slaves', being treated with brutality and rudeness.

This situation was impacted historically, through needs for legal changes, and practically, through the need for pragmatism. First, the apprentice laws of 1802 (the Health and Morals of Apprentices Act) and 1844 (Factory Act) limited abuses. Second, the transfer of factories from rural regions near waterfalls to cities, catalyzed by the replacement of waterpower by steam, enabled labor to be composed by children and women of the same family as the adult male worker. The increase in the size of machines and the regulation of child labor, known as 'factory laws', also changed the age profile of workers.

Marx considered these laws as a society's response to working conditions and as an effect of working-class pressures on the state, which had educational ramifications. In chapter II of *The Communist Manifesto*, written in 1848, when listing the measures that should be adopted after the seizure of power by the workers, Marx advocates the unification of education with material production, placing as a condition, the 'public and free education of all children. Elimination of child labor in the factories in its present form. Combination of education with material production, etc.' (Marx & Engels, 1996, p. 87).

The intention was thus to restore to the expropriated classes a superior form of education, linked to the new and more advanced relations of production, and this was a subject that Manacorda (2010) shows us crossed from the I to the IV Congress of the International. Marx (1866) exposed in writing his Instructions to the Delegates at the 1st Congress, held in Geneva, the proposal about the working-class education, which should encompass intellectual, physical, and technological education. In 1875, in his *Critique of the Gotha Program*, Marx reinforced the demand for an early link between education and productive work, as one of the most powerful means of transforming society. He subordinated it to the strict regulation of the duration of work according to different ages (Marx, 2012, p. 39).

Marx (1999, pp. 548–49) recognized in the utopian socialists an influence on his pedagogical thinking:

> From the factory system, as we can follow particularly in the writings of Robert Owen, was born the germ of the instruction of the future, which will unite for all children beyond a certain age productive labor with instruction and gymnastics, not only as a method for increasing social production, but also as the only method for forming fully developed men.

Understanding the principle of the union between production and instruction, or between teaching and work, in Marx and Engels requires, therefore, that we understand labor as a contradictory, vital human activity. It is the producer of misery and wealth, resulting from the interposition of merchandise, and the division of labor in the human being-nature-human being relationship. Although, under relations of exploitation, scientific-technological development, as the foundation of industrial production, is, at the same time, development of the human productive forces. As a result, development of the human being itself: 'the development of science, this ideal and at the same time practical wealth, is only one aspect, one form, in which is manifested the development of the human productive forces, i.e., of wealth' (Marx, 2011, p. 589).

However, under the limits of capital, the improvement of the productive forces, of universal wealth, of knowledge, and so forth occurs under the alienation of the worker, under 'conditions of an alien wealth and his own poverty'. But this contradiction produces, at the same time, the real conditions of its own overcoming, which presupposes, concretely, 'the understanding of his own history as a process and the knowledge of nature (existing also as practical power over it) as his real body' (ibid., p. 591). Put another way, it requires the worker to appropriate the totality of the productive forces, against the rule of capital. Marx identified polytechnic schools as a contradiction in this sense.

6.4 Polytechnic Education: A Concept Constructed by Capital-Labor Contradiction

Polytechnic education is not an abstract product of consciousness, but a concrete practice that brought virtuous contradictions to work, since the advancement of productive forces required to combine instruction and production.

> The polytechnic and agronomic schools are factors in this process of transformation that have developed spontaneously at the base of modern industry; also factors in this metamorphosis are the vocational schools where the children of the workers receive some technological instruction and are initiated in the practical handling of different instruments of production. The factory legislation has wrested from capital the first and insufficient concession to combine primary education with factory work. (Marx, 1999, pp. 552–53)

The pedagogical effectiveness of this combination has been attested, as Marx argues when speaking of the 'petty' but necessary provisions of the factory law regarding the education of children as an indispensable condition for their employment:

> Its success demonstrated, first of all, the possibility of combining education and gymnastics with manual labor, and, consequently, manual labor with education and gymnastics. The factory inspectors soon discovered, through the testimonies of the schoolmasters, that the children employed in the factories, although only half attending school, learned as much and often more than the regular pupils who had full daily attendance. (Marx, 1999, p. 548)

If the polytechnic schools would be 'spontaneous' products of modern industry, since the 'factory legislation snatched from capital the first and insufficient concession to combine primary instruction with factory work', the conquest of political power by the workers would bring the adoption of technological teaching in the workers' school, with a theoretical and practical core. Thus, we see the principles on which workers' education should be prepared: intellectual education; physical education, as given in gymnasium schools and by military drill; technological instruction, which imparts the general principles of all production processes and, at the same time, initiates the child and young people in the practical use and handling of the elementary instruments of all trades.

This is the project of polytechnic education in the work's perspective. This type of education, by providing the working class with the appropriation of the totality of the productive forces and by developing its capacities in all directions, will raise it to a higher level than the bourgeoisie (Marx, 1866). Here we are a powerful mediation against alienation, and for the benefit of both emancipation and demands that degrading working conditions be abolished:

> The polytechnic training, which was advocated by proletarian writers, must compensate for the drawbacks that are derived from the division of labor, which prevents its apprentices from attaining a thorough knowledge of their trade. On this point, one has always started from what the bourgeoisie understands by polytechnic formation, which has produced erroneous interpretations (...) On the one hand, it is necessary to modify the social conditions in order to create a new educational system; on the other hand, a new educational system is lacking to be able to modify the social conditions. Consequently, it is necessary to start from the present situation. (Marx, 2011, p. 138)

6.5 The Legacy of Marx and Engels for Working-Class Education

The leader of the Russian Revolution, Lenin, took Marx's theses about the union of instruction and labor for the organization of the school institutions of the first socialist state and enunciated them in the draft of the party program in 1917.

> Free, compulsory, general and polytechnic education (which familiarizes both in theory and practice with all the main branches of production) for all children of both sexes up to the age of 16; a close connection of education with the children's productive social work. (Lenin, *apud* Krupskaya, 2017, p. 175)

The conditions for its existence, previously systematized by Marx, would be stated thus by the leader: 'one will move on to the suppression of the division of labor among men, to education, instruction, preparation of onilaterally developed and onilaterally prepared men, of men capable of doing everything' (*apud* Manacorda, 2006, p. 315).

Twenty years before Lenin's critique of the 'petty-bourgeois utopian tendencies of the populists', he stated:

> It is not possible to conceive the ideal of a future society without combining instruction with the productive work of the young generation. Neither education in isolation from productive work, nor productive work in isolation from education, could be brought up to the present level of technique and the present state of scientific knowledge. (ibid., p. 314)

There are very significant passages on the subject in texts by Krupskaya (2017). When talking about 'polytechnism', the challenges of the school in face of the development of productive forces are evident, especially considering the curiosity and interest aroused in children, and that this should be stimulated by schools, thus creating favorable conditions for polytechnic education. The content of such education would consist not only in the acquisition of various skills by the students or in the teaching of modern and high forms of useful techniques, but also in the reproduction of a global system in whose basis lies the study of technique in its different forms. This is realized in its development and in all its mediations, from 'natural technological' to the technology of materials and the means of production. These are its mechanisms and energetic driving forces.

Polytechnic education is not limited to the study of the natural sciences and their laws that are appropriated by men as a productive force. It is also important to know the historical determinations of social relations. Productive labor, no matter in which sector of economy, has its foundations and techniques based on parts of sciences, but it has others historical determinations. For example, what problems led to the development of certain products and technologies? What political and economic disputes were involved for such development to be driven? Why and how does the spatial distribution of production occur?

The relations between workers, with the hierarchical structure of production and with society, also have their own history and express mediations of the class struggle, which shape ways of life and kinds of consciousness—a culture, we could say, or the social superstructure—that condense past, present, and perspectives of future. These issues belong to the social totality and manifest themselves at particularly productive processes and relationships. So, we conclude that production is a material and social process, and each one constitutes a particularity of the social totality. Here, we are a principle of polytechnic education: integration between particularity and social totality that requires studying all areas of knowledge—nature and social science, philosophy, languages, and art, linked to production and all social practices.

Therefore, 'polytechnism' is not about some specific teaching subject, but it should permeate all disciplines. It should be reflected in the selection of material from the natural and social sciences and in deep articulation between them. Its content should engage with practical activities and with the teaching of labor, which, then, can acquire a polytechnic character. This explains why the polytechnic school differs from a professional school.

> Because it has its center of gravity in the understanding of work processes, in the development of the ability to unite in a single whole theory and practice, in the ability to understand the interdependence of known phenomena, while the center of gravity of the vocational school passes through the training of students in work skills. (Krupskaya, 2017. p. 153)

This school, the Soviet educator lucidly explains, 'forms a fully developed worker, which capitalism does not need'. Therefore, on the one hand, under capitalism, the polytechnic school cannot fully unfold; but on the other hand, together with Lenin, there was a conviction of the fundamental importance of polytechnic education to help create the basis for a classless society (ibid., pp. 154–76).

In the 1930s, the question of the unitary school, polytechnic education, and the educational principle of labor became a fundamental theme for the Italian philosopher and militant Antonio Gramsci, who addressed it densely in the notebooks written in prison, especially Notebook 12. The school organization—as the private apparatus of hegemony—assumes relevance in the construction of the unity of manual and intellectual labor, and of economy and culture: 'the diverse distribution of the various types of schools (classical and professional) in the "economic" territory and the diverse aspirations of the various categories of these layers determine, or shape, the production of the various branches of intellectual specialization' (Gramsci, 2001, p. 49).

In the context in which he writes, Gramsci identifies a school crisis in the phenomenon of differentiation and particularization manifested in the creation of schools of different levels for specialized branches and professions, which emerge in coexistence with the old traditional 'humanistic' school. This crisis would be part of a broader and general organic crisis in the development of the capitalist mode of production, given the need for a new type of urban intellectual required by industrialism.

While he recognized the need for the formation of 'new type' intellectuals, Gramsci also criticized the disappearance, in Italy in the 1930s, of the 'disinterested' (or not immediately interested, as he understood the relationship between intellectuals and production, one that immediately aims at professional education) and the 'formative' school. He was concerned, at that time, with the educational duality, characterized, on the one hand, by the existence of a small number of traditional schools aimed at an elite that would not need to prepare for professional practice and, on the other, by the expansion of specialized professional schools, through which the destiny and future activity of students was predetermined. This phenomenon leads Gramsci (2001, p. 33) to propose a solution that 'rationally' should be followed, aimed at a:

> single initial school of general, humanistic, formative culture. One that equanimously balances the development of the ability to work manually (technically, industrially) and the development of intellectual work skills. From this single type of school, through repeated experiences of professional orientation, one will move on to one of the specialized schools or to productive work.

One can infer from the writings of our Italian thinker that the unitary school would be essentially humanistic and of general culture. However, he calls attention to the fact that his 'humanism' should be understood in a broad and not only in a traditional sense. This kind of humanism has a philosophical and historical foundation, found in the unity between *homo faber* and *homo sapiens*, which, at the time he wrote, was already mediated by science as a productive force, in an industrialist and technological society of the industrial revolutions.

In pedagogical terms, we find in Gramsci's analysis of the elementary school, the defense of education guided by the unity of the world of things and the world of men. The child would be introduced to the former through the study of scientific notions (today, the natural sciences and mathematics) and to the latter through the learning of rights and duties, through which they would learn about state life and civil society (the human and social sciences and philosophy). A complete education would also imply the study of languages, which Gramsci addresses when discussing the place of Latin in elementary school, even though he recognizes in industrialism the tendency to its suppression. Art is also fundamental in this organization, besides the development of corporal discipline for the dedication to studies. In this approach, we find the historicity of knowledge as a pedagogical principle, which can be achieved with the following questions mentioned earlier: What problems led to the development of certain products, knowledges, and technologies? What political and economic disputes were involved for such development to be driven?

Therefore, the educational principle in Gramsci, based on the proposals of Marx, Engels, and Lenin, is based on the dialectical unity between the natural sciences and the human and social sciences, which is condensed in labor. The formation of a new kind of human being free from traditional conceptions of the world implies, on the one hand, learning the laws of nature and, on the other, learning the civil and state laws produced by society. The latter, in turn, organize this one in a way that is historically more adequate to the interaction between man and nature in the social production of existence. It is not an abstract unity—exclusive to the level of thought or to academic activities—but a concrete one, which materializes in human labor. This is 'the very form through which man actively participates in the life of nature, with a view to transforming and socializing it ever more deeply and extensively' (Gramsci, 2001, p. 43). It is good to remember that Gramsci has the prospect of the formation leaders, including state cadres, who, according to him, should have a minimum of general culture to create or judge solutions of a technical-political nature.

Here lies the educational principle of labor since it cannot be realized in all its power of expansion and productivity without the knowledge of the laws of nature and society. Rather, the apprehension of the laws of nature is aimed at expanding human capacities to transform them according to their needs, while the laws of society are not external impositions or only coercion, but products of the contradiction between needs and freedoms:

> The concept and fact of labor (of theoretical-practical activity) is the educational principle immanent in the elementary school, since the social and state order (rights and duties) is introduced and identified in the natural order by labor. The concept of the balance between social order and natural order on the foundation of labor, of man's theoretical-practical activity, creates the first elements of an

intuition of the world free from all magic or witchcraft, and provides the starting point for the later development of a historical-dialectical conception of the world, for the understanding of movement and becoming, for the appreciation of the sum of efforts and sacrifices that the present cost the past and that the future costs the present, for the conception of the present as the synthesis of the past, of all past generations, which is projected into the future. (Gramsci, 2001, p. 43)

Based on the above, we conclude that Gramsci reinforces the understanding of work as the first mediation between human beings and nature, from which, as we saw earlier, the production of existence through the division of labor becomes social. By the principle of work, the human becomes aware of being a producer of his own existence in historically given conditions ('present as the synthesis of the past that is projected into the future'). These imply possibilities of emancipation since the satisfaction of needs expands freedom. But, at the same time, under the logic of private property, the working class remains confined to the realm of necessity as it does not produce directly for itself, but for capital (Marx, 2008).

Through work, therefore, the human being acquires the consciousness that the contradiction between necessity and freedom is both ontological, inherent to the human being, and historical since it is determined by the social relations of production. This consciousness is a condition for the development of the historical-dialectical conception of the world. For these reasons, Gramsci enunciates the concept and fact of work—thought and action—as the educational principle immanent in the elementary school. Once again, we can see that this does not mean making the school professionalizing at an early stage, since such a philosophical elaboration has as its project human formation in the perspective of emancipation and not the simple qualification of the workforce.

In the same way, Krupskaya, in her time, criticized the tendency of the Commissariat of Public Education to institute an early professionalization in school; of a monotechnical character instead of a polytechnical education, we must emphasize that the educational principle of labor does not allow us to defend professional schools as sufficient for the education of the working class. In these schools, unlike the integration that should exist between all subjects and the unity between theory and practice that characterizes polytechnism, the learning of the 'laws of nature' is reduced to instrumentality. Moreover, the learning of the 'laws of society' is reduced to their coercive character. At the same time, in traditional schools, general culture is confused with elite culture and intellectual labor with the exclusive property of the dominant class.

The occurrence of an imbalance like that is, in Gramsci's analysis, a 'degeneration', manifested in the enthusiasm for professional schools that were concerned with satisfying immediate practical interests, to the detriment of the immediately disinterested, formative school. The school delimited by its immediate interest in practical specialties perpetuates and crystallizes social differences. Even if its purposes seem democratic because they would aim to qualify the manual laborer, the peasant, and so forth, this is not enough. In Gramsci's words:

> the democratic tendency, intrinsically, cannot consist only in a manual worker becoming qualified, but in every "citizen" being able to become a "ruler" and that society places him, albeit "abstractly", in the general conditions under which he can do so: political democracy tends to make rulers and ruled (in the sense of government with the consent of the ruled) coincide, assuring every ruled the free learning of the skills and general technical preparation necessary for the purpose of governing. (Gramsci, 2001, p. 50)

It is precisely with the dual logic of the human being, of knowledge, and of formation that the philosopher breaks, on the ballast of his predecessors, configuring a new conception that shapes formal education against the educational principle of work and the organization of the unitary school. Thus, for Gramsci, instead of multiplying the types of professional schools, we should create a single type of preparatory school (elementary-middle school) that would lead young people to the threshold of professional choice. These would be trained as people capable of thinking, studying, directing or controlling those who direct.

Gramsci was clear about the practical organization of this type of school. Its task would be to insert young people into social activity after having brought them to a certain degree of maturity, capacity, and autonomy for intellectual creation. For this reason, the last phase of this school would be decisive, because, together with the fundamental values of humanism provided by general culture, it would develop the intellectual discipline and moral autonomy of the students necessary for further specialization. This could follow the paths of university studies, which he understands as scientific studies, or of productive practice. Moreover, beyond the moral element typical of the traditional school, or the active student practice proposed by the new pedagogies that followed it, the unitary school would seek to fuse discipline and moral and intellectual autonomy with theoretical and methodological mastery of the sciences, in order to develop in the student the ability to produce knowledge.

In this, Gramsci criticizes the Italian educational reforms, on the one hand, in relation to the proliferation of professional schools and, on the other, in the adherence to the model of the active school, as a means to counteract the traditional, Jesuitical school. For him, in the Italy of his time, this project was in a 'romantic' phase, 'in which the elements of the struggle against the mechanical and Jesuitical school were morbidly dilated by contrast and polemic: it is necessary to enter the "classical", rational phase, finding in the ends to be achieved the natural source for elaborating the methods and forms' (Gramsci, 2001, p. 37). This does not mean that he denied the active participation of young people in the educational process. What he rejected was the spontaneity and non-directedness of the educational project. Therefore, Gramsci goes beyond the idea of activity and states that the unitarian school is also creative.

6.6 Final Considerations: The School of the 'Crossing Over' in Brazil as a Synthesis of Historical Contradictions in the Struggle for Working-Class Education

Labor as an educational principle is at the base of an ontological, epistemological, and pedagogical conception that aims to provide subjects with an understanding of the historical process of scientific, technological, and cultural production of social groups. This is an understanding considered as socially developed and appropriated knowledge for the transformation of the natural conditions of life and for the expansion of human capabilities, potentialities, and meanings. At the same time, it is through the apprehension of the historical contents of labor, determined by the mode of production in which it is carried out, that social relations can be understood. Within them, this understanding extends to the conditions of exploitation of human labor, as well as its relation to the mode of being of education. This understanding is indispensable to the struggle to overcome alienation and to build a new kind of society.

Our existence, however, takes place in concrete social formations, also economically configured by the mode of production, and with historical characteristics corresponding to the level of advance of the productive forces and the contradictions of the social relations of production. Such characteristics place specific demands of technical-scientific mastery on society, so that humans become capable of producing their existence through insertion in these contexts. Therefore, labor becomes an educational principle also in this sense. It is these demands that become the foundations of productive activities, whose specialized exercise has historically configured the world of professions.

Omnilateral education implies the apprehension of the world by men through the knowledge of the properties of the real world (science), of valuation (ethics), and of symbolization (art), which has been recognized as knowledge of general education. Polytechnism, at the same time, are expressed by giving students access to the scientific-technological, sociohistorical, and cultural foundations of modern production, from which they can make professional choices.

In this regard, Gramsci argues that the phase of study or professional work after elementary school is characterized by intellectual self-discipline and unlimited moral autonomy. These, necessary for further specialization, 'whether of a scientific nature (university studies) or of an immediately practical-productive nature (industry, bureaucracy, commerce, etc.)', together with the fundamental values of 'humanism', and the 'study and learning of creative methods in science and in life', must be developed in last phase of the unitary school. That function must no longer be 'a university monopoly or being left to chance in practical life' (Gramsci, 2001, p. 39).

Here, the difference between technical and polytechnic education manifests itself, since in the first sense the professional choice is previously determined and the conceptual and technical foundations presented refer not to production as a whole, but to a specific sector. For this reason, the knowledge selected for this purpose is usually identified as specific training content of a professionalizing nature as opposed to general training.

When Gramsci updated the Marxian program of education in opposition to the Gentile reform in fascist Italy, he opposed any separation within the educational system, whether between elementary, middle, and high schools or between these and the professional school. And, as we could see with the arguments above, the unitary school would not be professionalizing. Brazilian Marxist educators were certain of this when they formulated the draft Law of Guidelines and Bases for National Education in 1988 (Saviani, 1997).

The possibility of secondary education being vocational resulted from discussions with society. Even so, the version of the law project that admitted such a possibility conditioned it to guarantee the general education of students. This was a consistent movement in Brazil in the 1980s, but weakened under the hegemony of neoliberalism also in this nation. In this context, during the government of Fernando Henrique Cardoso, the objective was to separate professional education from basic education, thus facilitating its privatization and making it, for children of the working class, an alternative to non-continuity of studies in higher education.

The reference for the selection of knowledge to be taught at school would no longer be the sciences, languages, philosophy, and the arts, but the competences that students should develop to adapt to neoliberal sociability. It was the period of diffusion of the Pedagogy of Competences (Ramos, 2001), which is currently taken up by the Secondary Education Common Curriculum National Base (BNCC). National education, therefore, tended to reproduce what Gramsci criticized in Italy in the 1930s: the proliferation of professional schools under more adverse conditions—not the responsibility of the state, but of entrepreneurs.

The struggle for the right of the working class to basic and professional education under these conditions imposed the defense of integration between these two educational modalities, which was only possible in 2004, in the context of the government of Luís Inácio Lula da Silva, with the Integrated High School project from the perspective of polytechnic education. So, the professionalizing finality that is aggregated in the proposal of integrated education in Brazil expresses the historical form of the struggle for the construction of the unitary and polytechnic school in this society. Knowing that its contradictions are not of a logical order (product of thought), but of a dialectical order (product of concrete reality), it achieves this in two ways.

First, the defense of professional education, integrated into general education and guided by the educational thought of Marx and Engels, of Lenin and the Soviet educators, and also of Gramsci, understands that the link between education and production enables the materialization of the educational principle of labor in school. The curriculum helps to show that the production of human existence is made by the relations between the needs of existence and the conditions to satisfy them, manifested through the class struggle in specific historical times and spaces.

The link between education and production in integrated education is not linked to the interests of the market. Although it seems contradictory to Gramsci's statements, in this type of school, students are led to make vocational training choices at the beginning of high school; but the moral and intellectual development advocated by the philosopher is intrinsic to this project. Its ontological, epistemological, pedagogical, and methodological foundations are the same as those of the unitary and polytechnic school, to which Lenin attributed fundamental importance in helping to create the basis for a classless society. When they finish their studies, having learned the dynamics of productive work, as the Soviet leader advocated, the students can move on to productive activity and/or continue their studies even in other specialties, as the Italian philosopher also advocated. In this way, the school's project of inserting young people in social activity is fulfilled, starting from a true moral, intellectual, and scientific maturation that will guide them in their subsequent choices.

Second, Gramsci did not project the unitary school ideally, but he knew, for example, that economic conditions could compel young people to immediate productive collaboration, which, for Marx and Engels in the context of capitalism, and for Lenin in the construction of socialism, could be a virtuous contradiction. This is because, in this way, the unity of natural sciences and social sciences, and the unity of theory and practice, were realized as foundations of social praxis. They contained the power to raise the knowledge of the working class above that of the bourgeois class. The condition for this was both in the factory and educational legislation, as we saw in Marx and Engels, and in the obligation of the state to assume the expenses that previously would have been the responsibility of families. As a result, education budgets increased, and the infrastructure and conditions of the schools were completely changed. These were principles already present in Marx's (1866) Instructions to the Delegates of the Provisional General Council and taken up in a clear way by Antonio Gramsci.

For these reasons, a consistent policy of professionalization in high school in Brazil, if it is conditioned to the conception of unity of labor, science, and culture, can be the way to organize Brazilian education based on the project of a unitary and polytechnic school, having labor as its educational principle. As a synthesis, we can affirm, with Frigotto et al. (2005), that the integration of high school with professional education is a social and historical need in the contemporary Brazilian society for workers' children. The construction of a new society requires facing concrete contradictions. The integrated high school project is one of them. For this reason, we understand it as a journey toward polytechnic education in Brazil in the 2000s.

Acknowledgments Thanks to the National Research Council (CNPq) and the Carlos Chagas Filho Research Support Foundation of the State of Rio de Janeiro (Faperj) for financial support for research on the subject developed by the author.

Disclosure Statement The author does not have any financial interest or benefit that has arisen from the direct applications of this research.

Note

1. In this text, the word 'labor' will tend to be used to express generic human production, reserving for the word 'work' the material production in its historical forms.

References

Fernandes, F. (2009). *Dependent Capitalism and Social Classes in Latin America*. Global.
Frigotto, G., Ciavatta, M., & Ramos, M. (2005). *Integrated High School: Conception and Contradictions*. Cortez.
Engels, F. (2010). *The Situation of the Working Class in England*. Boitempo.
Gramsci, A. (2001). *Prison Notebooks, Volume 2*. Civilização Brasileira.
Krupskaya, N. K. (2017). *The Construction of Socialist Pedagogy. Selected Writings*. Expressão Popular.
Lukács, G. (1981). *For an Ontology of Social Being* (I. Tonet, Trans.). Editori Riuniti.
Manacorda, M. (2006). *History of Education*. Cortez.
Manacorda, M. (2010). *Marx and Modern Pedagogy*. Alínea.
Marx, K. (1999). *The Capital. Critique of Political Economy: Book 1*. Civilização Brasileira.
Marx, K. (2008). *The Capital. Critique of Political Economy: Book 3*. Civilização Brasileira.
Marx, K. (2001). *Economic-Philosophical Manuscripts of 1844*. Martin Claret.
Marx, K. G. (2011). *Economic Manuscripts of 1857–1858: Sketches of the Critique of Political Economy*. Boitempo; Ed. UFRJ.
Marx, K. G. (1866). *Instructions for Delegates of the Provisional General Council*. Edições Aventes. Retrieved November, 10, 2022, from https://www.marxists.org/portugues/marx/1866/08/instrucoes.htm
Marx, K. G. (2012). *Instructions for Delegates of the Provisional General Council*. Edições Aventes. Retrieved November 10, 2012, from Critique of the Gotha Program. Boitempo.
Marx, K., & Engels, F. (1991). *The German Ideology*. Hucitec.
Marx, K., & Engels, F. (1996). *Communist Party Manifesto*. Vozes.
Ramos, M. (2001). *Skills Pedagogy: Autonomy or Adaptation*. Cortez.
Saviani, D. (2007). Work and Education: Ontological and Historical Foundations. *Brazilian Journal of Education.*, *12*(34), 152–165.
Saviani, D. (1997). *The New Education Law. LDB: Trajectories and Limits*. Autores Associados.

CHAPTER 7

Liberation Theology, Marxism and Education

Luis Martínez Andrade and Allan Coelho

7.1 Introduction

During the second half of the twentieth century, theoretical and political proposals were developed in Latin America that not only criticized the destructive dynamics of capitalist modernity but also delineated other forms of social organization. Among these proposals, we can mention the case of Latin American liberation theology (TdLL). For sociologist Michael Löwy (2019), Latin American liberation theology is the intellectual and spiritual expression of a deeper movement known as Liberationist Christianity. Indeed, Michael Löwy underlines the importance of the anti-capitalist and anti-imperialist ethos of the social movements of the 1950s: this movement involved significant sectors of the church (priests, religious orders, bishops), lay religious movements (Catholic Action, Christian University Youth, Young Christian Workers), popularly based pastoral networks, Christian base communities (CBCs) and several popular organizations created by CBCs activists: women's clubs, neighborhood associations, peasant or workers' unions and so forth. Liberation theology was therefore the result of a social praxis that preceded it. Here, although the Vatican II Council (1962–1965) was important for the *aggiornamento* of the Catholic Church, the role of the 1959 Cuban Revolution in many generations of Latin American militants cannot be ignored (Tamayo, 2019; Reed, 2020).

L. M. Andrade (✉)
Université Catholique de Louvain, Ottignies-Louvain-la-Neuve, Belgium
e-mail: l.martinez@uclouvain.be

A. Coelho
Universidade São Francisco-USF, Bragança Paulista, Brazil

© The Editor(s) (if applicable) and The Author(s), under exclusive license to Springer Nature Switzerland AG 2023
R. Hall et al. (eds.), *The Palgrave International Handbook of Marxism and Education*, Marxism and Education,
https://doi.org/10.1007/978-3-031-37252-0_7

On the other hand, the role of the Christian base communities (CBCs) and the 'Paulo Freire method' (Brandão, 2011) were crucial not only for the process of *conscientization*[1] of the subjects but also for the creation of a new political culture. In fact, mainly Latin American social movements have their roots in the political-pedagogical work of CBCs. The book *The Gospel in Solentiname* by the priest and poet Ernesto Cardenal (2006) is an example of the relationship between the process of conscientization, liberation theology and social praxis (Reed, 2020, 60). Liberation was not understood individually, but in community. From a reading of the Bible, in light of their experience, the members of the CBCs experienced a process of reconstruction of political subjectivity that led them to participate actively in social, political or community work. This chapter is organized in three parts. First, we look at some characteristics of liberation theology, then we look at how Karl Marx's theory of fetishism (Marx & Engels, 1960) was incorporated by some liberation theologians (Dussel, 1985; Hinkelammert, 1986) and, finally, we analyze the link between liberation theology and education.

7.2 Gods and Idols War

Liberation theology, a modern discourse on faith, issues a relentless critique of modernity (Martínez Andrade, 2017). However, this critique should not be considered anti-modern, or worse, postmodern, as this would imply overlooking its main characteristics: defense of civil freedoms, positive use of social sciences, critique against the privatization of faith, critique of progress as the ideology of the hegemonic social formation and the vindication of political projects for the transformation of society (Löwy, 2019). Liberation theology is also a critical and utopian political theology (Martínez Andrade, 2019). Although this theological current has its own characteristics (criticism of the idolatry of the market, denunciation of the socioeconomic structures of oppression, defence of the life of the poor because of its theological identification with Christ who suffers, etc.), it is not homogeneous. As a result, there are important and heated debates on sociopolitical or theological issues, both due to epistemic differences and theoretical differences (Martínez Andrade, 2015).

> The Latin American liberation theology's point of departure is therefore entirely different from that of the European Imperial orthodoxy theologies. In contrast to the latter, whose theological locus is the infidel or atheist, the *locus theologicus* of liberation theologies is the poor, the nonperson. Liberation theology's *Ausganspunkt*, its whence, is the immense and still growing poverty of the 'wretched of the earth'. Liberation theology begins not with the discovery of unbelief and scepticism but with the discovery of the 'absent ones of history', the despised Others. Its interlocutor is not the unbeliever but the hungry person, not the one who questions God, but the one whose carnality and survival is *the* question. While European theologies look at history through the prism of progress/modernization and atheism/theism, liberation theologies look at history from its

'underside' (Gutiérrez, Dussel) through the prisms of oppression/liberation and idolatry/God of life. (Mendieta, 1997, p. 263)

For the Brazilian theologian João Batista Libanio (2006, p. 17), Western utopian thought has its roots in the Old Testament, and in that sense, the people of Israel were born of utopia and hope. For this reason, the role of the prophets was central since, through their voice, the potency of messianism was unfolded anew. Messianism implies two dimensions: an apocalyptic and a critical one. Liberation theology keeps its distance from the former since it undermines any capacity for individual action. From the second, messianism assumes its subversive impulse with the aim of transforming reality. Messianism as a utopian and critical force thus becomes one of the main hermeneutical elements of this theology (Rossi, 2002; Díaz Núñez, 2005; Tamayo, 2017).[2]

Liberation theologians consider that every system or every society where a form of domination and oppression prevails creates false gods that legitimise or justify it. Theology is thus not only an 'epistemic conceptualization of the sacred' (Dussel, 1992, p. 42) but also a terrain of struggle (Richard, 1975). When there is a social formation based on inequalities, injustices and exploitation, prophetic denunciation emerges in all its forms (Comblin, 2009). Liberation theologians have carried out a radical exegesis of the critique of idolatry in the Old Testament. According to the theologian Paul Richard (1975), idolatry has two different meanings in the Old Testament: one that refers to the true God who abhors human sacrifice and representations, and the other that directs worship to offer offerings to false gods. To clarify the two meanings, the theologian quotes from the Book of Exodus are as follows:

> I am the Lord your God, who brought you out of Egypt, out of the land of slavery. You shall have no other gods before me. You shall not make for yourself an image in the form of anything in heaven above or on the earth beneath or in the waters below. (Exodus 20:2–4)

For Paul Richard, the prohibition of idolatry is based on the liberating character of Yahweh: whoever has been liberated cannot be an idolater. Thus, idolatry is always related to the manipulation of religious symbols to establish social relations of subjection and legitimize forms of oppression. In other words, only slaves and oppressors are idolaters. Hence, all men and women who have been freed from slavery practice the act of idolatry the moment they accept submission to a corrupt power. Richard bases his interpretation on Exodus chapter 32, that is, the passage where the people of Israel ask Aaron the following: 'Come, make us gods who will go before us. As for this fellow Moses who brought us up out of Egypt, we don't know what has happened to him' (32:1). Aaron then asks them to give him all the gold and carves a golden calf to be worshipped by them (32:6). Shortly afterward, Moses comes down from the mountain and punishes the people: approximately three thousand men are killed (32:28). Richard suggests that the real problem lies in the notion of the transcendence of God, since the golden calf did not represent God: it was about building the seat, the throne, the symbol of his presence. The key to understanding what was at stake was the opposition between the presence of the idol and the absence of Moses. When the people question the role of Moses (of the guide who won their trust and led them to liberation), they reject the liberating god. In other words, people prefer to opt for a God who comforts rather than one who liberates. God's transcendence lies in the project of liberating a people. By assuming oppression, idolatry becomes concrete. For Paul Richard, the meaning of the term idolatry is expressed in the worship of false gods or foreign gods.

For the Nicaraguan theologian Jorge Pixley (1989), liberation marks the difference between the true God and false gods. From this perspective, knowledge of Yahweh is directly linked to the sovereignty of the people of Israel. Liberation from slavery is for them a true confession of faith (Deuteronomy 26:5–9). Idolatry is concretized precisely in submission to an oppressive power. The people, marked by the sign of sin, must then reveal themselves and rise up. This is a particularly interesting point for liberation theology, since this emancipation can obviously be violent. It is not therefore an apology for violence per se but an insistence on the role of the subversive violence of prophecy as the *Word of God* that interrogates, criticizes and denounces the structure of oppression. Although the young Karl Marx of the *Theses On Feuerbach* was not unknown to liberation theologians (Dri, 1996; Dussel, 2017), we think that it is the Marx of the *Capital: A Critique of Political Economy*, through his theory of fetishism, that awakened the interest of some liberation theologians, for example, Franz Hinkelammert (1986), Enrique Dussel (2017) and Jung Mo Sung (2006).

Liberation theology is a theology of life (Barros & Betto, 2009). For the feminist theologian Maria Clara Lucchetti Bingemer, 'whoever fights for life encounters God in history and finds herself before God in history' (Bingemer, 2021, p. 45). For his part, the Brazilian philosopher and theologian Allan Coelho (2021) argue that the distinction between the gods of life and fetishes is crucial to understanding the critique of capitalist modernity made by liberation theologians. In fact, some theoretical-political concerns of liberation theology have transformed in recent years, but the defense of life (human and nonhuman) remains central to its discourse.

7.3 Theory of Fetishism

Following the military *coup d'état* in Chile led by Augusto Pinochet on 11 September 1973, the German economist and liberation theologian Franz Hinkelammert decided to return to his country and spend some years there: from 1973 to 1976. During those years, Franz Hinkelammert developed a friendship with the economist and dependency theorist André Gunder Frank. Moreover, this period was significant in Hinkelammert's work, as it allows us to understand not only his assimilation of Karl Marx's work, especially *Capital*, but also his critique of the dynamics of capitalist modernity. For the Bolivian philosopher Juan José Bautista (2007, p. 34), the texts *Economy and Revolution* (1967), *Latin American Underdevelopment* (1968), *Ideologies of Development and Dialectics of History* (1968) and *Surplus Value and Dynamic Interest. A Model for the Dynamic Theory of Capital* (1969) represent a shift toward philosophical interests. For our part, we argue that it is in the articles 'Fetishism of commodities, money and capital' (1971) and 'Mercantile relations in socialist society as a questioning of the Marxist critique of religion' (1973), originally published in the journal *Cuadernos de la Realidad Nacional* of the Catholic University of Santiago de Chile, where a critical use of *Capital* in Franz Hinkelammert's reflections on the notion of fetishism and the concept of investment can be observed. In this respect, Franz Hinkelammert (2021, p. 45) writes:

> In the line of Marx's thought, the analysis can be followed by an evaluation of the end of liberation, which he contrasts with this anti-man, who is the abstract man, mystified by religion. Taking a denomination that he used even before writing *The Capital*, it is about the concrete man, in the name of which Marx attacks this abstract man. Basically, the whole dialectic of *The Capital* can be understood as a dialectic between abstract and concrete categories. Use value as a concrete category, exchange value as abstract, concrete labour and abstract labour, labour process and valorisation process, technical and organic composition of capital, and so on. On all these levels, Marx develops his concept of the concrete and therefore of the concrete man as opposed to the abstract.

In 1976, Franz Hinkelammert returned to Latin America. Although he was invited to settle in Mexico City or Caracas, he decided to live in San José, Costa Rica. Together with the Brazilian theologian Hugo Assmann and other Chilean colleagues, he founded the *Departamento Ecuménico de Investigaciones* (DEI). The activities of this research center began in 1977, with the aim of training researchers and leaders close to the liberation movements to develop a systematic discussion of current issues. In 1977, Franz Hinkelammert published *The Ideological Weapons of Death: A Theological Critique of Capitalism*, in which Marx's theory of fetishism is updated in light of contemporary sociocultural and economic transformations. For Franz Hinkelammert, 'Capital fetishism is not limited simply to the mystification of value. Inasmuch as all the dynamism of human creativity and potential are present in the dynamism of value, capital claims for its future the highest dreams of humankind. This it does projecting the process of technology toward and infinitely distant future' (Hinkelammert, 1986, p. 41). Among the themes addressed in this work are the defense of concrete life, the denunciation of the effect of 'inversion' in the production of commodities, that is, the process in which objects become (apparently) subjects and producers become objects, the overcoming of the concept of superstructure and the concept of 'bad infinity', a Hegelian concept present in the Marxist analysis of the fetishism of money and capital (Hinkelammert, 1986).

For Jung Mo Sung (2002, p. 31), one of the main contributions of *The Ideological Weapons of Death* lies in the fact that it shows how the fetish is the spirit of institutions and, in this sense, the task of theology is to distinguish between the fetish and the spirit. In this regard, Jung Mo Sung (2008, p. 72) notes, 'this book marks a turning point in liberation theology'.

It is interesting to mention that since the Cuban Revolution (1959), a new generation of Marxist researchers—including liberation theologians—began to take an interest in Marx's *Economic and Philosophic Manuscripts of 1844* (Illades, 2018). Within liberation theology, the analysis of the link between economics and religion has been at the heart of the work of the members of DEI since at least the late 1970s. For the members of this group, the main topics of study are the fetishism of the market, the role of mythical reason and, above all, the idolatry of modern societies. Unlike European political theology, liberation theology recognized that the problem in Latin America and the Caribbean was not atheism but idolatry (Martínez Andrade, 2015).

In 1981, the book *La lucha de los dioses: los ídolos de la opresión y la búsqueda del Dios Liberador* was published by some members of the DEI. Although there are hardly any explicit references to Karl Marx, his presence can be perceived through the concepts of exploitation, proletariat or fetish in the texts of Jon Sobrino, Javier Jiménez Limón and Franz Hinkelammert. However, it is with the 1989 publication of *An idolatria do mercado: Ensaio sobre Economia e Teologia* by Hugo Assmann and Franz Hinkelammert (1989) that the DEI takes an important step in the analysis of capitalism not only as a system of fetishized appearances but also as a religion of everyday life that demands sacrifices. The authors traced the traces of theology in economic discourse and showed its impact on the social and environmental milieu. For Hugo Assmann and Franz Hinkelammert, economics is a kind of secular theology with its own apostles and theologians. By examining the main tenets of liberal economic theory (including its transcendental notions such as the invisible hand, the general equilibrium and the total market), these theologians unveiled the religious aspects hidden behind the scientific and secular appearance of the apologia of capitalist economics. We thus note not only a creative reception of Marx's work, especially *Capital*, in Franz Hinkelammert's reflections but also a contribution, from Latin American thought to Marxism.

> The first line of critique of a neoliberal political economy can be summarized as follows: rationalization by competitiveness and efficiency (profitability) reveals profonde irrationality or rationality. Efficiency is not efficient. Upon reducing rationality to rentability, the present economic system transforms itself into irrationality. It unties destructive processes that cannot be controlled from the parameters of rationality that it has chosen. The exclusion of a growing number of persons from the economic systema, the destruction of the natural bases of life, the distortion of all social relationships and, consequently, of actual mercantile relations are the nonintentional results of this reduction of rationality to rentability. The market laws of total capitalism destroy society and its natural environment.

By making absolute these laws by way of the myth of the automatism of the market, these destructive tendencies become uncontrollable and covert themselves into a threat to human survival itself. (Hinkelammert, 1997, p. 45)

In the early 1990s, the liberation theologian Hugo Assmann analyzed the logic of exclusion fostered by neoliberal globalization. Without moving away from the Marxist perspective, the Brazilian theologian continued to insist on the need to conceive of capitalism as the 'religion of everyday life' (Assmann, 1994, p. 83). Thus, the Brazilian theologian examined the market messianism of neoliberal discourse and pointed to the presence of the sacrificial dynamics of capitalist modernity. In line with Marx's approach that contrasts the logic of capital with the rationality of life (Hinkelammert, 2021), for Assmann, economic rationality is diametrically opposed to the solidarity of the God of life. For him (Assmann, 1994, p. 123), 'The concrete human being as being-of-needs and desires, as living corporeality, is not taken into account by the categories of economic thought'.

Currently, we can see an extension of the DEI school in the work of Jung Mo Sung (2018) and Allan da Silva Coelho (2021), who, in the line of Karl Marx, have examined not only the new mythical structure of capitalism but also the spirit of capitalism, as a rationalization of asceticism, in contemporary society. A disciple of the Methodist theologian Julio de Santa Ana, Jung Mo Sung undertook a critique of liberation theology, starting from its epistemological principles, to show the absence of reflections on the economy. By approaching postcolonial and decolonial proposals, Jung Mo Sung has enriched the development of liberation theology in terms of the critique of idolatry, the religious character of capitalism and the neoliberal myth. While Karl Marx analyzes capitalism as 'the religion of everyday life' (Marx, 1998) in the framework of English industrial society, theologian Jung Mo Sung examines the implications of capitalism as a mythical structure, that is, as a material narrative that legitimizes the sacrificial dynamics of capitalism in both developed and underdeveloped societies. Drawing on the contributions of dependency theory, Jung Mo Sung observes the socioeconomic consequences in Latin America: dependency structure, underdevelopment and overexploitation (Frank, 1967).

Most likely, here, we can observe an important difference with the dependency theory of the 1960s regarding environmental issues. While dependency theorists questioned the relationship between center and periphery, unfortunately, they did not question the idea of growth. In this regard, Ulrich Duchrow and Franz Hinkelammert mention that

During the 1970s, as people became increasingly aware of the problem of the destruction of the environment, a criticism of growth as a starting point developed within dependency theory. This criticism did not lead to the condemnation of growth as such, but it did address the realization that economic growth cannot be the supreme value of economic and social policy and that it may not be regarded as the engine of economic and social progress. Naturally, this led to conflict with the ideologies of globalization, which more than ever propagated economic growth -together with formal efficiency and competition- as the highest value of human existence. It was as if the growing awareness that the environment was being destroyed even increased the readiness of the representatives of globalization to continue its destruction. (Duchrow & Hinkelammert, 2004, p. 151)

If the destructive dynamics of capital can be observed in developed societies (Harvey, 2003), in the societies of the periphery, it acquires terrifying features. Indeed, impoverished populations (Indigenous and Afro-descendant) are generally seen as *nonpersons*, that is, as disposable beings. In the book *Capitalism as Religion: Walter Benjamin and Liberation Theologians*, Allan Coelho addresses, from an interdisciplinary perspective, some fundamental themes for the social sciences (secularisation process, sociology of consumption and advertising), philosophy ('myth of modernity', coloniality of power/knowledge) and theology (conflict between gods/idols, notion of faith, theology of debt, Abrahamic myth). Coelho's book is inscribed in the intellectual and political project of critical theory since it distances itself from 'the methodologies of bourgeois science that claim to be neutral and abstract' (Coelho, 2021, p. 27) while explaining the ambivalent dynamics of capitalism, that is, the terrible consequences of the exploitation of bodies and nature mixed with the 'illusions' that this model of civilization provokes in people. The seductive power of commodities expresses the spiritual-religious dimension of capitalism. However, the author points not only to the role of capital in the destruction of the (physical and social) conditions for the reproduction of life (human and nonhuman) but also to the responsibility of the state, which, through the criminalization of social movements and the implementation of austerity policies (mystique of death), consolidates the current social formation.

In another vein, Allan Coelho (2021, p. 148) argues that although the assertion that capitalism as a religion is radical, what is truly significant is to show that this system is a 'religion of the fetish', that is, a religion with a sacrificial aspect. To this end, Coelho takes up certain approaches from *Capital* and the DEI school (analysis of the logic of sacrifice through the myth of Iphigenia, the link between sacrifice and the utopian ideal, idolatry of the market, critique of the law that justifies domination, theology of debt, the transformation of Christian orthodoxy) to offer us his own theological-political exegesis of great depth. We read in *Capital* the following:

> For a society of commodity producers, whose general social relation of production consists in the fact that they treat their products as commodities, hence as values, and in this material ... form bring their individual private labors into relation with each other as homogenous human labor, Christianity with its religious cult of man in the abstract, more particularly in its bourgeois development, i.e., in Protestantism, Deism, etc., is the most fitting form of religion. (Marx, 1977, p. 172)

Thus, following Max Weber (1993), Coelho develops different 'ideal types' with the aim of understanding a religious mode of operation in the economic sphere. In this sense, the author establishes a distinction between an allegorical approach (expressed in the work of Paul Lafargue) and a dialectical approach (proposed by Walter Benjamin and the liberation theologians) with regard to the analysis of capitalism as religion. On the other hand, the theme of the 'spirit of capitalism' (as the rationalization of asceticism) is studied by the author to refer to the subjugation of modern-instrumental reason in the process of capital accumulation. In this way, Coelho notes the relevance of the theory of fetishism expounded in *Capital* to understand the process of alienation.

> We see here, on the one hand, how the exchange of commodities breaks through all the individual and local limitations of the direct exchange of products and develops the metabolic process of human labor. On the other hand, there develops a whole network of social connections of natural origins, entirely beyond the control of the human agents. (Marx, 1977, p. 207)

Although the approach to Marxism on the part of liberation theologians was not homogeneous or had the same intensity, some Marxist concepts and categories were incorporated into the proposals of some of their exponents (McGovern, 1989; Martínez Andrade, 2018). For instance, while the theologian Gustavo Gutiérrez (1988) was inspired by some ideas of the German philosopher Ernst Bloch and the Peruvian thinker José Carlos Mariátegui, in the case of the Brazilian theologian Leonardo Boff (2008, p. 151), we note the presence of some ideas of Antonio Gramsci. Liberation theologians moved away from the dichotomy between base and superstructure posed by some Marxist currents; for these theologians, the relationship between religion, economy and politics had to be understood dialectically. For instance, while some Marxist theorists reduced the phenomenon of religion to opium, Gustavo Gutiérrez recovered the emancipatory and utopian potential of religion. In the same way, Leonardo Boff takes up both the Gramscian idea of the necessary form of the concrete historical bloc and that of the class struggle as a cultural struggle (Gramsci, 1987).

7.4 Popular Education for Liberation

In the line of Karl Marx (1977), liberation theologians understand capitalism as 'the religion of everyday life', and, in that sense, they are convinced that capitalist society is founded on abstraction. Although the young Marx's notion of alienation was important for the critique of the phantasmagoria of capitalism, we believe that the theory of fetishism was central to the denunciation of capitalism as an idolatrous system. In the case of the Brazilian pedagogue Paulo Freire, the notion of alienation is central to his work *Pedagogy of Oppressed*. According to Matthias Preiswerk (1998, p. 38), a Methodist pastor, the emergence of popular education in the 1960s coincided with the birth of Latin

American liberation theology. In this sense, Paulo Freire is central to understanding the link between popular education and liberation theology. Originally from the city of Recife, Paulo Freire is currently presented as one of the main theorists of critical pedagogy. However, it seems that Freire has been considered more as a pedagogue than as a critical thinker. For Brazilian scholar João Colares de Mota Neto (2016), Freire's work is at the origin of what is now known as the decolonial turn (Restrepo & Rojas, 2010). Indeed, the thought and work of Paulo Freire allows us not only to rethink the role of dialogue in critical education (Sung, 2006, p. 30) but also to articulate the main constitutive elements of Liberationist Christianity (Coelho & Malafatti, 2021) in which certain values (solidarity, struggle for dignity, social justice) shape a counterhegemonic discourse and practice (Cunha, 2018).

Although Paulo Freire's work is vast, in this text, we will focus on his book *Pedagogy of Oppressed*, since in this book, the Brazilian thinker not only quotes Marxist authors (Karl Marx, Rosa Luxemburg, Georg Lukács, Karel Kosík, Lucien Goldmann, Gajo Petrovic, Erich Fromm, among others) but also raises important issues for an anti-colonial critical theory. In *Pedagogy of Oppressed*, it is interesting how Paulo Freire coincides with some of Frantz Fanon's theses, for example, in the role of revolutionary violence to rescue the subjectivity of colonized subjects, in the need to move away from Eurocentrism to build one's own thinking and, of course, in the urgency of destroying the structural racism of the capitalist system. On the other hand, we agree with the Brazilian scholar Ana Mae Barbosa (2021, p. 40), who argues that '*Pedagogy of the Oppressed* is a treatise on epistemology'. Needless to say, *Pedagogy of Oppressed* has more than twenty translations and is one of the most cited works in the social sciences (Arriada et al., 2017, p. 18).

Written in exile, *Pedagogy of Oppressed* is a work that has its origins in Freire's experience at the Brazilian Industrial Social Services (SESI) in Recife. According to Mota Neto (2016, p. 152), between 1946 and 1954, Paulo Freire carried out his first literacy experiences that would lead him to the elaboration, in 1961, of what is known as the 'Paulo Freire method'. This experience was crucial in his conception of popular culture and in the work of *conscientization* of the popular classes. In fact, Mota Neto (2016, 158) observes a rupture in Freire's thought, through his *Pedagogy of Oppressed*, as his incorporation of Marxism becomes evident: interest in the notion of social class, oppression and exploitation. In this regard, Mota Neto (2016, p. 175) argues that

> The book *Pedagogy of Oppressed* marks a turning point in Paulo Freire's thought, not so much because he abandoned the ideas he defended in his previous books but because he radicalized them through a clearly more politicized and progressive reading of history associated, on the intellectual level, with unorthodox Marxism and, on the level of political strategy, with the socialist project of the democratic left.

In the prologue of *Pedagogy of Oppressed*, it can be seen that the author addresses both Christians and Marxists (Freire, 2000, p. 37) to underline the role of dialogue with the people and, in accordance with some of Walter Benjamin's and Rosa Luxemburg's approaches, considers that the subject of knowledge is the subject that struggles. Let us recall that for liberation theology, the process of conscientization is central to politicizing the desalination of social actors. In fact, the work of the Christian base communities went in this direction. Sociologist Jean-Pierre Reed (2020) examined the importance of Paulo Freire's method, employed by Christian base communities, during the development of the Nicaraguan Revolution of 1979.

> The radical, committed to human liberation, does not become the prisoner of a "circle of certainty" within which reality is also imprisoned. In contrast, the more radical the person is, the more fully he or she enters reality so that, knowing it better, he or she can better transform it. This individual is not afraid to confront, listen, or see the world unveiled. This person is not afraid to meet the people or to enter into dialogue with them. This person does not consider himself or herself the proprietor of history or of all people, or the liberator of the oppressed; but he or she does commit himself or herself, within history, to fight at their side. (Freire, 2000, p. 39)

At the beginning of the first chapter, Freire acknowledges the role of the oppressive structure of modern capitalist society that dehumanizes human beings. Far from assuming a supposed position of neutrality typical of traditional theory (Horkheimer, 1975), the Brazilian thinker points out the antagonism and social contradictions. Even overcoming the Eurocentrism of some members of the Frankfurt School (Martínez Andrade, 2021), Freire contextualizes the process of dehumanization suffered by colonized peoples. Drawing on the contributions of Frantz Fanon and Albert Memmi, the Brazilian thinker lays the foundations of an anti-colonial critical theory. The author of *Pedagogy of Oppressed* was interested in analyzing not only the sociocultural domination process of colonialism (cultural invasion, dehumanization) but also the way in which the colonized adopted the values of the ruling class through internal colonialism. Like the author of *The Wretched of the Earth* (Fanon, 2005), Paulo Freire observes the harmful effects of colonialism on the subjectivity of the colonized. Indeed, the colonized are not assumed to be human beings, but as things or beasts. In this sense, Freire (2000, p. 63) argues that 'Self-depreciation is another characteristic of the oppressed'.

On the other hand, and inspired by the work of Erich Fromm (1971), Freire considers the role of the subjects' *praxis* in the struggle against the necrophiliac forces of capitalist society to be fundamental. For the German sociologist, the syndrome of decay implies processes of love of death and malignant narcissism. In opposition to the syndrome of decay, Fromm proposes the term syndrome of growth. In this respect, Fromm (1971, p. 15) writes,

> I shall describe the syndrome of growth; this consists of love of life (as against love of death), love of man (as against narcissism), and independence (as against symbiotic-incestuous fixation). Only in a minority of people is either one of the two syndromes fully developed. However, there is no denying that each man goes forwards in the direction he has chosen: that of life or that of death; that of good or that of evil.

The notion of the syndrome of growth is echoed in Freire's idea of 'becoming more fully human'. We note, then, that the Brazilian thinker's active reception of the ideas of humanist Marxism and anti-colonial currents was crucial for his proposal of problem-posing education, which implies the revalorization of the subjectivity of human beings. If 'banking education' legitimizes class domination and conceives human beings as passive entities, problem-posing education contributes to rescuing their subjectivity. Therefore, dialogue and collaboration between educators/educators is crucial in pedagogical and sociopolitical processes.

> Once again, the two educational concepts and practices under analysis come into conflict. Banking education (for obvious reasons) attempts, by mythicizing reality, to conceal certain facts that explain the way human beings exist in the world; problem-posing education sets itself the task of demythologizing. Banking education resists dialogue; problem-posing education regards dialogue as indispensable to the act of cognition that unveils reality. Banking education treats students as objects of assistance; problem-posing education makes them critical thinkers. Banking education inhibits creativity and domesticates (although it cannot completely destroy) the *intentionality* of consciousness by isolating consciousness from the world, thereby denying people their ontological and historical vocation of becoming more fully human. Problem-posing education bases itself on creativity and stimulates true reflection and action upon reality, thereby responding to the vocation of persons as beings who are authentic only when engaged in inquiry and creative transformation. In sum, banking theory and practice, as immobilizing and fixating forces, fail to acknowledge men and women as historical beings; problem-posing theory and practice take peoples' historicity as their starting point. (Freire, 2000, pp. 83–84)

For his part, Jung Mo Sung is one of the liberation theologians who has managed to articulate the theology-economy binomial. This member of the 'DEI school' (Coelho & Sung, 2019), Jung Mo Sung, has also reflected on education. In his *Educating to Reenchant Life*, this theologian not only analyzed the theological-mystical characteristics of commodities in the neoliberal phase but also underlined the role of problematizing education in the transformation of society. Jung Mo Sung argues that although modern society is conceived as disenchanted and free of religious myths, in practice, through the logic of capitalist consumption, human life is re-enchanted by a fetishist spirit. Thus, capitalist myths become the new references in this process of re-enchantment. Jung Mo Sung therefore makes a distinction between the dehumanizing myths of capitalist religion (invisible hand, success, prestige, individualism, total market, etc.) and the humanizing myths of ethical religions.

It should be noted that for this theologian, by myths, we should understand all narratives that speak of gods, utopias and the meaning of life (Sung, 2006, p. 50). In this regard, Jung Mo Sung also analyzes the reconfiguration of education during the mythical and anthropological transformation (Sung, 2018) brought about by neoliberalism, articulating the subjectivity of the individual as a customer-consumer to the forms of capital accumulation in consumer society. This process not only reorients the deeper meanings of human life but also contributes to the accelerated environmental deterioration caused by a system that only seeks profit and the creation of surplus value. Jung Mo Sung's research is thus inscribed in the same critical tradition as Paulo Freire's work.

7.5 Conclusion

The emergence of Latin American liberation theology in the 1970s was simultaneous with popular education (Preiswerk, 1998), Orlando Fals Borda's participatory action research (Mota Neto, 2016) and the renewal of anti-colonial Marxism in Latin America and the Caribbean (Löwy, 1992; Cadet, 2020; Martínez Andrade, 2023). Undoubtedly, Paulo Freire's work brought together three important currents (liberation theology, heterodox Marxism and popular education) of Latin American critical thought. In this sense, the *Pedagogy of Oppressed* represents a touchstone of contemporary radical thought. Inspired by the 'Paulo Freire method' (Brandão, 2011), the liberation theologians Hugo Assmann (2001) and Jung Mo Sung (2006) continued to promote the critique of the capitalist logic expressed in commodity fetishism. In terms of the emergence of a new political culture, we can observe the importance of Paulo Freire in the literacy and political awareness campaigns of the first Sandinista government in Nicaragua (Reed, 2020) or, currently, in the Brazilian Landless Workers' Movement-MST (*Movimento dos Trabalhadores Rurais Sem Terra*). In fact, the 'Paulo Freire method' is a pillar in the conscientization process of the militants, mostly peasants, of this social movement (Caldart, 2004).

Marxism in Latin America has a long list of thinkers who produced original thought, for example, the Peruvian thinker José Carlos Mariátegui (Gonzalez, 2019). Subsequently, and thanks to the influence of the Cuban Revolution of 1959 (Löwy, 1992), Marxism was again renewed both theoretically and in the sociopolitical field. Categories such as exploitation, class struggle, ideology and *praxis* were central in the socioanalytical mediation of liberation theologians to account for the conditions of poverty in Latin American societies (Martínez Andrade, 2023). Similarly, the relationship with Marxism and liberation theology made it possible for Paulo Freire to elaborate a pedagogical, political and epistemological project of great depth. It is no coincidence that this Freirean project played a very important role in the revolutionary processes of the 1970s and 1980s, and still plays a central role in social movements today. In her most recent research, Aline Mesquita Corrêa (2022) shows the validity of the 'Paulo

Freire method' in the experiences of alternative pedagogy tested in contexts of sociopolitical resistance and affirms that the work of this Brazilian thinker serves not only to prefigure other modes of socialization but also to counter the cultural invasion of the coloniality of knowledge. The *Pedagogy of Oppressed*, developed in a context of strong social mobilization and social struggles to transform capitalist society in the name of the defense of the concrete life of all people, is one of the main references in the articulation between education, liberation theology and Marxism. It was widely disseminated throughout Latin America and was adopted by popular movements and by Christian base communities (CBCs) in different ways. It was also criticized for its incorporation of Marxism and its closeness to liberation theology. Nevertheless, it provided a foothold for a tradition that continues to provide a theoretical toolkit for those currently struggling against neoliberal capitalism.

Acknowledgments This work was supported by Universidade São Francisco (Itatiba) through the Visiting Professor Program during the second semester of 2022.

Disclosure Statement None of the co-authors has any financial interest or benefit that has arisen from the direct applications of this research.

Notes

1. The term *conscientização* refers to learning to perceive social, political and economic contradictions, and to take action against the oppressive elements of reality (Freire, 2000, p. 35). This term plays a structuring role in this tradition. Although it became famous in the work of Paulo Freire, especially in *Pedagogy of Oppressed*, it was a term used in the processes of grassroots formation by the team of the Catholic bishop Dom Helder Camara. In Paulo Freire, conscientization is not only the purpose of educational practice, but also its process, that is, the act by which human beings and social structures are transformed.
2. Despite the abundant presence of messianism in the formulations of liberation theology, some authors insist on differentiating Christianity from classical messianism. For instance, José Comblin affirms that in messianic logics, the final victory of the Messiah is the guarantee of his legitimacy and divine mandate. However, for Comblin, the victory is not proof of any justice, which must be founded not on final power, but on the lives of the poor. Comblin stated that: 'Christianity is not messianism: it uses themes of messianism to say something else' (Comblin, 1968, p. 80). Jung Mo Sung, Brazilian theologian, incorporates this perspective into his analysis of liberation theology (Sung, 2015, p. 66).

References

Arriada, E., Nogueira, G., & Zasso, S. M. (2017). Pedagogia do Oprimido: do manuscrito ao texto escrito. *Revista Brasileira de Alfabetização—ABAlf, 6*(1), 17–39.

Assmann, H. (1994). *Crítica à Lógica da Exclusão. Ensaios sobre Economia y Teología*. Paulus.

Assmann, H. (2001). *Reencantar a Educação. Rumo à sociedade aprendente*. Vozes.
Assmann, H., & Hinkelammert, F. (1989). *An Idolatria do Mercado. Ensaio sobre Economia e Teologia*. Vozes.
Barbosa, A. M. (2021). Paulo Freire: Desde o Recife. In A. M. Araujo (Ed.), *Testamento da Presença de Paulo Freire. O Educador do Brasil: Depoimentos e Testemunhos* (pp. 25–43). Paz & Terra.
Barros, M., & Betto, F. (2009). *O Amor Fecunda o Universo. Ecologia e Espiritualidade*. Agir.
Bautista, J. J. (2007). *Hacia una Crítica Ética del Pensamiento Latinoamericano. Introducción al Pensamiento Crítico de Franz. J. Hinkelammert*. Grito del sujeto.
Bingemer, M. C. (2021). Direitos Humanos, Direitos Divinos. In D. Ribeiro de Almeida & F. Soares (Eds.), *Fé Cristiana e Direitos Humanos*. Loyola.
Boff, L. (2008). *Ecologia, Mundialição, Espiritualidade*. Record.
Brandão, C. R. (2011). *O Que é Método Paulo Freire*. Brasiliense.
Cadet, J. J. (2020). *Le Marxisme haïtien: Marxismes et anticolonialisme en Haïti (1946–1986)*. Delga.
Caldart, R. S. (2004). *Pedagogia do Movimento Sem Terra*. Expressão Popular.
Cardenal, E. (2006). *El Evangelio en Solentiname*. Trotta.
Coelho, A. (2021). *Capitalismo como Religião. Walter Benjamin e os Teólogos da Libertação*. Recriar.
Coelho, A., & Malafatti, F. (2021). Paulo Freire e o Cristianismo da Libertação: Contribuição do Conceito de Visão Social de Mundo. *Práxis Educativa, 16*, 1–16.
Coelho, A., & Sung, J. M. (2019). Capitalismo como religião: uma revisão teórica da relação entre religião e economia na modernidad. *Horizonte, 53*, 651–675.
Comblin, J. (1968). *O provisório e o Definitivo*. Herder.
Comblin, J. (2009). *A Profecia na Igreja*. Paulos.
Corrêa, A. M. (2022). *Tendências (des)coloniais na Pedagogia da Alternância da Escola Família Agrícola de Santa Cruz do Sul*. Doctoral thesis, Department of Education, University of Santa Cruz do Sul, Santa Cruz do Sul.
Cunha, C. A. (2018). Apontamentos Introductorios sobre o Desafio Decolonial para as Teologias latino-americanas. *Theologica Xaveriana, 68*(185), 1–20.
Díaz Núñez, L. (2005). *La Teología de la Liberación Latinoamericana a Treinta Años de su Surgimiento. Balance y Perspectivas*. Universidad Autónoma del Estado de México.
Dri, R. (1996). Fétichisme, foi et idolâtrie chez Marx et les prophètes hébreux. In M. Löwy (Ed.), *Utopie. Théologie de la libération. Philosophie de l'émancipation* (pp. 33–51). PUF.
Duchrow, U., & Hinkelammert, F. (2004). *Property for People, Not for Profit. Alternatives to the Global Tyranny of Capital*. WCC.
Dussel, E. (1985). Marx ¿ateo? La Religión en el Joven Marx (1835–1849). In S. Cabral (Ed.), *Marxistas y Cristianos* (pp. 179–212). Universidad Autónoma de Puebla.
Dussel, E. (1992). *Historia de la Iglesia en América Latina. Medio Milenio de Coloniaje y Liberación (1492–1992)*. Esquila Misional.
Dussel, E. (2017). *Las Metáforas Teológicas de Marx*. Siglo XXI.
Fanon, F. (2005). *The Wretched of the Earth*. Grove Press.
Frank, A. G. (1967). *Capitalism and Underdevelopment in Latin America: Historical Studies of Chile and Brazil*. Monthly Review Press.
Freire, P. (2000). *Pedagogy of Oppressed*. Continuum.
Fromm, E. (1971). *The Heart of Man Its Genius for Good and Evil*. Harper & Row.

Gonzalez, M. (2019). *In the Red Corner. The Marxism of José Carlos Mariátegui*. Haymarket Books.
Gramsci, A. (1987). *Selections from Prison Notebooks*. International.
Gutiérrez, G. (1988). *A Theology of Liberation: History, Politics, and Salvation*. Orbis.
Harvey, D. (2003). *The New Imperialism*. Oxford University Press.
Hinkelammert, F. (1986). *The Ideological Weapons of Death: A Theological Critique of Capitalism*. Orbis.
Hinkelammert, F. (1997). Liberation Theology in the Economic and Social Context of Latin America. In D. Batstone & E. Mendieta (Eds.), *Liberation, Theologies, Postmodernity, and the Americas* (pp. 25–52). Routledge.
Hinkelammert, F. (2021). *La Crítica de las Ideologías frente a la Crítica de la Religión*. Clacso.
Horkheimer, M. (1975). *Critical Theory: Selected Essays*. Continuum.
Illades, C. (2018). *El Marxismo en México. Una Historia Intelectual*. Taurus.
Libanio, J. B. (2006). Teologia no limiar do Século XXI: Relevância e Função da Soter. In M. C. de Freitas (Ed.), *Teologia e Sociedade*. Paulinas.
Löwy, M. (1992). *Marxism in Latin America from 1909 to the Present: An Anthology*. Humanity Books.
Löwy, M. (2019). *La Lutte des Dieux. Christianisme de la Libération et Politique en Amérique Latine*. Van Dieren.
Martínez Andrade, L. (2015). *Religion Without Redemption: Social Contradictions and Awakened Dreams in Latin America*. Pluto Press.
Martínez Andrade, L. (2017). Liberation Theology: A Critique of Modernity. *Interventions: International Journal of Postcolonial Studies, 19*(5), 620–630.
Martínez Andrade, L. (2018). Le Marxisme dans la Théologie de la Libération Aujourd'hui. *Actuel Marx, 64*, 60–73.
Martínez Andrade, L. (2019). *Ecología y Teología de la Liberación. Crítica de la Modernidad/Colonialidad*. Herder.
Martínez Andrade, L. (2021). Luces y Sombras de la Escuela de Frankfurt. Materialidad Negativa y Exterioridad. *Laguna. Revista de Filosofía, 49*, 59–75.
Martínez Andrade, L. (2023). *Dialectique de la modernité et socialisme indo-américain. Essais d'histoire intellectuelle*. L'Harmattan.
Marx, K. (1977). *Capital* (Vol. 1). Vintage.
Marx, K. (1998). Capital: A Critique of Political Economy. Vol. III. In *Marx and Engels Collected Works* (Vol. 37). Progress Publishers.
Marx, K., & Engels, F. (1960). *Sur la Religion*. Editions Sociales.
McGovern, A. F. (1989). *Liberation Theology and Its Critics. Toward an Assessment*. Orbis Books.
Mendieta, E. (1997). From Christendom to Polycentric Oikonumé. Modernity, Postmodernity, and Liberation Theology. In D. Batstone & E. Mendieta (Eds.), *Liberation, Theologies, Postmodernity, and the Americas* (pp. 253–272). Routledge.
Mota Neto, J. C. (2016). *Por uma Pedagogia Decolonial na América Latina. Reflexões em torno do Pensamento de Paulo Freire e Orlando Fals Borda*. CRV.
Pixley, J. (1989). Dios Enjuicia a los Idolatras en la Historia Ídolos. In F. Hinkelammert & P. Richards (Eds.), *La Lucha de los dioses. Los Ídolos de la Opresión y la Búsqueda del Dios Liberador*. Departamento Ecuménico de Investigaciones.
Preiswerk, M. (1998). *Educação Popular e Teologia da Libertação*. Vozes.
Reed, J. P. (2020). *Sandinista Narratives. Religion, Sandinismo and the Emotions in the Making of the Nicaraguan Insurrection and Revolution*. Lexington.

Restrepo, E., & Rojas, A. (2010). *Inflexión Decolonial: Fuentes, Conceptos y Cuestionamientos*. Universidad del Cauca.
Richard, P. (1975). *Cristianismo, Lucha Ideológica y Nacionalidad Socialista*. Sígueme.
Rossi, L. A. (2002). *Messianismo e Modernidade: Repensando o Messianismo a partir das Victimas*. Paulos.
Sung, J. M. (2002). *Sujeito e Sociedades Complexas. Para Repensar os Horizontes Utópicos*. Vozes.
Sung, J. M. (2006). *Educar para Reencantar a Vida*. Vozes.
Sung, J. M. (2008). *Se Deus existe, por qué há Pobreza?* Reflexão.
Sung, J. M. (2015). *A Graça de Deus e a Loucura do Mundo*. Reflexão.
Sung, J. M. (2018). *Idolatria do Dinheiro e Direitos Humanos. Uma Crítica Teológica do Novo Mito do Capitalismo*. Paulus.
Tamayo, J. J. (2017). *Teologías del Sur. El Giro Descolonizador*. Trotta.
Tamayo, J. J. (2019). *De la Iglesia Colonial al Cristianismo Liberador en América Latina*. Tirant lo Blanch.
Weber, M. (1993). *The Sociology of Religion*. Beacon Press.

CHAPTER 8

Marxism and Adult Education

John D. Holst

8.1 Introduction

Adult education is a field of practice. We have theories and frameworks for major topics for adult education such as learning, teaching, and program planning, along with the actual practice of adult education. But if asked to define who is an adult educator, one thinks of those who organize learning for adults; we generally define ourselves based on our practice.

For a chapter on Marxism and adult education, perhaps it is fitting to begin with the question of who is a Marxist. A Marxist is one who uses Marxism in their interpretation of the world and who is also a member of a political organization that has Marxism at the center of its theoretical outlook and political work. To just carry around a set of Marxist ideas in one's head in order to interpret the world is insufficient to claim the label of a Marxist; one has to practice Marxism to be a Marxist. Using Marxism to solely interpret the world disregards the example set by Marx or Engels. Throughout their decades-long collaboration, they worked to establish revolutionary organizations in which they would put their ideas into practice and from which they would garner sharper ideas or interpretations of the world. Marx and Engels were researchers, but both were also revolutionaries in the sense that they formed and actively worked in revolutionary organizations.

My definition of what constitutes a Marxist raises a challenge and an important framework for the goals of this chapter. I will begin with a review of how the Marxist tradition has been used in adult education scholarship. Then, I will

J. D. Holst (✉)
Pennsylvania State University-University Park Campus, State College, PA, USA
e-mail: jdh91@psu.edu

outline a general framework for or tenets of a Marxist pedagogical practice. In order to make these tenets more concrete and contemporary, I will also look outside of academia to the educational work of Marxists in revolutionary organizations actively engaged in the theory and practice of revolutionary Marxist pedagogy. Finally, and drawing from my examples of revolutionary organizations and militants, I will outline a Marxist analysis of the main contours of contemporary capitalism and detail the implications of this for revolutionary adult education practice today.

8.2   Marxism in Adult Education

Just as in other fields, there is no unified Marxist approach to adult education. Moreover, there is no journal, conference, or formal organizational entity that brings together adult education scholars working within the Marxist tradition, in order to build a common research agenda or common approach to the practice of adult education. Nevertheless, we can identify specific scholars and research agendas informed by, and that contribute to, a Marxist approach to adult education.

While there is no identifiable Marxist entity within the field of adult education, there is the Radical Adult Education (RAE) tradition within or under which those who significantly or wholly draw on Marxism have generally placed themselves. The RAE tradition emerges as a recognizable subfield within adult education in the 1960s (Tawney, 1964) and 1970s (Lovett, 1988), but it traces its origins at least as far back as the 1800s to efforts of independent working-class education. Since this tradition, which was rooted in the long history of what came to be called old social movements (OSMs), suffered along with the decline of these working-class-based movements in the now over 40-year era of neoliberalism, critical adult education (e.g., Clover, 2018; English, 2014; Huttunen, 2007) has occasionally been used as an updated moniker for RAE. Even more so than critical adult education, the remnants of RAE, along with renewed social democratic to socialist and Marxist approaches to adult education, have emerged in what is now increasingly being referred to as the subfield of social movement learning (SML) (Atta & Holst, 2023; Kuk & Tarlau, 2020; Niesz et al., 2018). There is also a parallel and often convergent stream of scholarship and practice of popular education, informed significantly by the work of Paulo Freire, Latin American-based popular education, and individual, nation-based radical approaches to adult education outside of Latin America (e.g., Boughton, 2013; Crowther et al., 2005; Holst et al., 2021; von Kotze & Walters, 2017; Walters & Manicom, 1996). Recent scholarship in this tradition has also followed the trend of broader scholarship to address issues of colonialism and decoloniality (e.g., Choudry & Kapoor, 2010; Zainub, 2019).

In this transition from RAE to SML (Holst, 2018), the field of adult education has gained increasing examinations of race (e.g., Sheared et al., 2010; Peterson, 2002), gender (e.g., Butterwick & Elfert, 2015; DiFilippo, 2015; English, 2005; Narushima, 2004), and sexuality (e.g., Hill, 2004; Walker,

2009) while also losing, leaving behind, or forgetting the long and rich history of socialist and Marxist traditions (Boughton, 1997). Moreover, a part of this forgetting is the fact that, seemingly unbeknownst to many (new) social movement learning scholars, the long history of Marxist and socialist adult education and movements has frequently explored and addressed, in very still innovative ways, the nature of race and gender in capitalist societies. For example, nowhere in adult education do we have thorough analyses of the Caribbean Communist Claudia Jones' (2011) mid-twentieth-century movement-based theoretical work on African Americans as an oppressed nationality in the US, or her work on 'the triply-oppressed status' (p. 87) of African American women written 40 years before Kimberlé Crenshaw's (1989) use of the term intersectionality. Moreover, one has to go outside the field of adult education (Burden-Stelly & Dean, 2022) to read about the early to mid-twentieth-century adult education social movement-based work of African American Communist women such as Williana Burroughs, who was director of the Harlem Workers School, and Grace P. Campbell, who cofounded the People's Educational Forum.

More broadly, adult education also lacks any significant engagement with the theoretical and practical work played by Communists in the Black Caribbean, New York City, and Mexico, in understanding and combating imperialism, colonialism, and racism (Stevens, 2017). In terms of specific, nonformal, adult education work, the national network of the US Communist Party's schools (Gettleman, 2002) is rarely mentioned (see Boughton, 2013; Brookfield & Holst, 2010, for exceptions) and yet to be researched in the field of adult education. This, despite the fact that, throughout the 1930s–1950s, thousands of adults studied at these schools in classes taught by preeminent scholar activists such as Eleanor Flexner and W. E. B. DuBois.

The general lack of research on Communist, nonformal, working-class educational initiatives can also be extended to that of the early to mid-twentieth-century initiatives of socialist labor colleges. This is despite the fact that in the 1920s, as Dolgon and Roth (2020) and Barrow (1990) document, there were approximately 300 Labor colleges across the US in 31 states and 95 towns or cities. Excluding the extensive correspondence education conducted by some of these colleges that enrolled thousands of workers, the residential enrollment alone of these colleges exceeded 30,000. Admittedly, there has been some research in this area, but much of it is decades, or nearly a century, old (e.g., Dwyer, 1977; Hansome, 1931; Hodgen, 1925; Kornbluh, 1987; Kornbluh & Frederickson, 1984; London et al., 1980; Mire, 1956). A few exceptions in this area would be the recent work of Rueda (2021) on the twentieth-century case of Luis Emilio Recabarren in Chile, the work of Tamboukou (2017) on working-class women's education spanning historical cases from the US, the UK, and France, and the work from outside of adult education by Katz (2011) on the socialist pedagogy of Jewish garment workers in the US. In this recent work, we are also reminded of how Communist- and socialist-based working-class educators addressed innovatively the issues of race, gender, and imperialism. Sadly, the field of adult education has largely moved away from research on worker-led or, at least, union-led working-class education (see Ng, 2012, and Hanson, 2014, for exceptions), despite the US 'founding father' of adult education Eduard Lindeman co-authoring two books on workers' education (Anderson & Lindeman, 1927; Hader & Lindeman, 1929).

Having identified some of the holes in our scholarship in which we have yet to research, recover, or remember the rich tradition of Marxist or socialist adult working-class pedagogical thought and practice, we can identify a number of adult education scholars who, in the last few decades, have centered Marxism in their work. This, despite the fact that Frank Youngman's (Youngman, 1986, p. 3) comment that 'few authors' in adult education 'have taken an explicitly socialist perspective', still holds true today. The main themes that run through the Marxist literature in adult education center on identifying key concepts for a Marxist pedagogy (e.g., Allman, 1999, 2007; Carpenter & Mojab, 2011, Carpenter & Mojab, 2017); analyzing or presenting the most common themes in adult education such as learning, research, program planning, and pedagogy from a Marxist or socialist perspective (e.g., Brookfield & Holst, 2010; Youngman, 1986); providing frameworks for Marxist analysis and theoretical development of and for adult education (e.g., Allman, 2001; Cooper, 2020; Youngman, 2000); providing case studies or examples of Marxist-informed adult education (e.g., Boughton, 2005, 2010; Carpenter & Mojab, 2011; Foley, 1999; Hammond, 1998; Rueda, 2021); and analyzing working-class learning in workplaces, unions, and communities from Marxist-informed versions of situated learning (e.g., Lave, 2019) and cultural-historical activity theory (e.g., Cooper, 2020; Livingstone, Adams, and Sawchuk Livingstone et al., 2021; Livingstone & Sawchuk, 2004; Sawchuk, 2003). There are also numerous studies of Antonio Gramsci, often in conjunction with Freire, from an adult education perspective (e.g., Allman, 1999; Holst, 2002, 2010; Holst & Brookfield, 2017; Mayo, 1999; Vetter & Holst, 2017). Finally, beyond Gramsci, and the vast literature on Freire, which is beyond the scope of this chapter, there have also been efforts to detail the specific pedagogical principles and practices of revolutionary adult educators, such as Ernesto 'Che' Guevara (Holst, 2009), Luis Emilio Recabarren (Rueda, 2021), and Julius Nyerere (Mulenga, 2010).

If we consider the Marxist-informed literature in adult education as a whole, we can see a few key themes across this literature. First, the nature of consciousness is central to much of this work. As Allman (1999, p. 1) states succinctly in a paraphrase of Marx: if social transformation 'is a process through which people change not only their circumstances but themselves[,] ... consequently it must be an educational process'. This change of self for adult educators centers on consciousness, its nature, and how adult learning and education change consciousness. Moreover, the relationship between changing our consciousness while we change our circumstances is captured by Marx's concept of praxis, which is also a focal point for Marxist adult education. Praxis in the Marxist tradition is conceptualized dialectically; therefore, dialectics, and thinking dialectically, are also central to Marxist adult education. Conceptualized dialectically, praxis—human activity that changes consciousness and circumstances—leads to the centrality of understanding education in the social context. The social context for Marxist adult educators is one of understanding the centrality of the contradictions of capitalism in the shaping of this context, and how relations of gender, race, nationality, and sexuality play a central role in shaping how these contradictions play out in people's lived realities.

For Marxist adult educators, however, there is an understanding that the working class, the majority of people, in all its racial, national, gendered, and sexual diversity, is the focal point for a socialist pedagogy. In other words, Marxist adult education, while focusing its analysis on the social totality, also privileges the working class as those best socially situated for engaging in 'revolutionary social transformation' (Allman, 1999). Moreover, the major objective of Marxist adult education is challenging prevailing hegemony as a part of the broader project of developing the political independence of the working class.

8.3 Outlines of a Marxist (Adult) Education Pedagogy

To make the broad themes we can draw from Marxist adult education scholarship more concrete, I will present specific points that can inform a Marxist pedagogy, or stated slightly differently, I will present a pedagogical analysis of Marx and Engels informed by my own reading of their work, the Marxist tradition, and Marxist adult education scholarship. It is noteworthy to point out that in all the Marxist literature in adult education, it is only Michael Law (1992) who has detailed the actual educational work of Marx and Engels. Given the fact that Marx and Engels were engaged revolutionaries, and, therefore, educators, detailing their educational work, a task begun by Law (1992), is actually a task in need of further elaboration.

If we consider Marx and Engels' ideas pedagogically, we can summarize them with the following tenets.

1. Reality itself is revolutionary. Dialectics is not just about thinking or conceptualizing, it is also ontological; we live in a dialectical world that is in constant motion and change. This change in the natural and the social world (Bellamy Foster, 2000) is knowable and dialectical, and it has major implications for revolutionary educators. This is at the heart of Marx and Engels' (1948, p. 23) comment in the *Manifesto* that the theoretical conclusions of the Communists 'merely express, in general terms, actual relations springing from an existing class struggle'. In other words, revolution, as they say, is not the ideas of some 'would-be universal reformer' that need to be lectured into the minds of workers; rather, revolution is embedded in the very nature of society itself. Reality is revolutionary.

2. To be a revolutionary is to be a pedagogue of a particular type. A Marxist revolutionary is dedicated to the emancipation of the proletariat—to that class, as Marx (2000, p. 81) says in 1844, that is 'in civil society [*bürgerlichen Gesellschaft*] that is not a class of civil society'. Revolutionary pedagogy is praxis; it is changing consciousness while changing the concrete circumstances of working-class people. Consciousness (subjective conditions) and circumstances (objective conditions) must be dialectically conceptualized. In this way, pedagogical and practical work (praxis) is about understanding these conditions both in the here and now, and in terms of how practical work can create new consciousness and new concrete circumstances. Marta Harnecker (2015) succinctly states this by saying that the goal is to make the impossible possible—to make what seems impossible today possible tomorrow, through both pedagogical and practical work.
3. The work of the Marxist educator is one of developing a collective understanding—to be a pedagogue along with others—of the interconnectedness of real-world relations as a historically developing social totality. It is a collective understanding of the revolutionary nature of reality.
4. Central to this collective understanding is to identify those most likely to move the historical development of these actual relations forward and to work to advance this historical development in ways that emancipate the working class. In other words, Marxist educators work to actively change the world, to improve the conditions of the working class while simultaneously changing consciousness. This pedagogical work of Marxists is a form of participatory action research. There is no blueprint for revolutionary change; there is only the ever-evolving, historical development of the social totality in which we live. This must be under constant investigation, in order to identify those best positioned within the working class to make change and to identify those concrete changes that can be made, and which make the impossibilities of today, the possibilities of tomorrow.
5. The collective understanding developed through Marxist pedagogical work cannot be the work of individual heroes. Great leaders may emerge, but Marxist pedagogy has to take place within democratically run organizations that center Marxist principles and that develop leadership and organic intellectuals of the working class. It is only through organization that change, both in circumstances and in consciousness, can be maintained, built upon, and furthered in long-term historical processes.
6. A Marxist organization must have as its goal and foundational to its pedagogical work the political independence of the working class—an understanding that emancipation is economic, cultural, social, and ultimately political. There are no emancipatory circumstances or consciousness without the transfer of political power to the working class.

8.4 What Does a Marxist Pedagogy Look Like?

If reality itself is revolutionary, do we actually need revolutionary organizations or revolutionaries? Won't socialism happen on its own with an inevitable collapse of capitalism under the weight of its own contradictions? The natural and social world is in constant motion and change, but that change, particularly in the social world, is determined by human beings in interaction with each other, with what we create, and with the natural world. Marx most certainly outlined laws of motion of the social world, but the ultimate outcome of social change is up to human beings. Capitalist crises and the crisis of capitalism itself do not lead to any predetermined outcome, except perhaps the two options that Rosa Luxemburg (1970) outlined in 1916 of socialism or barbarism. Therefore, the organized intervention of revolutionary pedagogues is necessary to determine and influence the direction of social change. Moreover, Marx's laws of motion are starting points for the never-ending need to collectively investigate social change resulting from the motion of the social world.

In the hopes of making the major themes and tenets of Marxist pedagogy even more concrete, I will draw on some of my own case study work on revolutionary Marxist organizations (Holst, 2004) to provide specific examples of what these themes and tenets look like in practice. For clarity, I will numerically identify the six tenets in the following narrative using numbers in brackets.

The development of the *League of Revolutionaries for a New America* (LRNA) is an example of all six tenets I outlined earlier. LRNA was formed by members of the Communist Labor Party (CLP) in 1993. According to Nelson Peery (1995), the CLP was formed in 1974 by three main groups: (a) anti-revisionist Communists who were either expelled from or left the Communist Party USA (CPUSA) in the mid- to late 1950s, and who went on with other Marxists to form the California Communist League in 1968; (b) members of the League of Revolutionary Black Workers based mainly in the Detroit area; and (c) collectives of Mexican American revolutionaries in California and the Southwest of the US. The CLP was, and LRNA is, arguably the most racially diverse revolutionary organization in the US; from their founding, working-class African Americans and Latinx people have been the base of the organizations and have constituted a significant part of their leadership.

In a 1993 document, Peery details how members of the CLP, throughout the 1960s, 1970s, and particularly in the 1980s, grappled with understanding what they came to see as fundamental transformations in capitalism. Reality was showing itself to be revolutionary [1], and this was visible only through the CLP's, and later the LRNA's, ongoing direct study and research of the members' and other's own, lived working-class realities in auto plants, steel mills, other workplaces, and in their communities [3]. The working class was fundamentally transforming. What the CLP and later LRNA members were experiencing in their own lives, and coming to understand, was that the nature of technology was changing qualitatively from that of being labor-saving to labor-replacing. As Peery (1993, p. 2) says, 'we were seeing the science of society—Marxism, being vindicated before our eyes'.

This transformation of technology and the working class itself [4] meant that what they came to call a 'new class', or a transformed working class, was emerging, growing, and increasingly finding itself pushed out of the basic relationships of capitalist production and distribution: workers find jobs to get a wage/salary to buy what they need. Due to qualitatively new, microchip-based technology, a growing class was forming that had less and less access to stable employment in order to survive. This transformed work(less)ing class, as Peery (2002) would state later on, based on further collective study, was objectively revolutionary [4]. This growing 'workless' class's survival is based on the need for fundamentally new non-capitalist forms of production and distribution.

As those in the CLP began to conclude that capitalism was entering a new stage—an epoch of social revolution—a new organizational form was necessary. Therefore, the decision was made to disband the CLP and create LRNA that they described (Peery, 1993) as an organization of revolutionaries and not a vanguard party as they considered the CLP to be [5]. As Peery (1993, p. 3) put it, 'the new era is producing a new movement. For the first time, an actual practical communist movement of the workers is emerging. Production without work demands distribution without money. The cause of communism is practical'.

Given the collective analysis developed by the LRNA, the organization's main efforts have turned to education [6], with a central focus on the historical subject they have identified [2], like Marx (2000, p. 81), that is a class 'in civil society that is not a class of civil society'. The educational focus of LRNA is to help the transformed working class understand itself, to understand its own experience as a class increasingly on the margins of the basic relations of capitalism with decreasing access to work to get money to pay for basic survival necessities of housing, food, and healthcare. Peery (2002, p. 15) notes that those among the class fighting for survival can come to understand, with Marxist pedagogical practice [6], that 'these demands express the elementary understanding of how and why a new society has to be organized …. The main role of the conscious revolutionary is to help the fighters become conscious of what they are doing'. Given the social base of LRNA in the working class, and in particular, workers of color whose jobs have been disproportionately impacted by automation, Peery (1993, p. 8) argued that they are 'firmly inside this revolutionary sector of the [working] class'.

Therefore, the organizational structure [5] CLP members felt was most appropriate for the new era workers find themselves in, was a more open, education-focused organization rather than a vanguard party. The project of the new organization was one of class-consciousness (ibid.) of the revolutionary potential of the growing, precarious sector of the working class. The spontaneous action of the class would lead to reform struggles around the survival necessities of the class; no revolutionary organization would be necessary for this to take place. For the LRNA, the role of the revolutionary educator was to raise the consciousness of the workers beyond struggles for reform, to a consciousness of the revolutionary nature of their demands, which required a whole-going restructuring, revolution, of society by a politically independent working class [6].

8.5 Moving Forward

LRNA is just one example of what Marxist pedagogical principles can look like in contemporary practice. It is an example specific to the US; one can find other US examples such as that of the Freedom Road Socialist Organization (FRSO, 2022; Holst, 2004) or the Party of Liberation and Socialism (Liberation School, 2021). Nevertheless, what the LRNA is trying to understand through its decades-long, collective research and study of the nature of capitalism and the working class today has a certain universality to it, in the sense that what they are doing is what the Marxist tradition has always done. At its best, Marxist pedagogy is about a working-class-based, and working-class-led, collective, organized, and ongoing research process into the ever-changing nature of capitalism. Its goal is detailing the objective (circumstances) and subjective (consciousness) conditions and prospects for working-class emancipation.

Interestingly what the LRNA began identifying as early as the 1960s—qualitative changes in technology, generating qualitative changes in capitalism, and the lived realities of working-class people—is only in recent decades, and really recent years, being seriously considered by Marxist academics and policymakers more generally. What the LRNA has identified as the 'new class', or the growing sector of the working class and now even middle class that is finding it harder and harder to hold down full-time, stable employment, is what the International Labour Organization (ILO, 2019) calls 'informal workers'. In 2018, such workers made up 61% of the global labor market. Analogous to what the LRNA has identified as informality's disproportionate impact on working-class women and workers of color in the US, the ILO has identified informality's disproportional impact on women and the working class of Global South countries.

The reality of what the LRNA calls the new class has slowly been recognized by Marxist and left-wing academics and scholar activists, with various terminology. Mike Davis (2007) described the issue as a planet of slums. Bieler, Lindberg, and Pillay (2008, p. 266) identify a 'precarious and pauperized working class'. Lane (2010) uses the term informal proletariat, and Munck (2011), like Standing (2011), talks of the global precariat. Baptist (2010, p. 262) uses the term 'new poor', and David Harvey (2010) refers to the dispossessed. In Latin America, Gilberto Valdés (2006) speaks of the 'new social subject', Raúl Zibechi (2005, p. 13) of 'those without', and Braga (2018) of the precariat. In India, and globally, Vandana Shiva (2005) discusses the enclosures of the commons, while Phil Jones (2021) describes work without the worker.

This is not a complete list of scholars who have taken up this issue, and they are not of one mind. There are also Marxist scholars such as Kim Moody

(2017) who take exception to the notion of a growing precarious working class as overblown and not necessarily that new. Dyer-Witheford et al. (2019) have provided a maximalist and minimalist typology to try to capture the two major sides in this debate. Admittedly, some of this maximalist literature too easily characterizes a shiny new world of 'fully automated luxury communism' (Bastani, 2019). This maximalist position seems to overlook the hard-fought struggles ahead if the growingly precarious global working class is able to take state power and use environmentally sustainable labor-replacing technology for its own emancipation and that of the planet from capitalism. Most importantly, missing, however, in this debate among scholars on the 'rise of the robots' and growing precarity is precisely what the LRNA brings to this debate; namely, a serious engagement on Marxist political economy on this issue, and the serious implications this has for actual revolutionary education and practice among the very class scholars are debating about.

There is a group of Marxist political economists who have seriously approached the question of the qualitative nature of new, labor-replacing, microchip-, and now artificial intelligence-based technology, from the standpoint of Marx's (1967) labor theory of value, and his analysis of the law of tendential fall in the rate of profit (Marx, 1991). It is beyond the scope of this chapter, but the main argument is as follows: Marx's labor theory of value posits that it is only human labor that produces value, which can be realized as profit when produced commodities are sold. Technology or machines, or robots, are products of human labor, but they do not produce value in the production process. As more technology is used in production, or as Nelson Peery so succinctly puts it, when technology changes from being labor-saving to labor-replacing, less and less value-producing human labor is involved in production. With less labor involved in production, less surplus value or profit can be realized in production. Marx argued that increasing use of technology in production was a historical tendency and, therefore, led to a corresponding, historical fall in the rate of profit in capitalist production. Marxist political economists such as Carchedi and Roberts (2018, 2023), Smith (2010), and Kliman (2012), and their colleagues around the world, have shown this to be empirically true in countries across the world. There has been a steady overall fall in the rate of profit across the planet throughout the twentieth century, leading to not just crises in capitalism that we have seen periodically over the decades, but to an overall crisis in capitalism itself.

Let me begin to wrap up this discussion by bringing it back to Marx and adult education. What these Marxist political economists seem to fail to capture in all of this, unlike revolutionaries like Nelson Peery (2002) and Baptist and Rehmann (2011) and colleagues, is the revolutionary implications of this growing crisis of capitalism, both for the emancipation struggles of the working class and the role of education in these struggles. Use whatever aforementioned term you would like for the growing sector of humanity finding itself outside the basic relation for production and distribution of goods in capitalism: the working-class majority finds work to get a wage/salary, to buy what it needs to survive or thrive. With a growing sector of people outside this relation, they have no way to get what they need to survive. This is why Peery (1993) spoke of a practical movement for Communism. A growing sector of humanity has to fight for distribution without money, or it will die.

Communism—distribution based on need, not the ability to pay—becomes a practical solution to the day-to-day survival of a growing sector of the species. This is not about people's opinions of capitalism or socialism, which are moving in favor of socialism in the US (Carchedi & Roberts, 2023), but about meeting people's basic needs. Moreover, Marxist education, as envisioned by Marx and Engels (1948, p. 22) in the *Manifesto*, becomes increasingly relevant. Communists do not need to 'set up any sectarian principles of their own, by which to shape and mould the proletarian movement'. Communists, when communism becomes practical as it has today, need to work pedagogically to 'bring to the front the common interests of the entire proletariat' (ibid.) through an understanding of the nature of capitalism today or 'the line of march, the conditions, and the ultimate general results of the proletarian movement' (ibid.).

The field of adult education has been somewhat bifurcated in the past decades, and perhaps since its existence, between scholars and practitioners focused on workplace training and workplace learning. It has been tilted much more in favor of the interests of employers than workers, and scholars and practitioners interested in social justice, social change, and learning in social movements (Cunningham, 1993). In the broad scope of things, this bifurcation, in a sense, does not matter all that much. The growing precarity of humanity and the growing fragmentation and informality of work dramatically impact all of us involved in adult education. The question is really how we will work, and with whom will we work, to understand this reality and the implications for the work we do as educators.

In the Marxist debates over new technologies and the falling rate of profit, there is a tendency to freeze-frame what is otherwise a dynamic social totality in constant motion, and change and to say either 'see, the robots haven't taken over yet' or 'the rise of the robots are coming for you'. Marx and Engels set out to understand the laws of social motion not to understand solely the present, but to understand the trajectory of where we are headed. Understanding this trajectory is essential for revolutionaries and their educational work. That is why it is revolutionaries, organic intellectuals like Nelson Peery and Willie Baptist, who seem to capture much better the implications of the recent fundamental transformations of capitalism. As adult educators, we would do well to work alongside or at least build bridges with these revolutionaries in order to make our work relevant for the current and coming struggles for the emancipation of the working class. If we do that, then we will be Marxists.

Disclosure Statement The author has no financial interest or benefit that has arisen from the direct applications of this research.

References

Allman, P. (1999). *Revolutionary Social Transformation: Democratic Hopes, Political Possibilities, and Critical Education*. Bergin & Garvey.

Allman, P. (2001). *Critical Education against Global Capitalism: Karl Marx and Revolutionary Critical Education*. Bergin & Garvey.

Allman, P. (2007). *On Marx: An Introduction to the Revolutionary Intellect of Karl Marx*. Sense.

Anderson, M., & Lindeman, E. C. (1927). *Education through Experience*. The Workers Bureau Press.

Atta, M., & Holst, J. D. (2023). Deriving a Theory of Learning from Social Movement Practices: A Systematic Literature Review. *The European Journal for Research on the Education and Learning of Adults, 14*(1), 177–196. https://doi.org/10.3384/rela.2000-7426.4334

Baptist, W. (2010). A New and Unsettling Force: The Strategic Relevance of Rev. Dr. Martin Luther King Jr.'s Poor People's Campaign. *Interface, 2*(1), 262–270. http://groups.google.com/group/interface-articles/web/3Baptist.pdf

Baptist, W., & Rehmann, J. (2011). *Pedagogy of the Poor: Building the Movement to End Poverty*. Teachers College Press.

Barrow, C. W. (1990). Counter-Movement within the Labor Movement: Workers' Education and the American Federation of Labor, 1900–1937. *The Social Science Journal, 27*(4), 395–417.

Bastani, A. (2019). *Fully Automated Luxury Communism: A Manifesto*. Verso.

Bellamy Foster, J. (2000). *Marx's Ecology: Materialism and Nature*. Monthly Review Press.

Bieler, A., Lindberg, I., & Pillay, D. (2008). What Future for the Global Working Class? The Need for a New Historical Subject. In A. Bieler, I. Lindberg, & D. Pillay (Eds.), *Labour and the Challenges of Globalization*. Pluto.

Boughton, B. (1997). Does Popular Education Have a Past? In B. Boughton, T. Brown, & G. Foley (Eds.), *New Directions in Australian Adult Education* (pp. 1–27). University of Technology Sydney-Centre for Popular Education.

Boughton, B. (2005). "The Workers' University": Australia's Marx Schools and the International Communist Movement's Contribution to Popular Education. In J. Crowther, V. Galloway, & I. Martin (Eds.), *Popular Education: Engaging the Academy* (pp. 100–109). NIACE.

Boughton, B. (2010). Back to the Future? Timor-Leste, Cuba and the Return of the Mass Literacy Campaign. *Literacy and Numeracy Studies, 18*(2), 23–40. http://epress.lib.uts.edu.au/journals/index.php/lnj/article/view/1898

Boughton, B. (2013). Popular Education and the 'Party Line'. *Globalisation, Societies and Education, 11*(2), 239–257.

Braga, R. (2018). *The Politics of the Precariat* (S. Purdy, Trans.). Haymarket Books.

Brookfield, S. D., & Holst, J. D. (2010). *Radicalizing Learning: Adult Education for a Just World*. Jossey-Bass.

Burden-Stelly, C., & Dean, J. (Eds.). (2022). *Organize, Fight, Win: Black Communist Women's Political Writing*. Verso.

Butterwick, S., & Elfert, M. (2015). Women Social Activists of Atlantic Canada: Stories of Re-enchantment, Authenticity, and Hope. *Canadian Journal for the Study of Adult Education, 27*(1), 65–82. https://cjsae.library.dal.ca/index.php/cjsae/article/view/3338

Carchedi, G., & Roberts, M. (2023). *Capitalism in the 21st Century: Through the Prism of Value*. Pluto Press.
Carchedi, G., & Roberts, M. (Eds.). (2018). *World in Crisis: A Global Analysis of Marx's Law of Profitability*. Haymarket Books.
Carpenter, S., & Mojab, S. (Eds.). (2011). *Educating from Marx: Race, Gender, and Learning*. Palgrave Macmillan.
Carpenter, S., & Mojab, S. (2017). *Revolutionary Learning: Marxism, Feminism, and Knowledge*. Pluto Press.
Choudry, A., & Kapoor, D. (Eds.). (2010). *Learning from the Ground Up: Global Perspectives on Social Movements and Knowledge Production*. Palgrave Macmillan.
Clover, D. E. (2018). Critical Adult Education and the Art Gallery Museum. *International Journal of Lifelong Education*, 37(1), 88–102. https://doi.org/10.1080/02601370.2017.1397785
Cooper, L. (2020). *Workers' Education in the Global South: Radical Adult Education at the Crossroads*. Brill.
Crenshaw, K. W. (1989). Demarginalizing the Intersection of Race and Sex: A Black Feminist Critique of Antidiscrimination Doctrine, Feminist Theory, And Antiracist Politics. *University of Chicago Legal Forum*, 1989(1), 139–167. https://chicagounbound.uchicago.edu/cgi/viewcontent.cgi?article=1052&context=uclf
Crowther, J., Galloway, V., & Martin, I. (Eds.). (2005). Popular Education: Engaging the Academy. *International Perspectives*. NIACE.
Cunningham, P. M. (1993). Let's Get Real. *Journal of Adult Education*, 22(1), 3–15.
Davis, M. (2007). *Planet of Slums*. Verso.
DiFilippo, S. H. (2015). Resistance and Relearning: Women's Experiences Choosing Midwifery and Home Birth in Ontario, Canada. *Canadian Journal for the Study of Adult Education*, 27(3), 43–63. https://cjsae.library.dal.ca/index.php/cjsae/article/view/3902
Dolgon, C., & Roth, R. (2020). Labor Education Programs: Radical Beginnings, Mccarthyist Backlash, and the Rise of Neoliberal Education. In T. S. Rocco, M. C. Smith, R. C. Mizzi, L. R. Merriweather, & J. D. Hawley (Eds.), *The Handbook of Adult and Continuing Education* (pp. 287–296). Stylus.
Dwyer, R. E. (1977). *Labor Education in the U.S.: An Annotated Bibliography*. The Scarecrow Press.
Dyer-Witheford, N., Kjøsen, A. M., & Steinhoff, J. (2019). *Inhuman Power: Artificial Intelligence and the Future of Capitalism*. Pluto Press.
English, L. M. (2005). Third-Space Practitioners: Women Educating for Justice in the Global South. *Adult Education Quarterly*, 55(2), 85–100. https://doi.org/10.1177/0741713604271851
English, L. M. (2014). Financial Literacy: A Critical Adult Education Appraisal. *New Directions for Adult and Continuing Education*, 141, 47–55. https://doi.org/10.1002/ace.20084
Foley, G. (1999). *Learning in Social Action*. Zed.
Freedom Road Socialist Organization. (2022). *The Political Program of Freedom Road Socialist Organization*. Author.
Gettleman, M. E. (2002). 'No Varsity Teams': New York's Jefferson School of Social Science, 1943–1956. *Science and Society*, 66(3), 336–359. https://doi.org/10.1521/siso.66.3.336.21020
Hader, J. J., & Lindeman, E. C. (1929). *What Do Workers Study?* The Workers Education Bureau Press.

Hammond, J. L. (1998). *Fighting to Learning: Popular Education and the Guerrilla War in El Salvador*. Rutgers University Press.
Hansome, M. (1931). *World Workers' Education Movements: Their Social Significance*. Columbia University Press.
Hanson, C. (2014). 'I Learned I Am a Feminist': Lessons for Adult Learning from Participatory Action Research with Union Women. *Canadian Journal for the Study of Adult Education, 27*(1), 49–64. Retrieved from https://cjsae.library.dal.ca/index.php/cjsae/article/view/3361
Harnecker, M. (2015). *A World to Build: New Paths toward Twenty-First Century Socialism* (F. Fuentes, Trans.). Monthly Review Press.
Harvey, D. (2010). Organizing for the Anti-capitalist Transition. *Interface, 2*(1), 243–261. http://groups.google.com/group/interface-articles/web/3Harvey.pdf
Hill, R. J. (2004). Activism as Practice: Some Queer Considerations. *New Directions for Adult & Continuing Education, 102*, 85–94. https://doi.org/10.1002/ace.141
Hodgen, M. T. (1925). *Workers' Education in England and the United States*. Trench, Trubner and Co.
Holst, J. D. (2002). *Social Movements, Civil Society, and Radical Adult Education*. Bergin & Garvey.
Holst, J. D. (2004). Globalization and Education within Two Revolutionary Organizations in The United States of America: A Gramscian Analysis. *Adult Education Quarterly, 55*(1), 23–40. https://doi.org/10.1177/0741713604268895
Holst, J. D. (2009). The Pedagogy of Ernesto Che Guevara. *International Journal of Lifelong Education, 28*(2), 149–173. https://doi.org/10.1080/02601370902757026
Holst, J. D. (2010). The Revolutionary Party in Gramsci's Pre-prison Educational and Political Theory and Practice. In P. Mayo (Ed.), *Gramsci and Educational Thought* (pp. 38–56). Wiley Blackwell.
Holst, J. D. (2018). From Radical Adult Education to Social Movement Learning. In M. Milana, J. Holford, S. Webb, P. Jarvis, & R. Waller (Eds.), *International Handbook of Adult and Lifelong Education and Learning* (pp. 75–92). Palgrave Macmillan.
Holst, J. D., & Brookfield, S. D. (2017). Catharsis: Antonio Gramsci, Pedagogy, and the Political Independence of the Working Class. In N. Pizzolato & J. D. Holst (Eds.), *Antonio Gramsci: A Pedagogy to Change the World* (pp. 197–220). Springer.
Holst, J. D., Rueda, M. A., Gerónimo-López, K., Ramos Concha, G. & Acuña Collado, V., Eds. (2021). Lifelong Learning and Adult Education in Latin American and Caribbean Social Movements. *New Directions for Adult & Continuing Education*, 171–172. https://onlinelibrary.wiley.com/toc/15360717/2021/2021/171-172
Huttunen, R. (2007). Critical Adult Education and the Political-Philosophical Debate between Nancy Fraser and Axel Honneth. *Educational Theory, 57*(4), 423–433. https://doi.org/10.1111/j.1741-5446.2007.00266.x
International Labour Organization. (2019). *World Employment Social Outlook: Trends 2019*. Author.
Jones, C. (2011). *Claudia Jones: Beyond Containment* (C. B. Davies, Ed.). Ayebia Clarke Publishing.
Jones, P. (2021). *Work without the Worker: Labor in the Age of Platform Capitalism*. Verso.
Katz, D. (2011). *All Together Different: Yiddish Socialists, Garment Workers, and the Labor Roots of Multiculturalism*. New York University Press.

Kliman, A. (2012). *The Failure of Capitalist Production: Underlying Causes of the Great Recession*. Pluto Press.

Kornbluh, J. L. (1987). *A New Deal for Workers' Education: The Workers' Service Program, 1933–1942*. University of Illinois Press.

Kornbluh, J. L., & Frederickson, M. (Eds.). (1984). *Sisterhood and Solidarity: Workers' Education for Women, 1914–1984*. Temple University Press.

Kuk, H.-S., & Tarlau, R. (2020). The Confluence of Popular Education and Social Movement Studies into Social Movement Learning: A Systematic Literature Review. *International Journal of Lifelong Education, 39*(5–6), 591–604. https://doi.org/10.1080/02601370.2020.1845833

Lane, M. (2010). Indonesia and the Fall of Suharto: Proletarian Politics in the "Planet of Slums" Era. *WorkingUSA, 13*(2), 185–200. https://doi.org/10.1111/j.1743-4580.2010.00282.x

Lave, J. (2019). *Learning and Everyday Life*. Cambridge University Press.

Law, M. (1992) *Engels, Marx, and Radical Adult Education: A Rereading of a Tradition*. Paper presented at the annual Adult Education Research Conference, State College, PA, USA.

Liberation School. (2021). *Revolutionary Education: Theory and Practice for Socialist Organizers* (N. Brown, Ed.). Liberation Media.

Livingstone, D. W., & Sawchuk, P. H. (2004). *Hidden Knowledge: Organized Labor in the Information Age*. Rowman & Littlefield.

Livingstone, D. W., Adams, T. L., & Sawchuk, P. H. (2021). *Professional Power and Skill Use in the "Knowledge Economy"*. Brill.

London, S. H., Tarr, E. R., & Wilson, J. F. (Eds.). (1980). *The Re-education of the American Working Class*. Greenwood Press.

Lovett, T. (Ed.). (1988). *Radical Approaches to Adult Education: A Reader*. Routledge.

Luxemburg, R. (1970). The Junius Pamphlet: The Crisis in Social Democracy. In M. A. Waters (Ed.), *Rosa Luxemburg Speaks* (pp. 353–453). Pathfinder Press.

Marx, K. (1967). *Capital, Vol. 1*. International Publishers.

Marx, K. (1991). *Capital, Vol. 3*. Penguin.

Marx, K. (2000). *Selected Writings* (2nd ed.) (D. McLellan, Ed.). Oxford University Press.

Marx, K., & Engels, F. (1948). *The Communist Manifesto*. International Publishers.

Mayo, P. (1999). *Gramsci, Freire, & Adult Education: Possibilities for Transformative Action*. Zed.

Mire, J. (1956). *Labor Education: A Study Report on Needs, Programs, and Approaches*. Inter-University Labor Education Committee.

Moody, K. (2017). *On New Terrain: How Capital Is Reshaping the Battleground of Class War*. Haymarket Books.

Mulenga, D. C. (2010). Mwalimu Julius Nyerere: A Critical Review of His Contributions to Adult Education and Postcolonialism. *International Journal of Lifelong Education, 20*(6), 446–470. https://doi.org/10.1080/02601370110088436

Munck, R. (2011). Beyond North and South: Migration, Informalization, and Trade Union Revitalization. *Workingusa, 14*(1), 5–18. https://doi.org/10.1111/j.1743-4580.2010.00317.x

Narushima, M. (2004). A Gaggle of Raging Grannies: The Empowerment of Older Canadian Women through Social Activism. *International Journal of Lifelong Education, 23*(1), 23–42. https://doi.org/10.1080/0260137032000172042

Ng, W. (2012). Pedagogy of Solidarity: Educating for an Interracial Working-Class Movement. *Journal of Workplace Learning*, 24(7/8), 528–537. https://doi.org/10.1108/13665621211261007

Niesz, T., Korora, A. M., Walkuski, C. B., & Foot, R. E. (2018). Social Movements and Educational Research: Toward a United Field of Scholarship. *Teachers College Record*, 120(3), 1–41. https://doi.org/10.1177/016146811812000305

Peery, N. (1993). *Entering an Epoch of Social Revolution*. Workers Press.

Peery, N. (1995, September 4). The LRNA Is an Organization of Revolutionaries. The People's Tribune (Online Edition), 22(28). https://www.marxists.org/history/erol/ncm-7/lrna.htm

Peery, N. (2002). *The Future Is Up to Us: A Revolutionary Taking Politics with the American People*. Speakers for a New America.

Peterson, E. A. (Ed.). (2002). *Freedom Road: Adult Education for African Americans*. Krieger.

Rueda, M. A. (2021). *The Educational Philosophy of Luis Emilio Recabarren: Pioneering Working-Class Education in Latin America*. Routledge.

Sawchuk, P. H. (2003). *Adult Learning and Technology in Working-Class Life*. Cambridge University Press.

Sheared, V., Johnson-Bailey, J., Colin, S. A. J., III, Peterson, E., & Brookfield, S. D. (Eds.). (2010). *The Handbook of Race and Adult Education*. Jossey-Bass.

Shiva, V. (2005). *Earth Democracy: Justice, Sustainability, and Peace*. South End Press.

Smith, M. E. G. (2010). *Global Capitalism in Crisis: Karl Marx and the Decay of the Profit System*. Fernwood Publishing.

Standing, G. (2011). *The Precariat: The New Dangerous Class*. Bloomsbury.

Stevens, M. (2017). *Red International and Black Caribbean: Communists in New York City, Mexico, and the West Indies, 1919–1039*. Pluto Press.

Tamboukou, M. (2017). *Women Workers' Education, Life Narratives, and Politics: Geographies, Histories, Pedagogies*. Palgrave Macmillan.

Tawney, R. H. (1964). *The Radical Tradition* (R. Hinden, Ed.). Pantheon Books.

Valdés, G. (2006). *El Sistema de dominación múltiple. Hacia un nuevo paradigma emancipatorio en América Latina*. Unpublished Doctoral Dissertation. Instituto de Filosofía, La Habana, Cuba.

Vetter, M. A., & Holst, J. D. (2017). A Pedagogy for Power: Antonio Gramsci and Luis Emilio Recabarren on the Educational Role of Working-Class Organizations. In N. Pizzolato & J. D. Holst (Eds.), *Antonio Gramsci: A Pedagogy to Change the World* (pp. 89–106). Springer.

von Kotze, A., & Walters, S. (Eds.). (2017). *Forging Solidarity: Popular Education at Work*. Sense.

Walker, W. (2009). Adult Learning in the Queer Nation: A Foucauldian Analysis of Educational Strategies for Social Change. *New Horizons in Adult Education and Human Resource Development*, 23(3), 10–17. https://doi.org/10.1002/nha3.10346

Walters, S., & Manicom, L. (Eds.). (1996). *Gender in Popular Education*. Zed.

Youngman, F. (1986). *Adult Education and Socialist Pedagogy*. Croom Helm.

Youngman, F. (2000). *The Political Economy of Adult Education and Development*. Zed.

Zainub, A. (Ed.). (2019). *Decolonization and Anti-colonial Praxis*. Sense.

Zibechi, R. (2005). Subterranean Echoes: Resistance and Politics "desde el sótano". *Socialism and Democracy*, 19(3), 13–39. https://doi.org/10.1080/08854300500257922

CHAPTER 9

In-Against-Beyond Metrics-Driven University: A Marxist Critique of the Capitalist Imposition of Measure on Academic Labor

Jakub Krzeski

9.1 Introduction

Standardization, quantification and measurement are all hallmarks of our time. Enough so that some are ready to call our age the age of surveillance capitalism (Zuboff, 2020), marking an important shift in capital's ability to capture even those sectors of production, that is, immaterial or biopolitical labor (Lazzarato, 1996), which some believe lie outside or beyond measure (Hardt & Negri, 2011). The subjection of academic labor by these processes marks a particular case in this wider process of transformations within the capitalist mode of production. Yet, as a particular case, it asserts also a singular meaning. This is because the subordination of new production sectors occurs through the subjection of the logic internal to the subjected sector, in order to seek ways of profit from it (Szadkowski, 2016a). Therefore, the critical perspective on the capitalist imposition of measure on academic labor developed in this chapter will follow the general Marxian understanding of critique. At the same time, it will attempt to adapt it to the singularity of capital's operation within the science and higher education (HE) sector.

The Marxist approach is developed here as an intervention in the polarized debate on the critique of measure and its operation in science and higher education. The intervention aims at overcoming two poles. The first can be

J. Krzeski (✉)
Nicolaus Copernicus University, Toruń, Poland
e-mail: j.krzeski@umk.pl

© The Editor(s) (if applicable) and The Author(s), under exclusive license to Springer Nature Switzerland AG 2023
R. Hall et al. (eds.), *The Palgrave International Handbook of Marxism and Education*, Marxism and Education,
https://doi.org/10.1007/978-3-031-37252-0_9

described as the reformist approach. It is founded on the belief that irrespective of our intentions, the processes of quantification have gone so far that metrics are here to stay. What is left is to spread and promote the responsible use of metrics (Wilsdon, 2016). Initiatives undertaken by the scientific and academic publishing community such as the San Francisco Declaration on Research Assessment (DORA) (Hatch & Curry, 2018) or Leiden Manifesto (Hicks et al., 2015) are perfect examples. They draw attention to the misuse of metrics in different assessments and evaluations of academics and propose general guidelines for their responsible use. One example would be advocating for rejecting measures of journal quality for evaluation of individual academics.

The second pole focuses upon the rejection of measure. This, in turn, is driven by the conviction that rankings, benchmarking and productivity measures in a fundamental way temper with the time fabric of academia. This catalyzes acceleration (Vostal, 2016), and as a result we can hear calls for a slowdown (The Slow Science Academy, 2010; Berg & Seeber, 2016). Here, it is assumed that knowledge cannot be truly produced—both in teaching and in research—under the general imperative of benchmark evaluation. As measures are one of the key driving forces of acceleration, the vision of a return to peaceful academic labor undisturbed by the mounting pressure and demands of the market seems to be the obvious answer.

This chapter argues that the Marxist perspective must establish its point of departure precisely in the refutation of these two approaches, which are unable to provide a critical approach toward the problem of the imposition of measures on academic labor. In the first case, reformism manifests itself only in soothing discontents brought by continuous standardization, measurement and surveillance of academic labor. By focusing solely on how metrics should be applied to a given situation, we never inquire into the particular set of social relations that are constitutive of this process in the first place. Here, reformists and university managers have much in common. They both believe that there is no alternative. Moreover, there are cases such as global university rankings where reformist critique is immediately co-opted by ranking providers, as a means of making ranking more resilient (Hamann & Ringel, 2023).

The second pole offers a more radical answer. Tired of decades of mounting market pressure, rejectionist academics seek alternatives by retreating to the depths of their offices and severing the ties with the knowledge economy (The Slow Science Academy, 2010). But as Isabelle Stengers warns, there is a trap in these approach in the form of romanticization of the past (2018). In turn, the alternative can be only brought about by reinstating the separation of academics from the buzz of the outside world. In contrast, the task of Marxist critique will therefore be not only to offer an alternative but more importantly to construct it through bridging the gap between academic and nonacademic labor.

Taking the two described perspectives as a point of reference, we can indicate the focal points of the Marxist critical approach toward the imposition of measures on academic labor. First, the focus is on the social relations constitutive of the current predicament. Although the history of the capitalist organization of knowledge production is long (Freudenthal & McLaughlin, 2009; Bernal, 2012; Arboledas-Lérida, 2020), the imposition of measures on academic labor marks a distinct moment in this history. This is often referred to as the subsumption of academic labor under capital (Hall & Bowles, 2016; Szadkowski, 2016b). The history of the imposition of capitalist measures on academic labor is, therefore, a part of a larger history in which capital subordinates activities within academia, and gradually begins to intervene directly in the social relations of production within the knowledge production sectors.

If this is the case, the Marxist approach toward the imposition of capitalist measures on academic labor must entail the critique of the political economy of measure. Yet, Marx was never interested in providing merely the theory of capitalist reproduction. His penetrating insight into the capitalist mode of production was remarkable in so far as it was developed with a clear focus—severing and transcending the capitalist relation (Lebowitz, 2003). In turn, measures have to be accounted for as a site of struggle and antagonism between capital and (academic) labor (De Angelis & Harvie, 2009). Finally, the alternative. A Marxist approach toward claims that struggles around measures are not only against the current predicament, but are also pushing the horizon of possibility. They force us to account for the following: What lies beyond knowledge production mediated by capitalist measure (Szadkowski, 2019)? Does postcapitalist knowledge requires rejection or the development of noncapitalist measure? (Krzeski, 2021).

9.2 Marx and the Double Perspective on Measure

The history of all hitherto existing measures is the history of class struggles. Long before the conditions of possibility for humans "to exchange and to order these exchanges" were mediated globally and "subjected to time and to the great exterior necessity" (Foucault, 2005, p. 244), measures were far more local and tangible affair. Yet because they were so closely related to the subjective and particular dimensions of our lives—humans' bodies and their environments—they were prone to all different sorts of metrological conflicts and being instrumentalized as weapons in class struggles. The very form the measure took gave rise to a situation in which the stronger dominated the weaker, imposing their measure on them (Kula, 2014). It is only the construction of universal and conventional measures that carried the promise to once and for all put an end to this situation. However, as Witold Kula famously observed, for the metric and universal metrological system to prevail, "two conditions had to be satisfied: the equality of men before the law, and the alienation of the commodity" (Kula, 2014, p. 123). Capitalism is, therefore, an important condition of possibility for the universality of measure.

But Marx's project marks an important intervention in the promise of the universalism of abstract measures. With Marx, we are endowed with the theory that not only accounts for the failure of this promise but how, in the capitalist mode of production, the struggle over measure is reproduced in its distinct form. Note that such struggle asserts a potential double meaning, as it implies that the particular measure can be weaponized by the capitalist and worker class alike. However, transition to the capitalist mode of production, with socially necessary labor time as a measure of abstract labor, poses some immediate problems when we try to grasp the double function of measure. First and foremost, *Capital* (Marx, 1978)—the usual point of reference for Marx's labor theory of value—presents this problem from a one-sided perspective, which privileges capital (Lebowitz, 2003). This, in turn, often results in Marx's freezing class struggle for his analysis. In effect, the political reading of capitalist measure requires additional support.

The *Grundrisse* offers a more dynamic picture. This is one of the reasons why some Marxists interested in developing theory from the workers' perspective either resorted to Marx's earlier formulation of his critique of political economy (Negri, 1991) or reread key passages from *Capital* politically by resorting to *Grundrisse* (Cleaver, 1994). The problem of measure is pivotal to this discussion. In the famous passage often referred to as "The fragment on the machines," Marx envisioned a situation in which "as soon as labour in the direct form has ceased to be the great well-spring of wealth, labour time ceases and must cease to be its measure, and hence exchange value [must cease to be the measure] of use-value" (Marx, 1973, pp. 705–706).

On the one hand, the increasing role of science in developing fixed capital to shorten necessary labor produced conditions of possibility for the demise of the law of value. On the other hand, it created favorable circumstances for the development of the social individual, who can finally enjoy social wealth due to the amount of free time liberated in this process. This opposition is formulated as a direct response to the inability of capital to impose work through its measure and, hence, realize the value (Cleaver, 1994). When taken together with the growing needs of the social individual, new circumstances arise, in which "the measure of wealth is then not any longer, in any way, labour time, but rather disposable time" (Marx, 1973, p. 708). This, in turn, has some powerful consequences for developing a Marxist approach toward measure, both generally and in HE. As Marx's argument is making a clear distinction between capitalist and noncapitalist measure, the relation between measure and communism becomes less antithetical than one may assume from the outset.

But although political, this reading relies on an important ontological assumption. It requires our conceiving of living labor as always pushing against and overflowing capitalist forms and measures, which—as John Holloway puts it—are nothing more than a procrustean bed. The content, what the measures attempt to contain, exists, in turn, "not only in but also against and beyond its form" (Holloway, 2015, p. 24). What are the grounds for such reading and why do they involve pondering on an ontological layer of Marx's argument? In his famous introduction to the *Grundrisse*, Marx opens his remarks on the method by inspecting the subject presupposed by the eighteenth-century classical political economist and exposes this subject as an isolated individual. In line with his "relational" thinking about subjectivity—already present in the

6th thesis on Feuerbach (Marx, 1969; cf. Balibar, 2017)—he argues that the standpoint of an isolated individual is inadequate for understating material production as it completely omits what is constitutive to the producing individual (Marx, 1973, p. 18). This argument is ontological in so far as it posits the element which is primary and precedes any form of appearance. It is also what eventually leads Marx to propose a different standpoint, one of a social individual, that accounts for what produces the individual.

Yet, this argument can be pushed even further as an important question arises. Is this relational basis and condition of possibility for all production autonomous from capital and governed by its logic, or does capital structure this dimension in its great quest to establish full dominance over the living? Holloway and other autonomist Marxists would argue for the former (Holloway, 2015), ontologizing the very impossibility of capital's full domination. Here again, the Marx of the *Grundrisse* comes to the fore and provides an important insight into the relation between the ontological grounding of production and how it appears in a particular and historical form under the capitalist mode of production.

> In fact, however, when the limited bourgeois form is stripped away, what is wealth other than the universality of human needs, capacities, pleasures, productive forces etc., created through universal exchange? The full development of human mastery over the forces of nature, those of so-called nature as well as of humanity's own nature? The absolute working-out of his creative potentialities, with no presupposition other than the previous historic development, which makes this totality of development, i.e. the development of all human powers as such the end in itself, not as measured on a predetermined yardstick? (Marx, 1973, p. 488)

"The absolute working out" is nothing more than the movement of pushing against capitalist forms, and the reason behind this content are the overflowing measures imposed on it. Yet, one has to be careful here. Although such a reading brings some level of optimism as it exposes the very condition of capitalist production as existing not only within, but at the same against and beyond its rule (Szadkowski & Krzeski, 2019a), it nonetheless highlights the continuous exploitation and corruption of wealth from the side of capital. To combat exploitation and corruption, we first need to uncover wealth from underneath its historical appearances. Hence, we now begin ontological reflection and work of denaturalization (Szadkowski & Krzeski, 2019b).

9.3 Measure and the Tension Between the Social and Isolated Individual

The critique of the measure of academic labor questions the hidden presuppositions that linger in the shadow of continuous standardization, quantification, measurement and surveillance of academic labor. In other words, in what sense are those assumptions constitutive of the functioning of capitalist measure within science and HE? Why did academia, despite the well-known discontents, naturalize capitalist measures as a key driving force behind knowledge production? To answer these questions, those assumptions have to be revealed in their ideological function. In Marx's argument, the very subject put forward by classical political economy—the isolated individual—was tasked with concealing something fundamental to the sphere of production, namely that production as such is a social endeavor (Marx, 1973). A critique of capitalist measure within science and HE sector must make this very problem its starting point. The question is how the tension between the isolated and social individual reproduces itself in the measurement of academic labor.

To grasp this tension, a short historical detour is needed. Although the origins of modern bibliometrics are most usually traced to the works of Derek J. de Solla Price and Eugene Garfield in the 50s and 60s (Wouters, 1999), there is strong evidence that quantitative research into science and scientific publications goes back earlier. Long before the establishment of the Institute for Scientific Information and the publication of the first Science Citation Index by Garfield, which eventually led to the creation of the journal impact factor, it was American psychologists who began systematic counting of scientific publications (Godin, 2006a). What is, however, of special interest is where these ideas originated. Namely the works of Francis Galton, the founding father of eugenics. Galton was himself interested in the hereditary aspects of the great men of science as he was afraid of their decline and insufficient support (Godin, 2007). Genius for him was an inborn natural trait of some human beings, which should not be wasted, but cultivated and reproduced.

Bringing the eugenicist origin of bibliometrics to the fore should not lead to simple moral panic, but rather be inspected precisely from the perspective of ontological inquiry. The question it raises focuses upon the assumptions made about knowledge and science as they are rooted in eugenics. At issue is the extent to which—and this is an open-ended question—these assumptions were naturalized in modern ideas of quantifying heterogeneous knowledge for its valorization. Knowledge is a social endeavor, and yet this story is instructive in how it has made the individual with inherent talent a point of reference to understand its organization, advancements and progress. This is also precisely the tension pointed out by Marx—of the isolated versus the social individual—reproduced in the quest to measure the productivity of knowledge production.

Contemporary productivity measures imposed on academic labor have long been exposed as one of the key drivers of competition at all levels of science and HE sectors. From individual academics and institutions, to the competition of national systems themselves, the commensuration of academic labor allows for constant benchmarking and vertical stratification (Reitz, 2017). Competition, as its object, has an elusive notion of excellence (Moore et al., 2017) that lacks its very substance (Readings, 1996) and is constructed purely through productivity measures (Münch, 2014). This picture already reveals some important assumptions. Stratification and benchmarking act as a signal mechanism, locating places where excellence resides. As such, they are a cornerstone of the distribution of funds, which are allocated to those that excel in the global struggle for excellence.

However, the elusive notion of excellence, having its roots in eugenicist founding fathers of bibliometrics, posits the individual as a proper (un)bearer of excellence. This, in turn, becomes the primary unit of analysis for quantifying each activity that takes place within science and HE sectors. Such an assumption, resting on the ontological primacy of the individual (Szadkowski & Krzeski, 2019b; Szadkowski & Krzeski, 2022), creates tensions with the social aspect of knowledge production. Knowledge production, as such, has little to do with producing isolated individuals. Rather, in line with Marx's argument about the social individual, individualization is something that occurs by being embedded in social relations. The same is true for knowledge production, as

> an isolated investigator is impossible. … An isolated investigator without bias and tradition, without forces of mental society acting upon him, and without the effect of the evolution of that society, would be blind and thoughtless. (Fleck, 1935)

The global struggle for excellence is the exact opposite. At its premise, it doesn't conceive knowledge production as an ecosystem of relations that enable prominent scholars to emerge, but ties the individual to the notion of excellence, and asks to what extent a given individual expresses the excellence constructed through measures. From this standpoint, we can already see how the tension between social and isolated individuals is reproduced within the problem of the measure of academic labor. From this perspective, indicators reflect (in a reversed, individualizing form) nothing more than the power of a given researcher, journal or scholarly piece to create a relationship (Szadkowski & Krzeski, 2019b). The task of ontology is to account for this reversal and bring the repressed social individual to the fore.

9.4 The Emergence of the Metrological System Controlled by the Capital

Ontology needs to encounter history. We need to ask how exactly capital became, first, entangled in the process of measuring academic labor, and then how it took control over the metrological system? The history of this process still demands to be written. However, we can point to several important moments in the subordination of the measure of quality to the interests of capital. To understand this process is to understand how this task became important not only for academics themselves, but also for the state and commercial entities directly engaged in the science and HE sector on a global scale.

The late 1970s and the transition to post-Fordism overlap with a shift in the mode of HE governance and the rise of the evaluative state in Western Europe, which displaces the central bureaucracy in this role (Neave, 2012). With the coming of the evaluative state, the sector's evaluation is no longer dependent on *ex ante* means, but *ex post* evaluation takes hold in two ways. First is in the coordination of massification and teaching, and the coordination of research. Hence, there is the growing need to produce an enormous amount of calculable data, upon which states become more and more dependent in coordinating sector activity. Although this process occurs primarily on a national level, it serves as an important precondition for capital accumulation (Krzeski, 2022), as the evaluative state plays the role of capital accumulation facilitator. Second, the rise of a certain economic imaginary resulted in a wide set of real developments, strategies and policies in (higher) education, such as the Bologna process (Jessop, 2008). In the knowledge-based economy, which at least since the 1990s dominated the discourse of such international organizations as the OECD, we can find another important source of the state's dependence on data and statistics. This shapes science policy discourse (Godin, 2006b), alongside acting as a benchmark in an ongoing competition between nation-states (Jessop, 2008).

The European Union's Lisbon Strategy is a perfect example of this process of turning Europe into the most competitive, knowledge-based economy. It is a strategy that was informed by the logic of excellence, according to which real science surmounts to excellent science (Nowotny, 2006, cf. Flink & Peter, 2018). In turn, whole science and HE systems as well as individual institutions joined in this global pursuit of excellence (Münch, 2014). However, excellence proved to be an extremely elusive concept (see. Readings, 1996; Lamont, 2009), hence the need for all different proxies, most often coming in the form of bibliometric indicators (Moore et al., 2017).

A second example comes in the form of university rankings. They are, to a great extent, an effect of organizational performance discourse which took hold primarily in the US in the late 1960s and 1970s, which was preoccupied with the question of evidencing quality through quantitative means (Wilbers & Brankovic, 2021). But university rankings as a truly global phenomenon took off later, with the first global university ranking established in 2003 (Hazelkorn, 2011). Although the methodologies of global university rankings vary, they all rely on quantitative data complied about particular university activities. Taken together, all those processes contribute to and feed one another, resulting in the ever-expanding metricization of science and HE. As a result, we may call the contemporary university a metrics-driven university.

However, the Marxist critique cannot restrict itself to the aforementioned processes. Acknowledging the effects of the discursive strength of neoliberalism promoted by the state and supranational agencies, which translates into science and educational policy, can't overshadow the fact that simultaneously the sector is penetrated by capitalist entities to an ever greater degree. The growing presence of capitalist entities and the evaluative state are two sides of the same coin. This is because the evaluative state is a capitalist state in so far as it facilitates capital accumulation. Evaluative homogeneity—the main product of the evaluative state—is acting as a leveler within the sector. It decreases the level of heterogeneity within a given national or regional system (Krzeski et al., 2022). In effect, different actors within the system—be it academics, students or administration staff—all share the same point of reference in the form of given standards and criteria when performing their tasks.

This is where the capitalist comes to the fore as it is performing these activities that become continuously mediated by different capitalist enterprises present in the science and HE sector. The scale of this mediation can most vividly be seen once the process of integration of academic infrastructure is inspected. As Posada and Chen had demonstrated, companies like Elsevier and Wiley develop their products in such a way as to cover the whole research and teaching process (2018). This is important because for the last two decades, we have witnessed a process of dynamic and aggressive acquisitions of new scientific journals from large, academic publishing companies. The scale of this process allows us to speak about the oligopoly of academic publishers (Larivière et al., 2015), with revenues unlike many other industries (Puehringer et al., 2021; Grossmann & Brembs, 2021). Elsevier and its parent company Relx Group are at the forefront of this process.

Simultaneously, this process is strengthened by the position of providers of data on scholarly communication—with Scopus and Web of Science as the two commercially most widely recognized databases. These not only serve as the point of reference for academics, but more importantly as a point of reference for all sorts of evaluation, stratification and benchmarking within the sector. What makes Elsevier such an illustrative case is the fact that publishing in a narrow sense is only a part of their operations. What makes Elsevier unique is the fact that it combines the two functions, by being at the same time one of the biggest academic publishers and an owner of Scopus. As such, it is one of the companies which was most successful in benefiting from transformations of global academic labor (Szadkowski, 2019).

Elsevier allows us also to give tangible meaning to what we referred to previously as capital mediating relations within the system. Academics all around the globe not only publish in Elsevier journals, but more importantly make countless decisions informed by the data and metrics provided by Elsevier. Those metrics foreshadow their decisions on publication venues and possible scientific cooperation. Even the effects of relying on those metrics can be traced epistemologically, that is, to what themes are worthy of scientific pursuit. In turn, we see a sort of loophole in which academics constantly reproduce this mediation and become increasingly dependent on information produced by these data providers. In effect, what we are dealing with is a process of emergence and stabilization of the metrological system in scholarly communication that is controlled and sustained by capital.

This is the most fundamental premise from which Marxist critique must depart. It approaches this problem genealogically—how valuation mechanisms immanent to the sector were gradually made subservient to the capitalist enterprise. For example, how competition between scientists for the primacy of discovery was instrumentalized for the vertical stratification of institutions and even whole, national systems. Yet this premise has to be developed in three further areas. First, the metrological system sustained by capital has to be critiqued in relation to Marxist political economy.

9.5   IN: OR THE CRITIQUE OF THE POLITICAL ECONOMY OF MEASURE

An attempt to establish the (critique of) political economy of measure within the science and HE systems is still a relatively new quest. Not because the political economy is estranged from the problem of measure, but because the imposition of measure on science and HE systems is still something relatively new. Although we can trace the genealogy of performance-based metrics to the beginning of the twentieth century (Godin, 2006a), evaluative purposes were asserted much later, at least in Western science and HE systems. As we have seen, it is only with the shift in the mode of sector coordination that the gradual process of transition from *ex ante* to *ex post* evaluation was initiated. This was a process that consisted of quantification, standardization and surveillance of academic labor or, in other words, homogenization and commensuration of heterogeneous knowledge and different activities of its production and reproduction (Espeland & Stevens, 1998; De Angelis & Harvie, 2009).

How this process is addressed defines a clean break between mainstream and Marxist approaches toward (critique of) political economy of measure within science and HE sectors. If, for the former, homogenization and commensuration is merely a precondition for introducing markets and quasi-markets, for the former to remain at the level of exchange is merely to stay at the level of appearance. Homogenization, therefore, has to be grasped through its fundamental role, not as a precondition for market relations but for establishing capitalist relations within the sector.

The pioneering work on the Marxist critique of the political economy of measure within the science and HE system was done primarily by Massimo De Angelis and David Harvie (2009). As part of the larger debate on cognitive capitalism, they made a strong argument against the premature optimism of authors such as Antonio Negri, who believed that immaterial labor—knowledge production included—is beyond measure, with capital increasingly struggling to measure it. Drawing mainly on the British system and Research Excellence Framework, De Angelis and Harvie convincingly showed that this is not necessarily the case. In fact, through engagement with an evaluation of academic labor, they were able to show that capital is getting more and more proficient in (re)imposing the law of value through measuring immaterial labor. The (re)imposition of the law of value within the sector occurs on two simultaneous levels. The diachronic process—continuous pressure to squeeze more for less—reduces socially necessary labor time of immaterial production both in teaching and research. Simultaneously, the synchronic process—quantification, stratification, benchmarking—makes the heterogenous reality of science and HE commensurate.

Taking these two processes together reveals both how the law of value operates within the sector, as a technical issue, and also as a category of struggle. In that sense, De Angelis and Harvie's approach is precisely two-sided, as the measure has to be grasped through capital's struggle to impose it as well as through the circulation of struggles against that measure, both within and outside the university. But this two-sided perspective leads to further questions. First, what is the direct link between the measurement practice and the functioning of capital within the science and HE sector? Second, on what basis can we try to reconnect measure with the circulation of struggles within and beyond the sector?

Even though De Angelis and Harvie's work on the (re)imposition of value was pivotal to the Marxist critique of capitalist measure within the HE sector, it did not produce any form of consensus. Consecutive works not only highlighted different aspects of the academic metrological system, but in doing so, they reveal major theoretical differences. The closest to De Angelis and Harvie is Krystian Szadkowski (2016, 2019). He starts his critique with a critical reference to his predecessors, pointing out that the major weakness of their proposition lies in the inability to directly connect the measurement of academic labor with the presence of capital within the sector. Building on autonomist Marxist traditions, Szadkowski claims that "measure allows a social and socially-created heterogeneous wealth of relations (the common) to be revealed as value" (Szadkowski, 2019, pp. 125–26; see also Szadkowski's chapter in this volume on the common). This central thought is then developed through direct engagement with actions of capitalist data providers such as Clarivate or Elsevier to fill the gap revealed in the proposition of De Angelis and Harvie.

However, if Szadkowski builds on De Angelis and Harvie's propositions, others dismiss it altogether. This is the case of Luis Arboledas-Lérida, who critiques them for their political reading of (re)imposition of the law of value. Concentrating on scholarly communication and the role of the so-called Altmetrics, he claims that the coercive nature of research impact metric is not an effect of how capital employs measure, but rather "research impact metrics are immanent to the capitalist relationship of production" (Arboledas-Lérida, 2021, p. 463). Of course, Szadkowski and Arboledas-Lérida do not exhaust the Marxist debate over the role of measure in establishing capitalist relations within academia. Yet, as they are clear opposites of each other, they mark the boundaries of this debate.

But this debate carries with it one important problem, which we only touched upon when discussing Marx's double perspective on measure, and his point that disposable time could become the measure of wealth once the capitalist law of value collapses. Fragments that suggest that for Marx, communism is not necessarily beyond all measure (Marx, 1973). Further Marxist critiques of the political economy of a capitalist measure imposed on academic labor reflect this problem when they approach the territory of transcending capitalist organization of science and HE. For example, Szadkowski concludes his work on productive and unproductive labor by stating that "the creation of knowledge without the mediation of capital—knowledge that would contribute to the common and shared wealth—seems to require the final abandonment of the measure, or at least some form of its significant modification" (Szadkowski, 2019, p. 127). Although he seems to be torn on whether such a modification is possible, there are strong arguments for making such an effort. John Welsh, another Marxist scholar who devoted his work to the audit culture and the critique of the political economy of HE, claims that reversion to the pre-measured reality is in itself a reactionary endeavor. Instead of rejecting the measure, one can go in another direction as "there is a dialectical way through the quantification moment in capitalist civilisation" (Welsh, 2021, p. 922). In other words, the sublation of capitalist measure does not necessarily entail the sublation of measure. Rather, it provides it with a different logic and subsumes it under radically different ends. This is in no way an automatic movement of transition. Hence, in what follows we will take a look at struggles that are organized around the problem of measure.

9.6 Against: Or Academic Struggles Around Measure

Academics around the globe continuously question the current prevalence of metrics-driven academia from different positions. Connecting those critiques and the resulting resistance strategies with insight produced by the critique of the political economy of measure has, however, barely started. There are several obstacles to this task. For one, measure is often connected to affective dimensions (Beer, 2016; Lupton, 2016; Moore et al., 2017)—how it makes us feel, and by doing so, how it catalyzes overworking and burnout in the case of academia (Burrows, 2012). From this perspective, struggles against measure take the form of a struggle for a better work culture within academia. Both the rejection of measure and calls for responsible use of metrics are supposed to lead to this goal. Moreover, connecting measure to the relentless marketization of science and HE translates to longing for stronger public control over the sector, which would temper the market and its discontents. From a Marxist perspective, what is missing is the antagonistic nature of capitalist relation to which the problem of measure ultimately points.

This leads to another problem. The individualizing function of capitalist measure stands against collective action against it. Feldman and Sandoval refer to this process as creating a very particular form of an academic self (2018), which frames success and failure as purely personal. Measure is pivotal to this process, as metric power (Beer, 2016) constantly produces and reproduces subjects complying on an affective level. Measures stimulate the body and make it feel in a certain way—it produces anxiety (Burrows, 2012; Espeland & Sauder, 2016) and an academic self that is always on its toes. This is a self in which relations to others are expressed primarily through comparisons facilitated by measure.

To some extent, Marxist perspectives share this insight, as this argument is echoed in the tension between isolated and social individuals, and in highlighting the crucial role the production of subjectivity (Mezzadra, 2018; Read, 2022) plays in the reproduction of capitalist social relations. As Lebowitz puts it, "All other things equal, the people produced within particular relations of production tend to be premises for the reproduction of those relations" (2021, p. 80). From this perspective, it can be argued that one of the greatest accomplishments of capital is its growing ability to align the subject's desire with its own goals (Lordon, 2014), and measure is definitely at the forefront of this process. However, this raises the question of how complete is this process? Is metric power completely totalizing, and ultimately producing full obedience to the logic imposed through it, or is there a space for the abolition of the separation it produces?

The Marxist answer to these questions is clear. Despite the sheer force and cunning of capital, its rule is never complete. Yet we face a fundamental difficulty. As we have seen through the critique of the political economy of measure, capital reproduces itself on the practices immanent to academia to such an extent that collective action becomes more and more challenging. It corrupts the common that underpins academic endeavor, making it increasingly hard to see through the individualized academic self as artificially created and reproduced. In effect, resistance to the capitalist measure of academic labor often takes individualized rather than collective forms. Hence, the talk of micro-resistance (Anderson, 2008) manifests itself in minimal or noncompliance with managerial demands, or refusing to participate in student evaluations, staff surveys, workload interviews and other managerial exercises (Feldman & Sandoval, 2018). Critique, in turn, has to reconnect those individual struggles, and connect them to the collective realm of forging new relations between laboring subjects within academia.

Thus, the "Against" moment of critique finds its footing in those struggles which attempt to reclaim HE and create alternatives within the sector subsumed under capital. Whereas individual resistance has little chance of overcoming the separation of workers within HE sectors, building alternatives is necessarily a collective endeavor. Thus, efforts to create cooperative universities (Neary & Winn, 2016), especially those built around the common in its non-corrupted form (Szadkowski, 2019; Szadkowski & Krzeski, 2019a), show the most promise in that task. What is of interest is that the cooperative university suggests not only a complete reconceptualization of academic labor and relations within the university, but it also reimagines the role of HE in society. As Joss Winn puts it, "according to the individual's capacity, the teacher is also a student, an administrator, a cleaner, etc., and a cooperative university need not do everything that a conventional university aims to do" (Winn, 2015, p. 47).

Although it does not constitute of itself a post-capitalist, knowledge production institution, the values that drive the cooperative seem nonetheless crucial. Engaging in such initiatives is of pivotal importance for challenging capitalist individualization in science, and acts as a condition of possibility for the counter-production of subjectivity. Moreover, although they do not challenge capitalist measures of academic labor directly, how academic labor is organized within those institutions provides an important point of reference for answering a fundamental question—whether the Marxist critique of capitalist measures can advocate for a different measure.

9.7 Beyond the Capitalist Measure of Academic Labor

Critique cannot be satisfied by simple restitution of the *status quo* and returning measure to the control of the academic community for several reasons. First, it has to account for the great promise inscribed in the homogenization of measure—as a technology of communication, conventional measure facilitated human cooperation on an unprecedented scale (Kula, 2014). The argument raised by David Harvey regarding the ill-advised romanticization of the free association of producers, which disregards completely capital's advancements in coordinating production and distribution on a planetary scale, seems to echo this argument (Harvey, 2013). Academia is truly a global affair.

This, in turn, requires not only political but also enormous technological imagination to not bury knowledge production in localities. We are not talking about technological utopias here. Rather, critiques of the capitalist oligopolies that sustain and control academic metrological systems point out that, technologically speaking, we already have an infrastructure for scholarly communication beyond the mediations of companies such as Elsevier (Brembs et al., 2021). The problem seems to lie in terms of who is capable actor for bringing this change and in whose hands the new infrastructure should rest.

There is also another dimension to the ambivalence of measure that has to be accounted for when thinking about the alternative, one connected directly to the question of power relations. Part of the promise inscribed in the conventional measure was putting an end to the domination of a stronger individual who was able to impose measure upon the weaker. This has failed. Yet in the context of science and HE, it has to be recognized that homogenous measure destabilized local power relations and neo-feudal hierarchies. Rendering capitalist measure void cannot afford to bring back a situation in which control over measures lies in the hands of an academic oligarchy at the expense of other groups that constitute academia. Going beyond the capitalist measure of academic labor entails bringing plural perspectives together.

This is precisely the point to which we referred when claiming, with John Welsh, that there is a dialectical move beyond the current quantification moment. It can be introduced as dissociating the measure from endless homogenization and commensuration of knowledge reality for its capitalist valorization. The point of support for this task seems to be in the reversal of the demand that lies at the root of the universalization of measures—no longer "one measure for all time!" (Kula, 2014) but rather metrological pluralism. In other words, this task can be described as opening the metrological system for more perspectives than the quantitative advancement of knowledge hijacked by capital's quest for its endless self-valorization.

Such a task is by no means utopian. We do already have examples of organizing production by subjugating labor to multiple measures. For example, in commoning, as Massimo De Angelis observed, "social cooperation occurs notwithstanding the fact that diverse social activities are subjected not to the one measure of profit, but rather to the plural measure of a community that reproduces itself, its relations and its resources" (De Angelis, 2017, p. 221). Notice the stress that commoning puts on different members and different positionalities within a given community. Here precisely lies an important difference—it is no longer the problem of bringing the measure back under the control of an academic oligarchy, but rather rethinking different parts of the academic community and ways to overcome the opposition between academic community itself and the lay public. One can object to such an answer and point out that such a reversal and establishing metrological pluralism is nothing else than going back to the situation we tried to transcend in the first place. After all, remember that abstract measures were introduced to put an end to the situation in which the stronger imposed their measure on the weaker. Doesn't metrological pluralism bring this situation back? This is the crux of the whole matter, which goes back to the dialectical nature of sublating the current capitalist quantification moment. Taken out of context, the answer to the above question has to be yes. However, one cannot take this isolation. In the course of this chapter, we have stressed the importance of the subjective dimension. Here, it becomes clear why this is the case, as it is due to subjective dimension that we can give a negative answer to the above question.

9.8 Conclusion

Taken together, as culmination of the critical movement, the task of going beyond the imposition of capitalist measure ultimately ceases to be a technical matter—substituting one measure for another one. It rather becomes a task of creating different sets of social relations—social relations that render inequalities between different parts of the community void (Toscano, 2011). Social relations in which the heterogeneity of social wealth and heterogeneous concrete activities are no longer subsumed as equal under the capitalist measure in a form of a predetermined yardstick (Marx, 1973, p. 488).

But what exactly would render inequalities void in the context of knowledge production mean? After all, one can argue that certain hierarchies are necessary for knowledge production. Hierarchies play a crucial role in the process of production and reproduction of knowledge-producing communities, such as the socialization process to a given discipline, and they are instrumental to the division of epistemic labor. Notice, however, that rendering inequalities void in going beyond the capitalist organization of knowledge production does not entail the complete dissolution of hierarchies. Nor does it advocate for some kind of abstract equality among constitutive parts of knowledge production communities. Rather, emphasis is placed on creating such social relations that would prevent a situation in which inequalities are subsumed as equal under one homogenous and abstract measure. This, in turn, is possible only if hierarchies themselves are not fixed, but are subject to renegotiation, and constructed according to changing and not determined needs. In other words, this demands creating social relations that advance knowledge production through transindividual and collective power, and not through competition between individuals struggling to set their mark upon the given body of knowledge. If this task requires a great deal of imagination, it is precisely because it violates the most sacred underpinnings of knowledge production and forces us to think beyond them.

In the course of this chapter, we have established four crucial components of the Marxist approach toward the problem of capitalist imposition of measure upon academic labor: the tension between isolated and social individual; critique of the political economy of measure; struggles around measure; and alternatives to capitalist measures of academic labor. Taken together as the movement of critique, they reveal the richness of relations and the reality that lies behind individualist measure, that is, the common. Rather than referring beyond material reality, to the values that sanction it, the common is the material basis of all practices of knowledge production, including scientific knowledge as its particular form (Roggero, 2011).

It follows that the alternative to the capitalist measure of academic labor has to contribute to the creation of such social relations, in which differences, the heterogeneity of social wealth and heterogeneous concrete activities are no longer subsumed as equal in a form of a predetermined yardstick. In other words, it would require the creation of knowledge without capital's mediation (Szadkowski, 2019). Here, knowledge production is rooted in different principles, those of solidarity and sharing, as well as subordinated to radically different objectives—social and cooperative use of knowledge, rather than its appropriation and valorization (Hall, 2014). The pursuit of this goal will inevitably not be achieved through the reformist position toward measure, nor through the demand for autonomy and separation of the science and HE sectors from the lay society.

Acknowledgment I want to express deep gratitude to editors for their comments and support. Special thanks are due to Krystian Szadkowski for an ongoing critical dialogue that inspired and continue to inspire me in different academic endeavors. All standard caveats apply.

Disclosure Statement The author has no financial interest or benefit that has arisen from the direct applications of this research. FundingThe work of Jakub Krzeski was financially supported by the National Science Centre in Poland (NCN), Grant number UMO-2019/33/N/HS6/00434

References

Anderson, G. (2008). Mapping Academic Resistance in the Managerial University. *Organization, 15*(2), 251–270.

Arboledas-Lérida, L. (2020). Capital and the Scientific Endeavour. An Appraisal of Some Marxist Contributions to the Debate on the Commodification of Science. *Critique, 48*(4), 321–367.

Arboledas-Lérida, L. (2021). On the Coercive Nature of Research Impact Metrics: The Case Study of Altmetrics and Science Communication. *Social Epistemology, 35*(5), 461–474.

Balibar, E. (2017). *The Philosophy of Marx*. Verso Books.

Beer, D. (2016). *Metric Power*. Palgrave Macmillan.

Berg, M., & Seeber, B. K. (2016). *The Slow Professor: Challenging the Culture of Speed in the Academy*. University of Toronto Press.

Bernal, J. D. (2012). *Science in History*. Faber & Faber.

Brembs, B., Huneman, P., Schönbrodt, F., Nilsonne, G., Susi, T., Siems, R., et al. (2021). Replacing Academic Journals. *Zenodo*.

Burrows, R. (2012). Living with the H-Index? Metric Assemblages in the Contemporary Academy. *The Sociological Review, 60*(2), 355–372.

Cleaver, H. (1994). *Reading Capital Politically*. Antitheses Press.

De Angelis, M. (2017). *Omnia Sunt Communia: On the Commons and the Transformation to Postcapitalism*. Bloomsbury Publishing.

De Angelis, M., & Harvie, D. (2009). 'Cognitive Capitalism' and the Rat-Race: How Capital Measures Immaterial Labour in British Universities. *Historical Materialism, 17*(3), 3–30.

Espeland, W. N., & Sauder, M. (2016). *Engines of anxiety: Academic rankings, reputation, and accountability*. Russell Sage Foundation.

Espeland, W. N., & Stevens, M. L. (1998). Commensuration as a Social Process. *Annual Review of Sociology, 24*(1), 313–343.

Feldman, Z., & Sandoval, M. (2018). Metric Power and the Academic Self: Neoliberalism, Knowledge and Resistance in the British University. *TripleC: Communication, Capitalism & Critique, 16*(1), 214–233.

Fleck, L. (1935). *Scientific Observation and Perception in General* (Eds. R. S. Cohen & Th. Schnelle), 1986, pp. 59–78.

Flink, T., & Peter, T. (2018). Excellence and Frontier Research as Travelling Concepts in Science Policymaking. *Minerva, 56*, 431–452.

Foucault, M. (2005). *The Order of Things*. Routledge.

Freudenthal, G., & McLaughlin, P. (Eds.). (2009). *The Social and Economic Roots of the Scientific Revolution: Texts by Boris Hessen and Henryk Grossmann*. Springer Science & Business Media.

Godin, B. (2006a). On the Origins of Bibliometrics. *Scientometrics, 68*(1), 109–133.

Godin, B. (2006b). The Knowledge-Based Economy: Conceptual Framework or Buzzword? *The Journal of Technology Transfer, 31*, 17–30.

Godin, B. (2007). From Eugenics to Scientometrics: Galton, Cattell, and Men of Science. *Social Studies of Science, 37*(5), 691–728.

Grossmann, A., & Brembs, B. (2021). Current Market Rates for Scholarly Publishing Services [Version 2; Peer Review: 2 Approved]. *F1000Research, 10*, 20.

Hall, R. (2014). On the Abolition of Academic Labour: The Relationship Between Intellectual Workers and Mass Intellectuality. *tripleC: Communication, Capitalism & Critique, 12*(2), 822–837.

Hall, R., & Bowles, K. (2016). Re-Engineering Higher Education: The Subsumption of Academic Labour and the Exploitation of Anxiety. *Workplace: A Journal for Academic Labor, 28*.

Hamann, J., & Ringel, L. (2023). The Discursive Resilience of University Rankings. *Higher Education*, 1–19.

Hardt, M., & Negri, A. (2011). *Commonwealth*. Harvard University Press.

Harvey, D. (2013). *A companion to Marx's Capital, volume II*. Verso Books.

Hatch, A., & Curry, S. (2018). Evaluation Woes: We're on it, Responds DORA. *Nature, 559*(7712), 32–33.

Hazelkorn, E. (2011). Measuring World-Class Excellence and the Global Obsession with Rankings. In *Handbook on Globalization and Higher Education*. Edward Elgar Publishing.

Hicks, D., Wouters, P., Waltman, L., De Rijcke, S., & Rafols, I. (2015). Bibliometrics: The Leiden Manifesto for Research Metrics. *Nature, 520*(7548), 429–431.

Holloway, J. (2015). Read Capital: The First Sentence; or, Capital Starts with Wealth, Not with the Commodity. *Historical Materialism, 23*(3), 3–26.

Jessop, B. (2008). A Cultural Political Economy of Competitiveness and Its Implications for Higher Education. In *Education and the Knowledge-Based Economy in Europe* (pp. 11–39). Brill.

Krzeski, J. (2021). How to Imagine a Non-Capitalist Measure? Going Beyond the Value Production with Spinoza's Concept of Expression. *Critique, 49*(3–4), 325–342.

Krzeski, J. (2022). Power and Agency Within the Evaluative State: A Strategic-Relational Approach to Quantification of Higher Education. *Educational Philosophy and Theory*, 1–14.

Krzeski, J., Szadkowski, K., & Kulczycki, E. (2022). Creating Evaluative Homogeneity: Experience of Constructing a National Journal Ranking. *Research Evaluation, 31*(3), 410–422.

Kula, W. (2014). *Measures and Men*. Princeton University Press.

Lamont, M. (2009). *How Professors Think: Inside the Curious World of Academic Judgment*. Harvard University Press.

Larivière, V., Haustein, S., & Mongeon, P. (2015). The Oligopoly of Academic Publishers in the Digital Era. *PLoS One, 10*(6), e0127502.

Lazzarato, M. (1996). Immaterial Labor. *Radical Thought in Italy: A Potential Politics, 1996*, 133–147.

Lebowitz, M. A. (2003). *Beyond Capital?* Palgrave Macmillan.

Lebowitz, M. A. (2021). *Between Capitalism and Community*. Monthly Review Press.

Lordon, F. (2014). *Willing Slaves of Capital: Spinoza and Marx on Desire*. Verso Books.

Lupton, D. (2016). *The Quantified Self*. John Wiley & Sons.

Marx, K. (1969). Theses on Feuerbach. In *Marx/Engels Selected Works* (Vol. 1). Progress Publishers.

Marx, K. (1973). *Grundrisse: Foundations of the Critique of Political Economy*. Penguin Books.

Marx, K. (1978). *Capital: A Critique of Political Economy. Volume One* (Trans. B. Fowkes). Penguin Books.

Mezzadra, S. (2018). *In the Marxian Workshops: Producing Subjects*. Rowman & Littlefield.

Moore, S., Neylon, C., Paul Eve, M., Paul O'Donnell, D., & Pattinson, D. (2017). "Excellence R Us": University Research and the Fetishisation of Excellence. *Palgrave Communications, 3*(1), 1–13.
Münch, R. (2014). *Academic Capitalism: Universities in the Global Struggle for Excellence*. Routledge.
Neary, M., & Winn, J. (2016). Beyond Public and Private: A Framework for Co-Operative Higher Education.
Neave, G. (2012). *The Evaluative State, Institutional Autonomy and Re-Engineering Higher Education in Western Europe: The Prince and His Pleasure*. Springer.
Negri, A. (1991). *Marx Beyond Marx: Lessons on the Grundrisse*. Autonomedia/Pluto.
Nowotny, H. (Ed.). (2006). *Cultures of Technology and the Quest for Innovation* (Vol. 9). Berghahn Books.
Posada, A., & Chen, G. (2018). *Inequality in Knowledge Production: The Integration of Academic Infrastructure by Big Publishers*. ELPUB.
Puehringer, S., Rath, J., & Griesebner, T. (2021). The Political Economy of Academic Publishing: On the Commodification of a Public Good. *PLoS One, 16*(6), e0253226.
Read, J. (2022). The Production of Subjectivity: From Transindividuality to the Commons. In *The Production of Subjectivity: Marx and Philosophy* (pp. 342–363). Brill.
Readings, B. (1996). *The University in Ruins*. Harvard University Press.
Reitz, T. (2017). Academic Hierarchies in Neo-Feudal Capitalism: How Status Competition Processes Trust and Facilitates the Appropriation of Knowledge. *Higher Education, 73*, 871–886.
Roggero, G. (2011). *The Production of Living Knowledge: The Crisis of the University and the Transformation of Labor in Europe and North America*. Temple University Press.
Stengers, I. (2018). *Another Science is Possible: A Manifesto for Slow Science*. John Wiley & Sons.
Szadkowski, K. (2016a). Socially Necessary Impact/Time: Notes on the Acceleration of Academic Labor, Metrics and the Transnational Association of Capitals.
Szadkowski, K. (2016b). Towards an Orthodox Marxian Reading of Subsumption (s) of Academic Labour Under Capital. *Workplace: A Journal for Academic Labor, 28*.
Szadkowski, K. (2019). An Autonomist Marxist Perspective on Productive and Un-Productive Academic Labour. *TripleC: Communication, Capitalism & Critique. Open Access Journal for a Global Sustainable Information Society, 17*(1), 111–131.
Szadkowski, K., & Krzeski, J. (2019a). In, Against, and Beyond: A Marxist Critique for Higher Education in Crisis. *Social Epistemology, 33*(6), 463–476.
Szadkowski, K., & Krzeski, J. (2019b). Political Ontologies of the Future University: Individual, Public, Common. *Philosophy and Theory in Higher Education, 1*(3), 29–49.
Szadkowski, K., & Krzeski, J. (2022). Conceptualizing Capitalist Transformations of Universities: Marx's Relevance for Higher Education Research. *Critique, 50*(1), 185–203.
The Slow Science Academy. (2010). *The Slow Science Manifesto*. http://slow-science.org/slow-science-manifesto.pdf
Toscano, A. (2011). Divine management. *Angelaki, 16*(3), 125–136.
Vostal, F. (2016). *Accelerating Academia: The Changing Structure of Academic Time*. Palgrave Macmillan.
Welsh, J. (2021). Stratifying Academia: Ranking, Oligarchy and the Market-Myth in Academic Audit Regimes. *Social Anthropology/Anthropologie sociale, 29*(4), 907–927.

Wilbers, S., & Brankovic, J. (2021). The Emergence of University Rankings: A Historical-Sociological Account. *Higher Education*, 1–18.

Wilsdon, J. (2016). The Metric Tide: Independent Review of the Role of Metrics in Research Assessment and Management.

Winn, J. (2015). The Co-Operative University: Labour, Property and Pedagogy. *Power and Education, 7*(1), 39–55.

Wouters, P. (1999). *The Citation Culture*. Universiteit van Amsterdam.

Zuboff, S. (2020). *The Age of Surveillance Capitalism: The Fight for a Human Future at the New Frontier of Power*. PublicAffairs.

CHAPTER 10

Classroom as a Site of Class Struggle

Raju J. Das

10.1 Introduction

According to Rosengarten (2014, 135), the author of *Revolutionary Marxism of Antonio Gramsci*, intellectual understanding involves five activities: intellectuals 'examine, clarify, argue, advocate, and theorise points of view related to areas of broad general interest'. Unfortunately, the author skips the work of asking questions, or critique. An intellectual understanding that prompts critique or questioning reveals the objective reasons for humanity's problems (poverty, inequality, global warming, etc.) and helps people see that many existing ideas that are being propagated about the causes of these problems and about the current social order are inadequate (on a critical discussion on the notion of critique, see Das, 2014).

Questioning is a medium through which we clarify our own thinking as well as others'. It is a medium through which we oppose the current social order too: we oppose not only the objective processes that create humanity's major problems but also the ideas that the system inculcates in us, the ideas that weaken our ability to fight the system. Cultivating a culture of questioning the world is especially important in the current times when the fascistic forces are curtailing the freedom to speak and criticize.

An important space for questioning is academia, which is a vital part of the intellectual arena. Academia is like a machine-producing machine, as Gramsci (1971, 15) would say, as would Althusser, Marx, Lewontin, and others discussed below. After all, as they train their students, university teachers, the

R. J. Das (✉)
York University, Toronto, ON, Canada
e-mail: rajudas@yorku.ca

© The Editor(s) (if applicable) and The Author(s), under exclusive license to Springer Nature Switzerland AG 2023
R. Hall et al. (eds.), *The Palgrave International Handbook of Marxism and Education*, Marxism and Education,
https://doi.org/10.1007/978-3-031-37252-0_10

people who specialize in thinking, produce thinking-people. In this chapter, I mainly focus on the classroom aspect of academia.

Students asking questions to their educators is a form of their active participation in the learning process, which is otherwise a process of alienation: their active participation should be seen as a necessary part of their self-education. Besides, the vast majority of students are also future *workers*; many of them are already workers as they need to earn money to fund their education. So, developing a critical perspective on society, of which questioning is an important component, is crucial to students' own intellectual and working lives and to the lives of their co-workers who may not be students and with whom they interact. When students question their educators, this might also contribute to their educators' re-education, and thus contribute, to some extent, to a non-alienated collaborative learning environment.

Viewing the classroom as a site of class struggle has many advantages. Three might be mentioned here. First, students in the classroom perform a kind of labor which is alienated (Cleaver, 2006). It is alienated in part because they receive an education which does not quite reflect their own material conditions and their own intellectual interest. This happens in a system which treats them as current/future workers *for* capitalists. They are also required to study in an environment which is competitive and antagonistic.[1] Second, given that education is increasingly produced and sold as a commodity, university teachers' labor produces value and surplus value, so they are productive laborers who, like other productive laborers, experience alienation which involves teaching under multiple constraints imposed by the system; the latter might prompt class struggle on their part which can open up ways in which they (along with their students) may both refuse capitalist work and create space for alternative educational projects that better meet their own needs (Cleaver, 2006; Harvie, 2006).[2] Third, as Lenin (1918) says, it is a bourgeois lie that 'schools could stand above politics and serve society as a whole'. True education of the working class is a deeply political process. He also claims that socialists' 'work in the sphere of education is part of the struggle for overthrowing the bourgeoisie' and that 'the revolutionary struggle [is] the finishing school for the [masses]' (ibid.).[3]

The remainder of the chapter is split into four sections.[4] Section 10.2 provides brief clarifications about the nature of capitalist class society and ideological class struggle from above and from below, in academia, including especially, the classroom. Section 10.3 presents a series of questions from the standpoint of the students who can oppose the ideas circulating in the academic classrooms as a part of their ideological class struggle from below. These questions concern professors' philosophical worldviews as well as their views on the nature of society, and on what is to be done to change society. Section 10.4 suggests that questioning is not enough, so students should make a series of demands on the academic system to improve the quality of their education and their working lives. This section also discusses the ways in which students and teachers can create alternative spaces for critical education. The final section summarizes the chapter and draws political implications of the class struggle from below in academia for the fight for a democratic society beyond capitalism.

10.2 Classes, Capitalism, Class Struggle, and Classroom

Academia in general, and the classroom in particular, can only be understood when it is seen as a part of society. And the most important attribute of the current society is that it is a class society. So one must begin with class theory.[5] Classes exist when one group, a minority, effectively controls society's productive resources and appropriates the surplus labor (or surplus product) from the majority who do not have control over these resources. Relations between classes are consequently antagonistic relations, whereby the ruling class benefits at the expense of the exploited classes. Given this, class struggle is always a possibility, which is also concretely expressed from time to time.

For the last 10,000 years or so, society has remained class-divided. The modern society—capitalism—is the most developed form of class society. Capitalism is a society dominated by market relations, a society where nearly all the use-values (wealth) take the form of commodity (Marx, 1887, 27). Indeed, in capitalism, the things people need to reproduce themselves (i.e. means of subsistence such as food and shelter and large parts of education and healthcare systems) and means of production (land, mines, factories, machines, etc.) are bought and sold as is people's ability to work. Capitalism is more than a market society: it is a society where wage workers are separated (and where large sections of small-scale property-owners are still in the process of being separated) from their control over property and from the surplus value that they produce and are alienated from the everyday process of production itself. The working masses lack effective control over state power too. For their continuation, class relations require—and reinforce—oppression of people based on gender, race, and other such identities. Given capitalism's internal class antagonism, class struggle is always immanent in capitalism. Like all previous forms of class society, capitalism is to be seen as a transient stage in human history, and not the end of humanity's evolution, although when, whether, and how capitalism is/will be transcended depends on the outcome of class struggle (Das, 2022a).

It is mistaken to equate class struggle to the struggle of the exploited or the working masses (wage/salary workers and small-scale producers). Class struggle is class struggle both from below and from above. Class struggle from below is when the exploited class fights in its own interest, that is, when common people engage in struggles to improve their conditions, economically and politically. This happens in two ways: common people, the working masses, fight against the symptoms of the system for temporary economic and political reforms (trade union struggle, or a lower stage of class struggle), and they fight for the abolition of wage-slavery and for the seizure of capitalist state power (a higher stage of class struggle, which includes the lower stage of struggle). Lower-class opposition to capitalism indeed takes forms of opposition to market relations; private property relations; exploitation relations and relations of dispossession of small-scale producers; relations of imperialist subjugation of the South and the concrete effects of all these capitalist relations (e.g. poverty, inequality, low wages, and attacks on union rights).

Class struggle from above is when the ruling class engages in its struggles to counter the opposition from the exploited masses and to defend and expand its class power to continue to monopolize society's productive resources and use them to make profit at the expense of the masses, and to politically subjugate them by using state power which fundamentally belongs to the ruling class.

As already indicated, class struggle takes material, that is, political-economic, form. It also takes ideological form. So, class struggle occurs over *interests* and *ideas*, respectively. Class struggle takes a material from when there is a fight over the opposed class-*interests*, which are both economic and political. In its material form, struggle happens not only in the workplaces (e.g. fight over wages) but also in the wider political sphere (e.g. struggles over democratic rights or the resources for public services). Class struggle takes an ideological form when it happens in the realm of ideas, which, ultimately, concern opposed class-interests. Ideas are system-opposing and system-supporting. As Lenin (1902, 23) said: 'in a society torn by class antagonisms there can never be a non-class or an above-class ideology', so ideas in the modern society, are, ultimately, socialist or bourgeois.

Marx's *Capital volume 1* provides a theory of objective class relations and subjective class struggle (Das, 2017). Ideological struggle is a necessary condition for a successful struggle over economic interests. 'Without revolutionary theory there can be no revolutionary movement' (Lenin, 1902, 12). One can also say that without ideas in support of bourgeois society, the latter cannot be reproduced. Not surprisingly, Marx's social theory (historical materialism) focuses not only on economic interests of different classes and class-fractions, but also on the 'ideological forms in which [people] become conscious of [the] conflict [over economic interests] and fight it out' (Marx, 1859). Marx's political economy illustrates this.

In capitalism, productive resources (means of production) are controlled by the top 1–10%, so the vast majority are economically forced to rely on wage-work and thus experience 'dull economic compulsion' (Marx, 1887, 523). It is not enough for the minority-class to control/monopolize resources (or money capital), however. To serve as capital, money has to be a part of a circuit, M-C-M$'$: capitalists invest money to make more money by buying labor power and productive resources and by appropriating surplus value from workers. This is the economic aspect of the capital circuit. It has a political aspect too. For capitalism to be reproduced, it is not enough that capitalists control capital and invest it to appropriate surplus value which they reinvest in successive cycles of accumulation.

The potential lower-class opposition, including to surplus value production and private property, must be averted too. Doing so requires potential and/or actual use of coercive state power (e.g. police against workers on the picket-lines) as well as providing some cheap revocable concessions. But neither (dull) economic compulsion nor (brutal) extra-economic compulsion nor (cheap) concessions are enough: additionally, the capitalist class and its state must ensure that common people possess *ideas* which make them freely/voluntarily accept the existing relations and mechanisms of society as natural or as, more or less, inherently good for all.

Capitalism requires that common people believe that even if the current world has some problems, a world beyond capitalist production and exchange is not possible, for capitalism is the final destination of human history. There is a need to naturalize capitalism, and to neutralize (or minimize) the potential for lower-class opposition to capitalism. In short, for the reproduction of capitalism, it is necessary that there be a 'working class, which by *education*, tradition, habit, looks upon the conditions of that mode of production as self-evident laws of Nature' (Marx, 1887, 523; italics mine). Capital not only manufactures commodities for profit. It also manufactures consent of common people for the voluntary acceptance of the system of commodity production for private profit by utilizing various institutions (e.g. the state apparatus).

Ideological Class Struggle from Above in Academia

Marx forgot to say that much of this education and habit formation happens in the academic classroom (and in other parts of the *educational* system). Indeed, 'The structure of social relations in education develops the types of personal demeanour, modes of self-presentation, self-image, and social-class identifications which are the crucial ingredients of job adequacy' (Hill, 2017, 44). Thus the academia in general, and the classroom in particular, serve as a space for disseminating ideas necessary to reproduce a working class that more or less accepts capitalism.

The ideological struggle from above is launched through a set of 'ideological state apparatuses' or ISA (Althusser, 2001). The education system is 'the dominant ideological State apparatus in capitalist social formations' (ibid., 104). This is where students learn the knowledges that not only help them become workers for capitalists but also willingly accept capitalist production and exchange as the normal state of affairs. Capitalism tends to reduce 'intellectual activity to serving the needs of the labour process, subordinate as it is to capital, and thus eliminating the critical component of reflexive thought' (O'Neill & Wayne, 2017b, 169). Or, as Hill (2017, 46) says, 'education systems are … locked into and … supportive of the current requirements of the capitalism'.

Generally, professors propagate bourgeois ideology, a set of ideas (a combination of truths, half-truths, and lies) that, more or less, justify the reproduction of capitalism as it is, or as it is slightly modified. According to the Marxist biologist Lewontin (1979, 25), 'The university is a factory that makes weapons—ideological weapons—for class struggle, for class warfare, and trains people in their use' (ibid.). For example, in a typical economics classroom, lectures naturalize capitalism, idealize its so-called free market, and present empiricist quantitative analyses of a system as the best that humanity could achieve (Heller, 2016). Similarly, in emphasizing the role of distance (*spatial/geographical* forms of human activities) and *natural* environment, geography classrooms disseminate ideas that under-emphasize the role of exploitative processes in and across societies and that provide descriptive features about different places and regions without much discussion of underlying spatially invariant class relations. Biology teaches biological determinism, the idea 'that everything is in our genes, that differences in status, wealth and power are inevitable' (Lewontin, 1979, 26). Biological determinism offers a reason why it is impossible to build a communist society, 'in which, despite the [biological] differences, everyone would get the same psychic and material benefits from society' (ibid.).

The ruling class, along with its state, utilizes a two-pronged strategy of ideological class struggle in academia, including in the classroom. Firstly, it directly or indirectly controls, to a large extent, the material basis of the university (university funding). This allows the ruling class to, more or less, control the production of ideas about the natural and social world and their dissemination in the classroom. Much emphasis is given to technical and business-organization-oriented education aimed at improving productive forces (e.g. skilled workers, better machines, better methods of management) to increase the rate of surplus value relative to labor compensation. Education in support of capitalist values is prioritized too. The classroom caters to the capitalist class, covertly and overtly. After all,

> The class which has the means of material production at its disposal, has control at the same time over the means of mental production, so that thereby, generally speaking, the ideas of those who lack the means of mental production are subject to it. (Marx & Engels, 1845)

Such ideas are presented in the classroom regularly. This tendency has become particularly strong since the turn to capitalism's neoliberal form in the post-1970s world (Clawson & Leiblum, 2008, 16).

Secondly, academia, including the classroom, blunts the system-opposing ideas, in particular Marxism. Broadly in service to the university on behalf of the ruling class and its state, and aware of the (possibility of) class struggle from below, most professors and administrators 'speak in the class-free, technocratic language of professional competence', while they 'have no particular difficulty judging Marxism and Marxists in class terms' (Horton, 1977, 79) which they suppress in the classroom, sometimes covertly, sometimes, overtly. 'There is a well-known saying that if geometrical axioms affected human interests attempts would certainly be made to refute them' (Lenin, 1908). This applies to

Marxism, which is a class-focused scientific theory of the need for, and obstacles to, communist society. Marxism 'directly serves to enlighten and organise the advanced class [i.e. the working class] in modern society', and it 'indicates the tasks facing this class and demonstrates the inevitable [need for the] replacement ... of the present system by a new order', that is, communism, which is why 'this doctrine has had to fight for every step forward in the course of its life' (Lenin, 1908; see also Das, 2019, 2020). A result of all the ruling class struggle in academia against communism is the fact that students receive an education that fails to help them understand the world scientifically (or objectively) and critically, that is, to understand the world in a manner that grasps the root of social-ecological problems of humanity.

Ideological Class Struggle from Below in Academia

Just as the sites of material production are the sites of class struggle from below, the sites of ideological production are sites of class struggle from below too. The system-reproducing ideas that represent ideological class struggle from above are challenged by ideological class struggle from below. After all, society has contested the idea that, for example, if a capitalist has paid the worker enough to have the energy to work for 24 hours, the worker should work for 24 hours. And the academia in general, and the classroom in particular, serve as a space, however limited, for disseminating these ideas.

The ideas propagated in the classroom in support of the capitalist class and/or its state can be, and are, challenged by students who are not only students but also 'future workers' (and indeed by those few professors who are the organic intellectuals of ordinary people). If the academia is a weapons factory, 'engaged in the manufacture [and distribution] of ideological instruments of class domination', class struggle from below by progressive teachers and students can and 'must make its weapons useless, prevent their use on the battlefield of class warfare', especially, in the classroom, and they must 'attempt to create other weapons—counter weapons—that can be put into the hands of people', including in the classroom, 'on the other side of the class struggle' (Lewontin, 1979, 26).

Firstly, progressives and Marxists (i.e. counter-hegemonic intellectuals) 'must demystify and destroy the obfuscation which is part of the ruling class ideological weaponry' (ibid.). As experts who study the natural and social worlds, through teaching activities, they must talk about the natural and the social world 'as it really is' (ibid., 27). Secondly, there is a need to create 'alternatives [radical ideas] that cannot be used by the weapon-makers of the university' and thus 'to create [intellectual] weapons that can be used by our side in the class struggle' (p. 27). There is a need to disseminate these ideas in the classroom. Ideological class struggle from below must unpack—demystify—how academia has been a site of class struggle from above. The ideological class struggle from below within academia, including in the classroom, must reveal the fundamental problems with it. These problems produce an unsatisfactory education for the students. There is space only for discussing what can be broadly called philosophical problems.

To understand anything properly, one has to have a theory, a theory that says, among other things, that an object, X, by virtue of its internal structure and by virtue of its relations to other objects within the overall system of which X is a part, causes Y (or is a necessary condition for Y), other things constant. It is theory that helps one connect the different parts of society, or the different concepts, one to another. Theory, the production of which requires a mastery over existing ideas and a constructive critique of these ideas, helps us derive generalized lessons from historical experiences (good and bad), and to produce a coherent picture of society. And, one has to be committed to the idea that scientifically produced knowledge is superior to claims based on superstition, personal belief, feeling, intuition, personal/group identity, and so on.

Many educators do not, however, believe in the need for theoretical thinking. There are many educators, in STEM and also outside STEM, who are just keen on their students to see the world for themselves, either in the laboratory or in the field (a city, a forest, etc.) without a proper theory. But without a theory, one may see many things without really seeing anything (much). And, with the post-modernist turn, the commitment to facts, reason, theorizing at the level of social totality, including its long-term dynamics, and the scientific character of knowledge, has been weak in academia including in classroom lectures.

Theory—or, broadly, intellectual thinking—is linked to political action (Das, 2019, 2022b). Professors in the classroom are generally not explicit about their own political stance (i.e. their views on what needs to be done about the things we study). They hardly talk about the connection between their political stance and their intellectual ideas that they offer in the classroom, when in fact there *is* such a connection. Indeed,

> If it is possible to place a given person's general type of thought on the basis of his [or her] relation to concrete practical problems, it is also possible to predict approximately, knowing his [her] general type of thought, how a given individual will approach one or another practical question. (Trotsky, 1942, 49)

To adequately explain the world, one has to agree on certain other principles too. These include the idea that: (a) there are objectively existing structures of relations and processes, whose contingent reproduction is then influenced by how people think and act; (b) things in our life are not creations of thought, although ideas can play important role in social change. Employing such principles—which put the accent on the materiality of life and its contradictory character—will compel an honest, scientifically focused thinker to critically examine the topic of the class character of society and the state, a topic that includes crucial issues such as the control over the means of production by a minority-class, the nature of the state, people's collective agency as it is rooted in relations of production and exchange (Das, 2017, 2022c).

But this does not generally happen in the classroom. As a site of class struggle from above, the university has been dominantly a place of what Gramsci called 'traditional intellectuals' who falsely consider their intellectual pursuit as independent from any social class, while producing ideas that help the reproduction of capitalist society. 'Scholarly work has been, and is still often, understood as "objective," "detached," and "disinterested"' (Hosseini, 2021).

Given the general absence of a commitment to a theoretical understanding of society at its root and of an emphasis on the material and contradictory aspects of social life, not only research but also classroom teaching suffers. Indeed, classroom academic practices often focus on a) the purely environmental or biological issues in isolation from social-class issues, or b) the individual human being (or culturally defined groups of individuals) abstracted from their contradictory social-material relations (i.e. class relations) or c) the intricate empirical complexity of a place (e.g. a particular city) or a part of society (e.g. a particular economic activity) without saying anything (much) about society as a whole. Often society is divided by professors in their lectures into numerous groups (e.g. women, refugees, indigenous peoples, heterosexual people). These divisions *are* important as they point to the subjugation of large segments of humanity. However, the academic approach emphasizing difference that is constantly propagated in the classroom fails to recognize that the various identity groups are related to one another in terms of their conditions of living, and that each of them is connected to the overall contradiction-ridden social-material (=class) character of society. Underlying the sectoral intellectual approach taught in the classroom is the political idea that society as a whole cannot be changed and that only small parts (e.g. some of the conditions of women or of Blacks, or of the incarcerated) can be changed, and, that too, in ameliorative ways.

In the classroom, critical approaches *are* offered. This is evident from the widespread use of such terms as critical sociology and critical human geography, but such critique is often confined to the critique of, for example, special oppression (mainly non-material) of certain groups rather than the critique of the total society or social totality—capital*ism*, a society that thrives on special oppression. And any critique of capitalism is often a (rather mild) critique of a specific *form* of capitalism (e.g. neoliberalism) or of its excesses (e.g. very low wages here, extreme form of ecological degradation there), which can be regulated and changed (a little).

So, in general, classroom-discussions fail to help students to critically theorize the *totality* of capitalist society, in terms of its major dimensions (economic, political, cultural, ecological, and geographical), and to empirically study that totality, from the standpoint of not only describing/explaining it and thus scientifically finding an order in society that stems from the objective material-social conditions, but also radically transcending the society.

10.3 What Kind of Questions for What Kind of Society and Education?

In the light of the foregoing discussion, let me provide some examples of questions that students themselves might consider asking their educators as a part of their ideological class struggle from below, including especially, in the classroom. With some justification, it can be said that: educators *as a group* (and especially, those with tenure) must be (re)educated. Marx (1845) indeed said as much: 'it is essential to educate the educator himself'. Educators must be humble enough to listen to students' questions and be prepared to be educated by them. Students—as learners and as future workers—must be courageous enough to assume the role of educators. To ask the kinds of questions I suggest that students ask, I invite them to consider assuming the role of what Gramsci calls organic intellectuals of the working masses.

Questions About the Science of Society

What is the main (major) social division—cleavage—in the current society? How would you respond to the idea that the major contradiction/division is between the two major classes—that is, between the vast majority of men and women who have little/no control over the means of production (e.g. land, mines, factories, department stores and research labs) and a small minority, which do? Do you think that the major division in society is between: men and women; non-whites and whites; foreign-born and native-born; indigenous communities and their settler colonizers; and so on? If one of these latter divisions is the primary one, what is the objective social origin of that division?

Do you agree that the wealth of those who control society's means of production (say, top 1–10% of wealth-owners) comes basically from the fact that workers receive in the form of wages/salary only a part of the value they produce, and secondarily, from small-scale producers not obtaining a remunerative price for the fruits of their labor? Are poverty and inequality unfortunate by-products of capitalism or are they inherent to it? Is there still something called imperialism, or, is imperialism an outdated concept, because there are increasing geographical flows of commodities and capital? Can capitalist production and exchange happen without significant environmental damage?

What is the state's fundamental role in society? Do you agree that state's main role is to preserve the existing property relations on the basis of the actual use and/or the threat to use force, cheap and limited material concessions and ideological interventions, in order to make common people actively or passively accept the current social arrangements? Or, is the state above the two basic classes?

Do you believe that society's major problems will be solved if common people work harder and have better moral values and help each other based on norms of trust and reciprocity? How would you respond to the idea that genetic or neural differences explain inequality in people's achievements? Do you think that humanity's major problems will be solved by unfettered market mechanisms which allow private property owners to do business as they like? Or, do you believe that while the socio-economic conditions under which people live should be, more or less, left to the market, the state should intervene only when market failures occur? Do you think that the state should look after the poor and the marginalized who are excluded from the limited opportunities that the market provides?

What is your conception of a good society that informs your classroom lectures and writings? Do you imagine a future society that is a slightly better form of capitalism, that is, a capitalism, where there is slightly more economic equality, there is a little less environmental damage, there is less oppression of women and racialized minorities, and there is greater balance in development between cities and villages and among them? Or do you imagine a future society that is *fundamentally* different from the existing one, that is, a communist society that is beyond the imperative of profit-making (on the part of big corporations/banks), where there is economic and political democracy, and where major productive resources are democratically and collectively controlled by men and women of different races and nationalities to directly meet human needs in an egalitarian, peaceful, ecologically sane, and geographically equitable manner and where the distinction between manual and mental labor and between rural and urban areas is gradually abolished? And, if society has to change in fundamental ways, which group of people—students, women, capitalists, government officials, peasants, people of the Global South, racially oppressed groups, or the working class, leading the small-scale producers and specially oppressed groups—is the most important agent in such a project, and why, and how exactly can they replace the current social order?

Philosophical Questions

Given that our philosophical views shape our thinking, what sorts of philosophical views do you hold? More specifically: Do you think that there are things in the social world (e.g. stock market, built environment, forests, factories, the need to go to work for a wage) that are, more or less, independent of how we think about them right now, or do they exist, more or less, as social-mental constructions? Is it possible to assess a society merely based on how people think about themselves and about the society as a whole; in other words, is it possible to combat 'the real existing world when one is 'merely combating the phrases of this world' (Marx & Engels, 1845)?

What do you make of the idea that human beings must first of all eat, drink, have shelter, clothing, healthcare, transit, and so on, before they can engage in politics, science, art, religion, and watch movies on Netflix and give Zoom lectures? In other words, what do you make of the idea that material conditions which exist under objective social relations are the primary explanation of things happening in our lives, even while material conditions are affected by discursive aspects of society? Do you believe in the doctrine of equal validity, that all ideas about a given object or process are equally valid? To what extent is adequate knowledge based on reason and evidence as opposed to mere intuition, feelings, and beliefs? Is scientific knowledge superior to other ways of knowing?

Do you think that the nature of a thing/process depends on its relations to other things/processes, that the relations in the world form totalities, which change over time, and that major societal changes are driven by their internal contradictions in society? While you talk about change, do you recognize that change is both gradual change, and change-by-leap, which happens when quantitative change gets transformed into qualitative change? Do you agree that at this current stage of human society, changing the parts requires changing the whole and that there are severe limits to quantitative, that is, gradual (reformist), change?

How correct is it to assume that social processes operate on the head of a pin, that is, that their outcomes are the same everywhere? Why indeed is university instruction often so geographically parochial? Why is it that a) social processes in Western Europe and North America are often taken as the norm, and b) ideas that explain what happens in these regions at a rather concrete level often remain the main academic focus in the classroom? Why is it not adequately recognized that what happens in the 'Western societies' is deeply connected to what happens in the Global periphery (where most people of the world live), and *vice versa*. Why do the reading lists used in the classroom include literature more or less from the western countries rather than what Marx calls in the *Manifesto* 'a world literature' (Das, 2022a). Conversely, why is it that an idea developed in Europe must necessarily be seen as having limited relevance to the less developed world? Isn't there a distinction between relatively abstract ideas, whether they happen to have been developed in the UK or India, that have wider social-geographical applicability and relatively concrete concepts that do not?

10.4 Going Beyond Questioning: And Educating—The Educators

Mere critique—questioning—of the professors is not enough, however. Students should also consider making demands on academia and on society in order to improve their life inside the classroom and outside. They should demand rights to question their educators without covert/overt retaliation from them and/or the state. They should demand curricular change to make it possible for them to receive rigorous theoretical training based on scientific temper. They must demand selective 'de-colonization', diversity and de-bourgeois-fication of the classroom: their educators must not only come from various social-cultural and geographical backgrounds but also must teach ideas that do not treat capitalism and class relations including private property as eternal. Students must demand that curriculum must reflect the interests of the majority (the masses), that is, people of different races, nationalities, genders, etc., who must work for wage or/and who must sell small amounts of goods/services to feed themselves, many of whom are brutalized by police and subjected to all kinds of social-cultural discrimination.

Students must take responsibility for their own education too by taking a part of their education outside of the classroom. They could, for example, form reading groups where they read books/articles/blogs on certain topics on their own and outside of the classroom, because these readings and topics are typically excluded—or are given only lip service—in the classroom.[6] Often the best of academic ideas is originally from non-academic scholars—for example, radical and communist scholars, and anti-war and environmental activists—who, unlike most academics, produce ideas as a part of their effort to change the world.

Another major source of education is, of course, the *intent* of students (the students as young intellectuals and as future workers) to radically change the society in which they receive education, and, where possible, their actual *participation* in the process of change—both on campus and off-campus. Students must demand an immediate stop to the commodification and creeping corporate control over education and its bureaucratization. They must demand that classroom has no place for pseudo-scientific, religious, and irrational hyper-nationalist ideas. Obstacles that students will face when they make these demands will be an enormous source of their own education.

After years of education, students accumulate a huge amount of debt. As well, the majority of the students will remain un- or under-employed, or they will be employed without a living wage or job security. These *material* facts cannot but adversely impact their education. An important part of student politics must therefore be a demand that all able-bodied men and woman obtain secure employment with an inflation-adjusted living wage and without any social-cultural discrimination. Students cannot receive a good education if it is delivered by people who are insecurely employed on meager wages and/or by those who do not enjoy freedom of expression. So, students must also demand that their teachers have a secure job and enjoy adequate compensation, and enjoy academic freedom. What is required is that student politics must be a part of a broader 'alliance' of forces including workers, small-scale producers, educators, and all those who fight against attacks on livelihood and democratic rights.

10.5 Conclusion

Class struggle is a necessary aspect of a class-divided society. While ordinary people engage in struggles to improve their conditions, the ruling class engages in struggles to defend its privileges. Thus, class struggle is *from below* and *from above*. And, class struggle occurs over the opposed class-*interests*, and in the sphere of *ideas* which, ultimately, concern the interests of opposed classes.

The need for ideological class struggle from above arises from the fact that common people must, more or less, voluntarily possess ideas which make them accept the existing exploitative conditions as natural or as inherently good for all. But the system-supporting ideas are challenged too, which is how ideological class struggle from below happens. Academia, including the classroom, is a major site of ideological struggle, from above and from below. To say that the university is not a space of the production of pro-capitalist ideas 'would be to adopt the liberal Enlightenment fantasy of the university as a free space beyond the workings of power', and that 'educational institutions play no part in economic exploitation and state domination' (Mills, 2014).

Generally, professors teach ideas that, more or less, justify the reproduction of capitalism as it is or in slightly modified forms, and give the impression that the classroom is class-neutral. These ideas can be challenged by students who are not only students but also 'future workers' (and by those few professors who are the organic intellectuals of ordinary people). Given the fascistic threat, and given massive inequality in a crisis-ridden society which underlies that threat, professors and students cannot assume the role of neutral observers. Without class struggle from below, whatever limited legitimacy academia has in the eyes of the masses will be risked. The ideological class struggle from below, in which students have a crucial role to play, must delegitimize the idea in that the classroom is class-neutral. As long as there is capitalism how can ideas about capitalism remain class-neutral?

I have emphasized the importance of theory in education, and have said that to develop a theoretical understanding, one needs to develop a culture of questioning. But there is a caveat. As Althusser (1970, 9) said: 'It is essential to learn with theory—but at the same time and crucially, it is essential to learn with the masses'. Students, as future workers (and many are already workers), have much in common with working people outside of the university. These people—their suffering and their struggles—are an immense source of learning. When students and workers fight for their rights together, that fight benefits both and that fight becomes a source of education for students.

Theory, including its criticisms, is necessary. But it is not enough to change society, including the educational experience of students in it. Questioning professors is not enough. Nor is mere educational change involving the introduction of more progressive curriculum enough: 'educational change cannot overthrow capitalism' (Hill, 2017, 47). 'The weapon of criticism', in itself, to paraphrase Marx (1844), that progressive students/educators (and others) may wield 'cannot … replace criticism by weapons' in the hands of the masses, for the material force of the capitalist structure must be overthrown by the material force of the political power of class-conscious organized masses. But that does not mean that the weapon of revolutionary or radical theory, to which progressive students/teachers can collaboratively contribute as a part of their ideological class struggle from below, is impotent: indeed, when students succeed in their demand that professors teach them ideas that help them understand the world at its root—that is, understand how it is that the root of society's problems ultimately is in the class relations and in the political obstacles to the fight for the communist society—and when those ideas from the classroom slowly cross the boundaries of the classroom to grip the minds of the masses, then those ideas from the classroom can become 'a material force'.

Radical ideas in the classroom can produce room for class-struggle. The university generally does not teach these ideas, however. An ideological transitional demand[7] must therefore be made by students and progressive educators that the university do this. And attempts must also be made by students toward their self-education in the radical ideas, through their study-groups independent of the bourgeois professoriate and, when possible, through the collaboration with communist and radical activist-scholars, within and outside the classroom.

The emancipation of the students and the youth from the capitalist form of education, including capitalist ideology offered in the classroom (and elsewhere), must be an act of self-education, as a part of ideological and political class struggle from below within academia and outside, just as '[T]he emancipation of the working classes must be conquered by the working classes themselves' (International Workingmen's Association, 1864).

Disclosure Statement The author has no financial interest or benefit that has arisen from the direct applications of this research.

Notes

1. Students' alienation is from their work: this results primarily from studying what they are told to study. Their alienation is from the product of their labor: this results from their schoolwork being merely something they do because their educators or future employers require it and therefore the abilities they acquire. They are alienated from other workers, and this results from competition among students and antagonism toward professors. And they are alienated from species-being: 'this means the lack of freedom to realize one's own self-determined social being, both individually and collectively' (Cleaver, 2006).
2. This chapter has not adequately emphasized teachers' alienation and its implication for class struggle.
3. The last two points are specifically developed in Sect. 10.4.
4. The chapter is a much shorter version of Das (2023).
5. I discuss class theory in Das (2017). Also see O'Neill and Wayne (2017a) and Wright (2005).
6. My current/former graduate students at York University and I have been educating ourselves by forming a reading group which has been holding intellectual meetings (which are open for all).
7. These demands link workers' present conditions and present level of consciousness to the project of seizure of state power (Trotsky, 1942).

REFERENCES

Althusser, L. (1970). Philosophy as a Revolutionary Weapon. *New Left Review, 64*, 3–11.
Althusser, L. (2001). *Lenin and Philosophy and Other Essays*. Monthly Review Press.
Clawson, D., & Leiblum, M. (2008). Class Struggle in Higher Education. *Equity & Excellence in Education, 41*(1), 12–30. https://doi.org/10.1080/10665680701776241
Cleaver, H. (2006). On Schoolwork and the Struggle Against It. Retrieved April 1, 2023, from https://la.utexas.edu/users/hcleaver/OnSchoolwork200606.pdf
Das, R. (2014). *A Contribution to the Critique of Contemporary Capitalism: Theoretical and International Perspectives*. Nova Science Publishers.
Das, R. (2017). *Marxist Class Theory for a Sceptical World*. Brill.
Das, R. (2019). Revolutionary Theory, Academia and Marxist Political Parties. *Links: International Journal of Socialist Renewal*. Retrieved May 10, 2022, from http://links.org.au/revolutionary-theory-academia-and-marxist-political-parties
Das, R. (2020). The Marginalization of Marxism in Academia. *Monthly Review Online*. Retrieved May 10, 2022, from https://mronline.org/2020/02/06/the-marginalization-of-marxism-in-academia/
Das, R. (2022a). On *The Communist Manifesto*: Ideas for the Newly-Radicalizing Public. *World Review of Political Economy, 13*(2), 209–244.
Das, R. (2022b). Theory and Class Struggle: A Dialectical Approach. *Links: International Journal of Socialist Renewal*. Retrieved May 12, 2022, from http://links.org.au/theory-and-class-struggle-dialectical-approach
Das, R. (2022c). *Marx's Capital, Capitalism and Limits to the State: Theoretical Considerations*. Routledge.
Das, R. (2023). Capitalism, Class Struggle and/in Academia. *Critical Sociology, Advance Online Publication*. https://doi.org/10.1177/08969205231152560
Gramsci, A. (1971). *Selections from Prison Notebooks* (Ed. Q. Hoare & G. Smit). International Publishers.
Harvie, D. (2006). Value Production and Struggle in the Classroom: Teachers Within, Against and Beyond Capital. *Capital & Class, 30*(1), 1–32.
Heller, H. (2016). *The Transformations of Higher Education in the United States since 1945*. University of Chicago Press.
Hill, D. (2017). Social Class and Education. In D. O'Neill & M. Wayne (Eds.), *Considering Class* (pp. 31–50). Brill.
Horton, J. (1977). A Contribution to the Critique of Academic Marxism: Or How the Intellectuals Liquidate Class Struggle. *Synthesis, 2*(1/2), 78–104.
Hosseini, M. (2021). What is Left in the Neoliberal University? *New Politics*. https://newpol.org/what-is-left-in-the-neoliberal-university/
International Workingmen's Association. (1864). General Rules. https://www.marxists.org/history/international/iwma/documents/1864/rules.htm
Lenin, V. (1902). *What is to Be Done*. Retrieved May 20, 2022, from https://www.marxists.org/archive/lenin/works/download/what-itd.pdf
Lenin, V. (1908). Marxism and Revisionism. Retrieved May 10, 2022, from https://www.marxists.org/archive/lenin/works/1908/apr/03.htm
Lenin, V. (1918). Speech at the First All-Russia Congress on Education. Retrieved May 10, 2022, from https://www.marxists.org/archive/lenin/works/1918/aug/28.htm
Lewontin, R. (1979). Marxists and the University. *New Political Science, 1*(2–3), 25–30.

Marx, K. (1844). The Introduction to Contribution To The Critique of Hegel's Philosophy of Right. Retrieved May 20, 2022, from https://www.marxists.org/archive/marx/works/1844/df-jahrbucher/law-abs.htm

Marx, K. (1845). Theses On Feuerbach. Retrieved May 20, 2022, from https://www.marxists.org/archive/marx/works/1845/theses/theses.htm

Marx, K. (1859). *A Contribution to the Critique of Political Economy: Preface*, https://www.marxists.org/archive/marx/works/1859/critique-pol-economy/preface.htm

Marx, K. (1887). *Capital volume 1*. https://www.marxists.org/archive/marx/works/download/pdf/Capital-Volume-I.pdf

Marx, K., & Engels, F. (1845). *German Ideology*. Retrieved May 25, 2022, from https://www.marxists.org/archive/marx/works/download/Marx_The_German_Ideology.pdf

Mills, N. (2014). Louis Althusser & Academic Marxism. *Against the Current*. Retrieved June 10, 2022, from https://againstthecurrent.org/atc173/p4298/

O'Neill, D., & Wayne, M. (2017a). *Considering Class*. Brill.

O'Neill, D., & Wayne, M. (2017b). On Intellectuals. In D. O'Neill & M. Wayne (Eds.), *Considering Class* (pp. 166–184). Brill.

Rosengarten, F. (2014). *The Revolutionary Marxism of Antonio Gramsci*. Brill.

Trotsky, L. (1942). In Defense of Marxism. *Marxists.org*. Retrieved June 30, 2022, from https://www.marxists.org/archive/trotsky/idom/dm/dom.pdf

Wright, C. (2005). *Approaches to Class Analysis*. Cambridge University Press.

CHAPTER 11

Science Communication, Competitive Project-Based Funding and the Formal Subsumption of Academic Labor Under Capital

Luis Arboledas-Lérida

11.1 Introduction

Science communication (SC, hereinafter) has become a central aspect of the academic enterprise (Bucchi & Trench, 2021). SC initiatives have been growing steadily all around the world since the 1980s—a trend which has intensified in the last two decades (Guenther & Joubert, 2017). Universities, private companies, journalists, professional science communicators and even scientists themselves—they are all entangled one way or another in the so-called social conversation around science (Bucchi & Trench, 2021). Science policymakers have also become very supportive of SC. But, as a matter of course, it has not happened out of a sudden 'enthusiasm towards the democratization of knowledge' on their part (Weingart et al., 2021). Rather, an economic issue is at stake here: more and better SC is expected to lead to a more skilled workforce, on the one hand, and to greater public support toward innovation and technology-driven societal change, on the other (Davies, 2021; Weingart et al., 2021; Thorpe & Gregory, 2010).

It comes as no surprise that, in this thriving milieu, critical research in SC does not abound. In several respects, a pre-critical attitude toward SC prevails among most scholars and practitioners of SC. As an example, Davies (2021)

L. Arboledas-Lérida (✉)
University of Seville, Seville, Spain
e-mail: larboledas@us.es

found that both groups of SC experts tend to concur with the view that SC is a cultural achievement and the outcome of social progress, and that it should enhance democracy and generate economic growth. 'Economy', 'society' or 'democracy' must be read here as the equivalent of those empty abstractions that classic political economy resorted to in order to *obfuscate* the economic foundations on which the whole social edifice stands—in a word, the capitalist relations of production (Marx, 1986, p. 37). Such naive views attests to the general lack of critical attitudes that permeates the whole field of SC studies (Wynne, 2014).

However, SC is far from being neutral or 'innocent' (Davies & Horst, 2016, p. 216). As a social form, it is marked by the distinctive features of the relations of production which bind human beings in the process of production and reproduction of life. SC is a particular dimension of the system of social production based on capital, a *mode of existence* of the capitalist relations of production.[1]

Some scholars have only recently started to address SC in its historical determinacy, in its connection with capitalism. It has been argued along these lines that SC reflects those 'capitalist pressures' which grip contemporary academic knowledge production (Davies & Horst, 2016, p. 124; see also Thorpe, 2020; and Thorpe & Gregory, 2010). The commodification of academic research has inaugurated a new SC regime, ironically termed as 'Public Understanding of Science Inc.' (Bauer & Gregory, 2007, p. 44). Changes in the *content* of SC under the 'PUS Inc.' regime have been well researched: as it has been pressed into the service of profit-making by science-intensive companies, SC 'reads and looks like advertising' (Gregory, 2016).[2] Universities are also more likely to engage in relations with the media and the public, since they aim to raise their public profile and, over time, translate their higher reputation into more endowments (Väliverronen, 2021).

However, much less has been said about how 'capitalistic pressures' and the commodification of academic research transform the *forms* taken on by SC. Attention regarding this should be paid to the 'cultural shift' among *academics themselves* in relation to their participation in SC activities (Rose et al., 2020). Whereas during most part of the twentieth century scientists were highly reluctant to engaging with publics (Bensaude-Vincent, 2001; Dunwoody, 2020; Hanauska, 2020), they have assumed nowadays that SC is a basic component of their professional duties and of the scientific activity (Dudo, 2015; Fecher & Hebing, 2021). Survey data from the US and the UK show that the greatest majority of scientists participate regularly in SC activities (data reported in Loroño-Leturiondo & Davies, 2018; Rose et al., 2020). Besides, they devote to SC activities an increasing amount of time (Sommer, 2019).

Undoubtedly, SC grows as academics engage more frequently in SC activities. But, in what sense does this phenomenon relate to the 'capitalist pressures' under which academic knowledge production is today? Or, to put it another way, to what extent is the growing involvement of academics in SC activities an expression of the commodification of academic research? This chapter looks for the mediating link that goes from the ongoing transformation of the economic foundations of contemporary academia, namely, the commodification of academic research, to the 'cultural shift' experimented by the academic community in relation to SC activities. To this end, it examines project-based science communication—possibly the modality of SC in which academics engage the most (Gertrúdix et al., 2021).

The examination of project-based SC will allow to understand that the 'capitalist pressures' contained in this form of SC are those concerning the *formal subsumption of academic labor under capital*. For project-based SC is premised on a very particular funding arrangement, namely, competitive project-based funding (CPBF, hereinafter). The distinctive character of CPBF is that it builds on, reproduces and deepens the separation of academic labor from its conditions of production. Such a split, at its turn, asserts itself in the *economic dependence* of academic institutions on the sale of the products of their research activity through CPBF. Given such a standpoint, the chapter proposes to examine CPBF in the light of the Marxist category of 'formal subsumption of labor under capital' and the determinants of the capitalist relations of production that it captures.

The chapter is divided as follows: the next section discusses project-based SC and the factors that have led to the growing involvement of academics in this particular form of public communication of scientific matters. Section 11.3, in turn, focuses on the funding arrangement that makes project-based SC possible, namely, CPBF. It will be shown that CPBF is an integral component of a broader orientation for research policy which aims at making universities more economically autonomous, so that the significance of CPBF can be better grasped in its connection to the commodification of academic research. Sections 11.4 and 11.5 will explore this issue further, analyzing CPBF through the Marxist category of 'formal subsumption of labor under capital'. This examination unfolds in a twofold movement: Section 11.4 draws on Karl Marx's observations on the formal subsumption of labor under capital to reconstruct its main features; on this basis, Section 11.5 looks more closely at the relationship between funding bodies and academic institutions that CPBF articulates, in order to determine whether a process of formal subsumption of academic labor under capital operates there. Section 11.6 recapitulates the main findings and concludes.

11.2 Project-Based Science Communication

Science policy has become a key agent in the promotion of SC activities. According to the views expressed in policy documents, policymakers support SC in the expectation that it can lead to innovation and economic growth (Conceição et al., 2020; Weingart et al., 2021), be it by re-skilling the workforce or by preempting any opposition or resistance toward technology-driven societal change (Davies, 2021; Weingart et al., 2021).[3] It comes as no surprise, therefore, that one of the most widely accepted definitions of SC *explicitly* states that it should be used to generate personal positive attitudes toward science (Burns et al., 2003).

This 'policy push' in SC finds a more concrete expression, among others, in the requirements set by funding agencies regarding SC activities—project-based SC. Most funding agencies around the world now ask their grantees to carry out SC activities alongside their core research tasks (Palmer & Schibeci, 2014). Academics must perform these tasks because they are *contractually obliged to do so* (Gertrúdix et al., 2021). Some funding agencies have gone as far as making SC an *eligibility criterion* to fund research projects. One of those is the European Commission (EC). Under its current Framework Programme for Research and Innovation, *Horizon Europe*, research proposals lacking a convincing communication plan will be *dropped from the selection process* with no further ado, no matter how 'excellent' they might be in other respects. And *Horizon Europe* is the world's largest funding program for R&D, with an unsurpassed budget of €95.5 billion for seven years (2020–2027). Given such a financial muscle, EC's *Horizon Europe* shapes to a great extent the international scene of R&D, both within the European research area and beyond (through international partnerships).

Of course, the European Union is a particular constellation of capital accumulation, and its traditionally proactive approach to project-based SC (Conceição et al., 2020) is not common to all funding bodies. Project-based SC is, so to speak, 'country-sensitive': different funding bodies understand SC in a slightly different manner (Palmer & Schibeci, 2014), depending on the pressing needs that SC activities are expected to address in each particular case. Less affluent countries approach SC in the same way as more developed ones did decades ago, namely, as a form of 'public instruction' and 'science education' (ibid.). By contrast, funding agencies in more economically developed nations emphasize the contribution of SC to the social legitimation of science and the need to build 'trust' and 'confidence' in science (Palmer & Schibeci, 2014; see also Conceição et al., 2020; Weingart et al., 2021). These differences are mediated, as it were, by the global dynamics of capital accumulation and the role played by each country in the international division of labor. But the crucial point is that project-based SC is a *general* feature of the contemporary systems of R&D (see Palmer & Schibeci, 2014). This already allows, in the author's view, to grasp project-based SC according to its simpler or more general determinants (*real* determinants at any rate), as this chapter does.[4]

Project-based SC pertains to a new reality of R&D funding. It is an undeniable fact that funding agencies are one of the chief drivers of the current growth of SC activities (Entradas & Santos, 2021) because they hold the power to impose project-based SC on academics. Project-based SC translates into *reality* that which is often claimed about SC, namely, that it is no longer an option for scientists, but a duty or responsibility that they must comply with (Bennet et al., 2020). More precisely, it is the *relations of production* that project-based SC condenses what has made project-based SC compulsory for academics. But scholarship has made little progress with respect to the economic reality underpinning project-based SC and on which the power of funding agencies over academics is based. Such circumstance is strikingly enough, given that SC is a social practice to which the academic community has been indifferent, and even reluctant, for more than a century, when science started to be professionalized (Bensaude-Vincent, 2001; Dunwoody, 2020; Hanauska, 2020;)—and changes in such deeply internalized attitudes do not occur by chance; powerful forces must be at work here.

The aforementioned CPBF is the funding mechanism that vests funding agencies with their power *vis-à-vis* academics. To better understand how project-based SC has become a responsibility for academics, the analysis should turn its attention to CPBF itself, as it sets the conditions for project-based SC to emerge and develop in the first place. It shall be seen below that CPBF is *not* a funding mechanism merely intended for effective allocation of public resources to R&D activities (as the OECD [2018] would have it). Rather, CPBF is a 'game-changer' in terms of public funding of academic research, for its distinctive feature is that public money is allotted on the basis of *competition* between research proposals, and, through them, between researchers and research teams, and between academic institutions. CPBF is as much the culmination as it is the catalyst of a whole series of transformations in the social relations of production developing in the field of academic knowledge production. It is, in a word, one of the most important nodal points in the chain of processes leading to the commodification of academic research and to the *formal subsumption of academic labor under capital*.

11.3 Competitive Project-Based Funding and the Commodification of Academic Research

Alongside the declining of public funds to R&D activities in absolute and relative terms (Reale, 2017), there have also been important modifications as regards the mechanisms for the allocation of funds used by governments. 'Project funding' or 'grant funding' stands as one of the most prominent features of contemporary systems of R&D funding (Lepori et al., 2007; Raudla et al., 2015; Reale, 2017). This funding mechanism has not completely replaced traditional 'institutional funding' (or 'block funding', as it is also called), but it has largely eclipsed the latter, as project funding has grown at the expense of institutional funding in most countries (OECD, 2018). This shift toward grant funding has happened in a context in which most science policy has been primarily oriented to make academic institutions more financially autonomous from capitalist states (Slaughter & Cantwell, 2012)—and the widespread adoption of grant funding in R&D is intimately connected to such a broader tendency.

The distinctiveness of CPBF as a funding mechanism lies in *competition*. 'Project funding is always allocated through competitive bid' (Reale, 2017, p. 47). Research proposals compete among one another in those calls for projects organized by funding agencies. However, as long as commodities 'cannot go to the market and make exchanges of their own account' (Marx, 1996, p. 94), research proposals do not participate themselves in competitive calls either. The real contenders are academics and their research teams, and, standing behind them, academic institutions. Competitive calls for projects put academics and universities to compete. The winner will be the one that demonstrates that it can deliver the expected outcomes in the most cost-efficient way (Geuna, 2001). Competition is a key aspect to understand how CPBF relates to the commodification of academic research, for competition can only take place between producers (individual or institutional) who are indifferent to one another and who can only exert influence over others in an indirect way, through competition. Such a form of organizing social (academic, in this case) labor could only take place when social production is *commodity production*, and the commodity appears as the general mediator which holds the whole social process together.

Participating in competitive calls in order to obtain funding may seem quite *natural* in contemporary academia, but it has not always been the prevailing funding mechanism, nor has competition always been the process through which funds were allocated to academic institutions. Back in time, states distributed funds among academic institutions 'with no strings attached' (Geuna, 2001; Hallonsten, 2021), on the basis of the number of faculty and/or students (Hicks, 2012). Academics themselves were left to distribute these funds internally, on the assumption that they had the knowledge, experience and capacity to take the best decision regarding the appropriate use of that public funding (Hallonsten, 2021; see also De Oliveira, 2013).

CPBF gained momentum as a funding mechanism in both the US and the UK around the 1980s and soon spread worldwide (Geuna, 2001). Since then, the share of CPBF in total R&D public expenditure has grown steadily, and it has now become the second largest mechanism for allocating public funds to R&D activities, next to institutional funding (Lepori et al., 2007; Raudla et al., 2015). CPBF represents roughly one-third of public spending in science in most OECD countries; however, Australia and Chile stand as borderline cases, for CPBF amounts there to 75 percent of the total public spending (OECD, 2018, p. 15). In the US, CPBF is estimated to represent two-thirds of global federal spending in R&D (Reale, 2017, p. 36). The European continent has its 'extreme' cases as well: Estonian universities get more than 80 percent of their funds from CPBF (Raudla et al., 2015; Reale, 2017, p. 38). In Belgium, the Czech Republic and Portugal, CPBF overtakes institutional funding as the primary mechanism for the allocation of public funds to R&D activities (Reale, 2017, p. 38). It is also worth noting that the volume of public investment, channeled through CPBF as a percentage of total governmental spending in R&D, has grown in most countries since the beginning of the twenty-first century (Lepori et al., 2007; Reale, 2017, pp. 41–2).

But these figures do not reflect the real influence and pervasiveness of CPBF. The rise of CPBF has been accompanied by the adoption of performance-based research funding systems (PRFSs, hereinafter) (Hicks, 2012; Wang et al., 2020). PRFSs basically involve governments conditioning part of the institutional funding transferred to universities on meeting pre-defined *performance thresholds*. These performance targets are multiple and may vary significantly between different cases, but always include teaching- and research-related items. The key point is that *grant funding features prominently* among the targets set in terms of research activities (Hicks, 2012; Wang et al., 2020). It means that, rather perversely, the system rewards with more institutional funding those universities that have raised more money through CPBF, which is usually public funding as well. PRFS therefore acts as an echo chamber for CPBF, amplifying its relevance for the R&D system as a whole—universities are *doubly* dependent on grant funding. Given the extent to which CPBF shapes the research activities of universities, some authors interpret it as another instrument for governments to steer and govern academic institutions 'at a distance' (Marginson, 2013).

The enthusiastic reception of CPBF by science policymakers does not mean that CPBF comes without drawbacks. On the contrary, CPBF is problematic for the R&D system as a whole in several respects. To start with, CPBF is a vector of precariousness for academics, particularly early-stage researchers (Franssen & de Rijcke, 2019). For universities as institutions, it means more financial instability and greater risk of market failure (Raudla et al., 2015). Apart from that, empirically evidence has demonstrated that CPBF reinforces the 'Matthew effect' in science, so that the distribution of funds is highly skewed toward those researchers, research teams and institutions who have been successful in previous competitive calls (Bol et al., 2018). Other problems shown by CPBF concern the time burden for academics, as writing proposals is a very time-consuming task (Ioannidis, 2011); its conservative character, for it encourages risk-avoiding approaches to research (Franssen et al., 2018); or the 'projectification' or rise of 'project mentalities' among academics that comes with the increasing importance of CPBF as a funding mechanism (OECD, 2018, p. 22; Ylijoki, 2016).

Some scholars find it rather intriguing that policymakers continue to embrace CPBF despite all the problems that it generates (e.g., Wang et al., 2018). This circumstance would come as no surprise if CPBF were understood in the broader context of contemporary science policy and the new economic foundations of higher education in general and of academic science specifically. But this dimension of CPBF, namely, its connection with the commodification of academic research, has not been investigated in any significant extent. It can be hypothesized that this lack of interest in CPBF, as part of the unfolding of capitalist relations of production in academia, reflects, at least partially, that most critical studies in higher education remain trapped in the public/private dichotomy, as Szadkowski and Krzeski (2022) aptly comment. Arguably, CPBF may have been overlooked given that most funding bodies are *public* funding agencies and that the money channeled through CPBF is mostly *public money* (Lepori et al., 2007; OECD, 2018). A glaring illustration of this circumstance is that one of the most comprehensive contributions to date to the debate on the commodification of academic science (Radder, 2010) mentions CPBF *once*, and only in passing (Resnik, 2010, p. 75).

Unfortunately, Marxian scholarship has not paid much attention to CPBF either. Marxist authors investigating the new reality of academic labor have already drawn attention to the fact that there are several mechanisms through which capitalist relations of production penetrate the academy, reengineering it as a site of surplus value production (Hall & Bowles, 2016). But CPBF has been overlooked by the Marxist literature that has built on such an important insight. Attention has been paid instead to some other aspects, highly relevant in their own account, such as 'metrification' of academic activity as a moment of the commodification of academic research and the subjection of academic labor to the rule of capital (Harvie and De Angelis, 2009; Szadkowski, 2016b). Interesting remarks have also been made in relation to the digitalization of academic labor and how such a dynamic may have transformed the material and social conditions of production in academia (Allmer, 2019; Woodcock, 2018). Moreover, the encroachment of capital into the academic enterprise has led to the recuperation and actualization of Marxist theory in relation to the value-producing and, hence, surplus value-producing condition of academic workers (e.g., Harvie, 2006; Szadkowski, 2019). For all that, however, the novel funding mechanisms and funding arrangements at work in contemporary knowledge production have not been systematically researched with the aid of Marxist theory. This chapter should then be seen as a first step to fill that gap, for, as explained above, it casts light on CPBF with the use of the Marxist category 'formal subsumption of labor under capital'.[5]

11.4 Formal Subsumption of Academic Labor Under Capital

Marx calls 'formal subsumption of labor under capital' the process through which labor is stripped of its objective conditions of production and is thereby subjected to the rule of capital. The formal subsumption of labor under capital involves that the producer[6] can no longer reproduce herself/himself except through *exchange against capital*. The formal subsumption of labor under capital involves that the means of production are, 'completely or at least in part', a property alien to the producers themselves (Marx, 1994, p. 95). But the subsumption of labor under capital is a dynamic process and not something given once and for all, so that

> the more completely these *conditions of labour* confront him as the property of another, the more completely is *the relation of capital and wage labour* present *formally*, hence the more complete the formal subsumption of labour under capital. (Marx, 1994, p. 95; emphasis in the original)

Formal subsumption is both the *process* through which labor is severed from its objective conditions of production and the *outcome* of that process.

Marx never tires of stressing that the full development of *commodity production* is not possible unless the split between labor and the conditions of production is completed. Considered as a process, the formal subsumption of labor under capital encompasses, *in the same movement*, the separation of labor from its conditions of production *and* the unfolding of *commodity production* or *production oriented toward exchange-value*. This is the reason why 'the exchange value of the product becomes the decisive purpose' of social production when labor becomes formally subsumed under capital (ibid.). Elsewhere, Marx notes that *the capital–labor relation* must be presupposed for exchange-value and the commodity-form to appear on the surface of economic life, standing, as it were, *immanently within* commodity production and market exchange (Marx, 1986).

The co-occurrence of the formal subsumption of labor and commodity production is a relevant point concerning the economic foundations of CPBF. As it shall be seen below, the economic dependence of academic institutions on commodity production and exchange against funding agencies is the materialization, the *mode of existence*, in the meaning used throughout this chapter for this expression (see endnote 1), of the split between the academic community and its objective conditions of production.[7] At this point, the remark must be made that the domination of capital over academic labor cannot be understood as something *different* from the generalization of commodity production. Putting it otherwise, the appearance of the commodity-form as the general mediator in academic knowledge production is in fact the *concrete expression* of the capitalist transformations endured by academic labor (on this, see Szadkowski & Krzeski, 2022). For one thing, the capital–labor relation is '*the ultimate development* of the value-relation and of production resting on value' (Marx, 1986, p. 90; our emphasis).

In its simplicity, the formal subsumption of labor under capital is a different form taken by the compulsion to perform surplus labor (Marx, 1994, p. 95). This *compulsion* is a common feature of any mode of production based on class divisions—continuous relative overproduction is indispensable for the reproduction of any kind of society, regardless of the social relations of production governing it (Chattopadhyay, 2019, p. 53). But capitalism carries it out 'in a manner more favourable to production' (Marx, 1994, p. 122), insofar as it heightens the continuity and intensity of labor (ibid., p. 102).

The difference of the formal subsumption as a form of enforcing surplus labor on producers is twofold. In comparison to the *real subsumption* of labor under capital, 'the labour process continues exactly as it did before—from the technological point of view' (ibid., p. 95), so capital subordinates already existing labor processes 'formed on the basis of various earlier processes of production' (ibid., p. 425). Real subsumption, on the contrary, 'creates a change in the shape of material production' (ibid., p. 106), bringing about a complete and a constant revolution in the mode of production itself, in the productivity of labor and in the relation between capitalist and worker (ibid., p. 439). The contrast between the two can be more easily seen in their connection with the forms of surplus value. *Absolute* surplus value belongs to the formal subsumption of labor under capital—if the mode of production remains the same from the technological point of view, surplus value can only be extracted through the extension of the working day (ibid., p. 426). *Relative* surplus value, on the other hand, comes with the real subsumption of labor under capital, for technological development increases the productivity of labor and this, in turn, cheapens labour-power—it takes relatively less socially necessary labor time to produce the means of subsistence for the workers (ibid., p. 95).

The difference between the formal subsumption of labor and previous forms of enforcing surplus labor on producers consists of the removal of 'all patriarchal and political admixtures from the relation of exploitation' when labor becomes formally subsumed under the yoke of capital (ibid., p. 102). Needless to say, the laborer remains as *economically dependent* on the non-laborer as before—the formal subsumption does not get rid of such a dependence, nor could it. But the crux of the matter is that this economic dependence is realized in and through *commodity exchange* (ibid., p. 95). The laborer and the non-laborer find each other in the market as *commodity owners*, that is, as free individuals between whom there is no other relation than that of buyer and seller (ibid.). When the political and patriarchal admixtures are stripped away, as it were, only the relation of exploitation remains (ibid., p. 430). These remarks reinforce the statement made earlier about the co-occurrence of the formal subsumption of labor and commodity production: what Marx is outlining here is that the formal subsumption of labor implies the *emergence, reproduction and development* of commodity production.

This brief reconstruction of the determinants captured by the category 'formal subsumption of labor under capital' lays the ground for a closer examination of the functioning of CPBF and the economic nature of the relationship between universities and funding agencies which proceeds through it. It shall then be seen that CPBF is one of the most important mechanisms through which the formal subsumption of academic labor under capital is realized, as the relationship between those two parties is actually a *commodity relationship* which is based on, reproduces and immanently deepens the separation of the academic community from its conditions of production.

11.5　Formal Subsumption of Academic Labor Under Capital Through Competitive Project-Based Funding

According to Marx, 'the manner in which the capitalist mode of production expands and subjects to itself spheres of production as yet not subject to it… entirely reproduces the manner in which it arises altogether' (ibid., p. 327). For our present purpose, this can only mean that the commodification of academic research must necessarily entail the *formal subsumption of academic labor* under capital, or what is the same, the separation of academic labor from its conditions of production. After all, capital can *only* subject academic labor to its domination if the latter confronts its objective conditions of production as an alien property, so that the reproduction of the academic community is rendered impossible unless it engages in commodity production and exchange. CPBF is one of the mechanisms that sets apart academic labor from its conditions of production.

The distinction between 'funding agency' and 'performing agency' (above all, universities) contains the whole secret of the economic foundations of CPBF. It is implied in this differentiation that both entities are *autonomous* and *reciprocally independent and indifferent to each another*. This situation sharply contrasts with the previous state of things, when universities belonged to the capitalist state or were treated as such. At any rate, for the production of academic science to take place, universities and funding bodies must come into contact one way or another, regardless of their mutual independence and reciprocal indifference. The point is that the very separation between the two entails that such a material exchange can only be established in an indirect form—more specifically, through the *commodity-form*. Universities and funding bodies relate to each other as *commodity owners*.[8]

The commodity that funding agencies personify is money, the universal representative of social wealth in capitalist society.[9] This money stands for all those conditions of production that performing agencies can no longer avail themselves *without exchange* with funding agencies. Funding agencies are therefore the *purchasers* of the products of academic knowledge production. This is one side of the commodity relationship. Academic institutions are on the other side, acting as performing agencies as they represent mostly labor and the remaining conditions of production that funding bodies have not yet taken possession of. They *sell* the products of scientific activity.

CPBF thus articulates the sale between performing agencies and funding agencies, so 'getting funds' reads here as 'selling'. When granting funds to projects, funding bodies are actually buying the outcomes of that laboring activity, whatever their material embodiment (technological innovation, technical intervention, evidence-based policy papers, etc.).[10] Performing agencies, on the contrary, participate in the competitive calls organized by funding agencies because they are *economically dependent* on the sale of the products of their labor—universities have no choice but to exchange their work and their products with funding agencies in order to obtain, in the form of money, those conditions of production necessary to maintain their productive operations running.

As it corresponds to the formal subsumption of academic labor, the economic dependence of academic institutions on exchange, hence, on CPBF and funding agencies, is not blended with 'political or patriarchal admixtures' of any sort. Academic institutions are fully autonomous in their condition as commodity owners. They depend on CPBF *in general*, but not on *particular* funding bodies. Universities can sell the products of their labor to any funding agency, be it domestic or from abroad. This aspect of CPBF is crucial to understand that CPBF self-expands, not only reproducing, but also deepening, the split between labor and its conditions of production. For now, it suffices to underline that CPBF *immanently reproduces* the economic dependence of academic institutions on sale and on funding agencies: once the exchange between the parties has come to an end, academic institutions find themselves in the same situation as they were in the first place, namely, in the same incapacity to reproduce themselves through means different from exchange and, accordingly, in the same dependence on exchange and on funding agencies' money.

From the perspective of the funding agencies, CPBF is the form taken by their *purchasing power*. Through CPBF, they buy those use-values (read here, products of academic labor) they are interested in. If performing agencies want to stand a chance in the competition for funding, they must adhere to the criteria set by funding agencies in their competitive calls for projects—once projects are funded, partners are contractually committed to deliver the expected outcomes, and that includes the design and implementation of a plan for the communication of the project and its results (see Sect. 11.2). Therefore, project-based SC forms part of the use-value of the commodity, the qualitative properties of the research activity and its results, that funding agencies purchase. As performing agencies would not receive funding and would not be in conditions to sustain their productive activities and were unable to provide the promised outcomes, CPBF allows funding bodies to align academic research with their own political priorities (Lepori et al., 2007; Wang et al., 2020)—including the enforcement of project-based SC—since performing agencies would not be funded and could not sustain their productive activities if they did not deliver the promised outcomes.

By putting research proposals in competition against one another, funding agencies ensure that those use-values they purchase only embody socially necessary labor time[11]—CPBF stimulates cost-efficient behavior among potential tenders of research grants (Geuna, 2001); *doing more with less* is the general motto when it comes to CPBF, in full accord with the underlying rationale of the formal subsumption of labor under capital (see Marx, 1994, pp. 429–30). However, it is also important to highlight that funding bodies *do not* lay down any particular clauses as regards the technological or organizational dispositions of the process of knowledge production; this aspect is left to the discretion of the academic community. Therefore, funding agencies take the academic laboring process as it stands and do not try to revolutionize it through labor-saving technological innovations. This is further evidence that CPBF operates at the level of the *formal*, rather than the *real*, subsumption of academic labor under capital (see ibid., pp. 95–6, 102–03). If changes do occur due to cost-efficient behaviors adopted by contenders in competitive calls, 'these modifications can only be the gradual *consequences* of the subsumption of given, traditional labour processes under capital' (ibid., p. 436; emphasis in the original). This circumstance could be attributed to the fact that the formal subsumption of academic labor under capital is still an ongoing process, so that the transition from the *partial* to the *complete* separation of academic labor from its conditions of production has not been made yet.

As representatives of money, incarnated social wealth in its general form (Marx, 1996, p. 80), funding bodies are all powerful *vis-à-vis* performing agencies. In fact, the fate of most academic institutions falls into their hands. But CPBF presupposes *competition*, as stressed earlier. And competition operates *at both ends* of the commodity relationship and not only between funders and performers. Funding agencies can maintain their control over academic knowledge production *if* they can act in their capacity as money owners, and depending on the size of their budget. CPBF thus means that funding agencies exert control over academic production by spending money alone. The more money they spent, the greater their control over academic production will be, both in intensive and extensive terms—*and vice versa*.

This explains why capitalist states have favored CPBF as a funding scheme and why more public funds relative to overall public R&D spending are channeled through it (Lepori et al., 2007; Reale, 2017). Academic institutions are made increasingly dependent on CPBF and on commodity exchange, but they are not dependent on particular funding bodies. Leveraging on their autonomy as commodity owners, academic institutions can seek funding wherever more money is available, and the chances of success in competitive calls are correspondingly higher. Nation-states have to channel more money through CPBF than other countries in order to ensure that their own national academic institutions do not perform R&D for the benefit of *foreign* constellations of capital accumulation.[12]

Competition is at the core of CPBF for it articulates a relationship between formally autonomous and reciprocally independent commodity owners. And this competition sets CPBF in motion, as it has been seen. CPBF expands and grows in importance as a funding mechanism because of its intrinsically competitive character—*CPBF immanently generates CPBF*. Needless to say, this self-expansion of CPBF has as its main result a *growing* dependence of academic institutions on funding agencies' money and on CPBF. A larger sum of money administered by funding agencies means that the latter own and control a greater number of conditions of academic knowledge production. The more money is channeled through CPBF, the more often academic institutions must enter into exchange with funding agencies or, saying it otherwise, get grant money by taking part in competitive calls for projects. On the flip side of the coin, global competition among constellations of capital accumulation pushes governments and nation-states to increase funds allotted to R&D activities through CPBF in order not to be surpassed by rivals and, if possible, to overtake them by offering advantageous conditions when it comes to funding R&D activities—imperialistic rivalries and conflicts are transferred to the realm of academic knowledge production through CPBF.

In short, CPBF not only *reproduces* the split between academic labor and its conditions of production but *deepens* it. The more the CPBF expands, the more complete this separation becomes; the more exchange-value is elevated to the ultimate purpose governing academic production; and, by the same token, the more complete is the formal subsumption of academic labor under capital.

11.6 Conclusion

Neither SC in general nor project-based SC in particular are 'innocent'. One way or another, both reflect the 'capitalist pressures' that the academic enterprise is under nowadays. But project-based SC is a distinctive form of SC in that those 'capitalist pressures' have *not* reshaped a pre-existing form of SC. On the contrary, project-based SC has emerged and developed *because of* these 'capitalist pressures'. Project-based SC exists *in and through* the growing dominance of capital over academic labor—more precisely, in and through the *formal subsumption of academic labor under capital*. It does not reflect 'societal progress' or 'cultural development', as some experts in SC would have it (see Davies, 2021), but plain and simple dominance of capital over higher education and academic science.

This chapter has uncovered the connection between project-based SC and the unfolding of the capitalist relations of production by drawing on the theoretical foundations of Marxism. More precisely, the economic reality underlying project-based SC has been investigated, and light has been cast on CPBF (the funding mechanism on which project-based SC is based) by drawing on the Marxist category 'formal subsumption of labor under capital'. This chapter can be thus seen as a contribution to that thriving strand of scholarship that addresses the commodification of higher education and academic research from a Marxist standpoint.

Given the thrust that funding agencies have recently given to SC activities, academics must carry out SC activities alongside their core research responsibilities if they want to conduct research at all. Funding agencies are the chief driver of the 'cultural shift' toward SC among academics, since drafting and implementing communication plans have become a requirement in most competitive calls for projects. Funding agencies hold this power to impose project-based SC on academics because of CPBF—and the enforcement of project-based SC through CPBF is already indicative of the nature of the relationship between funding agencies and academic institutions that CPBF establishes. Project-based SC attests to the fact that CPBF is *not* simply another funding mechanism for the allocation of public money. On the contrary, as this chapter has demonstrated, it is one of the chief drivers of the *commodification of academic research*, namely, the encroachment of the commodity-form into the core of academic knowledge production; the development of exchange-value as the main purpose of research activities in academia; and, by the same token, the penetration and further development of the capitalist relations of production within the academic enterprise.

The analysis of CPBF through the lenses of Marxist scholarship has helped to elucidate that the relationship between funding agencies and academic institutions that it arranges is actually a *commodity relationship*. Through CPBF, funding agencies buy the outcomes of the research activity organized and performed by academic institutions. Therefore, CPBF represents for academic institutions the sale of the products of their labor. Academic institutions participate in competitive calls for projects arranged by funding agencies because they *need to do so*—they could hardly maintain the productive activities running otherwise. CPBF condenses in itself the new reality of academic knowledge production: academic institutions are *economically dependent* on sale and exchange and hence on the money held by funding agencies, for this money represents the conditions of production that universities can no longer avail themselves *without* entering into exchange with funding agencies.

The dependence of academic institutions on CPBF is the concrete form that the split between the academic community and its objective conditions of production takes. CPBF would not be a funding arrangement, nor would funding agencies hold any power over academics, research teams and academic institutions, were the academic community in conditions to reproduce itself independently—without exchange. So, CPBF is based on the severance of academic labor from its conditions of production. But CPBF *reproduces* this split, as nothing else but the economic dependence remains after the exchange between funding agencies' money and universities' labor comes to a close. By turning its presuppositions into results, CPBF always renews the need for academic institutions to participate in competitive calls for projects organized by funding agencies in order to obtain grant money.

Worse still, the more money is channeled through CPBF, the more complete the split between the academic community and its conditions of production becomes. If more conditions of production fall on the side of funding agencies in the form of money—a larger budget represents a larger number of means of production—the independent reproduction of the academic community is further undermined. And it is worth noting that CPBF expands as a funding mechanism according to its own laws of motion, for *competition* drives CPBF forward and competition is, as a point of fact, the most significant property of CPBF as a funding arrangement. CPBF is *immanently* leading to the more complete formal subsumption of academic labor under capital and, by the same token, to the imposition of project-based SC as a duty or responsibility from which academics cannot evade.

Acknowledgments This work has been possible with the support of a fellowship granted by the University of Seville under its VI Framework Programme for Research and Knowledge Transfer (VI PPITUS). The author wants to show his gratitude to the editors of this *Handbook*, for their guidance, support and feedback on previous versions of this chapter. Any errors are the sole responsibility of the author.

Disclosure Statement None of the co-authors has any financial interest or benefit that has arisen from the direct applications of this research.

Notes

1. In this context, 'mode of existence' should be understood in a dialectic fashion, namely, as a form that 'necessarily grows out of the content itself' (Rubin 1928/ Rubin, 1973, p. 117), or, alternatively, if the emphasis is placed on content, a form is the mode of existence of a given content if the content is immanent in the form itself (Starosta, 2016, p. 93).
2. The coronavirus pandemic has provided a remarkable example of such an instrumentalization of SC: in the worst days of the global pandemic, the tandems Pfizer-BioNTech and Oxford-AstraZeneca, along with Moderna, announced the efficiency (in terms of immunized population) of their respective vaccines *prior* to any independent validation of these results—something *at odds* with the usual procedure in science. Stock-options of all these companies skyrocketed following their respective announcements. For Pfizer's CEO, it also resulted in personal enrichment: his own stock options in Pfizer were sold *after* the efficacy of the company's mRNA vaccine (90%) was ommunicated to the press (Reuters, November 11, 2020).
3. 'Innovation' is the fashionable term for technological transformation intended to the cheapening of labor-power and the extraction of growing quantities of surplus labor from workers. See Marx (1996, pp. 374–420) for a detailed account about how technological change (referred to as 'machinery') becomes a means for the production of relative surplus value through the enhancement of labor productivity and the cheapening of labor power to which it leads.
4. In the oft-quoted methodological introduction to *Grundrisse*, Marx noted that labor as such, the 'very simple category' of labor, can be understood in this general determinacy because this 'abstraction' has become *a practical reality*—capitalist society is characterized by the multiplicity and changeability of labors and by the adaptability of the laboring population to them (Marx, 1986, pp. 40–1). A similar consideration applies in this investigation: project-based SC can be grasped in its simplicity or generality because it is a request common to many funding agencies of R&D; it has been generalized as a responsibility imposed on academics conducting research with third-party funding all over the world.
5. In the author's view, the notion of formal subsumption is the most appropriate one for grasping the economic significance of CPBF and how it realizes the domination of capital over labor. But the author is aware of previous Marxist studies that have pointed to other forms of subsumption that may be at work in contemporary academia (on this, see Szadkowski, 2016).
6. Marx is thinking of the individual worker. But, as the following section will show, it can also be applied to the collective worker, namely, the institutional academic producer.
7. Public funding without strings attached meant for the academic community that it held the capacity to distribute these resources internally, following its own judgment. Accordingly, the academic community could relate to these conditions of production as if they were *its property*—the academic community itself was the *real producer*; it was a *real productive community*. The prevalence of peer review as the main form of decision-making in academic activity is, perhaps, the

most outstanding remnant of that past situation. In the business world, it is hardly conceivable that people from one company would make decisions with direct and immediate effects on the performance of other companies. But this is exactly what happens in science: 'juries of equals' are made up of experts from different backgrounds and institutional affiliations, and they make decisions which concern the performance of institutions other than their own (when reviewing papers, in tenure committees and so forth). Evaluation committees are the concrete instantiation of the academic community as such, which organizes and regulates academic labor through them. It is outside the scope of this chapter to explore this point further.

8. That the capitalist state acts as a commodity owner may appear strange at first glance, but it is not. This issue was already investigated by Marxist revolutionary Paul Mattick (1969/Mattick, 2020) in relation to 'state-induced production', namely, when the capitalist state sustains unprofitable production by buying commodities from private capitals. All in all, the capitalist state is as good a buyer as any other for the individual capitalist—provided that the latter can realize the normal profit through this sale. Crucially, Mattick does not understand this *economic* function of the capitalist state as *opposed* to its *political* role. This resonates with the statement made by Blanke et al. (1978) in the context of the 'State-derivation' debate, as they argued that the capitalist state can only perform its function as the political representative of the capitalist class by means of law (and its enforcement) and money.

9. About money as the *particular commodity* that plays 'within the world of commodities the part of the universal equivalent' and which, therefore, assumes the condition of universal representative of social wealth in capitalist society, see Marx (1996, pp. 80–1).

10. In some cases, the outcome of the laboring activity can hardly be distinguished from the laboring activity itself. This circumstance is immaterial for the attribute of CPBF at stake here.

11. Socially necessary labor time is defined as the time 'that is required to produce an article under the normal conditions of production, and with the average degree of skill and intensity prevalent' in a determined epoch (Marx, 1996, p. 49).

12. This is glaringly illustrated by the situation faced by the UK nowadays, after its exclusion from *Horizon Europe*. UK-based academic institutions are no longer eligible for funding in this funding scheme. UK government has been then forced to make a provision of hundreds of millions of euros to fund projects led by national institutions that had been already chosen for funding in *Horizon Europe*, under the threat of a 'brain drain' (McKie, 27 February, McKie, 2022). In the long run, this temporary 'Plan B' must become a national funding scheme in its own right (O'Grady, 21 July, O'Grady, 2022). It goes without saying that the UK alone cannot offset the concentrated purchasing capacity of twenty-seven countries, including some G7 ones, and the attendant benefits that come along with it (international collaboration, greater academic impact, etc.). This awkward situation is further compounded by the fact that the UK economy is stagnating and that the country hosts some of the world-leading academic institutions.

References

Allmer, T. (2019). Academic Labour, Digital Media and Capitalism. *Critical Sociology*, 45(4–5), 599–615. https://doi.org/10.1177/0896920517735669

Bauer, M. W., & Gregory, J. (2007). From Journalism to Corporate Communication in post-war Britain. In M. W. Bauer & M. Bucchi (Eds.), *Journalism, Science and Society Science Communication between News and Public Relations* (pp. 34–51). Routledge.

Bennet, N., Dudo, A., Yuan, S., & Besley, J. (2020). Scientists, Trainers, and the Strategic Communication of Science. In T. P. Newman (Ed.), *Theory and Best Practices in Science Communication Training* (pp. 9–31). Routledge.

Bensaude-Vincent, B. (2001). A Genealogy of the Increasing Gap Between Science and the Public. *Public Understanding of Science*, 10, 99–113.

Blanke, B., Jürgens, U., & Kastendiek, H. (1978). On the Current Marxist Discussion on the Analysis of Form and Function of the Bourgeois State. In J. Holloway & S. Picciotto (Eds.), *State and Capital: A Marxist Debate* (pp. 108–147). Edward Arnold Publishers.

Bol, T., de Vaan, M., & van de Rijt, A. (2018). The Matthew Effect in Science Funding. *PNAS*, 115(19), 4887–4890. https://doi.org/10.1073/pnas.1719557115

Bucchi, M., & Trench, B. (2021). Rethinking Science Communication as the Social Conversation Around Science. *Journal of Science Communication*, 20(3), Y01. https://doi.org/10.22323/2.20030401

Burns, T. W., O'Connor, D. J., & Stocklmayer, S. M. (2003). Science Communication: A Contemporary Definition. *Public Understanding of Science*, 12(2), 183–202. https://doi.org/10.1177/09636625030122004

Chattopadhyay, P. (2019). *Socialism and Commodity Production. Essay in Marx Revival*.

Conceição, C. P., Ávila, P., Celho, A. R., & Costal, A. F. (2020). European Action Plans for Science-society Relations: Changing Buzzwords, Changing the Agenda. *Minerva*, 58, 1–24. https://doi.org/10.1007/s11024-019-09380-7

Davies, S. (2021). An Empirical and Conceptual Note on Science Communication's Role in Society. *Science Communication*, 43(1), 116–133. https://doi.org/10.1177/1075547020971642

Davies, S., & Horst, M. (2016). *Science Communication: Culture, Identity and Citizenship*. Palgrave Macmillan.

De Oliveira, M. B. (2013). On the Commodification of Science: The Programmatic Dimension. *Science & Education*, 22(11), 2463–2483.

Dudo, A. (2015). Scientists, the Media, and the Public Communication of Science. *Sociology Compass*, 9, 761–775. https://doi.org/10.1111/soc4.12298

Dunwoody, S. (2020). Science Journalism. In A. Leßmöllmann, M. Dascal, & T. Gloning (Eds.), *Science Communication* (pp. 417–438). De Gruyter Mouton.

Entradas, M., & Santos, J. M. (2021). Returns of Research Funding are Maximised in Media Visibility for Excellent Institutes. *Humanities and Social Sciences Communications*, 8, 216. https://doi.org/10.1057/s41599-021-00884-w

Fecher, B., & Hebing, M. (2021). How Do Researchers Approach Societal Impact? *PLoS ONE*, 16(7), e0254006. https://doi.org/10.1371/journal.pone.0254006

Franssen, T., & de Rijcke, S. (2019). The Rise of Project Funding and its Effects on the Social Structure of Academia. In F. Cannizzo & N. Osbaldiston (Eds.), *The Social Structure of Global Academia* (pp. 144–161). Routledge.

Franssen, T., Scholten, W., Hessels, L. K., & de Rickje, S. (2018). The Drawbacks of Project Funding for Epistemic Innovation: Comparing Institutional Affordances and Constraints of Different Types of Research Funding. *Minerva, 56*, 11–33. https://doi.org/10.1007/s11024-017-9338-9

Gertrúdix, M., Rajas, M., Romero-Luis, J., & Carbonell-Alcocer, A. (2021). Comunicación científica en el espacio digital. Acciones de difusión de proyectos de investigación del programa H2020. *Profesional de la Información, 30*(1). https://doi.org/10.3145/epi.2021.ene.04

Geuna, A. (2001). The Changing Rationale for European University Research Funding: Are There Negative Unintended Consequences? *Journal of Economic Issues, 35*(3), 607–632. https://doi.org/10.1080/00213624.2001.11506393

Gregory, J. (2016). The Price of Trust—A Response to Weingart and Guenther. *Journal of Science Communication, 15*(6), Y01. https://doi.org/10.22323/2.15060401

Guenther, L., & Joubert, M. (2017). Science Communication as a Field of Research: Identifying Trends, Challenges and Gaps by Analysing Research Papers. *JCOM, 16*(2), A02. https://doi.org/10.22323/2.16020202

Hall, R., & Bowles, K. (2016). Re-engineering Higher Education: The Subsumption of Labour and the Exploitation of Anxiety. *Workplace, 28*, 30–47.

Hallonsten, O. (2021). Stop Evaluating Science: A Historical-sociological Argument. *Social Science Information, 60*(1), 7–26. https://doi.org/10.1177/0539018421992204

Hanauska, M. (2020). Historical Aspects of External Science Communication. In A. Leßmöllmann, M. Dascal, & T. Gloning (Eds.), *Science Communication* (pp. 585–600). De Gruyter Mouton.

Harvie, D. (2006). Value Production and Struggle in the Classroom: Teachers Within, Against and beyond capital. *Capital & Class, 30*(1), 1–32. https://doi.org/10.1177/030981680608800102

Harvie, D., & De Angelis, M. (2009). 'Cognitive Capitalism' and the Rat-Race: How Capital Measures Immaterial Labour in British Universities. *Historical Materialism, 17*(3), 3–30. https://doi.org/10.1163/146544609X12469428108420

Hicks, D. (2012). Performance-based University Research Funding System. *Research Policy, 41*, 251–261. https://doi.org/10.1016/j.respol.2011.09.007

Ioannidis, J. (2011). Fund people not projects. *Nature, 477*, 529–531. https://doi.org/10.1038/477529a

Lepori, B., van den Besselaar, P., Dinges, M., Potì, B., Reale, E., Slipersæter, S., Thèves, J., & van der Meulen, B. (2007). Comparing the Evolution of National Research Policies: What Patterns of Change? *Science and Public Policy, 34*(6), 372–388. https://doi.org/10.3152/030234207X234578

Loroño-Leturiondo, M., & Davies, S. (2018). Responsibility and Science Communication: Scientists' Experiences of and Perspectives on Public Communication Activities. *Journal of Responsible Innovation, 5*(2), 170–185. https://doi.org/10.1080/23299460.2018.1434739

Marginson, S. (2013). The Impossibility of Capitalist Markets in Higher Education. *Journal of Education Policy, 28*(3), 353–370. https://doi.org/10.1080/02680939.2012.747109

Marx, K. (1986). *Economic Manuscripts of 1857–1858. Vol. 29 of Marx and Engels Collected Works*. Lawrence and Wishart.

Marx, K. (1994). *Economic Manuscripts of 1861–1863. Vol. 34 of Marx and Engels Collected Works*. Lawrence and Wishart.

Marx, K. (1996). *Capital: A Critique of Political Economy. Volume I. Vol. 35 of Marx and Engels Collected Works*. Lawrence and Wishart.

Mattick, P. (2020 [1969]). *Marx and Keynes. The Limits of the Mixed Economy*. Pattern Books.

McKie, R. (2022, February 27). UK Scientists Fear Brain Drain as Brexit Rows put Research at Risk. *The Guardian*. Retrieved December 19, 2022, from https://www.theguardian.com/science/2022/feb/27/uk-scientists-fear-brain-drain-as-brexit-rows-put-research-at-risk

O'Grady, C. (2022, July 21). U.K. Outlines 'Plan B' Research Funding to Skirt EU Impasse. *Science*. Retrieved December 19, 2022, from https://www.science.org/content/article/u-k-outlines-plan-b-research-funding-skirt-eu-impasse

Organization for Economic Cooperation and Development. (2018). *Effective Operation of Competitive Research Funding Systems* (OECD Science, Technology and Industry Policy Papers No. 57). Retrieved October 20, 2022, from https://www.oecd-ilibrary.org/industry-and-services/effective-operation-of-competitive-research-funding-systems_2ae8c0dc-en

Palmer, S. E., & Schibeci, R. A. (2014). What Conceptions of Science Communication are Espoused by Science Research Funding Bodies? *Public Understanding of Science*, *23*(5), 511–527. https://doi.org/10.1177/0963662512455295

Radder, H. (2010). *The commodification of academic research: Science and the contemporary university*. Pittsburgh: University of Pittsburgh Press.

Raudla, R., Karo, E., Valdmaa, K., & Kattel, R. (2015). Implications of Project-based Funding of Research on Budgeting and Financial Management in Public Universities. *Higher Education*, *70*, 957–971. https://doi.org/10.1007/s10734-015-9875-9

Reale, E. (2017). *Analysis of National Public Research Funding (PREF)—Final Report*. Retrieved November 15, 2022, from https://doi.org/10.2760/19140

Resnik, D. (2010). Financial Interests and the Norms of Academic Science. In H. Radder (Ed.), *The Commodification of Academic Research: Science and the Contemporary University* (pp. 65–89). University of Pittsburgh Press.

Reuters. (2020, November 11). CEO Sells Stock Worth $5.6 mln on Same Day as Pfizer's COVID-19 Vaccine Update. Retrieved January 9, 2023, from https://www.reuters.com/article/pfizer-albert-bourla-stake-idCNL4N2HX334

Rose, K. M., Markowitz, E. M., & Brossard, D. (2020). Scientists' Incentives and Attitudes Toward Public Communication. *PNAS*, *117*(3), 1274–1276. https://doi.org/10.1073/pnas.1916740117

Rubin, I.I. (1973 [1928]). *Essays on Marx's Theory of Value*. Black Rose Books.

Slaughter, S., & Cantwell, B. (2012). Transatlantic Moves to the Market: The United States and the European Union. *Higher Education*, *63*, 583–606. https://doi.org/10.1007/s10734-011-9460-9

Sommer, D. (2019, October 8–11). *Trends in Research Communications: When, Why and How Do Researchers Communicate Their Work, and Where Do They Need More Help?* [Conference presentation] 6:AM Altmetrics Conference, Stirling, United Kingdom.

Starosta, G. (2016). *Marx's* Capital, *Method and Revolutionary Subjectivity*. Brill.

Szadkowski, K. (2016). Socially Necessary Impact/Time: Notes on the Acceleration of Academic Labor, Metrics and the Transnational Association of Capitals. *Theory of Science*, *38*(1), 53–85.

Szadkowski, K. (2016b). Towards an Orthodox Marxian Reading of Subsumption(s) of Academic Labour under Capital. *Workplace*, *28*, 9–29.

Szadkowski, K. (2019). An Autonomist Marxist Perspective on Productive and Unproductive Academic Labour. *tripleC, 17*(1), 111–131.

Szadkowski, K., & Krzeski, J. (2022). Conceptualizing Capitalist Transformations of Universities: Marx's Relevance for Higher Education Research. *Critique, 50*(1), 185–203. https://doi.org/10.1080/03017605.2022.2050536

Thorpe, C. (2020). Science, Technology, and Life Politics Beyond the Market. *Journal of Responsible Innovation, 7*, 53–73. https://doi.org/10.1080/2329946 0.2020.1816363

Thorpe, C., & Gregory, J. (2010). Producing the Post-Fordist Public: The Political Economy of Public Engagement with Science. *Science as Culture, 19*(3), 273–301. https://doi.org/10.1080/09505430903194504

Väliverronen, E. (2021). Mediatisation of Science and the Rise of Promotional Culture. In M. Bucchi & B. Trench (Eds.), *Routledge Handbook of Public Communication of Science and Technology* (3rd ed., pp. 129–146). Routledge.

Wang, J., Lee, Y., & Walsh, J. P. (2018). Funding Model and Creativity in Science: Competitive Versus Block Funding and Status Contingency Effects. *Research Policy, 47*(6), 1070–1083. https://doi.org/10.1016/j.respol.2018.03.014

Wang, L., Wang, X., Niclas, F., & Philipsen, N. J. (2020). The Effect of Competitive Public Funding on Scientific Output: A Comparison between China and the EU. *Research Evaluation, 29*(4), 418–430. https://doi.org/10.1093/reseval/rvaa023

Weingart, P., Joubert, M., & Connoway, K. (2021). Public Engagement with Science—Origins, Motives and Impact in Academic Literature and Science Policy. *PLoS ONE, 16*(7), e0254201. https://doi.org/10.1371/journal.pone.0254201

Woodcock, J. (2018). Digital Labour in the University: Understanding the Transformations of Academic Work in the UK. *tripleC, 16*(1), 129–142.

Wynne, B. (2014). Further Disorientation in the Hall of Mirrors. *Public Understanding of Science, 23*(1), 60–70. https://doi.org/10.1177/0963662513505397

Ylijoki, O.-H. (2016). Projectification and Conflicting Temporalities in Academic Knowledge Production. *Theory of Science, 38*(1), 7–26.

CHAPTER 12

Commodification, the Violence of Abstraction, and Socially Necessary Labor Time: A Marxist Analysis of High-Stakes Testing and Capitalist Education in the United States

Wayne Au

12.1 Introduction

High-stakes, standardized testing is ubiquitous as the central tool for major educational reforms and policies, particularly those structured to embody forms of capitalist production, competition, and accumulation around the globe. In this chapter, I use several Marxist concepts to explore the role of high-stakes, standardized tests within such capitalist-oriented reforms and policies in the United States in particular. First, I begin with a short, materialist history of the rise of standardized testing in the United States—from its beginnings with I.Q. testing and adoption into industrial capitalist models of schooling to its modern use as a tool for generating data that are used to reinforce market-based educational reforms. I then go on to detail how these tests operate as a mechanism for the abstraction, decontextualization, and commodification of students to support capitalist models of schooling and education. I end this chapter by arguing that, instead of measuring teaching and learning, modern-day high-stakes standardized tests actually measure socially necessary labor time—or the amount of social labor functionally congealed within students as a measure of our general investment of social resources in students.

W. Au (✉)
University of Washington Bothell, Bothell, WA, USA
e-mail: wayneau@uw.edu

12.2 A Brief, Materialist History of Standardized, High-Stakes Tests in the United States

The origins of modern-day high-stakes standardized testing in the United States can be drawn directly to France, where, in 1904, psychologist Alfred Binet had developed a test to assess if young children had a developmental disability. By dividing the test-determined mental age of a child by their biological age, Binet asserted that we could surmise an "intelligence quotient"—or, I.Q.—of the child. Even though Binet never connected the idea of I.Q. with biological or inherited intelligence, and he only intended it to be used as a general measurement of where a child was developmentally, a number of U.S. psychologists seized upon the idea of I.Q. testing. In the process, U.S. psychologists like Goddard, Terman, and Yerkes conformed this new form of assessment to their own underlying presumptions about humans and human ability (Au, 2023; Gould, 1996). For instance, after testing millions of U.S. military recruits during World War I, Yerkes used the test data to conclude that lighter-skinned Western and Northern Europeans were more intelligent than darker-hued Eastern and Southern Europeans and that Black Americans were the least intelligent of all peoples. These findings, and others based on these test scores, also played into burgeoning eugenics movement in the United States during that time, where an increasing number of white Americans believed that traits such as intelligence and criminality were based on genetic inheritance—a belief that, in its turn, was then used to justify arguments that rich, white men were biologically superior to all others (Au, 2023; Selden, 1999).

These psychological test designers, specifically Terman, found willing partners in the growing public school system. During this time period, the U.S. public school system was growing exponentially. Fourteen million immigrants entered the United States between 1865 and 1900, and a million a year more came for several years after 1900 (Callahan, 1964). It has been estimated that between 1890 and 1917, the U.S. population nearly doubled, with 9 million immigrants entering the United States in the first decade of the 1900s alone. Between 1920 and 1930, student enrollment in public schools rose by 22%, from 23.3 million to 28.3 million students (Chapman, 1988).

In order to handle the growing numbers of public school students, districts began to try and scale up efficiency of educational production, so to speak, such that schools were increasingly modeled along the lines of factory production. As early as 1910, public high schools generally adopted the policy of moving students through five or six class periods of 45–60 minutes a day, making the experience similar to movement along a factory process line. Increases in school size also meant increases in teaching loads as well, where high school teachers commonly taught between 150 and 200 different students a day and class sizes averaged 30–34 students (Callahan, 1964). This shift toward a more factory-like public education system also was part of a broader, institutionalized framing of education along the lines of capitalist production and business principles too. During this time period in the United States, local school boards wielded significant power to determine local policies, and research shows that these boards were dominated by white, male businessmen (Counts, 1927; Nearing, 1917; Timar & Tyack, 1999).

The potent mix of a growing public school system in search of efficiency, the rise of industrial capitalism and the subsequent logics that schools should be run like businesses, and the belief that intelligence was biologically based and measured "objectively" through these tests, made standardized testing very appealing to those in power. Terman, then a Stanford University professor of psychology and under the sponsorship of the National Academy of Sciences, adapted the above-mentioned army tests into the National Intelligence Tests for schoolchildren in 1919, and by 1920, over 400,000 copies of these tests had been sold nationwide. Terman and others also created the Stanford Achievement Test in 1922, and by late 1925, he reported sales of this test to be near 1.5 million copies. Further, a 1925 survey of 215 cities with populations over 10,000 found that 64% of these cities used intelligence tests to classify and sort elementary students; 56% used the tests to classify and sort junior high school students; and 41% did the same for high school students. Another survey of superintendents of school districts in cities with populations over 10,000 people, completed in 1926, produced similar results. Marketing Terman's own later-developed intelligence test, the Terman Group Test, the World Book Company reported annual sales of over 775,000 tests by 1928 (Chapman, 1988). By 1932, a total of 112 of 150 large city school systems in the United States had begun to use intelligence testing to place students into ability groups, and colleges had also begun to use these tests to justify admissions as well (Haney, 1984).

Standardized Testing, I.Q., and White Supremacist Eugenics

The adoption of these early standardized tests also validated eugenic notions of I.Q. and found a willing audience among eugenicists in the United States (Selden, 1999). This fact illustrates how the entanglement of issues of class stratification, white supremacy, and schooling were (and are) in the United States (Au, 2023). For instance, writing about what he saw as the frequent appearance of a lack of intelligence in Black and Brown Americans, Terman (1916, pp. 91–92) observed:

> The fact that one meets this type with such frequency among Indians, Mexicans, and negroes suggests quite forcibly that the whole question of racial differences in mental traits will have to be taken up anew and by experimental methods…Children of this group should be segregated in special classes and be given instruction which is concrete and practical. They cannot master, but they can often be made efficient workers, able to look out for themselves. There is no possibility at present of convincing society that they should not be allowed to reproduce, although from a eugenic point of view they constitute a grave problem because of their unusually prolific breeding.

With regard to schooling, he added:

> Among laboring men and servant girls there are thousands like them [feeble-minded individuals]. They are the world's "hewers of wood and drawers of water." And yet, as far as intelligence is concerned, the tests have told the truth. ... No amount of school instruction will ever make them intelligent voters or capable voters in the true sense of the word. (Ibid., p. 91)

Terman's tests (both the co-developed Stanford Achievement Test and his own Terman Group Test) became popular in schools as districts rushed to use this technology to start stratifying student populations and tracking them according to these racist I.Q. test scores (Chapman, 1988; Haney, 1984). In the U.S. West and Southwest during the 1920s, for instance, this led to major cities like Los Angeles, Houston, Phoenix, El Paso, and San Antonio using I.Q. tests to create special tracks of education specifically for Mexican American public school students (Blanton, 2003).

The SAT college entrance exam also shares this history. The SAT has gone by a few names over the last century. It started as the Scholastic Aptitude Test when it was first administered in 1926. It eventually was renamed the Scholastic Assessment Test in the 1990s, and now it doesn't stand for anything but the SAT (Boeckenstedt, 2020; Rosner, 2012; Viera, 2018). The SAT has its origins in the very same Army I.Q. tests administered by Yerkes over 100 years ago, where one of his assistants, Carl Brigham, adapted them into a college admissions exam. At the time, Brigham, like Yerkes, was a eugenicist who believed that I.Q. was biological. For instance, in his 1923 book, *A Study of American Intelligence*, based on I.Q. testing, he argued:

> The decline of American intelligence will be more rapid than the decline of the intelligence of European national groups, owing to the presence here of the negro. These are the plain, if somewhat ugly, facts that our study shows. The deterioration of American intelligence is not inevitable, however, if public action can be aroused to prevent it. (as quoted in Viera, 2018, n.p.)

Brigham eventually recanted this position, admitting that the idea the "tests measured native intelligence purely and simply without regard to training or school" was "one of the most glorious fallacies in the history of science" (as quoted in Creighton, 2006, n.p.), and even regretting that he created the SAT in the first place (Creighton, 2006; Lemann, 1999). Regardless, this legacy of eugenic racism (and classism) has carried through to the modern-day SAT, which produces scores that essentially mirror race, class, and educational backgrounds of those taking the test (Boeckenstedt, 2020; Viera, 2018), in part because of biases in the test question selection process (Kidder & Rosner, 2002; Santelices & Wilson, 2010).

High-Stakes Testing and Modern U.S. Federal Education Policy

The publication of *A Nation at Risk: The Imperative for Education Reform* (National Commission on Excellence in Education, 1983) is the starting point for the turn toward high-stakes, standardized testing in U.S. federal education policy (Nichols & Berliner, 2007). The Reagan-era report called reformers to arms and essentially blamed the possibility of impending nuclear war on the supposed failures of U.S. public education. *A Nation at Risk* made several recommendations for school reform in the United States, among them an increase in graduation requirements, specific content recommendations for graduation requirements, higher standards and expectations for all students, the establishment of core knowledge requirements (which the report called "New Basics"), higher educational standards for teachers, and for teacher salaries to be based on student test performance. Within a year of the report's publication, 54 state-level commissions on education were created, and 26 states raised graduation requirements. Three years after publication, 35 states instituted state education reforms that revolved around testing and increased course loads for students (Kornhaber & Orfield, 2001). By 1994, a total of 43 states implemented statewide assessments for k-5, and by the year 2000, every state but Iowa administered a state-mandated test (Jones et al., 2003).

In 2002, the U.S. federal government reauthorized the Elementary and Secondary Education Act, naming it the No Child Left Behind Act (NCLB) (U.S. Department of Education, 2002). As a policy, NCLB was built around high-stakes, standardized testing as the main tool to spur educational reform by mandating all students be tested in grades 3–8, and once in high school in reading and math by 2006, and that by 2008, students be tested at least once at the elementary, middle, and high school levels in science. Under NCLB, all students would be expected to be testing at 100% proficiency by the year 2014 or face significant sanctions (Karp, 2006). NCLB was extended well into the Obama administration without full reauthorization or major revision due to gridlock in U.S. federal politics (Karp, 2014, 2016). Unable to pass a new, signature federal education law, with the support of leaders in the business community, the Obama administration instead created the Race to the Top competitive grant program. In order to apply for money from this federal grant program, states had to commit to a series of educational reforms, including developing systems of teacher and principal evaluation based on high-stakes tests, developing data systems to support tracking student test scores for these evaluations, adopting the Common Core State Standards (CCSS) to provide a national baseline for high-stakes tests, and identifying the lowest-performing schools for "turn around" through strategies of firing staff, charter school conversion, or closure, among other reforms (Au, 2023; U.S. Department of Education, 2009). The Obama administration did eventually reauthorize its own version of U.S. federal education law in 2015, the Every Student Succeeds Act (ESSA). While ESSA was different from its predecessor in some ways, as Karp (2016, n.p.) observes, "Although NCLB represented a massive wrong turn in federal education policy, ESSA is more like a change in drivers than a U-turn. The major elements of test and punish reform remain in place, but they are largely turned over to the states."

The current policy apparatus of using test scores to determine rewards and sanctions in U.S. education policy is, just like over 100 years ago, central to maintaining a system of education built around the logics of capitalist production and competition. Not surprisingly, while there is no space to fully address it here, major corporations, their associated philanthropies (the Bill & Melinda Gates Foundation, for example), and nonprofit organizations often funded by these philanthropies and run by CEOs connected to major corporations, all played central roles in the formation of these capitalist education policies and reliance on high-stakes testing in recent decades (Au, 2023). As an example, in a pre-NCLB campaign speech delivered to the conservative Manhattan Institute think-tank, former U.S. President George W. Bush (1999, n.p.) said:

> Federal funds will no longer flow to failure. Schools that do not teach and will not change must have some final point of accountability. A moment of truth, when their Title 1 funds are divided up and given to parents, for tutoring or a charter school or some other hopeful option. In the best case, schools that are failing will rise to the challenge and regain the confidence of parents. In the worst case, we will offer scholarships to America's neediest children.

As another example, in his campaign for the widespread adoption of the CCSS in the United States ten years later, Microsoft billionaire Bill Gates Jr. (2009, n.p.) remarked:

> When the tests are aligned to the common standards, the curriculum will line up as well—and that will unleash powerful market forces in the service of better teaching. For the first time, there will be a large base of customers eager to buy products that can help every kid learn and every teacher get better.

High-stakes testing is central in framing education as a capitalist enterprise because the data produced by the tests are used as *the* metric for determining value, which, in turn, is used for comparison and competition in the educational marketplace (Au, 2023). Within these logics, "good" teachers and schools produce high test scores in students, "bad" teachers and schools produce low test scores in students, parents can use the data to then make choices about where to send their children (a.k.a. where the investment of their public monies should go), "bad" teachers can receive low evaluations and be fired, "bad" schools with low test scores will lose market share, be converted to charter schools and/or be closed, and "good" schools with high test scores will remain open and be successful. The tests and their scores allow education to be reconstructed around a simple model of commodity production, consumption, and marketplace competition akin to Adam Smith's invisible hand of the free market (Fabricant & Fine, 2013).

One concrete extension of this system of high-stakes testing is the control of both student and teacher labor. Functionally what happens is that, in response to the pressures of the tests, schools and teachers shape their curriculum and instruction to meet the test requirements. In doing so, teachers are compelled to "teach to the test" and restructure their pedagogies toward rote lectures and alter their curriculum toward more memorization to cover tested content (Au, 2007, 2023). Elsewhere, I've labeled this phenomenon "Teaching Under the New Taylorism" (Au, 2011) because of the rise of scripted curriculum that not only tells teachers what textbook page or lesson they must be teaching on a particular day, but sometimes even tells teachers exactly what they can and cannot say in the classroom. Of course, these kinds of test-compelled changes to curriculum and pedagogy ultimately control what and how students are learning too, as they find themselves being directed to perform educational labor that is aimed solely at what the tests require (Hikida & Taylor, 2020; Jennings & Bearak, 2014). Importantly, we must also recognize that the legacies of white supremacy intervene here as well, since research has consistently found that working class, Black and Latinx students in particular, have experienced the most stringent teaching to the test (Au, 2016; McNeil, 2005; Valenzuela et al., 2007), including the removal of non-Eurocentric, anti-racist curriculum from their classrooms (Au, 2009, 2023).

12.3 High-Stakes Testing, Commodification, and the Violence of Abstraction

The process of turning education—students, teachers, schools, and learning—into a number vis-à-vis high-stakes testing enables education to be viewed as a capitalist endeavor, shaping schooling akin to factory production lines, making comparisons, ranking everything, and treating it all like a competitive marketplace. The key to this process is the abstracting of the more complex, individuated contexts of students into a more generalized, decontextualized, or abstracted form articulated as a simplified number or data point. In turn, this allows for students (and schools and teachers) to be viewed as commodities with differentiated values within an idealized educational marketplace. High-stakes, standardized tests act as a specific kind of tool to facilitate this transformation of people and learning into numerical commodities.

In *Capital* Volume 1, Marx (1967) discusses how commodities are made up of two types of value: use value and exchange value. Use value is concrete in that it refers to the actual use of a thing. If you have a chair, for instance, you can use it to sit on. That is its use value. Exchange value is what you can get in exchange for a thing. In the case of your chair, it is what you can get in exchange for it in terms of money or something else deemed of similar value. Importantly then, once we consider something's exchange value, we are forced to abstract from the thing itself. That is to say, once you decide to sell your chair, you have to make a leap to viewing the chair (the concrete thing) as equivalent to something else that is not the actual chair, like money. This is a process of abstraction. Critical to the current analysis of high-stakes testing and commodification of people and learning, using Marx's analysis we see that high-stakes tests are created and used in such a way as to create an exchange value between students, teachers, schools, districts, and nations. The tests have to turn the people and institutions into commensurate objects for comparison within a policy field that treats education as a capitalist enterprise. This is a process of abstraction built upon positivistic notions of objective measurement and decontextualization (Au, 2023).

The whole basis for standardized testing is to be able to make (supposedly) fair and objective comparisons between students, teachers, schools, districts, states, and countries. To do so, we give the same test, in as standardized conditions as possible (same amount of time allotted, same exact directions read out loud, maybe using the same computer program, in a quiet-as-possible space), to different students in different classrooms in different regions. The whole premise is that minimizing contextual differences allows us to make valid and meaningful comparisons between students taking the same test in different contexts. Researchers, policymakers, and laypeople can then meaningfully assert that one student outperformed another student based on test scores. In essence, in order to operate as a tool for comparison, standardized tests are designed to deny large amounts of local context, local variability, or local difference, in order to establish a common measurement that can reach across a wide range of locations/contexts. Without such a denial of context, it would be impossible to compare students, teachers, schools, and countries using these scores.

Consequently, in our use of standardized tests to make comparisons and judgments, there is a built-in assumption that the tests themselves are objective, because objectivity would mean that there are no local, individual conditions or factors that would corrupt validity of the scores. Within that paradigm, extenuating circumstances of contextual factors simply do not exist for the test scores. This decontextualization is a literal abstraction of humans from their defining contexts, and it serves as the basis for standardized testing as a technology for transforming whole people and complex processes into numbers. As Lipman (2004, p. 172) explains in her study of the impact of high-stakes testing policies in Chicago schools:

> Students, as well as teachers, with all their varied talents and challenges, were reduced to a test score. And schools, as well as their communities, in all their complexity—their failings, inadequacies, strong points, superb and weak teachers, ethical commitments to collective uplift, their energy, demoralization, courage, potential, and setbacks—were blended, homogenized, and reduced to a stanine score.

In the process of the quantification of student knowledge, students themselves are quantified as a number. This quantification lies at the heart of the tests themselves, which turns real people and real social conditions into easily measurable and comparable numbers and categories. De Lissovoy and McLaren (2003, p. 133) point out how this is required to create commensurability:

> The key principle at work in the use of standardized tests, which is also what allows them to serve as the mechanism for accountability initiatives, is the reduction of learning and knowledge to a number, i.e. a score. Once this takes place, scores can be compared, statistically analysed and variously manipulated....In reducing learning to a test score, policy makers seek to make the knowledge of disparate individuals commensurable.

Standardized tests thus, by definition, objectify students by reducing them into decontextualized numerical objects for comparison, and by reducing students to numbers, standardized testing creates the capacity to view students as things, as quantities apart from their human qualities (Au, 2023; McNeil, 2005). This objectification is the key link to understanding the fundamental connections between systems of standardized testing and the application of logics of capitalism to education.

Standardized Testing and Commodity Fetishism

The objectification-through-quantification of students using standardized testing conceptually allows students to be seen as products and for education to be conceived of within the paradigm of capitalist production. In this way, standardized testing essentially *commodifies* students, literally turning them into commodities to be produced, inspected, and compared (Au, 2023; Berlak, 2000). In turn, this commodification of students and education enables systems of education to be framed akin to systems of commerce, because the logics of capitalist production require commodities to be produced, assessed, compared, and exchanged on the market (Brosio, 1994; Marx, 1967). This quantified and abstracted view of the production of commodities (whether students or material goods) is problematic, however, because it hides the actual human relations that exist in the process of their production, as well as in the products themselves. This phenomenon, as Marx (1967, p. 72) explains, is a "mysterious" thing that happens in the process of production and exchange of commodities under capitalism:

> A commodity is therefore a mysterious thing, simply because in it the social character of [human] labour appears...as an objective character stamped upon the product of that labour: because the relation of the producers to the sum total of their own labour is presented to them as a social relation, existing not between themselves, but between the products of their labour. This is the reason why the products of labour become commodities, social things whose qualities are at the same time perceptible and imperceptible by the senses.

Here, Marx is explaining how, under capitalism, when we deal with commodities, we see them as having characteristics that exist separately from the social and material relations that went into the production of that commodity. As a rough example to illustrate: when we get a new cell phone or computer, the logics of capitalism compel us to not consider the abusive child labor (Amnesty International, 2016) or the massive environmental damage that goes into lithium mining for our rechargeable batteries (Katwala, 2018). As such, the labor and resources that "live" inside commodities are hidden because we see commodities as things unto themselves and not as the collection of relations and resources that went into their production. Marx (1967) goes on to explain that things thus appear as relations between products of labor as opposed to relations between people. This disconnection of labor from commodities, this mysterious relationship between labor itself and the products of labor under capitalism, is what Marx calls commodity fetishism.

Marx's (1967) concept of commodity fetishism provides a window into how students are viewed within the capitalist logics of standardized testing. Students are commodified as soon as a commitment is made to the assumptions of standardized test as objective. This is evident in the abstract quantification of students as test scores, where their value in the educational marketplace is measured by the scores themselves. This value is determined through the measurement, categorization, and comparison of students-as-commodities, for they gain or lose their value only in relation to other students (other commodities). Those with higher test scores are more highly valued and can gain more highly valued credentials and diplomas, thus further increasing their value within the educational and employment marketplaces. Likewise, those with lower test scores are similarly commodified with lower value and for lower-level work (Au, 2023; Lapayese, 2007).

Within systems of standardized testing, then, the value of students is therefore not to be found in their humanity. Rather, students' values are found in their test scores—objectified, commodified, one-dimensional, and highly abstracted versions of the human beings sitting in a classroom. Thus, what is lost in this vision of commodified students, what is fetishized in this process, are the networks of social and environmental relations that constitute students' very being as humans. Hence, students' lives, home cultures, histories, educational differences, and socioeconomic conditions mean nothing within the logics of high-stakes, standardized testing. The realities of local conditions or specific contexts that impact, affect, and shape student performance are denied by regimes of standardized testing. Consequently, distancing test scores from the realities of students' lives and school conditions, systems of high-stakes testing effectively mask the existence of social relations and structural inequalities exploitation that persist in their lives (Au, 2023; McNeil, 2000).

This process of commodification of students, the abstraction of their being into quantified numbers for comparison within a system of capitalist-styled educational competition, is itself a form of violence, because, in Marx's (1842, n.p.) terms, it takes living, breathing humans and replaces them with the "immoral, irrational, and soulless abstraction of a particular material object and a particular consciousness which is slavishly subordinated to this object." In this regard, I strenuously agree with Day (2016, p. 9, *original emphasis*) when she remarks, "Where I locate the principal violence of capitalism is in the very way it abstracts (or rendered homogeneous as commensurable units of labor) highly differentiated gendered and racialized labor *in order to create value.*"

The value creation of commensurable units for comparison through high-stakes, standardized testing is an act of capitalistic violence against students. It is especially important to recognize that this violence is highly racialized as well (Au, 2018; Mayorga et al., 2020), where research consistently shows that low-income, students of color face more test-restricted forms of knowledge, curriculum, and pedagogy at significantly higher rates than their affluent, white peers—a phenomenon that ultimately restricts what student cultural and racial identities are deemed worthy to include in test-influenced classrooms (Au, 2023).

12.4 High-Stakes Testing, Correlations, and Measurement

Given that high-stakes, standardized tests rely on abstraction, decontextualization, and commodification of students' humanity in order to function as an "objective" tool of measurement, then it is important to recognize that perhaps testing advocates do not really understand what these tests are actually measuring. It is often presumed that our tests are measuring learning causally. That is, we teach content here, and that causes the student to learn over there. Then, we are supposedly measuring that causal relationship with the standardized test. The thing is, none of our standardized testing measures causality. They instead sample what a student is supposed to have learned (or a teacher is supposed to have taught), and then that sample is used to *infer* how much of the total the student learned. They only measure an inference based on a sample, and based on this inference, we presume that a correlation exists between how the student performed on the test and what they've learned. Our standardized tests actually measure indirect correlations, not direct causality (Amrein-Beardsley, 2014; Popham, 2001).

What many don't realize is that there are many different correlations we find with high-stakes test scores, and without a doubt, the strongest correlation we see with standardized test scores is poverty (Weber, 2016). As Berliner (2013, p. 5) explains:

> Virtually every scholar of teaching and schooling knows that when the variance in student scores on achievement tests is examined along with the many potential factors that may have contributed to those test scores, school effects account for about 20% of the variation in achievement test scores.... On the other hand, out-of-school variables account for about 60% of the variance that can be accounted for in student achievement. In aggregate, such factors as family income; the

neighborhood's sense of collective efficacy, violence rate, and average income; medical and dental care available and used; level of food insecurity; number of moves a family makes over the course of a child's school years;…provision of high-quality early education in the neighborhood; language spoken at home; and so forth, all substantially affect school achievement.

We also know that poverty overlaps disproportionately with race in the United States (National Poverty Center, 2017), and this reality maps onto many race-based disparities in test scores as well. For instance, data from the SAT college entrance test have consistently, across decades, shown a near perfect symmetry of race and economic class disparities in scores (Boeckenstedt, 2020). Ultimately, as Amrein-Beardsley (2014, p. 209) explains, "Correlations between student test scores and students' demographic and environmental backgrounds are so strong that one (i.e., students' demographics) can effectively be used to predict the other (i.e., students' test scores), even before the students take the tests, with near perfect precision." High-stakes standardized tests may not be very good at measuring teaching and learning, but they are really good at measuring poverty and family educational attainment.

In addition to poverty, standardized test scores also correlate with a whole host of other things as well. For instance, two studies have found a correlation between the amount of greenness from trees around the school (more trees and in the spring season) and slightly higher test scores (Kuo et al., 2018; Wu et al., 2014). Another study found a correlation between test scores and cardiorespiratory fitness (Garber et al., 2018), and other studies have noted the correlation between temperatures and test score performance (Chang & Kajackaite, 2019; Goodman et al., 2018). Studies have also found correlations between stress, cortisol levels, and lower test scores (Adam et al., 2017; Heissel et al., 2021), while other studies have also drawn correlations between levels of cognitive fatigue and test scores (Sievertsen et al., 2016). Based on the above research, while we cannot necessarily say that high-stakes, standardized tests measure learning, we can say that at a minimum they measure family poverty levels, how much tree cover there is on school grounds, the temperatures experienced by students, stress experienced by students both at school and at home, student cardiorespiratory fitness, and levels of cognitive fatigue. Based on the above evidence, I propose that our tests might be measuring something else altogether—what Marx (1967) referred to as "socially necessary labor time."

12.5 Measuring Socially Necessary Labor Time

As I discussed earlier in this chapter, through the processes of decontextualization and abstraction (separating students from the complex material realities and disparities of resources in their lives), standardized tests commodify students. This, in turn, enables systems of education policy to be structured in the form of capitalist markets, where students can be compared via test scores and where the scores set their values in the educational marketplace. Marx's examination of how that labor related to the value of commodities in capitalist exchanges is helpful here. In Marx's (Marx, 1967, pp. 39–40) analysis, commodities

> in which equal quantities of labour are embodied, or which can be produced in the same time, have the same value. The value of one commodity is to the value of any other, as the labour-time necessary for the production of the one is to that necessary for the production of the other.

He goes on to add, "As values, all commodities are only definite masses of congealed labour time" (p. 40). Using this framing, we can see the test-determined student-commodities as embodying "congealed labour time"—what we might say is the labor of social, family, institutional, and community resources that have gone into producing the student taking the test. It would then follow that relatively equal amounts of labor and time would likely produce commodities of equal value or, in this case, students with similar test scores (Au, 2023). Marx (1967, p. 40) further acknowledges that differences in the labor and resources used to produce commodities produce different values:

> The value of a commodity would therefore remain constant, if the labour-time required for its production also remained constant. But the latter changes with every variation in the productiveness of labour. This productiveness is determined by various circumstances, amongst others, by the average amount of skill of the [workers], the state of science, and the degree of its practical application, the social organisation of production, the extent and capabilities of the means of production, and physical conditions.

Applied to the test-derived commodification of students, we can start to understand that the "various circumstances" such as physical conditions, teacher's skill, what we understand about teaching and learning, the social relations that go into learning, and the resources that go into learning thereby influence the "value" created in students. This, in turn, leads to the concept of socially necessary labor time, where: "We see then that that which determines the magnitude of the value of any article is the amount of labour socially necessary, or the labour-time socially necessary for its production" (ibid., p. 39). Given that high-stakes, standardized test scores correlate most strongly with economic class and factors connected to the social, economic, and biological health of students' families and communities (Berliner, 2013), I would argue that our tests are measuring the differential social resources accrued within students. Or, put in terms of Marx's critique of capitalism, because kids with fewer resources in their lives effectively embody less congealed social labor (or because kids with more resources in their lives effectively embody more congealed social labor), our tests are measuring the highly differential and disparate socially necessary labor time used to produce different groups of students.

In essence, standardized tests are very broad measures of a broadly socioeconomic process of resource distribution and are terrible for measuring anything at the individual level.

12.6   Conclusion

For most Marxists, it is obvious that a school system developed under capitalism would not only be structured by policies and forms associated with capitalist production and competition (Bowles & Gintis, 1976), but also rely on a tool of measurement—high-stakes, standardized testing—that turns students into abstract commodities to support a capitalist paradigm (Au, 2018). Indeed, I would argue that this is exactly why we need Marxist analyses of high-stakes, standardized testing, as they (and the policies they are attached to) ultimately do the same things to students and teachers as capitalism does to labor and commodities. As such, in this chapter, I have sought to deepen our understanding of how these tests transform teachers and students into things as part of a process of violent abstraction and commodification. Further, I have argued that rather than measuring teaching or learning, the tests actually argue socially necessary labor time. That is to say, the tests measure the accrual of social labor in a child's education.

There is, of course, resistance to high-stakes, standardized testing and it's forced commodification of students, teachers, and education. Some of that resistance is simply the day-to-day decisions of classroom teachers deciding to "go rogue" and depart from test-mandated curriculum because they know it would be in the best interests of their students (e.g., Hikida & Taylor, 2020). There is also more broadly organized resistance, for instance, in the case of the teachers, parents, and students at Garfield High School in Seattle, WA. In 2013, the teachers at Garfield announced that they would be refusing to administer a standardized test that they thought was harmful to students' education and a waste of resources. Parents joined this resistance and offered their public support for this labor action. Students also joined through protest, official endorsement of the action, refusing to take the mandated test, and, in some cases, sitting for the test but actively sabotaging the test scores (Hagopian, 2014). There have also been significant national movements by U.S. parents to have their children opt out of taking the tests (Chen et al., 2021; Pizmony-Levy & Saraisky, 2016, 2021).

Importantly, we need to recognize that other forms of assessment exist that challenge the capitalist framing of high-stakes, standardized tests. Some of these include:

- Student self-assessments: In student self-assessments, students reflect on the work they've done and potentially articulate whether or not (and how) that work meets their own or their teacher's expectations.
- Teacher observations: This can include acting as ethnographers in their own or in others' classrooms, where a trusted colleague might observe some teaching and offer specific feedback at the request of another col-

league or teachers keeping their own field notes to help remember and assess how particular students are doing and/or how well a lesson worked, among others.

- Portfolios and public defenses of student work: In this assessment, students spend a significant amount of time (sometimes weeks) building a portfolio of work that they think reflects their learning and also meets whatever requirements or expectations that have been established. These portfolios not only include student curation of work, but also student meta-reflection on the work relative to how and why it meets expectations and represents their learning. Then students are asked to do a public defense of their portfolios to an audience that can include teachers, peers, parents, and community members (Meier & Knoester, 2017).

There are other examples, but the point here is to emphasize a few key differences of these kinds of assessments compared to high-stakes, standardized tests and their focus on commodification, comparison, and market-based education reform. So, while standardized testing focuses on efficiency and producing simplified numbers for comparison, anti-capitalist assessments are purposefully inefficient and attempt to look more deeply into learning and expressions of learning. This lack of efficiency also implies that teachers need more time, space, and control of their labor to work on these assessments, as they are much more individualized to students and classrooms. Further, while standardized tests are framed as a singular event to capture learning, assessments that challenge capitalism are interested in demonstrating processes of learning in and of itself. That is to say that, in doing a portfolio for instance, students are learning in the process of creating that portfolio and defending their work. Unlike high-stakes testing, these kinds of assessments also make no claim to being objective, and they are not useful for making comparisons, doing rankings, or otherwise treating students as marketplace competitors. Rather, these assessments are much more hyper-local, subjective to what students have learned in their specific classrooms and communities, and are designed for them to have increased power over the demonstration of their own learning (Au, 2023).

Just as we know that resistant, anti-capitalist forms of education are possible, we also know that resistant, anti-capitalist forms of assessment are possible. However, maintaining these anti-capitalist forms of assessment in a sea of systems built around high-stakes, standardized testing means constantly working against the tide, constantly struggling to keep our humanizing and potentially liberating assessments alive (Au, 2018, 2023). This leaves us with the same dialectic as always: anti-capitalist assessments help us glimpse the possibility of new and different educational worlds, but we're going to need a new anti-capitalist world to truly give up our reliance on high-stakes, standardized testing for good.

Disclosure Statement The author received no financial support for this research and does not have any financial interest or benefit from the application of this research.

References

Adam, E. K., Heissel, J. A., Hittner, E. F., Doleac, J. L., Meer, J., & Figlio, D. (2017). Adolescent Cortisol Responses to High-Stakes Testing in School-Based Settings. *Psychoneuroendocrinology, 83*, 85. https://doi.org/10.1016/j.psyneuen.2017.07.465

Amnesty International. (2016, January 19). *Exposed: Child Labour Behind Smart Phone and Electric Car Batteries*. Amnesty International. Retrieved October 27, 2021, from https://www.amnesty.org/en/latest/news/2016/01/child-labour-behind-smart-phone-and-electric-car-batteries/

Amrein-Beardsley, A. (2014). *Rethinking Value-Added Models in Education: Critical Perspectives on Tests and Assessment-Based Accountability*. Routledge.

Au, W. (2007). High-Stakes Testing and Curricular Control: A Qualitative Metasynthesis. *Educational Researcher, 36*(5), 258–267.

Au, W. (2009). High-Stakes Testing and Discursive Control: The Triple Bind for Nonstandard Student Identities. *Multicultural Perspectives, 11*(2), 65–71.

Au, W. (2011). Teaching Under the New Taylorism: High-Stakes Testing and the Standardization of the 21st Century Curriculum. *Journal of Curriculum Studies, 43*(1), 25–45. https://doi.org/10.1080/00220272.2010.521261

Au, W. (2016). Meritocracy 2.0: High-Stakes, Standardized Testing as a Racial Project of Neoliberal Multiculturalism. *Educational Policy, 30*(1), 39–62. https://doi.org/10.1177/0895904815614916

Au, W. (2018). *A Marxist Education: Learning to Change the World*. Haymarket Books.

Au, W. (2023). *Unequal by Design: High-Stakes Testing and the Standardization of Inequality* (2nd ed.). Routledge.

Berlak, H. (2000). Cultural Politics, the Science of Assessment and Democratic Renewal of Public Education. In A. Filer (Ed.), *Assessment: Social Practice and Social Product* (pp. 189–207). RoutledgeFalmer.

Berliner, D. C. (2013). Effects of Inequality and Poverty vs. Teachers and Schooling on America's Youth. *Teachers College Record, 115*(12). https://doi.org/10.1177/016146811311501203

Blanton, C. K. (2003). From Intellectual Deficiency to Cultural Deficiency: Mexican Americans, Testing, and Public School Policy in the American Southwest, 1920–1940. *Pacific Historical Review, 72*(1), 39–62.

Boeckenstedt, J. (2020, January 10). Some Final Thoughts on the SAT and ACT. *Jon Boeckenstedt's Admissions Weblog*. Retrieved October 30, 2021, from https://jon-boeckenstedt.net/2020/01/10/some-final-thoughts-on-the-sat-and-act/?fbclid=IwAR0ZBvh7hPkbbniDlD8Arnigl-xhKu5-ubb3fx2vlhvkefO42tPs9penL0c

Bowles, S., & Gintis, H. (1976). *Schooling in Capitalist America: Educational Reform and the Contradictions of Economic Life* (1st ed.). Basic Books.

Brosio, R. A. (1994). *A Radical Democratic Critique of Capitalist Education* (1st ed.). Peter Lang.

Bush, G. W. (1999, October 5). *The Future of Educational Reform*. Retrieved May 2, 2014, from http://www.manhattan-institute.org/html/bush_speech.htm

Callahan, R. E. (1964). *Education and the Cult of Efficiency: A Study of the Social Forces That Have Shaped the Administration of the Public Schools* (First Phoenix Edition). University of Chicago Press.

Chang, T. Y., & Kajackaite, A. (2019). Battle for the Thermostat: Gender and the Effect of Temperature on Cognitive Performance. *PLoS ONE, 14*(5), 1–10. https://doi.org/10.1371/journal.pone.0216362

Chapman, P. D. (1988). *Schools as Sorters: Lewis M. Terman, Applied Psychology, and the Intelligence Testing Movement, 1890–1930*. New York University Press.

Chen, Z., Hursh, D., & Lingard, B. (2021). The Opt-Out Movement in New York: A Grassroots Movement to Eliminate HGH-Stakes Testing and Promote Whole Child Public Schooling. *Teachers College Record, 123*(5), 1–22. https://doi.org/10.1177/016146812112300504

Counts, G. S. (1927). *The Social Composition of Boards of Education: A Study in the Social Control of Public Education*. Arno Press & The New York Times.

Creighton, J. V. (2006, March 13). It Doesn't Test for Success. *Los Angeles Times*. https://www.latimes.com/archives/la-xpm-2006-mar-13-oe-creighton13-story.html

Day, I. (2016). *Alien Capital: Asian Racialization and the Logic of Settler Colonial Capitalism*. Duke University Press.

De Lissovoy, N., & McLaren, P. (2003). Educational "accountability" and the Violence of Capital: A Marxian Reading. *Journal of Educational Policy, 18*(2), 131–143.

Fabricant, M., & Fine, M. (2013). *The Changing Politics of Education: Privatization and the Dispossessed Lives Left Behind*. Paradigm Publishers.

Garber, M. D., Stanhope, K. K., Cheung, P., & Gazmararian, J. A. (2018). Effect of Cardiorespiratory Fitness on Academic Achievement Is Stronger in High-SES Elementary Schools Compared to Low. *Journal of School Health, 88*(10), 707–716.

Gates Jr., B. (2009, July 21). *Speech Delivered to the National Conference of State Legislatures*. National Conference of State Legislatures. Retrieved May 5, 2014, from http://www.gatesfoundation.org/media-center/speeches/2009/07/bill-gates-national-conference-of-state-legislatures-ncsl

Goodman, J., Hurwitz, M., Park, J., & Smith, J. (2018). *Heat and Learning*. Working Paper No. 24639. National Bureau of Economic Research. http://www.nber.org/papers/w24639

Gould, S. J. (1996). *The Mismeasure of Man* (Rev. and expanded.). Norton.

Hagopian, J. (2014). Our Destination Is Not on the MAP. In *More Than a Score: The New Uprising Against High-Stakes Testing* (pp. 31–47). Haymarket Books.

Haney, W. (1984). Testing Reasoning and Reasoning About Testing. *Review of Educational Research, 54*(4), 597–654.

Heissel, J. A., Adam, E. K., Doleac, J. L., Figlio, D., & Meer, J. (2021). Testing, Stress, and Performance: How Students Respond Physiologically to High-Stakes Testing. *Education Finance and Policy, 16*(2), 183–208. https://doi.org/10.1162/edfp_a_00306

Hikida, M., & Taylor, L. A. (2020). "As the test collapses in": Teaching and Learning Amid High-Stakes Testing in Two Urban Elementary Classrooms. *Urban Education*, 1–29. https://doi.org/10.1177/0042085920902263

Jennings, J. L., & Bearak, J. M. (2014). "Teaching to the test" in the NCLB Era: How Test Predictability Affects Our Understanding of Student Performance. *Educational Researcher, 43*(8), 381–389. https://doi.org/10.3102/0013189X14554449

Jones, G. M., Jones, B. D., & Hargrove, T. Y. (2003). *The Unintended Consequences of High-Stakes Testing*. Rowman & Littlefield Publishers, Inc.

Karp, S. (2006). Bandaids Or Bulldozers?: What's Next for NCLB. *Rethinking Schools, 20*(3). Retrieved May 2, 2014, from https://rethinkingschools.org/articles/band-aids-or-bulldozers/

Karp, S. (2014). The Problems with the Common Core. *Rethinking Schools, 28*(2). Retrieved May 2, 2014, from http://www.rethinkingschools.org/archive/28_02/28_02_karp.shtml

Karp, S. (2016). ESSA: NCLB Repackaged. *Rethinking Schools, 30*(3). Retrieved February 17, 2017, from http://www.rethinkingschools.org/archive/30_03/30-3_karp.shtml

Katwala, A. (2018, May 8). The Spiralling Environmental Cost of Our Lithium Battery Addiction. *Wired*. Retrieved October 27, 2021, from https://www.wired.co.uk/article/lithium-batteries-environment-impact

Kidder, W. C., & Rosner, J. (2002). How the SAT Creates "built-in headwinds": An Educational and Legal Analysis of Disparate Impact. *Santa Clara Law Review, 43*, 131–212.

Kornhaber, M. L., & Orfield, G. (2001). High-Stakes Testing Policies: Examining Their Assumptions and Consequences. In G. Orfield & M. L. Kornhaber (Eds.), *Raising Standards Or Raising Barriers?: Inequality and High-Stakes Testing in Public Education* (pp. 1–18). Century Foundation Press.

Kuo, M., Browning, M. H. E. M., Sachdeva, S., Lee, K., & Westphal, L. (2018). Might School Performance Grown on Trees? Examining the Link Between "greenness" and Academic Achievement in Urban, High-Poverty Schools. *Frontiers in Psychology, 9*(1669), 1–14.

Lapayese, Y. V. (2007). Understanding and Undermining the Racio-Economic Agenda of No Child Left Behind: Using Critical Race Methodology to Investigate the Labor of Bilingual Children. *Race, Ethnicity, and Education, 10*(3), 309–321.

Lemann, N. (1999). *The Big Test: The Secret History of the American Meritocracy*. Farrar, Straus, and Giroux.

Lipman, P. (2004). *High Stakes Education: Inequality, Globalization, and Urban School Reform*. RoutledgeFalmer.

Marx, K. (1842). *Debates on the Law on the Theft of Wood*. Articles from the Rheinische Zeitung. Retrieved January 12, 2023, from https://www.marxists.org/archive/marx/works/download/Marx_Rheinishe_Zeitung.pdf

Marx, K. (1967). *Capital: A Critique of Political Economy* (S. M. & E. Aveling, Trans.; Vol. 1). International Publishers.

Mayorga, E., Aggarwal, U., & Picower, B. (Eds.). (2020). *What's Race Got to Do with It: How Current School Reform Policy Maintains Racial and Economic Inequality* (2nd ed.). Peter Lang.

McNeil, L. M. (2000). *Contradictions of School Reform: Educational Costs of Standardized Testing*. Routledge.

McNeil, L. M. (2005). Faking Equity: High-Stakes Testing and the Education of Latino Youth. In A. Valenzuela (Ed.), *Leaving Children Behind: How "Texas-style" Accountability Fails Latino Youth* (pp. 57–112). State University of New York.

Meier, D., & Knoester, M. (2017). *Beyond Testing: Seven Assessments of Students and Schools More Effective Than Standardized Tests*. Teachers College Press.

National Commission on Excellence in Education. (1983). *A Nation at Risk: The Imperative for Educational Reform* (p. 65). United States Department of Education.

National Poverty Center. (2017). *Poverty in the United States: Frequently Asked Questions*. National Poverty Center: Poverty Facts. http://www.npc.umich.edu/poverty/

Nearing, S. (1917). Who's Who on Our Boards of Education. *School and Society, V*.

Nichols, S. L., & Berliner, D. C. (2007). *Collateral Damage: How High-Stakes Testing Corrupts America's Schools*. Harvard Education Press.

Pizmony-Levy, O., & Saraisky, N. G. (2016). *Who Opts Out and Why? Results from a National Survey on Opting Out of Standardized Tests*. Teachers College, Columbia University. Retrieved November 16, 2021, from https://www.google.com/url?sa=t&rct=j&q=&esrc=s&source=web&cd=&cad=rja&uact=8&ved=2ahUKEwiZ0K6dwp30AhWGDjQIHdKhBwUQFnoECCEQAQ&url=https%3A%2F%2Fwww.tc.columbia.edu%2Fmedia%2Fnews%2Fdocs%2FOpt_Out_National-Survey%2D%2D%2D%2DFINAL-FULL-REPORT.pdf&usg=AOvVaw1YySXYhIfgOv2LUV7sbY-k

Pizmony-Levy, O., & Saraisky, N. G. (2021). Why Did They Protest? Stability and Change in the Opt-Out Movement, 2016–2018. *Teachers College Record, 123*(5), 1–30. https://doi.org/0.1177/016146812112300503

Popham, W. J. (2001). *The Truth About Testing: An Educator's Call to Action*. Association for Supervision and Curriculum Development (ASCD).

Rosner, J. (2012). The SAT: Quantifying the Unfairness Behind the Bubbles. In J. A. Soares (Ed.), *SAT Wars*. Teachers College Press.

Santelices, M. V., & Wilson, M. (2010). Unfair Treatment?: The Case of Freedle, the SAT, and the Standardization Approach to Differential Item Functioning. *Harvard Educational Review, 80*(1), 106–133.

Selden, S. (1999). *Inheriting Shame: The Story of Eugenics and Racism in America*. Teachers College Press.

Sievertsen, H. H., Gino, F., & Piovesan, M. (2016). Cognitive Fatigue Influences Students' Performance on Standardized Tests. *PNAS, 113*(10), 2621–2624. https://doi.org/www.pnas.org/cgi/doe/10.1073/pnas.1516947113

Terman, L. (1916). *The Measure of Intelligence*. Houghton Mifflin.

Timar, T., & Tyack, D. (1999). *The Invisible Hand of Ideology: Perspectives from the History of School Governance* (SE-99-3; p. 23). Education Commission of the States. http://www.ecs.org/clearinghouse/13/55/1355.doc

U.S. Department of Education. (2002). *No Child Left Behind: A Desktop Reference*. U.S. Department of Education, Office of the Under Secretary. Educational Resources and Information Center (ERIC).

U.S. Department of Education. (2009). *Race to the Top Program Executive Summary*. U.S.

Valenzuela, A., Prieto, L., & Hamilton, M. P. (2007). No Child Left Behind and Minority Youth: What the Qualitative Evidence Suggests. *Anthropology & Education Quarterly, 38*(1), 1–8.

Viera, M. (2018, October 1). The History of HTE SAT Is Mired in Racism and Elitism. *Teen Vogue*. https://www.teenvogue.com/story/the-history-of-the-sat-is-mired-in-racism-and-elitism

Weber, M. (2016, April 27). The PARCC Silly Season. *Jersey Jazzman*. http://jersey-jazzman.blogspot.com/2016/04/the-parcc-silly-season.html

Wu, C.-D., McNeely, E., Cedeno-Laurent, J. G., Pan, W.-C., Adamkiewicz, G., Dominici, F., Lung, S.-C. C. L., Su, H.-J., & Spengler, J. D. (2014). Linking Student Performance in Massachusetts Elementary Schools with the "greenness" of School Surroundings Using Remote Sensing. *PLoS ONE, 9*(10), 1–9. https://doi.org/10.1371/journal.pone.0108548

CHAPTER 13

The Reproduction of Capitalism in Education: Althusser and the Educational Ideological State Apparatus

Toni Ruuska

13.1 Introduction

Steve McQueen's *Small Axe* (2020) drama film series deals with the topics of discrimination, marginalization, and racism in the 1960s–1980s London. The final film of the series five, *Education*, tells a story of fictional characters, but one that is based on real-life experiences of the immigrants from the West Indies in the 1960s and early 1970s. The film's protagonist Kingsley is a clever and lively 12-year-old boy, who has trouble to read. The school offers little assistance to Kingsley; on the contrary, he is targeted due to his background. In one of the opening scenes, an English teacher mistreats Kingsley in class as he struggles to read. Because his reading is not on the expected level, Kingsley scores low in I.Q. tests, and thus the headmaster sends him to "a special school", where children are mostly neglected, even abandoned.

Luckily for Kingsley, he has loving, if strict, mother and caring sister, whose consciousness, regarding Kingsley's educational neglect, is raised by local politicians and activists. They find out that these kinds of procedures are systemic, and that there is nothing special about the school Kingsley has been sent to, and instead it is a "school" for the "educationally subnormal". In this part of the film, Bernard Coard's educational pamphlet, *How the West Indian Child Is*

T. Ruuska (✉)
University of Helsinki, Helsinki, Finland
e-mail: toni.ruuska@helsinki.fi

© The Editor(s) (if applicable) and The Author(s), under exclusive license to Springer Nature Switzerland AG 2023
R. Hall et al. (eds.), *The Palgrave International Handbook of Marxism and Education*, Marxism and Education,
https://doi.org/10.1007/978-3-031-37252-0_13

Made Educationally Sub-normal in the British School System (1971/2021), is read carefully by Kingsley's mother and sister. Eventually the sister, Stephanie, also reads the text out loud to their father, who is, like many others of his generation, illiterate. With help, the mother tries to bring Kingsley back to the school from where he was sent off.

In parallel, Kingsley and Stephanie start attending to a weekend school, organized on a voluntary basis, with individual needs-based teaching, and exploration of the roots and untold histories of the pupils. In an empowering scene, the weekend schoolteacher asks from the students, 'What do you all know about our ancestors?', and one of the students answer, 'That we were slaves'. The teacher quickly shakes the response off by saying, 'That is what they want us to know'. After this the class embarks on the histories of African warrior princesses and past kingdoms, as we learn that the past can be used to demoralize but also to empower. As for Kingsley, with individual assistance, support, and inspiration, he picks up on his reading and the film ends with a touching scene where he reads a text out loud as the family is gathered around their dining table.

McQueen's depiction clearly highlights not only the worst side of education, that is, the systemic and structural discrimination, and neglect of children, but also the emancipatory and empowering potential of it. For this collected volume and beyond, the film raises essential questions on education as it brings forward the different qualities of schooling, but also the wider institutional and economic-political context where education takes place. Now, if the liberal take on education is the "great equalizer", Marxist education scholars (e.g., Bowles & Gintis, 1976; Carnoy & Levin, 1985; Cole, 2008) criticize this, especially in capitalist contexts, by noting that education tends to reflect the surrounding society, and its power relations. It surely matters how, when, where, and for what one is educated. If a society, its legislation, relations of production and ownership are organized or even based on inequality, discrimination, and class, education cannot be expected to deliver equality. And as capitalist societies are based on competition, merit, and thus winners over losers, it should not be a radical statement to argue that education reflects these cultural traits and produces unequal outcomes.

In Marxist literature on education (e.g., Anyon, 1997; Au, 2018; Cole, 2008; Gottesman, 2016), education is broadly understood as a field of contested ideas, where the dominant ideas, of a particular era, speak the loudest. The founders, Marx and Engels, did not write much on education but when they did, they remained critical of the liberal bourgeois understanding of it (see Cole, 2008, pp. 29–30). In *The German Ideology* (1998, p. 67) they famously argued that 'the class which has the means of material production at its disposal, consequently also controls the means of mental production, so that the ideas of those who lack the means of mental production are on the whole subject to it'. Apply this to schools and one gets the sense that instead of being "pure" or "impartial", the schools are places where the ideas and ideologies of the dominant classes are reflected, and communicated to, and adopted by the students. Marxist, but also non-Marxist critical education scholars (e.g., Althusser, 2014; Bourdieu & Passeron, 1990; Bowles & Gintis, 1976; Freire 1970/1996) maintain that education, in the way we know it in the late Western industrial capitalist societies, is not based on equality, but is rather a process of screening, selection, and (social) reproduction.

To explore the connections between education and capitalism, I have found the work of Louis Althusser (1918–1990) to be eye-opening (see, e.g., *On the Reproduction of Capitalism*, 2014). In his work the concept of *reproduction* is central. By portraying the reproduction of capitalism, in which Althusser's conception of education is paramount, this chapter describes education a process of capitalist subjection to dominant ideology, norms, and attitudes, or, in other words, as the process of indoctrination to the capitalist society. This is claimed because the micro world of education (increasingly) mirrors the logics and needs of capital (see Ruuska, 2017). Consequently, education in capitalism commits students for careerism and meritocratic competition, creates pressure to succeed, and rewards submission and hard work for instrumental aims.

In the next section, I briefly go through how capitalism is reproduced. In the following section I present Althusser's remarks on *Ideological State Apparatuses* and education, before contemplating the sudden demise of both structuralism and the Althusserian approach to critical social and education theory. I also argue that reproduction theories in the field of education should be reconsidered in the 2020s educational context, but with certain reservations and updates. A reconsideration is in need, I argue, to deepen our understanding of the repercussions and outcomes of capitalist schooling, and how social structures, and institutions—in capitalism—contribute to socio-economic inequality.

13.2 Reproduction of Capitalism: A Brief Synthesis[1]

To change Kingsley's and others situation of systemic discrimination, neglect, and questionable social reproduction, we need to first understand the prevailing socio-economic dynamics, power relations, and socio-political structures that are reflected in education. Marxist education studies are explicit in this approach, as it insists, for instance, that we need to study education together with capitalism (or more generally education together with the wider societal structures and dynamics), to confront the problems of capitalist education.

Karl Marx was the first to "recognize", to name, and to deeply analyze the mode of production we today know as capitalism. It is well known that he did not just rigorously describe its components and dynamic logic but actively took the initiative to dismantle the whole system. Marx understood that capitalism is a paradoxical and unstable (or crisis prone) mode of production; for instance, the other side of accumulated wealth is socio-economic inequality, or poverty amid plenty (see, e.g., Harvey, 2014; Wright, 2010).

Capitalism has both remained the same and changed through ages. The industrial form of capitalism expanded its scope and influence from regional and continental contexts to eventually become a world-system (e.g., Malm, 2016; Wallerstein, 2004). The capital system (Mészáros, 2010) is a way to organize production of commodities, their distribution and exchange around private property and the profit motive. In terms of monetized "economic value" it has been very productive in utilizing cheap means of production, especially since it was coupled with the stored energy of sunlight in the form of fossil fuels, and their burning in combustion engines (Malm, 2016). By looking at its history, we can note that capitalism has been dynamic and flexible—there and have been several different versions of it; in fact to such a scale that it would perhaps be more sensible to speak about *capitalisms* (Wright, 2010). Nevertheless, some things have remained the same or are recognizable in its varying forms, such as private property, market exchange and competition, wage labor, surplus creation, and profit maximization. Yet, and as Wallerstein (2013, pp. 10–11) argues, the listing of characteristics of capitalism does not take us far in understanding its nature. Its fundamental logic and dynamic reveals itself, not in its characteristics, but in its processes, namely in the movements of capital (see also Harvey, 2014).

The most important systemic and processual trait of capitalism, according to Marx (1867/1973a), Wallerstein (e.g., 2013), and others, is the perpetual requirement for capital to accumulate. The endless demand for capital accumulation comes along with the need to invest, produce, and consume ever more. Worryingly for the questions of sustainability, capitalism cannot be downsized or halted without crisis. And its internal imperative for expansion is seemingly catastrophic, as the perpetual and exponential growth in production and consumption disrupts ecosystems and degrades the conditions of life now planetarily (e.g., Foster, 2009; Moore, 2015). Thus, in capitalism, the unprecedented material and monetary wealth has been coupled with socio-economic inequality, cultural imperialism, climate change, and mass extinction (Escobar, 1995; Foster, 2009; Wright, 2010).

Capitalism is, therefore, a deeply paradoxical way to organize production and distribution of commodities around commodification, profit maximization and wealth creation, investments, competition, and productivity enhancements. To be sure, none of it is reproduced without a proper regulation, nation states (or other safeguarding bodies), and supporting political-societal institutions, and of course, the individuals reproduced as workers and consumers in schools, universities, and at home. In my previous work I have used the term *socio-ideological structures* to highlight the bodies and parties that are not directly involved in the sphere of production, but nonetheless are vital in supporting and preserving capital accumulation and circulation (see Ruuska, 2017, 2019). The nation state and its institutions are among the most important ones, and education perhaps the most prominent of state institutions. But as we are dealing with a world-system, the political influence and power to steer the global economy that the transnational capitalist class, including their lobbying organizations, and many international organizations (such as UN, EU,

OECD, IMF, World Bank, and others) have, should be included in the analysis too (see Robinson, 2014).

By utilizing the concept of reproduction, we may address and examine these processual conditions, bodies, structures, and actions which enable the continuation of capitalism. Although it is the sphere of production, and the underlying relations of production and class, that define capitalism, the economic actors are dependent on reasonably stable socio-political conditions and the support of legislators, politicians, and societal institutions. They are also dependent on many services and infrastructures the states provide, such as educated workers, paved roads, (air)ports, and healthcare services, but also dependable on the state-monopolized "legal" violence, that is, the police, and the army. Regarding education per se, the economic actors need disciplined and skilled employees, but also the educational infrastructure, like schools, universities, educational technologies, student support services, and even the state-monopolized violence—think cops and security guards on campus, and mass surveillance technologies.

Reproduction as a Concept

In the first volume of *Capital* (1867/1973a) Marx applied the term "reproduction" to first describe how a *single* owner of the means of production continues his operation in a successful manner. In the second volume (1885/1973b) he portrayed the process of *extended* reproduction, as he explored the prospects for economic growth and the systemic economic factors for the continuance of capitalism. In addition, Morrow and Torres (1995, p. 122) have claimed that two other distinctions can be made based on Marx's exposition of reproduction. They are *complex* reproduction, and *transformation*. For our purposes, the former deals with questions how in capitalist societies societal stability is produced and maintained, and in our case how education contributes to social reproduction, and to the circulation and accumulation of capital. While the processes of single and extended reproduction have been studied at length in Marxist political economy, complex reproduction has received limited attention. There are, however, notable exceptions.

Antonio Gramsci (1971) was one of the early Marxists who paid attention to the wider socio-political dynamics regarding domination, ruling, and leadership, during the first decades of the twentieth century. Although he did not use the term "reproduction", he is nevertheless considered important for reproduction theorizing (see Giroux, 1983), especially because of his *cultural hegemony* conception, and due to his influence on Louis Althusser (e.g., Rehmann, 2014; Thomas, 2010). Hegemony, for Gramsci, is not only produced by authority, but also through cultural leadership. The dominant class, or historic bloc, rules in two ways: it leads the allied, and dominates the subordinate (ibid., p. 57). Hegemony, however, does not necessarily mean submission, because hegemony is never fully realized, but the subordinate classes and class fractions are often also powerless and disorganized (Lears, 1985, pp. 569–570).

Moreover, Gramsci argued that the dominant ideas are repeated and disseminated in what he termed *hegemonic apparatuses*; the dominant classes secure their power and position through various state institutions and structures, which communicate their ideas and aspirations to the wider public (see Thomas, 2010, pp. 223–224).

To combine the economic to the political, Balibar writes in *Reading Capital* (Althusser and Balibar 1968/2009, pp. 289–290) that the study of reproduction in capitalism entails the examination of three interconnected factors. The first is the recognition of the factors that secure the continuance of production. The second is the study and analysis of the intertwined relations of economic actors. The third is the portrayal and analysis of the interconnected relations between the factors of production, economic actors, and various societal structures and institutions, because the concept of reproduction implies also to the continuance of non-economic conditions and their stability. In a posthumous edited and collected volume *On the Reproduction of Capitalism* (2014)[2] Althusser utilizes the reproduction concept to study the continuation of capitalist relations of production. According to the analysis, all societies, and communities, whether capitalist or not, must reproduce conditions of production and livelihoods. For Althusser (2014, pp. 47–48) this entails the reproduction of: (1) the productive forces; and (2) the existing relations of production. According to both Althusser and Balibar, the reproduction of the conditions of production is not only a matter of production, but a more complex phenomenon and process, where the state and its institutions have an active role.

State (and) Capitalism

Historically, nation states have offered the legislative and socio-economic conditions for economic actors, as they have organized the workforce, and provided legal framework and stability to the markets (e.g., Calhoun, 2013). Marxist social and political scientists have, since the days of Marx and Engels, argued that the state is always the state of the dominant class(es) (see, e.g., Althusser, 2014, p. 80). Hence it is only logical to assume that the ideas, benefits, and practices of the dominant classes are reflected in state policy and its institutions.

Again here, we run counter to the hegemonic liberal-democratic take on things, and this time regarding the state. A liberal perception of the state tends to associate it with the rule of law, representative democracy, and reform, instead of perceiving the state as condensation, or a reflection, of class relations and domination of the capital system (Mészáros, 2010, 2022). As Mészaros argues in his posthumous *Beyond Leviathan* (2022), the liberals normally avoid the whole question of "might is right" as practiced by capitalist states, and refrain from seeing the state as hierarchical and repressive form of the necessary political command structure, which all class societies ought to have in some form or another. Although states are social relations and remain contested (see Poulantzas, 2000), they have been, throughout their history, susceptible for unequal and short-sighted policies that favor some over many. As Mészáros (2022) argues, (capitalist) states have been vulnerable for concentration of power, authoritarian rule, and warmongering, as the ruling elites have tried to consolidate their position and secure their (geo)political interest.

Even if we take a less critical stance towards the state, it is evident that state-regulated institutions, such as education and healthcare, but also the repressive apparatuses, the police, and the army, provide beneficial services for the agents of capital, and contribute to continuity and the needed sense of stability that, for instance, investors are looking for. State education, for instance, creates conditions for succession and the means to control the complex processes of reproduction in industrialized societies through education policy, and state-funded schools and educational programs. To be sure, states are always contradictory and paradoxical, and do not exist solely for the agents of capital (Poulantzas, 2000). However, what could perhaps be claimed is that, during the past decades, and in the post-bipolar world, the states have become "more capitalistic". And as we live the time of hegemonic global capitalism (Mészáros, 2010; Robinson, 2014) it is only reasonable to assume that capitalist ideas, practices, and norms steer and influence state policies and institutions around the world.

Now, and if the hegemony of capital is deeply felt in contemporary societies, we should ask, how does this reflect to education? It is here, I think, where Althusser's polemical remarks on Ideological State Apparatus hit the nerve.

13.3 Education in Capitalism: Althusser and Educational Ideological State Apparatus

Louis Althusser (1918–1990) was a French philosopher, and one of the leading thinkers, if not founders, of the stream called structural Marxism (e.g., Anderson, 1983; Gottesman, 2016; Resch, 1992), which is a critical body of literature examining and theorizing the outcomes and problems of capitalism, state institutions, and other socio-economic structures. It is well known that Althusser was influenced by Gramsci's ideas on class power and domination (see, e.g., Rehmann, 2014; Thomas, 2010). However, Althusser famously rejected Gramsci's hegemony conception (Balibar, 2014, p. xv). Instead of perceiving, for instance, communication of the dominant ideology by the newspapers, in a top-down format, Althusser turned the limelight elsewhere, and argued that the ideas and ideology of the dominant class(es) were indoctrinated and passed on in what he called Ideological State Apparatuses, and in particular what he termed the *educational Ideological State Apparatus* (2014, p. 243; see also Bidet, 2014, p. xxv).

In his essay *Ideology and Ideological State Apparatuses* (first published in 1970) and in *On the Reproduction of Capitalism* (Althusser, 2014, first published posthumously in French in 1995), Althusser argued that the reproduction of labor should be investigated separately from other means of production.

In his attempt to draft a theory of reproduction of the relations of production, Althusser (2014) separated Repressive State Apparatuses (RSAs) from Ideological State Apparatuses (ISAs). To the RSAs he placed the state administration, police, army, legislation, courts, and prisons. As for the ISAs, religion and religious institutions, education, family, law, parliamentary politics,[3] worker unions and lobbyists, communications (media and entertainment), and culture (art, literature, sports, etc.) are listed (ibid., p. 243).[4]

The ISAs are not defined by the monopoly of violence and repression, like the RSAs are, but the interests and ideology of the dominant classes. Althusser (ibid., p. 137, italics in the original) argues that what makes them ISAs is above all '*the ideology that is realized in them*. This ideology, being the dominant ideology, *is that of the dominant class, the class that holds state power* and directly and imperiously commands the Repressive State Apparatus'. The ISAs are not the instigators of the dominant ideology or the capitalist business as usual, but intermediaries who *pass* on these messages, practices, and norms, disregarding the relative autonomy dispersed quality of these institutions. ISAs are, of course, not monoliths or immutable, but objects and places of class struggle, which reflect the current socio-political status, orientation, and contextual differences (see the *Note on the ISAs*, ibid., pp. 218–220).

One of the key arguments that Althusser puts in place is that the school has superseded the church as the main ISA. Thus, for him, the capitalist school system is the most prominent intermediary in passing the dominant ideology to the next generation of workers, owners, and managers. Ideology (see e.g. Rehmann, 2014) is not only goal-oriented ideas (e.g., private ownership and its preservation), or specific attitudes (e.g., 'the poor are lazy'), practices (e.g., wage labor), norms (e.g., compulsory education) but also a mixture of worldviews (e.g., market liberalism) and beliefs (e.g., 'private sector is more efficient than the public sector'). For Althusser (2014, p. 184), ideology has also a material dimension, which crystallizes, for instance, in the form(at) of state education (e.g., the physical layout and structure of a classroom, and school buildings).

Considering the needs of the capitalist mode of production, the workers need to be competent, but also ready to submit themselves to be part of specialized, and complex production system, where their bargaining power is limited and working conditions, and opportunities, vary greatly. Consequently, Althusser asks, where does the reproduction of skillful but also submissive and properly socialized labor force take place? Eminently he responds that this does not happen, primarily, in the workplace, but prior to this, in the capitalist school system, and also in the other ISAs. In a long footnote (ibid., pp. 37–38) he claims, by following Marx's notes on extended reproduction, that what happens in a capitalist enterprise is something that happens in the capitalist system more generally, concerning the social "distribution" and "penning in" of people to certain tasks and posts. Althusser (ibid.) writes that no single economic actor is really in control of his operation, or what happens in the capitalist economy more generally. In other words, the most events that occur are beyond his influence, but, nevertheless, people are available to be exploited to produce profit, because it is 'the capitalist school system corresponding to the capitalist class's systems of exploitation, *not some other school system*' (ibid., emphasis in the original).

As Althusser (ibid., p. 51) stresses, the schools do not just teach the general skills and know-how, that is, mathematics and statistics, but also social norms and attitudes: 'the reproduction of labour-power requires not only that its qualifications be reproduced, but that its submission to the rules of respect for the established order be reproduced at the same time'. He (ibid.) notes that 'people also learn at school, the "rules" of good behavior [...]. These are rules of professional ethics and professional conscience: that is, to put it plainly, rules of respect for the social and technical division of labour, and, in the final analysis, the rules of the order established by class domination'.

Althusser (ibid., p. 146) notes that many of the 'contrasting virtues', such as modesty, resignation, submissiveness, confidence, and arrogance, are of course acquired elsewhere too, in families, the church, army, popular culture, or even in sports stadiums. Yet, as he (ibid.) states, 'no other ISA, however, has a captive audience of all the children of the capitalist social formation at its beck and call (and—this is the least it can do—at no cost to them) for as many years as the schools do'. Althusser (ibid., p. 251) also claims that for most people the educational ISA goes unnoticed, in its dominant role, because 'hardly anyone lends an ear to its music: it is so silent!' He (ibid.) argues that the capitalist school takes 'children from every class at infant-school age, and then for years, the years in which the child is most "vulnerable", squeezed between the family state apparatus and the educational state apparatus, it drums in to them, whether it uses new or old methods, a certain amount of "know-how" wrapped in the ruling ideology'.

Again, to contrast the liberal perception of education, Marxist reproduction theorists, following Althusser's work, have made the claim that education in capitalism, or in other class societies, *is not about equality but inequality* (Willis, 1983, p. 110). While it is true that education is nowadays available to increasing numbers of people around the world, this does not make education necessarily equal or good. On the contrary, education in capitalism has rather become a merit "scanner" of sorts, which screens and separates the winners from others through meritocratic competition with questionable outcomes (e.g., Pulkki, 2017). Willis (1983, p. 110) writes:

> education's main purpose of the social integration of a class society could be achieved only by preparing most kids for an unequal future, and by insuring their personal underdevelopment. Far from productive roles in the economy simply waiting to be 'fairly' filled by the products of education, the 'Reproduction' perspective reserved this to suggest that capitalist production and its roles required certain educational outcomes.

In the contemporary meritocratic societies, it is seemingly the educational apparatus where the future holders of different societal positions receive their know-how and prestige but are also nurtured to the capitalist norms, attitudes, and practices. From this point of view, it is very difficult to perceive education as something "pure", "impartial", or the "great equalizer". To follow Althusser and other reproduction theorists, we should rather try to understand the "correspondence" of education and capital accumulation (see Bowles & Gintis, 1976), to explore how the hegemony of capital affects, steers, and influences education and also to analyze how these processes undermine, or corrupt, democratic and egalitarian reorganization of education.

On this matter, it is peculiar that the complex and ambiguous relation of the state, education, and capital has seldom been treated in critical education studies (Morrow & Torres, 1995, p. 348). There are, however, undertakings that have tried to tackle these questions. For instance, Carnoy and Levin (1985, p. 50) have stated that the contradictory role of the capitalist state is evident in the field of education. They write that 'schools are part of social conflict. Education is at once the result of contradictions and the source of new contradictions. It is an arena of conflict over the production of knowledge, ideology, and employment, a place where social movements try to meet their needs and business attempts to reproduce its hegemony' (ibid.). Education is a condensation of class and power struggles, in this reading, which uphold histories of academic tradition, varying pedagogic ideals, and economic and political interests originating from various sources. This is one of the key things that Marxist education scholars are arguing, in addition to the worrying finding that education, in the period of global capitalism, has been impregnated by capitalist ideals and intensifying competition. Instead of attacking education per se, the point is rather to argue that the current outlook and the priorities that steer contemporary education should be questioned and changed in their entirety.

Taking this back to the beginning, and to Kingsley's situation, we should note that there is really nothing surprising in the seemingly scandalous treatment of "subnormal" children in the 1970s London, or Paris in Althusser's case. To put it plainly, this is how capitalist meritocracy works in capitalist schooling. The sharpest and most "appropriate" types, according to conduct, skills, and ethnicity, get ahead, while others reproduce their underprivileged positions, sometimes for generations. It is only by pressuring the legislators and decision-makers how active citizens and their organizations can improve the fates of vulnerable children, unless we are willing to touch and change the whole system of social reproduction and manufactured inequality, to something entirely different. It is not education, in a general sense, that disappoints us and our children, but rather the education in the class society that is destined to fail.

13.4 THE SUDDEN DISAPPEARANCE OF STRUCTURALISM

One could note that it is unfortunate that Althusser's arguments continue to maintain their validity. Perhaps it could be even claimed that their weight of evidence—in support of them—is even greater in the 2020s context. For instance, if we look at the changes that have happened in the Finnish higher education during the past decades, where a significant reorganization has taken place from a democratic and all-around education to innovation, competition, and capital accumulation (see Ruuska, 2017), it is evident that Althusser's remarks have sustained their explanatory power. At the same time, it must be mentioned that due to the fragmentary and unfinished nature of his work, on education and reproduction, there are number of concerns that have to be acknowledged.

Althusserian reproduction theorizing deals primarily with societal structures. And, as already said, he represents a structuralist approach to Marxist social and economic theory (see, e.g., Anderson, 1983; Resch, 1992; Wright, 1987). He was one of the champions of that stream of literary in the 1960s and 1970s, but today many have never even heard of him, while structuralist theory has fallen off the radar too. The late Erik Olin Wright (1987, p. 14) writes:

> By the late 1960s, he [Althusser] was a powerful intellectual force within the French left, and by the early 1970s, as translations of his work and that of his followers became readily available, Althusserian Marxism was one of the leading tendencies on the left in the English-speaking world. By the mid-1980s that influence—at least explicitly—had almost entirely disappeared.

There are, of course, many interlinking and overlapping reasons for the sudden "disappearance". Some of them may relate to the actual scholarly work, or to Althusser's long-term mental health problems, which tragically led to the death of his wife, and understandably tarnished his reputation, but it also seems that many of the academic reasons fall into more ambiguous and circumstantial category. Let's visit the academic critique, very shortly, and then come back to the political and cultural contingencies.

As Althusser (2014, p. 218) writes in the *Note on the ISAs*, the accusation that was most leveled at his 1969–1970 essay on the ISAs was "functionalism". In short, the functionalist accusation was based on a reading, which assumed that Althusser would have 'defined organs by their function alone, their immediate functions, thus *immobilizing* society within ideological institutions charged with functions of subjection' (ibid.). This kind of "non-dialectical interpretation", for instance to education, would, of course, exclude the possibility and existence of class struggle within the ISAs (ibid.), meaning that teachers, pupils, or university faculty would have no choice, but to submit to the iron rule of capitalism, and to the ideology of the dominant classes. However, a close reading of the 1970 ISA essay and his later *Note on the ISAs* affirms that Althusser, like Marx, acknowledged the '*primacy of the class struggle*' (ibid.), and thus also the schools and universities, as sites of contestation.

Overall, the functionalist, or very narrow, reading of Althusser's thesis seems to be symptomatic of the post-1970s reading and analysis (e.g. Resch, 1992). It is certainly true that Althusser's structural approach is rigid, and for instance his conception of the state and schooling are quite mechanistic. In *Political*

Power and Social Classes (1978), Poulantzas criticizes Althusser's dualistic categorization of state apparatuses as being too schematic. His (ibid., p. 33) argument is that Althusser allocates functions to state institutions in an essentialist way and overlooks the fact that state apparatuses can 'assume new functions either as additions to, or in exchange form, old ones'. While Althusser's account on socialization and subjection to capitalism, in schools, is in many ways convincing, it is apparent that Althusser's RSA/ISA framing omits the state's specific role in the constitution of the relations of production, and reduces it to repression and ideology. This denotes that he is not able to explain how the nation state is involved in the economic reproduction and various processes of capital accumulation (see Mészáros, 2022; Poulantzas, 2000; Ruuska, 2017).[5]

Moreover, as Anderson (1983, p. 38) writes, Althusser's radical structuralism, or 'theoretical antihumanism', is in danger of abolishing the subject. The structures, in structuralism or more generally in macro-theoretical approaches, are ubiquitous and powerful, so it is no wonder that the subject(s) is many times bypassed (or psychologically demoralized), if these remarks are not supplemented or discussed with theories of agency in a dialectical manner. However, it is also problematic if structural approaches are side-lined completely, which has been the case in post-1980s Marxism, and, of course, more widely in social theory, because we then may easily lose track of the prime motors of the (capitalist) society and economy.

Like the functionalist accusation, the supposed lack of room for agency in Althusser's theories has been used during the past decades, and to my understanding, to exclude the whole body of his work, compared, for instance, to how widely Gramsci's or Bourdieu's conceptions are used in critical education studies (Collins, 2009; Giroux, 1983; Gottesman, 2016). It is true that if one, for instance, searches for a comprehensive theory of ideology from Althusser, one is not able find it, because his remarks on ideology are much too sporadic (e.g., Rehmann, 2014). To some extent this applies to his work on education as well, but is this not symptomatic of many other Marxists as well? Marx's and Gramsci's scholarship is at times patchy too, but patchiness should not be a reason for a complete abandonment, but for critique, debate, and renewal.

In retrospect, we can argue multiple reasons for the demise of structuralism, which are linked to wider trends in social sciences (the so-called cultural turn), but also to the overall decline of Marxist scholarship, and the rising global hegemony of capitalism (see, e.g., Anderson, 1983; Gottesman, 2016). As Gottesman (2016, pp. 46–47) has noted, the rise of neoconservatism and neoliberalism, the continuing attacks on the working class, and the withering away of civil rights gains by the end of the 1970s and early 1980s shifted the political landscape and radical vision of the left globally (see also Jones, 2013). Similarly, as the 1980s progressed, critical education scholars altered their political position from revolution to reform, and their theoretical focus to cultural critique, strategic resistance, and agency in schools, instead of favoring radical social reconstruction, political mass struggles, or macro-theoretical critiques on capital (Gottesman, 2016, p. 47).

Gottesman (ibid.) claims that educational scholars increasingly 'preferred a cultural Marxist lens that looked at the ideological structure and content of schooling as opposed to the political economic Marxist lens that theorized capital and assessed quantifiable inputs and outcomes of schooling's reproductive tendencies'. In this context it is no wonder that Althusser's remarks on reproduction were considered mechanistic and overlooking agency. More importantly, it appears that his arguments simply became too radical to be defended in the post-structuralist, and post-socialist, or rather increasingly proto-capitalist, academia. After all, Althusser was a radical, and one of the last public intellectuals who, at the same time as he held a chair in the university, was involved in communist party politics that sought to overthrow the bourgeois establishment.

Since the days of Althusser, the academic-based critique of the capitalist business as usual has become increasingly more toothless, as schooling and university work increasingly resemble academic capitalism (e.g., Cantwell & Kauppinen, 2014), and as the ways to resist the hegemony of capital in academia have become difficult, and marginal (see, e.g., Allen, 2017; Cleaver, 2006; Giroux, 2014), even hopeless (Hall, 2021). But although Althusser and reproduction theorizing were brushed aside from critical education studies, the problems of inequality and oppression that come along with capitalism have not disappeared.

However, to theorize reproduction of capitalism in the twenty-first century and to consider re-heating some of the radical debates, there need to be updates to the nation-state-centered approach to reproduction (Ruuska, 2017, 2019). Gramsci (1971), Althusser (2014), and Poulantzas (2000), too, perceived domination and reproduction mainly from a single state standpoint, yet, in the twenty-first-century context, the integrated capitalist world economy, and the influence of transnational corporations and international organizations (such as IMF, EU, OECD, World Bank), must be incorporated to the framework (see Robinson, 2014). The globalization of capitalism and the integration of international policy have had a definitive impact also on education. For instance, OECD's PISA testing, or the Bologna Process, has restructured education from nation-centric phenomenon to a forum of international competition and prestige, but also turned it to a commodity (see Ruuska, 2017).

In the Finnish context, education scholars (e.g., Kauppinen, 2012; Rinne, 2004; Välimaa & Hoffman, 2008) have argued that transformation in Finnish higher education has been closely linked to the development of supranational higher education policy. As a result, Finnish higher education has become more EU- and OECD-like, rather than being national or Nordic (Rinne, 2004). Consequently, the reproduction of capitalism, and education's involvement in the process, should be theorized dialectically, to encapsulate both national and transnational aspects of it in the contemporary context.

13.5 Conclusion

For all the Kingsleys in the world, Marxist education scholars have bad news: education does not produce equality in capitalism; it reproduces the hegemony of capital. Education can surely be emancipatory and empowering for most but does not do it in class societies. To have education that could be considered the great equalizer, the society cannot be based on merit and competition, which then translates to manufactured inequality via the educational system. To move past this, and to have an equal society, education, or future, requires the dismantling of the hegemony of capitalism. None of this has changed from the days of Marx, which should also tell us that Marx, Marxism, and also Althusser's structuralist interpretation of it are still valid and critical for the struggle against systemic socio-economic inequality, discrimination, and marginalization.

Althusser's account on the educational ISA may be polemical, but it is also compelling portrayal of education in capitalism. However, we should not be demoralized by it, or the picture it paints, but be encouraged to rebel and to push beyond the world of inequality in schooling. Guided by the malaise of the capitalist curriculum, and empowered by, for instance, Freirean pedagogy of the oppressed, there is a whole world of education that remains underexplored, which could feel like the moment when Kingsley and Stephanie attend to the weekend school in Steve McQueen's film *Education*. It reminded us that education is never pre-fixed, nor is it pure or impartial, but also that education can be fair, inclusive, and inspiring, as long as people remain curious and stay in the struggle for a better world (of education).

Disclosure Statement The author has no financial interest or benefit that has arisen from the direct applications of this research.

Notes

1. For a more elaborate treatment on the reproduction of capitalism, see Althusser (2014); Poulantzas (2000); Robinson (2014); Ruuska (2017).
2. First published in French as *Sur la reproduction* in 1995.
3. In the *Note to the ISAs*, Althusser corrects the widespread misconception, namely the understanding that political parties are automatically ISAs. He (2014, p. 221, emphasis in the original) writes: 'I have never written that a political party is an Ideological State Apparatus. I have even said (only briefly, I admit) *something quite different*: that political parties are merely *the "component parts"* of a specific Ideological State Apparatus, the *political* Ideological State Apparatus, which "realizes" the dominant class's political ideology in, let us say, its "constitutional regime" (the "fundamental laws" under the monarchy of the Ancient Régime, the *Parlement*, and so on; the parliamentary-representative regime under the bourgeoisie in its "liberal" phases)'.
4. Note also that the legal state apparatus is represented in them both due to the difference in the formulation and execution of law.
5. Elsewhere, I have put forward an argument, which states that in order to understand the reproduction of capitalism in the twenty-first century, we need to have a dialogue between Gramsci, Althusser, and Poulantzas (Ruuska, 2017; Ruuska, 2019).

References

Allen, A. (2017). *The Cynical Educator*. Mayfly Books.
Althusser, L. (2014). *On the Reproduction of Capitalism: Ideology and Ideological State Apparatuses* (G. M. Goshgarian, Trans.). Verso. (Original Work Published 1995).
Althusser, L., & Balibar, E. (2009). *Reading Capital* (B. Brewster, Trans.). Verso. (Original Work Published 1968)
Anderson, P. (1983). *In the Tracks of Historical Materialism*. Verso.
Anyon, J. (1997). *Ghetto Schooling: A Political Economy of Urban Educational Reform*. Teachers College Press.
Au, W. (2018). *A Marxist Education: Learning to Change the World*. Haymarket Books.
Balibar, E. (2014). Preface. In L. Althusser (Ed.), *On the Reproduction of Capitalism: Ideology and Ideological State Apparatuses* (G. M. Goshgarian, Trans.). Verso. (Original Work Published 1995).
Bidet, J. (2014). Introduction. In L. Althusser (Ed.), *On the Reproduction of Capitalism: Ideology and Ideological State Apparatuses* (G. M. Goshgarian, Trans.). Verso. (Original Work Published 1995).
Bourdieu, P., & Passeron, J. (1990). *Reproduction in Education, Society and Culture* (2nd ed., R. Nice, Trans.). SAGE. (Original Work Published 1970).
Bowles, S., & Gintis, H. (1976). *Schooling in Capitalist America: Educational Reform and the Contradictions of Economic Life*. Basic Books.
Calhoun, C. (2013). What Threatens Capitalism Now? In I. Wallerstein, R. Collins, M. Mann, G. Derluguian, & C. Calhoun (Eds.), *Does Capitalism Have a Future?* Oxford University Press.
Cantwell, B., & Kauppinen, I. (2014). *Academic Capitalism in the Age of Globalization*. John Hopkins University Press.
Carnoy, M., & Levin, H. M. (1985). *Schooling and Work in the Democratic State*. Stanford University Press.
Cleaver, H. (2006). *On Schoolwork and the Struggle Against It*. libcom.org.
Coard, B. (2021). *How the West Indian Child Is Made Educationally Sub-Normal in the British School System* (5th ed.). Reprint, Independently Published. (Originally Published in 1971).
Cole, M. (2008). *Marxism and Educational Theory: Origins and Issues*. Routledge.
Collins, J. (2009). Social Reproduction in Classrooms and Schools. *Annual Review of Anthropology, 38*, 33–48.
Escobar, A. (1995). *Encountering Development*. Princeton University Press.
Foster, J. B. (2009). *Ecological Revolution – Making Peace with the Planet*. Monthly Review Press.
Freire, P. (1996). Pedagogy of the Oppressed (M. B. Ramos, Trans.). Penguin Books. (Originally Published in 1970).
Giroux, H. A. (1983). Theories of Reproduction and Resistance in the New Sociology of Education: A Critical Analysis. *Harvard Educational Review, 53*(3), 257–293.
Giroux, H. A. (2014). *Neoliberalism's War on Higher Education*. Haymarket Books.
Gottesman, I. (2016). *The Critical Turn in Education: From Marxist Critique to Poststructuralist Feminism to Critical Theories of Race*. Routledge.
Gramsci, A. (1971). *Selections from the Prison Notebooks*. International Publishers.
Hall, R. (2021). *The Hopeless University: Intellectual Work at the end of The End of History*. Mayfly Books.

Harvey, D. (2014). *Seventeen Contradictions and the End of Capitalism*. Oxford University Press.
Jones, D. S. (2013). *Masters of the Universe. Hayek, Friedman and the Birth of Neoliberal Politics*. Princeton University Press.
Kauppinen, I. (2012). Towards Transnational Academic Capitalism. *Higher Education, 64*(4), 543–556.
Lears, T. J. J. (1985). The Concept of Cultural Hegemony: Problems and Possibilities. *The American Historical Review, 90*(3), 567–593.
Malm, A. (2016). *Fossil Capital: The Rise of Steam Power and the Roots of Global Warming*. Verso.
Marx, K. (1973a). *Capital: A Critique of Political Economy, Volume 1: The Process of Capitalist Production* (S. Moore & E. Aveling, Trans.). International Publishers. (Originally Published in 1867).
Marx, K. (1973b). *Capital: A Critique of Political Economy, Volume 2: The Process of Circulation of Capital* (S. Moore & E. Aveling, Trans.). International Publishers. (Originally Published in 1885).
Marx, K., & Engels, F. (1998). The German Ideology (Unknown, Trans.) Prometheus Books. (Originally Published in 1846).
Mészáros, I. (2010). *Beyond Capital: Toward a Theory of Transition*. Monthly Review Press.
Mészáros, I. (2022). *Beyond Leviathan: Critique of the State*. Monthly Review Press.
Moore, J. W. (2015). *Capitalism in the Web of Life: Ecology and the Accumulation of Capital*. Verso.
Morrow, R. A., & Torres, C. A. (1995). *Social Theory and Education: A Critique of Theories of Social and Cultural Reproduction*. SUNY Press.
Poulantzas, N. (1978). *Political Power and Social Classes* (T. O'Hagan, Trans.). New Left Books. (Originally Published in 1970).
Poulantzas, N. (2000). *State, Power, Socialism* (P. Camiller, Trans.). Translated by P. Camiller. Verso. (Originally Published in 1978).
Pulkki, J. (2017). *On the Educational Problems of Competition: Virtues to the 21st Century*. Tampere University Press.
Rehmann, J. (2014). *Theories of Ideology: The Powers of Alienation and Subjection*. Haymarket Books.
Resch, R. P. (1992). *Althusser and the Renewal of Marxist Social Theory*. University of California Press.
Rinne, R. (2004). Searching for the Rainbow: Changing the Course of Finnish Higher Education. In I. Fägerlind & G. Strömqvist (Eds.), *Reforming Higher Education in the Nordic Countries – Studies of Change in Denmark, Finland, Iceland, Norway and Sweden*.
Robinson, W. I. (2014). *Global Capitalism and the Crisis of Humanity*. Cambridge University Press.
Ruuska, T. (2017). *The Reproduction of Capitalism in the 21st Century: Higher Education and Ecological Crisis*. Aalto University Publication Series, Unigrafia Oy.
Ruuska, T. (2019). *Reproduction Revisited: Capitalism, Higher Education and Ecological Crisis*. Mayfly Books.
Thomas, P. D. (2010). *The Gramscian Moment: Philosophy, Hegemony and Marxism*. Haymarket Books.
Välimaa, J., & Hoffman, D. (2008). Knowledge Society Discourse and Higher Education. *Higher Education, 56*(3), 265–285.

Wallerstein, I. (2004). *World-Systems Analysis: An Introduction*. Duke University Press.
Wallerstein, I. (2013). Structural Crisis, or Why Capitalists May No Longer Find Capitalism Re-warding. In I. Wallerstein, R. Collins, M. Mann, G. Derluguian, & C. Calhoun (Eds.), *Does Capitalism Have a Future?* Oxford University Press.
Willis, P. (1983). Cultural Production and Theories of Reproduction. In L. Barton & S. Walker (Eds.), *Race, Class and Education*. Groom-Helm.
Wright, E. O. (1987). The Intellectual Saga of Althusserian Marxism. A Review of Benton, T., The Rise and Fall of Structure Marxism: Althusser and His Influence. *Contemporary Sociology, 16*(1), 14–15.
Wright, E. O. (2010). *Envisioning Real Utopias*. Verso.

PART II

Against: Emerging Currents in Marxism and Education

CHAPTER 14

Critique of the Political Economy of Education: Methodological Notes for the Analysis of Global Educational Reforms

Inny Accioly

14.1 Introduction

Several critical studies on global educational reforms in recent decades have pointed to the growing phenomenon of privatization of education. The studies, in general, investigate how privatization occurs, the actors involved (Think Tanks, Foundations, non-governmental organizations), its effects on human formation, the role of the state, and the transfer of educational policies between countries (Ball, 2012; Saltman, 2015; Steiner-Khamsi, 2004; Verger et al., 2016).

Investigations into educational reforms contribute to the analysis of the dynamics of capitalist accumulation, in which education is converted into a lucrative market while playing a central role in the adequacy of the labor-power to the regime of bourgeois domination. One of the problems faced by such investigations is the wide naturalization of the categories of the bourgeois economy. In common sense terms, the privatization of education and its control by corporations is seen as something positive if reforms focus on efficiency in the use of public budget, employability, quality, and accountability.

This chapter starts from Marx's critique of Political Economy to remove the 'mystical veil'—using Marx's words (2013, p. 154)—that envelops these categories. This conceals the social relations underlying the process of wealth

I. Accioly (✉)
Fluminense Federal University, Rio de Janeiro, Brazil
e-mail: innyaccioly@gmail.com

production, and makes it difficult to understand the exploitation of labor intrinsic to the production of wealth in the societies where educational reforms are implemented. The chapter argues for the validity of Marx's critique of Political Economy, both as a method for analyzing the Political Economy of Education that underlies global educational reforms and for fighting against them. The chapter presents Marx's critique of the classical authors of Political Economy and the method that emerged from his critical studies. It then presents a critique of the Political Economy of Education, the issue of increasing worker productivity, human capital theory, and the international division of labor. Finally, it presents methodological elements to be considered in educational policy research, taking as an example the educational reforms in Mozambique.

14.2 THE CRITIQUE OF POLITICAL ECONOMY AND THE METHOD OF INVESTIGATION

The critique of Political Economy was fundamental for Marx in developing his social theory. This critique is the result of intense work of reading the classical authors, intellectual elaboration, and experimentation. It was in this process that Marx developed a method of research and exposition (dialectical historical materialism) that provides the elaboration of updated analyses, since the starting and ending point of the investigation is precisely the movement of reality, expressed in the actuality of social phenomena (Ranieri, 2018).

In his *Economic and Philosophical Manuscripts of 1844*, Marx (1844/2004, p. 79, our translation) explains how he confronted Political Economy:

> We have proceeded from the premises of political economy. We have accepted its language and its laws. We presupposed private property, the separation of labor, capital and land, and of wages, profit of capital and rent of land—likewise division of labor, competition, the concept of exchange value, etc. On the basis of political economy itself, in its own words, we have shown that the worker sinks to the level of a commodity and becomes indeed the most wretched of commodities; that the wretchedness of the worker is in inverse proportion to the power and magnitude of his production; that the necessary result of competition is the accumulation of capital in a few hands, and thus the restoration of monopoly in a more terrible form.

Marx's critique did not occur by the simple, theoretical negation of the classical authors, but meant their overcoming, incorporating their achievements, showing their limits, and deconstructing their mistakes. Marx understood that in order to transform the degrading social conditions that plague the working class, an accurate analysis of the society in which these conditions are produced is necessary. In this sense, Marx noted that 'the anatomy of bourgeois society must be sought in Political Economy' (Marx, 1859/2008, p. 47, our translation).

Adam Smith (1723–1790) and David Ricardo (1772–1823) are the main authors that Marx takes as references for his critique of Political Economy. In their works (despite the differences between the authors), it is possible to identify central characteristics of this body of theory that had been elaborated for about 200 years (Netto & Braz, 2006). Focusing their attention on issues related to labor, value, and money, these authors sought to understand the set of social relations that were emerging in the crisis of the Old Regime and the rise of the capitalist mode of production. Smith and Ricardo expressed the ideology of the bourgeoisie at the forefront of the social struggles that resulted in a new system of domination, the class rule of the bourgeoisie.

As it consolidated its dominance, the bourgeoisie reformulated its emancipating ideals (liberty, equality, and fraternity) and became a class whose central interest is the conservation of its domination regime (Netto & Braz, 2006). Therefore, private property should remain as an unquestionable mediation. However, private property presupposes the existence of a number of individuals dispossessed of property, which institutes a model of society split into classes: on one side, those who possess nothing but their own labor-power, as their physical and intellectual capacities; on the other side, those who accumulate wealth by owning the means of production. Labor-power, when put in motion, is a commodity capable of generating surplus value for the owners of the means of production, the bourgeois class.

What motivated Marx to study the theorists of Political Economy was his active involvement with the workers' struggle and the observation that the exploitation of labor-power is the general rule of capitalist society (Accioly, 2015). The generation of surplus value, 'which smiles at the capitalist with all the charm of a creation out of nothing' (Marx, 2013), is directly related to the exploitation of labor. This includes the appropriation of labor time, in which the worker toils beyond the limits of the work necessary for his or her self-support. It is a working time that, for the worker, does not create any value.

The bourgeoisie controls not only the process and product of labor, but it also seeks to control the worker's time in order to transform all life time into time geared toward the reproduction of capital (Harvey, 2013).

> 'What is a working day?' How long is the time during which Capital can consume the labor power whose daily value it pays? How long can the working day be extended beyond the working time necessary for the reproduction of labor power itself? To these questions, as we have seen, capital answers: the working day contains 24 full hours, less the few hours of rest without which the labor force would be absolutely incapable of performing its service again. From the outset, it is clear that the worker, during his entire life, is nothing but labor power, which is why all his available time is, by nature and by right, labor time, which belongs, therefore, to the self-valorization of capital. Time for human formation, for intellectual development, for the fulfillment of social functions, for social relations, for the free play of physical and intellectual vital forces, even the Sunday free time is pure futility! (Marx, 1867/2013, p. 337, our translation)

Marx revealed that time is the quantitative reality of labor, and the basis for the generation of value. Not by chance, the history of capitalist society is marked by struggles for the reduction of working hours, for the expansion of schooling time, for free time to access leisure and cultural goods. These struggles were fundamental for the establishment of labor rights, such as the regulation of the working day and the right to vacations.

In *Capital* (Marx, 1867/2013), Marx developed an analysis on the degree of labor exploitation that was observable throughout the nineteenth century. He noted that by appropriating the worker's time, capital usurps the time required for the consumption of fresh air and sunlight, hindering the healthy development of body and mind. As capitalistic exploitation of nature intensifies, degrading air quality, the access to fresh, clean air is restricted, especially for the non-white working class living in the urban peripheries (Bullard, 2000).

Throughout the twentieth and twenty-first centuries, the conditions of labor exploitation have intensified and taken on new nuances with the advance of technological development. A large number of workers are involved in labor relations mediated by apps and digital platforms, through which exploitation is covered up by the appearance of worker autonomy to manage their own time. Technology, a human creation with the potential to improve living conditions and grant free time, is used against the worker, breaking all limits of the working day. Marx had already pointed out this contradiction:

> Machinery, considered in itself, shortens working time, while, in capitalist use, it increases the working day; in itself, it facilitates work, while, in capitalist use, it increases its intensity; of itself it is a victory of man over the forces of nature, while, capitalistically used, it subjugates man through the forces of nature; of itself it increases the wealth of the producer, while, capitalistically used, it impoverishes him. (Marx, 1867/2013, p. 513, our translation)

It is certain that capital does not obey any ethical limits when it raises the level of exploitation of labor to the maximum. It is also true that exploitation is supported by legal relations that consider individuals equal and free to make choices, accumulate wealth, and consume commodities. In Marx's words, 'the wealth of societies where the capitalist mode of production reigns appears as a huge collection of commodities' (Marx, 1867/2013, p. 113, our translation). The mysticism surrounding the commodity form is an example of the way in which the economic forms of capitalism obscure the social relations underlying them, shrouding them in a 'mystical veil' (ibid., p. 154, our translation) that makes it difficult to understand how the exploitation of labor is intrinsic to the social process of wealth production.

Marx observed that the method used in investigations in Political Economy corroborated this mystical character. The investigations started from abstract categories such as 'population, nation, state, various states, etc.—, but always end with some general, abstract, determinate relations—division of labor, money, value, etc.—which they have discovered by analysis' (Marx, 1857/2010,

p. 111, our translation). In this way, society was explained through these abstract principles, which would rest at the core of its functioning.

Thus, the concept of 'population' is taken as the foundation and subject of the whole act of social production (Marx, 1857/2010). However, Marx points out that 'population' is a mere abstraction when the classes that constitute it are not considered, just as 'class' is an empty concept if one does not seek to know the elements on which the classes rest, such as 'wage labor', 'capital', and so on. These are elements that in turn presuppose exchange, division of labor (Marx, 2010).

Marx sought to refine these abstract principles by pursuing a method of inquiry that considers other historical moments to achieve the specificity of the present moment and does not consider these abstractions to be natural or eternal, but rather as transient and part of a complex totality in constant transformation. Methodologically, when investigating a certain political-economic-social system, it seems correct to start the investigation with what is supposed to be concrete. However, the empirical material, that which is immediately perceptible by our senses, never comes to our perception as it is. That which is in essence and that which appears to us are not identical, and it is necessary to investigate the relationship between the two in order to scientifically demonstrate the mediations between one form of existence and another (Pinheiro, 2018). Marx unveils that the 'concrete' is the synthesis of many determinations, that is, unity of the diverse (Marx, 2008). His method shows that if the form that the phenomenon manifests itself and its essence immediately coincided, scientific investigation would be superfluous.

Unlike investigations in natural sciences, in social research no microscope or chemical reagents can be used. It is necessary for the researcher to resort to the capacity for abstraction.

> In the analysis of economic forms, moreover, neither microscopes nor chemical reagents are of use. The force of abstraction must replace both. But in bourgeois society, the commodity-form of the product of labour—or value-form of the commodity—is the economic cell-form. To the superficial observer, the analysis of these forms seems to turn upon minutiae. It does in fact deal with minutiae, but they are of the same order as those dealt with in microscopic anatomy. [...] In the domain of Political Economy, free scientific inquiry meets not merely the same enemies as in all other domains. The peculiar nature of the materials it deals with, summons as foes into the field of battle the most violent, mean and malignant passions of the human breast, the Furies of private interest. The English Established Church, e.g., will more readily pardon an attack on 38 of its 39 articles than on 1/39 of its income. (Marx, 1867/2013, pp. 78–80, our translation)

In *Capital*, Marx reveals the synthesis resulting from a long process of investigation. He starts from the most visible form (that which seems concrete), and through the process of investigation, he unveils the mysteries that involve social reality within the capitalist mode of production. For Marx, the construction of theoretical knowledge must start from the empirical, from what is apparent and can be seen through the senses. Appearance is the starting point for knowledge, since it is the immediate way in which reality presents itself.

The categories of bourgeois economics, which permeate social-economic-political investigations, are forms of thought that appear to have an objective truth, and to the extent that they reflect real social relations, they are socially valid. However, at the same time that they reveal, they also conceal. For Marx, social-economic-political investigations must start from appearance and seek the intimate and dynamic structure of the phenomenon it seeks to understand, considering that social phenomena are as they are for a reason; they are parts that connect to a complex and contradictory totality, constantly in transformation (Costa & Accioly, 2017).

The construction of knowledge is understood as a movement of concretization that proceeds from phenomena to essence and from essence to phenomena, from the whole to the parts and from the parts to the whole, from totality to contradictions and from contradictions to totality. In this process of spiral correlations, concepts enter into reciprocal movement and elucidate each other, reaching concreteness (Kosík, 1976). Thus, the process of generating knowledge of reality must seek the synthesis of its innumerable contradictions. From the analysis of the relationship between parts and the whole, 'the concrete wealth of the dialectical contradictions develops increasingly within a unitary process, thus discovering the essence of the manifestations' (Kofler, 2010, p. 61, our translation).

Here it is essential to reaffirm that, for Marx, knowledge production is not neutral since it assumes the working class's perspective and aims to transform society radically. From this perspective, the production of knowledge in the field of education must consider the contradictions surrounding working-class education in the capitalist society that ultimately corroborate to maintain the bourgeois order. Therefore, it needs to take into consideration an analysis of the dynamics of class struggle in the context to be analyzed; the level of organization of the working class; the ethical-political forms of domination of the bourgeois class; the complex totality of global capitalism in its historical movement; the relations between states; and the relations between national bourgeoisies, ideologies, and the concrete bases that support them.

Here, it is important to note that ideologies are understood not as forms of thought expressed by a false consciousness that would lead to misunderstandings. Ideologies are supported by a firm material basis, which makes their critical analysis quite complex.

> Men are producers of their representations, of their ideas and, in effect, men are conditioned by the mode of production of their material life, by their material exchange and their further development in the social and political structure. [...] Consciousness can never be anything other than conscious being, and the being of men is their real-life process. [...] It is not consciousness that determines life, but life that determines consciousness. (Marx & Engels, 1993, pp. 36–37, our translation)

The mode of production and reproduction of material life is expressed in men's and women's beliefs and value systems, in their consciousness. At the same time that the materiality of concrete life is constructed by men and women, they develop their ideas and conceptions of the world by being immersed in this concrete materiality. In this way, 'life determines consciousness' (Marx & Engels, 1993, p. 37, our translation), in the sense that the materiality of life imposes itself on the ways men deal with their own lives. Therefore, educational theories and practices are generated in a close and contradictory relationship with the dynamics of class society, which encompasses the production, circulation, and appropriation of wealth. It is crucial to understand to what extent educational theories and practices support the workers' struggle for the socialization of wealth or to what extent they naturalize labor exploitation and the private ownership of socially produced wealth (including scientific and philosophical knowledge) and its concentration in the hands of a few.

14.3 Political Economy and Education

In Political Economy, since the worker's life time must be converted into time for the generation of value, schooling time, being non-working time, only makes sense if it contributes to increased productivity and accelerates the accumulation of capital. Thus, the debates about the importance of intellectual development and human creative capacities lose ground to narrow views that reduce education to mere training. The perspective of Ferguson (1723–1816), Smith's teacher quoted in Marx's work, is illustrative: 'Reflection and imagination are subject to error; but the habit of moving the foot or the hand depends on neither the one nor the other. For this reason, manufactures prosper most where the spirit is most dispensed with' (Marx, 1867/2013, p. 435, our translation).

Following this logic, Smith (2008) argued that one way to increase the worker's skill and productivity would be the division of the labor process, which would lead to the economic growth of a nation. Learning, thus, would take place through the repetition of simple tasks. However, Smith was not oblivious to the fact that the division of labor could motivate undesirable worker behavior, which would lead to productivity losses. Thus, the author argued that a minimum of instruction was necessary for workers to stay away from 'drunkenness,' 'brawling,' and 'debauchery' (Smith, 2008). For this man who is considered the father of liberalism, education should be provided within the limits of what was strictly necessary for the maintenance of social order.

Contrary to Smith, Charles Babbage (1791–1871) pointed out that the increase in productivity made possible by the division of labor would only be temporary (Tinel, 2012). However, it would enable the cheapening of the labor-power and increase the profitability of the employer (Babbage, 2009). Babbage, considered a forerunner of Frederick Winslow Taylor's (1856–1915) idea of 'scientific management,' known as Taylorism (Braverman, 1998), sought to observe how worker time was applied in the production process. He noted that skilled workers spent some of their work time performing simple tasks that would be below their skill level. As a result, the value of labor-power could be reduced if the labor process was divided so that tasks requiring high skills were assigned to a few skilled workers, and tasks requiring low technical skill were assigned to unskilled workers with very low pay (Babbage, 2009). Thus, the employer could select skill levels, get faster returns on the investment made in training and increase profits (Babbage, 2009; Mir-Artigues & Gonzalez-Calvet, 2007).

In this way, Babbage's principle became 'the underlying force governing all forms of labor in capitalist society, no matter in what configuration or at what hierarchical level' (Braverman, 1998, p. 57, our translation). A polarization is hereby created among the working class: on one side, workers with some qualification, whose time is valuable to a greater or lesser degree; on the other side, a mass of unskilled workers, whose time is worth almost nothing. 'This is the general law of the capitalist division of labor, which shapes not only labor but also populations' (Braverman, 1998, p. 58, our translation). In some parts of the world, the value of labor is so low that it is more profitable for industries to 'employ' (often with no labor rights and violating human rights) a large number of workers than to invest in machines to do the job.

For example, Rodney's historiographical work (Rodney, 1973) revealed that in most parts of Africa in the mid-twentieth century, 'Europeans who wanted to see a railroad built offered African workers the whip for wages and more whip for extra effort' (ibid., p. 327, our translation). One of the numerous examples was the construction of the Embakasi airport in the 1950s, when Kenya was a British colony: 'Thousands of people worked under armed guard, excavating a million tons of earth, filling craters with half a million tons of stone with nothing but shovels, stone hammers, and their bare hands' (ibid., p. 328, our translation). The expansion of capitalism on a global scale entailed diverse forms of 'free' slave labor (Fernandes, 1975), an apparently archaic way of working (in the face of global technological progress) that is not a detour on the path of an economy's development.

In fact, the development of the central capitalist economies is linked to the underdevelopment of the peripheral economies (Rodney, 1973)—former colonies that achieved formal independence but maintained structural economic dependence, that is reproduced by numerous coercive means (such as military threat and economic sanctions) and multiple ideological strategies of convincing adherence to the neoliberal political project. Besides suffering from the plundering of valuable metals and natural resources, the peripheral economies (especially in Africa and Latin America) are subject to economic mechanisms of unequal exchange (reflecting economic liberalization) in which national wealth outflows to central economies that hold the monopoly on the development of technologies that are, in turn, imported at high costs. The unequal exchange increases the peripheral economies' public debt, tying the public budget to the interest payment and debt amortization and subjugating the public budget to the agenda of neoliberal reforms designed by international agencies (Accioly et al., 2016). Increasing surplus production through the over-exploitation of the labor-power is the mechanism to ensure the internal dynamics of capital accumulation by the bourgeoisie (Marini, 1973). Increasing workers' productivity and reducing costs becomes a central problem for their ideologues.

That is why Babbage's (2009) principle of dividing the labor process by combining a few highly skilled workers with a mass of unskilled or low-skilled labor inspires educational theories and policies on a global scale. He is considered a precursor of the human capital theory (Rosenberg, 1994), which was developed by Schultz (1961) and Becker (1962) in the second half of the twentieth century, and underlies global educational reforms.

According to human capital theory, education has the purpose of endowing human beings with skills, knowledge, and attributes that increase their productivity, which would lead to economic growth and increased individual income (Becker, 1962; Schultz, 1961). The theory glosses over the fact that economic growth tends to accentuate income concentration, without benefiting workers (Accioly, 2018). Also, the division of labor in capitalism converted science, which is a power of the human spirit, into material power through industry. Knowledge was converted into a productive force and, therefore, into a means of production (Saviani, 2003). The private appropriation of scientific knowledge (such as patents) became a driving force of capital accumulation. In effect, private appropriation and the consequent monopolization of knowledge presuppose the expropriation of the working class from its access. Accordingly, from the human capital perspective (Schultz, 1961), spending on education should be done efficiently to maximize economic returns and avoid waste. Thus, public spending on schooling should occur within a maximum limit, which varies according to the market demands for labor-power in each era and in each geographical location.

In his time, Marx already pointed out that the 'necessary result of competition is the accumulation of capital in a few hands, and thus the restoration of monopoly in a more terrible form' (Marx 1844/Marx, 2004, p. 79, our translation). In the twenty-first century, the division of labor conceived by Babbage (2009) has reached extreme levels. The globalization of capital with wide liberalization of the economies, removal of barriers to capital mobility, and geographical fragmentation of production processes into global value chains (Chena et al., 2018) have brought about an international division of labor in which the degree of qualification of workers in each region of the planet is a critical factor for monopolized capital in its relentless pursuit to maximize profits.

For example, in the peripheral economies, global value chains corroborated an accumulation pattern primarily focused on extractive economic activities aimed at exporting commodities such as soy, timber, and coal, with a minimum degree of technological processing that does not demand a highly skilled labor-power. At the other end of global value chains, central economies vie for the monopoly of intellectual property and the high-tech development market.

In peripheral economies, local bourgeoisies, by appropriating the state apparatuses, establish alliances with bourgeois fractions of the central economies in order to maximize their profits (Fontes, 2010). The public budget is used in favor of private interests (such as tax exemptions for foreign corporations) to the detriment of investment in the public good. In doing so, the bourgeoisie claims that its actions are motivated by the good intention of generating jobs and improving the living conditions of the poor. At the same time, the bourgeoisie conducts reforms to reduce labor rights, transform educational systems, and apply the budget of educational policies according to the interests of capital accumulation. In his time, Marx already sounded the alarm about the benevolence of capitalists: 'the road to hell is paved with good intentions' (Marx 1867/Marx, 2013, p. 268, our translation).

Without disregarding that global capitalism is a complex and contradictory totality, the analysis of the international division of labor reveals that: a few workers receive qualifications of greater intellectual complexity so that they can develop ideas, theories, and technologies (usually in higher education and graduate school); some workers receive qualifications (not necessarily in higher education) so that they learn to perform tasks and use imported machines and technologies; a mass of workers receive rudimentary qualification for underemployment and informal labor; and large number of workers are left out of school (Accioly, 2018).

When analyzing the implementation of global educational reforms, this logic (that restricts access to higher education for a large part of the global population) emerges, at the same time that it is placed in contradiction when private educational corporations seek to profit from higher education offerings, often receiving state subsidies, charging tuition, and consequently excluding those who cannot afford it.

Besides being a lucrative market, schooling provides workers with skills that can contribute to increasing profits. Thus, school enrollments, education spending, school contents, and teaching methods are a target of interest for the bourgeoisie. On the other hand, since capitalist accumulation results in increased labor exploitation and expropriation of land and social rights (Fontes, 2010), it is faced with countless forms of working-class resistance, including education.

To dissuade resistance, the organic intellectuals of the bourgeoisie continuously elaborate ideas, reworking the ethical-political forms for the maintenance of hegemony (Gramsci, 2011). In this sense, organic intellectuals assume an important organizational function (Portelli, 1977) insofar as they act in the construction of consensus to achieve or maintain hegemony, which, it is important to emphasize, also encompasses multiple forms of coercion.

14.4 Investigating Global Educational Reforms

Research in education policy is permeated by debates about the relationship between education and economic growth, income distribution, equity, and gender, race, and ethnicity discrimination. Commonly, the research starts by analyzing data such as public and private school enrollment, illiteracy rates, gender and race disparity, educational budgets, success rates, and school dropouts. All these indexes are based on the concept of population, an abstraction that makes it possible to capture the phenomenon in its appearance. However, to understand the essence of the phenomenon (e.g., a certain action developed by the state for the education of the working class), it is necessary to dissect the abstraction, to situate it in the historical movement, and in the totality of global capitalism, in its actuality.

All over the world, educational reforms carry as common goals economic growth, creating opportunities for the poor, and increasing equity. For example, in 1990, international agencies and political leaders from around the world gathered in Jomtien (Thailand) for the World Conference on *Education for All*. The final report of the conference stated that the governments of poor countries should make a commitment to ensure children's basic learning needs. To achieve this goal, governments should conduct periodic performance assessments and partner with the private sector. Privatization is seen as a solution to improve quality, boost efficiency, or increase equity (or all of these things simultaneously) in the educational system (Verger et al., 2016).

In countries with high illiteracy rates and high numbers of out-of-school children and youth, increasing the public budget aimed at schooling the working class is extremely important. However, education conducted by the bourgeois state is necessarily crossed by the interests of the ruling class. In 'Critique of the Gotha Programme,' Marx warned about this issue:

> Does one believe that in today's society (and it alone is in question here) education can be equal for all classes? Or is it demanded that the upper classes must also be forcibly reduced to the modest education of the public school, the only education compatible with the economic conditions not only of the wage worker, but also of the peasant? (…) The government and the Church must rather be excluded from any influence on the school. (…) It is the State which, on the contrary, needs to receive a very strict education from the people. (Marx, 1875/2012, pp. 37–38, our translation)

After the World Conference on *Education for All*, capital appropriated the workers' demand for more schooling and began to direct educational policies, both to make schooling meet the demand for skills, and to turn public education into a lucrative market.

In African countries, the focus on meeting basic learning needs led to underfunding of higher education and research institutions. In the 1990s, the major funders of education in Africa, the US Agency for International Development (USAID), the Swedish International Development Agency (SIDA), and the World Bank allocated between 80 and 90% of resources exclusively to primary education (Brock-Utne, 2000).

Since the 1980s, the World Bank emerged as a collective, organic intellectual of the ruling class by funding research, reports, formulating policies, providing technical and financial assistance to governments, and consolidating databases on education policies around the world (Accioly, 2018). The ideas disseminated in World Bank publications have wide academic reach and corroborate to consolidate a consensus about what is the function of working-class schooling in Africa: to teach rudimentary reading skills and non-cognitive skills to increase productivity, and adapt workers to the capitalist market. The following quote is from an article published by the World Bank on skills and employability in Mozambique, a country in which a large part of the labor-power is engaged in subsistence family agriculture.

> Fundamental skills such as basic math and literacy are critical in all economic activities. Helping producers read and follow the instructions on a bag of fertilizer, for example, may be rudimentary, but a big step toward productivity gains. Technical skills, including occupational and professional skills, are important functional skills for pursuing an occupation. Finally, the importance of non-cognitive skills is increasingly recognized, particularly in modern jobs. These types of skills are relevant to economic activities in the labor market, and should be promoted through the educational system as well as labor market experiences. (Cho & Feda, 2015, p. 5)

Throughout the 1980s, the World Bank released reports with prescriptions for educational policies for economic growth in Sub-Saharan Africa (World Bank, 1981, 1987, 1989). The central argument was that economic growth would generate jobs, trigger social development and better living conditions for workers if governments implemented policies that prioritized primary education over secondary and higher education; reduced education spending; introduced tuition fees; reduced teacher salaries; increased pupil-teacher ratios; and instituted competency-based teacher training (ibid.).

These reports present policies for economic growth that are in stark contrast to those that had been adopted by countries that aligned themselves with the Soviet Union after national liberation. In Mozambique, the war of liberation from Portugal was followed by 16 years of civil war fomented by anti-communist opposition group, funded by the governments of South Africa and the United States (Accioly, 2018). Much of the public health and education systems were destroyed, and by the late 1980s the population faced extreme poverty, which motivated the government to enter into structural adjustment agreements with the International Monetary Fund to receive funding from international agencies. The situation of extreme financial dependence to develop social policies left the country tied to the prescriptions of the World Bank, which, in fact, are conditions to continue receiving funding.

The perspective of capital on the labor-power in Mozambique is expressed in World Bank publication:

> [In Mozambique,] labor costs are quite competitive: hourly wages are lower than in Kenya or Swaziland, but higher than in Ghana and Bangladesh. Even adjusted

for productivity differentials, labor in Mozambique is still competitive, but labor productivity needs to be increased. (World Bank, 2010, p. 13, our translation)

In line with human capital theory, schooling is considered necessary to increase the productivity of the labor-power. However, it should not contribute to generate expectations of wage increases. This would be the case if enrollment in higher education were expanded.

In this regard, World Bank publications in the 1980s criticize and discourage government spending on higher education in Africa: 'African governments spend as much for each university student as countries with per capita incomes three to eight times higher' (World Bank, 1981, p. 82, our translation). 'The costs of higher education are unnecessarily high. The pattern of financing higher education is socially unequal and economically inefficient' (World Bank, 1987, p. xvi, our translation). 'Since independence, African governments have placed great importance on Higher Education. Public subsidy of this level of education has contributed to increased demand' (World Bank, 1989, p. 22, our translation). The World Bank makes similar criticisms regarding public spending on higher education in Latin America, such as in Brazil (World Bank, 2017).

The educational reforms prescribed by the World Bank for Mozambique focus on meeting market demands without increasing enrollment in higher education. The guidelines are as follows: encourage the active participation of industry and business in the management of vocational training institutions; create a standardized, outcome-based training system with recognition of skills regardless of where they were acquired; design curriculum in modules, with external assessment; and advising students on their career plan (World Bank, 2006). The implementation of these measures would have the effect of leveraging economic growth and reducing unemployment.

However, the implementation of educational reforms in Mozambique over the first decades of the 2000s did not impact the high unemployment rate (Accioly, 2018). The period saw a reduction in per capita food production (Castel-Branco, 2013), increased reliance on food imports, and an increase in the population classified below the poverty line (International Monetary Fund, 2011), despite rapid GDP growth (7.5% per year between 2003 and 2012).

In the twenty-first century, Africa continues to play the role of provider of natural resources and a cheap labor-power for transnational corporations, which still rely on significant fiscal subsidies despite the terrible social and environmental impacts they unleash (Accioly, 2018). The unequal exchange—exporting wealth without social counterparts and importing high-cost goods and technologies—accentuates the economic dependence on foreign aid for education policies, which, in turn, must follow World Bank's guidelines. Since the guidelines reference the human capital theory, the development of technologies on African soil is strongly discouraged. Consequently, the focus is providing some workers with skills to apply imported technologies and be more productive and providing a mass of workers with skills for the informal labor market (Accioly, 2018). Acquiring these skills does not need to be in higher education since it does not involve complex knowledge. In addition, a large number of workers are left out of school.

Thus, in the international division of labor, the labor-power in Africa is thrown into the most impoverished levels of qualification. The school, therefore, moves away from its democratic role of 'socialization of systematized knowledge' (Saviani, 2011, 14, our translation), which is part of the political struggle for the socialization of wealth. It is no accident that educational reforms are articulated with other reforms that drive the expropriation of land, access to natural resources, and rights, which ultimately leads to the extreme precariousness of the working class's living conditions.

14.5   Concluding Remarks

In the *Critique of Political Economy*, Marx historicized the categories handled by the classics, breaking with the naturalization that presupposed them as eternal; and he could do so because he employed in his analysis a new method (the method of dialectical historical materialism). Performing an authentic, theoretical revolution, Marx left as a legacy a rich analysis of the laws of motion of the capital; this analysis constitutes the basis for understanding the dynamics of capitalist society, since, in this society, all social relations are subordinated to the command of capital.

Marx's own work was only possible because of the previous existence of classical Political Economy, since in it were found elements that, subjected to a historicizing treatment and considered under a new methodological perspective, signaled the movement and command of the capital (Netto & Braz, 2006). Based on Marx's method, investigations about educational reforms in the peripheries, implemented in the transition from the twentieth to the twenty-first century, end up scrutinizing some contradictions of contemporary capitalism. The foundations for the expansion of capital are private property, the legal equality of individuals, and the formal freedom of workers to sell their labor in exchange for a wage.

However, the movement of capital continually produces stratifications within the working class according to race, gender, ethnicity, level of schooling, and the type of schooling to which the worker has had access. The stratifications enhance the exploitation of labor to the same extent that they restrict the worker's freedom to sell their labor-power. Those strata of workers most dramatically expropriated from access to land, water, and labor rights are also dramatically expropriated from the right to scientific and philosophical knowledge, regardless of whether they have access to schooling or not. Schooling itself condemns workers to a limited range of functions that they may be able to perform in the labor market.

The idea that aligning education systems with the demands of the private business sector leads to increased employability and better living conditions is a reasonable one, since it is true that some workers gain individual benefits by having access to market-driven education. However, when we delve deeper into the phenomenon beyond appearance, the problem becomes more complex. As a driving force of capital accumulation, the private appropriation of scientific and philosophical knowledge remains untouched, even as workers' access to market-driven schooling increases. Analysis of the Mozambique case reveals that many workers cannot afford to attend school. Many workers who manage to attend school receive a rudimentary education for underemployment and the informal labor market; only a few workers afford to attend higher education (Accioly, 2018).

In the current stage of the international division of labor, in which the central economies dispute the monopoly of technology production, education is plunged into contradictions. At the same time that (a) education represents an expanding market with high potential for profitability as enrollment and schooling time increase, (b) school fulfills the function of providing the basic skills to increase productivity and adapt the worker to the ethical-political forms of class society; the capital, in its global movement to maximize profits, is impelled to restrict enrollment, schooling time, the level and nature of the skills to be acquired by workers.

As a consequence, schooling tends to no longer generate in working-class children and youth prospects for better living conditions in the future. This situation tends to keep children and young people out of school, which is a problem for the capitalist order, since they could move away from the sphere of influence of bourgeois ethics and norms, and start behaving in a dysfunctional way. Therefore, state apparatuses are used to firmly constrain any threats to private property, including private ownership of knowledge through patents and intellectual property contracts.

In peripheral economies, it is common to verify clandestine practices that involve the use of complex technologies developed to illegally take advantage of services provided by corporations (such as electricity, internet, cable television channels) or to steal goods. For example, in 2016 in Brazil, police investigations uncovered groups that were stealing millions of liters of oil from underground pipelines and refining gasoline clandestinely (G1, 2017). These activities demonstrate the popular creative potential in developing technologies that subvert the legal norms of capital.

The private appropriation of the knowledge socially produced throughout human history is a powerful form of domination. It must be emphasized that the looting of the African continent by the European colonizers was not only of goods but also of philosophical, scientific, and technological knowledge.

In this chapter, we argued the importance of Marx's method for investigating global educational reforms. The method makes it possible to go beyond appearances and unveil its multiple contradictions in the face of the international division of labor in globalized capitalism. Thus, investigations and struggles against the reforms and their deleterious effects must consider capitalism as a complex and contradictory totality; therefore, it should not be fragmented or focused only at the local level. For example, the fight against the commodification of higher education in Europe must join the fight for access to schooling in Africa and Latin America, where many children and young people are out of school. Likewise, they should be struggles for free, democratic, critical, and popular sovereignty-oriented schools. Access to schooling at all levels and scientific and philosophical knowledge is indeed essential in the political struggle to socialize wealth and end exploitation of labor.

Disclosure Statement The author has no financial interest or benefit that has arisen from the direct applications of this research.

References

Accioly, I. (2015). Ideologia do Desenvolvimento e do Consumo Sustentável na Educação Ambiental: Uma Análise das Políticas Públicas na Década da Educação para o Desenvolvimento Sustentável. In C. F. B. Loureiro & R. Lamosa (Eds.), *Educação Ambiental no Contexto Escolar: Um Balanço Crítico da Década da Educação para o Desenvolvimento Sustentável* (pp. 68–104). Quartet.

Accioly, I. (2018). *Educação e Capital-Imperialismo: As Influências Político-Pedagógicas Do Banco Mundial Nas Relações Entre Brasil E Moçambique*. Ph.D. Thesis, Universidade Federal do Rio de Janeiro, Rio de Janeiro.

Accioly, I., Gawryszewski, B., & Nascimento, L. (2016). Commodifying Education in a Dependent Capitalist Country. In R. Leher & I. Accioly (Eds.), *Commodifying Education: Theoretical and Methodological Aspects of Financialization of Education Policies in Brazil* (pp. 21–36). Sense Publishers.

Babbage, C. (2009). *On the Economy of Machinery and Manufactures*. Newyork: Cambridge University Press.

Ball, S. (2012). *Global Education Inc.: New Policy Networks and the Neoliberal Imaginary*. Routledge.

Becker, G. (1962). Investment in Human Capital: A Theoretical Analysis. *The Journal of Political Economy, 70*(5).

Braverman, H. (1998). *Labor and Monopoly Capital: The Degradation of Work in the Twentieth Century*. Monthly Review Press.

Brock-Utne, B. (2000). *Whose Education for All? The Recolonization of the African Mind*. Falmer Press.

Bullard, R. D. (2000). *Dumping in Dixie: Race, Class, and Environmental Quality*. Westview Press.

Castel-Branco. (2013). Refletindo Sobre Acumulação, Porosidade e Industrialização em Contexto de Economia Extrativa. *Desafios para Moçambique*. IESE.

Chena, P. I., Buccella, M. E., & Bosnic, C. (2018). Efectos de la financeirización en el cambio tecnológico en América Latina. In M. Abeles, E. P. Caldentey, & S. Valdecantos (Eds.), *Estudios sobre financeirización en América Latina. Libros de la CEPAL, n.152*. Comissión Económica para América Latina y el Caribe.

Cho, Y., & Feda, K. (2015). *Skills and Employability in Mozambique: Implications for Education and Training Policies*. World Bank.

Costa, C. A., & Accioly, I. (2017). A Formação Em Educação Ambiental Crítica Na Periferia Do Capitalismo. *Revista Trabalho, Política e Sociedade, 2*(2), 23–42.

Fernandes, F. (1975) *Sociedade de classes e subdesenvolvimento*.

Fontes, V. (2010). *O Brasil e o Capital-Imperialismo: Teoria e História*. EPSJV/ Editora UFRJ.
G1. (2017). Casos de furto de petróleo para refino clandestino disparam em 2017. *Portal G1*. Retrieved July 9, 2017, from https://g1.globo.com/rio-de-janeiro/noticia/casos-de-furto-de-petroleo-para-refino-clandestino-disparam-em-2017.ghtml
Gramsci, A. (2011). *Cadernos do cárcere, Vol. 3*. Civilização Brasileira.
Harvey, D. (2013). *Para entender o Capital, Livro I*. Boitempo.
International Monetary Fund. (2011). *Republic of Mozambique: Poverty Reduction Strategy Paper*. IMF.
Kofler, L. (2010). *História e dialética: Estudos sobre a metodologia da dialética marxista*. Rio de Janeiro: Editora UFRJ.
Kosík, K. (1976). *Dialética do Concreto*. Paz e Terra.
Marini, R. M. (1973). Dialéctica de la dependencia. In *América Latina, dependencia y globalización. Fundamentos conceptuales Ruy Mauro Marini. Antología y presentación Carlos Eduardo Martins*. Bogotá: Siglo del Hombre - CLACSO, 2008.
Marx, K. (2004). *Manuscritos Econômico-Filosóficos [1844]*. Boitempo Editorial.
Marx, K. (2008). *Prefácio [1859]. Contribuição à crítica da Economia Política*. Expressão Popular.
Marx, K. (2010). O método da economia política [1857]. Apresentação de João Quartim de Moraes e tradução de Fausto Castilho, *Crítica marxista*, n. 30.
Marx, K. (2012). *Crítica Do Programa De Gotha*. Boitempo Editorial.
Marx, K (2013). *O Capital: Crítica da Economia Política, livro I: O processo de produção do Capital [1867]*.. Boitempo Editorial.
Marx, K., & Engels, F. (1993). *A ideologia alemã (Feuerbach)*. Hucitec.
Mir-Artigues, P., & Gonzalez-Calvet, J. (2007). *Funds, Flows and Time: An Alternative Approach to the Microeconomic Analysis of Productive Activities*. New York: Springer.
Netto, J. P., & Braz, M. (2006). *Economia política: uma introdução crítica*.
Pinheiro, H. (2018). O método sintético de Marx em quatro atos: elementos para uma construção crítica do objeto teórico. In J. Ranieri (Ed.), *Além do véu de névoa: leituras e reflexões em torno de O Capital, de Karl Marx* (pp. 57–78). UNICAMP/IFCH.
Portelli, H. (1977). *Gramsci e o Bloco Histórico*. Paz e Terra.
Ranieri, J. (2018). Notas sobre Marx – a presença de Hegel e o lugar das determinações-da-reflexão para a constituição de uma teoria genética. In J. Ranieri (Ed.), *Além do véu de névoa: leituras e reflexões em torno de O Capital, de Karl Marx* (pp. 11–56). UNICAMP/IFCH.
Rodney, W. (1973). *How Europe Underdeveloped Africa*. Tanzanian Publishing House.
Rosenberg, N. (1994). Charles Babbage: pioneer economist. In *Rosenberg, N. Exploring the black box. Technology, economics, and history*. Cambridge: Cambridge University Press.
Saltman, K. J. (2015). *Capitalizing on Disaster: Taking and Breaking Public Schools*. Routledge.
Saviani, D. (2003). O choque teórico da politecnia. *Trabalho, Educação e Saúde*, *1*(1), 131–152.
Saviani, D. (2011). *Pedagogia Histórico-Crítica – primeiras aproximações*. Autores Associados.
Schultz, T. (1961). Investment in Human Capital. *The American Economic Review*, *51*(1).
Smith, A. (2008). *A Riqueza das Nações: Uma Biografia*. Zahar.

Steiner-Khamsi, G. (2004). *The Global Politics of Educational Borrowing and Lending*. Teachers College Press.
Tinel, B. (2012). Labour, Labour Power and the Division of Labour. In B. Fine & A. Saad-Filho (Eds.), *The Elgar Companion to Marxist Economics*. Edward Elgar.
Verger, A., Fontdevila, C., & Zancajo, A. (2016). *The Privatization of Education: A Political Economy of Global Education Reform*. Teachers College Press.
World Bank. (1981). *Accelerated Development in Sub-Saharan Africa: An Agenda for Action*. World Bank.
World Bank. (1987). *Education Policies for Sub-Saharan Africa: Adjustment, Revitalization, and Expansion*. World Bank, September.
World Bank. (1989). *Sub-Saharan Africa: From Crisis to Sustainable Growth – A Long-Term Perspective Study*. World Bank.
World Bank. (2006). Project Appraisal Document on A Proposed Credit in the Amount of Sdr 20.8 Million (Us$30 Million Equivalent) to The Government of Mozambique for A Technical and Vocational Education And Training Project. February 21, 2006.
World Bank. (2010). Eliminando as Barreiras para o Desenvolvimento Inclusivo: Sumário do Relatório Econômico de Moçambique. Washington: Banco Mundial.
World Bank. (2017). *A Fair Adjustment: Efficiency and Equity of Public Spending in Brazil*. World Bank.

CHAPTER 15

The Beginnings of Marxism and Workers' Education in the Spanish-Speaking Southern Cone: The Case of Chile

María Alicia Rueda

15.1 Introduction

The translation into Spanish of Marx's *Das Kapital* by the Argentinian Juan B. Justo, published in Spain in 1898, meant that the workers' organizations prospering in countries such as Argentina and Chile at the turn of the *twentieth* century could incorporate its reading into the ongoing educational activities in their mutual aid societies, resistance societies, trade unions, labor unions, and federations of workers. This did not mean that the socialists and other groups in both countries were unfamiliar with Marx before its publication, as the *Communist Manifesto* and other publications were known, particularly in Argentina, through the influx of European immigrants (Tarcus, 2013).

Although not limited to Spanish-speaking countries in the Southern Cone, such as Argentina and Chile, the Marxist-inspired education of workers to achieve power can be claimed to have been the distinct characteristic of the movements of the region at the start of the twentieth century. This is as

---

Portions of this chapter originally appeared in *The Educational Philosophy of Luis Emilio Recabarren: Pioneering Working-class Education in Latin America*, by María Alicia Rueda, © 2021, Routledge. Reproduced by permission of Taylor & Francis Group.

M. A. Rueda (✉)
University Park, PA, USA
e-mail: mavetter100@msn.com

© The Editor(s) (if applicable) and The Author(s), under exclusive license to Springer Nature Switzerland AG 2023
R. Hall et al. (eds.), *The Palgrave International Handbook of Marxism and Education*, Marxism and Education,
https://doi.org/10.1007/978-3-031-37252-0_15

contrasted with revolutionary endeavors in other Latin American regions and countries, such as the Mexican Revolution and Sandino's rebellion in Nicaragua (Devés, 1991).

In this chapter, I explore the presence of Marxism in workers' education conducted in Chile during the first quarter of the twentieth century by Luis Emilio Recabarren (1876–1924), founder of the Socialist Workers Party of Chile (POS) in 1912. In this context, I also examine the connections with Argentinian socialism and the influence of European Marxist thought on the education of Chilean workers as conducted in their organizations and press toward the independence, empowerment, agency, and ultimate triumph of the working class.

The educational efforts conducted in Chile by Luis Emilio Recabarren must be placed in the context of an era of British imperialism in the region. The exploitation of nitrates in the north of the country extended from the 1880s to the first quarter of the *twentieth* century. The workers Recabarren led belonged to an industrial working class—miners and associated trades—that contended with domestic capitalism as well as with imperialism. More than a hundred organizations were registered in the mining towns in the North between the 1890s and 1912, with an estimated total membership of 10,000 workers. These workers were involved in 150 strikes between 1884 and 1912 (Recabarren Rojas, 1954). The uniqueness of the Chilean experience in the Latin American context must be attributed in great part to the industrial nature of the mining working class, to the semi-colonial conditions in which that class labored, and to the understanding Recabarren had of the particularities of their labor from a Marxist perspective.

Although Recabarren has been portrayed as a 'self-taught' leader and organizer arising from the working class, the historical data point to a (lower) middle-class background and traditional schooling. Moreover, entering the trades as an apprentice typographer at age 14 provided him with access thereon to a variety of intellectual output—newspapers, pamphlets, books—as well as with exposure to the advanced working-class thinking and organization going on at the end of the nineteenth century in the trades. It can be assumed, and it has been confirmed by his comrades and fellow travelers, that Recabarren not only enjoyed a vast cultural background but also partook, with the advantage afforded by his trade, of a revolutionary working-class culture. In these regards, he exemplified the organic intellectual; this he was well-aware of, defining himself very early on as a 'revolutionary socialist' (1904/1985) and, later, as an ideologist equal to any of the socialist leaders he met and became acquainted with in Europe.

It should be noted that Marxist thought appeared early both in Argentina and in Chile. In Argentina, this is credited to an influx of European immigrants, some of them seeking refuge after the defeat of the Paris Commune (Tarcus, 2013). In Chile, there are claims (Jobet, 1972) that one of the founders of the *Sociedad de Igualdad* in 1850, Santiago Arcos, had read Victor Considerant's *Manifesto* of 1843/1847, and possibly became familiar, while in

France, with Marx and Engels' *Communist Manifesto* at the time of its very first publication in 1848. In terms of early accessibility to publications in Chile, Millas (1962) claimed that works by Marx could be found in bookstores in Santiago, Chile, as early as 1865, while Furci (1984) stated that the Morel and Valdes Bookshop catalogue of 1854 listed "even some early works by Karl Marx" (p. 24), among works by Proudhon, Saint Simon, and Le Blanc.

Some of the early influences of Argentinian socialism in Chile can be traced to the reception of the socialist newspaper *La Vanguardia* starting in 1896, two years after its founding in Argentina, and to the direct exchanges between intellectuals and organizers on both sides of the Andes through traveling and exiles. Most important in this context were Recabarren's two exiles in Argentina and his two trips to Europe in representation of the Southern Cone.

15.2 A Marxist Thinker, Organizer, and Educator

Luis Emilio Recabarren as a Marxist thinker has been the subject of, at times, intense debate. Portrayed in the literature as a workers' leader and socialist propagandist, as well as 'one of the first Marxist thinkers of Latin America' (Löwy, 1999, p. 4), his Marxist theoretical background and Marxist analyses have been argued for by several authors (Millas, 1962, 1987; Puiggrós, 2013; Ramírez Necochea, 2007a, 2007b; Vitale, 1987, 1994; Witker Velásquez, 1977), disputed at times (Loyola Tapia, 2000, 2007; Massardo, 2008; Salazar Vergara, 1992; Varas, 1983), and, at others, generally overlooked. There are those who have argued for the Argentinean influence on Recabarren and his development as a socialist thinker, through his contact with Justo and his participation in the Socialist Party of Argentina (PSA), during his exile there both between 1906 and 1908 (Grez Toso, 2011; Massardo, 2008; Pinto Vallejos, 2013; Varas, 1983) and between 1917 and 1918 (Loyola Tapia, 2011). Finally, there are those who have argued that he was not fully a Marxist nor a theoretician with a classical Marxist outlook (Varas, 1983).

Nevertheless, a close reading and textual analysis of his works (Rueda, 2021; Vetter, 2013) makes it evident that he was not only familiar with Marx's works from early on, but also that he strived to apply Marxist concepts to the analysis of the struggles of the Chilean working class, as well as to their education and organization.

15.3 First Marxist Approaches by Recabarren

It is in 1902 when a fundamental concept of Marxism appears first in Recabarren's writings: the emancipation of the working class by the workers themselves:

> Even though we live far away, separated by immense distances, we enjoy a community of ideas. … And those feelings and ideas are, my friend, the ones every

worker should have: *The emancipation of the workers achieved by the workers themselves.* (Recabarren, 1902/1985, p. 7)[1]

The sentence in italics (in the original) is a direct quote from the preamble to the *Provisional Rules of the Association* by Marx (as cited in Marx & Engels, 1985, p. 14): 'Considering, [t]hat the emancipation of the working classes must be conquered by the working classes themselves'.

Furthermore, Recabarren (1902/1985, pp. 8–9) writes:

> THE EMANCIPATION OF THE WORKERS MUST BE THE RESULT OF THE EFFORTS OF THE WORKERS THEMSELVES [emphasis in original], … the experience of years must mark for you a new conduct for the future … never again at the service of the owners, the bosses, the rich, … let's work but for ourselves.

From this point on, Recabarren's efforts will be fully dedicated to the education of the Chilean working class in pursuit of its own emancipation. This education, as conceptualized by him, rested on two pillars: the working-class organization and the working-class press. The working-class organization provided practical training in leadership and management, while the press allowed the workers to develop their own ideology as a class.

Recabarren himself moved away from civilizing notions of education present early on to revolutionary ones. Confronted with the Liberal plans of the elites for a 'popular education' that fostered schooling and technical training for the workers (Núñez, 1982), Recabarren proposed an education by the workers themselves in pursuit of their own objectives as a class. Between 1903 and 1905, stationed in a small port town in the north of Chile as director of *El Trabajo*, a recently founded paper by the *Mancomunal* of boatmen, he proposed to the workers of nearby mining towns and to those who worked in port-related activities to build a center in the middle of the Toco Desert. This center would house schools for adults and for children and provide a central place for the mining workers, and those in related trades, to engage in their own recreational and educational activities.

With the founding of the POS in 1912, an educational agenda was set in place and the locale that housed the party as well as the printing press of the newly founded El *Despertar de los Trabajadores* also became a gathering place for workers to conduct educational activities in their after-work hours. Elias Lafertte (1971, p. 86) documents the readings the mining workers engaged in at these incipient night schools:

> There they would read newspapers from Santiago, from Argentina and from Uruguay, and they could buy Recabarren's pamphlets. From France, we periodically got *L'Humanite*, which was the organ of the then French Socialist Party, directed by Jean Jaures; from Spain, we got *The Socialist*, that made familiar to us the names of Pablo Iglesias… *The Socialist* was our favorite newspaper.

In 1912 and coinciding with the founding of the POS and the newspaper *El Despertar*, Recabarren published a pamphlet titled *Socialism. What Is It and How Will It Be Accomplished?* In it, he outlined the major tenets of socialism, which he had been proposing in a variety of ways since 1907. The influence of Marxism becomes evident in concepts such as surplus value, from *Capital*, as well as the influence of evolutionary theories associated with the Second International. Furthermore, some philosophical Marxist concepts are present as Recabarren attempted to make distinctions between 'natural man' (man as a living organism indistinct from other living organisms) and 'species man' (exclusively human), as Marx (1959) had done in the *Economic and Philosophical Manuscripts* of 1844.

Recabarren posed socialism as a moral, civilizing force, one that would redeem and regenerate society in every aspect of its functioning, conducting it to its goal of happiness for all. In this context, Recabarren (1912/1976, p. 105) proposed that socialism itself was educational: a 'doctrine' (or theory) of human improvement, which, when put into practice, would be an agent for the civilizing of society and contribute to its evolutionary process. 'From a social point of view, it is a doctrine of justice and morality, … to suppress the unhappiness caused by the ill-organization (of society) and so that life is lived in perpetual happiness' (ibid.).

Recabarren claimed that all the ills of society stemmed from inequality and believed that it was in the economic realm where they must be resolved first for other changes to follow. According to him (ibid., p. 110), the economic system itself (capitalism) is immoral (therefore unnatural): 'From a human and moral point of view, mankind should not be involved in the exploitation of others'. He argued that only by changing private property into public property and eliminating private ownership of the means of production could human rights be ensured.

Two new Marxist elements in the theoretical framework of Recabarren were presented here: the necessity for the abolition of private ownership of the means of production, as Marx (1966) discussed in his *Critique of the Gotha Program*; and the concept of 'human rights' as distinct from civil rights, comparable to Marx's (2000) discussion in *On the Jewish Question*: 'There are inalienable rights, such as the right to life and the right to its fullest enjoyment, which cannot be either limited nor suppressed; it is on those rights that Socialism bases itself and reclaims them' (Recabarren, 1912/1976, p. 136).

Recabarren (ibid., p. 136) claimed that human rights are natural rights, in the sense that it is nature itself and its laws that dictated social duties:

> Humans are born by a will other than their own and from the moment of their birth they are entitled to the right to live. Human beings are born into society, which is then called upon not to destroy them or impede them of their means for survival. Every human who is born is destined to the survival of the species and it is this survival of our species that must guide us to take care of the life that is born. Faced with the circumstances presented to us by nature, we must obey its laws.

To this view of nature, which had its roots in the Enlightenment and Romanticism, and of human rights, which had a Judeo-Christian origin, Recabarren, as Marx had done, added the new element of 'human rights' as different from civil rights, or 'the rights of man'. According to Marx (2000, p. 61), the 'Rights of Man' do not go 'beyond egoistic man, man as he is in civil society, namely an individual withdrawn behind his private interests and whims and separated from the community'. In Recabarren, the concept of human rights as different from civil rights coincided with his views and judgment of the Chilean Republic established after Independence from Spain in 1810, and then in 1817 by a creole upper class. In 1910, Recabarren wrote *Rich and Poor at the Time of the Centennial*, to commemorate the date. With this essay, he attempted to prove that the republic had not only betrayed all its promises, but that civil rights had not been guaranteed for most of the population. Furthermore, even those afforded civil rights, such as the right to vote, did not enjoy or have their human rights guaranteed.

The civil rights of citizens established by the bourgeois constitutions, and the Chilean one was no exception, did not include basic human rights or natural rights, only the rights of civil participation. Furthermore, civil rights were to be strictly enjoyed by citizens. In most countries that underwent bourgeois revolutions, and established constitutions with the purpose of ensuring civil rights, amendments were devised to limit the concept of citizenship. Therefore, as Marx (2000, p. 61), challenging the Declaration of the Rights of Man of 1793, stated:

> [C]itizenship, the political community, is degraded by the political emancipators to a mere preservation of these so-called rights of man, that the citizen is declared to be the servant of egoistic man, the sphere in which man behaves as a communal being is degraded below the sphere in which man behaves as a partial being, finally that it is not man as a citizen but man as a bourgeois who is called the real and true man.

It follows that most workers, not considered 'men', enjoyed neither civil nor human rights. Echoing Marx, Recabarren (1910/1965c, p. 80) wrote: 'It is the bourgeoisie that has degraded the people politically. It has destroyed the citizen's dignity; it has defiled our sovereignty'.

In 1912, Recabarren (1912/1976, p. 132) expanded on these concepts, claiming socialism was based on love as 'the only moral and just base on which human life rests'. He also considered this notion of love as the motor of society to be a law of nature: 'Mutual love is a law of nature, as well as of reason, because the existence of humanity would be meaningless without it' (ibid.). Recabarren, like Marx (2000), proposed the idea that it is in mutual recognition (love) that humans see each other as equals and thus recognize themselves as species beings. Society was devoid of love because of exploitation, oppression, and tyranny; and, because of ignorance, inequality reigned:

> Socialism wants to eradicate inequalities to increase the wellbeing of all; and it wants to ameliorate as much as possible the inequalities imposed by nature when those affect human happiness. But the major inequality that affects humans today is social inequality and its resulting political and economic inequality. (Recabarren, 1912/1976, p. 133)

The transformation of private property into collective or common property would, according to Recabarren (ibid.), take care of the objective base of inequality, while education would resolve the subjective obstacle:

> The major obstacle for social equality today is the difference in culture and education, and in customs. That can be resolved by providing the means for education and cultivation and in a few years of active work, all lack of culture and manners will disappear.

15.4 The Educational and Revolutionary Role of the Organization

The working-class organization as educator of the working class in pursuit of its own emancipation as a class can be considered the foundational notion behind all the organizational activities Recabarren engaged in during his entire political life. This notion led him to organize unions, cooperatives, and eventually, a party, and, as a long-time general secretary of the Communist Party of Chile (CPCh) claimed, the educational role of the party is still part of Recabarren's legacy in the CPCh (Luis Corvalán, personal interview 2005).

As a member of the Democratic Party founded in 1887, and then as a founder of the POS in 1912, Recabarren founded, promoted, and led several different class organizations to which he consecutively assigned a leadership as well as an educational role. This was the case with *mancomunales*, trade unions, labor unions, cooperatives, federations, and, ultimately, the party itself.

The first organizations that Recabarren considered exemplary in providing leadership to the working class were the *mancomunales*. These organizations, a combination of mutual aid and resistance (to capitalism) societies, were founded early in the century by boatmen connected to mining activity in the North of Chile. Recabarren recognized their potential from their very beginnings and joined the one in the Tocopilla port in 1903. It was there, while directing the organization's paper *El Trabajo*, that he developed a theory of the importance of the local based on the experiences of a radical working-class organization combined with a progressive municipal government.

The notion that socialism could be achieved locally under such conditions remained a constant in his writings, even after Recabarren moved on to found and promote other organizations such as unions and a new party. Ten years later, and when the workers in Tocopilla had already developed socialist sections of the POS, Recabarren (1916/1986b, pp. 64–65) proudly reported on their educational activities as exemplary, highlighting the existence of a theater room, a small library, and an abundance of newspapers. Among the educational activities there was a theater group which put on socialist plays, and, while some schooling took place one night a week, there was also a night dedicated to political education.

Mancomunales spread through the country. In 1904 there were 15 *mancomunales* that grouped up to 20,000 workers in one federation (Artaza Barrios, 2006); by 1907, seven more had joined the federation (Barria, 1971). Starting in the North around mining, many of these organizations also sprung up in the agrarian South.

15.5 Unions and Union Action: The Argentinean Influence

Although the Marxist influence was present since the very early writings, Recabarren did not start defining an independent Socialist agenda until 1906–1907, when he traveled to Argentina and later to Europe. It was in contact with Argentinean Socialism that Recabarren's views on workers' organizations and their educational potential, as well as his socialist philosophical outlook, took shape as distinctly different from a republican democratic project.

In Argentina, Recabarren became directly acquainted with trade unions and powerful trade union activity. Scholars have stressed the theoretical influence of Justo and of the Socialist Party of Argentina (PSA) on Recabarren, through his participation as a party member and exposure to new readings and abundant press. Without dismissing those influences, reading Recabarren's writings of the period it becomes clear that what was pivotal for his views on working-class organizations was what he witnessed and was part of in the labor movement there.

In *The Nature of the Organization* (El Caracter de la Organización), Recabarren (1907/1986a, pp. 26–27) wrote to his Chilean cadre promoting the idea that the *mancomunales* moved toward the founding of full trade unions. Impressed by the success of strikes, Recabarren (ibid., p. 27) wrote: 'Here in Buenos Aires, we have four, six, up to eight strikes going on daily, organized by the trade unions, or by the workers of a particular workplace'. In announcing the so-called Unification Congress of the (Argentinean) Workers' General Union (usually referred to as the IV Unification Congress) to be held that year, he informed that a resolution had been made to declare 'a general strike in the whole Republic indefinitely' (ibid., p. 13) if the police were to attempt to interrupt the meetings. And, Recabarren (ibid.) added, 'If it takes place, the strike will be the most colossal in South America due to the actual revolutionary capacity of the workers'. In April 1907, statistics were published of a general strike that had taken place in Buenos Aires in January 1907. According to the study, close to 100,000 workers, organized in 51 trade unions, had participated in the strike.

Echoing the discussions in Europe resulting from the 1905 Russian Revolution (see Luxemburg's [1906/1970] *The Mass Strike, the Political Party and the Trade Unions* of 1906 for comparison), Recabarren (1907/1986a, p. 78) read a declaration at the IV Unification Congress that highlighted the educational value of the general strike:

> [C]onsidering that the general strike is genuinely a workers' weapon and the most effective … that it reveals to the workers in the most evident fashion the profound antagonism of interests that divides the two classes … that it strengthens the fighting spirit improving consciousness and strengthening the workers' organization … the IV Congress declares that the general strike is a superior and effective means and advises the proletariat to train and prepare for it … [I]t must take place spontaneously and at the very moment and under the circumstances that it might be required.

The similarities here point to a common Communist working-class culture and to the interconnectedness of the working-class struggles going on before WWI. For a leader such as Recabarren, establishing connections with his European counterparts became a must.

15.6 Socialist Party: The European Influence

In Europe, in 1907–1908, Recabarren came in direct contact with European socialism and had the opportunity to meet with Pablo Iglesias, the head of Spanish socialism. Jaime Massardo (2008, p. 20) claims that Iglesias and Spanish socialism had such an impact on Recabarren and Chilean socialism that the program of the POS, founded in 1912, turned out to be a replica of the program of the Socialist Party of Spain put together by Pablo Iglesias in 1880. If this were so, Recabarren would have been already familiar with such a program when he tried to register a Chilean Socialist Party (with an almost identical program as the one of 1912) at a meeting with Lenin during that same early trip to Europe.

This was the first attempt to make the Democratic Party a socialist party. With the suggestion of a name change to Socialist Democratic Party of Chile, Recabarren (1907/1986a, pp. 123–124) published a *Declaration of Principles*, to be studied and discussed and approved at the next convention of the party. Failing to split the Democratic Party, the declaration was again put forward in August 1909, in *El Socialista*, as the program of the Workers' Socialist Party (PSO), and more fully in 1912 as the program of the Socialist Workers Party (POS) in *El Despertar*. The fact that Recabarren promoted a socialist party program as early as 1907, insisting two more times after that, is evidence that he considered a working-class party an absolute necessity.

In Europe, Recabarren also became aware of **cooperatives** and their potential in the struggle against capitalism. He argued that capitalism itself had pushed the working class to find ways to survive; unions would push for better salaries, while cooperatives would resolve the commercial dependency on the middleman, gradually assuring the total independence of the working class. Furthermore, Recabarren (1916/1986b, p. 131) attributed this newly found knowledge in unions and cooperatives to the intelligence of workers. 'These weapons did not previously exist. They have been invented by the workers, who take care of them and improve them all the time. Our ideas are not, therefore, just projects or ideals: they are working realities in progress'.

Recabarren (ibid., p. 136) believed that it was largely through the cooperatives that the working class would be able to abolish private property and expropriate capital, at the same time socializing society and establishing a collective system:

> The day that all industries have fallen into the hands of socialists; the day that all intermediary actions of industry and commerce are in the hands of socialist cooperatives, won't in fact the capitalist class have disappeared, swallowed by cooperatives? The day the industrial system will be in the hands of the socialist cooperatives, that day industrial work will be simplified and reduced to the limits that are needed, providing for an effective economy that would increase social wellbeing and ensure peace all over the world.

Moreover, the cooperatives combined with the unions and with the party offered a ground for workers to train for the future society; they formed 'a positive school that provides the practical experience of THAT WHICH MUST BE life' [capitalized in the original] (ibid., 137). Nevertheless, Recabarren (ibid., p. 138), just as Marx (1866) had done when discussing cooperative labor and the future of unions, warned against contentment with immediate gains. Socialist action, he said, should have 'as the aim of its action the defeat of the patron class to replace the system of exploitation with one of cooperation'. Union and cooperative actions had to be, therefore, 'infused with socialist doctrine' to achieve their ultimate aims.

> Democracy is only a doctrine that aspires to the perfecting of the political customs of peoples and that establishes equality of means for those that can reach a certain level of progress. ... Socialism is an entirely different doctrine. Socialism is the transformation of the social organization by the abolition of private property and of the forces that sustain it. This is the only way that the exploitation of millions through the tyranny of salaries in its present form will stop. ... Democracy does not resolve social and working-class problems. (Recabarren, 1912/1986a, p. 183)

In the 'Manifesto of the Socialist Workers Party of Tarapacá', Recabarren (ibid.) established the fundamental role of the working class in society as well as addressed the international dimension of working-class struggles: 'Working-class life is today the focus of world attention, because workers are the soul of production and, therefore, they are the life of humanity itself' (ibid., p. 214). In the document, Recabarren attempted to explain that working-class struggles should not limit themselves to the organizing of cooperatives and of guilds and unions, but that the proletariat should strive for political power for itself. Again, as Marx (1866), Recabarren (ibid., p. 217) emphasized education as a key element in the pursuance of these purposes:

> In order that the people improve on their capacities and can struggle successfully, it is necessary to give the POS and the socialist unions the strength and resources that they need to teach the people through talks and books, with newspapers and social meetings. It is also necessary to always speak of socialism; it is necessary to talk to discuss, to discuss to convince, and to convince to increase the forces that will make the *idea* a reality.

Over the course of 1918, Recabarren successfully guided different workers' organizations to join together in one **Federation (FOCH)**. The resolutions of the First Regional Congress of the FOCH in 1919 were the ones previously adopted by the POS in 1918. Among other resolutions of importance, the congress included those that concerned education: the financing of speakers to travel around the country offering lectures; the ongoing combat against alcoholism; the struggle for free, lay, and obligatory primary education; and the creation of free cultural spaces, such as libraries and theaters (Recabarren, 1919/1987, p. 10). For Recabarren (ibid., p. 24), the importance of the FOCH resided in the collective power of workers through the organization:

> The objectives of unionizing will not be achieved but with the existence of a collective force, whose value will reside in the most perfect education of that force.
> Once that collective force has been educated in the objectives that have given rise to it, the application of such objectives must be a methodical and intelligent task.

Recabarren (ibid., p. 25) insisted that the organization of the society of the future was predicated on the education of workers, which would ensure the socialization of the instruments of labor and the abolition of salary. 'The Federation must not only be the force that raises salaries, but also the one to ensure its increase in time, and also the one that guarantees its disappearance when it is no longer necessary'. The collectivity, Recabarren argued (ibid.), should provide individual development—intellectual, moral, cultural—to each of its members. The collective force should be the result of that education.

In December 1921, at the Fourth Congress of the FOCH, its members voted to have the FOCH join the Red International of Labor Unions (RILU) and Recabarren was elected to represent it as its delegate to the RILU. The next three years were ones of great workers' mobilization and activities in the country. Workers organized into increasingly more cohesive organizations and there were great strikes in different sectors, such as by coal miners, dock workers, and fishermen. The FOCH became the major organizing force.

In January 1922, at its IV Congress, the POS, under Recabarren's leadership, became the Communist Party of Chile (PCCh). Echoing Marx and Engels in the *Communist Manifesto*, Recabarren (1922/1987, p. 154) wrote a couple of months later:

> What is the Communist Party? In the first place it is not and it will never be a political party, because it will never accept political relations with the parties of the capitalist class. We accept electoral participation as an instrument of struggle and strictly of a revolutionary character, never of a political character.

The role of the PCCh was educational:

> The Communist Party has as its immediate objective to train, orient, and provide scientific discipline to its members in order that they become the revolutionary vanguard of the people and, with its members present in all the unions, help direct the march of the proletariat towards the final triumph of our aspirations of abolishing the capitalist system with all its injustices and miseries. (ibid.)

When the PCCh joined the Third International, Recabarren and the party membership embraced the tenets of the Soviet Revolution and the Leninist views of the party, although Recabarren had argued in 1921 (1921/1965b, p. 52) that those views had long been his and the Chilean workers' much before the 1917 Revolution:

> I believe that the Soviet system is not any more advanced than everything we started preaching in Chile so many years ago. If these ideas have been printed in pamphlets, books and newspapers is because we, the workers, have been able to get our own resources to establish our own elements for combat, in other words, to have our own press.

15.7 The Educational and Revolutionary Role of the Working-Class Press

With the start of the *twentieth* century, journalism in Chile underwent a process of modernization, with an accent on news and objectivity often understood as nonpartisan or impartial. In this context, partisan working-class journalism became 'a source of ideological guidance, an organizational nucleus, a theoretical combatant, an agitator for social struggle, and a propagandist of solutions and objectives for the (working) class' (Arias Escobedo, 1970, p. 15).

The main ideologies vying for working-class support through the press at the start of the *twentieth* century were either democratic, as espoused by the Democratic Party, or anarchist, spread through their own abundant press. With Recabarren in the Democratic Party, several of the democratic newspapers claimed themselves socialist and working class. With the founding of the POS, the socialist press began to consolidate a different Marxist view that found its full expression in 1922 with its change to the CPCh (Arias Escobedo, 1970).

Recabarren collaborated in the founding or directing, or both, of the following newspapers: *La Democracia*, Santiago, 1900; *El Trabajo*, Tocopilla, 1903; *El Proletario*, Tocopilla, 1904; *La Vanguardia*, Antofagasta, 1906; *La Reforma*, Santiago, 1906; *El Grito Popular*, Iquique, 1911; *El Bonete*, Iquique, 1911; *El Despertar de los Trabajadores*, Iquique, 1912; *El Socialista*, Antofagasta, 1918; *La Federación Obrera* and *Justicia*, Santiago, 1921–1924 (Arias Escobedo, 1970; Cruzat & Devés, 1985, 1986a, 1986b, 1987). He also collaborated in the founding of the Argentinean newspaper *La Internacional*, in Buenos Aires, in 1917 (Cruzat & Devés, 1986b). A few of these papers were the most important and longest running in the working-class press. Recabarren, as the main writer and publisher of the democratic press between 1900 and 1912, and then of the socialist press between 1912 and 1924 (communist after 1922), was also published in all other venues of the working-class press in Chile.

Between 1900 and 1924, Recabarren's views of the role of the working-class press changed consecutively from civilizer to social emancipator, defender, guide, educator, tribune, and organizer of the working class. The civilizing role featured predominantly inside the project of the Democratic Party between 1898 and 1903; the social redemption (or emancipator) role appeared during the *mancomunal* years; the defender's role corresponded to the period between 1906 and 1912, when Recabarren struggled to provide an alternative press that did not fit the project of the Democratic Party any longer but did not agree with the anarchist press approaches. In 1912, with the paper *El Despertar de los Trabajadores*, Recabarren identified the working-class press as the educator of the working class, at the same time noting that *El Despertar* was the first socialist newspaper in Chile.

Finally, Recabarren (1920/1987, p. 67) addressed the need for a national paper to bring together all the organizational efforts going on in the country: a press that would connect and direct, 'that will spread the propaganda through an electric wire from north to south, as it were, and that will put all the social forces in intellectual contact'. That paper became the paper of the Federation of Chilean Workers (FOCH), *La Federación Obrera*, which, shortly before Recabarren's death, changed its name to *Justicia*.

The working-class press in general was highly democratic, and inclusive if publications furthered working-class interests. The newspaper offices in which Recabarren worked often included writers and journalists of different tendencies. Such was the case of the above-mentioned *La Federación Obrera*, where José Santos González Vera, a renowned Anarchist writer worked side by side with Recabarren. As the printing presses were usually located in headquarters, where workers from all over the country attended classes and held meetings, many workers were able to work on the press as well. González Vera (2005), the most cited source on Recabarren, was also the one to describe in detail the educational activities going on at the print shop of *La Federación Obrera*.

In 1918, Recabarren (1986b, pp. 150–151) wrote an article dedicated entirely to the working-class press, which, he said, 'performed the most interesting mission in daily human work all over the world'. Underlining what the press meant in the hands of workers, he also argued for its ultimate counter-hegemonic power:

> The press that is our press, which has seen the light to serve our purposes, ... that press, must be the object of all our efforts. ... We the workers have our own press, and it is our duty to perfect it to make of it a power capable of uniting all of those who dream of better days, but also those that do not think of anything today but might in the future.
>
> The day that we realize that tyranny can be more easily defeated through the press than through the arms, the day that we understand that exploitation and oppression can be reduced to nothing through the action of a people's press, then ... the press will become inseparable from our lives; ... the press is the decisive factor in the redemption of the oppressed, ... the press for us workers is our savior.

Summing up the role of the working-class press in *The Dawn of Revolution* (1921/1965b, pp. 52–54), Recabarren underlined the key role played by its independence:

> While the press was not in our hands, we were invisible, we lived in darkness, ignored; we could not develop our thinking. But the creation of the press reveals a genius in the thought of the workers. When they have said: 'Let us have a press, then we will be able to perfect our intelligences', then and only then have things started to change.
>
> This is what the people of Chile do, what the genuine working class does: with its enthusiasm, with its intelligence, with what it invents, it has a great aspiration to overcome the chaotic state of ignorance in which it is forced to live, and then it looks by itself for the necessary tools to develop its intellectual capacity.

15.8   Conclusion

Luis Emilio Recabarren as a Marxist shares that reputation in the region with several other Latin American intellectuals and revolutionaries, such as José Carlos Mariátegui in Perú and Julio Mella in Cuba. Although there is an absence of comparative studies, the massive working-class educational efforts of the period in Chile appear to bear no comparison anywhere else. As Devés (1991, p. 132) has pointed out, the working-class struggles in Chile, although they coincided with the popular struggles going on around the centennial in other regions, 'were conducted not by "caudillos" but by educators ... for whom no authentic popular struggle existed without education and organization'.

The educational and organizational efforts spanning 1900 to 1924 in Chile owe the revolutionary direction they took to Recabarren's practical leadership and Marxist ideological training. Recabarren's press writings and his most important essays gave a Marxist direction to workers in resistance and mutual aid societies. From self-help organizations, and resistance strikes that were often met with violence, the workers moved to class organizations in pursuit of their own emancipation and agency. Workers' education, previously understood as the civilizing of laborers, became the education of class subjects through participation in class organizations and through their own press.

Although highly localized, what characterized Recabarren's endeavors in Chile and in the region was their internationalism. This internationalism prospered during Recabarren's travels to Argentina and Europe, where connections were made with the major international working-class organizations of the period. In turn, the major ideas promoted in those organizations, primarily those of Marxism and Communism, made their way to the organizations and press in both countries, as well as to others in the Southern Cone such as Uruguay. To underscore the importance of these connections and influences, I must highlight the presence of delegations from Chile, Argentina, and Uruguay at the Fourth Congress of the Communist International in Moscow in 1922, with Recabarren in representation of Chile along with representatives of Argentina and Uruguay. This was the first time that official delegates of the recently founded Communist parties in all three countries attended the Congress.

As a result of his participation in the Congress, Recabarren (1923/1965a, p. 186) wrote *La Rusia Obrera y Campesina*, in which he left no doubt about his allegiance to the Soviet Revolution and to his ascribing to Marxist-Leninist thought. Furthermore, he wrote: 'I have returned from Russia more convinced than ever that it is urgent to hasten the Social Revolution that will put in the hands of the people all the powers for the construction of a Communist society'.

The lasting influence of the educational endeavors of the first quarter of the *twentieth* century in Chile could perhaps be best measured by the many times that the Chilean working class has come close to taking power. Most famously, this seemed possible under the socialist government of Salvador Allende (1970–1973). Further evidence of a legacy can be found in the number of working-class organizations and in the staying power of the working-class parties; as an example of the latter, the Communist Party of Chile (CPCh), in a Left party coalition in government today, traces its beginnings to the POS, founded by Recabarren in 1912. Nevertheless, this legacy has been, and continues to be, contentious. In the first place, Recabarren never advocated for the working-class to *be represented* in power, but rather for it to take power and lead a socialist process. Although he believed this could be achieved through education and peaceful means, believing that society led by the working class would naturally evolve into socialist relations and a communist future, Recabarren never called for a joining of bourgeois institutions to do so, as it has been conveniently claimed at different times by friends as well as by critics.

The current politics in Chile offer striking similarities with Recabarren's times. While during the first quarter of the *twentieth* century, the working class contended with Liberalism, Chileans today must contend with Neoliberalism. After Recabarren's untimely death at the end of 1924, the working class, organized in a constitutional assembly of salaried workers and intellectuals, wrote its own national Constitution '*La Constitucion Chica*' (Grez Toso, 2016), as it would later be called. And just as the working-class constitution was replaced with a bourgeois one in 1925 and forgotten, the Chilean political elite has once again triumphed over the massive protests of 2019 that led to the writing of a new constitution by a democratically elected popular assembly, and it is in the process of replacing it with one designed by Congress and a team of 'experts'. The one opportunity in perhaps a century for Chilean society to move forward has been squandered once more, and lessons must be drawn about the limits of spontaneous uprisings. Nevertheless, we can still speak of a Recabarrian legacy at the base that considers the education of workers a fundamental task of its organizations.

Disclosure Statement The author has no financial interest or benefit that has arisen from the direct applications of this research.

Note

1. All translations from the Spanish are by the author.

References

Arias Escobedo, O. (1970). *La prensa obrera en Chile: 1900–1930*. Universidad de Chile-Chillán.

Artaza Barrios, P. (2006). La Mancomunal de Obreros de Iquique: Su propuesta de vinculación entre movimiento social y politización popular, 1900–1909 [The Workers' mancomunal of Iquique: Its Goal of Combining Social Movement and Popular Politicization]. *Espacio Regional*, 3(1), 9–18. https://www.archivochile.com/Ideas_Autores/artazabp/artazabp0001.pdf

Barria, S. J. (1971). *El movimiento obrero en Chile*. Ediciones de la Universidad Técnica del Estado.

Cruzat, X., & Devés, E. (1985). Cronología Luis E. Recabarren S., 1876–1095. In Recabarren, *Escritos de Prensa* [Newspaper Writings] (Vol. I) (X. Cruzat & E. Devés, Eds.) (pp. vii–ix). Terranova.

Cruzat, X., & Devés, E. (1986a). Cronología L. Emilio Recabarren S., 1906–1913. In Recabarren, *Escritos de Prensa* [Newspaper Writings] (Vol. II) (X. Cruzat & E. Devés, Eds.) (pp. 1–2). Terranova.

Cruzat, X., & Devés, E. (1986b). Cronología de Luis E. Recabarren S., 1914–1918. In Recabarren, *Escritos de Prensa* [Newspaper Writings] (Vol. III) (X. Cruzat & E. Devés, Eds.) (pp. 1–3). Terranova.

Cruzat, X., & Devés, E. (1987). Cronología, 1919–1924. In Recabarren, *Escritos de Prensa* [Newspaper writings] (Vol. IV) (X. Cruzat & E. Devés, Eds.) (pp. 1–3). Terranova.

Devés, E. (1991). La cultura obrera ilustrada chilena y algunas ideas en torno al sentido de nuestro quehacer historiográfico. *Mapocho*, 30, 127–136. https://www.archivochile.com/Ideas_Autores/devese/devese0009.pdf

Furci, C. (1984). *The Chilean Communist Party and the Road to Socialism*. Zed Books.

González Vera, J. S. (2005). Luis Emilio Recabarren. In C. Soria (Ed.), *Letras anarquistas: Artículos periodísticos y otros escritos inéditos [Anarchist Letters: Newspaper*

Articles and Other Unpublished Writings] (pp. 255–262). Planeta. (Original Work Published 1950).
Grez Toso, S. (2011). *Historia del comunismo en Chile: La era de Recabarren (1912–1924)*. LOM.
Grez Toso, S. (2016). La Asamblea Constituyente de Asalariados e Intelectuales, Chile 1925: Entre el olvido y la mitificación. *Izquierdas, 29*, 1–48. https://doi.org/10.4067/S0718-50492016000400001
Jobet, J. C. (1972). Notas en torno a Santiago Arcos, Fermín Vivceta, Alejandro Escobar y Luis Emilio Recabarren. *Occidente, 236*, 53–60. http://www.bibliotecanacionaldigital.gob.cl/bnd/628/w3-article-223280.html
Lafertte, E. (1971). *Vida de un comunista*. Austral.
Löwy, M. (1999). *Marxism in Latin America from 1909 to the Present: An anthology*. Humanity Books.
Loyola Tapia, M. (2000). Recabarren: Su función mítica y notas para la comprensión de su pensamiento político'. In M. Loyola Tapia & J. Rojas (Eds.), *Por un rojo amanecer: Hacia una historia de los comunistas chilenos* (pp. 81–106). Valus.
Loyola Tapia, M. (2007). *La felicidad y la política en Luis Emilio Recabarren: ensayo de interpretación de su pensamiento*. LOM.
Loyola Tapia, M. (2011). Recabarren en Buenos Aires, 1916-1918: Una estadía teórica decisiva. *Revista Izquierdas, 10*, 30–38. http://www.redalyc.org/articulo.oa?id=360133450002
Luxemburg, R. (1970). The Mass Strike, the Political Party and the Trade Unions. In M. A. Waters (Ed.), *Rosa Luxemburg Speaks* (pp. 212–300). Pathfinder. (Original Work Published 1906).
Marx, K. (1866). Instructions for the Delegates of the Provisional General Council of the International Workingmen's Association. https://www.marxists.org/archive/marx/works/1866/08/instructions.htm
Marx, K. (1959). *Economic and Philosophical Manuscripts of 1844*. Progress Publishers.
Marx, K. (1966). In C. P. Dutt (Ed.), *Critique of the Gotha Programme*. International Publishers.
Marx, K. (2000). In D. McLellan (Ed.), *Selected Writings* (2nd ed.). Oxford University Press.
Marx, K., & Engels, F. (1985). *Collected Works* (Vol. 20). Progress Publishers.
Massardo, J. (2008). *La formación del imaginario político de Luis Emilio Recabarren: Contribución al estudio crítico de la cultura política de las clases subalternas de la sociedad chilena*. LOM.
Millas, O. (1962). Medio siglo de partido obrero en Chile. *Principios*, July–August, pp. 7–29.
Millas, O. (1987). *De O'Higgins a Allende: Páginas de la historia de Chile*. Michay.
Núñez, I. (1982). *Educación popular y movimiento obrero: Un estudio histórico*. PIIE.
Pinto Vallejos, J. (2013). *Luis Emilio Recabarren: Una biografía histórica*. LOM.
Puiggrós, A. (2013). *De Simón Rodríguez a Paulo Freire*. Colihue.
Ramírez Necochea, H. (2007a). Historia del movimiento obrero en Chile. In J. Punto Vallejos (Ed.), *Obras escogidas* (Vol. 1, pp. 267–524). LOM.
Ramírez Necochea, H. (2007b). Origen y formación del Partido Comunista de Chile. In J. Pinto Vallejos (Ed.), *Obras escogidas* (Vol. 2, pp. 151–467). LOM.
Recabarren, L. E. (1902/1985). *Escritos de prensa* (Vol. I) (X. Cruzat & E. Devés, Eds.). Terranova. (Original Works Published 1898, 1900, 1901, 1902, 1903, 1904, 1905).

Recabarren, L. E. (1904/1985). *Escritos de prensa* (Vol. I) (X. Cruzat & E. Devés, Eds.). Terranova. (Original Works Published 1898, 1900, 1901, 1902, 1903, 1904, 1905).

Recabarren, L. E. (1907/1986a). *Escritos de prensa* (Vol. II) (X. Cruzat & E. Devés, Eds.). Terranova. (Original Works Published 1906, 1907, 1908, 1909, 1912, 1913).

Recabarren, L. E. (1910/1965c). Ricos y pobres a través de un siglo de vida republicana. In J. C. Jobet, J. Barría, & L. Vitale (Eds.), *Obras Escogidas*, Tomo I, (pp. 57–98). Editorial Recabarren. (Original Work Published 1910).

Recabarren, L. E. (1912/1976). El socialismo. ¿Qué es, y cómo se realizará? In D. Castañeda Fuertes (Ed.), *Obras* (pp. 101–185). Havana, Cuba: Casa de las Americas.

Recabarren, L. E. (1912/1986a). *Escritos de prensa* (Vol. II) (X. Cruzat & E. Devés, Eds.). Terranova.

Recabarren, L. E. (1916/1986b). *Escritos de prensa* (Vol. III) (X. Cruzat & E. Devés, Eds.). Terranova. (Original Works Published 1914, 1915, 1916, 1917, 1918).

Recabarren, L. E. (1919/1987). *Escritos de prensa* (Vol. IV) (X. Cruzat & E. Devés, Eds.). Terranova. (Original Works Published 1919, 1920, 1921, 1922, 1923, 1924).

Recabarren, L. E. (1920/1987). *Escritos de prensa* (Vol. IV) (X. Cruzat & E. Devés, Eds.). Terranova. (Original Works Published 1919, 1920, 1921, 1922, 1923, 1924).

Recabarren, L. E. (1921/1965b). Los albores de la revolución social en Chile. In J. C. Jobet, J. Barría, & L. Vitale (Eds.), *Obras Escogidas*, Tomo I, (pp. 21–56). Editorial Recabarren. (Original Work Published 1921).

Recabarren, L. E. (1922/1987). *Escritos de prensa* (Vol. IV) (X. Cruzat & E. Devés, Eds.). Terranova. (Original Works Published 1919, 1920, 1921, 1922, 1923, 1924).

Recabarren, L. E. (1923/1965a). La Rusia Obrera y Campesina [The Russia of workers and peasants]. In J. C. Jobet, J. Barría, & L. Vitale (Eds.), *Obras Escogidas*, Tomo I [Selected works, Vol. I], (pp. 99–186). Editorial Recabarren. (Original Work Published 1923).

Recabarren Rojas, F. (1954). Historia del proletariado de Tarapacá y Antofagasta, 1884–1913 [History of the proletariat of Tarapacá and Antofagasta, 1884–1913]. Unpublished Master's Thesis, Universidad de Chile, Santiago de Chile.

Rueda, M. A. (2021). *The Educational Philosophy of Luis Emilio Recabarren: Pioneering Working-Class Education in Latin America*. Routledge.

Salazar Vergara, G. (1992). *Movimiento social, municipio y construcción de estado: El liderazgo de Recabarren (1910–1925)*. SUR, Centro de Estudios Sociales y Educación.

Tarcus, H. (2013). *Marx en la Argentina* (2nd. revised ed.). Siglo XXI.

Varas, A. (1983). *La formación del pensamiento político de Recabarren: Hipótesis para una investigación histórica*. Programa de la Facultad Latinoamericana de Ciencias Sociales (FLACSO).

Vetter, M. A. (2013). *Luis Emilio Recabarren: Educator of the Chilean Working Class*. Doctoral dissertation, Northern Illinois University.

Vitale, L. (1987). *Los precursores de la liberación nacional y social en América Latina*. Ediciones Al Frente.

Vitale, L. (1994). *Interpretación marxista de la historia de Chile: De la república parlamentaria a la república socialista, 1891–1932* (Vol. V). LOM.

Witker Velásquez, A. (1977). *Los trabajos y los días de Recabarren*. Nuestro Tiempo.

CHAPTER 16

Commodification and Financialization of Education in Brazil: Trends and Particularities of Dependent Capitalism

Roberto Leher and *Hellen Balbinotti Costa*

Conquering political power has therefore become the great duty of the working classes [...]. One element of success they possess: the number of their members. But this quantity only weighs in the balance if these members are united by a common articulation and guided by knowledge. (Marx, Inaugural Message of the International Workingmen's Association, 1864, quoted in Musto, 2014, p. 98)

16.1 Introduction

Education is one of the most strategic social rights for the working class, as is evident in the propositions that circulated in the International Workingmen's Association—IWA (1864; 1866; 1868, 1869[1]), in the acts and practices of the Paris Commune (1871), in all of the socialist revolutions of the twentieth

R. Leher (✉)
Federal University of Rio de Janeiro, Rio de Janeiro, Brazil

CNPQ, CNPq research fellow, Distrito Federal, Brazil

FAPERJ, Scientist of Our State Program-RJ, Rio de Janeiro, Brazil
e-mail: robertoleher@fe.ufrj.br

H. B. Costa
Federal University of Rio de Janeiro, Rio de Janeiro, Brazil

UFRJ, Faculty of Education, Rio de Janeiro, Brazil

© The Editor(s) (if applicable) and The Author(s), under exclusive license to Springer Nature Switzerland AG 2023
R. Hall et al. (eds.), *The Palgrave International Handbook of Marxism and Education*, Marxism and Education,
https://doi.org/10.1007/978-3-031-37252-0_16

century, as in the Russian revolution (1917), the Cuban revolution (1959), and the decolonization of Africa (1970–1980). Education has also been on the agenda of social reforms, as exemplified by the Constituent Assembly in Brazil (1987–1988), the student movements at the National Autonomous University in Mexico (1999), and the Penguin movement in Chile (2006). These struggles underpinned the legitimacy of demands in defense of the right to a common, lay, universal public school, as a duty of the State, which also emerged in dependent capitalist countries[2] (Fernandes, 1981).

As Fernandes (2008) points out, the bourgeois revolution in Brazil was *sui generis*; that is, it was a revolution without revolution, which explains why the universalization of basic social rights is so late, incomplete, unequal, and problematic. To understand the root of the problem it is necessary to establish the connections of dependent capitalism with the particularity of the bourgeois revolution in Brazil. Historically, the dominant bourgeois factions did not even lead a classic bourgeois educational project, like those arising from the French Revolution and from the liberal democratic propositions of the Enlightenment. The Brazilian universities are, broadly speaking, twentieth-century institutions, and the universalization of basic education is still an unfinished task, despite the achievements of the 1988 Constitution. In part, this is because of the historical and material development of the pillars of dependent capitalism. These are the brutal exploitation of labor and the structural mechanisms of worker expropriation, which assure the economic conditions of surplus value sharing that reproduce the partnership of the local bourgeois factions with the hegemonic imperialized factions (Fernandes, 1981), notably the money-trading capital operators referred to by Marx in Volume 3 of *Capital* (Marx, 2017), in conformity with the interests of the System of States that configure imperialism (NATO, IMF, World Bank, G-7, OECD).

Cultural and scientific heteronomy does not derive unilaterally from external imperialist imposition, but rather from the subordinate association of the local bourgeois factions that manage, on a daily basis, the bases of that heteronomy. It is surprising, therefore, that contemporary educational debates omit how those educational achievements are inseparable from anti-systemic struggles and from social reforms inscribed in class struggles. Possibly, such silencing has contributed to erase the core of these claims, namely the unitary school of labor (Gramsci, 2016), a slogan present since the Paris Commune. The Italian communist leader stated that public education should incorporate the educational principle of labor, the scientific foundations of technologies, and the praxis of labor. This aims to ensure an education that allows the proletariat to be the leader of the society of the future, which requires a school that refuses the disjunction between those who think and those who execute; between those who command and those who obey. The unitary school is committed to an omnilateral formation: scientific, technological, artistic, cultural, and always from *both* the social-historical perspective of knowledge *and* the praxis present in social work.

The profound changes in the correlation of forces since the 1990s have worked to the detriment of working class struggles. Even the achievements contained in the Constitutions of several countries, such as the right to free and public education, are being radically redefined in the context of the growing hegemony of austerity (Mattei, 2022) and of the bourgeois factions that operate in the financial sphere. It is in relation to these changes that this chapter brings contributions in the light of the class struggle, with particular emphasis on Brazil.

This is important because capital has achieved increasing influence over educational agendas and practices, introducing new preconditions that deny even the liberal-democratic pedagogy. It does this through the re-signification of scientific, cultural, and philosophical knowledge in rarefied competencies that reinforce capital's order (entrepreneurship, resilience, socioemotional dispositions); the establishment of significant evaluations that frame what should be taught in schools, and that establish competition through rankings; the spread of the ideology of meritocracy; and the relentless emptying of the content of teaching work, intellectually expropriating that material from systems and teaching platforms. In this chapter, the focus of the investigation and analysis is the economic movement of the commodification of education. Specifically, it focuses upon education as a commodity inscribed in the business engendered by financial groups that, by promoting acquisitions of school organizations, publishers, systems, and teaching platforms, are moving the entire, immense educational apparatus to stock exchanges and to the portfolio of investment funds, especially in the form of private equity.

16.2 Private Hegemonic Apparatuses and Neoliberal Education

In the period of hegemony of the neoliberal system of accumulation, the big bourgeoisie invested in the constitution of private corporate apparatus of hegemony (Fontes, 2021; Leher, 2018), precisely to spread a pro-systemic ethos in education. Vast, educational, counter-reform movements have been effected based on an ideology of austerity (Mattei, 2022). In this perspective, education is a matter for technocrats since, in the view of capital, it is the basis for the formation of human capital. This legitimizes the participation of (bourgeois) civil society in education by means of the aforementioned private corporate apparatus of hegemony (PCAH). In this view, the participation of teachers and students should be displaced to irrelevant spaces in the definition of educational policies, since their agendas, considered corporativist and anachronistic, are hostile to the process of calibrating education to the demands of business organizations.

In our argument, we aim for greater conceptual precision in relation to commodification, through which we understand how education is inserted into the movement of expanded reproduction of capital, involving the cycles of productive capital (Marx, 1867), monetary capital Marx, 1885), and commodity capital (Marx, 2017).

> It was in the context of the crisis of the so-called welfare state that the word 'commodification' was added in the dictionary in the mid-1970s. It corresponds, in English, to 'commodification', dated 1975 (Oxford[3]) or 1976 (Webster, Commodity, from the French commodities):[4] an economic good. (…) In general, dictionaries use as synonyms 'to become the object of commerce', 'commercialization', emphasizing its character as a commodity engendered by capital. (…) Commercialization of a service that, since the end of the 1990s, may be object of competition between local and multinational companies, even with ramifications with corporations that operate in the world market (accentuating its condition of merchandise, as expressed as of 1995 in the WTO's General Agreement on Trade in Services and in the Trade in Service Agreement—TISA). (Leher, 2022, p. 84)

As if in a pincer movement, the operators of capital are closing in on the totality of education. First, the PCAH act to obtain hegemony over what is taught in schools, and the corporations convert private non-profit institutions (philanthropic, community, confessional) into for-profit groups under the direction of investors. Second, at the same time, they throw their tentacles into textbook publishing and establish publicly traded branches for colonizing the business of teaching systems and teaching platforms that are already widely present in public schools. It is possible to postulate, therefore, that in the twenty-first century, capital achieves ideological influence through the material force reproduced by its PCAH. This develops directly, through the acquisition of schools, the production of teaching materials—systems and platforms—that circulate in public basic education networks, and the training of a large part of future teachers in empty, distance learning courses.

In the wake of the structural crisis of capitalism, and the deepening of social contradictions resulting from austerity, in another not irrelevant prism, the extreme right inserts schools in the theater of operations of the culture war. It acts in order to subordinate schools to reactionary family demands, in general through the precepts of religious fundamentalism, controlling the content of textbooks and teacher training programs, disqualifying diversity and criticism of racism, and propagating the crusade against the so-called gender ideology.

Both the PCAH and organizations of the extreme right are engaged in fighting the precepts of equality and integral, unitary, and omnilateral human formation. Recent high school reform in Brazil (equivalent to the 14–17 age group), implemented in 2016, after the illegitimate impeachment of former president Dilma Rousseff, with the support of PCAH and the far right, has exacerbated the social segregation of students by directing the poorest students toward a professionalization devoid of formative rigor. The hegemonic impetus for educational change also recommends an early, disciplinary split: either language, mathematics, natural sciences, or social sciences. This reform is being accompanied by new curricular bases that deny the new generations access to historical, social, scientific, technological and cultural knowledge.

> From the Factory system budded, as Robert Owen has shown us in detail, the germ of the education of the future, an education that will, in the case of every child over a given age, combine productive labour with instruction and gymnastics, not only as one of the methods of adding to the efficiency of production, but as the only method of producing fully developed human beings. (Marx, 1867)

It is not difficult to conclude that, in a multifaceted way, capital revolutionizes the place of education in the class struggle, a situation, as pointed out before, that has been little investigated in the academic educational field. In dependent capitalist countries, the PCAH, the commodification of education, and the practices of the extreme right generate a reality full of particularities and nuances, whose result confirms that diverse expressions of capital desire to appropriate every educational practice, to reinforce their specific agendas.

Moreover, it is possible to conclude that the commodification of education does not end in the sphere of economics, but composes the scope of the political economy of labor, involving the analysis of the correlation of forces in class struggles. This was pointed out by Antonio Gramsci in his Notebooks. In considering the relations of forces, the formation of consciousness requires education (although education in itself is insufficient), especially critical-historical pedagogy (literacy, social-historical training, criticism of religious and natural determinisms, familiarity with methodical thinking, etc.). In Gramsci's words:

> The consciousness of being part of a particular hegemonic force (i.e., political consciousness) is the first phase of a further, progressive self-consciousness, in which *theory and practice finally become unified*. Therefore, also the unity of theory and practice is not a mechanical fact, but a historical becoming, which has its elementary and primitive phase in the feeling of 'distinction,' of 'separation,' of almost instinctive independence, and progresses until *the actual and complete acquisition of a coherent and unitary conception of the world*. That is why attention must be drawn to the fact that the political development of the concept of hegemony represents, in addition to political-practical progress, a great philosophical progress, since it necessarily implies and presupposes an intellectual unity and an ethics appropriate to a *conception of reality that has overcome common sense and become critical, even if within still restricted limits*. (Gramsci, 2015, p. 90, *emphasis* by the authors)

Neoliberal hegemony has re-signified education as a technical practice, radically different from teaching and learning processes that contribute to political consciousness. In the name of false scientific evidence, they argue that educational matters should be run by technocrats imbued with the ideologies of austerity, which are deliberately anti-worker (Mattei, 2022). This is a relationship that exists throughout the world. It is possible to postulate that the force of the pedagogy of capital, in its various facets, by dehydrating the historical-critical formation of the working class, has contributed to its disorganization and depoliticization, strengthening the extreme right.

Indeed, despite the successive periods of economic crises that have shaken the world economy since the 1970s, social struggles and revolutionary processes against the order of capital have been localized and discontinuous. As Marx (1864) pointed out in his Inaugural Message, one of the main theoretical and practical challenges of revolutionary praxis is to try to understand the reasons why the working class, although vast in number (ILO: 3.3 billion 'workers' in 2022) and crucial to the expanded reproduction of capital (there is no profit without the extraction of surplus value from human labor), is not politically powerful enough in the context of class struggles. Because of course, a significant part of it is being won over to the ranks of the extreme right of a fascist nature, as seen in the Brazilian case after 2013.

Even after the tragedies caused by fascism in the 1920s and 1930s, the experience of the twentieth and twenty-first centuries allows us to postulate that, in contexts of crisis, many millions of subjects belonging to the working class have shown themselves to be susceptible to a common sense that is hostile to socialism and to the internationalism of struggles. This exacerbates the imperialist intentions of big capital. More specifically, it is imprudent to ignore the mental dispositions that lead expropriated and exploited workers to embrace proto-fascist, neo-fascist and, as can be seen from still apparently localized manifestations, explicitly Nazi ideals and practices. The theme of consciousness formation is therefore closely linked to a pedagogy critical of the currently, grossly conservative common sense, despite this being a 'contradictory, multiform, ambiguous concept' (Gramsci, 2015, p. 102). With Paulo Freire (1967), we can put on the political agenda the importance of confronting the conformist pedagogy of capital, in order to emulate the inventive imagination that is essential to confront the hegemony of capital. In this agenda, it is imperative to confront the commodification of education as a strategic dimension of the class struggle.

16.3 Particularity of the Commodification of Education in the Twenty-First Century

The commodification of education has been disrupting education worldwide since the 2000s. Unlike in the past, private education is not driven by family groups who invest in and exploit a particular educational service for profit. Although lagging behind in comparison to other sectors of the economy, in the twenty-first century, education definitely entered the 'upper stage of capitalism' referred to by Lenin in his classic on Imperialism (Lenin, 2008). This process hits basic and higher education (HE), public and private, with the force of a tsunami.

Commercialization and Financialization of Education

The theoretical problem of the commodification and financialization of education is referenced in concepts present in Lenin's work on Imperialism (Lenin, 2008) and in Marx (2017), especially in Volume III (Chapters 21–27). Based on these authors, this study examines the current characteristics of 'finance capital' and, as referenced in Volume III, especially the particularities of money-trading capital, highlighting interest-bearing capital (money as a commodity); and inextricably linked to this, the role of fictitious capital (stocks, bonds, etc.) lent by banks, pension funds, and owners of large sums of money to investment funds (private equity), aiming to secure additional money-capital.

As Marx penetratingly captured in Volume III, large sums of money-capital are now directed to money-trading businesses (interest-bearing capital) and these businesses, in connection with the processes of surplus value production, have gained relative autonomy. Through the expansion of fictitious capital, this has generated a new reality in capitalism that was originally apprehended by Hilferding (1985) and Lenin (2008). In today's capitalism, large sums of money-capital from individual and collective investors, such as pension funds and certain banking portfolios, are being driven towards investment funds. As is characteristic of finance operators, many of these investments in funds are made by owners of securities and backed by further securities. This entails a high degree of uncertainty about the future realization of value, and leads investors to demand an investment portfolio that ensures a high rate of return.

A characteristic of private equity funds is the directing of investments in businesses that are already consolidated, seeking to reduce the risk rate. In times full of uncertainty, as the events resulting from the worsening of the financial market crisis in 2008 have shown, they seek investments that have a connection with real assets (land, infrastructure companies, education, health, social security, etc.). Crucially, however, they only make investments in the productive capital circuit (in fixed capital, technologies, acquisitions of new related companies, and in labor force) if the rate of return is substantively favorable.

When investment funds carry out the acquisition and merger of educational groups, the first step is the restructuring of courses, closing those with low returns and creating general, basic cycle of educational circulation that covers several, not necessarily related, courses. In the Brazilian case, this restructuring involves the proliferation of distance learning courses. The central goal is to reduce the cost of the labor force, and investors push for mass layoffs, reduction of the workday with salary reduction, proliferation of task work, service provision, and outsourcing.

The assumption for the realization of value is always the intensification of labor exploitation. This tendency completely shatters any attempt to establish a minimum standard of quality in the courses offered, with the exception of very specific niches of courses for the high-income public. Groups like private equity investors seek to ensure a utilitarian training regime, which is presented as capable of increasing the human capital of the buyers of the commodity education.

Despite the low cost of tuition for distance learning degree courses, the return is high, since the investment in fixed capital is low. ICTs and the use of the Internet have fallen in cost, and the modality demands little expenditure on physical facilities, libraries, laboratories, and so on. Profound restructuring is carried out to reduce personnel costs through the concentration of administrative services and a sharp reduction in the teaching workforce. A small group of teachers can work in areas in which they are not specialists, by virtue of the scripted classes inserted in teaching systems and in work platforms. This breaks a principle that has structured education in previous centuries: that teaching presupposes knowledge of a given area and certain subjects.

Commodification in Brazil

From the deepening of the structural crisis, as a counter-tendency to the fall of the average rate of profits, new domains of social life have been expropriated by capital. In the Brazilian case, the commodification of education stands out. The advance of capital did not involve a change in the constitutional text, but is radically reconfiguring private education and, increasingly, entering the public institutions themselves. This ranges from curriculum guidelines to teacher training, from the organization of basic education to pedagogical material, from the use of public funds by capital and to the definition that the public can contemplate financial corporations operating in schools. It operates centrally, by the actual subordination of teaching work to capital—through education systems and work platforms linked to corporations, and structured corporately.

During the period of the corporate-military dictatorship (1964–1985), private HE experienced a strong expansion through the increased contribution of public funds (tax exemptions and the concession of educational credit subsidized by the State). The growth occurred through family-owned educational groups and formally non-profit.[5] Under the dictatorship, total enrolments in HE grew from less than 40% to more than 60% between 1964 and 1985. It must be acknowledged that the re-democratization (after 1985) did not reverse this trend, and the current percentage of private enrollments is 77.5%.

In the wake of the 2008 crisis, however, privatization took on new configurations. Needing to export surplus capital, important global investment funds— Actis; Advent; BlackRock; Capital World Investors; Cartesian Capital Group; Coronation; Credit Suisse; Devry; HSBC—Hong Kong and Shanghai Banking Corporation; Kohlberh Kravis Roberts (KKR); Oppenheimer, today Canadian Imperial Bank of Commerce; Singapore, among others, and also funds with relevant participation of local bourgeois fractions (Brazil), such as: Ascese; Banco BTG Pactual; Banco Pátria; BR Investimentos; GP Investimentos— redefined their business portfolios, in search of real assets to protect their investments in the crisis context. In the Brazilian case, these funds have shown special interest in educational business, as can be inferred from the feverish process of acquisitions and Initial Public Offerings (IPOs). This opens a new chapter in the history of the commodification and internationalization of the business of education in Brazil.

What is new, since 2008, is the conversion of large educational groups into Corporations (S.A.). In fact, large educational groups that were active in HE have gone public on the stock exchange for the first time. Between 2008 and 2021 about 400 acquisitions of educational groups were made, ensuring a prominent place for education, always among the ten sectors with the highest number of acquisitions. This involves millions of student enrollments and the movement of tens of billions of dollars in these transactions, and confirms an unprecedented monopolization of a sector that, until a decade ago, was characterized by enormous fragmentation. It is possible to affirm, based on the research conducted, that the change in the form of capital ownership has altered these institutions profoundly, in four radical ways.

1. The group becomes part of a set of other businesses under total or partial control of the investment funds, while some subordinate companies maintain their own legal personality: if it has low returns, it can be easily discarded by the funds, putting the company under permanent threat of decapitalization if it does not achieve the goals.
2. The center of power in educational institutions is no longer the rectory and academic councils, or even former sponsors. It is now concentrated in the Board of Directors, a locus where the voices of the majority investors prevail, thus subordinating educational decisions to the imperatives of those who demand short- and medium-term returns (this is evident in the movement of disinvestments of funds, generally around five years).
3. Short-term profit comes from restructuring, such as the creation of basic cycles, bringing together courses that may or may not have similarities. This leads to the closing down of courses with low profitability, and the creation of courses based on market image, for example, Information Systems, Game Design, Systems Analysis, Biomedicine, or courses associated with the image of social and economic prestige such as Law and Medicine. This is based on aggressive marketing in the media. It also emphasizes the centralization of administrative sectors, and laying off personnel from the sector. What follows is the dismissal of teachers from unprofitable courses with the intensification of teaching work by increasing the number of students per class.
4. The development of a proper business ethos in the management of educational organizations, including in pedagogical coordination, means that the teacher is now conceived as a collaborator who is paid per activity. Teachers cannot be rigorous in the evaluation of students, in order not to displease these 'clients,' and they must conform to pedagogical conceptions congruent with the emptiest, business common sense. This is supported by the ideology of human capital and the pedagogy of competencies.

These, and other changes, reconfigure the educational enterprise in such a way that it is possible to affirm the restructuring of the very character and nature of the educational business, now under complete subordination to the imperatives of capital. Managers, teachers, administrative staff, and students are now part of a business whose center of decision-making power is no longer accessible to any of these segments.

Private Higher Education

Such structural change in educational organizations under the control of the funds, involves profound changes in State legislation, notably the following.

1. Institutionalizing the for-profit sector (until the late 1980s, private institutions were said to be non-profit): there are in Brazil 2153 private HEIs, corresponding to 87.6% of the HEIs, a large part of which is formed by smaller units, called faculties (77%). According to the last higher education[6] census, private HEIs hold 77.5% of undergraduate enrollments. In 2021, about 3.7 million students were enrolled in distance learning courses, 95% in private HEIs, confirming the advancement of the commercialization of education in the country and the shrinking of public enrollments. In fact, from 2010 to 2020, the private sector grew 90% and the public network only 10.7%.
2. Instituting commercial freedom between buyers and sellers of educational merchandise, abolishing any law for readjusting school fees.
3. Making State evaluation more flexible favors the for-profit sector.
4. Defining flexible curricular guidelines with less scientific complexity.
5. Deregulating labor relations.
6. Expanding the autonomy of non-university institutions (faculties) through so-called University Centers that, despite not complying with the constitutional requirement of indissociability among teaching, research, and extension, are granted autonomous prerogatives similar to those of public universities in the creation of courses and campuses, and so on.
7. Building a discourse that education is a public good that, in the name of democratization, can be offered by both the market and the State, thus justifying the transfer of public funds to private-mercantile organizations.
8. Granting large tax exemptions and transferring large sums of public funds to educational corporations.

Indeed, the exponential growth of for-profit institutions would not have been possible without the participation of public resources passed on by the State that, in this way, induced commodification. As Lenin (2008) argues, financial capital is inseparable from the State. Also in education, besides the creation of the aforementioned legal bases that leveraged the sector, the State economic induction justified in the name of the democratization of education leveraged the profits of the private-mercantile sector, shielded by the ideological cloak of the public good.

This process happened mainly through the combination of heavy tax exemptions (University for All Program—Law No. 11.096/2005) with direct transfers of huge sums of public money through the issuing of debt bonds by the State to economic groups in the scope of the Student Financing Fund/FIES (exacerbating fictitious capital). Besides leveraging the educational sector to further financial dominance, this policy has generalized the indebtedness of the families of students who borrow from FIES, through loans that, although largely subsidized, must be repaid by the borrowers. While corporations appropriated the funds, the student consumers, who received mostly very insufficient education, making it difficult to get jobs, were left with the debts (Leher, 2020). The bulk of FIES' resources were appropriated by organized groups like S.A., especially Kroton, Estácio, among others. After the crisis of the said Fund, in 2015, the educational institutions themselves carried out vertical integration of capital with credit institutions, and started lending money at interest to students for the payment of their tuition fees.

In the Brazilian case, it is possible, therefore, to speak of a strict commodification of education, initially in the HE sector and, more recently, also in basic education (Leher, 2022). The result of this *sui generis* process of commodification is a huge private-mercantile sector. It was in this last sector that the unequivocal leadership of the S.A.s was consolidated, which, although few in number, are responsible for more than a third of Brazilian enrollments. The five publicly traded corporations—Ânima Holding, Bahema Educação S. A., Cogna Educação S. A., Cruzeiro do Sul Educacional S. A., Ser Educacional S. A., and Yduqs Participações S. A.—have more than one third of the private enrollments. The monopolization of higher education is undeniable: in 2002, the 20 largest groups had 14% of the market; in 2015, the 12 largest groups reached 44% of the market.

As a consequence of the Bolsonaro government's anti-university measures, especially the deep budget cuts between 2019 and 2020, public universities reduced their enrollments by 6%. There was also a strong shrinkage of face-to-face enrollments: between 2010 and 2020, distance learning enrollments grew 234%, while face-to-face courses had a minimal expansion of 2.3%. Only between 2019 and 2020 did in-person enrollments fall, by 9.4%. In 2020, the number of students in the distance learning modality exceeded 3 million students (35.8% of enrollments). Most new students entering HE will attend a distance learning course, indicating that face-to-face courses will likely be restricted to the more affluent public, especially in Medicine. The case of distance education is emblematic:

> Teachers who worked in the distance education sector of Laureate (which at one point reached 300 thousand students with only 300 professors) taught classes for 20 to 40 thousand students per semester and, according to recent records, 50 thousand students per semester[7] and online classes with 300 students in environ-

ments similar to call centers; For this reason, it is not surprising that the aforementioned corporation used robots to correct the assignments of students who took distance learning courses through the digital platform (blackboard)[8] (obviously, it is impossible for one teacher to correct 60 thousand assignments per semester!). All this in a context of complete disrespect to the authorial creation of professors. Once prepared (scripted), the course is reproduced in the subsidiaries of the educational group without any recognition of intellectual property rights. (Leher, 2022, p. 94)

Capital as educator of the popular mass is a disastrous phenomenon for the working classes. Between 2015 and 2021, the number of undergraduate (teacher training) students taking precarious distance learning courses doubled, from 30% to 61% (one million in distance learning and 640,000 face-to-face). At the same time, as highlighted, the education systems hegemonized by the PCAH are emptying the cultural and scientific training of basic education and, through work platforms, instituting ferocious expropriation of the intellectual labor of teachers, exacerbating the real subordination of labor to capital.[9]

16.4 Basic Education

The Brazilian public education network comprises more than 43 million enrollments distributed among a little more than 158,000 schools, among them municipal, State, and federal. The continuous downward trend in enrollments in public basic education over the last decade is remarkable, as well as the falling number of existing schools. Enrollment swung from around 44 million in 2010 to 38 million in 2022. The number of schools totaled 158,000 in 2010, falling to 137,000 in 2022.

The reduction in the public sector is offset by private growth. In 2010, private enrollments did not reach 15%; in 2022, they reached 19% of the total, adding a little more than nine million enrollments. The number of schools rose from 18% to 23% of the total in the same period, making 41,000 schools (INEP, 2022). Although with a delay and in a smaller proportion in relation to HE, private growth in basic education is led by the mercantile sector. Commodification does not end with the acquisition of schools, but includes publishers, systems, and teaching platforms that are being widely used in both the private and public networks.

The growth in the commodification of basic education has to do with the business strategy of educational groups organized in the form of holding companies, and the emergence of the lucrative business sector of teaching systems and teaching and work platforms. As noted above, diversification was a response to the FIES crisis that drastically reduced the transfer of public funds to the private mercantile sector. Initially, corporations sought to respond to the crisis through associations between the largest educational groups. However, the groups already had such size in the market that the Administrative Council for Economic Defense (Cade), in 2017, denied the merger request between the two largest education groups in HE, KROTON, now the COGNA holding company, and Estácio, now YDUCS. As an alternative, the educational groups dramatically expanded the offer of distance education and opened new markets in basic education. Starting in 2017, a business boom occurred in the basic education segment. The COGNA holding company purchased the largest basic education group in the country, Somos Educação, taking over 44 educational establishments that at the time served around 37,000 students, and the three main publishing houses owned by that group: Ática, Scipione, and Saraiva (Costa, 2020). This was a very important step for the market. Other companies, also backed by investment funds, were formed, such as Bahema Educação S.A., focusing on schools with a constructivist pedagogy tradition, and Grupo Eleva, headed by one of the richest men in the country, Jorge Paulo Leman, whose focus is the acquisition of premium schools for the children of the ruling class. Eleva is the result of the merger of two Rio de Janeiro education networks in 2013, Elite Rede de Ensino and Pensi Colégio e Curso, now owned by Cogna. In a few years, the group already had 115 school brands and three of its own brands (Cariello, 2021) and, according to the group, it enrolled around 117,000 students. However, in 2022, there was a restructuring of the Eleva group and Vasta (Cogna's holding company). The latter acquired Eleva's education system, which, in turn, acquired 52 schools that belonged to the Cogna group (to which Vasta is linked) (Cardial, 2022), with a long-term agreement to feed Eleva's schools with the system that now belongs to Vasta.

The groups organized as corporations that operate in the basic education segment, Arco Educação S.A., Afya Participações S.A., Vasta Plataform Limited (part of the Cogna holding), trade their shares on NASDAQ. It is these groups that concentrate on education systems and platform services. Bahema Educação S.A., the newest among the groups, trades its shares on the Brazilian stock exchange. The current configuration of these companies involves a large portfolio of educational products. They comprise textbooks, alongside teaching platforms that assume that the teacher performs teaching tasks and is not the intellectual organizer of the teaching and learning processes. The platforms and teaching systems organize the classes that will be taught, the students' activities, the tests that will be applied, and their correction. These are always referenced in the operationalization of the Common National Curricular Base and the New High School, which evidences the close relationship of forces between educational corporations and the performance of the PCAH already mentioned. It is important to point out that the business plan of these corporations envisions a market that covers all basic education, beginning with early childhood education, through elementary school, and finally high school. This is a schooling that covers the ages of 4 to 17, according to the legislation that established the compulsory nature of basic education (Adrião et al., 2016).

The period of the pandemic accelerated the action of these corporations in basic education, not in the form of a replacement of face-to-face school in favor of virtual education, but in the re-signification of school as a place where children attend in person (a requirement of working families). As families need face-to-face teaching in basic education, educational corporations are investing in teaching systems and work platforms to be used in schools, aiming to expand the exploitation of work and make control over the content of classes more systemic, expropriating teachers' knowledge. As a result, corporations are developing subsidiary companies to occupy this promising market niche, in search of new frontiers for profits. In the Brazilian case, companies in the sector are trading their shares on the NASDAQ.

Another necessary point to highlight is the presence of these groups in the public sector. Since such schools are publicly administered, the conglomerates mainly raise funds through the National Book and Teaching Material Program—a program aimed at the evaluation and distribution of books and teaching materials in public networks. The Cogna holding alone owns three of the largest publishing companies that participate in the bidding for the program. For this holding company, National Textbook Plan considered 'the most representative business' in the educational material sector. The corporations are currently targeting the market opened through high school reform, offering digital courses for vocational training. These new expressions of the commodification of education were also identified by Jessop (2018).

Subordinated to the empire of capital, in a short period of time, not only private education systems, but especially public education systems, are increasingly under the direct control of capital. This is radically reconfiguring what is thought and taught in schools, reaching a significant part of the nearly 50 million Brazilian students.

16.5 Conclusion

In the Brazilian case, public education is a late social right, due to the particularity of dependent capitalism that engendered a process of revolution without revolution. It was during the period of rising struggles and strong organization from below, in the 1970s and 1980s, that the conditions were created for the Federal Constitution of 1988. This ensured, in a comprehensive and structural way, public and free education as a right for all, and a duty of the State. Changes in the pattern of capital accumulation and in the correlation of forces, however, hindered the realization of a real national system of public education. As a result, the public space has given way to private initiatives, as demonstrated in this study.

The analysis of the commodification of education outlined here, from the Marxist perspective, allows us to conclude that Brazil is in the world vanguard of the process of real subordination of the right to education by capital. This is not due to the invisible hand of the market. The State is not an externality to this process. On the contrary, it is an organic and inseparable part of commodification.

Commodification imposes a multifaceted discontinuity in relation to the guarantee of this social right demanded by the working classes. It is possible to postulate that capital advances over public education when PCAH introduces a pedagogical ethos congruent with capital, whose matrix for domination is the conversion of education into practices of human capital formation. In this case, this is for simple work in dependent capitalism. This is reinforced by the practices of austerity policies, such as performance management, the establishment of operational and socio-emotional skills descriptors, the introduction of *sui generis* forms of fierce meritocracy, the deepening of the expropriation of teachers' knowledge. Together, these practices establish a process of subordination of education to capitalist imperatives.

As opposed to countries that have succeeded in establishing national, public education systems, in the Brazilian case, a growing process of occupation of enrollments by the private-mercantile sector linked to financial organizations is underway, especially through educational groups converted into corporations. In HE, not only are the great majority of young people enrolled in these organizations, but they have also been led to massive, distance learning courses that do not guarantee a university education. This is a problem that is systemically aggravated by the fact that the great majority of future teachers in basic education will also be trained by these organizations. The research also makes it clear that the hegemony of capital in basic education has material strength, because here, too, the branches of educational holdings, some of them with shares in NASDAQ, are expanding into services of teaching systems and work platforms in public schools. This is either through pedagogical materials referenced in the questioned Curricular Bases defined by the PCAH; teaching systems that organize the space-time of schools; work platforms for teachers or through so-called professionalizing digital courses for young people under the terms of the high school reform.

The commodification of education by large financialized corporations is a harsh reality worldwide: the main publishing houses are under the control of economic groups; information and communication technologies are strongly concentrated in the big techs; scientific journals and large databases belong to a select group of large companies; and a new educational market, that of teaching systems and teaching work platforms, increasingly directs the investments of educational holdings. Such investments are driven especially through distance learning and digital education, the latter generally through associations with telephony corporations. The characteristics of commercialization, however, are not uniform around the world. The reality of each country has particularities.

Tragically, Brazil is in the global vanguard of these new forms of financialized commodification that have no parallel in history. As pointed out, the reality of each country can only be understood considering the state and its policies, which means that it depends on the correlation of forces between social classes. Without the huge transfers of public funds to corporations, the magnitude of commodification would not be the same, and in countries where the struggles for public education have a greater historical basis, the obstacles to commodification have been more effective. However, the commodification of education is a process of global capitalism in which corporations, big techs, investment funds from different countries, stock market trading (such as NASDAQ), and guidelines from international organizations make up a totality.

This is why the fight for the demercantilization of education is necessarily a cause that requires recovering the perspective of internationalist struggles. International networks and coalitions are crucial, such as *The Initiative for Democratic Education in the Americas* (IDEA) Network. IDEA 'is a flexible network that brings together organizations in the Americas that share a commitment to protecting and improving public education, seen as essential to democratic development and the protection of human rights.' But broader coalitions that can express the great struggles of the working classes, following the example of 'The First International' organized by Marx, can allow for more effective responses on a global scale.

Faced with such attacks by capital, certain tasks are required. It is crucial that education workers and students appropriate, through the experiences of struggles, the critique of the political economy of labor so that, in the reorganization movement, they can constitute a new starting point for struggles in defense of public education. Only with broad coalitions of education unions, social movements, student collectives and, indispensably, representations of other fractions of the working classes will it be possible to put unitary education back on the political agenda of the country. The struggle for demercantilization is, substantively, an anti-capitalist struggle. It means, objectively, to remove education from the sphere of capital and, therefore, only the reorganization of working class struggles will be able to prevent the advance of the educational apartheid that is underway.

Acknowledgments The chapter was translated from Portuguese to English by **Silvia Iacovacci**.

Disclosure Statement Neither of the co-authors has any financial interest or benefit that has arisen from the direct applications of this research.

Notes

1. Karl MARX: Inaugural Message of the International Workingmen's Association, 1864; Resolutions of the Geneva Congress, 1866; VARIOUS: Resolutions of the Brussels Congress, 1868; Karl MARX: Discourses On Education in Modern Society, 1869, all available from MUSTO (2014).
2. Dependent capitalism, as Florestan Fernandes characterizes 'the peripheral and dependent form of monopoly capitalism (which inexorably and inextricably associates the "national" and "foreign" forms of finance capital).' 'It materializes through over-expropriation and autocracy, characterizing what Florestan Fernandes calls savage capitalism. It combines dependent economic growth with despotic misery and exclusion, and the absence of rights outside the dominant social sectors' (Cardoso, 1995).
3. Commodification,n. Second edition, 1989; online version November 2010. http://www.oed.com/view/Entry/37198.

4. https://www.merriam-webster.com/dictionary/commodification.
5. In Brazil, private for-profit institutions came into existence after the regulation of the Law of Directives and Bases of National Education in 1996. Until then, all higher education institutions were philanthropic, confessional, or community-based. Thus, the commercialization of education was camouflaged by philanthropy.
6. BRAZIL. Anísio Teixeira Brazilian Institute of Educational Studies and Research (INEP). Census of Higher Education. Brasília, DF, 2022. Available at: https://download.inep.gov.br/educacao_superior/censo_superior/documentos/2021/apresentacao_censo_da_educacao_superior_2021.pdf. Access on: 1/12/ 2022.
7. Gabriel Teixeira. Anísio Teixeira Seminar, PPGE/ UFRJ, 6/1/22, Holding in the education sector. https://www.youtube.com/watch?v=aPNDFev%2D%2Dew.
8. Thiago Domenici. Laureate uses robots in place of teachers without students knowing. Agência Pública, 04/30/2020, available at: https://apublica.org/2020/04/laureate-usa-robos-no-lugar-de-professores-sem-que-alunos-saibam/.
9. Thiago Domenici. Laureate: o raio-x de uma fraude para reconhecer uma graduação no MEC. Agência Pública, 13/11/2020. https://apublica.org/2020/11/laureate-o-raio-x-de-uma-fraude-para-reconhecer-uma-graduacao-no-mec/.

References

Adrião, T., et al. (2016). Grupos empresariais na educação básica pública brasileira: limites à efetivação do direito à educação. *Education and Society, 37*(134). https://doi.org/10.1590/ES0101-73302016157605

Cardial, E. (2022). Educação Básica em Alta nas fusões e aquisições. *Revista Educação*. Retrieved April 21, 2022, from https://revistaeducacao.com.br/2022/04/21/educacao-basica-fusoes/

Cardoso, M. L. (1995). Capitalismo Dependente, Autocracia Burguesa e Revolução Social em Florestan Fernandes. *Instituto de Estudos Avançados da Universidade de São Paulo*. Retrieved April 18, 2023, from http://www.iea.usp.br/publicacoes/textos/limoeirocardosoflorestan1.pdf/at_download/file

Cariello, L. N. (2021). Construindo Redes de Intelectuais Orgânicos: o programa de bolsas de estudo Lemann fellowship da Fundação Lemann (2007–2018). *Dissertação – PPGE História Social, Universidade Federal Fluminense*, Niterói.

Costa, H. B. (2020). Financeirização da educação básica: tendências 2010–2019. *Dissertação (Mestrado) – Programa de Pós-Graduação em Educação, Universidade Federal do Rio de Janeiro*, Rio de Janeiro.

Fernandes, F. (1981). *Sociedade de classes e subdesenvolvimento* (4th ed.). Zahar.

Fernandes, F. (2008). *A revolução burguesa no Brasil. Um ensaio de interpretação sociológica*. (5 a ed.)., 2 a reimpressão São Paulo: Globo.

Fontes, V. M. (2021). Pedagogia do Capital. In Dias, A. P., et al. (Orgs.) (Ed.), *Dicionário de Agroecologia e Educação* (p. 537). RJ e SP: EPSJV-Fiocruz e Expressão Popular.

Freire, P. (1967). *A educação como prática da liberdade*. Paz e Terra.

Gramsci, A. (2015). *Cadernos dos Cárcere*, V.1. Introdução ao estudo da filosofia. A filosofia de Benedetto Croce. 8 a edição. Trad. Carlos Nelson Coutinho. RJ: Civilização Brasileira.

Gramsci, A. (2016). *Cadernos dos Cárcere*, V.2. Os intelectuais. O princípio educativo. Jornalismo. 8 a ed. Trad. Carlos Nelson Coutinho. RJ: Civilização Brasileira.

Hilferding, R. (1985). *O capital financeiro*. Nova Cultural.

INEP. (2022). *Sinopse Estatística da Educação Básica*. Inep. Disponível em. Retrieved April 18, 2023, from http://portal.inep.gov.br/sinopses-estatisticas-da-educacao-basica

Jessop, B. (2018). On Academic Capitalism. *Critical Policy Studies, 12*(1), 104–109. https://www.tandfonline.com/doi/full/10.1080/19460171.2017.1403342

Leher, R. (2018). *Universidade e heteronomia cultural no capitalismo dependente: um estudo a partir de Florestan Fernandes*. Consequência.

Leher, R. (2020). Ler a crise, ler a mercantilização da educação. In Santos, M. R. S. et al. (Orgs.) (Ed.), *Políticas, gestão e direito à educação superior : novos modos de regulação e tendências em construção* (1st ed.). Fino Traço.

Leher, R. (2022). Mercantilização da educação, precarização do trabalho docente e o sentido histórico da pandemia Covid 19. *Revista de Políticas Públicas, 26*(Especial), 78–102. https://doi.org/10.18764/2178-2865.v26nEp78-102

Lenin, V. (2008). *O imperialismo* (4th ed.). Centauro.

Marx, K. (1864). *Inaugural Address and Provisional Rules of the International Working Men's Association, along with the "General Rules"*. Marxists.org. Retrieved April 18, 2023, from https://www.marxists.org/archive/marx/works/1864/10/27.htm

Marx, K. (1867). *Capital, Volume 1*. Chapter Fifteen: Machinery and Modern Industry. SECTION 9. The Factory Acts. Sanitary and Educational Clauses of the Same. Their General Extension in England. Marxists.org. Retrieved April 18, 2023, from https://www.marxists.org/archive/marx/works/1867-c1/ch15.htm#a218

Marx, K. (1885). *Capital, Volume II*. Marxists.org. Retrieved April 18, 2023, from https://www.marxists.org/archive/marx/works/1885-c2/index.htm

Marx, K. (2017). *Capital, Livro III* (2nd ed.). São Paulo.

Mattei, C. E. (2022). *The Capital Order How Economists Invented Austerity and Paved the Way to Fascism*. University of Chicago Press.

Musto, M. (Org.). (2014). *Trabalhadores, uni-vos!* Antologia política da I Internacional. Boitempo.

CHAPTER 17

Critical Environmental Education, Marxism and Environmental Conflicts: Some Contributions in the Light of Latin America

César Augusto Costa and Carlos Frederico Loureiro

17.1 Education, Human Formation and the Environmental Question in Capitalism

This chapter discusses the relationship between environmental education, from a critical theoretical perspective, and the environmental conflicts in Latin America, bringing theoretical contributions to the emancipatory and anti-systemic educational practice to those impacted by the intensification of capital. The theoretical-political bases that support our text are linked to the critical Marxist tradition in dialogue with Latin American thinkers, such as Maristela Svampa, Enrique Dussel, Carlos Frederico Loureiro, Virgínia Fontes, Carlos Walter Porto-Gonçalves, Roberto Leher, Michel Lowy, Henri Acselrad among others, who collate the environmental debate in Latin America in its social, political, historical, economic and cultural tensions against the logic of peripheral and dependent capitalism.

Having said this, it is convenient to enter in the conceptual discussion about education, as ontological process of formation of human beings that dialectically determines the way we create and satisfy needs, and establish the society-nature metabolism. Such factors indicate that for human beings to exist, they need to continuously produce their means of life. This imposes as a requirement for human existence the transformation of nature to the satisfaction of

C. A. Costa (✉) • C. F. Loureiro
Universidade Católica de Pelotas, Pelotas, Brazil
e-mail: fredericoloureiro89@gmail.com

© The Editor(s) (if applicable) and The Author(s), under exclusive license to Springer Nature Switzerland AG 2023
R. Hall et al. (eds.), *The Palgrave International Handbook of Marxism and Education*, Marxism and Education,
https://doi.org/10.1007/978-3-031-37252-0_17

material and symbolic needs. This process of transformation of nature and material production, called labor in Marx (2013), dialectically determines how we create and meet needs, establish the society-nature metabolism, produce culture, give meaning to life and our own way of being as individuals in society.

This ontological conception of human being implies affirming that the materiality of social processes cannot be seen in a mechanical way, because in the causal relations themselves the actions of social agents are inserted. Material determination should be understood as objective and objectified (historically produced) moments and conditions from which we start in our movement of transformation and constitution of people and of reality itself (Chasin, 2009). The social totality, in this line of reasoning, is a structured and historically determined complex, or rather, a complex of complexes whose specific parts (partial totalities) are related to each other, in a series of interrelationships and reciprocal determinations that constantly vary and modify themselves (Bottomore, 2001).

All work is social, thus, what is produced, learned and known needs to be transmitted and constantly recreated in the objectification-subjectivation[1] movement demands that each one of us performs. Being a being that becomes specific by its creative and intentional activity (praxis) in the world and in the relationship with the other, education becomes a requirement of human becoming. There is no society without education, in the sense that there is no social life without what humanity has produced (instruments, technology, science, art, behavior, customs, values, various knowledge, that is, culture) being transmitted, reproduced, expanded, socialized and transformed. In this way, "all society lives because each generation takes care of the formation of the next generation and transmits to it something of its experience, educates it. There is no society without work and without education" (Konder, 2000, p. 112).

Education, in this perspective, is the very movement of human formation, as human becoming, becoming human, under concrete relations and objective conditions (Freire, 2019). Put in these terms, education, which has in schooling its main form of producing sociability and cultures and transmitting knowledge and techniques in modern societies, is a social practice. As such, understanding the world, being aware of it, interpreting it, "being world", making value judgments and establishing linguistic codes are events that take place only in society. Thus, we can say that education is a social phenomenon that is inherent to the human condition and crosses all humanity in any historical time, but it is only formed in the materiality of historically determined societies, acquiring different configurations and social meanings.

We live, especially in the last two centuries, in a society that was constituted by the exploitation of labor and negation of the other in a movement of objectification of life (Lukács, 2013). Therefore, if our intention is to overcome this alienated social form, the educational action must be intentional and directed to a practice of freedom, which seeks the reflective knowledge and the experience of relationships without oppression, discrimination and mechanisms of expropriation inherent in the capitalist mode of production. This is not to be confused with manipulation of the educational act or with the search for an idealized human being. The negation of capitalist social relations is the affirmation of the human and historical possibility of transformation, of overcoming objectively destructive relations that have become universalized.

Social relations in capitalism are essentially mediated by alienated labor, which is realized as end and means, making them impersonal. Before, individuals depended on each other and produced in order to meet needs established by them in open relations. Now, individuals are faced with structures that objectify and the production of more value becomes an end in itself, making work a self-mediation (Postone, 2014).

Labor power is transformed into commodity and the purpose of social production becomes surplus value, that is, the material wealth obtained by the exploitation of the surplus labor in relations of worker expropriation. This not only inverts the meaning of the creation of the means of life and subordinates the material production of existence to the production of surplus value, but also demands: the social and technical division of labor; the ideological affirmation of the supremacy of instrumental rationality' the precarization of labor relations' and the hyper-specialization of knowledge and its fragmentation for purposes of effectiveness in the productive process of creating commodity. Thus, the private appropriation of the means of production, the dissociation between producer and product of labor, the need to expand the surplus of working time for the generation of surplus value and to promote scientific and technological development to ensure capitalist economic efficiency, establish an alienated totality.

Wealth, transformed into capital, has enabled a unique phenomenon. Poverty in the face of a monumental generation of economic, cultural and cognitive assets. The concentration of these assets has increased in the last century, with short intervals of modest decreases in inequality rates. This has condemned the majority of the population to deplorable living standards, especially when we consider that there is installed capacity to solve hunger, illiteracy, unhealthy conditions, some epidemic diseases and homelessness. If before scarcity was due to low productive capacity and technological and scientific development, now we have abundance bringing poverty as the reverse side of the same coin. The more society reveals its capacity to produce wealth, the more the contingent of those who are dispossessed of the material conditions of life increases.

The promises of happiness and satisfaction through the insatiable consumption of commodities, fostered by ideologies disseminated through education and communication to give an outlet to the gigantic production of goods—many absolutely superfluous. This generates a growing cycle between consuming, discarding, buying to satiate desires that only exist as we work harder to consume more. It is a society that transforms even leisure into merchandise, creating a spiral of frustration. With this, capitalism bases its acceptance on the promise of a comfort that is not universalized, of a meritocratic success that sharpens competitiveness and selfishness, and on the idea that economic growth is the only alternative for generating well-being and prosperity, even if this means sacrificing life—whether human or not.

Contemporary society has another unique feature: it is global. The capitalist mode of production became in the twentieth century the dominant and overwhelmingly expansive form of sociability and organization of the state and economy. Consumer goods, the organization of cities, technologies and habits are standardized according to Eurocentric parameters. With this, effects that were once localized become universalized and with unpredictable consequences. The mercantile exchange, the universal saleability of goods become the purpose and the meaning to which creative energies are directed. This alienated work establishes the metabolic failure in the society-nature relationship, the disrespect to natural cycles and reaches the carrying capacity of ecosystems in the interaction with the different sociabilities (Foster, 2005).

These forms of metabolic interaction with nature, established in the process of social work, lead to alienation, to estrangement in the relationship with the other. The alienated relationship imposes on the cognitive level what may be called a mechanism of dissociation: the loss of understanding of the social totality. The fragmentation propitiated by instrumental rationality and the social division of labor facilitates the mental separation of environmental impacts from their causes. Thus, the established norm and the way it is produced become legitimate or unproblematized, and criticism, a misplaced questioning.

What we are affirming with the exposition made so far is that the problems and questions posed in contemporaneity are configured in certain ways in capitalism that are not equivalent to what was socially established in any other society and that such forms need to be faced concretely by education. More than that, we are saying that the current environmental crisis is the expression of a deep societal crisis, historically determined, with magnitude and universality never seen before, exactly because it is intrinsic to the expansion movement of the capitalist mode of production of reducing life to the status of merchandise.

In view of the conceptual aspects above, the chapter goes on to discuss the relationship between environmental education from a critical perspective, and the existing environmental conflicts in Latin America, bringing theoretical contributions to emancipatory educational practice in this context in three major moments. In the first, we discuss the category of environmental conflicts, as a requirement of the capitalist mode of production, whose element is determinant in the process of destruction of nature. In this, the sociometabolism of capital reinforces social inequalities and reduces the possibility of survival of social groups that live in different ways, that are non-restricted, with nature. In the second moment, we reinforce that such conceptual aspects of environmental conflicts are reflected in the horizon of dependent capitalism and the process of coloniality of knowledge and power in Latin America. Finally, we explain how the social struggles of workers, native peoples and traditional peoples are constituted and waged with a view to the liberation of peoples, a final synthesis is made, explaining the intentionalities of environmental education in these Latin American emancipatory struggles.

17.2 The Pedagogy of Environmental Conflict

An environmental conflict is configured when two or more social agents have divergent needs and interests, characterized in the processes of use and appropriation of nature, and put unequally in society (Aceslrad, 2004). Thus, not all forms of material and symbolic use of nature generate conflict, since there are cultural and economic practices that do not directly threaten the dominant normativity and the expansion of commodified economic relations. Here there are risks and damages whose forms of confrontation can be consensual. With this, we can say that, in theory, not every human creative act in the reproduction of their ways of life, under the dominance of capitalist sociability, generates conflict. However, every objectified conflict is associated with territorial changes that make it impossible or difficult to maintain ways of life made marginal in an unequal and hierarchical social structure.

There are environmental conflicts, in short, because certain ways of life are impeded in their right to exist to the detriment of other ways that are affirmed as valid for all people by force of the unequal power of those who live this way, that is, in function of the place of domination that they possess and exercise over others. There are environmental conflicts because, strictly speaking, the process of destruction of nature reinforces social inequalities and reduces the possibility of survival of social groups that live in differentiated, more territorialized ways with nature.

Environmental conflict, thought in these structural terms, is not a disrespectful dispute between people, a lack of communication and tolerance, although these are phenomenal aspects that are consolidated in the social process. It is not caused by a matter of misunderstanding or ill will of one person towards another. Environmental conflicts, which have, therefore, in the appropriation and use of nature as their object of dispute, are a structural condition of an unequal society. Without confronting them, there is no democracy and no possibility of overcoming the alienated social relations that constitute us.

In this way, dealing with conflict pedagogically is related to the recognition that solidarity, equality, tolerance and dialogue can only be promoted by confronting and overcoming social relations that promote domination and exploitation. One cannot be in solidarity just because one wishes to be or speaks in that direction. Being in solidarity is not a matter of discourse. Solidarity and the just treatment of the other pass through creating just relations—and this cannot happen ignoring the conflictive basis of a class society. Therefore, conflict, being part of the structure of society, is pedagogically indispensable because it brings the content to the concrete and to everyday life. In other words, it is a dimension of social life that needs to be recognized in order to be addressed.

When the conflictive dimension is addressed, it becomes possible to understand that environmental problems and issues are not neutral or possible to be solved only by technical intervention or by "ecologically correct" personal behavior. The historicity becomes constitutive of the pedagogical activity, and it is no longer enough to see the problem or the voluntarism to solve it, being vital the problematization that leads to the knowledge of its causal dynamics and the social agents involved.

This politicizes education and requires its subjects to position themselves in relation to projects for society and sustainability. The need to position oneself leads to a reflective practice of reality, to a complex understanding of the responsibilities and rights of individuals, groups, and classes, and to a practice that acts both in daily life and in the political organization for social struggles. Following the path of our argumentation, we analyze the context of the logic of extractivism in the face of environmental conflicts in the Latin American context.

17.3 Situating the Logic of Extractivism: Between Environmental Struggles and Conflicts in Latin America

In Brazil, the environment as a "common good" is a constitutional condition, in which nature can only be appropriated for purposes of fulfillment for the collectivity, as explained in Article 225 of the Brazilian Federal Constitution of 1988:

> Everyone has the right to an ecologically balanced environment, an asset for common use by the people and essential to a healthy quality of life, imposing on the public authorities and the collectivity the duty to defend and preserve it for present and future generations.

For our text, this concept is of interest when we refer to the State's obligation to ensure the "common" character of the environment in a class society (Loureiro, 2012).

Therefore, we know that the legal-state instruments should meet the needs of all, but they are far from being something only established by law. Thus, according to Loureiro: "Their objectifications depend directly on the public-private tensions in the Brazilian state and the guarantee of communal appropriations of nature, partially ensured in legislation" (2012, p. 43). Thus, the environment as a political category does not remain immune to discussion, even for its universalistic sense (what unites us around the planet). That is, in the face of democratic premises, the universalistic sense of what is public does not mean treating everyone in an abstract way, since it would represent in practice the legal-institutional dimension of a State that reduces social inequalities to the sphere of private life. On the other hand, it demands that individual and political freedoms are established through the materialization of dignified conditions (freedom-need), treating the different needs and capacities equally. Without delay, we reiterate that:

a public space, and the environment as a common good, become universally effective when the criticism and organized dissent of the working classes and the expropriated (including traditional populations and communities) can be installed as equals in the demand for rights, in the definition of the institutions that govern social coexistence and the norms that shape the uses and appropriations of nature. Thus, there is only public space to the extent that the socially unequal find themselves as autonomous subjects and political protagonists and there is only environment as a common good to the extent that access to the wealth produced and to nature is fair, and the various ways of organizing based on sustainable economic and cultural processes are respected. (Loureiro, 2012, p. 46)

In historical terms, the debate about the "common good" is fundamental, given that after five centuries of the configuration of a dependent capitalism, Latin America continues to serve the hegemonic interests of industrialized capitalist countries through the supply of raw materials (Gonçalves, 2016). According to Galeano (2013, p. 5): "we continue to applaud the kidnapping of natural goods with which God, or the Devil, has distinguished us, and thus we work for our doom and contribute to the extermination of what little nature we have left".

Regarding the colonial exploitation process for the process of environmental conflicts and its relationship in dependent capitalism, it had its consequences (Costa & Loureiro, 2018). In addition to the extermination and slavery of native and black populations, expropriated in their knowledge and territories, centuries of exploitation of nature and its "gifts" extracted from the soil and subsoil ensured the primitive accumulation of capital in Europe (Marx, 2013). For Dussel (2001, pp. 372–373):

The mining wealth (silver and gold) was simply owned by the colonists, had to pay a tribute to the crown, and passed on to Europe where it was poured into the brand new world market (the first truly world market, and whose first "currency" was the silver extracted by the Indians of Mexico or Peru, or the African slaves, later, in Minas Gerais in Brazil). When the mercantilism of metals and tropical products is transformed into industrial capitalism (around 1750), the World-System at its "center" will begin the accumulation of value added in Europe itself, and will restructure the colonial contract, under English hegemony with the beginning of an unequal exchange with textile production. Around 1870, the accumulation of wealth and technology allowed the expansion of Imperialism, installing territorial railroads and sailing the oceans with coal-fired steamships. Large areas (Argentina, Canada, Australia, etc.) will be incorporated by the gigantic extraction of agricultural and mining production. The "periphery" will always remain in an asymmetrical position.

According to Dussel (1984), Latin America received the impact of the conquest not only at the political level of domination, economic of exploitation, ideological, but also technical. These factors inaugurate a long history of dependency, as a region dominated by a capitalist world market which is the fruit of Latin American labor from 1492 to the present. Thus, the model of export extractivism that has expanded, based on large enterprises, strengthens strategies of territorial control and accumulation by dispossession (Harvey, 2003).

One of the consequences of the current extractivist inflection has been the explosion of environmental conflicts, visible in the dynamization of ancestral struggles for land, in the hands of indigenous and peasant social movements, as well as in the emergence of new forms of mobilization and citizen participation focused on the defense of natural assets. Thus, the process of environmentalization of social struggles in Latin America (Acselrad, 2010) includes a vast and heterogeneous group of collectives and modalities of resistance to the brutality of the forms of expropriation determined by the socio-metabolism of capital, which are being configured as a broader network of organizations, in which eco-territorial movements are not the only protagonists. From our perspective, what is new is the articulation between different actors (social, indigenous, peasant, and socioenvironmental movements, nongovernmental organizations, environmentalists, intellectuals, and cultural collectives), which has translated into a dialogue of knowledge and disciplines, characterized both by the elaboration of knowledge that is independent of dominant discourses and by the valuing of local knowledge, much of which has indigenous and peasant roots (Svampa, 2012).

Harvey (2003) points out that the accumulation of capital has two elements. The surplus value generated by the subordination of use value to exchange value, in relations of expropriation founded on private ownership of the means ensuring economic production (knowledge, technology, natural resources, etc.). Thus, accumulation is an economic process, which has as a determining aspect a transaction between the capitalist and the salaried worker and the current forms of precariousness of labor relations (pejotization, uberization, outsourcing, etc.). The other point refers to the relations between capitalism and non-capitalist modes of production, which are beginning to emerge on the international scene. In terms of the processes of environmental and territorial expropriation, what does this indicate? Harvey (2003, p. 121) understands that:

> A closer examination of Marx's description of primitive accumulation reveals a wide range of processes. There is the commodification and privatization of land and the violent expulsion of peasant populations; the conversion of various forms of property rights (common, collective, state, etc.) into exclusive private property rights; the suppression of peasants' rights to common [shared] lands; the conversion of property rights into exclusive private property rights.) into exclusive private property rights; the suppression of peasant rights to common [shared] lands; the commodification of labor power and the suppression of alternative (indigenous) forms of production and consumption; colonial, neo-colonial, and imperial processes of appropriation of assets (including natural resources); the monetization of exchange and taxation, particularly of land; the slave trade; and usury, national debt, and ultimately the credit system as radical means of primitive accumulation.

In this way, the state, with its monopoly of violence and its definitions of legality, plays a central role in these social processes, establishing intertwined territorial capitalist logics of power, even if they do not necessarily converge. Thus:

> All the characteristics of primitive accumulation that Marx mentions remain strongly present in the historical geography of capitalism to this day. The expulsion of peasant populations and the formation of a landless proletariat has accelerated in countries like Mexico and India in the last three decades; many resources once shared, like water, have been privatized (often at the insistence of the World Bank) and inserted into the capitalist logic of accumulation; alternative forms (indigenous and even, in the case of the United States, home-made goods) of production and consumption have been suppressed. Nationalized industries have been privatized. Agribusiness has replaced family farming. And slavery has not disappeared (particularly in the sex trade). (Harvey, 2003, p. 121)

According to Harvey (2003), capitalism internalizes predatory practices making possible the accumulation by spoliation in various ways, because there is a determinant *modus operandi*, whose centrality lies in the expanded reproduction of capital. Therefore, the mixture of coercion and consent in the scope of these activities bargained in and by the State vary, making the hegemony of capital constructed through financial mechanisms the royal road of capitalist development. "The umbilical cord that links accumulation by spoliation and expanded reproduction is what finance capital and credit institutions give it, as always with the support of the powers of the state" (Harvey, 2003, p. 214).

We remember that the constitutive crises of capitalism do not indicate its "fragility" or automatically lead to its overcoming, which depends on social engagement in the struggles against this form of sociability (Fontes & Miranda, 2014) that impacts the peoples, especially in Latin America. Thus, we can point out that for Dussel (1984, p. 97):

> In effect, Anglo-Saxon neocolonialism is based, in reality, on exports of products manufactured by the industrial revolution and on imports of raw materials or matter for its highly developed technological work. The use value of both exchanges-material subtract of exchange value- has a poietic-productive meaning: it is a matter of matter of labor or products of labor. In unequal exchange consists practical injustice or exploitation; in poietic inequality lies the real possibility of such domination. The technological instance is thus discovered at the heart of political and economic, and equally ideological, domination.

Thus, the expropriations are not only reproduced, but also amplified, because the urbanized populations have long been faced with the violence of expropriation characteristic of capitalist expansion, now under new specificities. Here, we highlight the withdrawal of rights linked to the exercise of labor, henceforth exercised even without contracts. This also includes the flattening of conquered social rights, flexibilization of labor laws, and continuous reduction of the rights to health and education, each of which are privatized and converted into a way to valorize value (Fontes & Miranda, 2014).

Looking at the processes of expropriation/concentration, one of the most harmful is the current expropriation of almost all of humanity of elements that have always been part of the repertoire of socio-metabolic exchanges, those that occur between societies and nature, as well as the expropriation of fundamental aspects of biological life itself. We point to the dissemination of transgenic seeds, capable of colonizing native seeds without knowing what effects such transgenic foods may have on humans and other living beings (rice, corn, wheat and soybeans) in different quadrants of the planet. For Fontes and Miranda (2014, p. 310):

> All the elements of this scenario express the international logic marked by the unequal and combined expansion of capitalism. This inequality deepens in the socio-environmental terrain, as the dominant classes of industrialized countries simultaneously seek to extort their workers internally (through the production of high value-added commodities) and seize sources of raw materials in other countries, whose production processes generate greater socio-environmental impact. The scale of international inequality seems to deepen as even the bourgeoisies of late industrialized countries embrace large-scale *commodity* production, exacerbating social, economic and environmental injustice and inequality.

Thus, socio-environmental damage has a greater impact on the Southern hemisphere due to the economic relations configured in the globalization of capitalism. In Dussel's (1984) view, international capitalism is now experiencing a crisis, perhaps the deepest in its history. We must be aware of how this crisis is faced and what it represents at the level of science and technology. However, what we see is that in these cases the question of technology is faced with concrete problems that are not human, which could be summarized in relation to the question of the exhaustion of renewable resources in a perspective of continuous growth. The ecological preservation threatened by capitalist development itself (Dussel, 1984). Therefore, we can point out that:

> The requirements of new technology in the process of internationalization of production and in the productive processes required by world capitalist accumulation, and its close connection to the demands of global control. In this case, technology is a necessary mediation within the capitalist system directly linked to greater profitability. (Dussel, 1984, p. 231)

We will finish our reflection by indicating the contributions of critical environmental education in Latin America to the dynamics of environmental conflicts.

17.4 Final Considerations: For a Critical Environmental Education in Facing Environmental Conflicts in Latin America

From the foregoing, what contributions could critical environmental education bring to the Latin American environmental debate? From a critical perspective, Environmental Education (EE) contributes to the understanding of reality, which encompasses the "representation of the thing" (appearance/phenomenon) and the "thing itself" (essence/concept), and to the transformation of society and education in the process of human formation (Mészáros, 2005). Thus, critical EE articulates the conception of education as a process of omnilateral human formation with the following preconceptions: a conception of environment based on social, historical and political development; and, the environment understood as concrete thought, as "synthesis of multiple determinations" (Loureiro et al., 2009). For Loureiro et al. (2009, p. 89):

> In this conception of education, the approach to programmatic content or knowledge to be built requires us to consider, as an important pedagogical resource, the reality experienced by educators and students in their places of study, living and working, highlighting the cultural diversity and social exclusion that characterize society. This pedagogy is based on the understanding that the social relations of domination and capitalist exploitation are internalized, as the dominant ideology that informs a reading / stance on everyday life, and are materialized in social and environmental problems.

Contextualizing historically the environmental discussion in Latin America, we take into account that the Latin American continent still sees itself as European-Latin, hiding and silencing social groups that were far from Latinity, except for suffering the imperial developments that so markedly characterize the Eurocentric tradition (Porto-Gonçalves, 2009). Thus, it is an opposition to what the original peoples of Abya Yala[2] (known as Latin America) want to affirm by adopting a name by which they seek to reappropriate the territory that was undermined to them, in a not definitive way. Thus, the expression still leaves out Afro-descendants. This implies considering that:

> It will not be invisibilizing this tension that we will be able to overcome the contradictions that inhabit us as an in-body-created history for 500 years. The experience currently underway in Bolivia and Ecuador, countries where the indigenous protagonism is indisputable, shows that it is possible, with interculturality, to overcome the limitations of American cultural studies and its multiculturalism, and postmodernism, which keeps each monkey in its own branch and gives rise to harmful essentialist fundamentalisms. After all, it is possible to overcome xenophobia of racist inspiration from other epistemic and political projects, and this implies accepting that the liberal tradition with its individualist principle has colour and place of origin: Europe. In short, this tradition is provincial and, like all bad provincialism, thinks that its world is The World. And the worst

provincialism is that which, holding power, tries to present itself as universal, forgetting the pluriversality of the world. (Porto-Gonçalves, 2009, pp. 27–28)

We note that the concept of progress for the environmental debate is a concept identified with the ideals of a Eurocentered bourgeoisie, which sought to affirm the superiority of its societal project in the face of an "old and archaic" mode of organization that needed to be overcome for the consolidation of the market and private property. This civilizational project was affirmed based on European illustrated science as the only truth and rationally superior, capable of instituting the negation of other knowledge linked to traditional and communal forms of property (Loureiro, 2012, 2019).

In recent years, the struggles of social movements in Latin America and the Caribbean have stood out for confronting and exposing the disparities in productive processes with agribusiness, the cellulose industry, mining, extensive livestock farming, and the privatization of water. Certainly, it materialized the environmental debate and brought it to the political field and to the economic world as had never been seen before. For Mészáros (2002), the valorization of capital makes social violence inseparable from environmental violence. That is, objective conditions propitiated that the "environmental" was incorporated into social struggles as relevant elements for the understanding of environmental conflicts, since the dispute for natural goods and their control in use is inherent to capitalist private property (Loureiro, 2012).

Here, it is interesting to note that political ecology certainly has many contributions to this discussion, since its differential is not in the acceptance of nature as a condition for production, but in the way in which it is qualified. For this critical reference, one cannot speak of the existence of populations without considering an established territoriality. That is, before one thinks of the economic activity of a group and its social viability. Factors that need to be seen and contextualized in which ecosystem and limits, and in which territory, since this concept refers to the idea of *nature + culture* (Porto-Gonçalves, 2009). Loureiro (2012, p. 30) exemplifies that:

> The extractivist rubber tappers can only be understood through the work they perform in a specific type of forest, in a direct relationship with a species that conditions not only the economy generated, but the very culture and organization of this group. Mode of production and way of life define themselves dialectically, therefore. It is not without reason that the so-called traditional communities and populations and other groups whose ways of life are clearly defined by their relationship with nature and oppose worldviews that commodify life and the society-nature dichotomy (quilombolas, small farmers, extractivists, river dwellers, caiçaras, etc.) have become a strong object of study and subjects of environmentalist political practice.

We must consider what is emerging specifically in Latin American countries, where such ecological concerns do not have a conformist tone in the context of dependent capitalism (Fernandes, 1975). Among peasants and indigenous communities, we have observed relevant mobilizations in defense of environmental issues, all the more necessary because it is to the periphery of capitalism that the most violent and destructive forms of production of nature are exported, with impacts on the health of these populations.

We understand that the movement of capital demands the transformation of all natural common goods into merchandise, which leads to the destruction of nature. In this way, oil zones in Latin America, abandoned by multinationals after years of exploitation, poisoned and looted, leaving a trail of destruction as well as disease among the inhabitants.

According to Lowy (2014, p. 62), "it is therefore perfectly understandable that the populations that live in more direct contact with the environment are the first victims of this ecocide, and try to oppose, sometimes successfully, the destructive expansion of capital." This is a position defended by Porto-Gonçalves (2009), who points out that the struggle for territory takes on a central character, from a theoretical-political perspective, to the extent that the subjective, cultural dimension is allied to the material dimension—water, biodiversity, land. Territory is thus *nature + culture*, since the struggle for territory becomes explicit in its epistemic and political implications in the face of the new frontiers of expansion of capitalism (Porto-Gonçalves, 2009).

Neoliberal globalization is inscribed as part of the social struggles. In fact, it denies to a large extent part of the demands posed by different social movements and their struggles. Thus, globalization and its entire process of transformations that has been going on since the 1970s seems to gain more evident form when seen in the light of the social conflicts that have triggered in subsequent decades (Porto-Gonçalves, 2015). Watching the process of neoliberal globalization in this bias is relevant to understand the complex and contradictory historical process in which it establishes the environmental challenge, seeking alternative ways out of it. For Porto-Gonçalves (2015, p. 20):

> In these last 30–40 years of neoliberal globalization we have been facing a devastation of the planet without precedent in all of human history, a period in which, paradoxically, there has been more talk about nature and in which the environmental challenge itself has been posed as such. Hence it is fundamental that we understand the nature of the globalization process and how this process does or does not imply the globalization of nature.

We see, therefore, that the process of globalization brings in itself the globalization of the exploitation of nature with profits and waste distributed unevenly. Also that allied to it, globalization is at the same time the domination of nature and the domination of some men over other men, of European culture over other cultures and peoples, and of men over women (Porto-Gonçalves, 2015). Historically, there is no shortage of arguments that this domination occurred for natural reasons, to the extent that certain races would be inferior. "European modernity invented coloniality and raciality (the basis of slavery) and, thus, this triad—modernity-coloniality-raciality—continues crossing, until today, the social and power practices" (Porto-Gonçalves, 2015, p. 25). From reflecting on the insurgent character to the logic of Latin American capitalism, we point out that:

> The anti-systemic social movements, critical of neodevelopmentalism, have forged self-organized educational experiences, such as rural education, agroecology and the Florestan Fernandes National School (MST), in quilombola communities, extractive reserves and the peripheries, in cultural initiatives such as hiphop, funk, etc. The indigenous peoples (AbyaYala) of Latin America have been spreading another civilizing horizon, expressed in the Good Life, radically critical of neodevelopment and green capitalism. Internationalist initiatives like CLOC-Via Campesina forge other economic and social horizons that reject expropriation and exploitation, as well as the coloniality of knowledge. In the struggles against the commodification of nature and all spheres of life, another hegemony is being forged [...]. If the struggle for food sovereignty requires confronting agribusiness and historical-critical and libertarian education requires combating the commodification of education, also the dignity of workers in factories, supermarkets, telemarketing centers, requires the denial of their conditions of disposable factors of production, a process that objectifies the work and, consequently, women and men. (Leher, 2013, p. 229)

Starting from the theoretical-political reflection aligned in Dussel and the debate made, we place ourselves in favor of a "Politics of Liberation", which is distinct from a "Politics of domination" (Dussel, 2007). We understand that as the people (the totality of the population as a whole, workers, poor, blacks, women, native and traditional peoples, vulnerable, marginalized social groups) hold an "ethical-political meaning", since they present themselves as sociopolitical subjects of liberation, mostly denied by the dominators (Dussel, 1982).

For all the above reasons and based on the Marxist method of understanding and intervention in reality, the objectives of critical EE consist in referencing that, in the field of social and environmental policies, the Brazilian State's actions occur through conjunctures, being necessary to the expropriated classes and social groups, intervene in a qualified way in the systematization of these policies, as a means to overcome their use for private purposes, ensuring the universalization of rights (Loureiro et al., 2009).

In light of the Latin American environmental debate, defending critical EA in line with a Politics of Liberation (Dussel, 2007), implies considering environmental resistances/insurgencies: the extractive reserves of Xapuri (inherited from Chico Mendes), the Zapatista Movement (Chiapas in Mexico), the Water and Gas War (Bolivia); the Movement of those Affected by Dams (MAB), the Landless Movement (struggle for agrarian reform), the Via campesina, the Homeless Workers' Movement (MTST), the indigenous movement (struggle for land), the struggle of artisanal fishermen and quilombolas/black movement; the struggles of those affected by the Vale/Samarco mining projects, among others, against the advance of the capitalist development project in the region.

In light of the discussion held at the level of Latin American movements, the dimension of critical EE is a pedagogical approach that problematizes the societal contexts in their interface with nature, because it is not possible to conceive environmental problems apart from social conflicts. Given that the constituent cause of the environmental issue has its origin in social relations, the model of society and capitalist development, for the critical perspective assumed in this work, it is not enough to fight for a new culture in the relationship between human beings and nature; it is necessary to fight at the same time for a new society (Loureiro & Layrargues, 2013).

Acknowledgements Work carried out with the support of the National Council for Scientific and Technological Development (CNPq/Brazil).

Disclosure Statement Neither of the authors has any financial interest or benefit that has arisen from the direct applications of this research.

Notes

1. For Costa and Loureiro (2014, p. 137), the realization of work is only effective in an inseparable movement in two planes: subjective (processed within the subject) and objective (resulting in the material transformation of nature), in which its effectuation constitutes an objectification of the subject who acts. Work reveals how these two categories are articulated, since social being originates in the synthesis between subjectivity and objectivity. Through practical activity what was once in consciousness (now is outside it), transformed into an object.
2. Abya Yala, in the language of the Kuna people, means Mature Land, Living Land or Land in Bloom and is synonymous with America (Porto-Gonçalves, 2009).

References

Aceslrad, H. (2004). *Conflitos Ambientais No Brasil*. Relume Dumará.
Acselrad, H. (2010). The Environmentalization of Social Struggles—The Case of the Environmental Justice Movement. *Advanced Studies, 24*(68), 103–119.
Bottomore, T. (Ed.). (2001). *Dicionário do pensamento marxista*. Jorge Zahar Editor.
Chasin, J. (2009). *Marx: Ontological Status and Methodological Resolution*. Boitempo.
Costa, C. A., & Loureiro, C. F. (2018). Environmental Question, Neoextractivism and Peripheral Capitalism: A Political Reading in Enrique Dussel. *SER Social, 20*(42), 164–181.
Dussel, E. (1982). *Para una ética de la liberación latinoamericana*. Vozes.
Dussel, E. (1984). *Filosofia de la Producción*. Nuova America.
Dussel, E. (2001). *Hacia una filosofia política crítica*. Editorial Desclée de Brouwer.
Dussel, E. (2007). *20 Theses on Politics* (R, Rodrigues, Trans.). CLACSO and Expressão Popular.

Fernandes, F. (1975). *Capitalismo dependente e classes sociais na América Latina*. Zahar.
Fontes, V., & Miranda, A. (2014). Pensamento crítico e as populações do campo, da floresta, das águas e... das cidades. *Tempus, actas de saúde colet, Brasília, 8*(2), 305–316.
Foster, J. B. (2005). *Marx's Ecology: Materialism and Nature*. Civilização Brasileira.
Freire, P. (2019). *Pedagogy of the Oppressed*. Paz e Terra.
Galeano, E. (2013). *The Open Veins of Latin America*. L&PM.
Gonçalves, R. (2016, July/December). 'Extractivist Capitalism in Latin America and the Contradictions of Large-scale Mining in Brazil'. Cadernos Prolam/USP, 15(29), 38–55.
Harvey, D. (2003). *The New Imperialism*. Loyola.
Konder, L. (2000). *A construção da proposta pedagógica do SESC-Rio*. Editora SENAC.
Leher, R. (2013). Hegemonia, contra-hegemonia e problemática socioambiental. In: L. A. Ferraro Júnior (Org.). Encontros e caminhos: formação de educadores ambientais e coletivos educadores (1st ed., Vol. 3, pp. 221–232). Ministry of Environment—Division of Environmental Education, 2014.
Loureiro, C. F. (2012). *Sustentabilidade e Educação: o olhar da ecologia política*. Cortez.
Loureiro, C. F. (2014). Historical-dialectical Materialism and Environmental Education Research. *Research in Environmental Education, 9*(1), 53–68.
Loureiro, C. F. (2019). *Questão ambiental: questões de vida*. Cortez.
Loureiro, C. F., & Layrargues, P. (2013, January/April). Political Ecology, Environmental Justice and Critical Environmental Education: Perspectives of Counter-hegemonic Alliance. Trab. Educ. Saúde, Rio de Janeiro, *11*(1), 53–71.
Loureiro, C. F., Trein, E., Tozoni-Reis, M., & Novick, V. (2009, January/April). Contributions of Marxist Theory for Critical Environmental Education. Cad. Cedes, Campinas, *29*(77), 81–97.
Lowy, M. (2014). Indigenous Ecosocial Struggles in Latin America. *Revista Critica Marxista, 38*, 61–70.
Lukács, G. (2013). Para uma ontologia do ser social. Vol. 1 e 2. Boitempo.
Marx, K. (2013). *Capital. Book I* (R. Enderle, Trans.). Boitempo.
Mészáros, I. (2002). *Para além do capital*. Boitempo.
Mészáros, I. (2005). *A educação para além do capital*. Boitempo.
Porto-Gonçalves, C. W. (2009, July/December). Between America and Abya Yala—Tensions of Territorialities. Desenvolvimento e Meio Ambiente, 20, 25–30.
Porto-Gonçalves, C. W. (2015). *A Globalização da natureza e a natureza da globalização*. Civilização brasileira.
Postone, M. (2014). *Tempo, trabalho e dominação social*. Boitempo.
Svampa, M. (2012, November). Consenso de los commodities, giro ecoterritorial y pensamiento crítico en América Latina. OSAL, Año XIII N° 32, 16–38.

CHAPTER 18

Green Marxism, Ecocentric Pedagogies and De-capitalization/Decolonization

Sayan Dey

18.1 Introduction: Marxism Is ~~Red~~ Green

all progress in capitalistic agriculture is a progress in the art, not only of robbing the labourer, but of robbing the soil; all progress in increasing the fertility of the soil for a given time, is a progress towards ruining the lasting sources of that fertility. (Marx cited in Benton, 2018)

Usually, the understanding and interpretation of Marxism and Marxist ideas are restricted within the functional parameters of the human civilization. To elaborate further, the notions of class structures, sociopolitical hierarchies and economic violence within the paradigm of Marxism are centrally understood with respect to the relationships between human communities. A majority of Marxism-centered public discussions, protest movements and classroom teachings have been structured on the sufferings, violence and crisis of certain sections of the human society. The necessity of building Marxist narratives on the violation, demonization and the capitalization/colonization of nature has been systemically ignored.

Before proceeding further, I would like to briefly discuss what I mean by Marxist narratives on the violation, demonization and the capitalization/colonization of nature. The aspects of class structures, economic violence and sociopolitical hierarchies not only involve the human beings but also the

S. Dey (✉)
School of Liberal Arts, Alliance University, Bangalore, India
e-mail: sayan.dey@alliance.edu.in

© The Editor(s) (if applicable) and The Author(s), under exclusive license to Springer Nature Switzerland AG 2023
R. Hall et al. (eds.), *The Palgrave International Handbook of Marxism and Education*, Marxism and Education,
https://doi.org/10.1007/978-3-031-37252-0_18

natural environment. Marx (as cited above) in *Capital* shared how the global project of colonialism/capitalism[1] was founded on the violation of both humans and the natural environment. However, prior to the evolution of green Marxism, not much importance was given to the inclusion of the natural environment within Marxist discourses. Marx's arguments about the connection between the exploitation of the human civilization and the natural environment have mostly been rejected and ignored. For instance, Australian ecofeminist Val Plumwood, in her book *Feminism and the Mastery of Nature* (1993, p. 244), completely rejected Marx's ideological consciousness toward the natural environment and has heavily critiqued the ecocentric interpretation of Marxist ideas as a mere reinterpretation of Marx's 'radically unsatisfactory materials.' She also adds that it is logically impossible to understand Marxist theory through the ecological lens.

This rejection is highly problematic. It is true that Marx does not engage with the aspects of capitalization/colonization and commodification of the natural environment in a direct and detailed way, but his consistent reference to the violation of nature along with the human civilization cannot be denounced. Scholars like Paul Burkett (*Marx and Nature*), Howard Parsons (*Marx and Engels on Ecology*), Jean-Guy Vaillancourt ('Marxism and Ecology'), Steven Vogel ('Marxism and Alienation from Nature'), Ted Benton (*The Greening of Marxism*), Kohei Saito (*Karl Marx's Ecosocialism*), Madhav Gadgil (*Ecological Journeys*), Ramachandra Guha (*Environmentalism*), Ashish Kothari (*Pluriverse*), and many others have highlighted the ecological references in Marx's works. Moreover, they have also argued for the necessity of re-reading and re-implementing Marxist ideas in an ecological manner and how green Marxism can counter the issue of ecological imbalance through ecocentric knowledge production. Besides these aspects, my socio-cultural positionality also contributed toward the development of this chapter.

I was born to a family of Marxist activists in Calcutta.[2] During my childhood days, one of my uncles, who was an active member of the Communist Party of India (Marxist), would often tell me stories about how the humans evolved and how they were nurtured in the natural environment. He would share the ways in which the economically privileged people disrupted the culture of nature-human cohabitation and selectively destroyed humans and the natural environment[3] to fulfill their political and commercial motives. Later on, whenever my uncle shared stories about the history of Marxist revolution in West Bengal and other parts of the world, he would emphasize on how the violence of colonialism/capitalism should be understood as 'an evolving totality of capital, power and nature' (Moore, 2017b, p. 288). He would reflect on the ways in which the existential patterns of the natural environment can teach the human civilization about class equality, economic inclusivity and sociopolitical de-hierarchization. He would also take me out for walks in forest areas and agricultural fields that were located near his house and would narrate stories on how the human society can successfully adopt the cooperative and collaborative existential patterns of nature.

Such ecocentric narratives widely contributed toward my reading of Karl Marx as an ecocentric thinker and my interest toward the paradigm of green Marxism. But, despite the evolution of green Marxism as a social, political and economic paradigm across the globe, it continues to remain ignored in India. The application of Marxist principles in contemporary India ignores the possibilities of implementing Marxist thoughts through the lens of the existential and functional patterns of the natural environment. In fact, this ignorance is not only limited within India, but across other parts of South Asia as well. Today, the rapid rise of rightwing political ideologies in South Asia and its toxic capitalistic impact through the limitless expansion of industries, mines, pipelines and flyovers at the cost of violating the ecocentric livelihoods of the indigenous communities and the natural environment further necessitate the development of green Marxism as a collective and urgent project.

In the context of the handbook, the discussions on green Marxism in this chapter exclusively engage with the necessity of shaping ecocentric pedagogies in the educational institutions of South Asia, and how the ecocentric pedagogical approaches can provide 'a fundamentally more coherent approach to practical ecological politics' (Moog & Stones, 2009, p. 40). In order to ensure an in-depth analysis, the geographical focus of this chapter has been limited within India and Bhutan. These two countries within South Asia have been specifically chosen because the author is from India and actively collaborates with environment researchers and activists from India and Bhutan.

The chapter is divided into five sections. The first section, 'Introduction,' lays the theoretical and thematic foundation of this chapter by discussing the factors that provoked the author to develop this chapter and how the Marxist ideas of class relations, power structures and market economy are not only related to the human civilization, but also to the natural environment. The second section, 'Research Method,' outlines the method through which the research was conducted across India and Bhutan. The third section, 'Ecocentric Pedagogies and Green Marxism,' reflects on the necessity of developing ecocentric pedagogies as a part of green Marxist approaches in South Asia, to challenge the anti-ecological capitalistic education system on the one side and dismantle the hierarchies in class relations and power structures on the other. The theoretical arguments in the third section have been experientially argued in the fourth section titled 'Case Studies.' In this section, case studies on selective ecocentric educational institutions in India and Bhutan unpack how green Marxist principles can be applied in daily modes of teaching and learning. The section also discusses how green Marxist ideas create possibilities in addressing class and economic hierarchies. On the basis of the arguments in the previous sections, the final section, 'Conclusion,' discusses how green Marxist principles of teaching and learning can lead to social, cultural, political and economic de-capitalization/decolonization.

18.2 Research Method

In this chapter, the study has been conducted by selectively identifying ecocentric educational institutions in India and Bhutan. In Bhutan, the study was conducted physically between August 2019 and January 2021, and for the educational institutions in India, the study was conducted online. After identifying the institutions, necessary information about the ecologically sustainable educational practices of the institutions was collected through personal conversations with students and teachers (in Bhutan), from websites and from different conversation pieces and articles. Along with collecting information, online interviews with faculties from different private universities in India were also conducted. The study focused on the green Marxist concepts of 'contradictions of capitalism,' 'capitalocene,' 'eco-pedagogy,' 'eco-curriculums' and 'class relationships.'

The interviews and the field work experiences have engaged with these green Marxist concepts by discussing the different socio-historical consequences of the conflicts between the celebrators of capitalistic education systems and the celebrators of the ecocentric education systems. In the following sections it is found how the celebrators of capitalistic education systems defend the violent contradictions of capitalism and the catastrophic impacts of capitalocene by preserving the anti-ecological and profitmaking knowledge structures on the one side and dismissing every effort to build eco-pedagogies and eco-curriculums on the other.

18.3 Ecocentric Pedagogies and Green Marxism

The project of European colonization in South Asia (as in other parts of the world) extracted, exploited and commodified not only human bodies, but also the objects of nature, like land, water, minerals, forests, and created agricultural products. During the British colonial era in India, the Zamindari System was introduced by British official Charles Cornwallis under the Permanent Settlement Act in 1793. The Act socio-economically divided the Indian society into British colonizers, zamindars and peasants. In order to gain the support of the economically privileged Indians, the British allowed a group of high-caste and high-class landowners to forcefully dislocate the peasants from their own lands and reduce them to slavery. This colonial strategy, on the one side, socio-economically compartmentalized the Indian society, and on the other side, silenced the grievances of the peasantry that were associated with their displacement from agricultural and forestlands. The sufferings of the peasantry in India in the hands of the British colonizers and zamindars led to the outbreak of peasant movements [Champaran Satyagraha (1917), Kheda Satyagraha (1918), Moplah Rebellion (1921), Bardoli Satyagraha (1928), etc.] at different points of time. The peasant movements against the Zamindari System marked the onset of Marxist revolution in India. During the movements, the peasants voiced themselves not only against socio-economic catastrophes, but also against ecological catastrophes. The movements highlighted how the violation of the natural environment and human societies are interconnected.

With the passage of time, as the colonial imperial regimes translated into commercial regimes, the commodification of the natural environment in South Asia gained further impetus. While, historically, in South Asia, a lot of Marxist theoretical narratives exist on the issues of commodification of land, feudal authority and displacement of peasants, the displacement of the natural environment by the industrial forces is not much talked about within the paradigm of Marxism. Today, in South Asia, the practice of commodification and industrialization expands beyond the factories and into the educational institutions: by designing syllabuses and pedagogies that focus less on the ecological values and more on seeking jobs and making commercial profits; by creating physical infrastructures in the forms of laboratories and research centers which are accessible to a set of selective academic disciplines like business, management, science and technology that regulate the functioning of the global markets; and by systemically marginalizing[4] scholarships in humanities and social sciences that facilitate discussions and activisms on the importance of building anti-capitalistic and ecocentric knowledge spaces in daily life.

The commodification and industrialization of the educational system in South Asia have led to the evolution of widely two forms of institutions—profit-oriented institutions and job-oriented institutions. Their functional patterns highlight the violent contradictions of capitalism and the catastrophic impacts of capitalocene. A lot of schools and higher educational institutions in South Asia function as profitmaking units through minting degrees and certificates in lieu of high admission fees. In such institutions, the construction of high-tech classrooms, airconditioned community halls and massive food courts is considered more important than the quality of syllabus structures, the pedagogical patterns and the practical outcome of learning (Marginson, 2004; Rikowski, 2004; Thompson, 2015; Brown, 2018). There are also a lot of educational institutions that exclusively focus on job-centric methods of teaching and learning. The students in such institutions are taught that their only purpose of studying and getting degrees is to get high-salaried jobs.

Obviously, one of the many purposes of teaching and learning is to gain relevant degrees and jobs, but when the focus of knowledge production lies exclusively in producing degrees and seeking jobs over anything else, then the higher education system is nothing more than a 'marketable product' which is 'rated, bought and sold by standard units' and 'reduced to staple equivalence by impersonal, mechanical tests' (Mbembe, 2016, p. 30). The higher education system as a marketable product performs what Karl Marx argued as the first contradiction of capitalism. According to Marx, the first contradiction of capitalism is that the capitalists believe that the only way to maintain profit is to recklessly indulge in labor exploitation. But, in reality, such an approach reduces the profit rate. In a similar manner, market-centric educational institutions may create more jobs for their students, but the quality of knowledges and scholarships; the social, cultural and economic standards of jobs; and the ecological and humanitarian values of existence are widely affected.

The marketability of the higher education system is strategically maintained through social, cultural, communal, commercial and geographical hierarchies. A lot of educational institutions are illegally constructed on farmlands and unclaimed natural spaces (HT Corresponden, 2021; Special Correspondent, 2021; Rajput, 2022). Along with the educational institutions, a lot of commercial hubs are constructed near the institutions for the welfare of the students and staff by destroying the natural environment. Such educational institutions prefer socio-economically privileged students and staff belonging to high class and high caste (especially in India) and who can consistently contribute to their profitmaking agenda, rather than people from indigenous communities who have been illegally uprooted from their lands and who would stand as a barrier to their infrastructural, pedagogical and curricular values. The construction of educational institutions through destroying the natural environment unpacks the catastrophe of capitalocene, during which 'cultural ecology and ecological culture are expressed in the social relations of material production, distribution, exchange and consumption' (O'Connor, 1998, p. 46). Such an expression regards the natural environment as 'cheap' (Moore, 2017a, p. 602) and builds educational institutions as an 'accumulation strategy' (ibid.) by normalizing the destruction of the natural environment for profit-centric knowledge production.

The interviews further reveal the normalization and violence of capitalism on the natural environment. As a part of the interviews, I selectively interacted with five faculty members[5] who are based at different private universities across India. The question that I asked them is: Is the capitalization of education system harmful for ecological development in contemporary India? A faculty from a recently established private university in Faridabad[6] shared how much important it is to build schools and higher educational institutions in the rural areas of India so that the village people can get 'a taste of progress and development' (Participant A, 2022). Another faculty from a private university in Kanpur[7] shared that 'only the construction of more private educational institutions in the rural areas of India can develop the country in an inclusive manner' (Participant B, 2022). The other three participants, in the name of socio-economic modernization and development, also voiced their support in favor of capitalization and privatization of the Indian education system. The act of constructing private universities in the rural areas of India[8] in the name of modernization and development is equivalent to the act of bulldozing the natural environment and building devastative knowledge systems from its debris.

In spite of evidences that the capitalization/colonization of education system is leading to ecological violence (Bell, 2015; Klees, 2017; Skordoulis, 2010; Bainbridge, 2020), why do individuals and institutions continue to support it? This question invites us to investigate how 'formal education has become ensnared in the mire of capitalist productivity' by concealing the 'educationally-induced destruction of planetary systems that support human flourishing' (Bainbridge, 2020, p. 737) and has generated a false consciousness that colonization was over with the judicial independence of the colonies. Such a false consciousness has allowed the national bourgeoisie in the postcolonial nations to 'step into the shoes of the former European settlement' (Fanon, 1963, p. 149) and preserve and reconfigure the brutal foundations of colonialism/capitalism.

Historically, it has been necessary for colonialism/capitalism to disrupt indigenous education systems because the strategies to prevent ecological catastrophe and to preserve the natural environment by the native indigenous communities are 'incompatible with the expansive and destructive logic of capitalism' (Skordoulis, 2010, p. 35). As a result, the expansive, destructive and extractivist policies of colonialism/capitalism across different segments of human civilization and the natural environment invite us to address multiple civilizational and ecological issues in an intersectional manner. The dialectics of the nature-society system need to be collapsed and the aspects of environmental destruction, class hierarchies, power structures, natural calamities, violent pedagogical practices and profitmaking curricular structures need to be addressed in an interwoven manner.

To elaborate further, during teaching and learning in the schools and higher educational institutions it is important to understand the functional aspects of the human civilization and the functional aspects of the natural environment together and not as separate and hierarchical entities. The capitalistic modes of knowledge system have been teaching that the nature and the humans share a hierarchical relationship, where humans dominate, regulate and guide the natural environment for its wellbeing. In order to counter such a problematic knowledge system, the development of green Marxism within the teaching and learning spaces in the schools and higher educational institutions became crucial. The paradigm of green Marxism invites us to re-assess the violence of colonialism/capitalism in intersectional and entangled ways, and revive the ecologically sustainable knowledge systems in South Asia and other parts of the world. The phenomenon of green Marxism was founded on the necessity of 'promoting and advancing global ecological health' alongside the wellbeing of the citizens (Boxley, 2022, p. 305).

Apart from the failure of Marxist ideas to engage with the histories of ecological violence in India and other parts of South Asia, environmental education has failed to generate 'transformative educational discourse practice' (Gruenewald, 2015, p. 72). David Gruenewald also adds that in order to meet the profitmaking ambitions, the field of environmental education has been disciplined by detaching ecology from its 'human-related histories of unequal social, economic and ontological relations' (Trisos et al., 2021, p. 1205). To explain further, since the initiation of ecological violence and enslavement by the European colonizers, several resistant movements were generated by the indigenous communities and later on by various community organizations. But, those movements were not shaped within the paradigm of Marxism. It was only in the late 1960s and early 1970s, with the rise of green Marxist consciousness in Europe, that the peasant movements against land, labor, economic and ecological violation in South Asia were being structured and executed through the phenomenological lens of Marxism.

For instance, the Chipko Movement in India, which was organized by the Uttarakhand Sangharsh Vahini,[9] played a crucial role in making Marxist activists in India and other parts of South Asia realize that 'it is the relationship among human beings which determines the relationship between humans and the forests' (Omvedt, 1984, p. 1865). Besides making individuals and institutions realize the necessity of reconfiguring Marxism through ecological viewpoints, this movement was also a phenomenal step to decolonize the paradigm of green Marxism. Through this movement, the scholarships on green Marxism were no more restricted exclusively within the white elite institutional spaces of Europe and the United States, but also evolved within the resistant movements of the laborers, peasants and indigenous communities of the Global South.

This geopolitical, epistemological and ontological shift of knowledge production from the Global North to the Global South has the potential to decolonize the curricular and pedagogical patterns of teaching, learning and understanding green Marxism in India and other parts of South Asia in two major ways. Firstly, by interpreting the various crises of the human civilization and the natural environment in the local respective contexts of the Global South and not in the distant contexts of the Global North, and secondly, by broadening the theoretical and philosophical understanding of green Marxism beyond the Euro-North American-centric textbooks and critically acknowledging the intentions and outcomes of the ecological movements in the Global South as green Marxist scholarships.

Prior to the Chipko Movement, green Marxism was believed to be 'the preserve of the White, highly educated middle class' (Boxley, 2022, p. 306). The movement was led by the peasantry in Uttarakhand[10] and the leadership of the peasants dismantled the Eurocentric myth of white ownership. But, unfortunately, in the schools and higher educational institutions of South Asia, the interpretation of the peasant movements is mostly restricted within the enclaves of historical, political and socio-economic narratives, without ecologically contextualizing them. This colonial tradition of separating the nature and society needs to be dismissed, and the relationship between human society and the natural environment needs to be collaboratively perceived as 'society-in-nature' (Moore, 2017b, p. 286). So, the purpose of discussing green Marxist practices with respect to ecocentric pedagogies in this chapter is not only to position the narratives of ecological development within the discourses of Left politics in South Asia, but also to de-capitalize/decolonize the paradigm of Marxism in general.

In the following section, the curricular and pedagogical practices from selective ecocentric educational institutions of India and Bhutan have been discussed and the specific green Marxist educational concepts that are addressed in the discussions are 'eco-curriculums,' 'eco-pedagogies' and 'class relationships.' The section also analyzes how ecocentric curricular and pedagogical practices have the potential to develop long-term plans for tackling ecological catastrophes on the one side and addressing hierarchies in class relationships, social dynamics and power structures on the other.

18.4 Case Studies: Selective Instances of Practical Applications

In this section the curricular and pedagogical practices of two ecocentric institutions have been elaborately discussed. They are Barefoot College and Green School System.

Barefoot College

The Barefoot College was founded in the Tilonia District of Rajasthan by Sanjit 'Bunker' Roy in 1972. Initially, the college was founded as Social Work and Research Center (RWRC) in 1972, after conducting a thorough survey of the state of water supply in 100 drought-prone areas in Rajasthan. During the survey, Roy and his team realized that solving the water supply problem alone won't improve the existential state of the villages because the villages are infected with multiple forms of caste, class, social, economic and political hierarchies. Therefore, it was crucial to empower the villagers toward sustainable development. So, along with improving the water and irrigation facilities of the villages, RWRC started teaching and training the villagers about the various ways in which people from diverse caste, class, gender and economic backgrounds can collaboratively work toward the infrastructural development of the villages. The villagers started learning about the essential medical treatments, hygienic lifestyles, solar power facilities, water conservation and technology.

The training allowed the villagers to realize that in order to co-exist and contribute toward the development of their respective communities they need to function together in a de-hierarchical way. During the training, the villagers were also taught to perform developmental activities in such a manner so that the natural environment is not harmed. So, irrespective of caste, class, gender and economic differences, the villagers have been working together by installing solar power devices, digging irrigation channels, building food banks and initiating local radio stations, without disrupting the existential patterns of the natural environment. In this way, the training has been making the villagers ecologically self-dependent and has been reducing their dependency on the ego-centric, mechanical and exploitative forces of colonialism/capitalism.

But, this project of expanding the college center into a de-hierarchical, inclusive and ecologically sustainable training space was underpinned by multiple forms of caste, class, religious, communal, gender, geographical and economic challenges. A social survey revealed that Tilonia alone houses 'fourteen different castes with very specific social traditions' (O'Brien, 2015, p. 9). With the evolution of this project in Tilonia, a selective group of high-caste people have been trying their best to use this project as a medium to fulfill their self-centered, socio-economic schemes and to continue to marginalize the low-caste people. Such a redundant cultural attitude is anti-ecological in nature because the caste hierarchies also systemically contribute toward the depletion of the natural environment. The depletion takes place when the high-caste and socio-economically privileged people uproot the low-caste and outcaste indigenous communities from the natural environment for constructing educational institutions, shopping centers and housing complexes. This is not only physical uprooting, but also a form of social, cultural and pedagogical uprooting, due to which indigenous educational patterns and knowledge systems get erased. In fact, historically, since the precolonial era, this is how caste-based violence and ecological violence have been interrelatedly performed in India.

Despite these challenges, the college started growing with the active participation of the villagers from different caste, class, economic and gender backgrounds, who were trained in medical sciences, health knowledges, solar power technologies, irrigation technologies, water conservation techniques and other forms of sustainable needs, not only for the sake of self-empowerment but also to be the regulators of social, cultural, economic and political change for fellow villagers.

Such an initiative has been disintegrating the hierarchies in class relationships, social dynamics and economic structures on the one side and dismantling the 'class-exploitative, crises-ridden, lop-sided [and] wealth-concentrative nature' of mainstream education systems on the other (Westra, 2007, p. 219). Except for a training campus in Tilonia, the college exists in a decentralized and physically non-shapeable state without any other campus. The pedagogical patterns in Barefoot College encourage the students to self-develop through learning in an ecologically sustainable manner. Let us look into an example, which shows how students of Barefoot College have been collaboratively and co-creatively working toward evading class, caste and economic hierarchies through ecocentric knowledge systems.

Nilanjana Bhowmick, in one of her articles, narrates the story of a 19-year-old Dalit woman named Santosh Devi, who has been a victim of severe caste, gender and economic discrimination since her childhood. Before joining Barefoot College, Devi was solely identified as an outcast. The high-caste males in her village did not consider her socio-culturally suitable to be respected and economically capable to contribute toward the development of her village. But, after learning about developing solar panels and graduating from the college, she is looked up to as a solar engineer. While talking about her transformed identity status among the high caste people in Tilonia, Devi says: 'For them, I am a solar engineer who can repair and install the light installations. From looking down on the ground when higher caste people passed to looking them in the eye, I never imagined this would have been possible' (cited in Bhowmick, 2011). This experience of Santosh Devi not only socio-economically empowers her, but also interrogates the violent 'expansion of capitalist "civilisation"'

(Cordova & Bailey, 2020, p. 5). Her contribution as a solar engineer bulldozes the caste, class and economic prejudices of her village and shows how nature-based knowledge systems can address the capitalism-sponsored socio-economic hierarchies in the human society.

The transformative experiences of Santosh Devi and the practical ways in which they have contributed to the sustainable development of her community are stimulated by the following practices:

(a) Ecological self-sustainability: Karl Marx's concept of communism enables us understand 'how intertwined the issue of ecological sustainability is with the creation of a rich, many-sided society in which sustainability of human and nature relationships—rather than the mere pursuit of wealth for its own sake—has become the central principle of social organization' (Foster, 1997, p. 290). On a similar note, the green Marxist modes of teaching and learning methodologies in the college, instead of encouraging the students to depend on the unsustainable, industrially manufactured, and ecologically harmful objects for their daily survival, motivate them to learn and live with the resources that they find in the natural environment. Such a practice enables the students to be self-sustainable, respect each other, respect the natural environment, gain knowledge in an ecologically practical way and utilize the natural resources optimally. The optimal usage of natural resources as a green Marxist existential practice teaches the students how to utilize natural resources to address the basic needs of life and not to indulge in the capitalistic exercise of 'unlimited use of natural resources' and overproducing commodities (Dijk, 2015). These pedagogical exercises also allow the college students to interrogate the capitalistic profitmaking systems of knowledge production, and the practices of class, caste and economic hierarchies. The ecocentric curriculums and pedagogies teach the students to design developmental strategies, shape class relationships and nurture economic sensibilities through the functional patterns of the natural environment and not at the cost of it.

(b) Making collective decisions: Collaborations and co-creations are the two most crucial principles that govern the pedagogical and curricular practices of Barefoot College. After completing their training in the college, the students become self-empowered and self-reliant, and extend their training to other villagers. To remove 'both formal and informal hierarchies' (O'Brien, 2015, p. 11), all the staffs in the college equally participate in the decision-making processes. The graduating students, irrespective of their caste, class and economic status, collaborate to form Village Education Committees (VECs) to monitor the selection of teachers for the schools. These selections are held in the Tilonia campus of the college, and enable communal supervision of the teaching and learning procedures in the college (ibid.).

Despite trying to colonize the ecosystem, 'the capitalist economy remains fundamentally dependent on nature' (Lievens, n.d., p. 10). Every effort to 'make abstraction from this dependence inexorably leads to the exhaustion of nature' (Lievens, p. 10). The green Marxist curricular and pedagogical patterns of Barefoot College outline how collaborations with the natural environment can assist in removing the hierarchies in class, caste, economic and social structures.

Green School System

In *My Green School* (2014), Thakur S Powdyel argues that green is not just a color but a phenomenon of ecological sustainability in daily life. The functional pattern of the Green School system is analogous to the functional pattern of green Marxist pedagogies. As the green Marxist pedagogies provoke the learners to analyze the class identities like 'bourgeoisie' and 'proletariat' and interpret class relationships, economic relationships, power structures and political ideologies through the ethical, functional and existential values of the natural environment, the Green School system of Bhutan also encourages the students to do the same. The system teaches the students that socio-economic modernization and development need to be initiated without marginalizing indigenous knowledge values and without getting entrapped into the violent and divisive policies of capitalism. As a part of the Gross National Happiness (GNH) phenomenon, the Green School system in Bhutan was founded in 2003 by the former Education Minister of Bhutan Thakur S Powdyel in collaboration with the fourth king of Bhutan, Jigme Singye Wangchuck. The central idea behind the development of this phenomenal practice across the country is to 'educate the youth to use the natural environment as the integrating context for learning and also use the local natural environment to teach students concepts in all disciplines, while emphasizing hands-on real-world learning experiences' (Drakpa & Dorji, 2013, p. 314).

The Green School system is underlined with eight principles (Powdyel, 2014), and they are natural greenery (integrating the pedagogical and the curricular patterns of a school with the natural environment to learn and share knowledges in collaboration with nature); social greenery (the involvement of the students and teachers in maintaining the physical greenery of school campuses and learning and teaching through it); cultural greenery (realizing the richness of diverse cultures through close association with the natural environment); intellectual Greenery (curating intellectual systems through the nature-based, non-chronological, non-linear, de-hierarchical and spontaneous forms of knowledge production as portrayed by the natural environment); academic greenery (building bridges between written texts and environmental contexts); aesthetic greenery (understanding the differences between appearance and reality through the ecological knowledge systems); spiritual greenery (blending spiritual values with rational thinking through the functional features of the natural environment) and moral greenery (creating collaborative and collective societies based on the cohabitational existential patterns of the natural environment).

Through the eight principles, the students learn both within the four-walled westernized classrooms and in the open spaces of the natural environment. As a part of the Green School System, the school tutors in Bhutan ensure the simultaneous practice of text-based learning and context-based learning of the students. On the one side, the students are taught modern/Western science, technology, mathematics, literature, geography and other subjects inside the classrooms and laboratories. On the other side, they are taken to the agricultural fields, dairy farms, fruit orchards and forests that are located within the school campuses. Unlike the hierarchical tutor-centric dictation technique of the capitalistic education system, the Green School system allows the teachers and students to learn with each other in a decentralized manner. The students learn not only from the professional degree-holders, but also from the community elders who have imbibed knowledges from their ancestors.

Such a collaborative teaching-learning system fractures the social, economic and class hierarchies and weaves green Marxist economies of caring and sharing, where, irrespective of educational qualifications, class positions, economic conditions and geographical locations, individuals can co-participate in the knowledge production processes. Though, generally, in capitalist profitmaking spaces, activities like agriculture and dairy farming leads to the commodification of nature, in Bhutan the students are taught how these activities can be performed beyond 'experimenting' with nature and as a way of learning with and about nature through caring and sharing. Instead of selling the agricultural and dairy products in the market, the school authorities use them for self-consumption and distribution amongst the villagers. Such self-sustainable practices of caring and sharing also invite individuals to reorganize societal relationships in a horizontal way by making the learners realize that in order to make a society ecologically sustainable it is important to not treat the natural environment as a commercial object and not treat the humans differentially on the basis of their economic status.

As an example, let us analyze the pedagogical and curricular frameworks practiced in the Yonphula Lower Secondary School (YLSS). In YLSS, the students from the very first day of their school are taught how to weave a balance between textual and contextual knowledges. Besides the four-walled, digitally equipped, westernized classrooms, the school campus also consists of open fields with shades. In those open spaces, the students and the teachers break away from the classrooms' usual teacher-centric sitting patterns and sit in a circle. Within the circle, the teacher, instead of sitting in the center, sits with the students. Every day the classes are conducted both within the four-walled classrooms and in the open spaces. Such a way of teaching and learning makes the students believe that teaching and learning is a de-hierarchical, collaborative and co-creative process, where a teacher is a lifelong learner and vice versa. Besides, professional teachers, village elders are habitually invited to enlighten the students with ecocentric knowledge systems. The simultaneous involvement of the village elders and professional teachers erases the Euromodern capitalistic practice that only individuals with selective academic qualifications from selective educational institutions are qualified to teach and dismantles class hierarchies.

This habitual shift allows the students to build a bridge between text-based knowledges and community-based knowledges. When the students are given home tasks they are highly encouraged to complete them with their parents and grandparents. Such a collaborative teaching and learning process, respects the intellectual capability of four-walled classrooms and open natural spaces, acknowledges the knowledge values of trained teachers and community elders simultaneously, and celebrates the cultural values of nature and human civilizations. This is underlined with the green Marxist educational values of respecting the natural environment, the indigenous knowledge systems and the culture of socio-cultural cohabitation.

After the students complete their school and university degrees, the collaborative ecocentric systems of knowledge production are carried forward to their workplaces. For instance, every citizen of Bhutan, irrespective of their professional and gender affiliations, is trained as a civic volunteer (locally known as *desuups*). After a year of rigorous physical and psychological training, the civic volunteers, according to their knowledge expertise, are placed in different rural and urban regions of Bhutan, to assist the communities during any form of crises. During the outbreak of Covid-19, ministers, school teachers and staff, university teachers and staff, businessmen, shopkeepers, homemakers, retired army professionals and individuals from various other professions were trained to assist the people with food, groceries, medicines, transportation and other daily needs (Lamsang, 2020; Pem, 2020; Wangchuk, 2022).

Such a collective and collaborative system of shouldering socio-cultural responsibilities not only dilutes the capitalism-based layers of class, profession and economy, where different economic and professional backgrounds are structured in a pyramidal fashion, but also unfolds how the de-hierarchical and cohabitational existential characteristics of the natural environment can be habitually inherited to regulate the class and economic relationships in the human society. These green Marxist educational practices of 'cohabitation [and co-learning] between natural and human habitats' (Lawson & Nguyen-Van, 2020, p. 2) can also be found in different educational institutions in Pakistan (Clean Green School Programme), Bangladesh (earth architecture), Nepal (Eco-Smart School Program) and Sri Lanka (Thomas Gall School).

The Clean Green School Program (CGSP) in Pakistan is a part of the Prime Minister's Clean Green Pakistan Movement (CGPM) and it focuses in designing and redesigning curricular and pedagogical practices in the schools in a way so that students can gain knowledges about the climate and the natural environment and reconfigure the socio-economic relationships through the green Marxist ecocentric values of caring and sharing. As a part of CGSP, the students learn 'behaviours and practical skills to reduce their environmental footprint' (CGSP, n.d.). The students also learn to 'extend learning beyond the classroom to develop responsible attitudes and commitment, both at home and in the broader community' (ibid.).Such a learning process in Pakistan enables the students to practically understand the values and applications of the green Marxist concepts of eco-curriculums and eco-pedagogies.

The community-based ecologically sustainable learning process can be found in the eco-friendly schools of Bangladesh as well. In the year 2005, the first eco-friendly school in Bangladesh was built. In collaboration with architects Anna Aeringer (from Austria) and Eike Roswag (from Germany), the elderly villagers, young women and men, children, architects, business and local craftsmen from the Rudrapur district came together to build a handmade school through using local 'earthbound materials' (Architecture, n.d.). The materials like 'loam and straw were combined with lighter elements like bamboo sticks and nylon lashing to create an environmentally sustainable foundation' (ibid.). The collaborative effort toward building environmentally sustainable spaces of knowledge production in Rudrapur has encouraged individuals from different class and economic backgrounds to co-participate in a de-hierarchical manner, and to re-think and re-interrogate the existing hierarchies in class and economic relationships. This ecocentric process of re-thinking and re-interrogating the class and economic hierarchies in Bangladesh is underpinned with green Marxist pedagogical intentions of reshaping class and socio-economic relationships according to the cohabitational principles of the natural environment.

Similar to Bangladesh, Nepal has also been making efforts to build environmentally sustainable spaces of knowledge production. In collaboration with Wildlife Conservation Nepal (WCN) and Nepal Prakriti Pathshala (NPP), the Eco-Smart School Program was launched by the Government of Nepal in 2016. As a part of the program, school teachers and students across Nepal are invited to attend workshops and training courses throughout the year about eco-friendly initiatives like 'practicing waste and water management, implementing school gardens, [and] becoming energy efficient' (Wildlife Conservation Nepal, 2021). The workshops and training courses are conducted through 'hands on experience to practice sustainable lifestyles beyond text books' (ibid.) and the pedagogy focuses on 'outdoor education' (ibid.). The workshop and training spaces are chosen within the natural environmental spaces that are under WCN, like nature parks and villages, and serve as a socio-economic melting pot, where teachers and students from different class, caste, religious and economic backgrounds learn with each other. The ecocentric educational practices of the Eco-Smart School Program in Nepal uphold the green Marxist educational values by implementing eco-pedagogies and eco-curriculums on the one side and dismantling the social, cultural and economic hierarchies in class relationships on the other.

Sri Lanka's commitment to build eco-friendly educational institutions is no different from other South Asian countries and their eco-friendly initiatives are also reflective of green Marxist educational ideologies. For instance, the Thomas Gall School was launched in Sri Lanka by the Foundation for

Environmental Education in 2021. This is the first eco-school in Sri Lanka, where all the subjects are learnt with 'sustainability at the core' and the teachers and students engage in 'topic-based learning that infuses lifelong skills to create lifelong environmentally conscious people' (Daily, 2021). The ecologically sustainable and the environmentally conscious ways of learning enable individuals to implement the ideological values of green Marxism by interrogating the class hierarchies in Sri Lanka as based on social, cultural and economic status, and the capitalistic educational policies of the educational institutions. The application of the green Marxist educational values can also be located through the eco-curriculum and the eco-pedagogy of the Thomas Gall School, where the processes of teaching and learning the academic disciplines are interwoven with the knowledge values of the natural environment. The ecocentric curricular and pedagogical patterns in the school offer 'a learning environment that encourages awareness, curiosity, empathy, love, passion, tolerance and much more' and trains students to 'appreciate and accept others as equals and respect their environment and community around them' (ibid.). The values of empathy, awareness, love, curiosity, passion and tolerance are integral aspects of the functional system of the natural environment and green Marxist pedagogies.

The green Marxist curricular and pedagogical practices of these ecocentric educational institutions remind us that the natural environment is not meant to be treated as a profitmaking commodity to 'serve human needs' (Veinovic & Stanisic, 2018, p. 16) and should not be exploited 'for the benefit of mankind' (Boslaugh, 2011, p. 15). The curricular and teaching-learning systems of majority of the educational institutions in South Asia need to be de-capitalized/decolonized by reconfiguring the curricular structures with respect to the modern-day issues of the natural environment. The reconfigurations should be done in such a manner so that the teachers and learners can understand the ways to utilize ecocentric knowledge systems to interpret economic and class relationships in their respective contexts. Based on the case studies, the final section of the chapter discusses how green Marxist pedagogical practices may lead to de-capitalization/decolonization of educational institutions in South Asia.

18.5 Conclusion: De-capitalization/Decolonization

In this chapter the necessity of re-reading Marx with respect to the concerns of the natural environment and re-interrogating the 'undergoing states of eco-planetary crisis' has been elaborately discussed (Wilson, 2022, p. 6). The discussions in this chapter outline how green Marxist pedagogies enable individuals to 'connect the exploitation of nature with the alienation and exploitation of workers under a class system' (Boxley, 2022, p. 312). To elaborate further, the process of collaboratively analyzing the phenomena of ecological violence and class structures unfolds how the 'economic power of the ruling class over the working class is played out in the appearance of power over nature' (ibid., p. 312). The chapter also reflects on how the existential patterns of the natural environment can be inherited to de-capitalize/decolonize the education system in South Asia, with a specific focus on India and Bhutan.

The green Marxist practices of the ecocentric educational institutions in South Asia reminds us that the curricular and pedagogical strategies in the contemporary educational institutions need to be re-designed beyond the narrow enclaves of profitmaking and material gaining to encompass what Donna J. Haraway in her book *Staying with Trouble* (2016, p. 58) argues as the philosophy of 'sympoiesis.' With respect to the philosophy of sympoiesis, Haraway (ibid.) in the book argues that no living communities can live and produce knowledge on their own and that every living community is a part of 'complex, dynamic, responsive, situated, [and] historical systems.' This philosophy of existential cooperation and cohabitation of the natural environment needs to be imbibed within the habitual patterns of teaching and learning in the educational institutions through perceiving the nature-human relationship in an entangled manner. The green Marxist practices of teaching and learning, as discussed in the previous section, contribute toward de-capitalization/decolonization in the following ways:

(a) Shifting from society and nature to society-in-nature: The green Marxist curricular and pedagogical practices of the ecocentric educational institutions in South Asia, by disintegrating teacher-student hierarchies and building ecologically sustainable, praxis-based pedagogies, have been making efforts to erase the nature-human dichotomy and address the class and economic hierarchies through the co-existential functional patterns of the natural environment. The co-teaching and co-learning processes in Barefoot College (India), Yonphula Lower Secondary School (Bhutan), and the ecocentric educational institutions in Pakistan, Bangladesh, Nepal and Sri Lanka invite individuals to perceive the human society within the existence of the natural environment. The ecocentric educational institutions also teach how the concerns of the natural environment should be understood in symbiosis with the concerns of the human society and vice versa.

(b) From education-for-economy to education-for-ecology: The discussions on green Marxist knowledge-making practices in this chapter also engage with the necessity and processes to make a shift from 'education-for-economy' toward 'education for ecology.' The shift is underpinned with the green Marxist eco-pedagogical, epistemological, ontological and methodological practices of analyzing environmental injustices, ecological injustices, class injustices and socio-economic injustices in an intersectional way. As a green Marxist exercise, the discussions in this chapter invite the readers to reanalyze the Marxist concepts of 'class relationships,' 'socio-economic relationships,' 'bourgeoisie,' 'proletariat' and the 'contradictions of capitalism' with respect to the existential, cultural and functional patterns of the natural environment. A job-centric education system turns a society into a reckless profitmaking machine, where the sole purpose of knowledge production is to get degrees, jobs and contribute toward economic development at the cost of exploiting and abusing the natural environment. The ecocentric curriculums and pedagogies not only interpret the human society as a part of the natural environment, but also try to build a new model of sustainable civilization which Simon Boxley (2022, p. 311) identifies as 'integral ecology.' The phenomenon of integral ecology challenges the capitalism-based social, cultural and economic structures of knowledge production and makes us realize that economic and class relationships cannot be de-hierarchized without practicing ecological sustainability.

(c) <u>From degree-based scholarship to apprentice-based scholarship</u>: Besides re-locating and re-interpreting the human society within the natural environment and shifting the capital-centric education systems toward ecocentric education systems, green Marxist principles of teaching and learning also encourage apprentice-based scholarship over degree-based scholarship, where the ecologically sustainable practical applications of knowledges are valued more than restrictive and instrumental accreditations. As already discussed in the previous sections, within degree-based scholarships, accreditations are centrally designed to fetch jobs and don't guarantee the ecologically sustainable development of individuals. The sustainable development of the individuals can only be ensured through ecocentric apprentice-based scholarships. Unlike degree-based scholarships, the apprentice-based scholarships consider the values of both accreditations and praxis-based learning as equally important. The curriculums and pedagogies in the ecocentric educational institutions generate collective spaces for activist-scholarships by encouraging 'community-based research' and exposing the teachers and learners to 'different ways of knowing and observing the world' (de Wit et al., 2020, p. 333). Through collaborating with communities and the natural environment, the apprentice-based ecocentric pedagogies counter the Euromodern practice of granting legitimacy and authority to selective knowledge systems and make us realize that 'all "scholarly knowledge" is not our own: we simply, organize, filter, and renew knowledge that communities and activists already have' (ibid.).

Altogether, it is through green Marxist educational practices that the teachers and learners can 'liberate and reconcile with earth' and 'build a new sensibility towards life' (Kahn, 2010, p. 17). But, the practice of building ecocentric curriculums and pedagogies should not be restricted within a few educational institutions. It needs to be adopted across every educational institution in South Asia and the world so that the de-hierarchical cohabitation of the natural and the human civilizations can be essentialized, a richer set of connections with eco-systems and the non-human world can be developed, and socio-culturally diverse, economically inclusive and ecologically sustainable knowledges can be collectively produced, without relying on the manipulative policies of the self-profiting governing institutions.

The conversations in this chapter do not conclude here. They just briefly pause to contemplate, reorganize, diversify and continue till the planetary vision of building ecologically sustainable societies with the coexistence of the human communities and the natural environment is realized. In order to continue with the applications of green Marxist curriculums and pedagogies, it would be crucial to further explore how, besides building alternative educational institutions in India and other parts of South Asia, eco-pedagogical and eco-curricular practices of teaching and learning in open-air classrooms; learning different subjects through hands-on experiences in nature and reconfiguring socio-economic relationships and class structures on the basis of the functional patterns of the natural environment can be recovered, redeveloped and regularized within the mainstream educational institutions through teaching, learning, research, community development initiatives and infrastructural transformations.

Acknowledgments I would acknowledge the support of all the students and staffs at Yonphula Centenary College, Bhutan, without whose support and cooperation this project would not have taken any shape. I would also like to express my gratitude to the editors of this volume for curating this amazing project and making me a part of it.

Disclosure Statement The author has no financial interest or benefit that has arisen from the direct applications of this research.

Notes

1. In this chapter, the word 'colonialism' has been used together with 'capitalism' because, historically, the evolution of capitalism took place through the expropriative and appropriative activities of European colonialism. So, the paradigms of colonialism and capitalism are inseparable. Due to the same reason, the words 'capitalization' and 'de-capitalization' has been used together with 'colonization' and 'decolonization' respectively.
2. The city of Calcutta (now Kolkata) is located in the Indian state of West Bengal. The state of West Bengal is located in the eastern part of India.
3. By selective destruction of human communities and nature, I mean how specific racial groups, gendered communities and geographical locations have been destroyed by the capitalistic forces across the world.
4. The systemic marginalization of humanities and social sciences take place in the higher educational institutions through not providing sufficient financial aids to conduct research; not creating sufficient academic and research exchange programs with other institutions; and not acknowledging the scholarships that are produced by the students and the faculties.
5. The participants were selected through random sampling and their participation was based on interest and availability. The author only interviewed participants from India, because no participants from Bhutan, for various personal, ethical and official reasons, gave their consent to be interviewed.
6. Faridabad is a city which is located in the western Indian state of Haryana.

7. Kanpur is a city which is located in the northern Indian state of Uttar Pradesh.
8. The universities in the rural areas in India are constructed on natural forests and agricultural lands, which are mostly taken away from the farmers and indigenous communities by force (Bahuguna et al., 2016).
9. A social work organization based in the state of Uttar Pradesh in India. The organization was established in 1977 and is responsible for spreading eco-consciousness and for protecting the natural environment against human violation.
10. A state located in North India.

References

Architecture. (n.d.). *Earth Architecture: Handmade School in Bangladesh*. Retrieved August 10, 2022, from https://www.designboom.com/architecture/earth-architecture-handmade-school-bangladesh/

Bahuguna, K, Ramnath, M., Shrivastava, K. S., Mahapatra, R., Suchitra, M., & Chakravartty, A. (2016). *Indigenous People in India and the Web of Indifference*. Retrieved January 8, 2023, from https://www.downtoearth.org.in/coverage/governance/indigenous-people-in-india-and-the-web-of-indifference-55223

Bainbridge, A. (2020). Digging Our Own Grave: A Marxian Consideration of Formal Education as a Destructive Enterprise. *International Review of Education, 66*, 737–753.

Bell, K. (2015). Can the Capitalist Economic System Deliver Environmental Justice? *Environmental Research Letters, 10*(12). Retrieved August 2, 2022, from https://iopscience.iop.org/article/10.1088/1748-9326/10/12/125017

Benton, T. (2018). *What Karl Marx Has to Say About Today's Environmental Problems*. [online]. Retrieved July 31, 2022, from https://theconversation.com/what-karl-marx-has-to-say-about-todays-environmental-problems-97479

Bhowmick, N. (2011). *The Women of India's Barefoot College Bring Light to Remote Villages*. Retrieved August 8, 2022, from https://www.theguardian.com/global-development/2011/jun/24/india-barefoot-college-solar-power-training

Boslaugh, S. (2011). Anthropocentrism. In J. Newman & P. Robbins (Eds.), *Green Ethics and Philosophy: An A-to-Z Guide* (pp. 15–17). SAGE Publications.

Boxley, S. (2022). Green Marxism. In A. Maisuria (Ed.), *Encyclopaedia of Marxism and Education* (pp. 302–320). Leiden.

Brown, M. (2018). *Is There a Marxist Perspective on Education?* Retrieved January 8, 2023, from https://www.culturematters.org.uk/index.php/culture/education/item/2819-is-there-a-marxist-perspective-on-education

CGSP. (n.d.). *Clean Green School Programme*. Retrieved August 10, 2022, from https://www.wateraid.org/pk/clean-green-school-programme

Cordova, J. P. P., & Bailey, D. J. (2020). Decolonising Green Marxism: Capitalism, Decolonialism and Radical Environmental Politics. *Capital and Class, 45*(1), 3–9.

Daily, F. T. (2021). *Thomas Gall School, Sri Lanka's First Eco-School*. Retrieved August 10, 2022, from https://www.ft.lk/education/Thomas-Gall-School-Sri-Lanka-s-first-eco-school/10515-717324

de Wit, M. M., Shattuck, A., Iles, A., Graddy-Lovelace, G., Roman-Alcalá, A., & Chappell, M. J. (2020). Operating Principles for Collective Scholar-Activism: Early

Insights from the Agroecology Research-Action Collective. *Journal of Agriculture, Food Systems and Community Development, 10*(2), 319–337.

Dijk, A. V. (2015). *The Green Marx*. Retrieved January 9, 2023, from https://www.greeneuropeanjournal.eu/the-green-marx/

Drakpa, D., & Dorji, R. (2013). Green School for Green Bhutan: Relationship with Gross National Happiness in Chukha Dzongkhag. *Indo-Bhutan International Conference Proceedings On Gross National Happiness, 2*, 314–324.

Fanon, F. (1963). *The Wretched of the Earth*. Grove Press.

Foster, J. B. (1997). THE CRISIS OF THE EARTH: Marx's Theory of Ecological Sustainability as a Nature—Imposed Necessity for Human Production. *Organization and Environment, 10*(3), 278–295.

Gruenewald, A. D. (2015). A Foucauldian Analysis of Environmental Education: Toward the Socioecological Challenge of the Earth Charter. *Curriculum Inquiry, 34*(1), 71–107.

Haraway, D. J. (2016). *Staying with the Trouble: Making Kin in the Chthulucene*. Duke University Press.

HT Correspondent. (2021). *Farmhouse Owners Get Notices for Illegal Construction on Aravalli Land*. [online]. Retrieved August 2, 2022, from https://www.hindustantimes.com/cities/gurugram-news/farmhouse-owners-get-notices-for-illegal-construction-on-aravalli-land-101614967206685.html

Kahn, R. (2010). *Critical Pedagogy, Ecoliteracy, and Planetary Crisis: The Ecopedagogy Movement*. Peter Lang.

Klees, S. (2017). Beyond Neoliberalism: Reflections on Capitalism and Education. *Policy Futures in Education, 18*(1), 9–29.

Lamsang, T. (2020). *Why ex-PM Dasho Tshering Tobgay Joined De-Suung and His Learnings From It*. [online]. Retrieved August 9, 2022, from https://thebhutanese.bt/why-ex-pm-dasho-tshering-tobgay-joined-de-suung-and-his-learnings-from-it/

Lawson, L. A., & Nguyen-Van, P. (2020). Is There a Peaceful Cohabitation Between Human and Natural Habitats? Assessing Global Patterns of Species Loss. *Global Ecology and Conservation, 23*, 1–20.

Lievens, M. (n.d.). *Towards an Eco-Marxism*. Retrieved August 8, 2022, from https://core.ac.uk/download/pdf/34477961.pdf

Marginson, S. (2004). A Revised Marxist Political Economy of National Education Markets. *Policy Futures in Education, 2*(3-4), 439–453.

Mbembe, A. (2016). Decolonizing the University: New Directions. *Arts and Humanities in Higher Education, 15*(1), 29–45.

Moog, S., & Stones, R. (2009). *Nature, Social Relations and Human Needs: Essays in Honour of Ted Benton*. Palgrave Macmillan.

Moore, J. W. (2017a). The Capitalocene, Part I: On the Nature and Origins of Our Ecological Crisis. *The Journal of Peasant Studies, 44*(3), 594–630.

Moore, J. W. (2017b). Metabolic Rift or Metabolic Shift? Dialectics, Nature, and the world-Historical Method. *Theory and Society, 46*, 285–318.

O'Brien, C. (2015). Sustainable Happiness: How Happiness Studies Can Contribute to a More Sustainable Future. *Canadian Psychology, 49*(4), 289–295.

O'Connor, J. (1998). *Natural Causes: Essays in Ecological Marxism*. Guilford.

Omvedt, G. (1984). Ecology and Social Movements. *Economic and Political Weekly, 19*(44), 1865–1867.

Participant A. (2022, July 22). Online Interview.

Participant B. (2022, July 22). Online Interview.

Pem, D. (2020). *Desuups in Service of the Nation*. [online]. Retrieved August 9, 2022, from https://thebhutanese.bt/desuups-in-service-of-the-nation/

Plumwood, V. (1993). *Feminism and the Mastery of Mastery of Nature*. Routledge.

Powdyel, T. S. (2014). *My Green School: An Outline for Human and Societal Flourishing*. Newsy Advertisement and Media.

Rajput, V. 2022. *Illegal Construction on Yamuna Floodplains: Farmers to Fast Unto Death in Protest*. Retrieved August 2, 2022, from https://www.hindustantimes.com/cities/noida-news/illegal-construction-on-yamuna-floodplains-farmers-to-fast-unto-death-in-protest-101648148903398.html

Rikowski, G. (2004). Marx and the Education of the Future. *Policy Futures in Education, 2*(3-4), 565–577.

Skordoulis, C. D. (2010). Critical Environmental Education with a Ecosocialist Vision. In A. S. Gkiolmas & C. D. Skordoulis (Eds.), *Towards Critical Environmental Education* (pp. 35–50). Springer.

Special Correspondent. (2021). *Faridabad to Demolish All Illegal Structures on PLPA Notified Land*. [online]. Retrieved August 2, 2022, from https://www.thehindu.com/news/cities/Delhi/faridabad-to-demolish-all-illegal-structures-on-plpa-notified-land/article35596961.ece

Thompson, K. (2015). *The Marxist Perspective in Education*. Retrieved January 8, 2023, from https://revisesociology.com/2015/01/27/marxist-perspective-education/

Trisos, C. H., Auerbach, J., & Katti, M. (2021). Decoloniality and Anti-oppressive Practices for a More Ethical Ecology. *Nature Ecology and Evolution, 5*, 1205–1212.

Veinovic, Z. P., & Stanisic, J. M. (2018). From Anthropocentrism to Eocentrism in Teaching Science and Social Studies. *Иновације у настави, XXXI*(4), 15–30.

Wangchuk, K. (2022). *1631 Desuups Complete Training*. [online]. Retrieved August 9, 2022, from https://kuenselonline.com/1631-desuups-complete-training/

Westra, R. (2007). *Green* Marxism and the Institutional Structure of a Global Socialist Future. In R. Albritton et al. (Eds.), *Political Economy and Global Capitalism: The 21st Century, Present and Future* (pp. 219–236). Anthem Press.

Wildlife Conservation Nepal. (2021). *Eco-Smart School Program*. Retrieved August 10, 2022, from https://wcn.org.np/what-we-do/1-ecosmart-school-program/18/

Wilson, R. S. (2022). Introduction: Worlding Asia Pacific into Oceania—Worlding Concepts, Tactics, and Transfigurations against the Anthropocene. In S. S. Chou et al. (Eds.), *Geo-Spatiality in Asian and Oceanic Literature and Culture: Worlding Asia in the Anthropocene* (Ithaca: Cornell University Press) (Vol. 2022, pp. 1–31).

CHAPTER 19

Indian Problem to Indian Solution: Using a Racio-Marxist Lens to Expose the Invisible War in Education

Linda Orie

19.1 Introduction

Yellow, pink, pink, yellow, pink, yellow, green, yellow, pink, green, pink, pink, more pink. No blue, not one single blue. Frustrated, I put down my multi-tipped highlighter as Einstein's famous definition of insanity came to mind. I refilled my coffee and prepared myself for yet another student data team meeting where we would discuss how 'low' our kids are, throw our hands up in the air, and swap stories about how nothing worked to motivate our yellows and pinks, those kids who stubbornly scored 'basic' or 'minimal' on standardized measures of academic achievement. Save the few, green 'proficient' students and occasional blue, 'advanced' student, coded data sheets year after year revealed a depressing picture of yellows and pinks at data meetings. These felt more like pity parties where predominantly white teachers and administrators banged their heads against the cold, white, cinderblock walls of the tribal school. Sick to my stomach, I attended the meetings hoping someday the conversation would shift from all the things most of our students lacked to the invisible assets and talents they possessed—it never did.

American Indian (AI) public school students' racially disproportionate academic and social-educational performance, objectified and commodified as

L. Orie (✉)
University of Wisconsin-Madison, Madison, WI, USA
e-mail: orie@wisc.edu

© The Editor(s) (if applicable) and The Author(s), under exclusive license to Springer Nature Switzerland AG 2023
R. Hall et al. (eds.), *The Palgrave International Handbook of Marxism and Education*, Marxism and Education,
https://doi.org/10.1007/978-3-031-37252-0_19

grades, standardized test scores, and behavioral records, act as dehumanizing measures that consistently devalue these students as a racialized, classized group. This legacy of the settler-colonial school system has created systems of flat representation, devoid of AI students' historical and cultural struggles toward educational sovereignty, within schools' predominantly white, middle-class, assimilation-based academic and social norms. Traditional public school methods of ranking students by grade point average, comparing academic success of AI students with white students, and judging AI students' behavior against white norms have produced persistent patterns of racial disproportionality which are often seen as individual/family/community deficits, and not artifacts of historical hegemony and forced assimilation. This chapter examines how education for AI (also referred to as Indigenous) youth remains a problem in the eyes of dominant educators perpetuating cycles of failure and deficit-based outcomes using standardized measures compared to white, middle-class performance. After providing historical context from the Indian boarding school era, this chapter will explore mechanisms of racialized perceptions that lead to devaluation of Black and Brown youth in schools, a legacy of settler-colonial education.

19.2 Assimilation: The Indian Problem Then Is the Indian Problem Now

Before its inception, the United States has grappled with its 'Indian Problem,' dealing with multitudes of Indigenous Peoples living throughout 'wild' places eyed by European missionaries, colonists, and, later, settlers. Considering white men's insatiable greed for land, resources, minerals, and other bounties on Indigenous lands, leaders like Carl Schurz advanced assimilation into individualistic, capitalist American ways of life as the answer for all Indians. 'The circumstances surrounding them place before the Indians this stern alternative: extermination or civilization,' asserts Schurz (1881, p. 7), who asks the perennial white man's question, 'Can Indians be civilized?' (ibid.).

As Indian boarding schools continued their missions, following General Richard Henry Pratt's dictum to 'Kill the Indian, save the man' (Pratt, 2003) at the turn of the twentieth century, official government reports contained testimony of Indian agents and others tasked with oversight of the education of Indigenous children from a multitude of tribal nations across the United States. Initially funded by monies from the US War Department, Indian boarding and residential schools acted as ideological arms of the US war machine, deploying weapons like Bibles, paper and pencil, and chalk and blackboards in the hands of teachers tasked with the daunting goal of assimilating Indian children into respectable, clean, hard-working, and moral Christian adults.

In the 1903 Report of the Superintendent of Indian Schools, the question arises, 'Is there an Indian problem? If so, what is it, why is it, and where is it?' E.T. Hamer, industrial teacher from Siletz, Oregon answers, 'I would say the problem is to make the Indians, as individuals and as a race, self-supporting, self-respecting and respectable citizens ... he should be removed from a state of dependence to one of independence' (Miller, 1903, p. 36).

Leaders of Indian Education used a strategic plan not only to educate the Indians in reading, writing, and arithmetic, but also endeavored to make individual property owners out of collectivist tribal peoples who had no concept of personal ownership prior to European contact. With the overarching goal of civilizing the Indian into an economically successful property owner who could earn a living independent of government subsidies, the curriculum of Indian schools focused on teaching trades and domestic skills. Like Pratt envisioned decades prior, Indian children learned trades and useful domestic skills to prepare them for a distinctly American industrial and agricultural future. In the 1903 Report of the Superintendent of Indian Schools, W.P. Campbell, assistant superintendent of Salem School in Chemawa, Oregon, asserts:

> To train the head and heart and not the hand is to stop short of the best success and the product is a useless citizen. The industrial education idea is growing and will soon take its proper place in the front ranks ... and our large schools should be stepping-stones for the students into the body politic. (ibid.)

Superintendent of the Indian school at Chilocco, Oklahoma, S.M. M'Cowan reminds the Lake Mohonk Conference (1905, p. 72) that all this benevolent schooling comes at a high cost to the US government, and spending too much money on the Indians has not made them into what the whites expected:

> Our pernicious, wicked kindness is worse, ten thousand times more harmful than others' harshness. The old, uneducated Indian will not accept our civilization, just as the Chinaman will not. It is foolish, absurd, to think he will. For 400 years we have done our best to absorb him without educating him, yet he is no more one of us today in thought, hopes and ambition than the caged wolf who eats from our hand, but would burrow in his native wilds snarling in glee if he could.

M'Cowan and others, dissatisfied with Indians' lack of becoming appropriately absorbed, even after all the time, money, and efforts by whites to Christianize, school, and thereby change them from collectivist hunter/gatherers into individual landowners/farmers, viewed these investments as wasteful, directly connecting the lack of expected results with inherent defects and unwillingness of Indians to change.

Assimilation into the melting pot of America was, and still is, the White Answer to the Indian Problem. Then and now, assimilation remains the main goal, with compulsory education and mainstream American culture/media the dominant ideological forces threatening Indigenous youth today. As long as American public education measures and compares Indigenous youth's school performance using white standards administered in settler-colonial-white supremacist-capitalist (SCWSC) mainstream frames of perception, Indians will always be a problem and whites with their capitalist ways of life, self-ordained as solutions.

19.3 Looking at the Indian Problem Through Critical Race and Marxist Lenses

Ray (2019), paraphrasing Marx (1867/2004), defines 'race not as a thing but as a relationship between persons mediated through things. This definition of race eschews biological essentialism and highlights that race is constructed relationally via the distribution of social, psychological, and material resources' (ibid., pp. 29–30). Using concepts within Critical Race and Marxist theories, I now attempt to address the Indian Problem by shifting readers' focus to the colonial-capitalist, inherently classist and racist roots of our current public education model, which delimits, reduces, objectifies, and commodifies student performance into quantitative measures compared always to white, middle-class norms. The master-cycle of alienation inherent within capitalistic systems of production, examined in Marx's (1844) *Economic and Philosophic Manuscripts of 1844*, can be applied to modern American schools as sites of capitalist production.

Marx's explanation of various forms of alienation within capitalist production, along with examination of use versus exchange value and fetishism of commodities in *Capital Volume One, Part One: Commodities and Money* (1867/2004), illuminates how objectifying and commodifying non-white academic and social performance in schools reifies non-white subjugation. I argue that this systemic practice is so ingrained in American educational institutions, it is invisible, ubiquitous, and for those reasons *the* most pervasive and insidious threat to AI and other minoritized students' humanity and survival. As the losers of the public education game, AI students' lower scores predictably contrast their white peers' success, reifying and recreating systems of alienation of students furthest from white ideals.

According to Marx (1867/2004), alienation marks capitalist production in several ways as workers are forced to create products that estrange their humanity from their labor, as both their labor and the products of their labor are controlled and manipulated by others. Bourgeoisie controllers of capitalist production determine what is produced, as well as the conditions of production including where, when, and how the proletariat expend their labor. Synthesizing human labor with natural materials, the why of production revolves around capitalistic profit, leading to erasure (through alienation) of the individual workers' human identities and lives whose labor made production possible. In the factory model of schooling, all students' labor is similarly externalized, objectified, and alienated from them, as their academic and social performance become commodities. However, the predictable bifurcation of human experience within alienating capitalist systems cleaves along class lines. In *The Holy Family*, Marx and Engels (1845) describe:

> The propertied class and the class of the proletariat present the same human self-estrangement. But the former class feels at ease and strengthened in this self-estrangement, it recognizes estrangement as *its own power* and has in it the

semblance of a human existence. The class of the proletariat feels annihilated in estrangement; it sees in it its own powerlessness and the reality of an inhuman existence.[1]

Moreover, as capitalist production yields commodities which are assigned objective values based on their exchange value: 'by equating their different products to each other in exchange as values, they equate their different kinds of labour as human labour. ... Value, transforms every product of labour into a social hieroglyphic' (Marx, 1867/2004, pp. 166–67) As teachers, administrators, parents and students decipher these social hieroglyphics, what do they find? The seemingly objective commodification of school performance in the form of standardized test scores, grades distributed along the bell curve, and behavioral reports all of which mask the underlying 'secret' (ibid.) of commodity fetishism—human labor's equivalence through abstraction.

To make the system of commodities' exchange values possible, differential human labor must become commensurable, assumed equivalent during the process of abstraction, alienated from not only the individual workers themselves, but also their particular social and material contexts. Standardized curricula and evaluation assume uniform human labor inputs, equivalency in abstraction through the objectification/commodification process, and historically determined social-material relations among laborers masquerade as simple exchange value. Thus, a student's labor in the learning factory of schooling is only valuable as a commodity, in relation to other commodities' relative values which the capitalist mode of production via commodification requires abstraction and assumed equivalence of human labor. The resulting valuations (or devaluations) of particular commodities obscure material, social, and historical inequities embedded within labor, manifesting as objective, quantifiable measures of students' aptitudes within the assimilatory system.

Aggregated white, middle-class students' scores (values) starkly contrast with non-white, underclass students' scores (values relative to whites' scores), reifying and normalizing settler-colonial, white supremacist hegemony as legitimate contemporary artifacts. SCWSC domination in schools and the larger economy requires subjugation of non-white Others' academic performance to perpetuate ideologies of relative value and differential investment in children, where 'the sky's the limit' for apt pupils while the less apt become fodder for the SCWSC war machine. AI students and other non-white Black and Brown youth are still fighting the war leveraged on their ancestors now, though this war has been made invisible through generations of reification within assimilatory systems of capitalist production in schools and the larger economy.

19.4 Racial Capitalism as a Conceptual Framework

Thinking about how racism in America operates like capitalism, with almost the same level of ubiquity and invisibility, helps foreground not only how pervasive and important it is to us all, but also how both systems operate from similar ideologies about the relationship between diverse people's humanity and the naturalized socioeconomic world. Robinson (2020) uses the term 'racial capitalism' to refer to the development of racism's permeation of social structures emergent from capitalism. Integrating a racial lens with Marxism helps reveal the inner workings of the normalized functions of human devaluation, in both economic and social organization.

Devaluation of entire racialized groups' humanity requires social stratification, wherein those at the bottom are valued according to what they can potentially produce within existing or emerging industries. Marx's (1867/2004, p. 291) description of capitalist production describes how human lives (time, energy, labor) participating in capitalist systems become, or manifest, into capital via the production of surplus-value through extraction of surplus-labor and 'the subordination of labour to capital.'

By exploring the connection between this transformation and subordination of labor to capital and its racially and socioeconomically disproportionate effects via manipulation by powerful agents of capitalism, one may see that the racism system works like our capitalist system. These intertwined systems directly manifest patterns of production and consumption in which certain demographic groups, whose humanity has been devalued, provide a constant supply of cheap labor. This aids in production of more and more capital, benefiting the powerful agents who control these cycles. Moreover, I argue that these same certain demographic groups, who not only spend a substantial portion of their lives producing capital, also experience/produce (in both bodies and minds) disproportionate amounts of human suffering, disease, dysfunction, and strife. These have also become lucrative sites for capitalist profit in our modern information age. Capital's birth becomes humanity's death as the vampires direct and control production: 'Capital is dead labour, that vampire-like, only lives by sucking living labour' (Marx, 1867/2004, p. 342). As a means of producing more and more capital and profit, producing increasing numbers and appetites of consumers to buy goods and services is also a main goal, feeding the system from the other end, via consumption.

Racial capitalist processes begin early in our experiences with the social world, where we learn our places and value to society through the institution of schooling. This chapter attempts to uncover the inner mechanisms of what the author calls the Invisible War Machine, which is driven by dehumanizing processes perpetuated by dominating SCWSC frames of perception which objectify and commodify youth's school performance into standardized, comparative measures. This three-dimensional (3D) to two-dimensional (2D) representation and comparative value to idealized models of white behavior and academic achievement in schools perpetuates cycles of Black and Brown children's failure, continuing deficit and need-based approaches that reify normalized white supremacist structures and ideology. Racialized, non-white, Othered children's subordinate outcomes to those of middle-class, white peers lead to inequitable socioeconomic opportunities and assure a large, undereducated population ready for vampiric exploitation by Capital. American schooling's predictable racialized and classized achievement gap inequalities and other social inequalities are explained and justified by social scientists' applying the SCWSC gaze—placing dysfunction in individuals and cultures, rather than racialized, capitalist systems.

19.5 Making the Invisible War Machine Visible

Bonilla-Silva and Zuberi (2008) use the terms *white logic* and *white methods* to describe how the physical and social sciences have actively helped create racial stratification as a scientifically legitimate and socially acceptable concept, helping create and justify racialized outcomes and experiences using the self-endowed power of human objectivity. This power of assumed objectivity and the power of objectification of everything entering its perceptual field have historically been controlled by white capitalists, who use this god-like perspective to control the production of knowledge as well as cycles of production and consumption of goods and services. The *white racial frame* as described by Feagin (2020) similarly theorizes how the same white logic and methods called out by Bonilla-Silva and Zuberi (2008), and James (2008), reveal how white supremacist, dominant perspectives operate under the assumption that their perceptions, evaluations, and explanations are purely objective. This is then presented as the most correct and justified conclusion about the nature of the unjust relationship between whites and non-white Others. Feagin's (2020) concept of the white (supremacist) racial frame illustrates how human perception by powerful elites self-justifies as it produces and exploits patterns of human suffering, war, environmental degradation, cultural and genetic erasure, and other hegemonic effects that become normalized and accepted as part of everyday life.

The biological and social evolutionary paradigm provided the intellectual and scientific basis for colonial thought, as Seth (2009, p. 374) explains: 'The racialised practices of colonial administration … drew heavily on the content and status of Darwinian biology and natural history. The history of almost all modern science, it has become clear, must be understood as "science in a colonial context".' If science was the means of colonial investigation into the Other resulting in recommendations for action, the ends was the overarching civilizing mission. Seth (ibid.) asserts:

> As part of the civilising mission, science played two contradictory roles in colonial discourse, at once making clear to the 'natives' the kind of knowledge that they lacked (which omission justified colonialism itself) and holding out the hope that such knowledge could be theirs.

This cruel and ironic contradiction within science as both colonizer and teacher of Indigenous Peoples can be seen as the tremendous effect of the power placed on what counted as knowledge. Colonial authorities counted their own epistemologies, cultures, languages, religions, and ways of being as exemplars of the highest forms of human civilization on Earth, and all Other (non-white/non-European) epistemologies were subjugated, trivialized, and dismissed. As indicated by Said (1978, p. 7), 'the major component in European culture is precisely what made that culture hegemonic both in and outside Europe: the idea of European identity as a superior one in comparison with all the non-European peoples and cultures.'

The invisible war over educating our children has been centuries-long struggle to maintain our full humanity in the eyes of powerful whites bent on assimilating racialized Others. Omi and Winant (2014) point to the connection between race-making and Othering, which is a process not solely based on racial distinctions. Along with race, other perceived distinctions like gender, class, religion, age, sexuality, among others 'are frequently evoked to justify structures of inequality, differential treatment, subordinate status, and in some cases violent conflict and war' (ibid., p. 105). The invisible war over Indigenous education is so old, omnipresent, and tireless, it has become unquestioned and embraced as normal. To help deal with the psychological trauma of uncovering the invisible war, it is helpful to separate the dehumanizing, evil effects powerful European elites have created and perpetuated on others through their colonial-capitalist ideologies, by theorizing colonial power as a machine (Mitchell, 1991).

Through considering the power, physical and ideological control which colonial agents wielded on Indigenous Peoples through countless generations evokes a timeless, ubiquitous, terrible machine that is everywhere and nowhere at the same time. Since the dawn of the spirit and embodied actions of colonialism and capitalism, necessary ideological developments that led to those belief structures and their quasi-omnipresent reign required Europeans to elevate their humanity in order to subjugate Others. Harris (2020, pp. 2–3) points out:

> Power organizes hierarchies. Inequality is not the product of dysfunctional culture, or the biology—the 'comorbidities'—of misbehaving, undisciplined bodies: rather, racial regimes construct and exploit vulnerabilities. These are preexisting conditions, embodiments, material manifestations of exploitation. This is a feature of racial capitalism.

19.6 Who's Looking? War Machine's Gaze Devalues and Dehumanizes the Other

Separating single human lives or identities from SCWSC ideologies and actions leads us to imagine the SCWSC machine as subject with gigantic eyes of mirrors. Constantly reflecting everything using this comparative frame continuously creates and re-creates settler-colonial illusions of white supremacy. Through these illusions, no Other can possibly be 'better' than any white settler, on any dimension or aspect of life, without qualifying this brilliance using more settler-colonial fantasies (also based on white supremacist ideology). The concept of 'better' itself remains one of the most foundational ideological constructs of the SCWSC gaze, arranging objectified human beings along an increasingly dehuman continuum of value, based on their social and material worth to the colonial-capitalist machine. As Foster et al. (2020) point out, 'Marx invariably saw such indigenous and noncapitalist societies as reflective of a long struggle for free human development, one which included the fight for survival of indigenous societies and control over their own lands and lives.'

Repeatedly creating the object of the Indian and Indian Problem within the SCWSC ideological-perceptual lens (with evaluation as its iris, contracting and relaxing to let varying, selected amounts and types of information in) is inherently comparative to itself only. Set up using racial/class/religious/other sociocultural categorical comparisons as its framework, the SCWSC lens yields subjects' creations of Indigenous (and other non-white) dehumanized objects as reflections of the SCWSC gaze. These reflections reify settler-colonial, capitalist conquest of Indigenous Peoples through objectification and commodification of learning within the standardized curricula and measurement inherent in modern American education systems. As the factory model of schooling perpetuates differentially valued products, Marxian analysis points to the importance of examining the fetishism of commodities, which originates in 'the peculiar social character of the labour that produces them' (Marx, 1867/2004, p. 165).

As a composite of the a-historical, a-material, alienated human labor of learning, commodities like grades and test scores produced within standardized measures assume equality of material conditions and social relations among producers, masking the inherent inequality on which normative white success has been made possible in the United States. As commodification demands this assumption of commensurability and thus equality of human labor within exchange value actions, US schools devalue and dehumanize non-white students by assessing their learning using standardized, white-normed measures. American Indian and other non-white students' efforts toward this assimilationist model of learning (objectified and commodified as low grades and test scores) provide educators operating within the SCWSC mindset evidence of Indigenous Peoples' subjugation, conquest, inferiority, and less-human nature, perpetuating the cycle of non-white failure and justification for low investment in non-white communities. This flattening, decontextualizing, and ahistoricizing function of the SCWSC machine, driven and controlled by the SCWSC gaze, posits deficits among racialized children as inherently intrinsic, rather than socially/historically constructed by colonial-capitalist forces.

Hundreds of years of colonization and domination by those beholden to this gaze have created a perceptual filter, a way of looking at the world and human interaction with Others and the environment through white supremacist, imperialistic assumptions. This filter created by the SCWSC lens has established a ubiquitous blind spot that is so old, so powerful, and so accepted by the mainstream that it often goes unnoticed and unquestioned.

19.7 Functions of the SCWSC Machine

For the SCWSC gaze to maintain its power, direction, and control over subjects' perceptual frame, obsequious lookers are required to devalue and dehumanize Others to maintain their ideological and material hegemony. Subjects' use of microaggressions, biases, and other semi-conscious actions helps reveal the sometimes-veiled system of white supremacy/colonial power always operating in the background of US settler-colonial (public) schools. Teachers of Indian children, hypnotized by the SCWSC gaze and acting within this perceptual frame, unknowingly (or sometimes knowingly) do violence, create harm, perpetuate false imprisonment, abuse, neglect, dehumanization, and other crimes against body, mind, and spirit. These most often go unnoticed, unacknowledged, and are therefore made invisible within the SCWSC school system. Indian children a hundred years ago and today live the first part of their lives greatly affected by public schooling, under the gaze of an almost exclusively white teaching force.

Through standardized curricula written from the SCWSC ideological frame, imperialist notions of Manifest Destiny and justified colonial exploitation and continual vampiric sucking of life from labor reify the failure of AI and other Black and Brown people in assimilatory education systems. Here, learning factories' reliable creation of non-white deviance and academic failure in the form of 2D, commodified grades, test scores, behavior reports (all compared to white 'peers') serve a planned, two-fold purpose. First, filling in the lower rungs on standardized measures and bell curves, this reifies, contrasts, and provides comparative 'evidence' of white and middle-class success, advancing the privileged few at the expense of the faceless many. Second, this faceless mass of youth, whose humanity has been devalued, objectified, and exchanged as a commodity, become prepared for economic and social exploitation. As Marx (1867/2004) describes the fetishism that demands the illusion of equality of labor among workers, objectification and commodification of youth's school performance flattens hundreds of years of SCWSC exploitation into reified codes where the predictable many are headed to feed capital and the conditions of production of future capital.

Worse, this dehumanizing, alienating cycle of recreating SCWSC domination and hegemony has not only created the learning factory commodity system itself and perpetuated it by preserving the status quo; this systematic oppression has been internalized by many stakeholders in education. This leads to attitudes of learned helplessness and limiting Othered youth's academic and social potential. As Pratt and other architects of the first government schools for Indians envisioned and prepared AI people for lives of vocational, agricultural, or domestic work, today's schools largely ensure a ready 'surplus army' (Marx, 1867/2004)[2] of workers and prisoners to feed the SCWSC war machine, growing capital at the expense of entire lineages and ethnic groups, social classes whose ancestors' labor, land, and lives themselves built this nation.

Conceptualizing how the often-invisible control mechanism works in the SCWSC gaze helps us to think about Indian children in early US boarding schools and today's Black and Indigenous/Brown minoritized Others. Then and now, as youth attend schools, they are being forcibly put into a world *behind the mirror*, where settler-colonialism, white supremacy, and capitalism form the ideological frame. The mirror itself forms the eyes of the ubiquitous machine that evaluates our children, consumes our hopes, fuels our fears, desires, appetites, and choices—manipulating and controlling us by producing illusions. Those in power maintain control over us by controlling these illusions, projections, and reflections of white supremacy and evaluative hegemony, which hypnotize us into thinking all we are and deserve are the lookist labels we find in the eyes of the SCWSC machine. As a function of this perceptual filter formed by white supremacist, capitalist ideology, non-white Others face lookism. This is a mode of prejudice or discrimination grounded in physical appearance measured against societal ideals of beauty, activated simply by attending public schools and interacting with whites. All minoritized Others are automatically positioned as less-than, simply by being forced to see themselves in the SCWSC mirror; always being forced to compare ourselves to imagined, idealized notions of white success, goodness, beauty, and ways of being and representing knowledge.

19.8 War Over White Control of Cycles of Production and Consumption

Each time the Indian is recreated as an object of white settler intervention and control, comparative frames mask their inherently inequitable histories and historically accumulated experiences by objectifying learning and academic success as measurable commodities. Actions within the public education system, like standardizing and commodifying artifacts of learning, enact the motives and intention of the SCWSC ideologies influencing settlers' choices and proclivities. This includes their designs for and evaluations of planned progress in assimilating the Indian into white, middle-class norms by controlling what students can produce and consume within school walls. Is this reification of SCWSC dominance not also true today? Students who are successful at participating in settler-colonial schools and meeting SCWSC expectations for academic achievement and social acceptance (privileged reflections of whiteness) become somehow commensurable with racialized, minoritized Others within the commodity fetishism produced by capitalist production. Multiple facets of compulsory, government-funded schooling including top-down governance through funding, regulation, and maintenance of material (i.e., curricula, disciplinary protocols) and social structures alienate those furthest from white ideals, and dissolve minoritized people's agency within assimilatory systems.

Marxian analysis is helpful to uncover capitalist assumptions of the commensurability and homogeneity of human labor as workers create commodities for exchange (Marx, 1867/2004). Marx's (1875/1970) critique of the 'bourgeois right,' or concept of 'equal right' based upon standardized measures invented and wielded in capitalist modes of production, may be applied to dominant systems of education wherein the social relations of students' labor appear as relations among its products/commodities (i.e., standardized test scores, grades along a bell curve). Debunking notions of equal right connect to their correlates within SCWSC schools—the illusions that human learning outcomes are objective reflections of the same, equivalent human labor and interactions within the system. Differential exchange value resulting from commodity fetishism reifies settler-colonial domination by masquerading as evidence of the inherent defects of racialized, minoritized Others.

Evaluations reviewed throughout the primary sources (Annual Report of the Commissioner of Indian Affairs to the Secretary of the Interior, 1908; Lake Mohonk Conference of Friends of the Indian and Other Dependent Peoples, 1905; Miller, 1903) gave anecdotal and general accounts of the overall functioning of Indian schools, and tables enumerated attendance, financial expenditures, personnel data, and other material facts. Projects to be undertaken and challenges encountered were occasionally described, but details about individual students' achievements were not included in these broad government reports. Every section of primary sources reviewed for this chapter only included whites' perspectives; Indigenous voices did not populate the assessments nor inform the experience of the human objects of the Indian school system. This one-sided representation overwhelmingly present in these primary sources should be explored in contemporary public schools—are student, family, and community perspectives included in government or school reports?

Indigenous Peoples' conspicuous authorial absence from these reports demonstrates their lack of administrative control and evaluative powers within early government schools, yet AI youth's deviance from white norms and racialized difference are continually foregrounded in deficit language. Largely, this is still true today as AI and other Black and Brown youth continually are described in terms of what they are not. The floating target of normative white academic and behavioral success reliably produces patterns of failure among minoritized youth, as their assimilation is always unfinished under the SCWSC gaze. Black and Brown students' failure and alienation from academic success should be considered as a reliable byproduct of the larger settler-colonial-capitalist system that ensures minoritized people's socioeconomic status remain below that of whites, and is not simply just a measure of their deficits. Marx (1867/2004, pp. 782, 784) points to capitalist accumulation's production of 'a relatively redundant population of labourers ... a surplus population,' as a 'disposable industrial reserve army, that belongs to capital ... [and] creates ... a mass of human material always ready for exploitation.'

As capitalist societies like the United States require an abundance of cheap labor in the form of a less-educated underclass, it also requires this same underclass to fuel consumption such that our bodies and minds become productive sites of suffering ready for capitalist profit. For example, avoidable health problems like diabetes, heart disease, substance abuse, and cancer disproportionately affect AIs and correlate with lower levels of education and lower socioeconomic status. In a sense, we are the cattle that feed the capitalist machine through forced control of cycles of production and consumption, beginning with objectification of our youth in public schools, and ending with shorter lifespans marked by physical and mental suffering as we are fed upon by ubiquitous, unseen capitalist forces.

Invoking a Marxian analysis of the four manifestations of alienation (Hall, 2018; Marx, 1844), not in industrial factories producing goods, but in historical and modern learning factories of assimilatory, standardized education, foregrounds its productive and ideological value to the capitalist machine. First, through severing control, agency, and connections among academic products produced directly by students and as entire communities and ethnic groups, students are alienated from the things they create within the system. Standardized curricula, evaluative systems, behavioral reports, attendance records, participation in extracurricular activities, and other easily comparable and exchangeable, societal markers of value and potential value control stakeholders' perception of minoritized students' performance and place in the larger system. The fetishism of these commodities erases the inherent inequality necessary to uphold the system, requiring illusions of commensurability as a sense-making presupposition. Through forced participation in government schools, these commodified products of AI and other Black and Brown youth reify white dominance, myths of meritocracy, and continued underfunding and devaluation of minoritized students' full humanity.

Second, as AI students are schooled through SCWSC institutions, they are also alienated from their bodies, minds, spirits, cultures, and communities as they are forced to reproduce what is expected by the curricula and standards. With little to no control over educational structures, direction of learning, culturally congruent approaches to communicating information and learning from others, AI and other minoritized students are alienated from the learning process itself. Third, this leads to low effort, expectations, interest, motivation, growth, and other important factors of school success, and as such they are also alienated from each other and differing demographic groups in many ways. Tribal people with rich interconnections to extended families, clans, and the natural world are forced to become individuals and individualistic, to compete with peers and strive to be the 'best' by assimilating into white, middle-class values that undergird school culture. Teachers stuck in the SCWSC perceptual frame cannot see these rich, complicated connections and do not bring them into the learning endeavor, rendering them invisible or absent, and leaving deficits the only intelligible explanation for AI failure. These 'social hieroglyphics,' as predictably decoded by educators, simultaneously inscribe non-white, non-middle-class failure and SCWSC success, and are then exchanged as differing forms of value for different social and racial groups.

Fourth, Black and Brown youth's deficits, commodified as standardized measures of achievement and social success (markers of assimilation and control), alienate these Othered youth from what Marx called their 'species-being' (Marx, 1844). Uniting, and thereby affirming the inherent worth of different racial groups' humanity under the biological designation of one species, our use of Marxian analysis points out the severing of connections of all workers to the natural world, the original and ultimate source of survival prior (and subsequent?) to capitalism's reign. Perhaps the case of Indigenous youth most immediately illustrates this last form of alienation in the current era, as standardized curricula immediately conflict with the home and community cultures, ways of being, values, and epistemologies carried by these youth and under constant threat in dominant institutions of schooling.

19.9 Indigenous Strategies for Decolonialization of Public Schools

Foregrounding Relationships

Prashad (2022) concludes, 'Decolonial thought … cannot go beyond post-Marxism, failing to see the necessity of decolonizing the conditions of social production,' which is prerequisite to decolonizing the mind. This prioritizing of transformations in 'the conditions of social production that reinforce the colonial mentality' (ibid.) in capitalist systems can be approached using shifts toward decolonizing perspectives from Indigenous lenses, which privilege relationships grounded in reciprocity among concepts, people, things, and places over the concepts, people, things, and places themselves (Kimmerer, 2013). Those intent on contributing to decolonizing efforts must foreground relationships as a way of beginning to see and act in a different, future decolonized world. As a decolonial-ideological move against the inherent objectification our people have been subjected to since contact with Europeans, foregrounding and working on multiple relationships attempts to reconcile historical traumas and heal connections between groups and individuals across racial lines and all species of life. Indigenous Peoples' reciprocal relationships with land, mineral resources, other human beings, plants, animals, air, and water shared in a place for thousands of years still exist and must be honored and normalized, replacing SCWSC objectification and alienation in economic as well as educational contexts.

As Veracini (2017, p. 7) asserts, 'If settler colonialism is a mode of domination premised on a particular relationship, its undoing will be a relationship. This is not a metaphor. This is what happens after land is returned and substantive sovereignty is acknowledged.' If individualistic white settlers dominated and controlled aspects of the world to legitimize and disseminate colonization, then 'Decolonization will be a collective, indigenous-led endeavor' (ibid.). According to Veracini (ibid., pp. 2, 4), settler-colonial studies must 'focus on settlers and what they do in order to undo settler colonialism,' including settler-colonialists' logic of elimination, which 'remains the dialectical counterpart of indigenous sovereignty.' Turning Pratt's infamous quote around, Veracini (ibid., p. 10) proposes to metaphorically 'kill settlers' to 'save their humanity' aiming to 'turn the descendants of invaders, including their political descendants, into resources for decolonization.' Here, to save their humanity, Veracini's Pratt-like proposal posits settlers (who may be white or non-white) as the object of intervention; this key shift reverses settler-colonial logic. In the larger historical (present) assimilatory systems of settler-colonialism that held (hold) Indian removal as their main objective, Indigenous youth's presence posed (continues to be) a problem for settlers in general and settler-colonial (public) schools.

Settler-Colonial Replacement to Indigenous Futurity

According to Wolfe (2006, p. 388), settler-colonialism 'destroys to replace,' revealing white settlers' ultimate goal of finally being able to claim native status to the places in which they desire to reside. This includes, of course, full use and control rights over land, water, plants, animals, and other natural resources present in these places. Wolfe (2006, pp. 394, 390) asserts, 'Settler colonialism was foundational to modernity' and is 'a structure rather than an event.' Wolfe (ibid.) connects overt genocide via physical murder, and Indian removal by the US government of the eighteenth and nineteenth centuries, with government-run, Indian boarding schools that also sought to eliminate the Native through epistemic and cultural erasure. I further argue that the unfinished settler-colonial project of the Indian boarding schools continues to this day, inherently built into American public schools in myriad ways.

Tuck and Gaztambide-Fernández (2013, p. 73) theorize the settler-colonial *curricular project of replacement*, 'which aims to vanish Indigenous peoples and replace them with settlers, who see themselves as the rightful claimants to land, and indeed, as indigenous.' The unwavering desire of settlers to become the sole owners of Indigenous land requires severing original inhabitants' relationships to the land itself, and retelling history from white supremacist perspectives that justified invasion and conquest. Teaching history from the SCWSC perspective, inscribed through the curriculum and communicated by state-sanctioned agents, amounts to a larger pedagogic project on a societal scale. This biased and incomplete historical outline of how the United States came to be, the mainstay of the settler-colonial curricular project of replacement, is described as 'intent on relieving the inherent anxiety of settler dislocation from stolen land' (ibid., p. 78).

Conflict over Indigenous land and current and future control over associated resources must be recognized as the central concern in decolonial efforts. Revealing patterns of the omission of Indigenous perspectives within and control over school curricula and policy begins to address this conflict, and the largely invisible injustice that perpetuates Indigenous alienation in schools. It is important to critically examine the opportunity cost of educational hegemony and commodification by first recognizing and confronting the advance of

American public assimilatory education at the expense of marginalized communities' chosen approaches, forms, traditions, values, and place-based methods of education in reciprocity with the natural environment. Interdependently developed by Indigenous nations and self-sustaining social networks, long before colonizers created Indian boarding schools, parents' and communal rearing of children in Indigenous cultures endured and resisted total erasure by compulsory schooling. As decolonial efforts to reconceptualize, re-write, and populate the curricular representations of knowledge and accepted canons of study with Indigenous epistemologies and approaches, it becomes more difficult to disappear the Native. Those who claim to use decolonialism as an ideology or method must overcome their settler anxiety, and reconcile their own participation, first, in the settler-colonial curricular project of replacement, and second, in the dominant stance on settler futurity. According to Tuck and Gaztambide-Fernández (2013, p. 80), this:

> always indivisibly means the continued and complete eradication of the original inhabitants of contested land. Anything that seeks to recuperate and not interrupt settler colonialism, to reform the settlement and incorporate Indigenous peoples into the multicultural settler colonial nation state is fettered to settler futurity.

Focusing on how epistemic erasure is perpetuated and reified in standardized curricula and enacted through pedagogy based in SCWSC perspectives, settler-colonial projects of replacement are directed and materialized by dominant agents sanctioned to uphold and gatekeep academic achievement to preserve white privilege. Recognizing how success within assimilatory schooling systems amounts to portable 'Whiteness as property' (Harris, 1993, p. 1709) that reifies non-white, non-middle-class subordination in the propertyless races, the commodified nature of material learning artifacts exposes the disappearance and negative participation of marginalized Others within compulsory school systems. Hierarchical, stratified social reproduction created by schooling, along class and race lines requires reproduction of the conditions of capitalist production, namely, a surplus source of labor-power. This human experience in the space of alienation as undifferentiated and dehumanized surplus value, a mainstay of capitalist production, is also the space of settler futurity made possible by the settler-colonial project of replacement's vampiric 'sucking of living labor' (Marx, 1867/2004, p. 342) by capital.

Critically examining patterns of the effects of colonial power requires a unification and collapsing of the human experience of time. This is an Indigenous worldview and approach to life explained by Cusicanqui (2012, p. 96), as follows: 'The indigenous world does not conceive of history as linear; the past/future is contained in the present. The regression or progression, the repetition or overcoming of the past is at play in each conjecture and is dependent more on our acts than on our words.' Here lies the path out of the grasp of the SCWSC frame—what we *do* now (more so than what we say or write) creates our future, keeping in mind our past also informs our future. This reminds us that for Marx (1844), '[Socialism] proceeds from the *theoretically and practically sensuous consciousness* of man and of nature as the *essence*.' This move toward reviving the basis of human interaction with place and the multitude of plants, animals, and other beings advances transformation of social relations of production by combating capitalistic processes of alienation of man from his 'species-being' (ibid.).

Our reflection and action, coupled with democratic evaluation and sovereign control by those most oppressed by SCWSC ideology, will synthesize into place-based, decolonizing praxis. Cusicanqui (2012, p. 100) plainly asserts, 'There can be no discourse of decolonization, no theory of decolonization, without a decolonizing practice.' Action absent intentional, decolonizing practice and attempts toward decolonizing means and ends must drive real, material change as well as spiritual, ideological change that includes evidence of societal transformation from the perspectives of the abject, minoritized Others.

Tuck and Yang's (2012, p. 1) important reminder that 'Decolonization brings about the repatriation of Indigenous land and life; it is not a metaphor for other things we want to do to improve our societies and schools' makes a clear connection between the unchanging, ultimate settler-colonial goal of ridding desired lands from Indigenous Peoples, and modern settlers' desire to reconcile historical injustice. White and other settlers looking for a way out of the perennial Indian Problem hastily apply the term 'decolonization' metaphorically to name aspects about their approach, practice, method, or aspiration as educators, when their very presence in the place of potential Others (who come from the communities served by the school and mirror students' demographics) remains a problem from the Indigenous perspective. 'The desire to reconcile is just as relentless as the desire to disappear the Native; it is a desire to not have to deal with this (Indian) problem anymore' (Tuck & Yang, 2012, p. 9).

Browning the Curriculum and Rematriation

Using critical lenses, browning the curriculum as decolonizing praxis uncovers the settler-colonial foundations of American public education, by making connections between larger sociopolitical historical power relations and everyday people's lives. Through changing the object in curricula systems from assimilation to decolonization, browning curriculum opens the door to authentic, non-white cultural infusion within existing school curricula, alongside the invention of new, decolonial curricula. Tuck and Gaztambide-Fernández (2013, p. 84) explain the decolonizing function of 'browning' the curriculum: 'Browning highlights the present absences and invokes the ghosts of curriculum's past and futures, unsettling settler futurity.' Allowing time, energy, and curricular space to do this will require sweeping changes to how schools conceptualize curriculum and personnel-resource allocation.

An entire rethinking and restructuring of the localized manifestations of the approach and spirit of education and all its reflections of the SCWSC machine must be called out, to track the violence inherent in institutions of compulsory education which feed the capitalist war machine with our very lives. Challenging zero-sum game expectations grounded in competitive societal interactions moves us away from thinking and acting as if one group's futurity must come at the expense of many Others.' Can AI and other devalued Black and Brown youth ever be seen as more than what they never were, are not, and never can be, as demanded by the SCWSC gaze? Through overcoming our own species-alienation, by uncovering normalized, ubiquitous constraints perpetuated by the SCWSC gaze, we begin to revalue hitherto devalued human beings and their communities through reconnection and restoration of relationships across humans, environment, and collapsing of time.

Overturning centuries of SCWSC alienation via dehumanization through the commodity fetishism inherent in schooling must reveal the secret of the illusion that undergirds cycles of reification. Inequitable historical material experiences do not disappear by employing a standardized measure, driven by commodity fetishism. Instead, the exchange value differentially stamped on commodities reifies the social relations of production (Marx, 1867/2004). SCWSC control of cycles of production of evaluative measures and 'evidence' of academic success create the necessary conditions of production for the next generation. This perpetuates the forced consumption of the material and social-ideological curriculum of the institution and reifies white, middle-class hegemony.

After breaking illusions generated by SCWSC frames of perception, standardized measures' power to commodify and compare minoritized youth is exposed. AI and other minoritized youth begin to regain full humanity as they step from behind the mirror, empowered to control their own futurity as agentic creators. Though we may remain haunted by settler-colonial ghosts while schools work through the decolonial transition, stubborn ghosts and the living who embody and act in the settler-colonial spirit will help future generations recognize, name, and finally rid public schools of minoritized children's SCWSC nightmare. Indigenous Peoples who bring previously undervalued, dismissed visions of education will create decolonial alternatives, previously precluded by their planned, conspicuous absence.

One key present absence in teacher education identified by McCoy and Villeneuve (2020) provides an example of the generative utility of browning as a decolonial strategy. The conspicuous absence of non-white teachers, administrators, and other educators in public schools today was not always so. Returning to the topic of early Indian schools, McCoy and Villeneuve (ibid.) use a historical-critical lens to describe seven stories from various Native American nations that illuminate how Indigenous People have repurposed schooling to advance Indigenous interests, since the 1830s. Surprisingly, by the turn of the century, hundreds of Indian teachers and teacher training programs existed: 'Between 1884 and 1909, the government hired 134 Indigenous people as industrial teachers, assistant teachers, and teachers in the six industrial board schools that had offered teaching departments, over half of which were women' (ibid., pp. 502–03). This important realization begs the question, if substantial numbers of Indigenous teachers were certified and employed in government schools over 100 years ago, why not today and what could the field gain by raising a new generation of Indigenous educators?

Accompanying a flood of changes that will ensue after the door to decolonizing praxis opens, increasingly diverse hands will take the wheel of the curricular vehicle through a process Eve Tuck (2011) calls 'rematriation.' According to Tuck (ibid., p. 37), 'A rematriation of curriculum studies is concerned with the redistribution of power, knowledge, and place, and the dismantling of settler colonialism.' Tuck and Gaztambide-Fernández (2013, p. 84) describe rematriation's focus: 'it, by design, aims to undercut and undermine the legacy of settler colonialism in curriculum.' To do this, employing the reversal tactic is essential for replacing paternalistic precedent and unsettling the foundations of settler-colonialism. By employing the relational, ecological lens of rematriation in place of the objectifying, instrumental lens of the patriarchal SCWSC gaze, alienation is overcome through a return to relationships and human revaluation through unity and redistribution of power and control of knowledge production. As Indigenous worldviews and cultures gain presence and change educational systems' structures and approaches to learning, relationships become foregrounded and people with diverse epistemologies gain power.

Given our global, crisis-level challenges shared in the present time, an ecological approach reversing SCWSC tactics and assumptions has the potential to transform the curriculum and schooling for all. When Othered, silenced, overlooked and denied perspectives are affirmed and included, given leadership and design power, minoritized people wield real, material, and ideological power, advancing their important roles in humanity's 'survivance' (Vizenor, 2008). They are encouraged to not only bring their unique ideas and new approaches in problem-solving to public schools, but to lead with the wealth of human technology they bring, revolutionizing teaching and learning. In the decolonial era, they will light the path forward we will walk together.

Centralizing the Perceptual Shift: 2D Illusions to 3D Realities

Before decolonization efforts can be realized, educators and researchers must first reflect upon their own perceptions to be able to see how they have been controlled by the SCWSC machine's gaze. In attempts to shift the illusion of individualized Indigenous failure to system failure, I insist readers must first shift reflections from the SCWSC mirror to consider Indigenous Peoples' lived realities as entire worlds behind (and controlled by) the mirror. Only then will decolonizing approaches be able to change the way educators see Indigenous students' current performance and future trajectories. Decolonial perspectives demand data be seen and acted upon from Indigenous perspectives, flipping school power orientations of evaluation, control, and design, from using strictly SCWSC ideologies to realizing decolonial and anti-colonial ideologies.

To make the flipping action possible, I recommend an unsettling of familiar beliefs and expectations using an exercise with a mirror. Look closely into a mirror and wave with your right hand, noticing the image that appears in the mirror is waving with its left hand. In regular household (planar) mirrors, the images ever-created and re-created are distortions of reality, reflecting light against material objects in such a way that flips each image/perception from front to back—the image you see in the mirror is not exactly the same as a camera or person 'sees,' but its mirror opposite. That image, as a 2D reproduction of you, looks like it is waving with the same hand you are because you are moving your right hand and the 2D image's hand is moving also on the right side of the mirror. However, if this image-person was real, living in three dimensions, looking at you somehow, from behind the mirror, s/he/they is/are waving at you with her/his/their left hand—proof that the 2D image is not you and the virtual image is an illusion.

Seeing that now-strange, mirror-image replica of yourself in the mirror, waving to you with its opposite hand, helps call attention to the importance of seeing images/representations of ourselves, our actions, and ideologies always as reflections of SCWSC ideology, on which most human mainstream success has been made possible in the United States. Though that image in the mirror looks and acts like you, it is not you (nor could it ever be all of you), but a flip-flopped, reversed virtual representation of your material body, from your perspective. As in regular household (planar) mirrors, these images ever-created and re-created in the SCWSC frame are distortions of reality.

Making the familiar strange to disrupt the power of the SCWSC gaze helps white educators unsettle common perceptions about minoritized students, families, and communities. When mainstream educators finally realize their assimilatory actions may actually hurt and impede Indigenous Peoples' success, rather than helping, they may begin to value Indigenous perspectives and moves toward decolonizing public schools. This process also requires a great deal of reflection and dialogue with Others who have been oppressed so long, they may also need liberating through this perceptual shift. I argue that this paradigmatic perceptual shift is a necessary first step in fighting for those whose humanity is frozen in racist perceptions maintained by the ubiquitous SCWSC frame that only sees and recreates illusions from its own perspective.

Marxist humanist approaches demand the same shift from commodification and exploitation of humans and their labor to affirmation of their inherent humanity (Marx, 1844). As Marx (ibid.) asserts, 'But natural science has invaded and transformed human life all the more *practically* through the medium of industry; and has prepared human emancipation, although its immediate effect had to be the furthering of the dehumanization of man.' Fundamental perceptual shifts from the SCWSC gaze to Indigenous, decolonial frames of perception reverse this industrial transformation back toward rehumanization and 'human emancipation' (ibid.).

19.10 Conclusion: The Indian Solution, Smashing Reflections Frozen in Settler-Colonial-Capitalist Mirrors

When we look closer, shift our way of seeing to using the perspective of that Other who is standing behind the settler-colonial mirror, we finally see how backward, inverted and therefore incorrect that powerful image is. When we make the SCWSC, two-dimensional plane mirror unfamiliar to ourselves, we can begin to question the images created from that ideological framework. When we consider how long all-white researchers and educators have been the most powerful seers/lookers and evaluators of non-white children, modern scholars of education and other subjects should begin to question the images and persistent patterns consistently created and re-created. These keep circulating the same flat, predictable, 2D representation of reality that depicts non-white, non–middle class, non-mainstream Other children as broken, deficient, needing help, less-than, all as compared to their white peers' physical and ideological performance in the material world. The dominance of this performance is reproduced and reified as necessary products of material manifestations of the social relations of labor within SCWSC-dominated schools, using standardized curricula and evaluative methods also all created from SCWSC perspectives.

Seeing only these representations, and these flat, reversed reflections of reality so often, normalizes us into thinking that they are real. In reality, when we acknowledge them as illusions, we realize that these are mere representations of reality produced within settler-colonial capitalist mirrors of white supremacy, and that there are entire worlds beyond the mirror. More importantly, there are entire societies of Others who have been stuck there, behind the mirror, limited, controlled, and frozen into 2D reflections of inferiority by those powerful enough to control the mirror. When white mainstream educators are brave enough to step out from the mirror they have enjoyed their whole lives, they might humbly attempt to see the world from the eyes of the disempowered, abject Other. They might finally help the children of centuries-long, white supremacist, colonial violence see these incorrect images for what they truly are: twisted and incomplete, flat representations, created purposefully to control and disempower. Brave educators willing to bear the discomfort of stepping into Others' real, 3D worlds and perspectives help us capture these evil, frozen, timeless distortions of reality and one by one, smash them.

Inverting and reframing reified instantiations of Indigenous and other minoritized youth's deficits into solution-based, revalued, and centralized opportunities for systemic change opens new possibilities for decolonial praxis in education. Further, critically examining, exploring, and advancing non-capitalistic approaches to education creates space for potential new, humanist worlds to emerge from decolonial praxis. Rather than preventing Indigenous Peoples' non-commodifiable, inherently invaluable relationships to land and life inform institutionalized education through severing these via alienation,

Marxian analysis and adaptation of critique of capital to historic and current models of education help shape how we may make this invisible war over cycles of production and consumption visible.

Addressing SCWSC ideology requires the conscious praxis of shifting from the usual, ubiquitous SCWSC gaze to being open to Others' perspectives, and demands the reconciling of one's own participation in settler futurity, regardless of race. If the power is (and has been) yours, give it. If the power has been kept from you, take it. Where you see dull, cheap, ordinary bits of broken coal and gather us as fuel for your settler-colonial, capitalist war machine, we know ourselves as diamonds here! We are those same bits of broken carbon, having stuck closer and closer together under tremendous heat, weight, and pressure of history's struggle—we are harder than anything and able to withstand anything as one; able to cut through your lies and resist your consumption.

Decolonial praxis conceptualizes the Indigenous as the Indian Solution—legitimate, central and necessary, rather than deviant, marginal, and surplus. Ripping *Capital*'s vampire parasitism off of living labor may become possible when all facets of humanity are deemed unexploitable. Unifying and revaluing the Othereds' experiences in mainstream society through tracing tracks of the SCWSC war machine through generations of capitalist hegemony offer a way to centralize and reposition marginalized educational stakeholders as fully human, not as commodified objects assigned differential value as exchanged and contrasted with 'peers.'

Systemic change-work using decolonizing frameworks like Indigenous Learning Lab (Bal et al., 2021) begins with identifying stakeholders who have been othered by local SCWSC gaze at the transformation site. It brings them together in a constructive, problem-solving team, where they learn from each other's perspectives and experiences, sharing power to create. Educators ready for change and committed to discovering how they unknowingly perpetuate the ills of the SCWSC gaze must stand together in doing the work of separating dehumanizing SCWSC machinery from present school functioning and ideology. Only then may the fetishism of commodified learning entrenched in settler-colonial schools be revealed, and minoritized Others allowed for once to define themselves by who, and how they are, rather than measured by who and how they are not reflections of SCWSC ideals. Empowering and sharing design, directive, and evaluative control over various aspects of school functioning in culturally respectful ways allows minoritized Others to be recognized as fully human, as they build a new system in which commodification, reification and the resulting erasure of Black and Brown futurity are revealed and transformed.

As the expansive space opens where opposing gazes meet, the same machine living within the SCWSC mirror in all of us begins to become visible. As the machine becomes unmasked, It loses its hypnotic power required to maintain control. As Foucault (1978, p. 86) illuminated, 'power is tolerable only on condition that it mask a substantial part of itself. Its success is proportional to its ability to hide its own mechanisms.'

Empowering decolonial perspectives allows those whose humanity remains frozen in SCWSC reflections to advance their own sovereign powers of creation by shattering false illusions. Tracing the patterns of effects of those acting as part of the SCWSC machinery across generations and throughout the globe forces the machine into our purview where we can finally see It and call It by its name. To the SCWSC ideological machine we say:

> We see you, though you will never truly see us. We've followed your tracks and can see you for what you are by what you've done and continue to do to our children and futures. We are not afraid anymore to be what you are not, denying the anti-human in all of us.

Disclosure Statement The author has no financial interest or benefit that has arisen from the direct applications of this research.

Notes

1. This is taken from Chapter IV, 'Critical Criticism' as the Tranquillity of Knowledge, or 'Critical Criticism' as Herr Edgar.
2. See Chapter 25 of *Capital* for a discussion of the progressive reduction of a relative surplus population or industrial reserve army.

References

Annual Report of the Commissioner of Indian Affairs to the Secretary of the Interior. (1908). *Reports of the Department of the Interior (1908) Vol. 2: Indian Affairs Territories*. Government Printing Office, Washington, DC.

Bal, A., Bird Bear, A., Ko, D., & Orie, L. (2021). Indigenous Learning Lab: Inclusive Knowledge-Production and Systemic Design Toward Indigenous Prolepsis. In W. Cavendish & J. F. Samson (Eds.), *An Intersectionality-Based Policy Analysis Framework in Education Policy and Research* (pp. 122–150). Teachers College Press.

Bonilla-Silva, E., & Zuberi, T. (2008). Toward a Definition of White Logic and White Methods. In E. Bonilla-Silva & T. Zuberi (Eds.), *White Logic, White Methods: Racism and Methodology* (pp. 3–30). Rowman & Littlefield.

Cusicanqui, S. R. (2012). Ch'ixinakax utxiwa: A Reflection on the Practices and Discourses of Decolonization. *South Atlantic Quarterly, 111*(1), 95–109. https://doi.org/10.1215/00382876-1472612

Feagin, J. R. (2020). *The White Racial Frame: Centuries of Racial Framing and Counter-Framing* (3rd ed.). Routledge.

Foster, J. B., Clark, B., & Holleman, H. (2020). Marx and the Indigenous. *Monthly Review*. Retrieved May 7, 2023, from https://monthlyreview.org/2020/02/01/marx-and-the-indigenous/

Foucault, M. (1978). *The History of Sexuality, Volume 1: An Introduction* (R. Hurley, Trans.). Pantheon Books.

Hall, R. (2018). *The Alienated Academic: The Struggle for Autonomy Inside the University*. Palgrave Macmillan.

Harris, C. I. (1993). Whiteness as Property. *Harvard Law Review, 106*(8), 1707–1791. Retrieved May 7, 2023, from https://harvardlawreview.org/print/no-volume/whiteness-as-property/

Harris, C. I. (2020). Reflections on Whiteness as Property. *Harvard Law Review Forum, 134*(1), 1–10. Retrieved May 7, 2023, from https://harvardlawreview.org/forum/vol-133/reflections-on-whiteness-as-property/

James, A. (2008). Making Sense of Race and Racial Classification. In E. Bonilla-Silva & T. Zuberi (Eds.), *White Logic, White Methods: Racism and Methodology* (pp. 31–46). Rowman & Littlefield.

Kimmerer, R. (2013). *Braiding Sweetgrass: Indigenous Wisdom, Scientific Knowledge and the Teachings of Plants.* Milkweed editions.

Lake Mohonk Conference of Friends of the Indian and Other Dependent Peoples. (1905). Proceedings of the 23rd Annual Meeting of the Lake Mohonk Conference of Friends of the Indian and Other Dependent Peoples. The Conference.

Marx, K. (1844). Economic and Philosophic Manuscripts of 1844. *Marxists.org.* Retrieved May 7, 2023, from https://www.marxists.org/archive/marx/works/1844/manuscripts/preface.htm.

Marx, K. (1867/2004). *Capital, Volume 1: A Critique of Political Economy.* Penguin.

Marx, K. (1875/1970). Critique of the Gotha Programme. In *Marx and Engels Selected Works* (vol. 3, pp. 13–30). Progress Publishers.

Marx, K., & Engels, F. (1845). The Holy Family or Critique of Critical Criticism. Against Bruno Bauer and Company. *Marxists.org.* Retrieved May 7, 2023, from https://www.marxists.org/archive/marx/works/1845/holy-family/index.htm

McCoy, M., & Villeneuve, M. (2020). Reconceiving Schooling: Centering Indigenous Experimentation in Indian Education History. *History of Education Quarterly, 60*(4), 487–519. https://doi.org/10.1017/heq.2020.53

Miller, M. (1903). *Report of the Superintendent of Indian Schools.* Government Printing Office.

Mitchell, T. (1991). *Colonising Egypt: With a New Preface.* University of California Press.

Omi, M., & Winant, H. (2014). *Racial Formation in the United States* (3rd ed.). Routledge.

Prashad, V. (2022). On Marxism and Decolonization. *Monthly Review.* Retrieved May 7, 2023, from https://mronline.org/2022/07/16/on-marxism-and-decolonisation/

Pratt, R. H. (2003). *Battlefield and Classroom: Four Decades with the American Indian, 1867–1904.* University of Oklahoma Press.

Ray, V. (2019). A Theory of Racialized Organizations. *American Sociological Review, 84*(1), 26–53. https://doi.org/10.1177/0003122418822335

Robinson, C. J. (2020). *Black Marxism. The Making of the Black Radical Tradition* (3rd ed.). University of North Carolina Press.

Said, E. (1978). *Orientalism.* Pantheon Books.

Schurz, C. (1881). Present Aspects of the Indian Problem. *The North American Review, 133*(296), 1–24. Retrieved May 7, 2023, from https://www.jstor.org/stable/25100977

Seth, S. (2009). Putting Knowledge in Its Place: Science, Colonialism, and the Postcolonial. *Postcolonial Studies, 12*(4), 373–388. https://doi.org/10.1080/13688790903350633

Tuck, E. (2011). Rematriating Curriculum Studies. *Journal of Curriculum and Pedagogy, 8*(1), 34–37. https://doi.org/10.1080/15505170.2011.572521

Tuck, E., & Gaztambide-Fernández, R. A. (2013). Curriculum, Replacement, and Settler Futurity. *Journal of Curriculum Theorizing, 29*(1). Retrieved May 7, 2023, from https://journal.jctonline.org/index.php/jct/article/view/411

Tuck, E., & Yang, K. W. (2012) Decolonization Is Not a Metaphor. *Decolonization: Indigeneity, Education & Society, 1*(1), 1–40. Retrieved May 7, 2023, from https://jps.library.utoronto.ca/index.php/des/article/view/18630.

Veracini, L. (2017). Decolonizing Settler Colonialism: Kill the Settler in Him and Save the Man. *American Indian Culture and Research Journal, 41*(1), 1–18. https://doi.org/10.17953/aicrj.41.1.veracini

Vizenor, G. (Ed.). (2008). *Survivance: Narratives of Native Presence.* University of Nebraska Press.

Wolfe, P. (2006). Settler Colonialism and the Elimination of the Native. *Journal of Genocide Research, 8*(4), 387–409. https://doi.org/10.1080/14623520601056240

CHAPTER 20

Re-reading Socialist Art: The Potential of Queer Marxism in Education

Bogdan Popa

20.1 INTRODUCTION

Queer Marxism is a theoretical approach that integrates queer concerns within a broader theoretical framework of historical materialism. Queer Marxism emerges from a theoretical tradition of trying to think together these two directions of social critique (Hennessey, 2000; Floyd, 2009; Liu, 2015; Popa, 2021). Petrus Liu's (2022, pp. 63–70) classificatory model of five types of queer Marxism offers a cogent analysis that identifies key theoretical and interdisciplinary innovations in political and cultural theory. In his view, the model of queering Marxism (as exemplified, for instance, by Eve Sedgwick's *Between Men* (Sedgwick, 2015)) seeks to insert into a theoretical tradition deemed economistic a focus on sexuality and gender by showing that even the most arid texts contain queer potentialities. Rather than working exclusively with concepts such as capital, superstructure, overdetermination, queer Marxism aims to introduce sexuality and gender as modalities to historicize political economy. A second model works the other way around by materializing queer theory and considering how queer and trans theorists need to tackle aspects of economic exploitation (among many examples, we find the work of Aizura, 2018).

Differently put, queer and trans people live a life of exploitation as well, and a Marxist analysis helps queer theory to make its claims broader and popular.

B. Popa (✉)
Transilvania University, Brașov, Romania
e-mail: george.popa@unitbv.ro

The third approach changes the focus from the working class to a different collective subject, which departs from a dated understanding of the worker as factory worker. Given its new understanding of the exploited, Holly Lewis (2022) proposes for instance "a politics of everybody" and Kevin Floyd (2009) "substitutes the queer for the proletariat in an updated cultural Marxism" (Liu, 2022, p. 66). A fourth model moves between analyses of intersectional models (such as triad class, race, and sexuality) and a biting queer of color critique (Ferguson, 2003; Muñoz, 2009), which recenters on the materiality of race and class and challenges the normativity of white middle class subject in queer theory. Finally, an analysis inspired by world system theories interrogates the historical emergence of sexual knowledge (Kahan, 2019) and practices of sodomy (Chitty, 2020). The last model of queer Marxism integrates Foucauldian and Wallersteinian theories to make globally relevant a critique about sexual identities.

While Liu is right to insist on a materialist turn in queer studies, my article adds to this theoretical orientation a focus on the intersection between Eastern European socialism and education. I discuss the contrast between Marxist theory and queer theory to conceptualize a different approach to queer Marxism in pedagogy.

In chapter four of Keti Chukhrov's (2020) book, which is titled "Gender and the social paradigm," the Georgian-Russian philosopher and literary theorist takes aim at dominant theories that sought to find subversive manifestations of gender and sexuality during Soviet socialism. In her formulation, "lexicons of emancipation in formerly socialist societies" could be the same as those in the West, "only if they are separated from allegedly authoritarian structures" (2020, p. 122). In other words, Chukhrov criticizes the uninterrogated translation of lexicons of subversion from Western epistemologies to socialist states. Her assumption is that Marxism in socialist states had functioned within a different conceptual and epistemological framework, which represents a serious obstacle in finding queer performativity during socialism. This re-reading of the distinct nature of socialist regimes has important consequences not only on a historical interpretation of Eastern European socialism but also on a Marxist theory of pedagogy. Gender theory offers a subversive space for creating different power relations, yet for Chukhrov such space is still capitalistic.[1] According to Chukhrov, only really existing socialism has offered an alternative to capitalism. Such argument has a devastating impact on theories of queer education since their emancipatory practices are severely curtailed by their embeddedness in capitalism.[2]

The problem with Chukhrov's analysis is her premise: historical socialism was a historical formation that was thoroughly anti-capitalistic. Instead of debating what socialism really was, I see the history of socialism primarily as a debating ground for today's concerns. To insert discussions about the past in discussions about queer Marxism, this chapter argues that queer Marxism in socialist Romania offers an important theoretical lesson for educational purposes.

In Part I, I provide a theoretical genealogy to Chukhrov's opposition between socialism and gender theory by emphasizing the distinctness of two conceptual vocabularies. The difference can be located at the level of conceptual language. Among Marx's concepts, we find alienation, communism, private property, bourgeois economics, need, the development of human senses. These ideas work in a Hegelian tradition of critique by emphasizing the historical and universal potential of everyone to lead an emancipated life. By contrast, many concepts in queer theory have their genealogy in readings of Foucault by Judith Butler, Eve Sedgwick, and José Esteban Muñoz. Queer thinkers work with ideas such as performativity, relations of domination, power differentials, and practices of liberating the self from social constraints (Popa, 2021). As opposed to early theories in queer theory, among newer critical concepts in critical education studies, we find terms such as genderification (the flattening of all gender diversity according to the normal),[3] heteroprofessionalism ("queer exclusion through discourses of professionalism"),[4] bullying, postgay (the understanding that liberal societies are tolerant and diverse that they overcome rigid gay identities),[5] and queer thrival ("to ask that we investigate, uncover, and invent ways of thriving upon and amid our surviving").[6]

While the gap between queer theory and Marxism seems unbridgeable, my argument refutes such a conclusion. In Part II, I draw on a Romanian film about a queer adolescent in socialist Romania in the 1980s to show the potential of queer Marxism. I concentrate on a socialist film about a queer adolescent "For your sake, Anca". Bullying, genderification and queer thrival are contemporary modalities to conceptualize and understand Anca's actions. Because they are primarily conceptualized in an individualist and ahistorical mode of looking at human agency, I offer a reading that focuses on the socialist dimensions of the film. I concentrate not only on a historical argument about class and class formation in Romania, but I also emphasize the need to develop a wide range of sensorial capacities through play. By discussing critically Chukhrov's arguments and using a queer Marxist lens, I show that a deeper understanding of history and relations of exploitation can lead to stronger conceptualization of educational strategies. In Part 3, I explain how a dialectical conception of queer Marxism offers not only a critique of narrow ethical concerns, but of a critique of queer ideas that do not consider the emancipatory dimensions of education.

20.2 Part I: A Conceptual History

Queer and Marxist pedagogy have been conceptualized as two antagonistic and historically determinate political conceptions. While seeking to overcome the alienation of human beings, Karl Marx argued that a system designed to lead to a humane life is rooted in the critique of private property and the capitalist system of production.[7] In queer pedagogy, the fight against the normal, which is shaped by heteronormativity and a straight curriculum, is the problem to be tackled. In Marx's theory, a system of education needs to emphasize the sociality of our perceptions and social modes of understanding the world. That transformation calls for the development of all senses, which is an act countering the primary problem in capitalism, the exacerbation of one sense. By focusing on one sense, which is that of having and possessing goods, capitalism creates truncated human beings. In queer pedagogy, what seems to matter the most is the normalization of students, who are in danger of assimilating a false narrative about themselves as normal heterosexual members of society.

Chukhrov considers such models to be irreconcilable, given that she contrasts socialist education, which is encapsulated by this formulation "to be faithful to the idea of socialism," and gender theory, which means "subverting heteronormative norms." Socialism emerged from a different cultural and political economy, which was "not to exclude the ill, the insane, or the corrupt person, but to transform him/her through his/her conscience, supraconsciousness and belief, and instigate his/her own decision in becoming adequate to communism, in being converted into it."[8] As a result, one of the most famous schools in Soviet time, the Makarenko school, derived from the fact that "those who put to shame and instruct are not supervisors, though, but one's equals" (2020, p. 128). In the words of Anton Makarenko, one of the most influential theorists of pedagogy in Soviet Union, education was primarily a collective task.[9] As he also argued, a productivist approach to becoming communist was an anti-capitalist program that could lead to world revolution.[10] As Chukhrov (2020, p. 129) comments on Makarenko's theory of education, the main contradictions in socialism were not about how "to get away from or subvert power," but that people had a hard time being faithful to the idea of socialism. Yet are socialist and queer frameworks irreconcilable? Perhaps we should start by engaging in conceptual history to see if that's the case.

20.3 The Critique of Alienation

In *Economic and Philosophical Manuscripts* Marx's critique of liberal political economy juxtaposes an interrogation of alienation with the economic conditions of the working class. This is a key moment in Marx's development of an alternative to capitalism. In the section *Alienated labor*, Marx's analysis starts by showing how the premises of bourgeois political economy, including private property, the division of labor, and the concept of exchange value, led to the worker's alienation. In Marx's language, "The worker becomes a commodity that is all the cheaper the more commodities he creates" (Marx, 2000, p. 86). Private property is the basis of bourgeois economy. As a result, the object which labor produces, labor's product, confronts the worker as something alien, "as a power independent of the producer" (ibid.). This mechanism of appropriating labor leads to the estrangement of those who produce commodities. Not only do commodities become hard to appropriate but also labor: "labor itself becomes an object he can only have in his power with the greatest of efforts and at irregular intervals" (ibid., p. 87).

The world of capitalism leads to two major consequences. First, when the labor of the worker becomes external to them, it leads to a sense of powerlessness. In Marx's description, in the producer's work, "the externalization of the worker in his product implies not only that his labour becomes an object, an exterior existence but also that it exists outside him, independent and alien, and becomes a self-sufficient power opposite him, that the life that he has lent to the object affronts him, hostile and alien"(ibid.). Second, the objective product of his labor exists as something outside to oneself, or as alien. Marx captures this feeling of estrangement with this sentence: "the object confronts him as something hostile and alien" (ibid.). As a result, the spontaneous activity of human imagination, operates on the individual independently of him, that is, "operates as an alien, divine or diabolical activity" (ibid.). The upshot of the estrangement is that the collective life of humanity is separated from one's individual life and makes individual life the purpose of the life of the species (ibid.). Marx's solution to the problem of alienation is communism.[11] Communism is the positive expression of abolishing private property, and it involves a third stage, when the man returns completely to himself as a social being. In communism, Marx explains that social enjoyment exists not only in some direct form of communal activity and directly communal enjoyment, but also when a direct expression of sociability stems from the character of the activity. When one is active scientifically, one's activity is social.

Here is Marx's answer to the problem of human alienation (ibid., 100):

> Man appropriates his universal being in a universal manner, as a whole man. Each of his human relationships to the world—seeing, hearing, smell, tasting, feeling, thinking, contemplating, feeling, willing, acting, loving—in short all the organs of his individuality, just as the organs whose form is a directly communal one, are in their objective action, or their relation to the object, the appropriation of this object. The appropriation of human reality, their relationship to the object, is the confirmation of human reality. It is therefore as manifold as the determinations and activities of human nature. It is human effectiveness and suffering, for suffering, understood in the human sense, is an enjoyment of the self for man.

The implications of the critique of alienation on educational theory are tremendous. As Makarenko suggested, Marxist pedagogy means the transformation of human nature to develop a new social consciousness. Such transformation will lead to a different type of human relation which will part company with capitalism. While, in Marx's reading, communism could signify many things from the transformation of the state to the production a new human nature, communism for Marx means primarily the development of all organs or senses. The senses transform themselves when they become social organs, so that "the eye has become a *human* eye, just as its *object* has become a social, *human* object—an object made by man for man" (ibid.). In Marx's beautiful prose, "in practice the senses have become direct theoreticians" (ibid.). The appropriation of human nature is different from the appropriation of commodities, which can only lead to strengthening the dominance of private property. However, only through a historical process can alienation be abolished, and a more developed social consciousness emerge. Yet Marx's lesson is that the development of sense perception is a product of changes in technology and modes of production. As he put it, "the objectification of the human essence" is required "to create the *human sense* corresponding to the entire wealth of human and natural substance" (ibid.). Creating human senses is a key concern for a Marxist- driven political and educational practice. In *Theses on Feuerbach*, this critique focuses on Feuerbach's thinking, which remains for Marx abstract and does not theorize the practical activity of human senses.[12] The key to a new pedagogy is to link the transformation of human senses to the abolition of private property.

20.4 Queer Pedagogy

While the Marxist transformation of social consciousness had represented a key model for pedagogy, in the 1990s a new model of education had become influential, which draws its inspiration from queer studies.[13] I take as an important example Deborah Britzman's 1995 article, which focuses on the question of translating queer theory in education. The differences between a queer and Marxist view on education will shine through by comparing these modes of theorizing pedagogy and education. Written after the peak of the AIDS epidemic, Britzman's article seeks to challenge the effects of a global health event, which led teachers and professors to "put back into place boundaries at all costs" (Britzman, 1995, p. 152). In front of this return of boundaries and strict demarcations regarding objects of knowledge, Britzman finds in queer pedagogy a refusal of "normal practices and practices of normalcy" and "one interested in the imagination of a sociality unhinged from the dominant conceptual order" (ibid., 165). This is, after all, not unlike Marx's demand to re-appropriate human nature and rework new social relations. Recent discussions about forms of education dedicated to queer students have underlined the problem of "stop reading straight," which in Deborah Britzman's phrase, is explained as "to refuse the unremarked and obdurately unremarkable straight educational curriculum" (ibid.).

The difference from Marxism comes with two key moves. First, the queer argument is not about replacing a system of social relations, but of integration of non-normative subjects in a better educational setting. The argument is that new students with different experiences and standpoints, which are given by their queer positionality, can transform the system to create modalities adequately responding to new subjects. Britzman calls for an integration of the political experience of gay and lesbian subjects, "the redefinition of family," of "public economies of affectation and representations," and "for the right to an everyday not organized by violence, exclusion, medicalization, criminalization and an erasure" (ibid., p. 152).

There are two consequences resulting from this move, which signal the separation of queer theory from a Marxist thinking about pedagogy. One demands the importance to think ethically about difference, choice, and visibility. Such thinking will acknowledge that an education space is not made only for heteronormative subjects, but also for queer people. The difference from the Marxist model is striking because all subjects are affected by alienation, which shifts the focus on changing the rules of political economy. The transformation of educational spaces cannot be successful without a broader process of social and economic change, which would lead to a socialist economy. A second consequence is that subjectivity and its formation have to be considered primarily through an engagement with violence and the disciplinary techniques of forming subjectivity. Such an approach requires an investigation about how queer subjects are produced through traumatic means.

In Britzman's conceptualization, following D.A. Miller, queer means here "not a name, but the continual elision of one… [that disrupts a system of connotation]" (ibid., 153). What queer theory brings to pedagogy is "methods of imaging difference on its own terms: as eros, as desire, as the grounds of politicality" (ibid.). This inquiry derives from a different model of understanding knowledge, in contrast with traditional models that see Enlightenment as a continuous process of advancing knowledge. Queer pedagogy has a new demand. It insists that knowledge and ignorance "implicate each other," that they enforce some forms of knowledge and some forms of ignorance, and that ignorance is an effect of knowledge and not its opposite, "an originary or innocent state" (ibid., p. 154).

While in its early formulation queer pedagogy is considered to have a different theoretical model from Marxism, I will explain in part II the importance of thinking about a mixed model. A dialectical understanding of queer concerns is important to strengthen queer theory. Such theoretical effort can provide a different historical and socio-political background to queer theory, which can ground itself in a materialistic worldview.

20.5 Part II: Queer Marxism—Re-reading *For Your Sake, Anca*

My reading of the Romanian film *For your sake, Anca* aims to provide a model of queer Marxism, which brings in concerns from both queer and Marxist thinking. The film is a snapshot from the life of a queer teenager who undergoes a crisis in the early 1980s Romania. Anca/Ancu Visarion is an unusual adolescent who is described as not following the rules of her gender. From the first dialogues in the film, Anca is described to be at odds with norms of femininity. She performs plays about historical characters in the attic, plays soccer, and generally does not dress like a girl. But the film is giving us a broad and sociological understanding of her life within a particular social situation. She is in sixth grade. Her parents are working class and they move from a house to a new apartment. Anca is attracted to art in a manner that puts her at odds with the conventional perceptions of those around her. Here is how her mother comments on Anca's attraction to football: "We are making a fool of ourselves with you liking soccer. Why weren't you attracted to volleyball?" The contrast and the conflict of the film is made clear from the beginning. Anca does not obey the rules of becoming an adolescent girl, unlike her sister and colleagues who seem to resent and exclude her.

Anca/Ancu's queerness takes its shape in a socialist environment which is partly supportive of her actions. The director takes us first into a physics class where through various scenes we understand Anca's splendid imaginative power. In class, both Anca and the best student in class must answer questions from their teacher. We discover a stark contrast between the boy who repeats the lesson by heart and Anca's answers. The boy does not understand much from what he says, because he only repeats words mechanically. In turn, Anca understands the physics lesson at a direct practical level. During the practical explanations, the teacher cites from Marx to whom abstract thinking is useless without understanding its role in one's life. The example is one of oscillatory movement and how to account for various forces involved in calculating its trajectory. While the teacher explains the lesson, Anca is able to visualize herself in a swing and perceive the different components from the class' abstract formulas. Her imagination is very theatrical. The impact of the lesson is not at the abstract level, as Marx explained as in his critique of Feuerbach, but it shapes Anca's practical and sensuous activity. She lives her lessons, not just memorizes them, and transforms the educational content by thinking about it.

Cristiana Nicolae wonderfully moves between the real of the explanation and the imaginary world of Anca. In the next shot, Anca is called to an English class where students are taking an exam. She chooses to enter in class by pulling off a Chaplin routine and both the teacher and the students are delighted. The gender boundaries in this socialist school are easily trespassed.[14] The English teacher who is charmed by Anca's impersonation asks her: "Are you Chaplin's nephew?" The film moves into a new register when Anca is not only made to be a witness to a bullying scene but also when she tries to stop it. The plot is driven by a conflict between the family of the bully and Anca's decision to stand up for her colleague. First, we see how a young student is bullied by a bigger colleague. Anca intervenes to help the weaker boy. We later learn that the bully, Sorin, is a kid of a rich woman, who will later seek to punish Anca for her attitude. A teacher who's responsible for Anca's class, who does not like her boyish behavior, takes side of the bully. Her remarks after the fighting between Anca and the bully are indicative of her resentment: "You were getting in a fight again, didn't you? You do not want to behave in a civilized manner?" She has already decided, without listening to what students wanted to tell her, that Anca is to blame for her behavior. Her anger about Anca's unruly ways gets translated into her manner of addressing the kids. While Ioana, the chief of the pioneers, and Sorin, are called by their first name, the teacher addresses Anca by her second name, Visarion.[15] Anca's actions are not judged in terms of their direct content, such as stopping the bullying of a colleague, but in relation to social evaluation of who the children were and to what social class did they belong to.

The situation at school triggers a crisis in the Visarion family. In Anca's household, tensions accumulate. Her mother is very angry with her husband because she does not get any help in raising children. She is shown as she talks to herself while her husband does not want to hear any of her snide remarks. Later that evening, Anca is not able to sleep. From a minor conflict with her sister, she starts to improvise a play. Chaplin is again imitated, and the viewer is asked to understand that Anca can use her theatrical inclinations and imagination to deal with difficult moments in school. Anca starts to reflect in her own manner about the tense situation in school. She talks with her sister about her desire not to go to school. She wants to become a clown in a circus. Before this crisis generated by the bullying scene, Anca was treated as a boy. She was able to create all sorts of theatrical scenarios and identity herself with various genders. While her father encouraged her, the new circumstances change the position of her parents. Anca decides to tell her parents that she does not want to go to school anymore. Her parents do not understand her demand and seem to be oblivious to Anca's difficult time in school. Anca has difficulties connecting with the girls her age who sometime reprimand her for playing soccer. She finds out that there is another kid in the neighborhood, Victor, who is treated as an outcast because he decided not to go to school anymore.

The film reveals the school not only as a set-up for violence, but also for human development. It offers a dialectical view of the possibilities of education, which stem from participating in environments that have positive and negative aspects. Anca gets a lot of sympathy from the physics teacher, who is thrilled by Anca's imaginative power. He gives her the highest mark in class. He seems to be Anca's only ally in an environment that cultivates a strong gender normativity. Yet, when she tries to explain abstract theoretical concepts, the students humiliate her. They laugh at her explanations. The teacher responsible with the group (*diriginta*) takes the side of the rich kid, Sorin. She humiliates Anca publicly and calls her "a savage."[16]

The dialectic of the film also emphasizes the role of models for students who are in crisis. These models can be not only artistic works (such as a Soviet film), but also real human presences. The pressures at school take their toll on the Visarion family. A key scene is the moment when they watch *The Forty First*, a Soviet film about a brave woman who kills her lover because he betrays socialist ideals. Her family is less than impressed with the film and her sister comments: "it is a pity that the end is not beautiful." Anca, in turn, remains completely mesmerized by the story. The family calls her to join the food table and continue to make fun of the film. "Come to the table, forget about the film, the guy died, just come to the table." Anca locks her door, and she begins to cry. The family get very anxious and do not know how to react. Her dad slaps as he tries to enforce the family rituals. They ask her to behave like her sister or other models of femininity at school. In reacting to her family's treatment, Anca starts an artistic scenario in her head where she behaves like a clown. She has huge ears, and her family is appalled by her becoming a comedian. This revenge scenario helps her overcome this scene, and she starts to laugh at the family table. Anca is not a complete outlier in the family, because her parents had strong theatrical inclinations. Her mother and dad acted in a play in the factory amateur group. The film shows how the family is connected to an older Marxist culture, which is on the process of being eliminated by a class of *new money*.

While the director revisits sympathetically an old Marxist culture, she also illuminates the struggles around Anca's perception as a non-normative rebel. The conflict in the film is with both new money and heteronormative demands on the youth. The film offers a way out by emphasizing the role of humane models and the power of imagination. Anca befriends an elegant woman, Alexandra Ioniță, who is single, has her own car, and went to the same school as Anca. In Anca's mind, the world of adults can be transfigured and transformed so that violence can be momentarily stopped. For instance, Anca notices that her new friend tries to help a group of boys playing soccer, which are bullied by neighbors. She fails to do so. Yet Anca reworks this incident in her imagination, which takes a different shape. In her mind, she lets a bird fly away while she is dressed as a clown.[17] Because she has multiple friendships and relations that helps her navigate the world, Anca refuses to become a victim of some of the abusive relations she is engaged in. A viewer at the time was called to understand that a non-normative adolescent needs a strong humane model and various relationships to be able to navigate a bullying environment.

20.6 Part III: Conclusion—Queer Marxism in Education

My reading of *For your sake, Anca* uses the conceptual language of queer and Marxist theory to reveal the broader implications of socialist pedagogy. Concepts such as bullying represent an important category to understand how Anca experiences the world. The character is abused by her teachers at school when she takes the side of a bullied colleague. The consequences were dire. Her anxiety in the world is strongly tied to a permanent threat of violence.

The analytic of bullying, however, has limitations in its explanatory power. The problem with bullying is that it is used to analyze relations of power among individuals without understanding the deeper historical roots of these acts. Queer theory needs historical materialism, as much as historical materialism needs queer theory. In contrast, the film connects aspects of individual and psychological life to a socialist mindset. It shows that bullying is part of a process by which socialist ideals of education are undermined by a different historical reality, which is the rise of a richer class. Well-endowed parents not only defend their abusive children but also generate a cycle of violence in schools.

This process is related to the commodification in schools where students are evaluated primarily through their participation to a class system. The violence and the response to it are shaped by privileging a monied class that benefited from such attitude. Anca, a student from a poor working-class family who goes to an elitist school in Bucharest, is not primarily a victim of individual violence, but of class and gender violence as manifested through attempts to punish and diminish her. Yet Anca fights for her capacity to act creatively in an environment that works to punish her. If the alienation of the world leads to commodification and violence, Anca is part of a web of human relations that functions in an emancipatory capacity. Such possibility is given by her actions because she develops her senses to appropriate social reality, as Marx argued. Anca's attempt is to become a social being, as opposed to bullies, which function as devices of commodification.

Like bullying, concepts such as genderification and queer thrival illuminate important parts of Anca's struggles as a student. Her love for play and theater is in deep contrast with the traditionally feminine concerns of her colleagues, as depicted in the film. While they are interested in making themselves pleasant to be liked by boys, Anca wants to play football with them. She sees herself not as fundamentally different from her male peers. The film captures an important moment in how feminized notion of gender gets to be imposed to girls at that age. Anca neither rejects girls' behavior, nor their preoccupation with fashion. A different subjectivity is articulated here where one is at the same time multiple things. She can flirt with Victor, and at the same time, play football with him. Because the gender lines are not clearly traced, Anca does not reject an identification with a female gender. She blurs the lines between what is and is not appropriate for a girl to do.

Anca's queer behavior is not a transhistorical quality of a subject. To the contrary, the film shows us the roots of her passion for theater and search for justice. Like Anca, her family acted in plays as part of a socialist program to raise the consciousness of the working class. We understand that Anca's socialist upbringing offered her the resources to develop herself as a queer subject. The fight against alienation is an important part of Anca's behavior. She wants to stay in school because that's the location where the products of her creative work can be rewarded. She wants education because she knows that is her social labor. While the working class has historically been distributed a smaller share of cultural enjoyment, Anca challenges this tradition. Because of the transgressions, she is abused by her teacher as a strategy to put her in her place. Students like Anca/Ancu are not supposed to enjoy pleasure or develop cultural tools to understand the world the way bourgeois students have access to. The notion of alienation is key to understand Anca's fight against genderification as a process of expanding capacities for a better human life. As Marx put it, if senses are theorists in practice, Anca's the pleasure in acting is a mode of appropriation the human essence. It is also a manner of fighting a system that seeks to develop a single sense, which is the sense of owning objects.

Queer thrival is also an important lens by which we can see Anca's development as a student. She needs a deep connection to theater and playing with her male peers to be able to survive a violent world, which she wants to correct and improve. While she protects a bullied kid and faces the consequences of her actions, the last scene leaves us with unsolved questions. Anca is described as a witness to a scene of violence: older men acted out violently because they were disturbed while playing backgammon. Alexandra Ioniţa, a respected and authoritative communist woman, intervenes to protect the students, but she cannot put an end to bullying.

Yet, despite the on-going violence against young students, the end of the film is not pessimistic. Anca's friendship with Victor is an important element of queer thrival. Because of this relationship, which has also elements of erotic attraction, Anca is shown as capable of trying to make it in a violent world. Anca's love for imaging different worlds, in reaction to the pain of witnessing or experiencing violence, is central element of queer thrival. A queer thrival cannot be in itself a goal because it depends on a political economy where some students can thrive and others cannot. Anca's fight within the system is for a society that allows for everyone to have the capacity to experience a *human sense*, which would correspond, as Marx says, "to the entire wealth of human and natural substance." It is not a coincidence that the Marxist physics professor helps Anca develop her abstract thinking, because he understood the importance of connecting high conceptual problems with mundane realities of the world. Queer thrival is in this Romanian socialist film a project of human emancipation which is aimed not only a special category of children, endowed with special talents, but to all. As revealed in Marxist pedagogy, capacities for human development can be developed for humanity as a species.

My proposal in this chapter, which I locate in a tradition of queer Marxism, calls for the overcoming of an antagonistic relation between Marxist and queer practices of education. I suggest that the film "For your sake, Anca" helps our thinking with both theoretical traditions. In dialectically working with queer and Marxist concepts, I argued that an arsenal of concepts from queer theory, while useful to understand some important dynamics in the film, do not expand to a broader understanding of causes and modalities of social alienation. The concept of bullying can identify important dynamics of power, but it needs to be supplemented with an understanding of conflicts between rich and working-class students in elite Romanian schools. The idea of genderification describes how a single gender can become normative across schools, but it stops short from explaining it as an outcome of a capitalistic emphasis on having property over one's body and gender. The term queer thrival offers an important insight into how queer students can develop their artistic and imaginary capacities. Yet while thrival and friendship are important features of a queer life, they seem to be allotted to a particular group of students who might be consider special. To the contrary, a Marxist theory that fights against alienation seeks to develop a humane sense for all so that everyone enjoins the achievements of human civilization.

A queer socialist conception of education should incorporate insights from queer theory on education, but it needs to expand to a broader critique of a political system and its underlying assumptions. On the one hand, it should move beyond an ethical critique of incorporating queer subjects into a more diverse society. In turn, what a socialist program asks is a focus on the critique of alienation, because the education concentrated on the sense of having represents a threat to both queer and non-queer students. Feelings of alienation within an entire educational system can be challenged by an investment in modalities to cultivate other senses, alongside an emphasis on the activity of producing artistic objects. On the other hand, queer Marxism also needs to distance itself from a program that too often concentrates on the role of ignorance in supporting forms of knowledge and techniques of education. Given the assumption that most educational practices presuppose a system of discipline and punish, the balance has shifted nowadays to a refusal of Enlightenment process of passing education from teachers to students. An important suggestion of my argument is that a re-evaluation of educational methods of state socialism might also lead to modalities of emancipating students and developing their artistic capacities.

Disclosure Statement The author has no financial interest or benefit that has arisen from the direct applications of this research.

Notes

1. In Chukhrov's interpretation of Judith Butler's critical analysis of gender, the analytic of gender subversion serves as modality to understand the relation between capitalist economy and a politics of the body. Gender and queer theory are not an alternative to capitalism, but an alternative which is constituted within capitalism's political economy. Subversive bodies have liberating effects only as part of an economy based on commodification: "the chief transformative potentiality of such a body is to provoke power by performative and subversive exposures of its trauma (the trauma caused by the confrontation with ideology and its apparatuses) and to treat such exposures as liberating" (Chukhrov, 2020, p. 125).
2. The goal in gender theory seems to be to normalize subversion and pathology rather than to transform the system: "the emancipatory demand in this case is not that society should integrate and normalize subversiveness, but rather that it should allow for the performance of subversiveness and pathology within a special, legally delimited site, separate from the accepted conventions of normality" (Chukhrov, 2020, p. 125).
3. For genderification, see Harris and Holman Jones (2016, pp. 117–127).
4. For heteroprofessionalism, see Mizzi (2016, p. 137).
5. See Lapointe (2016, p. 205).
6. See Greteman (2016, p. 310).
7. See Marx (2000), and especially: pp. 83–122 (selections from *Economic and Political Manuscripts*); 175–209 (selections from *The German Ideology*); and 472–481 (on "The fetishism of commodities," in *Capital, Volume 1*).
8. This approach was theorized by cultural theorists such as Kharkhordin (1999) and Alexey (2006), who drew in their interpretations on Foucault's ideas of

discipline and surveillance. As Chukhrov (2020, p. 127) tells us, "the Stalinist paradigm was not surveillance but rather putting to shame".
9. See Makarenko quoted in Pavlidis, 'Socialism', p.8.
10. "The Soviet collective defends the issue of world unity of the working humanity as a matter of principle. It is not merely a biotic unification of people, but a part of the humanity's battle front in the era of the world revolution", Makarenko quoted in Pavlidis, '*Socialism*', p.9.
11. Ibid, "Private Property and Communism", pp. 95–104.
12. Ibid., p. 171:"The chief defect of all hitherto existing materialism (that of Feuerbach included) is that the thing, reality, sensuousness, is conceived only in the form of the object or of contemplation, but not as sensuous human activity, practice, not subjectively."
13. See Popa (2021, pp. 97–131), for a historical account of the relation between Marxism and queer theory.
14. Nicolae has mentioned in an oral interview that her elementary school was modeled after a famous Soviet model, Zoia Kosmodemianskaia, and the school was famous on Bucharest for its progressive views.
15. The pioneers a term for the formal organization of the communist youth in socialist Romania.
16. In the scene where the mother of the bully seeks to take revenge on Anca the class differences are articulated through clothes. Anca's simple clothes are put in contrast with the outfit of the woman, who displays richness and defends her bullying boy. The students take Anca's side in the conflict, but *diriginta* decides to punish Anca by giving her extra duties.
17. The director moves from Anca's imaginary world to the actual scene in the backyard of her building. We get a sense that she wants to run away from this world because she says to Victor that she does not want to play football anymore. Victor then teases her and invites her to a football game. She manages in the end to reconcile with Victor and join a football game.

References

Aizura, A. (2018). *Mobile Subjects: Transnational Imaginaries of Gender Reassignment*. Duke University Press.

Alexey, Y. (2006). *Everything was Forever, Until it Was No More: The Last Soviet Generation*. Princeton University Press.

Britzman, D. (1995). Is there queer pedagogy? Or, stop reading straight. *Educational Theory, 45*(2), 151–165.

Chitty, C. (2020). *Sexual Hegemony: Statecraft, Sodomy, and Capital in the Rise of the World System*. Duke University Press.

Chukhrov, K. (2020). *Practicing the Good*. University of Minnesota Press.

Ferguson, R. (2003). *Aberrations in Black: Toward a Queer Critique of Color*. University of Minnesota Press.

Floyd, K. (2009). *The Reification of Desire: Toward a Queer Marxism*. University of Minnesota Press.

Greteman, A. (2016). Queer Thrival. In *Critical Concepts in Queer Studies and Education: An International Guide for the 21 Century* (pp. 309–317). Palgrave Macmillan.

Harris, A., & Jones, S. (2016). Genderification. In *Critical Concepts in Queer Studies and Education: An International Guide for the 21 Century* (pp. 117–127). Palgrave Macmillan.

Hennessey, R. (2000). *Profit and Pleasure: Sexual Identities in Late Capitalism.* Routledge.

Kahan, B. (2019). *The Book Of Minor Perverts: Sexology, Etiology, And The Emergences Of Sexuality.* University Of Chicago Press.

Kharkhordin, O. (1999). *The Collective and the Individual in Russia: A study of practices.* University of California Press.

Lapointe, A. (2016). Postgay. In *Critical Concepts in Queer Studies and Education: An International Guide for the 21 Century* (pp. 205–218). Palgrave Macmillan.

Lewis, H. (2022). *The Politics of Everybody: Feminism, Queer Theory, and Marxism at the Intersection: A Revised Edition.* Bloomsbury.

Liu, P. (2015). *Queer Marxism in Two Chinas.* Duke University Press.

Liu, P. (2022). *The Specter of Materialism. Queer theory and Marxism in the Age of the Beijing Consensus.* Duke University Press.

Marx, K. (2000). *Selected Writings* (D. McLellan, Ed.). Oxford University Press.

Mizzi, R. C. (2016). Heteroprofessionalism. In *Critical Concepts in Queer Studies and Education: An International Guide for the 21 Century* (pp. 137–147). Palgrave Macmillan.

Muñoz, J. E. (2009). *Cruising Utopia: The Then and There of Queer Futurity.* New York University Press.

Popa, B. (2021). *De-centering Queer Theory: Communist Sexuality in the Flow During and After the Cold War.* Manchester University Press.

Sedgwick, E. K. (2015). *Between Men. English Literature and Men Homosexual Desire.* Columbia University Press.

CHAPTER 21

Making Sense of Neoliberalism's New Nexus Between Work and Education, Teachers' Work, and Teachers' Labor Activism: Implications for Labor and the Left

Lois Weiner

21.1   The New Neoliberal Project[1]

A new iteration of the neoliberal project, driven by information technology and profits that are made from it, has already manifested itself globally in teachers' work and public education, from preschool through mass public higher education (Boninger et al., 2020; Kerssens & van Dijck, 2021; Klees et al., 2019; Lindh & Nolin, 2016; Williamson, 2018). No student is too young or too old for education to be "data-driven," with metrics for teaching and learning decided far from classrooms, with 'new models of curriculum provision …by a variety of commercial organizations, politically-connected entrepreneurs, teacher-creators, public and charitable institutions,' increasing commercial penetration into state schooling through a mixed economy of new providers and public/private partnerships (Williamson & Hogan, 2020, p. 28). Reports of world financial institutions, in particular the World Bank's World Development Reports (2018, 2019, 2020), articulate the project aims, expressed in rhetoric about ending world poverty. Language and concepts associated with a Left critique of neoliberalism are now embraced by a sector of the ruling class. For instance, the "New Democrats" think tank, identified with

L. Weiner (✉)
New Jersey City University, Jersey City, NJ, USA
e-mail: lweiner@njcu.edu

© The Editor(s) (if applicable) and The Author(s), under exclusive license to Springer Nature Switzerland AG 2023
R. Hall et al. (eds.), *The Palgrave International Handbook of Marxism and Education*, Marxism and Education,
https://doi.org/10.1007/978-3-031-37252-0_21

the Clinton wing of the Democratic Party, with offices in Washington D.C. and Brussels, has named itself the Progressive Policy Institute (PPI) and boasts creation of a new "neoliberal project" (Mortimer, 2020).

Scholarship of educational researchers about teachers' work, curriculum, and teachers' labor activism in the past two decades is often missing in analyses of these topics by academics, even those working in the critical tradition (Dandala, 2019; Weiner & Asselin, 2020). Often, critical scholarship about education not informed by work of educational researchers flattens or omits essential areas of study, like how school knowledge reflects and reinforces social inequality, including social class and curriculum (Anyon, 1980), and how neoliberal reforms in city schools relate to changes in capitalism globally (Lipman, 2011). Educational research that maps, how conditions outside the school and classroom walls connect to what occurs inside, alters how we analyze schooling's reproduction of capitalist social relations. This connects with Marx's work in *Capital* (Marx 1867/2004) and *The Grundrisse* (Marx 1857/1993) about the development of social relations of production as they are impacted by transformations in organizational and technological development. The question becomes not *whether* schools disrupt or reproduce unequal social relations but *how* they do so and *for whom*.

Although this chapter focuses on school reform, what occurs in classrooms and schools is not the only, nor arguably, the most influential education that occurs under capitalism. Social movements teach by exposing cultural and ideological assumptions, and they educate unions politically (Dyke & Muckian-Bates, forthcoming 2023; Mann, 2014); transformed unions educate their members and support formation of counter-hegemonic movements (Gutstein & Lipman, 2013; Nuñez et al., 2015). Learning occurs in families, and popular culture influences the way we speak, dress, eat, and think (Apple, 1999). Schools are workplaces that educate about class relations, alongside how unions can and do alter working conditions that directly affect students (Bascia & Rottman, 2011; Compton & Weiner, 2008; Stevenson, 2017).

Close analysis of teachers' work and labor activism challenges the widespread, inaccurate nostalgia for a working class of heterosexual, cis-gender, white men, toiling in industry. As we have seen in waves of teachers' strikes in the past decade, teachers can be among the most militant workers. Relatively recent research explains this militancy, relating it to activists' involvement in social justice movements, and a new commitment to what is called "social justice teacher unionism," (Dyke & Muckian-Bates, forthcoming 2023; Gautreaux, 2019; Stark & Spreen, 2020). Another set of factors explaining teachers' labor activism relate to teaching's location in the economy (Friedman, 2018). An often-ignored factor is gender, which Russom (2020) explains drove the 2018 teacher walkouts. Construction of the working class as white ignores the valuable history of Black teachers, mostly women, excluded from white professional associations and segregated teachers unions. They formed independent associations to protect themselves as workers and conditions for Black students (Houchen, 2020; Weiner et al., 2023, Forthcoming). Their legacy of union and political activism resonates with a new generation of Black teachers, who attempt to democratize their unions and build bridges to community (Owens, 2022) to challenge neoliberal policies.

21.2 Focusing on Education to Understand and Contest Changes in Work, Capitalism, and the New Neoliberal Project

The New Neoliberal Project and a Terrain of Reform

Educational reforms in the past three decades have reflected and reinforced tectonic shifts in capitalism and refashioning of work that started well before the Left named what was occurring as "neoliberalism." As I explain later in the rationale for using a social system framework for analyzing capitalism, education is located at the intersection of cultural, political, social, ideological, and economic forces. Because schooling is used to reproduce (or disrupt) existing social, political, and economic relations, what occurs in education is a naturally-occurring case study that illuminates alterations in the society that are in process or have been crystallized. Focusing on education shows how much of what is considered the "new normal" in capitalism is not new. Creation and deepening of new forms of control and privatization by edu-business, using information technology and new forms of privatization, actually began well before the pandemic, shortly before the 2008 financial collapse (Saltman, 2018; Williamson & Hogan, 2020). Huws and Frapporti (2021) also note 2008 as a turning point that clarified and accelerated changes to labor through digitalization. This connects to Marx's (1867/2004, p. 493) analysis of how technology is central in enabling humans to reimagine the world:

> Technology reveals the active relation of [humans] to nature, the direct process of the production of [their] life, and thereby it also lays bare the process of the production of the social relations of [their] life, and of the mental conceptions that flow from those relations.

One reason these changes have been difficult to trace is that conditions are metamorphosing as we identify and study them, a factor that makes publishing timely peer-reviewed research extraordinarily difficult (Huws & Frapporti, 2021).

A complete explanation of how changes in education reflect the ways capitalism has altered work globally with information technology goes well beyond this chapter, but a brief overview of alterations in the past three decades is needed, to clarify what aspects of the original neoliberal project in education persist and what has been changed. In the 1990s labor unions throughout the world were pressured to adopt changes to working conditions, including "lean production," to adapt to a changed global economy in which manufacturing would be contracted out and off-shored, moved to another country (Moody, 1997). Education reforms reflected this shift in pressures to teach the "new basic skills," which were linked to international assessments of students' work (Weiner, 2001).

As unions in the private sector accepted downsizing and concessions in what was defended as the only way to keep jobs from being off-shored, the rationale for public education became increasingly coupled to the economy, with curricular changes purportedly designed to make individual workers as well as the economy more competitive. In the U.S. the two national teachers unions, the American Federation of Teachers (AFT) and National Education Association (NEA), accepted this rationale for curriculum change and for offering concessions on teachers' pay and working conditions, shifting to "trust agreements" instead of contracts and the concept of "pay for performance," which later became merit pay, based on student performance on standardized tests (Weiner & Asselin, 2020).

International standards for learning established by world finance organizations, ostensibly reflecting demands of work in the new global economy, presented as a solution to inequality and poverty, and assessed with standardized tests, are central to neoliberal educational reforms (Benavot & Smith, 2020; Compton & Weiner, 2008). Because of neoliberalism's successful usurpation of the discourse about ending inequality, critical analysis about its purported solutions needs to acknowledge that social inequalities, including those heightened and publicized during the pandemic, are longstanding problems in which labor, teachers unions, and the education establishment have been complicit (Rothstein, 2014; Rousmaniere, 2001). No "golden age" of public education, nor of equality in the workplace and unions, exists for us restore.

Hence, the Left's challenge is developing a narrative and conceptual framework for informing resistance to capitalism's degradations of life and education, which not only acknowledge social oppression but, as I will explain, center it, along with an inclusive definition of the relationship between social classes and unions, based on understanding Marxism as a theory of revolutionary change (Draper, 1978, 1970/2004). This inclusive definition reminds us that Marx (1845, *emphasis* in original), in *The Theses on Feuerbach*, argued for concrete revolutionary activity that was personal and collective:

> The materialist doctrine that [humans] are products of circumstances and upbringing, and that, therefore, changed [humans] are products of changed circumstances and changed upbringing, forgets that it is [humans] who change circumstances and that the educator must himself be educated... The coincidence of the changing of circumstances and of human activity or self-change can be conceived and rationally understood only as *revolutionary practice.*

Neoliberal Reforms and Changes to Knowledge Work

Against such revolutionary self-change and praxis, neoliberal reforms defended standardized tests as not only the best but the only valid, reliable measures of student, teacher, and school performance, despite testing's racist origins and outcomes (Au, 2022). New curricular standards and testing were accompanied by policies to make education a profit center, fragment public control and oversight, and destroy the influence and power of teachers unions (Compton & Weiner, 2008). The fundamental outline of this project persists, globally: using standardized tests to control curriculum and teaching (Au, 2022); deepening of privatization through expansion of unregulated charter schools (Au & Ferrare, 2014; Green & Connery, 2019); and financing schools in ways that maximize profits and undercut democratic control (Saltman, 2018).

While parent and teacher activists' resistance to reforms associated with the original template has continued, especially in cities (Benson & Weiner, 2021), newer, even more invasive forms of privatization, including an expanded role for private equity in public/private partnerships (Private Equity Policy Project, 2022), are mostly under the radar of activists, unions, and researchers, as is the companion to privatization to increase profits—transformation of teaching and learning with educational technology. The Right's newest waves of political attacks on curriculum and school practices are often cast by opponents, as wholly separate from information technology's changes to education and work and new forms of privatization, but the two projects share a common goal: strengthening ruling class power to determine schooling's reproduction of capitalism.

Though changes to manufacturing, warehouses, and the global supply chain have been well-studied (Moody, 2018), less attention has been paid to parallel changes in cultural and knowledge work (Huws, 2014; Petrucci, 2021), including teaching. Even before the pandemic, knowledge and cultural workers experienced heightened intensification of labor, diminution of autonomy and creativity, standardization of work processes, pressure to 'perform according to the ever more stringent standards laid down from above (defined in terms of protocols, performance targets, and quality standards' (Huws, 2014, p. 40)). Indeed, the skills and attitudes employers demanded read like a classified ad for teachers before the pandemic: being 'digitally literate,' 'self-motivated,' being 'good team players,' and having a 'commitment to lifelong learning' (ibid.). Transnational corporations also wanted workers familiar with or able to master specific software packages and communicate with distant customers in a global market—as teachers did in the shift to remote learning in the pandemic.

The Need for Critical Scholarship of Educational Proletarianization

In retrospect, analyses of deprofessionalization and loss of autonomy due to the "new managerialism," including sophisticated scholarship that related these changes to gender and neoliberalism (Davies, 2003), needed to explore new modes of control and the role of information technology. One material cause of this lag is the absence of funding for critical scholarship about teachers' work, a problem teachers' unions might help address through collaboration with researchers. As one international project showed, these collaborations are labor-intensive, strain institutional boundaries, and produce useful findings (Couture et al., 2020). The British Columbia Teachers' Federation (BCTF) has combined critical research and members' insights about changes to their work to develop awareness and policies to contest their provincial government's collaboration with educational policies of the Organization for Economic Co-operation and Development (OECD) for curricular standards that contradict student needs (Gacoin, 2019). In response to evidence members needed help, the Alberta Teachers' Association (ATA) collected and analyzed empirical data from members and contextualized the findings in a study about "compassion fatigue" among teachers arising from caring for students amidst conditions under COVID (ATA & Kendrick, 2020; Kendrick, 2020). The Education International's sponsorship of research about Pearson (Sellar & Hogan, 2019), linked to a global campaign to stop Pearson's privatization efforts in Africa, shows the potential power of teachers unions to support quality research that can be applied internationally. In the U.S., the AFT and NEA fund little research directly. However, the National Education Policy Center (NEPC), which receives support from foundations AFT and NEA fund, has produced valuable materials about school privatization and dangers of ed-tech (NEPC, 2021), for example, about personalized learning (Boninger et al., 2020). Two large US teachers' unions that identify as committed to social justice, teacher unionism have refocused research on strategic concerns (personal correspondence 2022).

The absence of support for research has meant teachers' unions lag in understanding and addressing immediate dangers in neoliberalism's new iteration, one of which is "platformization" of services, seen in the ubiquity of "apps," accelerated in the pandemic in a vast swath of workplaces, including schools. Algorithms control work, assuming management functions previously handled by employers, making low-paid, contingent labor even more precarious and exploitative. Platforms break work down into modules, making workers' performance and time more easily controlled, degrading the skills needed to perform the job because the units are designed on the assumption no specific knowledge or skills are required to do the work (Schreyer, 2021). For venture capitalists, private equity, and tech startups, the work of teaching isn't substantially different from delivering a pizza or any other kind of service. We can see how educational technology is used to accelerate deprofessionalization and proletarianization of academic labor in the corporatized university, where contingent labor and adjunct faculty are used to deliver a lecture or a module with content that is predetermined (Ovetz, 2020).

Deprofessionalization occurs in primary and secondary teaching (preK-12 in the U.S.) when entry requirements are eliminated or diminished to address lack of capacity to staff schools, as occurred widely in the U.S. during the pandemic. For example, New Mexico school districts addressed the teacher and substitute shortage by using the National Guard, and in Oklahoma, the police. The conditions in higher education that Ovetz (2020) explores, and staffing in the pandemic, raise the question of what will happen to credentialing with teachers' use of platforms operating with preconstructed lessons broken into modules? Platformization can do to teaching what DoorDash has done to food delivery, especially if grading bots, already developed, perform assessments with predetermined criteria embedded in software schools already use or will purchase (Smith, 2022). These relate to modes of proletarianization that Marx (1857/1993, p. 705) also described and analyzed in his fragment on machines in *The Grundrisse*, where 'the human being comes to relate more as a watchman and regulator to the production process itself.' He also noted:

> The accumulation of knowledge and of skill, of the general productive forces of the social brain, is thus absorbed into capital, as opposed to labour, and hence appears as an attribute of capital, and more specifically of fixed capital [machinery] (ibid., p. 694).

Still another, newer source of profit in education, intensified and accelerated in the pandemic, is use of edtech for assessment of "social and emotional learning" (SEL). One international market research company reports $1.725 billion spent on SEL for the 2021–2022 school year, and growth for 2023, while slowed, will increase 22.9% thereafter (Simba Information, 2022). The report notes pushback to SEL as a factor in sales and profits, without explaining the origin. As Mahfouz (2022) explains in a report published by NEPC, social conservatives have organized against use of SEL as invasive, replacing parents' role in teaching children moral values. Mahfouz refutes assumptions and claims of this right-wing attack, defending schools' responsibility for students' social and emotional well-being. Yet the report omits exploration about use of data from SEL for profit, surveillance, and social control as I explain subsequently.

While unions focus on local and national educational policies, the global context in many respects provides a clearer picture of ruling class assumptions and aims for education, as seen in Klees et al.'s (2019) critique of the WDR in 2018, and also of the World Bank's System Approach for Better Education Results (SABER), more testing, and data collection to drive improved outcomes (Klees et al., 2020). The ways information technology is being used to alter work and education are explicit in World Development Reports produced well before the pandemic: "Learning to Realize Education's Promise" (2018); "The Changing Nature of Work" (2019); and "Data for Better Lives" (2020). The United Nations Educational, Scientific and Cultural Organization (UNESCO) has also supported more data collection to rectify problems of inequality in education, seen in its report about failures to educate special needs students during the pandemic (UNESCO, 2020). Evaluations of psychological, physical, emotional, and social health, completed in schools, are now linked to databases that store information on student and family health.

Funding new organizations that identify as supporters of social and racial justice and advocate for solutions for inequality advanced by edtech entrepreneurs is a key strategy in the push for adoption of more invasive and profitable technology. Activists who lead these groups often see alignment between their ideals, which their funders claim to support, and the answers foundations and think tanks funded by Silicon Valley and Wall Street advance. For instance, while educational justice groups argue against old forms of discipline as racist, opposing the "school to prison pipeline," their funders push (and profit from) new forms of control, linked to "national security" with private vendors who make big money from student data.

The invasiveness of the edtech control system puts the progressive demands of teachers, students, and unions committed to social justice in a new light. What does it mean to demand and even strike to hire "counselors, not cops," when counselors must complete assessments of students that are linked to health records that are bought, sold, and stored, for life? Ridding schools of police doesn't address the use of surveillance cameras that link images of students to their IDs—and larger databases being compiled. Moreover, the irony of teachers unions having advocated and fought so courageously for remote learning during the pandemic to save lives is that remote learning accelerated adoption of edtech platforms that give corporations vast new profits and more effective control of teachers' and students' behaviors, routinizing learning, and hence deskilling teachers' work, opening the door to frightening new ways to subvert professional ideals—and democracy.

Although the military, use of technology, and education have long been connected (Noble, 1998), tighter more direct connections have been forged. New school security guidelines, issued by the federal government under President Biden's appointee, show school safety is tied to antiterrorism strategies, an intensification of government, and capital's control of student bodies, data—and protection of Empire. Comprehensive school safety guidelines are now issued by the Cybersecurity and Infrastructure Security Agency (CISA), which is part of the US Division of Homeland Security (Kuykendall, 2022). CISA is headed by a Biden appointee, Jen Easterly, who was unanimously approved for the position. According to Easterly's biography on the CISA website, she headed the Firm Resilience and the Fusion Resilience Center at Morgan Stanley, where she was responsible for ensuring preparedness and response to operational risks to the Firm. She is also a member of the Council on Foreign Relations, whose membership and aims of expanding and protecting the US empire are described in "Who rules the World?" (Chomsky, 2016).

21.3 Theorizing Capitalism as a Social System

In retrospect, the term "neoliberalism," adopted as we made sense of capitalism's changes, missed the value of analyzing capitalism as a social system, as it had been previously by Marxists (Woods, 1995). I suggest that restoring use of this older conceptual frame clarifies and helps navigate tensions that have intensified in the past decade, fueled by the Right, between defending teachers' and others workers' economic rights and supporting struggles of social movements for equality and justice outside the workplace.

In an exchange about neoliberalism Michael Rustin (2012, p. 84) writes it is 'indeed the organizing principle of the great transformation of our times' and 'captures much of what needs to be understood' about the historical moment. Yet Rustin (ibid.) argues for a reversion to 'the antiquated term capitalism, as the name not merely of an ideology but of an ensemble of interrelated elements (modes of production, distribution, social control, socialisation, communication, military power, etc)' (p. 84). Theorizing capitalism as a social system integrates all spheres of human experience (Marx 1867/2004). It explains and reinforces—as we have been reminded, again, by social movements for justice and equality, especially Black Lives Matter—that all forms of social oppression, racism, patriarchy, anti-immigrant sentiment, heteronormativity, and ableism have been "baked into" capitalism's development.

A fundamental contradiction of capitalism is that as it changes, wreaking new harm, it also awakens new perceptions of and resistance to its damage, a process that most often occurs first outside the unions. Movements to make society more equal, just, and humane educate us about tacit assumptions about normalcy that obscure prejudices, inequalities, and physical dangers. A social system framework also allows for attention to how capitalism's political and economic engine, the drive for more profit and control of work, depends on control of work and workers. This gives the workplace and workers a strategic importance and power—not to be mistaken for a moral or political superiority—in challenges to the status quo (Moody, 2018). Workers must act collectively to make improvements in their conditions and pay, and while it's better if they understand how organizing at the workplace challenges the system, regardless of whether they do, the fact of their organizing creates a new kind of space in the system, introducing the idea of democracy at work and fulfillment of human needs that transcend the drive for profit.

Another advantage of restoring the concept of capitalism as a social system is how it illuminates why social hierarchies reflecting oppression outside work infect and permeate the workplace and workers' social relations on the job, and how life outside the workplace configures individual and collective identities, just as work shapes consciousness, too. This links to Marx's (1857/1993, p. 361) analysis of labor as 'the living, *form-giving fire*' governed by the relationship between labor-power as a commodity and 'living time' (Marx, 1993, p. 361). Material practice in the world shapes consciousness, socially and historically (Draper, 1978; Marx, 1845), and shapes human relations with the labor process, the products of labor, our ideas of what it means to be human, and ourselves (Marx 1844/1974). These are processes of alienation and estrangement that enable systemic, social oppression.

Social oppression undercuts solidarity and collective action on the job, which is why unions and workers have a very practical stake in making society more just and equal. When unions contend that workers' economic well-being is their first or primary responsibility (as is done in business unionism), they actually adopt capitalism's ideology: workers' purpose consists of making profits possible. In ignoring workers' lived experiences outside of work, unions not only undercut the power of workers' collective organization, they undercut the mutual learning and support so critical to building opposition to capitalism's toxic control over life. Even if unions try to wall off the workplace from the society, they find they must have a relationship with the state because rights to organize on the job are framed by the state's role in protecting capitalism and profit, because of unions' contradictory role under liberal capitalism: they protect workers' rights within a political system that constrains their power and authority. Inevitably, unions as organizations that must function within capitalism experience conservatizing pressures to insulate themselves and their resources, and to limit the aims and methods of struggle, so that the apparatus survives economic and political attacks.

The inherent counterweight is workers' self-organization, which demands that unions become democratic participatory organizations. Another counterweight to conservatizing pressures in the contradictory space that unions inhabit in capitalism is movements for social justice outside the workplace, which push unions to become involved in struggles beyond the economic realm, challenging capitalism directly on the terrain of social relations (Dyke & Muckian-Bates, forthcoming 2023; Mann, 2014; Moody, 2022; Russom, 2020). When we construct the fight for economic justice and the dignity of labor as themselves being social justice struggles, the challenge in labor organizing is to connect economic demands to aspirations of social movements outside the workplace, and in the case of teachers unions, outside the school walls.

21.4 Teacher Unionism's Unique Location and Contribution

Because teachers' work is located at the intersection of so many of the realms of capitalism when it is theorized as a social system, including culture, care work traditionally done by women, and knowledge production, connections to social movements' demands are fairly easy to recognize in classrooms. Yet disciplinary silo-ization in the academy as well as isolation between researchers and social movements diminish our capacity to apply theory to real-life struggles, disrupting the dialectic between theory and practice so often advocated and so seldom achieved. Teachers' labor activism provides an opportunity to bridge the divide because when workers are in motion, they are looking for ideas and support, and who better to help with ideas than researchers who examine teachers' work and understand labor's strategic role under capitalism?

Shortly before the teacher walkouts exploded into public view in 2018, an activist familiar with my work called to pick my brain about navigating the increasing tensions between the state affiliates of NEA and AFT, which represented only a tiny fraction of education workers, and the exploding number of teachers and school workers organizing for more funding for education and salaries. I suggested if the union were doing what it should, he and others wouldn't have to do what they were: the union should have been a vehicle for struggle. Instead it was passive, and even at times a barrier, because officers and staff defined union power as the existence of the apparatus and their personal access to politicians. The union was satisfied with the status quo. Therefore, given an understanding of the contradictory role of unions under capitalism, the question for activists wasn't *whether* the officials would betray the movement by cutting deals with politicians but *how and when* the betrayals would occur. While ideals and intentions of individual staff and officers influence their thinking and decision, the union apparatus is only as representative of workers' needs and wishes as we make it, because the union as an organization is embedded in capitalist political relations.

Although the program adopted by the Chicago Teachers Union (CTU) to prepare for and wage its 2012 strike (Gutstein & Lipman, 2013; Nuñez et al., 2015) has been adopted as a template by many unions (Gautreaux, 2019), I suggest a seminal contribution of the CTU's demands, articulated in "The Schools Chicago Students Deserve," is highlighted when we use the lens of capitalism as a social system. The explicit language and attention to racism, the apartheid of Chicago's school system, has been widely recognized as path breaking, and for good reason. It was a stunning challenge to the way unions traditionally cast their responsibilities. The program embedded demands for teachers' working conditions and improvements in pay and benefits in analysis that centered racism in education and society. The program and strike demands implicitly challenged the nexus between economic inequality and racism— social oppression, baked into capitalism.

Often overlooked was how the CTU used the contract to address capitalism's pressures to subject working-class students to a curriculum that prepared them for a life of drudgery: no art, no music, not even physical education. Insisting that "specials" be restored, hiring social workers and counselors, challenged capitalism's drive for profit, its driving logic and force, that life contains no space or time for play or attention to emotional and psychological needs. Finally, the union waged a strike for this program against a mayor with close contacts to the White House, during a presidential election. It thus openly challenged power relations in the society and pressures to have unions support the status quo. Without articulating this explicitly, perhaps without realizing it, the CTU developed a program and fought for demands that took on capitalism as a social system, a lens that can be applied to other unions and sectors.

In some occupations, making connections to movements fighting social oppression is more difficult, conceptually and in practice. However, when we critically examine conditions at work and examine workers' lives holistically, contextualizing our findings in a critical analysis of capitalism as a global social system, connections emerge. We see linkages between social oppression, working conditions, and political, social, and economy policies—and also how information technology is altering those connections. This reminds us that Marx argued for the revolutionary power of cooperative labor in society (Draper, 1970/2004). Capitalism educates us to compete against one another, acting on expectations and fears of scarcity, adopting the deficit paradigm, the premise that individuals, communities, and families are responsible for failure that is, in fact, caused by systemic issues that undercut success. As is true in classrooms, the deficit paradigm obscures mistakes in organizing, blaming individuals rather than critically scrutinizing what could be done differently, expanding the democratic spaces for member involvement, critique, and activity. Beyond the material limitations of time and human resources, the challenge for union activists, who want to integrate social justice demands and form alliances with social movements, is formulating campaigns and demands that are additive to struggles about economic concerns, that address fear and hostility that these other concerns are distractions or problems.

Capitalism educates us to compete against one another, acting on expectations and fears of scarcity. The antidote to that mindset is collective struggle for common goals, formulated with an eye to what people bring that is special, and how capitalism as a social system thwarts our achieving what we all need and deserve.

Disclosure Statement The author has no financial interest or benefit that has arisen from the direct applications of this research.

Note

1. This chapter adapts two chapters of my book in progress, previously published online in 2022, "Education reforms and capitalism's changes to work: Lesson for the Left", https://newpol.org/issue_post/education-reforms-and-capitalisms-changes-to-work/, in *New Politics*, 18(4); and "Capitalism and the changing classroom. Education 'reforms' through the neo-liberal lens, https://www.tempestmag.org/2022/04/capitalism-and-the-changing-classroom/, in Tempest.

References

Anyon, J. (1980). Social Class and the Hidden Curriculum of Work. *Journal of Education*, 162(1), 2–11.

Apple, M. W. (1999). Education, Culture, and Class Power: Basil Bernstein and the Neo-Marxist Sociology of Education, *Counterpoints*, 109, 137–163. Retrieved March 27, 2023, from http://www.jstor.org/stable/45136084

ATA & Kendrick, A. H. (2020). Compassion Fatigue, Emotional Labour and Educator Burnout: Research Study. Phase One Report: Academic Literature Review and Survey One Data Analysis. Retrieved March 27, 2023, from https://www.teachers.ab.ca/SiteCollectionDocuments/ATA/Publications/Research/COOR-101-30%20Compassion%20Fatigue%20Study.pdf

Au, W. (2022). *Unequal By Design: High-Stakes Testing and the Standardization of Inequality*. Taylor and Francis.

Au, W., & Ferrare, J. (2014). Sponsors of Policy: A Network Analysis of Wealthy Elites, Their Affiliated Philanthropies, and Charter School Reform in Washington State. *Teachers College Record*, 116(8), 1–24.

Bascia, N., & Rottman, C. (2011). What's So Important about Teachers' Working Conditions? The Fatal flaw in North American Educational Reform. *Journal of Education Policy*, 26(6), 787–802.

Benavot, A., & Smith, W. C. (2020). Reshaping Quality and Equity: Global Learning Metrics as a Ready-made Solution to a Manufactured Crisis. In A. Wulff (Ed.), *Grading Goal Four: Tensions, Threats, and Opportunities in the Sustainable Development Goal on Quality Education* (pp. 238–261). Brill.

Benson, K. E., & Weiner, L. (2021). Teachers Unions and Urban Education. Resistance Amidst Research Lacunae. In H. R. Milner & K. Lomotey (Eds.), *Handbook of Urban Education* (2nd ed., pp. 183–194). Routledge.

Boninger, F., Molnar, A., & Saldaña, C. (2020). Big Claims, Little Evidence, Lots of Money: The Reality Behind the Summit Learning Program and the Push to Adopt Digital Personalized Learning Platforms. University of Colorado, Boulder, School of Education. Retrieved March 27, 2023, from https://nepc.colorado.edu/publication/summit-2020

Chomsky, N. (2016). *Who Rules the World?* Metropolitan Books.

Compton, M., & Weiner, L. (Eds.). (2008). *The Global Assault on Teaching, Teachers, and Their Unions: Stories for Resistance.* Palgrave Macmillan.

Couture, J.-C., Grøttvik, R., & Sellars, S. (2020). A Profession Learning to Become: The Promise of Collaboration Between Teacher Organizations and Academia. *Paper Commissioned for the UNESCO Futures of Education Report.* Retrieved March 27, 2023, from https://unesdoc.unesco.org/ark:/48223/pf0000374156

Dandala, S. (2019). Teacher Social Justice Unionism and the Field of Industrial relations in the United States. *Journal of Labor and Society, 22,* 1–14.

Davies, B. (2003). Death to Critique and Dissent? The Policies and Practices of New Managerialism and of 'Evidence-Based Practice'. *Gender and Education, 15*(1), 91–103.

Draper, H. (1978). *Karl Marx's Theory of Revolution, Volume II. The Politics of Social Classes.* New York University Press.

Draper, H. (1970/2004). Marxism and Trade Unions (Transcripts of Speeches from the Center for Socialist History). *Marxists.org.* Retrieved March 27, 2023, from http://www.marxists.org/archive/draper/1970/tus/1-marx-tus.htm.

Dyke, E., & Muckian-Bates, B. (Forthcoming, 2023). *Rank-and-File Rebels: Theories of Power and Change in the 2018 Education Strikes.* Colorado State University Open Press.

Friedman, E. D. (2018). What's Behind the Teachers' Strikes? The Labor-movement Dynamic of Teacher Insurgencies. *Dollars and Sense.* Retrieved March 27, 2023, from http://dollarsandsense.org/archives/2018/0518edfriedman.html.

Gacoin, A. (2019). Navigating the Global "Transformation" of Education. BCTF Research Department. Retrieved March 27, 2023, from https://www.bctf.ca/publications/ResearchReports.aspx?id=55273

Gautreaux, M. (2019). Unionism: Contemplating a Radical Social Movement Unionism for the Post-Janus U.S. Labor Movement. In D. R. Ford (Ed.), *Keywords in Radical Philosophy and Education* (pp. 477–489). Brill Sense.

Global Education Monitoring. (2020). Global Education Monitoring Report: UNESCO Shows 40% of Poorest Countries Failed to Support Learners at Risk During COVID-19 Crisis and Urges Inclusion in Education. Retrieved March 27, 2023, from https://gem-report-2020.unesco.org/wp-content/uploads/2020/06/2020_Press_Release_EN.pdf

Green, P. C. I., & Connery, C. E. (2019). Charter Schools, Academy Schools, and Related-Party Transactions: Same Scams, Different Countries. *Arkansas Law Review, 72*(2), 407.

Gutstein, E., & Lipman, P. (2013). The Rebirth of the Chicago Teachers Union and Possibilities for a counter-hegemonic Education Movement. *Monthly Review*, 65(2). Retrieved March 27, 2023, from http://monthlyreview.org/2013/06/01/the-rebirth-of-the-chicago-teachers-union-and-possibilities-for-a-counter-hegemonic-education-movement

Houchen, D. F. (2020). An 'Organized Body of Intelligent Agents,' Black Teacher Activism During de jure Segregation: A Historical Case Study of the Florida State Teachers Association. *Journal of Negro Education*, 89(3), 267–281.

Huws, U. (2014). *Labor in the Global Digital Economy: The Cybertariat Comes of Age*. Monthly Review Press.

Huws, U., & Frapporti, M. (2021). Digitalisation, Labour and the Pandemic: Working Life in the Post-COVID-19 City. *Work Organisation, Labour & Globalisation*, 15(1), 7–10. https://doi.org/10.13169/workorgalaboglob.15.1.0007

Kendrick, A. (2020). *Compassion Fatigue, Emotional Labour and Educator Burnout: Research Study*. Retrieved March 27, 2023, from https://www.teachers.ab.ca/SiteCollectionDocuments/ATA/Publications/Research/COOR-101-30%20Compassion%20Fatigue%20Study.pdf

Kerssens, N., & van Dijck, J. (2021). The Platformization of Primary Education in The Netherlands. *Learning, Media and Technology*, 46(3), 250–263.

Klees, S. J., Ginsburg, M., Anwar, H., Baker Robbins, M., Bloom, H., Busacca, C., Corwith, A., Decoster, B., Fiore, A., Gasior, S., Le, H. M., Primo, L. H., & Reedy, T. D. (2020). The World Bank's SABER: A Critical Analysis. *Comparative Education Review*, 64(1), 46–65.

Klees, S. J., Stromquist, N. P., Samoff, J., & Vally, S. (2019). The 2018 World Development Report on Education: A Critical Analysis. *Development and Change*, 50(2), 603–620.

Kuykendall, K. (2022). Comprehensive K–12 School Security Guide, Online Assessment Tool Released. *Transforming Education through Technology*. Retrieved March 27, 2023, from https://thejournal.com/articles/2022/02/25/cisa-releases-updated-school-security-guide.aspx

Lindh, M., & Nolin, J. (2016). Information We Collect: Surveillance and Privacy in the Implementation of Google Apps for Education. *European Educational Research Journal*, 15(6), 644–663.

Lipman, P. (2011). *The New Political Economy of Urban Education: Neoliberalism, Race, and the Right to the City*. Taylor and Francis.

Mahfouz, J. (2022). NEPC Review: The Unexamined Rise of Therapeutic Education: How Social-Emotional Learning Extends K-12 Education's Reach into Students' Lives and Expands Teachers' Roles. Boulder, CO, National Education Policy Center. Retrieved March 27, 2023, from https://nepc.colorado.edu/thinktank/sel

Mann, K. (2014). Social Movement Literature and U.S. Labour: A Reassessment. *Studies in Social Justice*, 8(2), 165–179.

Marx, K. (1845). *Theses on Feuerbach*. Marxists.org. Retrieved March 27, 2023, from https://www.marxists.org/archive/marx/works/1845/theses/theses.htm

Marx, K. (1844/1974). *Economic and Philosophical Manuscripts*. Progress Publishers.

Marx, K. (1857/1993). *Grundrisse: Outline of the Critique of Political Economy*. Penguin.

Marx, K. (1867/2004). *Capital, Volume 1: A Critique of Political Economy*. Penguin.

Moody, K. (1997). *Workers in a Lean World. Unions in the International Economy*. Verso.

Moody, K. (2018). High Tech, Low Growth: Robots and the Future of Work. *Historical Materialism*, 26(4), 3–34.

Moody, K. (2022). *Breaking the Impasse*. Haymarket.
Mortimer, C. (2020, February 10). A New Chapter: The Neoliberal Project Joins PPI. Retrieved March 27, 2023, from https://www.progressivepolicy.org/blogs/a-new-chapter-the-neoliberal-project-joins-ppi/
NEPC. (2021). 'Dataveillance', Algorithmic Bias, and Other Concerns About Learning Management Systems. *National Education Policy Center Newsletter*. Retrieved March 27, 2023, from https://nepc.colorado.edu/publication/newsletter-dataveillance-012821
Noble, D. D. (1998). The Regime of Technology in Education. In L. E. Beyer & M. W. Apple (Eds.), *The Curriculum. Problems, Politics, and Possibilities* (pp. 267–283). SUNY Press.
Nuñez, I., Gregory, M., & Konkol, P. (2015). *Worth Striking For: Why Education Policy is Every Teacher's Concern. Lessons from Chicago*. Teachers College Press.
Ovetz, R. (2020). The Algorithmic University: On-Line Education, Learning Management Systems, and the Struggle Over Academic Labor. *Critical Sociology, 47*, 1–20.
Owens, L. Z. (2022). (Re)Forming Unions for Social Justice. A Critical Autoethnographic Inquiry into Racism, Democracy, and Teacher Leadership. *Critical Education, 13*(2) https://doi.org/10.14288/ce.v13i3.186607
Petrucci, L. L. (2021). Taylored Flexibility: Agile, Control, and the Software Labor Process. *Unpub. PhD*. Division of Graduate Studies, University of Oregon. Retrieved March 27, 2023, from https://scholarsbank.uoregon.edu/xmlui/handle/1794/26848
Private Equity Policy Project. (2022). Private Equity in Education: How Wall Street Profits from a Public Good. Retrieved March 27, 2023, from https://pestakeholder.org/wp-content/uploads/2022/12/Education-report-design_v3-1.pdf
Rothstein, R. (2014). Segregated Housing, Segregated Schools. *Education Week*. Retrieved March 27, 2023, from https://www.edweek.org/ew/articles/2014/03/26/26rothstein_ep.h33.html
Rousmaniere, K. (2001). White Silence: A Racial Biography of Margaret Haley. *Equity and Excellence in Education, 34*(2), 7–15.
Russom, G. (2020). The Teachers' Strikes of 2018–2019: A Gendered Rebellion. In R. K. Givan & A. S. Lang (Eds.), *Strike for the Common Good: Fighting for the Future of Public Education* (pp. 172–182). University of Michigan Press.
Rustin, M. (2012). The Crisis of a Social System. In J. Rutherford & S. Davison (Eds.), *Sounding on the Neoliberal Crisis* (pp. 80–87). London.
Saltman, K. J. (2018). *The Swindle of Innovative Educational Finance*. University of Minnesota Press.
Schreyer, J. (2021). Algorithmic Work Coordination and Workers' Voice in the COVID-19 Pandemic: The Case of Foodora/Lieferando. *Work Organisation, Labour & Globalisation, 15*(1), 69–84. https://doi.org/10.13169/workorgalaboglob.15.1.0069
Sellar, S., & Hogan, A. (2019). *Pearson 2025—Transforming Teaching and the Privatization of Education Data*. Retrieved March 27, 2023, from https://issuu.com/educationinternational/docs/2019_ei_gr_essay_pearson2025_eng_24
Simba Information. (2022). United States Social and Emotional Learning: 2022–2023. Retrieved March 27, 2023, from https://www.researchandmarkets.com/reports/5654263/united-states-social-and-emotional-learning

Smith, C. S. (2022). Is A.I. the Future of Test Prep? *New York Times* (Business). Retrieved March 27, 2023, from https://www.nytimes.com/2022/12/27/business/ai-education-app-riiid.html

Stark, L. W., & Spreen, C. A. (2020). Global Educator Movements: Teacher Struggles Against Neoliberalism and for Democracy and Justice. In R. K. Givan & A. S. Lang (Eds.), *Strike for the Common Good: Fighting for the Future of Public Education* (pp. 234–252). University of Michigan Press.

Stevenson, H. (2017). The 'Datafication' of Teaching: Can Teachers Speak Back to the Numbers? *Peabody Journal of Education, 92*(4), 537–557.

Weiner, L. (2001). Review of "Workers in a Lean World". *Educational Studies, 32*, 351–357.

Weiner, L., & Asselin, C. (2020). Learning from Lacunae in Research: Making Sense of Teachers' Labor Activism. *Multidisciplinary Journal of Educational Research, 10*(3), 226–270.

Weiner, L., Asselin, C., Owens, L. Z., Dyke, E. & Benson, K. E. (Forthcoming, 2023). Research on Teachers' Labor Activism and Teachers Unions: Implications for Educational Policy, Scholarship, and Activism. In: J. S. Lora Cohen-Vogel & P. Youngs (Eds), *American Educational Research Association Handbook of Education Policy Research* (2nd ed.). American Educational Research Association.

Williamson, B. (2018). Silicon Startup Schools: Technocracy, Algorithmic Technocracy, Imaginaries and Venture Philanthropy in Corporate Education Reform. *Critical Studies in Education, 59*(2), 218–236.

Williamson, B., & Hogan, A. (2020). Commercialisation and Privatisation in/of Education in the Context of Covid-19. Retrieved March 27, 2023, from https://issuu.com/educationinternational/docs/2020_eiresearch_gr_commercialisation_privatisation

Wood, E. M. (1995). *Democracy Against Capitalism*. Cambridge University Press.

World Bank. (2018). *World Development Report 2018: Learning to Realize Education's Promise*. World Bank.

World Bank. (2019). *World Development Report, 2019. The Changing Nature of Work*. World Bank.

World Bank. (2020). Concept Note. *The World Bank World Development Report 2021. Data for Better Lives*. The World Bank.

CHAPTER 22

Contemporary Student Movements and Capitalism. A Marxist Debate

Lorenzo Cini and Héctor Ríos-Jara

22.1 Introduction

Student movements have historically been a key factor in the transformation of modern societies. From the role that young intellectuals and students' societies played during the American Independence process and the French Revolution to the most recent student protests against austerity and climate change, students have been a relevant actor in social movements. Over the past century, students have massively arisen to challenge various institutions of capitalist societies. During the 1960s, students have globally mobilized to contest the elitist and authoritarian character of universities by foreseeing the crisis of Fordist capitalism and its logic of accumulation. Triggered by the 2008 financial crisis, in the early 2010s, student protests emerged in various world's regions to oppose the implementation of neoliberal policies in higher education (HE) and, more in general, the process of knowledge commodification.

Despite their historical importance, students and their political activism have been a controversial issue in the Marxist tradition. Although contemporary student activists have described themselves and their protests as anti-capitalist, Marxist intellectuals have developed different interpretations about both the role of students in class struggle and their revolutionary potential. One of the

L. Cini (✉)
University College Cork, Cork, Ireland
e-mail: LCini@ucc.ie

H. Ríos-Jara
Universidad Alberto Hurtado, Santiago, Chile
e-mail: hector.rios.18@ucl.ac.uk

reasons explaining the difficulties of Marxists in theorizing student protests as anti-capitalistic has to do with a 'foundational' bias of this tradition. Marx and Engels have built a revolutionary theory of social change, which assigned an almost exclusive centrality to workers in the class struggle. Whilst workers have been considered as the "grave-diggers" of capitalism, and the subject of social emancipation *per excellence,* students have never had a clear role in it.

For example, in exploring the view that Marx and Engels had of student activists during the revolts of 1836 and 1848, Draper (1977) found out that the two authors exhibited an ambivalent reading. They criticized the reactionary student factions defending the old regime during the revolts, while encouraging the student groups supporting the working class. Marx was also skeptical in promoting free HE. He described free education as a transference of worker's wealth to the bourgeoisie's offspring. Hence, Marx's analysis of student protests was in line with his theoretical view, in which students were not considered as pivotal in the revolutionary process. Such original omission of students as a relevant actor in social change has, then, impacted on all the successive Marxist interpretations of student movements.

In this chapter, we explore and compare the 1960s and 2010s global waves of student protest to purse two research objectives. First, we illustrate and cast light on their (anti)capitalistic character and their political claims. Second, we present and discuss how various Marxist theorists have interpreted students and their mobilizations in the process of capitalist change. We analyze both waves by using the Marxian concept of labor-power (and its relation to the capitalist production process) as a prism. For Marx, labor-power (also presented as living labor) is the set of (generic) mental and physical capabilities existing in physical form of a human being, whose exploitation is the only source of economic value in capitalism. In *Volume* I of *Capital,* Marx presents and discusses such conception of capitalist valorization of labor defined as labor theory of value. As he puts it: "the specific use-value which this commodity possesses of being a source not only of value, but of more value than it has itself" (Marx, 1867, p. 136). Put otherwise, for Marx, the exploitation of labor-power is the source of capitalist valorization and the center of its mode of production. Capitalism is, therefore, the specific production mode based on the valorization and appropriation of labor-power.

Building on this framework, we present and discuss the different Marxist interpretations of student protests that have considered student politics in relation to contemporary processes of capitalist valorization. We focus on the 1960s and 2010s global waves of student protests, which we regard as two theoretically and politically emblematic cases to analyze in relation to such processes. We structure and guide our chapter around two questions: (1) Can contemporary students be considered as labor-power in the capitalist economy? (2) Can their mobilizations be seen as fully anti-capitalistic and part of a broader conception of class struggle?

The chapter is structured as follows. In the first part, we analyze the historical context and the rise and fall of the 1960s student protests by illustrating their main political demands. Then we present and discuss the theoretical debate that such mobilizations spurred among various Marxist intellectuals and how these interpreted the role of student revolts in the then capitalist transformation. In the second part, we follow the same path for the 2010s student protests. We conclude the chapter with a final section where we discuss this comparison considering our research questions, and we identify some further challenges to theorize the political potential of contemporary student movements.

22.2 The Rise and Fall of the 1960s Protests

The wave of student protests of the 1960s included May 68 in France, student mobilizations in Germany between 1967 and 1969, the long cycle of social struggles in Italy and the United States (US), as well as the cases of student protests in Mexico, Praga, and Japan, among other cases (Barker, 2008; Ehrenreich & Ehrenreich, 1969). Despite the national differences, the literature has highlighted significant commonalities between the protests that give a distinctive meaning to the wave (Altbach, 1970; Barker, 2008).

Postwar Capitalism: The Golden Years

These student protests emerged in a period described as the golden age of capitalism (Hobsbawm, 1995). Particularly in countries like the US and Germany, the 30 years after the Second World War was a period of high economic prosperity and relative stability. Keynesian policies favored a strong state in the planning and coordination of the economy. National redistributive policies complemented industrial policies, which included rising wages and full employment. They also involved the creation of welfare regimes, which provided access to health, education, pension, and social care (Korpi, 1983). The combination meant a partial redistribution of wealth from capital toward labor within each nation and the experience of high living standards and job security for the working class.

The golden age was also a period of political stability. Democracies of developed countries stabilized around the imperative of national reconstruction. Consequently, the conflict between capital and labor tended to institutionalize and stopped being considered as a revolutionary threat. Mass parties managed to represent a vast spectrum of society, giving institutional representation to the labor movement in parliament and government. Strikes and protests arose, but they were used more strategically to achieve concrete aims and support institutional forces within the democratic game.

The distinctive features of the post-war period had a direct impact on HE. The developmental policies of industrial capitalism favored the expansion of universities as institutions oriented to the production of technology and skilled labor in economies in full expansion. The US, the United Kingdom, and West Germany introduced plans for university expansion, favoring the creation of new public institutions (Trow, 1973). The plans transformed the elitist HE systems into massive ones. However, not all countries invested enough in the process. In Italy and France, university massification meant more students but not enough funding. Consequently, the infrastructure and quality deteriorated, and students were exposed to overcrowded and outdated lectures (Barker, 2008).

University massification also meant a more complex student population. In the US, the advancement of the civil rights movement allowed access for people of color and women to universities. Nonetheless, they still suffered from institutional discrimination and segregation. In addition, the massification of universities did not mean a reform of the structure of governance of universities and the almost plenipotentiary powers of authorities. Most student efforts to demand reforms confronted authoritarian measures that enforce law and order. The absence of democratic mechanisms of participation and representation within the university forced students to radicalize their tactics, opting for more disruptive actions against authorities. Such action soon became an opposition to the police, government, imperialism, and different types of institutions that represented the power and authority of capitalist societies (Cohn-Bendit & Cohn-Bendit, 1968).

Students and the Revolutionary Anti-capitalism of the 1960s

There is consensus among scholars that the 68 protests did not have a shared pledge of demands (Altbach, 1970; Barker, 2008). The famous slogan at the Sorbonne, "be realistic, demand the impossible," captures the scope of transformation opened by protests and the lack of a coherent pledge among activists. Nevertheless, the 1960s protests acquired a distinctive emancipatory meaning that renewed the critique of capitalism and created a new political space for a left critical of capitalism and the experiences of real socialism (Cohn-Bendit & Cohn-Bendit, 1968). We briefly explore some of the distinctive critiques of capitalism developed by activists and how this critique related to the labor movement.

Most of the student activists declared themselves as anti-capitalists and revolutionaries. Students denounced capitalism as a system of exploitation and oppression. They considered capitalism to be an irrational form of society that only concentrate wealth and power in the hand of the bourgeoisie of the west, perpetuating the oppression of society inside and outside capitalist countries. However, the meaning of an anti-capitalist revolution was not crystalized in any concrete program of change or organization but in the constant exploration for new ways of protesting and organizing to subvert capitalist order (ibid.).

For example, one the most shared topics of contestation among activists was the opposition to disciplinary rules over political expression, sexual conduct, intellectual development, and other moral regulations within universities and broader society. For activists, conservatism, repression, and violence were integral to capitalist societies and despite the concrete role that each social sector played within the economy, all society was exposed to capitalist oppression. Authoritarian institutions placed students and other stratum of society in a situation of oppression as similar as that of workers. Universities, as much as the police, the media and political parties, were considered part of the bureaucracy governing capitalist societies. Like the Fordist factories that exploited workers, students saw universities, the police, the media, and political parties as disciplinary factories forcing society to reproduce capitalism and alienate humanity of its solidarity and creativity. From this perspective, the abolition of social classes was imagined as the result of the eradication of repressive institutions and the alienating culture of capitalism, which activists saw as the main cause of human oppression (Hayden, 1962).

The anti-capitalism of the 1960s represented a form of reimagining an alternative society by freeing the collective creativity of human beings. In this context, the revolution did not mean an armed insurgency against a certain regime but the physical and ideological disruption of any authority that constrained the collective exercise of freedom. In this critique, students reclaimed emancipatory values of freedom and democracy that they perceive as forgotten by the left parties and the labor movement. As consequence, students questioned the role that unions and left-wing parties were playing in reproducing capitalist bureaucracy. In their view, unions and political parties were another example of bureaucracy that alienated workers from their revolutionary potential. Indeed, during the protests, student activists denounced the control and repression that political parties and unions exercised over workers. In France, students denounced how the Socialist and Communist Parties prohibited workers to ally with students. Likewise, in the US, the lack of support from the Democrats to the civil right movement and anti-war protests was a point of conflict between students and party politics. In the activists' eyes, traditional left-wing parties and their unions were unwilling to challenge the system, as they were merely playing the game of the bourgeoisie, in taming workers' disruptive power, and keeping them away from other subaltern groups willing to oppose capitalism (Cohn-Bendit & Cohn-Bendit, 1968).

The Marxist Interpretations

The 1960s' protests were controversial among Marxist intellectuals. As protests started in universities, many intellectuals had direct interactions with activists, having immediate reactions toward the events. Despite close connections, there was a divisive view of the protests and its meaning for the left (Drake, 1997; Freyenhagen, 2014). For example, Althusser and Habermas were skeptical about the movement's revolutionary credentials. Althusser (Macciocchi & Althusser, 1973) criticized the vanguardist positions that students presumed, their lack of a strategic line of action, and the ideologies that a-critically they embraced. For him, the most important flaw of the movement actor was the lack of a structural power of students and the absence of a clear position on the revolutionary class struggle. Thus, he argued:

if a movement like the Workers' Movement deserves its title, that is because it is the Movement of a social class (the proletariat), and furthermore of the only objectively revolutionary class. The university students, secondary school students, and young intellectual workers do not constitute a class, but rather "middle strata" with a petty-bourgeois ideology. (ibid., p. 312)

Althusser described students as a part of the middle class, which was experiencing a crisis of dissatisfaction with capitalist ideology and their false prospects. In his view, students were not as exploited as workers, as their labor-power was not exposed to a process of commodification and to value extraction. Therefore, student oppression was to be seen as merely symbolic, and it did not take place in the core infrastructure of capital. For him, the lack of objective conditions of exploitation made the student movement a petty-bourgeois ideological revolt against the educational apparatuses of reproduction of capitalism rather than a revolutionary movement. This ideological revolt revealed a crisis of justification among different *bourgeois strata*, but not a revolutionary movement capable of taking a leading role in the class struggle. Accordingly, Althusser saw the effort to homogenize students and workers as a part of the same oppressed society as both theoretically wrong and political dangerous. First, it denied the strategic and leading role that workers, as a class, have within capitalist opposition. Second, it overestimated the role that students and their political ideas can have in the construction of the revolutionary movement.

In a similar fashion, Habermas (1987) also criticized the anti-capitalist attitudes of the movement, denying the real connection between the structural position of students, their practices, and their claims. Like Althusser, Habermas described student protests as a middle-class revolt driven by the rise of individual and postmaterial demands that industrial capitalism promised but never delivered. For him, the anti-capitalist attitudes of students were unrepresentative of most of the society that does not possess the level of wealth of the middle classes, and whose incomes depend on the commodification of their labor-power. For Habermas, the movement resulted from a psychosocial dissatisfaction amongst privileged sectors of the liberal elite concerning their culture and status. This was conveyed by contesting the conservative norms of the historical and material form of this specific capitalist society. However, students lacked organic connections with the main social subjects exposed to capitalist exploitation and oppression, being unable to represent or lead them.

By contrast, Marcuse celebrated the revolt and saw it as a paradigmatic event in class struggle (Leslie, 1999). Marcuse agreed with Habermas and Althusser about the absence of a structural position amongst students in relation to capitalist domination, and agreed that student labor-power is not directly exposed to exploitation like workers (Marcuse, 1969). However, in his view, the critique made by students of capitalist bureaucracy, culture and imperialism represented a symptomatic expression of the new contradictions of capitalism. It contained the potential for a broader social base for transformation that was able to go beyond the labor movement. This included peasants and people from former colonies of the then third world, as well as the unrealized promise of equality, prosperity, and freedom in the capitalist metropolis. Students were part of this broader social base of capitalism, and they played a strategic role in subverting the institutions and values of capitalism from within.

In addition, Marcuse (ibid.) highlighted the relevance of student protests as an effort to renew socialist values and practices that overcome the institutionalized expressions of the labor movement, by giving new emancipatory meanings to the concept of revolution and socialism. For him, the fact that students were not under the circuits of labor exploitation was an opportunity to unleash the emancipatory potential of social groups that remained at the margins of capitalism, and whose labor-power remained fresh and creative. For Marcuse, students could not replace the workers' movement as a key revolutionary subject. Yet, they could generate a "radical enlightenment, in theory, and by practice, and the development of cadres and nuclei for the struggle against the global structure of capitalism" (ibid., p. 33). From this perspective, students were not a revolutionary movement, but they were strategic agents of change with the potential to amplify the social base of the class struggle and imagine new forms and meanings of socialism.

Like Marcuse, Ernest Mandel (1968) also defended the revolutionary role of students. He saw in the students a form of alienated intellectual labor-power with the capacity to rebel against the capitalist domination inside and around universities. He recognized that students have a strategic role in the class struggle, since universities play a fundamental role in the production of technicians, professionals, and the scientific knowledge to continue advancing the capitalist development. For Mandel, the student contestation of university curricula, authorities, and mission meant a rejection of the capitalist view of HE and, more broadly, a critique of the functional role that knowledge and students played within capitalism.

However, like Althusser and Habermas, Mandel recognized that most university students came from the middle class, and they would have worked as white collars workers. But he also saw that growing sectors of the working class were accessing universities, and many prospective graduates would be precarious workers with a critical attitude toward capitalism that can grow politically. In addition, Mandel highlighted the unity of theory and practice that the student revolt achieved. Like for workers and other past movements, students rebelled against their immediate conditions of oppression within the university system and society at large, theorizing and acting against their political subordination within universities and their future condition of exploitation in the capitalist labor market. Although students did not have the same function of workers in Fordist capitalism, the 1960s students were able to contest university and other capitalist institutions and authorities. Consequently, their alliance with workers was not only plausible in principle, but also politically necessary since they could still play a relevant role in the revolutionary process.

22.3   On the 2010s Student Wave

The New Neoliberal Context of HE

At the beginning of the 1980s, the rise of neoliberalism, as a new model of capitalism and with a renewed ideology, had a significant impact on HE. Indeed, the neoliberal conception of education challenged the notion of right to education, replacing the expansion of public and free universities with a marketized view of delivering education (Berman, 2012). Drawing on the assumption of the higher efficiency of the private sector, the new HE approach promoted the discipline of the marketplace, the power of the consumer, and the engine of competition (McGettigan, 2013). Driving this process is capital's profit-searching activity, incessantly aimed at creating new terrains of valorization (Harvey, 2017; see also the original discussion on competition and creation of the world market economy in the *Third Volume* of *Capital*: Marx, 1894). Increasing the weight of families' expenditure while reducing state funding, the neoliberal conception placed universities in competition with each other for tuition fees and private funding. This process brought about significant institutional changes affecting the resources and opportunities for students, including: a) the commodification of services, with the introduction of tuition fees and loans, or the increase of their levels; b) the expansion of private HE institutions; c) managerialism, with mechanisms of competition and funding allocation conditional on the performance of criteria defined externally, and the introduction of cost-benefit and efficiency principles; and d) the marketization of curricula (see della Porta et al., 2020).

The neoliberal agenda in HE intensified the commodification of the sector by replacing public spending with private investments (Klemenčič, 2014). As public funds were drastically reduced, universities were increasingly operating like businesses and perpetually in search of monies via increased tuition fees and private investments (Smeltzer & Hearn, 2015). To achieve this, they invested more in marketing, brand management, and promotion. Privatization was a related trend, which also implied the proliferation of private—in some cases de facto, for-profit—institutions in competition with public ones. This transformed the function of the state from the provision of public services (such as education) to a regulator of (quasi)market competition, with the state contributing to financing HE and regulating the quality of the study courses offered by universities.

Managerialism was a related trend affecting the internal governance of the institution, with an increase in the number and decision-making power of managers and top-level administrators in governing bodies, at the expense of academics and professors (Ginsberg, 2011). While up to the 1970s the dominant idea was that universities were self-governing bodies, in the neoliberal approach universities must be responsive to numerous stakeholders, and quickly and efficiently adapt to their requests. The demands for adaptation to labor-market changes were especially relevant, as well as the claim of the rational administration of resources in a context dominated by austerity. As managerialism accompanied a marketization of curricula, the conception of the role of the university changed from creating culture and knowledge to preparing individuals for the labor market. In the 'new managerialism' approach, universities were considered as producing goods such as teaching, research, and services (Agasisti & Catalano, 2006). Changes in courses, curricula, and academic programs aimed to meet the demands of the business sector or to respond to requests made by supranational bureaucracies.

Finally, the impact of the economic crisis in 2008 further contributed to the acceleration of this process of marketization. Many governments across the world adopted one or more of these measures as a way out of the crisis, by pursuing the dominant political creed of the neoliberal and pro-austerity agenda. Austerity measures, following the crisis, accelerated the implementation of neoliberal reforms in countries where they previously did not exist. For example, after the 2008 crisis, countries like the UK, Canada, and Germany accelerated neoliberal reforms in their HE systems. Most of these changes were part of the austerity packages and necessitated the introduction of dramatic cuts in the public spending to the welfare system.

Student Critiques of the Neoliberal HE

The context described above is the backdrop against which a global wave of student protests arose and diffused in the second half of the 2010s. Indeed, the implementation of the market logic, whose intensity and depth varied across countries, created the re-emergence of significant distributive conflicts around HE and its policies. Insofar as market relations have colonized an increasing number of aspects of HE with their profit-led logic, various struggles for the decommodification of goods, services, and social relations have emerged. More specifically, most student protests have centered on the growing costs of postsecondary education for students and their families. The rise in the cost of HE has been driven by the escalation of tuition fees and the massification of student loans introduced in many countries around the world. The introduction of fees and loans meant the transference of the responsibility to fund HE from collective and corporate taxation toward individuals. There has been a change in the education of students, focused around a move from citizens entitled to a social right toward consumers responsible for their own decisions (Sukarieh & Tannock, 2015). Overall, the marketization of HE has triggered protests in a variety of locations, in both advanced and developing economies.

Fighting back against this process, student protests arose in several regions across the world, ranging from South Korea and India in Asia, Chile and Mexico in South America, Quebec and the US in North America, to South Africa and Nigeria in Africa, and Italy, the UK, and Germany in Europe (Brooks, 2016; Klemenčič, 2014). Their main demands were an end to the introduction (or increase) of student fees and the return to free education in a publicly funded system (Cini et al., 2021). Notably, these protests arose as a response to growing structural contradictions in the relationship that post-secondary education had with society and the economy at large. For decades now, post-secondary education has been promoted by governments around the world as the most important vehicle for individual social mobility, promising access to good jobs and high standards of living. Yet, at the same time, those students found themselves unable to obtain the high quality and high wage employment that they believed had been promised to them. The world's systems of post-secondary study have been pressured to deliver on promises they were not able to keep. Facing the personal and collective consequences of such broken promises, students have, thus, started mobilizing across the world.

Yet, for some observers, the protesters' claims were only framed in terms of the opportunities that further and HE can open for social and economic mobility at the individual-level (Sukarieh & Tannock, 2015). In such a view, most of the protesters' demands were not about radically transforming the substance of current post-secondary education systems, but 'focused instead either on preserving and defending current systems from proposed future restructuring and/or rolling conditions in these systems back to an earlier period of welfare state post-secondary education that saw its heyday during the 1950s and 1960s' (ibid., p. 126). In such interpretations, these mobilizations did not challenge the basic vision of the education for a model of social mobility, rather they simply challenged the structural obstacles students perceived to be threatening their ability to realize this vision for themselves.

By contrast, other observers provided a more nuanced, and less individualistic, picture of the 2010s student protests. For Caffentzis (2010), for instance, these protests had two souls: one that demanded free university education, reviving the dream of publicly financed mass scholarity, ostensibly proposing to return it to the model of the Keynesian era; and another that was in revolt against the university itself, calling for a mass exit from it, or aiming to transform the campus into a base for alternative knowledge production that is accessible to those outside its walls.

Regardless of the various and alternative interpretations of the 2010s mobilizations, we maintain that all these analyses depart and share the same starting point. The contextual factors from which such mobilizations have arisen saw the reappearance of students as political actors related to the emergence of a range of distributional conflicts stemming from the implementation of the neoliberal agenda in the field of HE. In other words, the rise and proliferation of these mobilizations can be seen as a collective response to the expansion of neoliberal capitalism and its political consequences for HE. Whether such a response is to be interpreted as a demand for class-based, social mobility, for individual co-optation in the system or, by contrast, more radically as an antisystemic challenge, is an open question that can only be answered in the fullness of time.

The Marxist Interpretations

Compared to the 1960s' student unrest, the Marxist readings of the 2010s' student protests have been less numerous in terms of volume and variety. Yet, intellectuals belonging to various neo-Marxist perspectives have utilized and revived specific Marxian concepts to make sense of these mobilizations by emphasizing their potential role in the overthrowing of neoliberal capitalism. Classical concepts serve as heuristics in this tradition, such as mode of production, valorization process, general intellect, and labor-power. These have been retaken and creatively adopted in such perspectives to account for the novel features of neoliberal capitalism and, in it, for the role played by students. All these interpretations see the current mode of production as a capitalist regime based upon the valorization of knowledge, in the sense that knowledge is considered as the key source of the accumulation process (see, for instance, Aronowitz, 2000; Hardt & Negri, 2009; Roggero, 2011; Slaughter & Rhoades, 2004; Soederberg, 2014). Put otherwise, knowledge is seen as the new raw material to be converted to products, processes, and services, which are then sold in the marketplace for a profit (Aronowitz, 2000; Slaughter & Rhoades, 2004). Accordingly, HE acquires a pivotal economic function in this mode of production, and universities are a major site for the process of knowledge commodification and, thus, key drivers of the global economy.

If knowledge is the central feature of the current mode of capitalist production, then 'knowledge workers' are seen as its central actors, almost portrayed as the new (revolutionary) class, and, therefore, at least according to the most radical neo-Marxist interpretations, also pivotal for its overthrowing. This is where the interpretations of the 2010's protests are mostly differentiated from the Marxist readings of the 1960's student revolts. Key to this divergence is the extended meaning given to the Marxian concept of labor-power in the new context based upon knowledge valorization. For these intellectuals, given the centrality of knowledge in contemporary relations of production, students must be already considered as labor-power (and not only as labor-power in formation), namely, as workers whose social activities are already immediately productive, namely, creating capitalist (surplus) value (partially building here on the Marxian concept of *general intellect* as formulated in the *Grundrisse*: see Marx, 1857). In such readings, students represent a key component of the class of knowledge workers and, thereby, their mobilizations against the commodification of HE, and neoliberalism more in general, must be read as a direct political contribution to the overthrowing of capitalism.

For Soederberg (2014), for instance, students must be considered as part of the new surplus labor-power, intrinsically connected to, and defined by, the current processes of credit-led accumulation. Capitalists today employ consumer credit as a means of creating new markets for interest- and fee-generating revenue, in order to further commodify HE. In her view, the burgeoning student loan industry, as essential part of the neoliberal shift away from public support for HE to placing the burden of financing on the individual, is a case in point of this accumulation process. According to Soederberg (ibid.), students do not only contribute to the expansion of the market of HE as consumers, but they also constitute a necessary condition for the expanded reproduction of the credit-led accumulation process as (surplus) workers.

The surplus working population (Marx, 1867) is, in fact, a highly dynamic and heterogeneous segment of the population that is comprised of underemployed and unemployed workers, which places downward pressure on existing wage levels, threatens employed laborers with layoffs, discourages labor organization, and increases the intensity of labor for those employed. In short, such a population is a ready supply of cheap workers that is profitable for capitalists. Seen from this angle, indebted students are to be regarded as surplus labor-power as well. Accumulating hefty debt loads, an ever-increasing share of the student population is, in fact, compelled to accept low-paid and precarious jobs, both during their years of study and for many years after their graduation, to repay their debts. Embedded in such a debt trap, these workers increase the ranks of the global reserve army of labor-power and, therefore, further spur the current process of capital accumulation. To halt this process and, with it, to overthrow neoliberal capitalism, indebted students, in coalition with other indebted actors, should rise-up and oppose the student and other loan industries. Indeed, this is the political meaning that Soederberg (2014) gives to the 2010's student protest wave.

The post-Workerist reading (Roggero, 2011), deriving from the Italian 1960s' *operaista* tradition (for a review, see Wright, 2002), has provided an even more radical interpretation of the 2010's student mobilizations, in terms of labor-power in revolt (Cini, 2019). Even more explicitly than Soederberg's theory, these Marxists—connected to the then operating *Edu-factory* collective, an international Marxist network of political militants and engaged academics considering HE as a new pivotal terrain of class struggle in contemporary capitalism (Dokuzović, 2016)—see students as knowledge-producing labor and part of the new cognitive class, which, if undertaking a process of politicization, will be able to reverse the process of knowledge commodification and transcend its mode of capitalist exploitation. More notably—for the post-Workerists—the social cooperation enacted by such a class in its cognitive activities promotes various circuits of knowledge production, both inside and outside the university context, and is the crucial source for the valorization process in the current mode of production. Lucarelli and Vercellone (2013, p. 10) define such a system of production as 'cognitive capitalism,' meaning 'a system of accumulation in which the cognitive dimension of labor becomes the dominant principle of value creation, whereas the main form of capital becomes the so-called immaterial and intellectual one.' Central to this regime is, thus, the exploitation of cognitive labor-power.

Drawing on the Marxian concept of *general intellect* (Marx, 1857), Roggero (2011) calls such labor-power 'living knowledge' to highlight that the main source of value production, knowledge, is embedded in the living labor of the subjects producing it, namely, students and other knowledge workers. In this view, and unlike the Marxian interpretation identifying the general intellect with the general social knowledge embodied in fixed capital (see Marx, 1857, pp. 704–706, but also Harvey, 2017 for a more recent, 'orthodox' interpretation), 'the general intellect is no longer objectified in dead knowledge [namely, the fixed capital] but formed in social cooperation and in the production of living knowledge: it is inseparable from the subjects that compose it' (Roggero, 2011, p. 25). In other words—for these Marxists—the general intellect, embodied today in the living knowledge of workers, can be, de facto, created and developed without the intervention of capital and of its structures of control and command. What is in permanent crisis in the knowledge-based society is, thus, the capitalist capacity of command over cognitive labor. By contrast, labor-power has potentially, in itself, the capacity to overthrow these parasitic, command structures, and instead to create an alternative social organization, based on the free production and circulation of knowledge. This is a society that Hardt and Negri (2009) call the 'common.' In this view, the 2010's student protests can be read as cognitive labor-power in revolt against neoliberal capitalism for the creation of a neo-communistic society, based on free knowledge-production.

22.4 Discussion and Conclusion

Our study compared the global waves of student protest of the 1960s and 2010s, to explore and evaluate their anti-capitalist character and discuss their (potential) role in processes of (anti)capitalist transformation. We did so by analyzing these students' main political demands and how specific Marxist intellectuals interpreted their mobilizations. In this final section, we summarize and discuss the main points of the chapter by explicitly answering the two questions that structured and guided our exposition. In doing so, we will be addressing the key similarities and differences between the two waves of protest. For the sake of analysis, we treat each question separately.

Starting with question 1: can contemporary students be considered as labor-power in the capitalist economy? In the chapter, we noted that identifying the specific capitalist formations in which these students were embedded during the two distinct protest waves was crucial to answer this question. The passage from Fordism to neoliberalism has in fact significantly impacted on the function of HE for each capitalist model, on the societal role of students as well as on their political claims of mobilization. In the aftermath of the 1960s' student mobilizations, HE institutions were, in fact, relatively isolated with respect to the Fordist economy and its logic of accumulation. In this sense, universities were still perceived as the key site where the future ruling class was educated. The 1960's student mobilizations aimed, thus, to demolish such enduring elitist and authoritarian institution to open it up to the offspring of the working class.

In terms of labor-power, students were, therefore, considered as a prospective, white collar, working population with only an ancillary function in the class struggle carried out by the industrial working-class. By contrast, the 2010's wave of student protests emerged in a completely different societal scenario, where the rise of a knowledge-based economy placed the role of HE and students at the center of the processes of capitalist valorization. In this sense, the latter mobilizations aimed to oppose the capitalist process of knowledge commodification and to overthrow its institutions, which were primarily geared to exploit a high-skilled and educated working population. In this interpretation, students were, thus, already considered as part of a broader class of cognitive labor-power, whose full exploitation was supposed to drive the economic growth of a knowledge-based society.

In relation to question 2: Can contemporary student mobilizations be seen as fully anti-capitalistic and part of a broader conception of class struggle? The comparison between two waves of student protests and their interpretations showed that student protests have remained a controversial phenomenon to read for the Marxist tradition. However, the theoretical and political dilemmas associated with the student protests have significantly evolved between the two waves. In the 1960s, the alliance between students and workers was predominantly seen as theoretically and politically problematic. Most of the Marxist scholars we considered did not recognize students as a strategic actor within capitalism and denied the existence of a revolutionary potential in their mobilizations. In the 2010's wave, the Marxist intellectuals we treated remarked, instead, on the significant role that students could have within the broader struggle against neoliberal capitalism, and in HE more specifically.

Partially building on the optimistic and progressive view of Marcuse and Mandel, the Marxist observers of 2010's student protests broadened the concept of class (struggle) and labor-power to stress the transformative power of students. Although their interpretations were diverse and not necessarily coherent, they all emphasized how changes in capitalist accumulation incorporated new social groups and new areas of society within the spectrum of exploitation (Marx, 1867), and how these transformations opened new opportunities for contestation. The neo-Marxist interpretations of the student movement followed the renewed efforts within this tradition to update the theory of labor exploitation, facing up a new model of accumulation based on knowledge, and to expand circuits of commodification, as well as the forms of labor-power's extraction. This interpretative aperture helped to redefine the contours of the revolutionary class and the meaning of labor, which recognizes students as well as other social groups within the category of labor. In doing so, these Marxists recognized the emancipatory potential of students and relevance of their politics.

However, a few challenges remain to be discussed to advance a more fine-grained analysis of the student protests and their anticapitalist potential. First, contemporary Marxist scholars are urged to develop a more systematic investigation of the role that education plays in the knowledge-based economy and in neoliberalism in general. Second and relatedly, it is important to identify the current function that students perform in capitalist societies, and the different forms of exploitation and subordination to which they are exposed, alongside the political opportunities that they may have under those circumstances. Finally, we need to explore what kinds of alliances and solidarity students can make today with the broader workers' movement. The recognition of the revolutionary potential of students would remain incomplete without theorizing how students relate to workers, and in which sense student politics can or cannot contribute to overthrowing capitalism.

Disclosure Statement None of the co-authors has any financial interest or benefit that has arisen from the direct applications of this research.

References

Agasisti, T., & Catalano, G. (2006). Governance Models of University Systems—Towards Quasi-Markets? Tendencies and Perspectives: A European Comparison. *Journal of Higher Education Policy and Management, 28*(3), 245–262.

Altbach, P. G. (1970). The International Student Movement. *Journal of Contemporary History, 5*(1), 156–174.

Aronowitz, S. (2000). *Knowledge Factory. Dismantling the Corporate University and Creating True Higher Education.* Beacon Press.

Barker, C. (2008). Some Reflections on Student Movements of the 1960s and Early 1970s. *Revista crítica de ciencias sociais, 81*(81), 43–91. https://doi.org/10.4000/rccs.646

Berman, E. P. (2012). *Creating the Market University: How Academic Science Became an Economic Engine.* Princeton University Press.

Brooks, R. (Ed.). (2016). *Student Politics and Protest: International Perspectives.* Routledge.

Caffentzis, G. (2010). *University Struggles at the End of the Edu-Deal.* Mute. www.metamute.org/editorial/articles/university-struggles-end-edu-deal

Cini, L. (2019). *The Contentious Politics of Higher Education. Struggles and Power Relations within English and Italian Universities.* Routldge.

Cini, L., della Porta, D., & Guzman-Concha, C. (Eds.). (2021). *Student Movements in Late Neoliberalism. Dynamics of Contention and their Consequences.* Palgrave Macmillan.

Cohn-Bendit, D., & Cohn-Bendit, G. (1968). *Obsolete Communism. The New Left-Wing Alternatives.* McGrow-Hill Book Company.

della Porta, D., Cini, L., & Guzman-Concha, C. (2020). *Contesting Higher Education: The Student Movements Against Neoliberal Universities.* Bristol University Press.

Dokuzović, D. (2016). *Struggles for Living Learning: Within Emergent Knowledge Economies and the Cognitivization of Capital and Movement.* Transversal Texts.

Drake, D. (1997). Sartre and May 1968: The Intellectual in Crisis. *Sartre Studies International, 3*(1), 43–65.

Draper, H. (1977). *Karl Marx's Theory of Revolution Vol. II* (Vol. 2). Aakar Books.

Ehrenreich, B., & Ehrenreich, J. (1969). *Long March, Short Spring: The Student Uprising at Home and Abroad / by Barbara and John Ehrenreich.* Monthly Review Press.

Freyenhagen, F. (2014). Adorno's Politics: Theory and Praxis in Germany's 1960s. *Philosophy and Social Criticism, 40*(9), 867–893. https://doi.org/10.1177/0191453714545198

Ginsberg, B. (2011). *The Fall of the Faculty: The Rise of the All-Administrative University and Why It Matters*. Oxford University Press.

Habermas, J. (1987). *Toward a Rational Society*. Polity Press.

Hardt, M., & Negri, A. (2009). *Commonwealth*. Harvard University Press.

Harvey, D. (2017). *Marx, Capital and the Madness of the Economic Reason*. Oxford University Press.

Hayden, T. (1962). The Port Huron Statement of the Students for a Democratic Society. *1*, 2006.

Hobsbawm, E. (1995). *Age of Extremes: The Short Twentieth Century, 1914–1991*. Abacus.

Klemenčič, M. (2014). Student Power in a Global Perspective and Contemporary Trends in Student Organising. *Studies in Higher Education, 39*(3), 396–411.

Korpi, W. (1983). *The Democratic Class Struggle*. Routledge and Kegan Paul.

Leslie, E. (1999). Introduction to Adorno/Marcuse—Correspondence on the German Student Movement. *New Left Review, 233*, 118–123.

Lucarelli, S., & Vercellone, C. (2013). The Thesis of Cognitive Capitalism. New Research Perspectives. An Introduction. *Knowledge Cultures, 1*(4).

Macciocchi, M. A., & Althusser, L. (1973). *Letters from inside the Italian Communist Party to Louis Althusser*. New Left Books.

Mandel, E. (1968). *The Revolutionary Student Movement: Theory and Practice*. Young Socialist Alliance.

Marcuse, H. (1969). Re-examination of the Concept of Revolution [in Marxist Theory]. *New Left review*, 27–34.

Marx, K. (1857). *Grundrisse: Foundations of the Critique of Political Economy*. Penguin Books.

Marx, K. (1867). *Capital. A Critique of Political Economy. Volume I. Book One: The Process of Production of Capital*. Progress Publishers.

Marx, K. (1894). *Capital Volume III. The Process of Capitalist Production as a Whole*. International Publishers.

McGettigan, A. (2013). *The Great University Gamble: Money, Markets and the Future of Higher Education*. Pluto Press.

Roggero, G. (2011). *The Production of Living Knowledge. The Crisis of the University and the Transformation of Labor in Europe and North America*. Temple University Press.

Slaughter, S., & Rhoades, G. (2004). *Academic Capitalism and the New Economy. Markets, States, and Higher Education*. The Johns Hopkins University Press.

Smeltzer, S., & Hearn, A. (2015). Student Rights in an Age of Austerity? "Security", Freedom of Expression and the Neoliberal University. *Social Movement Studies, 14*(3), 352–358.

Soederberg, S. (2014). *Debtfare States and the Poverty Industry. Money, Discipline and the Surplus Population*. Routledge.

Sukarieh, M., & Tannock, S. (2015). *Youth Rising? The Politics of Youth in the Global Economy*. Routledge.

Trow, M. (1973). *Problems in the Transition from Elite to Mass Higher Education*. Carnegie Commission on Higher Education.

Wright, S. (2002). *Storming Heaven: Class Composition and Struggle in Italian Autonomist Marxism*. PlutoPress.

PART III

Beyond: Marxism, Education and Alternatives

CHAPTER 23

Revisiting and Revitalizing Need as Non-dualist Foundation for a (R)evolutionary Pedagogy

Joel Lazarus

23.1 Autobiographical Preface

This chapter is an expression of my personal journey to understand how we can change. The question of change is always ultimately a pedagogical question—how we can *learn* to change. This journey has led me to inhabit the roles of student and teacher in multiple educational sites: schools, universities, and community spaces. It has led me to join others to exist and resist within and explore and imagine beyond current educational institutions.

Change begins with ourselves as individuals and as communities but, since we are each an integral part of the whole, personal change is also systemic change. This can be very challenging since education systems are not neutral mediums for pedagogical relations; they are tools for hegemonic control and are, increasingly, themselves sites of profound exploitation and thus profound insecurity and power inequalities.

Possibilities for change require effective pedagogical frameworks for individual and collective subjects to meet their needs for understanding, imagination, creation, connection, and participation and more. Central to my journey has been an experimental engagement with many such frameworks, all of which hold elements of great truth, beauty, and power. Over the past few years, through my work on a development and research project called "WorkFREE,"[1] I have engaged increasingly deeply with learning, using, and developing pedagogical frameworks focused on needs. I have come to believe that, since they

J. Lazarus (✉)
University of Bath, Bath, UK
e-mail: jl3779@bath.ac.uk

© The Editor(s) (if applicable) and The Author(s), under exclusive license to Springer Nature Switzerland AG 2023
R. Hall et al. (eds.), *The Palgrave International Handbook of Marxism and Education*, Marxism and Education,
https://doi.org/10.1007/978-3-031-37252-0_23

direct us to our most essential layers, needs-based pedagogical approaches hold the greatest emancipatory and transformative promise. This suggests that, concerning the question of change, questions of ontology, or of consciousness lie prior to the pedagogical question, i.e., before we ask "how can I/we change?" we must understand as much as we can about who or what this "I" or this "we" is. In this context, I have embraced needs frameworks inspired by Positive Psychology that recognize the I or we as living organisms (Maslow, 1971, 1999). This embrace opens the door not just to a universality of needs—we all have the same needs because we are all human organisms—but to a non-duality—we are all ultimately unique parts of the integral organism of Life or Earth.

In this chapter, I try to prize open a space within Marxist thinking in which to embrace a universality and non-duality of needs that I believe is vital to pursuing this promise. Consequently, the chapter is more theoretical than empirical. However, I try wherever possible to bring abstract concepts to life by relating them to current educational realities.

23.2 Introduction

Theory is fulfilled in a people only insofar as it is the fulfilment of the needs of that people ... Only a revolution of radical needs can be a radical revolution.' (Marx, 1970, p. 65)

The concept of needs is foundational to materialist philosophy. Springborg (1981) highlights the centrality of the concept in the materialist philosophy of pre-Socratic and later Stoic and Epicurean thinkers. Their lines of thought are revived and advanced by Western Enlightenment thinkers, most notable among them Jean-Jacques Rousseau (1997), and later G.W.F Hegel and early utopian socialists. Following this long line of ancient and modern thinkers, Karl Marx founded his own historical materialist philosophy and political economy on the concept of need. It underpins the "first premises" of the historical materialism that Marx, alongside Engels, first systematically presents in *The German Ideology*:

... life involves before everything else eating and drinking, habitation, clothing and many other things. The first historical act is thus the production of the means to satisfy these needs, the production of material life itself (Marx & Engels, 1976a, p. 7)

In short, it is impossible to conceive of a materialist and Marxist philosophy without reference to needs.

My objectives in this chapter are threefold. My first is to present the reader with an overview of a Marxian philosophy of need. By Marxian, I refer primarily to the philosophy of need encountered in Karl Marx's own writings, but also to subsequent contributions, particularly of those who came to be known as

"Neo-Marxist" (c.f. Fromm, 1956; Marcuse, 1964, 1998; Reich, 1997; Sartre, 1991). My second objective is to offer one specific critique of this Marxian philosophy of need, namely, the conflation of a needing subject with a needed object, a position derived from the basic postulate of objectification in materialist philosophy. Conceiving needs as objects leads Marx to historicize human needs as particular to given modes of production.

Thus, Marx (1970, p. 7) saw the transcendence of capitalism as achieved through an awakening of a consciousness of "radical needs" within the bearer of universal revolution, the proletariat, in response to capitalism's denial of these needs. I will argue that Marx's conflation of needing subject and needed object is a conflation of means and ends. This conflation obscures both the universality of our needs and therefore our universal nature or "species-life" (Marx, 1992, p. 221), and, consequently, alternative non-alienated ways of meeting our needs and thus actualizing our essential species-life, i.e., of pursuing communism.

My third objective, then, is to present a second brief overview, this time of two pedagogical frameworks, Human-Scale Development and Nonviolent Communication, that invite us to connect with our needs, and to imagine and pursue new, non-alienated ways of meeting them (Max-Neef, 1991, 1992; Rosenberg, 2003). I conclude with brief observations of how the ontologies of both HSD and NVC point to more nondualistic ways of experiencing the world and pursuing transformation. I address how these align completely with the ontologies of leading Marxist pedagogues, and how we can readily adopt a nondualistic interpretation of Marx's own ontological position; an interpretation that reopens space for what I call a (r)evolutionary praxis of needs. My overarching goal in this chapter is to kindle a curiosity or even an excitement in the reader around the power of a needs-based praxis, and to germinate thoughts about how this sits within the kind of intersectional, pedagogical praxes documented in many other chapters in this handbook.

23.3 An Overview of a Marxian Philosophy of Need

Marx's Ontology of Needs

As the quote above from *The German Ideology* makes clear, for Marx, a historical materialist "theory of genesis" is founded on a theory of needs and their satisfaction (Heller, 2018, p. 23). In his early writings, Marx (1992, p. 250) had noted that "… in the first place, labour, *life activity, productive life* itself appears to man only as a means for the satisfaction of a need, the need to preserve physical existence" [sic]. In this sense, life itself is "productive life," "life-producing life," and "appears only as a *means of life*" (ibid., p. 250) [sic]. Thus, if "free conscious activity constitutes the species-character of man" then human life activity is oriented toward the satisfaction of our needs (ibid., p. 250). To be alive is to need and to pursue the satisfaction of one's needs. However, for

Marx, needs are not unchanging universals, but are produced and thus expand alongside human, productive forces.

In the *Grundrisse*, Marx (1993, p. 1043) writes how "needs are themselves scant at the beginning. They too develop only with the forces of production" and that "it is precisely because total production rises that needs, desires, and claims also increase, and they increase in the same measure as production rises." Thus, needs become almost synonymous with objects—"needs are produced just as are products"—so that "regarded materially, wealth consists only in the manifold variety of needs (Marx, 1993, p. 418). This is a logical consequence of Marx's materialist ontology rooted in a radical dialecticism between being and object:

> A being which does not have its nature outside itself is not a natural being and plays no part in the system of nature. A being which has no object outside it would exist in a condition of solitude … As soon as I have an object, this object has me for its object. (Marx, 1992, p. 260)

Later, Marx (1844) gives an example of this materialist dialectic:

> The Sun is an object for the plant, an indispensable object which confirms its life, just as the plant is an object for the Sun, as expression of its life-awakening power and its objective essential power.

Heller (2018, p. 46) summarizes the centrality of objectification in Marx's materialism thus:

> Man's need and the object of the need are correlated: the need is always related to some concrete object or to an objective activity. The objects "bring about" the needs, and the needs bring about the objects. The need and its object are "moments," "sides" of one and the same complex.

For Marx, "the moment of production occupies first place: it is production which creates new needs" (Heller, 2018, p. 29). Springborg (1981) has highlighted how, in this aspect, Marx follows in the wake of Western materialist critics of civilization, ancient and modern. If needs are socially created' (Marx, 1993, p. 72), then the creation of an ever-expanding number of new needs are clearly "not given to man's biological constitution" (Heller, 2018, p. 48). This framing compels Marx to establish and explore distinctions between what he calls, variously, "natural" or "necessary" needs and the appearance of "so-called luxury needs" (Marx, 1993, p. 419), and how economic conditions turn initial, luxury needs, like "mechanisation and the use of chemicals" in agriculture, into "necessary needs" (Marx, 1993, p. 418). As a result, if the nature and scope of natural needs are socially determined then the dichotomy between natural and socially-created needs dissolves—*all* needs are social needs (Heller,

2018, p. 36). If this is the case then we must ask "how did Marx understand the 'structure of need' under capitalism?"

The Capitalist Structure of Needs

For Marx, needs under capitalism are structured, unsurprisingly, around two antagonistic poles of the basic survival needs of workers and the singular need of capital for self-valorization. If "the history of all hitherto existing society is the history of class struggles" (Marx & Engels, 1976b, p. 79), then even the most fundamental material needs become dependent "to a great extent on the level of civilization attained by a country; in particular they depend on the conditions in which, and consequently on the habits and expectations with which, the class of free workers has been formed" (Marx, 1976, p. 183). A "historical and moral element … enters into the determination" of natural needs (ibid., p. 183); natural needs become "necessary needs," necessity defined empirically according to "what needs ought to be satisfied so that the members of a given society or class should have the feeling and the conviction that their life—at a given level of the division of labour—is normal" (Heller, 2018, p. 37). Within capitalism, then, natural needs are coterminous with those necessities of life "habitually required by the average worker"; in short, "the value of labour power" (Marx, 1976, p. 407).

This historical structure of needs plays out through each of what Heller (2018, p. 28) lists as the "three [original] economic discoveries which Marx attributes to himself": "the discovery of the significance of use value"; "the theory that the worker sells to the capitalist not his labour but his labour power"; and "… the general category of surplus value." Heller (2018, p. 33) remarks that in each of these three fundamental Marxian "economic categories"—use value, labor power, and surplus value—"the concept of need plays the hidden but principal role."

The role of the concept of need in use value is not hidden at all. In just the second paragraph of Volume One of *Capital*, Marx defines a commodity's use value in terms of its capacity for need satisfaction. Later, in the *Grundrisse*, Marx (1993, p. 320) offers an unambiguous definition: "Where the need for a certain use value ceases, it ceases to be a use value. It is measured as a use value by the need for it." By beginning his first volume of *Capital* with a dissection of the commodity into its use and exchange values and by founding his conceptualizations of these two attributes in a theory of need, Marx reveals not just the mechanism by which the capitalist mode of production is reproduced, but, crucially, how it may be transcended. Patricia Springborg (1981, p. 1) argues that:

> … the whole thrust of [Marx's] distinction between use value and exchange value serves to remind us that whatever the mechanisms may be that allow us to inculcate a demand for the ever-increasing flow of commodities that capitalism produces, they stand in stark contrast to the needs of man under socialism.

Here, it is Marx's third "original" contribution to political economy—the category of surplus value—that comes to the fore, since the category of surplus value materially embodies and expresses need-satisfaction as social antagonism within capitalism. The greater the surplus value produced by workers for capital, the greater the rate of exploitation, i.e., the greater the needs of humanity are sacrificed to the need of capital and, thus, the more "necessary need" is reduced to a bare physiological and quantifiable minimum. Thus, the greater the rate of surplus value, the more forcefully we are confronted with the political (and therefore pedagogical) question of how the immense growth in productive powers, capable of producing the surplus that capital has summoned, can be directed toward meeting the needs of all human beings (Heller, 2018, p. 27). Thus, by founding his political economy on the concept of need, Marx highlights the vital dialectical realities of alienation (capitalism) and, therefore, the possibilities for transcending alienation (communism). Before we explore the nature of Marx's understanding of communism in the context of needs and their satisfaction, let us further examine the alienation of our needs under capitalism.

The Alienation of Needs Under Capitalism

Agnes Heller (2018, Ch.2) identifies four mechanisms by which our needs are alienated under capitalism: the impoverishment of our species-life; the inversion of means and ends; the quantification of quality; and the defeminization of the "general interest." In terms of the first of these, Marx (1992, p. 268) argues that "the rich man" is "the man in need of the totality of vital human expression; he is the man in whom his own realization exists as inner necessity, as need." In place of this totality of vital human expression, capitalism reduces human need to the need to possess. Both "crude practical needs" and luxury needs are all produced by capital in the pursuit of its own singular need for self-valorization (ibid., p. 268).

In practice, this involves the commodification of need-satisfaction and constitutes a profound and essential "estrangement" of our "physical and intellectual senses" and, thus, of human consciousness (Marx, 1992, p. 266). This process of means/ends inversion surely plays out in contemporary education within increasing intensity as young people advance through the years through the instrumentalization of education; the reduction of education as a positional good by which the attainment of appropriate qualifications and grades secure employment success which, in turn, functions to guarantee access to commodity-based need-satisfaction.

This impoverishment proceeds through an inverted form of relations of objectification, in which "every end becomes a mean and every means an end" (Heller, 2018, p. 34). Heller and Marx share a Kantian deontological ethics according to which, in non-alienated "normal" life, "the main end of man is other man" (ibid., p. 34). In contrast, under capitalism, human beings become mere "means towards the satisfaction of [our] private ends" (ibid., p. 34). For

Marx (1992, p. 268), money is crucial here, because it constitutes the totalizing alienating force separating each of us from our ultimate need for each other: "Money is the pimp between man's needs and his object, between his life and his means of life." Money alienates our interdependency, instead creating a "new dependence" on capital, thus transgressing multiple needs, not least for freedom (ibid., p. 271). Thus, "[t]he need for money is … the real need created by the modern economic system, and the only need it creates" (Marx, 1992, p. 271). Let us take, for example, the marketization of higher education over recent decades; a process defined by the expansion of areas of circulation in such forms as student fees, loans, and debt; rents to service providers; and institutional refinancing and corporate debt (cf. McGettigan, 2013; Hall, 2021).

By producing for exchange value: our concrete labor satisfies others' needs; the development of social productive forces serves not to lighten our burden, but to increase it; communal life is shaped by social ends perverted toward satisfying private means; and, in short, "[t]he very wealth of needs is converted from an end into a means" (Heller, 2018, p. 35).

The third structural process by which needs are alienated in capitalism is identified by Heller (2018, p. 34) as the "quality/quantity inversion." Under the reign of money, "everything can be bought, everything can be transformed into money" (Marx, 1993, p. 670). But, if something can be purchased with money, it is, by definition, alienable. Consequently, "inalienable, eternal possessions … break down in the face of money … Everything is to be had for 'hard cash'" (Marx, 1993, p. 671). This "quantification of quality" is "apocalyptic" since "it causes the 'atrophy' of the nonquantifiable to the point at which "[t]here is 'no higher or holier'" (Heller, 2018, p. 38; Marx, 1993, p. 671). Again, the notion of the quantification of quality should resonate with any teacher working within contemporary school, further or higher education, for it is the experience of the collapse of the quality of relationships inside classrooms within their representation as data, which is then framed as an objective, and thus accurate or truthful, totality.[2]

A final manifestation of alienation under the capitalist structure of need is identified by Heller (2018, p. 40) as the defeminization of the category of "interest." For Marx, "interest" expresses "the standpoint of bourgeois society" that constitutes "… the reduction of needs to greed" (Heller, 2018, p. 40). This is because "interests' are the private concerns and objectives of citizens pursued in the 'quasi-natural' realm of civil society" (ibid., p. 56). In this context, the "general interest" is "throughout history … created by individuals who are defined as 'private persons'" (Marx & Engels, 1976b, p. 81). Thus, under capitalism, the general interest expresses the private interests of the ruling class passed off as general to secure bourgeois hegemony. As such, the general interest constitutes "an alienated power resulting from the struggle between private interests, and thwarting the ends and aims of individual human beings" (Heller, 2018, p. 43). Thus, in place of relationships of need, "relations of interest dominate relationships between human beings" (Heller, 2018, p. 65). A society bound together by private interest is a society bound by "economic chains" (ibid., p. 41). Again, as an integral institution of civil society, the education system clearly plays a central form of alienation of the defeminization of the general interest.

This is manifested not just in school, college, and university curricula, but in dominant views of education like the instrumentalization of education referred to above. It is a hegemonic category that is clearly resisted by emerging anti-capitalist, intersectional, and decolonial counterhegemonic movements today. Thus, the alienation of needs under capitalism constitutes an impoverishment of humanity through the reduction of needs to possession. This impoverishment occurs through the inversion of means and ends, the quantification of quality, and the creation of a civil society that replaces mutual relations of need with those of competing private interest and a bourgeois defeminization of the "general interest."

The Doctrine of True and False Needs

Earlier, I argued that, by founding his political economy on the concept of need, Marx revealed not just the alienated structure of needs under capitalism, but the possibilities for transcending our alienation. What were the dialectical historical processes by which Marx envisaged the proletariat achieving revolutionary transformation from the "Is" of existing capitalist alienated life (extant reality) to the "Ought" of non-alienated communist life (utopian future)? Here, Agnes Heller (2018, p. 63) offers a succinct summary of Marx's theory of crossing this bridge from capitalist Is to communist Ought.

1. Capitalism is an antinomous society: its essence is alienation.
2. Capitalist society as a totality, as a "social body," produces not only alienation but the consciousness of alienation, in other words, radical needs.
3. This consciousness (radical needs) is necessarily generated by capitalism.
4. This consciousness (the complex of radical needs) already transcends capitalism by its existence, and its development makes it impossible for capitalism to remain the basis of production. The need to resolve the antinomy and the activity directed towards this end are therefore constituted in the collective Ought, in the consciousness that "exceeds its bounds."

Thus, for Marx, the potential for communist revolution was contingent on the awakening within the proletariat of a consciousness of their radical needs, an awakening dialectically provoked by the denial and alienation of these very needs by capital. According to this theory, it cannot be emphasized strongly enough that, just as our radical needs are inherent to, and their satisfaction is vital to actualizing, our species being, a revolutionary consciousness can only be authentically aroused and experienced *subjectively* through the material, psychological, and emotional experience of alienation. And yet, revolutionaries are impatient by nature and, in his later years, Marx himself overlooked this subjectivist principle at the heart of his dialectical materialism to countenance "the possibility of reaching communism by a circuitous route, 'jumping over' capitalism" (Marx in Heller, 2018, p. 52). What we find, both in the Soviet Union and later in China, Cuba, and other communist revolutionary states, are, indeed, conscious efforts by vanguard leaders to "jump over" capitalism. For a young Lenin, for example, the force of the energetic "spontaneity of the masses" (Is-ness) had to be hammered into coherent form by the "consciousness of the Social Democrats" in order to achieve its revolutionary potential (Ought-ness). He (Lenin, 2009, p. 375) argued that

> We have said that there could not have been Social-Democratic consciousness among the workers. It would have to be brought to them from without.

It was in the post-War era that Western revolutionaries were compelled to confront the "longevity and tenacity of the capitalist system" and to seek new explanations for the prolonged hibernation of a proletarian consciousness of radical needs (Springborg, 1981, p. 248). For some, this required a reconsideration of the foundational concept of alienation in Marx's thought, questioning whether it should be considered a category merely of labor or whether capitalism's endurance could be attributed to its capacity to manufacture subjectivities that created new forms of alienation, turning us into "one-dimensional" servants of capital (Marcuse, 1964). Thus, an investigation of capitalism was pursued through an experimental fusing of Marxism with Freudian psychoanalysis alongside sociological critiques of mass society (Packard, 1960; Mills, 2000,) by thinkers associated with the Frankfurt School who came to be known as "neo-Marxists."[3]

This theory crystallizes in the writing of Herbert Marcuse as the "doctrine of true and false needs." For Marcuse, we are imprisoned in the labyrinth of a false consciousness satisfied by false needs, and primarily the false needs of consumerism that we have internalized—we have been "bought off with golden chains" (Marcuse in Fitzgerald, 1985, p. 93). We are imprisoned because this false consciousness is a "consciousness of servitude" whereby we do not even realize we are not free (ibid., p. 92). This introjection of false needs is the all-pervading foundation of the most resilient and pernicious "non-terroristic" form of a technocratic, "totalitarian," "productive apparatus" that "obliterates the opposition between private and public existence, between individual and social needs" and serves to "institute new, more effective; and more pleasant forms of social control and social cohesion" (Marcuse, 1964, p. xv, xvi).

From this perspective, the "optimal goal of political activity"—what is to be done?—is self-evident. It is "the replacement of false needs by true ones (or the inculcation of true needs rather than false ones) and the abandonment of repressive satisfactions"; that is, the redefinition of needs (Fitzgerald, 1985, p. 92). But, who is to do it? Who is to establish our true needs and mobilize us toward their satisfaction? Just like Lenin before him, Marcuse (1964, p. 6) judges us, the masses, under the veil of false consciousness, ultimately incapable of determining and responding to our own true needs. Just like Lenin, Marcuse

(1964) identifies a minority of a higher consciousness, the intelligentsia, who must serve as the catalyst of historical change and "force men to be free" (Rousseau in Fitzgerald, 1985, p. 93). Thus, the Is-Ought bridge now takes the form of a process of mass "re-education into the truth" undertaken by an "educational dictatorship" (Marcuse in Fitzgerald, 1985, p. 93).

And *how* is this educational dictatorship to determine our true needs? This determination involves "standards of *priority* which refer to the optimal development of the individual, of all individuals, under the optimal utilization of the material and intellectual resources available to man" [sic] (Marcuse, 1964, p. 6). The practical details of this process are vague, but it clearly comprises a rationalistic determination of social priority of needs, and a calculation of optimal levels of their satisfaction conditional on (implicitly limited) accessible resources. Have we really escaped from the bureaucratic technocracy that Marcuse sought to overcome? How, asks Alisdair MacIntyre (1970, p. 72), has Herbert Marcuse "acquired the right to say of others what their true needs are? How has he escaped the indoctrination which affects others?"

We have journeyed across the first two-thirds of the twentieth century from an explicitly democratic and *subjectivist* universalist to an explicitly authoritarian, positivist, and *objectivist* theory of needs and consciousness. It is the latter position that triggered a wave of criticism in the 1970s and 1980s from liberal and conservative moral and political philosophers seeking to bury historical materialism.[4] Of greater concern for us is the response to this objectivist universalism in those same decades from radical thinkers.

The Rejection of Needs, the Rejection of Universalism

If we take the radical needs for human freedom and autonomy seriously, the doctrine of true and false needs appears not as a bridge, but as a dead-end. It is unsurprising and understandable, therefore, to see among anti-colonial, feminist, and postmodern thinkers of the latter decades of the twentieth century, a rejection of needs as emancipatory frame and a "general skepticism about the coherence of conceptions of rationality or reality which purport to be universal and objective" (Doyal & Gough, 1991, p. 1). I say understandable because fundamental to the mechanics of colonialism is, of course, the very ontological and material construction and imposition of "an inflated particular" as a "universality entirely incommensurable with it" that are fundamental to the constructive practices of hegemonic relations and that lead tragically to the "encouragement [of] a sense of inferiority and helplessness in the face of Western 'progress'" (Laclau in Zerilli, 2004, p. 88; Doyal & Gough, 1991, pp. 13–14; c.f. Fanon, 2008).

Thus, the position that "the concept of universal needs inevitably favours the dictatorial oppressor" became widespread and universalism was replaced with a concept of "human liberation … equated with reclaiming the right of oppressed groups to determine what preferences they will designate as needs" (Rist in Doyal & Gough, 1991, p. 14). Writing in the early 1990s, Doyal and

Gough cite a variety of anti-racist and feminist scholars insisting on a cultural uniqueness expressed and cherished by their communities that could never be understood by oppressive outsiders—a "radical separation" or an "entirely different ontology" that made black communities or societies unintelligible to white people or women fundamentally unintelligible to men (Dworkin and Stanley and Wise in Doyal & Gough, 1991, pp. 15–16).

I believe that this imposition of inflated particulars as universals defines contemporary education today, perhaps above all in the form of supposedly neutral data that function to construct a rationalistic, objectivist universalism not of needs, but of progress and thus of academic success and failure, of the good and the bad student, teacher, department, institution, or even national education system. This is a practice not of education as freedom, but of education as disciplinary and punitive control.

Behind this rejection of needs, then, is a deeper rejection of any praxis of universalism. Pivotal here, in the West at least, was the "discursive turn" toward poststructuralism that presented a major challenge to Marxian materialist, alongside structuralist ontology and politics. This was exemplified by the seminal "post-Marxist" contribution of Ernesto Laclau and Chantal Mouffe (2001) (Critchley & Marchant, 2004). For Laclau and Mouffe (2001, p. x), the objective world existed outside the world of meaning, which could never be universally determined. Instead, the "notion of the social" was an unendingly contingent, open "discursive space" of hegemonic contestation that antagonistic social groups struggled to control and stabilize by articulating meaning. Thus, poststructuralism expressed an ontological position that Laclau and Mouffe (2001, p. x) saw as "unthinkable within the ... ontological paradigms governing the field of Marxist discursivity." This ontological position explicitly rejected any possibility of a universalism. For poststructuralists, there is only unending antagonism in which discourses of utopian universalism are both impossible but necessary since their "non-solution is the very precondition of democracy" (Zerilli, 2004, p. 105). Thus, universalism is merely an "expression of the desire for a fullness that is always deferred" (Zerilli, 2004, p. 121).

If revolution is contingent on consciousness then, from my perspective, both neo-Marxism and post-Marxism drew necessary attention to the semiotic organs of manipulation of consumerist and hyper-individualist capitalism. Through the manufacture of desire and addiction, though they may not have colonized our very psyches, these manipulations alienate us in profound ways. Additionally, poststructuralism provided an essential counter to the preceding violence of objectivist universalism by emphasizing the "limit of all objectivity," the unending contingency and unfinished nature of the social and the human condition (Laclau & Mouffe, 2001, p. 122). And yet, any practitioner of radical pedagogy recognizes the classroom or community as the precise spaces in which the very *material* nature and consequences of structures not just of class, but also of race, gender, and other social antagonisms, can be understood.

However, this is also where the possibility of overcoming those intersecting antagonisms, of healing and unity, can be experienced through relational practices that reveal to us our universal species-life and even our ultimate oneness. For Doyal and Gough (1991), whose seminal *A Theory of Human Needs* articulated a powerful refutation of poststructuralist and anti-colonialist rejections of universalism and needs, the achievement of this universalism could be pursued in a rationalistic combination of Rawlsian liberal principles of distributional ethics and Habermasian "ideal speech" communicative acts (Rawls, 1973; Habermas, 1987).[5] Their pragmatic policy focus aimed at a democratization of what remained as a rationalist and objectivist universalism.

My first objective was to present the reader with an overview of a Marxian philosophy of need. From here, I made the case for the central importance of the praxis of needs, not just to class politics but also to radical politics in general. If revolution depends on a conscious awakening to our radical needs, and if a philosophy of needs itself ends in either the violent neo-Marxist, objectivist universalism of forcing us out of our false consciousness and false needs or in a post-Marxist and anti-colonial rejection of universal needs, then our cause looks bleak. I believe that there is a way to redeem an historical materialist philosophy and pedagogy of need—a subjectivist, universalist approach that begins with one very simple but inexpressibly crucial corrective. I believe that this corrective can redeem the universalism of needs and, therefore, its potential to serve a democratizing and emancipatory function in all educational settings in ways that transcend rationalism and objectivism.

23.4 THE ESSENTIAL CORRECTIVE: SEPARATING NEEDS FROM SATISFIERS

To reiterate, following materialists as ancient as Democritus and Epicurus, Marx saw in the processes of production and consumption that characterize and motivate life, an essential unity between needing subject and needed object. I believe that this essentially equates to the conflations of ends with their means—a truly fundamental ontological and, therefore, logical error. As I have shown, when we conflate needs with their objects of satisfaction, we fall into the interminable trap of having to determine whether a need is necessary or artificial and superfluous or even "false." Even Agnes Heller, the philosopher who dedicated herself to the most forensic consideration of Marx's philosophy of need, recognizes this dilemma. For Heller (2018, p. 21), Marx's "classification of needs on the basis of their objectifications, that is to say, on the basis of their objects in general" constitutes "the most problematical point" in his conceptualization of needs. She herself, however, cannot resolve this problem:

> The question is, whether it is possible to categorise needs (or the objects towards which they are directed) on the basis of their content and their quality, along with the categories of necessity and luxury, or whether it is solely and primarily effective demand that decides whether a need and the object related to it are a 'luxury'. (Heller, 2018, p. 25)

From my perspective, a universalist philosophy of need can only begin from a separation of need not just from object, but from what Chilean economist Manfred Max-Neef (1991, p. 17) called "satisfiers." Conceiving of satisfiers as mere objects expresses the very impoverishment of consciousness that Marx identified as a mechanism of capitalist alienation. Instead, we should conceive of satisfiers as expressive of the entire forces of production and cultural apparatus:

> Satisfiers are not the available economic goods. They are related, instead, to everything which, by virtue of representing forms of Being, Having, Doing, and Interacting, contributes to the actualization of human needs. Satisfiers may include, among other things, forms of organization, political structures, social practices, subjective conditions, values and norms, spaces, contexts, modes, types of behaviour and attitudes, all of which are in a permanent state of tension between consolidation and change. (Max-Neef, 1991, pp. 24-5)

This simple move opens up an alternative, materialist conceptualization of needs as universal and transhistorical (Max-Neef, 1991, p. 18). From this perspective, it is not needs but their satisfiers that are historically particular and produced (ibid., p. 18). By disentangling needs and satisfiers, means and ends, we are able to extricate ourselves from the morass of moral philosophy—the terrain of normative judgments and arbitrary classifications and typologies. This critique of a Marxist philosophy of need is an essential first step toward revitalizing needs as a universal and (largely) transhistorical category upon which to pursue what I will call a "(r)evolutionary" pedagogical praxis. I say "largely" because if needs were truly transhistorical then they would not be evolutionary and if they were not evolutionary they would not be essentially human or organismic.

A second step is to explore a humanist, "positive" psychology that, I believe, achieves far more in the reintegration of the evolutionary and the subjective, than the confused Freudian pursuits of the neo-Marxists or the discursive antagonist world of post-Marxists. This offers us conceptual paths for facilitating this revitalization (Rogers, 1995, 2004; Maslow, 1971, 1999). A third step is to integrate within a Marxian pedagogy, practical frameworks inspired by both Max-Neef and positive psychology. These seek to cultivate a universal and evolutionary personal and collective consciousness of needs, which empower participants to articulate and pursue their own strategies for meeting these needs. To this end, in this chapter, I outline two such needs-based theoretical and practical frameworks—Max-Neef's own Human-Scale Development and Marshall Rosenberg's (2003) Nonviolent Communication—with these attributes.

23.5 NEED-BASED PEDAGOGICAL FRAMEWORKS

Human-Scale Development (HSD) and Nonviolent Communication (NVC) both locate the diagnosis of our suffering and the prescription for our flourishing in the realm of human needs and function pedagogically to support participants not just in awakening to a consciousness of our universal radical needs, but in designing and pursuing strategies for satisfying or meeting them. What this means in practice is that participants in processes utilizing HSD and NVC frameworks are invited first to learn a new language of needs, next to apply that language to their own lives and identify their needs and how they are currently satisfied or thwarted, and then to imagine and ultimately to pursue new strategies for meeting unmet needs.

Human-Scale Development

HSD was developed in the late 1980s by a team of Latin American social scientists and philosophers led by Chilean economist Manfred Max-Neef. Theirs was a response to the brutal social consequences of Structural Adjustment Programmes imposed on the continent and the wider Third World in the wake of the US commercial bank debt crisis earlier that decade. Through iterative fieldwork experiences (Max-Neef, 1992), Max-Neef (1991, p. 18) identified nine "fundamental human needs" that were universal and transhistorical, "few, finite, and classifiable."

- Subsistence
- Protection
- Affection
- Understanding
- Participation
- Leisure
- Creation
- Identity
- Freedom

Max-Neef (1991, p. 31) also identified five separate types of satisfiers: "violators" of human needs, e.g., war; "inhibitors" that repress capacities for need-satisfaction, e.g., Taylorist production; "pseudo-satisfiers" that satisfy needs in a superficial and ultimately harmful way, e.g., charity; "singular satisfiers" that are usually technocratic interventions designed to satisfy one particular need, e.g., welfare programs; and, "synergic satisfiers" that are forms of social organization that meet multiple needs at once, e.g., a community allotment. Max-Neef saw detrimental satisfiers as invariably exogenously imposed, whereas synergic satisfiers were generated endogenously through participatory, democratic, dialogical community processes—processes that themselves met multiple human needs such as creation, participation, freedom, identity, and affection.

In this spirit and to this end, HSD was developed by Max-Neef and continues to be developed by other practitioners as a practical pedagogical framework to use for any community setting (Guillen-Royo, 2015; Aponte, 2022). The essence of this framework consists of the necessary first step of helping participants to learn the HSD language of needs and satisfiers. Once this vital conceptual step has been taken, participants are invited to explore how their needs are currently satisfied or not satisfied, what it would look like if they were satisfied, and, ultimately, to devise synergic satisfiers to move toward that optimal scenario. The praxis cycle then begins again with reflection.

Nonviolent Communication

Deeply informed by positive psychologists, above all Carl Rogers, Marshall Rosenberg (2003) developed his NVC framework in the historical context of the US civil rights movement of the 1960s. NVC offers us, in our personal and wider social relationships, a path to journey from a situation of violence in which our needs are denied, ignored, and unmet, to one where our needs are acknowledged, welcomed, and met. This path of nonviolence takes the form of a four-step process. The process begins with bringing our attention inwards in order to *observe* what is happening, and then to *feel* what we feel in relation to what we observe. These feelings point us toward underlying, unmet needs that help us to *make sense* of both the impact of events on us and the ultimate ends motivating our actions. Finally, we need to *formulate requests* to ourselves and to others in order for these needs to be met. NVC is a hugely successful needs-based framework for community transformation. It is practised in myriad settings in countries on all continents.

Shared Ontological Principles

Here, I briefly outline three main ontological principles that I believe HSD and NVC share and state why I believe these are so integral to realizing the transformative potential of education.

1. *Our birthright of self-reliance*

The principle of self-reliance, of reclaiming our birthright of taking responsibility for ourselves and each other is at the heart of both HSD and NVC. Max-Neef (1991, pp. 57–8) articulate this:

> Dependent relations from the international space to the local spaces, and from the technological to the cultural domain, generate and reinforce processes of dominance which frustrate the satisfaction of human needs. It is only by generating self-reliance, where people assume a leading role in different domains and

spaces, that it is possible to promote development processes with synergic effects that satisfy fundamental human needs.

Similarly, for Rosenberg, the journey from dependency and a spiritual state of infancy or "emotional slavery" to one of spiritual maturity or "emotional liberation" centers on the acceptance and assumption of responsibility.

> We accept full responsibility for our own intentions and actions, but not for the feelings of others. At this stage, we are aware that we can never meet our own needs at the expense of others. Emotional liberation involves stating clearly what we need in a way that communicates we are equally concerned that the needs of others be fulfilled. NVC is designed to support us in relating at this level. (Rosenberg, 2003, p. 72)

Jacques Ranciere was perhaps the most eloquent and vociferous critic of the "explicative order" definitive of modern education—the "myth of pedagogy" that produces a "world divided into knowing minds and ignorant ones, ... the intelligent and the stupid" and that creates an "enforced stultification" among learners (Ranciere, 1991, pp. 5, 7). His philosophy of education constitutes a fundamental critique of the learned dependency instantiated and introjected in education systems worldwide. It follows that the emancipatory and transformative potential of education lies in the rejection of the "master explicator" in favor of a democratic educational practice that meets all the needs and more that Max-Neef specifies based on a recognition that "understanding is never more than translating" meaning in ways relevant to one's own life (ibid., p. 12, 8).

2. From scarcity to abundance

A second shared principle lies in the objective of transitioning from a situation of perceived scarcity to one of abundance. For Max-Neef (1991, p. 42), the strategy for achieving this objective centers on a process of empowerment through which communities come to identify "synergic bridging satisfiers." These are practical strategies for creating new collective institutions for satisfying multiple needs. In doing so, participants escape from the mental prison of economism—the ontological belief that reality is a place of finite, scarce resources whose distribution is determined through competition—by identifying the "nonconventional," "endogenous," often non-material resources or "intangible" assets within their own community (Max-Neef, 1991, pp. 76, 80, 77)

> Unlike conventional economic resources which are characterized by scarcity, nonconventional resources are plentiful. They also have a tremendous capacity to preserve and transform social energy for processes of deep change. (Max-Neef, 1991, p. 79)

In NVC practice, the shift from scarcity to abundance begins with recognizing needs, one's own and those of others. "[B]ecoming aware of a need reduces the attachment to any particular strategy for satisfying it, the universe of possible outcomes expands with growing awareness in the system" (Kashtan, 2014, p. 107). "Abundance" here, then, expresses the actual wealth of possible options open to us once we loosen our attachments to particular satisfiers/strategies for meeting our needs.

The concept of structuring education around the principle of moving from ontological scarcity to the potential for abundance seems equally indispensable to me. It is a principle that constitutes the antithesis and antidote to all four forms of the capitalist alienation of need identified by Heller earlier that crystallize in education as the commodification of education, the quantification of the pedagogical relation, and the instrumentalization of education—all processes that involve the defeminization of economism and therefore of ontological scarcity.

3. *Systemic and non-dualistic ontological perspectives*

The understanding that self-actualization is a process by which the individual realizes herself in her contribution to the community or social totality is a long-standing tenet of radical social thought, and is expressed in Marx's concept of radical needs. For Max-Neef (1991, p. 60), "the articulation between the personal and social dimensions of development may be achieved through increasing levels of self-reliance." They identify a process of actualization that "necessarily and inevitably involves a deep transformation in the modes of social behavior and interaction." The outcome is "the transformation of the person-object into a person-subject"; a transformation from "homo economicus" to what they term "homo synergicus" (ibid., p. 90).

Proponents of NVC share a similar vision of restoration and reintegration, driven by a shift in consciousness beyond judgement of self and other, towards an alignment of needs and goals. Otto Scharmer (2009, p. 3) calls this consciousness shift the movement "from ego to eco." NVC goes further than HSD in articulating an essentially non-dualistic ontology and intentions. The Centre for Nonviolent Communication (CNVC) was founded by Marshall Rosenberg and has become the leading organization for the development and advancement of NVC worldwide. The CNVC "pursues the vision of a world where ... everyone values everyone's basic human needs and lives from a consciousness that connects with the universal life energy and natural oneness of all life." Similarly, it sees its vision as "contribut[ing] to more sustainable, compassionate, and 'life-serving' human relations in the realms of personal change, interpersonal relationship and in social systems and structures."[6]

HSD and NVC both articulate an ontology that recognizes not just the human being as organism, but as organism within a larger social, species, or even unified biological organism. This is an ontology that is denied inside the educational structures, cultures, and practices of the global North, which seek to individualize and commodify us, to produce "homo economicus," at all costs. If crossing the Is-Ought bridge is the journey beyond alienation then such an ontology seems indispensable to our journey and thus to education.

23.6 Conclusion: A Non-dualist Sense-Perception for a (R)evolutionary Praxis of Needs

By locating the revolutionary subject as not just the individual, but the community, the society, even human species-life, I believe that HSD and NVC comprise two praxeological frameworks founded on a subjectivist universalism that revitalizes a radical (r)evolutionary pedagogy of needs. A subjectivist universalist pedagogy of needs is founded on two core positions—a trans-rationalist epistemology and a nondualism.

Transrationalist Epistemology

Critical Marxist pedagogy shares with post-Marxism a recognition that we are infinitely "unfinished" (Freire, 2014, p. 8). It is a "conscious awareness of our incompleteness" that stimulates an "educability of being" (ibid., p. 8). Positive psychology, especially that of Maslow (1971), emphasizes most explicitly that which is clear but implicit in Marx—that, though we may be its most complex expressions, we are organisms, we are life. If this is so, then a Marxist pedagogy capable of empowering individuals and communities to awaken to a consciousness of our radical needs that Marx identified as vital to transcending capitalism must be founded on an epistemology that locates knowledge and understanding within the entire human organism or sensorium. It is *trans*rational epistemology because it is an epistemology that does not just (literally) incorporate the body into ways of knowing but sees the ways in which the body can know and understand as prior to and *beyond* the limits of the mind's own logic and reason.

A brief survey of seminal contributions to the field of critical pedagogy reveals a recognition of and advocacy for this holistic, transrational epistemology. For Paolo Freire (1998, p. 94), "consciousness does not end with rationality," but is "a totality-reason, feelings, emotions, desires; my body, conscious of the world and myself, seizes the world toward which it has an intention" (Freire, 1998, p. 94). Gloria Anzaldua (2015, p. 64) declared that "spirit and mind, soul and body, are one, and together they perceive a reality greater than the vision experienced in the ordinary world." For bell hooks, the classroom needed the "essential transformative energetic power of 'the erotic'—that 'moving force that propelled every life-form from a state of mere potentiality to actuality'" (hooks, 1994, p. 194).

Elsewhere, she underlines the primacy of the somatic in the transformative pedagogical power of the "passion of experience" that "encompasses many feelings but particularly suffering" and that is a "way of knowing that is often expressed through the body, what it knows, what has been deeply inscribed on it through experience." In their remarkable ethnographies of Latin American radical community pedagogical practices, Motta and Cole (2014, p. 168) identify "processes of collective knowledge construction [that] seek to overcome the dualisms between intellect and emotion, mind and body, and thought and action, so characteristic of the 'neo-liberal capitalist one-dimensional man'."

Nondualism

Like many of the decolonial praxes referred to here, a subjectivist universalist praxis of needs goes further still to open us to a universality that transcends mere recognition of shared experience and goals. This takes us towards the experience of the ultimate oneness of Life; we come to know not just what I, you, or even we need, but what is needed or what Life-as-us needs at any given moment. I believe that we can read Marx's remarkable interpretation of "sense-perception" from this non-dualistic position:

> Sense-perception (see Feuerbach) must be the basis of all science. Only when it proceeds from sense-perception in the two-fold form of sensuous consciousness and sensuous need—is it true science. All history is the history of preparing and developing 'man' to become the object of sensuous consciousness, and turning the requirements of 'man as man' into his needs. (Marx, 1992, p. 193)

What this means in practice, in the context of education, is the reintegration of the mind with the body in order to cultivate educational relationships and experiences that reawaken us to our species-being—"from ego to eco." Such practices involve a plethora of methods involving meditation, deep listening, and physical movement. From this ontological, experiential platform we can then deploy our reason in the service of meeting our essential needs.

I have presented the reader with an overview of a Marxian philosophy of need. I have critiqued the materialist conflation of needs and objects that defines it. I have proposed an alternative approach that, by separating needs and "satisfiers," revives a universalist approach to needs and revitalizes a radically democratic, *subjectivist* praxis of identifying our needs and pursuing alternative satisfiers. I have offered brief overviews of two frameworks, HSD and NVC that serve these pedagogical, transformative ends. Finally, I have argued that, if the goal of Marxist education is to serve humanity in evolving its consciousness to its radical needs, then theorists and practitioners of Marxist education should embrace transrational and nondualistic ontological and epistemological praxes, many of which are articulated and documented in multiple chapters of this handbook.

Acknowledgements I acknowledge funding from the European Research Council for the WorkFREE project which has allowed me to research and write this chapter.

Disclosure Statement I have no financial interest or benefit that has arisen from the direct applications of this research.

Notes

1. See www.work-free.net for information about the WorkFREE project.
2. I thank editor Richard Hall for making this important point.
3. Springborg (1981, p. 7) persuasively questions whether this is a genuine fusion. She identifies thinkers like Herbert Marcuse, Wilhelm Reich, and Erich Fromm as expounding a revisionist Marxist theory that sought to 'more or less supersede the labour theory of value as the central explanatory principle in the critique of capitalism'. Equally, she highlights their often crude and simplistic applications of Freudian psychoanalytical concepts (Springborg, 1981, Chap. 8 and 9).
4. See, for example, Flew, 1981; Gray, 1996; Nozick, 2001.
5. By Rawlsian distributive ethics, I refer to the abstract moral philosophy of optimal resource distribution put forward by liberal philosopher John Rawls in his *Theory of Justice* in 1973. By 'Habermasian ideal speech communication, I refer to the, again, abstract theory of optimal speech communication described by philosopher Jurgen Habermas in his *Theory of Communicative Action* of 1987.
6. See https://www.cnvc.org/about. Accessed 8th December, 2022.

References

Anzaldua, G. (2015). *Light in the Dark: Rewriting Identity, Spirituality, Reality*. Duke University Press.
Aponte, I. (2022). Communities as Hothouses for Regenerative Culture. In J. Blewitt (Ed.), *New Economy, New Systems: Radical Responses to Our Sustainability Crises* (pp. 195–223). Goodworks.
Critchley, S., & Marchant, O. (2004). *Laclau: A critical reader*. Routledge.
Doyal, L., & Gough, I. (1991). *A Theory of Human Need*. Macmillan.
Fanon, F. (2008). *Black Skin, White Masks*. Pluto.
Fitzgerald, R. (1985). Human Needs and Politics: The Ideas of Christian Bay and Herbert Marcuse. *Political Psychology*, 6, 87–108.
Flew, A. (1981). *The Politics of Procrustes: Contradictions of Enforced Equality*. Temple Smith.
Freire, P. (1998). *Pedagogy of the Heart*. Continuum.
Freire, P. (2014). *Pedagogy of Commitment*. Paradigm.
Fromm, E. (1956). *The Sane Society*. Routledge and Kegan Paul.
Gray, J. (1996). *Mill on Liberty: A Defence*. Routledge.
Guillen-Royo, M. (2015). *Sustainability and Wellbeing Human-Scale Development in Practice*. Routledge.
Habermas, J. (1987). *Theory of Communicative Action*. Polity.
Hall, R. (2021). *The Hopeless University: Intellectual Work at the End of the End of History*. Mayfly Books.
Heller, A. (2018). *The Theory of Need in Marx*. Verso.
hooks, b. (1994). *Teaching to Transgress: Education as the Practice of Freedom*. Routledge.

Kashtan, M. (2014). *Spinning Threads of Radical Aliveness: Transcending the Legacy of Separation in Our Individual Lives*. Fearless Heart Publications.
Laclau, E., & Mouffe, C. (2001). *Hegemony and Socialist Strategy: Towards a Radical Democratic Politics*. Verso.
Lenin, V. I. (2009). *Collected Works, Volume 5: May 1901–February 1902*. Progress Publishers.
MacIntyre, A. (1970). *Herbert Marcuse: An Exposition and Polemic*. Viking Press.
Marcuse, H. (1998). *Eros and Civilization a Philosophical Inquiry Into Freud with a Preface by Douglas Kellner*. Routledge.
Marcuse, H. (1964). *One-Dimensional Man: Studies in the Ideology of Advanced Industrial Society*. Routledge.
Marx, K. (1844). *Economic and Philosophical Manuscripts*. Retrieved March 22, 2023, from https://www.marxists.org/archive/marx/works/1844/manuscripts/hegel.htm
Marx, K. (1970). *Critique of Hegel's 'Philosophy of right'*. Cambridge University Press.
Marx, K. (1976). *Capital, Volume One*. Pelican Books.
Marx, K. (1992). *Early Writings*. Penguin.
Marx, K. (1993). *Grundrisse: Foundations of the Critique of Political Economy*. Penguin.
Marx, K., & Engels, F. (1976a). *The German Ideology*. Progress Publishers.
Marx, K., & Engels, F. (1976b). *The Communist Manifesto*. Penguin.
Maslow, A. (1971). *Farther Reaches of Human Nature*. Penguin.
Maslow, A. (1999). *Toward a Psychology of Being*. Wiley.
Max-Neef, M. (1991). *Human Scale Development: Conception, Application and Further Reflections*. Apex Press.
Max-Neef, M. (1992). *From the Outside Looking In: Experiences in Barefoot Economics*. Zed.
McGettigan, A. (2013). *The Great University Gamble: Money, Markets and the Future of Higher Education*. Pluto.
Mills, C. W. (2000). *The Power Elite*. Oxford University Press.
Motta, S., & Cole, M. (2014). *Constructing 21st Century Socialism in Latin America: The Role of Radical Education*. Palgrave Macmillan.
Nozick, R. (2001). *Anarchy, State, and Utopia*. Wiley-Blackwell.
Packard, V. (1960). *The Hidden Persuaders*. Penguin Books.
Ranciere, J. (1991). *The Ignorant Schoolmaster*. Stamford University Press.
Rawls, J. (1973). *A Theory of Justice*. Oxford University Press.
Reich, W. (1997). *The Mass Psychology of Fascism*. Souvenir Press.
Rogers, C. (1995). *A Way of Being*. Houghton Mifflin Co.
Rogers, C. (2004). *On Becoming a Person: A Therapist's View of Psychotherapy*. Constable.
Rosenberg, M. (2003). *Nonviolent Communication: A Language for Life*. PuddleDancer Press.
Rousseau, J.-J. (1997). *Rousseau: The Social Contract and Other Later Political Writings*. Cambridge University Press.
Sartre, J.-P. (1991). *Critique of Dialectical Reason*. Verso.
Scharmer, C. O. (2009). *Theory U Leading from the Futures as it Emerges: The Social Technology of Presencing*. Berrett-Koehler.
Springborg, P. (1981). *The Problem of Human Needs and the Critique of Civilisation*. Allen and Unwin.
Zerilli, L. M. G. (2004). This Universalism Which Is Not One. In S. Critchley & O. Marchart (Eds.), *Laclau: A Critical Reader*. Routledge.

CHAPTER 24

Reproduction in Struggle

David I. Backer

24.1 Introduction

For education researchers, social reproduction in the Marxist sense refers to how classes and their fractions maintain the continuity of their productive life. As Marxism generally examines workers' production in capitalism, as Tithi Bhattacharya (2017) puts it succinctly, social reproduction asks: Who produces the worker? This entry will introduce readers to various responses to this question. Yet the entry may sound strange to some. While social reproduction is having a resurgence in Marxist theory, in education it is largely considered an historical curiosity (Backer & Cairns, 2021). It was relegated to the dustbin through several fundamental critiques, namely of the theory's economic determinism and functionalism (Backer, 2022).

These critiques concluded that social reproduction was not a theory of class struggle. However, there were many varieties of the concept developed, some directly applied to education, that give the lie to social reproduction's being jettisoned. After an initial expression in Marx's *Capital*, there have been at least three streams of thinking about social reproduction flowing from it (interweaving, transmission, and carework). The entry foregrounds three lesser-known tendencies of social reproduction thinking that have been lost or underemphasized: Martin Carnoy's theory of mediation, Henri Lefebvre's account of the production of new relations of production, and Enrique Dussel's decolonial concept of analectics.

D. I. Backer (✉)
West Chester University, West Chester, PA, USA
e-mail: DBacker@wcupa.edu

24.2 Marx's Preservation as Reproduction

Readers will find the terms reproduction and social reproduction throughout the manuscripts of *Capital*, in Volumes One (2019), Two (1956), and Three (1959), the latter two written between 1861 and 1863, which Marx left incomplete but his writing and organizing partner Friedrich Engels edited. Morrow and Torres (1995), in *Social Theory in Education: A Critique of Theories of Social and Cultural Reproduction*, in defining social reproduction, cite Volume One where Marx writes: "When viewed as a connected whole, and as flowing on with incessant renewal, every social process of production is, at the same time, a process of reproduction" (p. 121, in Marx, 2019, vol.1, p. 531). This renewal "provides not only commodities, not only surplus value, but it also produces and reproduces the capitalist relation" (p. 122, in Marx, 2019, vol.1, pp. 541–2).

The concept also figures prominently in the second and third volumes of *Capital*, where the insight quoted above from the first volume gets elaborated. In these later writings social reproduction gets at the ways capital renews and expands in a capitalist economy. In the first sections of Volume Two covering the circulation of capital, Marx (1956, p. 36) writes the famous formula for how prices become commodities, which become money, and then turn (through exchange) into commodities with prices again:

> The circuit of productive capital has the general formula P ... C'—M'—C ... P. It signifies the periodical renewal of the functioning of productive capital, hence its reproduction, or its process of production as a process of reproduction aiming at the self-expansion of value; not only production but a periodical reproduction of surplus-value; the function of industrial capital in its productive form, and this function performed not once but periodically repeated, so that the renewal is determined by the starting-point.

Marx calls this "periodical renewal of the functioning of capital," or its "self-expansion," a simple process of reproduction, which David Harvey interprets as the same amount of value transferring between phases of production. Marx (1956) goes on to detail this value's reproduction on an extended scale as well. The passage above covers productive capital, which is the kind of capital that "consumes its own component parts for the purpose of transforming them into a mass of products of a higher value," (Marx, 1956, p. 22) such as the capital that goes into paying for labor and equipment needed to complete the labor. Later chapters articulate the simple reproduction (that is, periodical renewal and self-expansion) of surplus value and social capital.

This third type, social capital's simple reproduction, Marx calls "social reproduction." Whereas productive capital and surplus value are particular individual kinds of capital, these kinds of capital can also mix with one another to become social capital. When productive capital and surplus value become social capital they "intertwine, presuppose and necessitate one another"

(p. 215). Social capital, for Marx in Volume Two, is just this "interlacing' of capitals, or all the capitals in their aggregate (with a Hegelian flare) 'as a totality'" (p. 215). Social reproduction therefore is the renewal and self-expansion of these intertwined and interlaced kinds of capital.

It is interesting to note that in the analysis of productive capital's reproduction, Marx writes the term "preservation" to refer to what workers do when they nourish themselves to continue producing. "The wage-laborer lives only by the sale of his labor-power. Its preservation—his preservation—requires daily consumption. Hence payment for it must be continuously repeated at rather short intervals in order that he may be able to repeat acts [of selling his labor] …" To do this, he has to "repeat the purchases needed for his self-preservation" (p. 21). Marxist feminists in the twentieth century like Margaret Benston (1969), Maria Dalla Costa, and Sylvia Federici used the term reproduction in reference to this nourishment, yet Marx's usage of the term refers to the self-expansion of different kinds of capitals (productive, surplus, social).

The social reproduction theorists in education following Durkheim (Bourdieu & Passeron, 1979, 1990), use the term more in the sense of self-expansion but with a very different notion of what is self-expanding and renewing—namely, a larger social equilibrium in the form of a collective consciousness engaged in the division of labor, where certain cultural privileges get transmitted through educational institutions like universities, a form of symbolic violence. Finally, Louis Althusser would famously interpret social reproduction as being the ultimate condition of the conditions of production, naming education explicitly as the most effective ideological state apparatus in modern capitalist societies (Althusser, 2014; Backer, 2022).

These traditions of the concept are well-known, particularly the arguments against their functionalism and determinism, which, in its common form, claims that social reproduction theories such as Althusser's cast teachers, students, and others around schools as "mere puppets of controlling coercive and ideological structures" (Morrow, 2014, p. 708). Yet recent rereadings of Althusser's and others' accounts of social reproduction show these critiques lacking (Backer, 2022; Bhattacharya, 2017). In what follows, I will present three lesser-known articulations that cast social reproduction as a class struggle theory. The first is Richard Johnson's framework for reproduction-in-struggle.

24.3 Neither Structuralism Nor Culturalism Will Do: Johnson's Reproduction-in-Struggle

While not explicitly applied to education, Richard Johnson's (2018) "Histories of Culture/Theories of Ideology" includes a concept of reproduction-in-struggle that education researchers should consider seriously. The way Johnson accomplishes this reconceptualization of social reproduction as a class struggle theory is to navigate between the pitfalls of what was once the hottest debate in Marxist theory: whether Marxists should be culturalists focusing on the complex agentic actions in the realm of culture, or structuralists attending to the obdurate relations of exploitation and oppression constituting the structure of society. To the extent that critical pedagogy, and critical education generally, in their recent iterations, were configured by debates between culturalists and structuralists in England and France postwar, when giving an account of social reproduction as a class struggle theory we can turn to one of the most fascinating and under-studied attempts to synthesize the two paradigms: Johnson's.

First, Johnson (2018) names the tendencies he seeks to bring together. "On the one hand there is the older British tendency, formed in the breaks from Leavisite literary criticism and economistic Marxism, concerned primarily with the analysis of the history of cultural traditions, class experiences or literary forms" (ibid., p. 53). Johnson points to E. P. Thompson and Raymond Williams as scions of this "culturalist" (ibid.) tendency. He calls the second tendency "structuralist," for which Louis Althusser is the representative. While culturalist texts "take the form of specific histories" (ibid.) and are "written on the basis of definite pre-suppositions of an epistemological and theoretical kind" (ibid., p. 54), structuralist writings are "philosophical, formalistic and pitched, unrelentingly, at a high level of abstraction" (ibid., p. 53). Johnson sees the tendencies both co-existing and interrupting each other, being "in radical opposition to the extent that on some essential matters it is necessary to choose between them" (ibid., p. 54). But he also declares clearly, and in italics "*[n]either culturalism nor structuralism will do!*" (ibid.).

Different as they are, Johnson shows their common heritage "forged in the political opposition to Stalinism and in theoretical opposition to 'economism'" (ibid., p. 56). Both Thompson and Althusser "sought to vindicate Marxism out of a peculiarly hostile cold war climate … by developing (in very different ways) Marxist work on non-economic questions" (ibid., p. 57). Thompson sought to fill "a real silence in Marx on the subject of 'value-systems'". Each tendency uses load-bearing terms, each sharing a certain "catholicity" (Johnson, 2018, p. 58): culture and ideology. Each of these terms are capacious enough to include whole institutions and ways of life (ibid., p. 59). Both tendencies "are opposed to idealism" (59).

Each has strengths. Structuralism "provides more than a general justification of *historical* materialism: he also supplies us with notions that enrich historical understanding and our ability to analyze specific situation … in general, the theme of complex, structured and contradictory unities" (ibid., p. 60). Its abstract method has "a clarity and adequacy to the purpose (an alternative to economism) that all culturalist formulations lack" (ibid., p. 64). Overall, "structuralism's central contribution is to re-assert Marx's own sense of the objective force of social relations and their salience over merely experiential categories" (ibid., p. 70). On the other hand, culturalism's "main imperative is to respect the authenticity, rationality, and validity of the experiences of cultures that are addressed" (ibid., p. 60). These experiences "are understood fundamentally as class experiences" and "there is a primary concern with the cultures of subordinate or oppressed classes which are seen as having a particular authenticity and dignity and yet are in need of recovery within the historical record" (ibid., p. 60). In particular, Thompson "insists on the validity, according to their experience, of the utopian, millenarian or insurrectionary aspirations of groups ... and seeks to 'rescue' them from 'the enormous condescension of posterity'" (ibid., p. 61). There's a value in the culturalist project to "grasp social phenomena in their own terms, in their forms of appearance in the world" (ibid., p. 65). The tendency "stands as a corrective to all unilateral notions of 'control' or 'ideological domination'" (ibid., p. 66).

Each have weaknesses, however. When it comes to structuralism "it is simply not fruitful to develop more and more sophisticated structuralist, semiological, linguistic, or psychoanalytic *theories*" that make no "reference to the analysis of particular situations" (ibid., p. 55). Its high level of abstraction can be violent (ibid., p. 61). While its terms are helpful "problems arise, however, when notions like 'determination in the last instance' or 'relative autonomy' acquire the status of a priori truths" (ibid., p. 64). Such *a priorism* can lead to "violent abstraction" (ibid.). Althusser has a tendency to critique texts for not being Marxist, but "it is not an adequate critique of any text to say that it is not Marxist" (ibid., p. 65). Structuralism "supplies no full alternative to culturalist practices" and can "radically simplify the social formation" and "slide into a functionalist account" (ibid., p. 67). The functionalist slide happens when structuralists "think of ideology or the ideological instance solely as a condition of existence for a given mode of production" (ibid., p. 69).

Yet when it comes to culturalism "there *is* a failure adequately to theorize the results of concrete studies and to make starting-points quite plain. There is a tendency to vacate the ground of determinations that do not show up in the experience of actors" (ibid., p. 55). "Cultural prefers to speak of an undifferentiated human praxis ... or of a 'dialectic' between being and consciousness ... Quite so, but the problem is *how*" (ibid., p. 62). The pronouncements of such dialectics are a "stretch" and a kind of "concession" (ibid., p. 63).

To Johnson, culturalism subscribes to "the theory of no-theory" (ibid.), where the category of '"experience" conflates the forms that present themselves as the raw material of cognition or which intrude upon material human existence with the (mental) means of their representation (ibid., p. 76). Culturalism refuses to make abstractions out of a fear of abstraction's violence "as a form of closure rather than a means to more complete knowledge" (ibid., p. 63). Yet "the refusal to make abstractions seriously weakens this position and renders its general conceptions vague and confused" (ibid.). In the end, "groups of individuals as 'people' cannot be the be-all and end-all of explanation" and it could be that "we can only understand their consciousness and their praxis via a detour that takes as its object the relations in which they stand" (ibid., p. 66). How to reconcile these strengths and weaknesses?

Johnson's proposal is to articulate a "more adequate account than that offered by "experience" to grasp the relation between economic and social relations and ideological practices ... and above all, a set of terms that permits us to understand ideological struggles in relation to what Antonio Gramsci called 'the necessities of production' without relapsing into a functionalism" (ibid., p. 71). Johnson proposes Gramsci as a compromise figure in his attempt to synthesize the culturalist and structuralist tendencies, focusing specifically on hegemony as an example of an account that is adequate for such a synthesis. But he makes an important point regarding hegemony before laying out that synthesis. "It is important to add that though Gramsci's 'hegemony' is now very familiar in English cultural theory, it has been appropriated, almost always, in a particular culturalist form" (ibid., p. 74). In this culturalist appropriation, hegemony "refers wholly to superstructural relations or cultural relations of authority" (ibid.). His proposal is to take a synthetic approach to the concept of hegemony rather than proceed with this culturalist appropriation, which is how he pivots to reproduction.

He understands the term "in Gramsci's own usage" to mean "the *relation between* structure and superstructure" where the "relation is that of massive disjunctions and unevenness" (ibid.). Hegemony in this sense "describes the practices by which some greater uniformity it sought" (ibid.). Johnson goes on to apply this compromise interpretation of Gramsci to reproduction: "reproduction, then, is here presented as a hard and constantly-resisted labor, a political and ideological work for capital and for the dominant classes, on very obstinate materials indeed" (ibid.). Thus, the synthetic concept of hegemony renders reproduction as a struggle. It collates the strengths of structuralism and humanism while accounting for their weaknesses. For example, "there are cultural elements to which capital is *relatively* indifferent and many of which it has great difficulty in changing and which remain massively and residually present" (ibid., p. 75).

Thus, the causality of reproduction is one of struggle: when culture is a result of ideology, this doesn't mean that ideology mechanically makes culture such that culture is a one-to-one reflection of ideology. Rather, for reproduction-as-struggle as a synthetic approach to structuralist and culturalist tendencies, we should "start by looking for contradictions, taboos, displacements rather than unities" (ibid., p. 76), where the concern is "the precise *forms* of the determination" rather than the "*fact* of a powerful relation between class position and culture" (ibid., p. 77). Again, while Johnson does not focus on education, this reproduction-as-struggle concept provides the necessary reconceptualization that opens the door for understanding what others, more explicitly focused on education, have laid out in a manner consistent with Johnson's framework, namely, Carnoy, Lefebvre, and Dussel.

24.4 Carnoy's Mediation

Martin Carnoy, the American political economist of education, provides a uniquely structural elaboration of social reproduction in education through his concept of mediation, which fits Johnson's criterion for adequacy. Trained in economics but influenced by anti-imperialists in the late 1960s, Carnoy's work has focused on education and cultural imperialism (1974), why Cuban students do better than most other students (2007), education and transitions to socialism in the third world (2014), and globalization (1999). After distinguishing himself by working as an organizer for Robert Kennedy's presidential campaign in the late 1960s, he completed an economic study of education in Mexican labor markets by doing direct field work (rare among economists), Carnoy turned his attention to Marxist theory and education, with an essay called "Education, Economy, and the State" (1982). After a deft intellectual history of Marxist theories of the state from Marx to Lenin to Gramsci, Althusser, and Poultanzas, and locating schooling within each of these, Carnoy—using the classic distinction between economic base and superstructure—argues that schools, as part of the superstructure, mediate contradictions in the economic base. This mediating action takes the form of contradictions and tensions in the process of struggle.

Simply put, Carnoy's (1982) theory of mediation is that "[s]truggle in the base leads to attempts to 'mediate' that struggle, and one of the ways that mediation takes place is through the public education system" (ibid., p. 114). Thus, the superstructure "softens" (ibid., p. 122) the contradictions in the base. School is part of that softening effect, mediating contradictions in the class struggle. Schools contribute to the ruling class's side of the class-struggle by mediating contradictions in the base. Reproduction is thus a key part of struggle in a complex and differentiated formation. Contradictions are present in schools from the wider class struggle, but they are not an overpowering presence. The schools can and do exert a force with, through, and even against those pressures from the struggle. The way they exert that force is through mediation, which manifests in contradictions.

Carnoy points to four such contradictions. The first is over-education. This is not the idea that, generally speaking, a populace has too much education. Rather, Carnoy's concept of over-education is relative to the economy. Over-education happens when the kind and amount of education supersedes labor market openings. In this case there is a mismatch between existing job opportunities and the school system set up to train, certify, and develop people to be ready for job opportunities in general. One way to think about this contradictory mismatch of over-education is the common sense that education leads to opportunity. This is "correct to some extent" (ibid., p. 119) because, to secure a position, you need education. At the same time, it is true that you do not get a job just because you are educated. Over-education is when a population attains a certain amount of skills through education while their economy does not have jobs available for them. Schools can mediate a contracting labor market through shifts in curriculum, teaching methods, technology, or other messages from the ruling class.

The second contradiction has to do with democracy, namely, that in school democracy is understood as a symbol. While Carnoy (ibid.) observes that schools are not democratic, students learn about democracy and "come to accept the abstract nature of democracy in their post-school, everyday lives" (ibid., p. 121). As students, many of us come to understand this hypocrisy between our supposedly democratic country and the obviously nondemocratic structures in the school. The contradiction occurs in the fact that this symbol of democracy maintains a promise of equality and participation. The symbol of democracy remains a horizon towards which students can always orient themselves. That horizon will always be dangerous for bourgeois hegemony, because it "does promote an ideology of individual and human rights. This mass ideology can be and is directed against big business as well as big government" (ibid., pp. 121–22).

My early research on the democratic connotations of classroom discussion is a pedagogical case school mediating this contradiction (Backer, 2018). On the one hand, discussion contains democratic meaning—it connotes participation and equality—while on the other hand, actual discussions are observably quite rare. Teachers largely maintain central control of classroom discussion, making these interactions more like recitations or question-answer sessions. The word discussion promises a democracy that goes unfulfilled. Yet the symbol of democracy can be taken up if teachers facilitate discussion in such a way as to increase participation and equality, dangerous as it might be for their careers.

Carnoy's third contradiction is that school is considered a legitimate institution whose purpose is largely understood as reproducing society. People recognize that school is where young people go to become productive members of society. Rather than limiting schools' autonomy, this legitimacy—an institution charged with preparing a society's future generations—imbues schools with power. Everyone in the social formation respects it in a certain way. This permits teachers, students, and others in the school community to extend the boundaries of what the capitalist economy or government expect, and even its mediating role itself. The intensity of the connection to its surrounding society, and its importance in maintaining that society, "gives the schools a formal autonomy from the base and the private hegemonic apparatuses," and this autonomy "allows teachers, administrators, and students to follow independent strategies which are not consistent with the mediation functions required for softening contradictions in the base" (Carnoy, 1982, p. 122).

Fourth, as the long tradition of youth subculture studies has shown, Carnoy claims youth culture itself is a contradiction in schooling. "The very bringing together of large numbers of youth in the same institution promotes the development of youth culture which may be inconsistent with social reproduction" (ibid.). Althusser noticed that schools bring together teachable young people into one institution that can, effectively, control the message. Yet in so doing, the institution takes a risk in bringing together large numbers of (from its point of view) untrained youth who can, as Paul Willis (1981) famously observed in *Learning to Labour*, block and break up that message.

Each of the four contradictions—over-education, democracy-as-symbol, reproduction, and youth culture—are mediations of conflicts within the mode of production, which in capitalism is defined by struggle. But schools are not a smoothly functioning machine keeping social cohesion. Each mediation, taking the form of a contradiction, has serious consequences for the material life of a society. When the number or kind of jobs available to an educated populace is inadequate to its education, that populace can feel a dissatisfaction. When a society promises democracy but delivers top-down control, its denizens might feel brow-beaten and disappointed. When young people get corralled into institutions whose purpose is unclear and does not consider their daily experiences, they might revolt or reject its programming. Dissatisfaction, disappointment, revolt, rejection, and anger permeate and fester in a social formation leading to "absenteeism, worker turnover, wildcat strikes, alcoholism and drug usage, deterioration of production quality" (Carnoy, 1982, p. 122). In our moment, the opioid epidemic would be an interesting case to examine. To what extent does such an epidemic owe its magnitude to over-education?

The contradictions have consequences within school as well. Over-education can cause "relaxation of educational standards" (ibid., p. 123) since, in a shrinking job market, what an education means deflates in value. Such relaxed standards can lead to a lack of discipline (ibid.). Relaxing standards and lack of discipline then threatens the legitimacy of the grading system, causing grade inflation, or "higher grades for relatively poorer quality work" (ibid.) and erosion of the school's legitimacy. There's a concomitant "falling commodity value of education" (ibid.). These impacts in schooling come back around in the world of work, when it comes to discipline in the workplace, for example.

Carnoy's theory of mediation answers, with fine-grained detail, the question of how schools are involved in the class struggle as apparatuses. They are mediators. The contradictions mentioned are manifestations of that class struggle in schools. Education is part of the class struggle because it is a terrain in the balance of forces "by dint of the organic relation between struggle in superstructure and struggle in the base" (ibid., p. 124). Importantly, mediation is uneven. To Carnoy, "actions in the schools have the potential to contribute positively to labor's position in the class struggle" (ibid.). Rather than a stultifying, flattening passivity, there is "a constellation of relations between the schools and the workplace," which means that schools can offer "either reinforcement or disruptive potential" due to "the independent dynamic of schools and their internal contradictions" (ibid.). Mediation in Carnoy's sense is a theory of social reproduction that captures the structural subtleties of education in Marxism in an agentic way, which Henri Lefebvre's does as well but in a much different manner.

24.5   Lefebvre's Production of New Relations

Another lesser-known Marxist concept of social reproduction in education may be found in the work of Left Hegelian Marxist philosopher and urbanist Henri Lefebvre's (1973) *The Survival of Capitalism: The Reproduction of the Relations of Production*. While not focused specifically on schools, Lefebvre (ibid., p. 46) focuses on reproduction in general, and in so doing offers a unique conception for education researchers in the Marxist tradition. He begins with the claim that "[i]t was in 1863 that Marx came up with the concept" of reproducing the relations of production:

> in a letter to Engels (6 July) in which Quesnay's famous economic table is mentioned. In Marx's opinion, this table was more than a mere summary of the circulation of goods and money. He believed it demonstrates how and why the process remains unbroken … According to Marx, the problem can therefore no longer be a simple one of the reproduction of the means of production, but the *reproduction of the relations of production.*

He actually calls this "Marx's last discovery" (ibid., p. 51), as he wrote this letter while drafting the unpublished chapters of the *Grundrisse*.[1] Harkening back to Marx's original formulation of social reproduction as preservation, Lefebvre is thus interested in the "renewal of capitalism" (ibid., p. 9) and "the ability of capitalism to maintain itself during and beyond its critical moments" (ibid., p. 70), but also how that renewal happens during "the repetition of everyday motions and actions" (ibid., p. 9). Lefebvre only mentions schooling briefly in this context, but to understand his reference to education as both a site of reproduction and struggle, we should first have an understanding of his broader concern and account.

The book is rife with examples of his interest in renewal, like sleep. "*Sleep* (resting time) plays a big part in the maintenance and reproduction of labour power" (ibid., p. 45). Lefebvre therefore wants to investigate the "maintenance of the essentials of social relations" but also "the regression, degradation, and transgression" of relations of production (ibid., p. 14). Further, and most importantly, he wants to make space for "the production of new relations" (ibid.). The idea of social space is one of his central contributions to Marxist thinking, and he draws from that contribution to talk about this central concern: "[s]ocial space is where the reproduction of the *relations* of production … is located" (ibid., p. 17).

Reproduction happens where "coherences … enter into conflict with one another" (ibid.), or from "the lived … to the living … by way of particularities and the chaos of things" (ibid., p. 16). His approach to the problem of the reproduction of relations of production is to articulate explicitly how capitalism maintains continuity in incoherent social space:

> The pursuit of cohesion in the mode of production does not preclude either its dissolution or its transformation; capitalism is changing and, as such, disintegrating, even in the process of realizing its own concept. Transgressions serve as geiger-counters, causing this process to appear in all its contradictory and dialectical totality … As an ensemble, they justify the hypothesis of a 'point of no return' (metamorphosis and/or self-destruction). (*ibid.*, p. 14)

Relations of production can dissolve, transform, or disintegrate as they reproduce. They can be transgressed, or brought to a point of no return where they metamorphosize and self-destruct. Talking about urban space, both large and small, local orders at the level of neighborhood, town, local communities, and even eco-systems (ibid., p. 27), Lefebvre emphasizes "a deeper conflictive relation" and "fragmentation" in the social formation, which he conceives as a "dialecticized, conflictive space ... where the reproduction of the relations of production is achieved. It is this space that produces reproduction, by introducing it into its multiple contradictions" (ibid., p. 19). In other words, while some

> former relations may degenerate or dissolve— e.g. the town, the natural and nature, the nation, everyday poverty, the family, 'culture', the commodity ... [o]thers are constituted in such a way that there is *production* of social relations within the re-production—e.g. the urban, the possibilities of the everyday, the differential. These new relations emerge from within those which are dissolving: they first appear as the negation of the latter, as the destroyers of the antecedents and conditions which hold them back. (*ibid*., p. 82)

In general, the "[a]im of this project is to produce a 'difference' which is different from any that can be inferred from the existing relations of production ... this difference can be produced through space as well as time" (ibid., p. 35). But there are criteria for producing such differences in the relations of production. There might be "substitution and displacement" of the relations of production that are actually "the total renewal of the previous relations of production under new names" (ibid., p. 39). Such a "*transition*" to "a new and qualitatively different society" does not follow "the political revolution, as it did in Marx's outline. It precedes it ... the new 'values' are not imposed: they are proposed" (ibid., p. 91).

As noted, while the book mentions education only here and there, Lefebvre does write that "when working-class and student youth ... reject the mode of production, the symptom turns into the cause, and reproduction (of the social relations) wavers" (ibid., p. 22). School, for Lefebvre, is a social space of conflict. He mentions French students and how they inaugurated a pedagogical critique of the university (ibid., p. 51):

> Gradually, beginning with the mass primary school, [the pedagogical critique] disclosed the characteristics of this teaching: the methods, the surroundings and organization of space, which reduce the pupil to passivity and get him used to working without joy (in spite of the spurious claims to have reintroduced 'living' education). Pedagogical space is repressive ... Imposed knowledge, ingurgitated by the pupils and regurgitated in exams, corresponds to the division of labor in bourgeois society, and therefore sustains it. (*ibid*., p. 52)

Yet school is conflicted and a site of struggle. Students, whom he characterizes as largely middle class, can "furnish us with an example of how ambiguities can turn into conflicts ... The lack of consistency and specificity which marks the middle classes as a swamp actually helps them to obtain 'positive' advantages, to score some points" (ibid., p. 25). This view of students as being able to score points on the terrain of school fits with his overall thesis on the reproduction of relations of production as dissolving, degenerating, and regenerating in new forms. "Learning, culture, the town— the roles which all these elements play are poorly perceived, poorly controlled, and under present conditions they are areas of dissolution rather than of transformation" (ibid., p. 97). For Lefebvre, the urban is a social space where this conflict happens: "the urban today is the location both of the reproduction of the former social relations and their decomposition, and of the formation of new relations and their contradictions" (97). Lefebvre's concept of social reproduction is urban-focused, agentic-structural, and focuses specifically on the ways relations of production actually exist, viz., reproduction in the contingent froth of history and everyday life.

24.6 Dussel's Analectics

Originally writing in the 1970s, the Argentinian philosopher of liberation Enrique Dussel (2019) set out his thinking on education in a short book on pedagogics that was recently translated into English, along with updates and comments by the author. As an influential thinker within the decolonial theoretical movement, Dussel conceptualized pedagogics as an ethic born out of a philosophy of liberation, decentering the European experience and democratizing epistemology so as to be communal rather than imperialistic. Specifically, by pedagogics, he means "the part of philosophy (along with ethics, politics, and economics) which considers face-to-face relationships: the parent—child, teacher—student, doctor—patient, philosopher—nonphilosopher, politician—citizen, etc." (2019, p. 47). Pedagogics explores the ways that these face-to-face interactions reproduce the oppressive dynamics of society or provide space for Otherness and what is not yet known.

The concept of childhood plays an outsized role in this schema. Influenced by the French philosopher Immanuel Levinas, Dussel understands the child as a radical newness in a world of sameness. A child is quintessentially Other and must be brought into the fold through various institutions such as family and school. Yet there is a dynamic at play, a sort of battleground, where different groups with different interests, histories, and goals attempt to absorb the child into their respective political, economic, cultural, and sexual practices. Augmenting the Hegelian and Marxist concept of dialectic, Dussel (ibid.) calls this dynamic an analectic: the interplay of Sameness and Otherness, represented respectively by what he calls a reigning and dominant interiority, on the one hand, and an alterity exterior to it on the other. The dominant interiority, or Sameness, is configured by ruling classes and—while he does not the term, it is fitting—reproduces that sameness throughout society, particularly in face-to-face interactions where there are inequalities of knowledge. Writing specifically of Latin America's relationship to other regions of the world, Dussel's analectic has a colonial logic. Sameness emanates outwards from imperial centers like the United States and Europe to peripheries like Latin American countries, having a broadly educational impact when it comes to educational governance, policy, and regulation, but also in the larger sense of pedagogic impact Dussel intends.

When an imperial center engages with a periphery, the parent-child analectic plays out pedagogically in myriad ways through the aforementioned dyadic relationships. Education is crucial in this process. Dussel argues that parents, educators, and policymakers have a fundamental choice. They can either welcome the exteriority of their respective pedagogical Others (children, students, the community) or reject that alterity by insisting that these Others assimilate into a reigning Sameness determined by the empire. Philosophically, Dussel articulates this pedagogics of liberation in a Figure that defines the *Ontological pedagogics of the schoolteacher's ego and orphanic entity* (ibid., p. 95, see below Fig. 24.1). Dussel first describes his pedagogics as an anti-pedagogy, using Levinasian terms such as idiosyncratic hyphenation and the terms ontology and Totality, referring to a kind of closed existential dominance, to talk about the dynamic of sameness and alterity in the education:

> This pedagogics of liberation is an anti-pedagogy existing within the system. Against Hegel, we might define our anti-pedagogy as 'the art of making unethical man (unsittlich).' Ontological pedagogics dominates because it considers the child–disciple an entity in which knowledge and attitudes must be deposited. These attitudes and knowledges compose 'the Same,' which the master or preceptor is. This domination (arrow b… [in Fig. 24.1]) includes the child in the Totality (arrow a in the same figure): it alienates him. In this case the child–disciple is that which is educable: the one who is educated is the fruit, an effect of educational causality … The pro-duct (the 'guided' in opposition to the view or

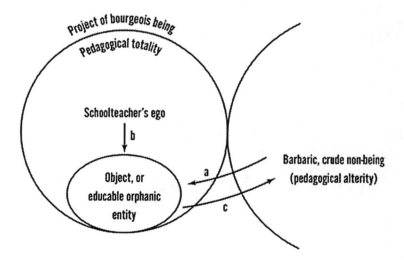

Fig. 24.1 Ontological pedagogics of the schoolteacher's ego and orphanic entity (special thanks to Vincent W.J. van Gerven Oei at punctum books for the permissions to reproduce this image, cited from Dussel (2019), where it was Figure 3)

reason which evaluates the result) is a formed, informed adult. This informed adult is constituted in accord with the fundamental pedagogical pro-ject: 'the Same' that the father, teacher, system already is. (*ibid.*, p. 105)

As Dussel makes clear in (Fig. 24.1),[2] this ontological totality is the bourgeois project of sameness, which includes a pedagogical totality. In that totality, the schoolteacher's ego comes to bear on the educable subject who, in the context of the bourgeois project, is considered orphanic since the school, as an institution, can displace parents, family, and community. Alterity refers to ways of being that do not fit within the bourgeois project, which educationally means a crude pedagogical alterity which students, specifically colonized subjects considered outside the empire, inhabit (Fig. 24.1).

The arrows, particularly arrows "a" and "c" represent the back and forth dynamic that holds between the student's pedagogical alterity and the bourgeois project, as well as the teacher's role in the reproduction of the latter's form of Sameness, within the totality. That dynamic, Dussel claims, in an analectic that occurs at the face-to-face level within the larger dialectic of social forces, such as the struggle between capital and labor. While Dussel does not characterize the theory in this way, a pedagogic that imposes the reigning colonial sameness of the bourgeois project on the student's pedagogical alterity reproduces ruling class hegemony. Liberation for Dussel entails an openness to the alterity of the Other in the analectic, which in the educational situation takes advantage of the contingency of the social formation to undermine that ruling class sameness in the colonial context. Decolonization then entails the systematic pedagogical recognition of students' alterity in the everyday analectic of the face-to-face educational situation. Thus, the contrast he makes between a dominating dialectic and a liberatory analectic (Fig. 24.2).

In "A Brief Note on Pedagogics," Dussel writes about the analectic between an indigenous student and her Spanish teacher in a Latin American context to provide a concrete example of this theory.

Dominating dia-lectic	versus	Liberatory ana-lectic
Conquistador's attitude	versus	Co-laborator's attitude
Divisive attitude	versus	Convergent attitude
Demobilizing attitude	versus	Mobilizing attitude
Manipulative attitude	versus	Organizing attitude
Attitude of cultural invasion	versus	Creative attitude[35]

Fig. 24.2 Dussel's contrast between a dominating dialectic and a liberatory analectic (special thanks to Vincent W.J. van Gerven Oei at punctum books for the permissions to reproduce this image, cited from Dussel (2019))

The teacher must learn the content of the youth's new projects ... The teacher should not say to an Indian student: 'You do not know how to speak. Learn how to speak Spanish [castellano].' The student in this instance goes home and lets her parents know the teacher is telling her she must learn to speak, because she does not know how to. Her mother says: 'But we speak our language.' 'Yes,' the student replies, 'but my teacher says that does not count.' That is domination! But if the teacher tells the student: 'You speak Quechua, Aymara, Maya, Otomí! I do not speak that language. You are bilingual, you are wiser than I am,' then the student goes back home to let her mother know the teacher thought she was wise. (*ibid.*, p. 100)

In this case, we see the fine-grained struggle of the maintenance of ruling class hegemony at the pedagogical level, what Dussel names the analectic. The teacher has the choice to be oppressive or liberatory, which, in Dussel's context, hinges on whether that teacher sides with the ruling colonial sameness at stake in the classroom situation. Appreciating the students' ability to speak an indigenous language, recognizing the student's alterity in the context of language education, satisfies the theory's criterion for liberation in that (de)colonial analectic.

Like Lefebvre, in Dussel's theory, we get a way to change or disrupt the reproduction of dominant relations of production in education and make these relations liberatory rather than oppressive. Like in Carnoy's theory, Dussel's theory helps clarify the fine-grained contradictions involved in everyday education from the structural perspective. Unlike either of these however, Dussel's analectics has a (de)colonial focus, bringing in the international dimension to the class struggle in education.

24.7 Conclusion

Social reproduction, in the Marxist tradition, refers to the preservation and maintenance of a capitalist society over time. There have been several views of social reproduction in education in this vein, three of which I have named intertwining, carework, and transmission in this entry. These views have, to greater and lesser extents, been critiqued for their determinism and functionalism, or for not being class struggle theories. Yet what distinguishes the Marxist concept of social reproduction in education is its focus on how ruling classes and their fractions, through educational institutions, maintain hegemony in the context of struggle. Several theories of social reproduction in education have brought this out, yet have gotten considerably less attention from researchers. Richard Johnson (2018) set the stage for what is perhaps the most advanced Marxist concept of social reproduction as reproduction-in-struggle, striking a balance between structuralism and culturalism. I have foregrounded three lesser-known accounts of social reproduction in education consistent with Johnson's formulation: Carnoy's theory of mediation, Lefebvre's account of the production of relations, and Dussel's decolonial analectics each of which capture the socially reproductive aspect of education amidst class struggle.

Disclosure Statement The author has no financial interest or benefit that has arisen from the direct applications of this research.

Notes

1. This letter mentioned by Lefebvre is from Marx to Engels from 6th July 1863 (MECW vol. 41 p. 483–487). The discovery of how reproduction of relations of production occurs by Marx is traditionally connected with him discussing the Quesnay's Tableau economique. Quesnay's contribution to the classical political economy's understanding of how surplus value circulate between the classes was considered a true milestone, which drew a clear line of demarcation between Marx's account and more classical political economy. I thank the editors for both finding the letter Lefebvre references and making clear its significance historically.
2. Special thanks to Vincent W.J. van Gerven Oei at punctum books for the permissions to reproduce both images cited from Dussel (2019).

References

Althusser, L. (2014). *On the Reproduction of Capitalism: Ideology and Ideological State Apparatuses*. Verso.

Backer, D. (2022). *Althusser and Education: Reassessing Critical Education*. Bloomsbury Academic.

Backer, D., & Cairns, K. (2021). Social Reproduction Theory Revisited. *British Journal of Sociological of Education, 42*(7), 1086–1104.

Backer, D. (2018). The Distortion of Discussion. *Issues in Teacher Education, 27*(1), 3–16.

Benston, M. (1969). The Political Economy of Women's Liberation. *Monthly Review, 41*(7), 31–44.

Bhattacharya, T. (2017). *Social Reproduction Theory: Remapping Class, Recentering Oppression*. Pluto Press.

Bourdieu, P., & Passeron, J. C. (1979). *The Inheritors: French Students and Their Relation to Culture*. Univ of Chicago Press.

Bourdieu, P., & Passeron, J.-C. (1990). *Reproduction in Education, Society and Culture* (Vol. 4). Sage.

Carnoy, M. (1999). *Globalization and Educational Reform: What Planners Need to Know*. UNESCO, International Institute for Educational Planning. Essay on Educational Change (2002) PDF.

Carnoy, M. (1974). *Education as Cultural Imperialism*. Longman.

Carnoy, M. (1982). Education, Economy and the State. In *Cultural and Economic Reproduction in Education* (pp. 79–126). Routledge.

Carnoy, M. (2014). *Education and Social Transition in the Third World*. Princeton University Press.

Carnoy, M., Gove, A. K., & Marshall, J. H. (2007). *Cuba's Academic Advantage: Why Students in Cuba Do Better in School*. Stanford University Press.

Dussel, E. (2019). *The Pedagogics of Liberation: A Latin American Philosophy of Education* (D. Backer, & C. Diego, Trans.). Punctum Books.
Johnson, R. (2018). Histories of Culture/Theories of Ideology: Notes on an Impasse. In *Routledge Revivals: Ideology and Cultural Production (1979)* (pp. 49–77). Routledge.
Lefebvre, H. (1973). *The Survival of Capitalism*. Allison and Busby.
Marx, K. (1956). *Capital: Volume Two*. Progress Publishers.
Marx, K. (2019). *Capital: Volume One*. Dover Publications.
Morrow, R. A. (2014). Reproduction Theories. In D. C. Phillips (Ed.), *Encyclopedia of Educational Philosophy and Theory* (pp. 706–711). Russell Sage.
Morrow, R. A., & Torres, C. A. (1995). *Social Theory and Education: A Critique of Theories of Social and Cultural Reproduction*. SUNY Press.
Willis, P. (1981). *Learning to Labor: How Working Class Kids Get Working Class Jobs*. Columbia University Press.

CHAPTER 25

State and Public Policy in Education: From the Weakness of the Public to an Agenda for Social Development and Redistribution

Felipe Ziotti Narita and Jeremiah Morelock

25.1 Introduction

One of the most salient political *tours de force* of modernity was the construction of the welfare state in the twentieth century. The idea of providing political and economic resources that could ensure well-being not only reshaped the notion of the *basic* needs of citizenship (with public infrastructures of health, education, etc.), but rather marked a promise of social cohesion guaranteed by public institutions (Habermas, 1996). As a reformist agenda, welfare policies aided the inclusion of working classes and underprivileged groups in central and peripheral countries (Arretche, 1995; Esping-Andersen, 1990), reshaping the very notion of the *social* (Toro, 2005) in light of the public commitment to a quality standard of living. Welfare public policies aim to modify the imbalances of the market (Briggs, 1962), above all, via labor regulation (by guaranteeing a minimum income) and ensuring that citizens can count on basic public services for their wellbeing (education, healthcare, housing, etc.).

Beginning in the 1980s, market pressures informed a redefinition of state responsibilities regarding welfare policies and social justice (Castañeda, 1993;

F. Z. Narita (✉)
São Paulo State University, São Paulo, Brazil
e-mail: felipe.narita@unesp.br

J. Morelock
Boston College's Woods College of Advancing Studies, Boston, MA, USA
e-mail: jeremiah.morelock@bc.edu

© The Editor(s) (if applicable) and The Author(s), under exclusive license to Springer Nature Switzerland AG 2023
R. Hall et al. (eds.), *The Palgrave International Handbook of Marxism and Education*, Marxism and Education,
https://doi.org/10.1007/978-3-031-37252-0_25

Rosanvallon, 1981). Especially in Latin America, which underwent structural market and state reforms in the wake of the fiscal crises of the 1980s, this process has been palpable in educational systems (Betancur, 2008; Narita et al., 2022). The pressures of oligopolies and the expanded presence of private actors in public schooling, from elementary school to higher education, point not only to the discourse of efficiency and performance, which marked the apex of the neoliberal political economy in the 1990s (Clarke & Pitelis, 1993), but also to the *weakness of the public* (Puiggrós & Narita, 2020). We are not dealing only with the classic model of privatization based on the transfer of public means of production to private ownership (O'Neil, 2009), but also with the strong presence of NGOs, foundations and corporations (Feldfeber et al., 2018; Garcia, 2018; González López & Parra Moreno, 2016; Kummer, 2019), emphasizing the role of civil society and private actors *amidst* public administration. In other words, more than a diminishing of the state, we are dealing with a liberal economic rationality that inserts private logics *into* public structures, reshaping the very notion of the public.

The incorporation of private management strategies into the public domain reinforced the need for adaptation to how capitalism has re-engineered learning environments. A large-scale study based on the databases from UNESCO and Latin American institutions (Verger et al., 2017) shows that privatization processes comprise charter schools (public institutions managed by private groups), educational vouchers (the families can chose among public and private schools in order to force competition among institutions), and tax breaks for schools and families to favor the private sector. The weakness of the public is not properly about the minimal state, but rather a complex political symbiosis between public structures and private actors that corrupt welfare policy and the commonwealth with private appropriation of public goods.

Moschetti et al. (2019) argue that we can divide the privatization processes into four axes. (1) Part of the structural reform of the state (educational reforms in the 1980s, in Chile, favored the vouchers systems). (2) Incremental reform as a set of diffuse policies that favored private initiatives (the *colegios en concesión* in Colombia, and the force of private groups of education in elementary and higher education in Brazil) (Gustavo Ortiz, 2021). (3) Privatization by default due to the limited capacity of state agency and public budget (Peru and Dominican Republic). (4) Public-private partnerships to broaden the school coverage in the most economical way possible (Argentina) or via experimental projects in countries where education is still dominated by public presence (Uruguay). Market relations tend to reinforce inequalities (Balarin, 2016; Ortiz et al., 2021), turning the access to cultural assets dependent on social asymmetries subsumed under capital valorization. As state and public responsibilities are transferred to private actors, education becomes a matter of training and profitability, its function narrowed to the development of human capital (Álvarez Aragon et al., 2010), and human beings are conceived as instruments to improve the production of goods and services.

We argue that these processes of privatization fit with the theory of human capital, which appeared in the 1960s in the works of the Chicago economist Gary Becker. This chapter builds from Marxist and decolonial perspectives to critique human capital theories in light of the geopolitics of knowledge, and to argue the need for public policy to reverse the structural social asymmetries and class cleavages in peripheral societies of Latin America. Marxism offers a relevant set of tools for analyzing this problem, since human capital theories tend to detach individuals from the social conditions that organize the production of society. On the one hand, human capital reinforces a rationality committed to optimize and naturalize market relations. On the other hand, Marxism unveils the logics of domination behind the discourse of market optimization. Decolonial theories, which have been discussed especially among Latin American scholars since the 1990s, also unveil forms of domination behind market ideology. Rather than classical Marxist "class" relations per se, decolonial theories state how market rationality reinforces structural asymmetries of social power between geopolitical/cultural regions. They reveal how peripheral societies are subjected to new forms of domination in the wake of the historical effects of coloniality, under the rhetoric of market efficiency and the integration of national economies into the global tendencies of capital. Public policy in education, as a counterpart of redistributive policy, can be conceived as a prospect of social development and emancipation committed to the quest for dignity and the denunciations of the contradictions of the discourse of citizenship in liberal democracies.

25.2 Human Capital and Education

A former Brazilian secretary of economics, Paulo Guedes, in one of his first speeches since he joined the administration of President Jair Bolsonaro in January 2019, stated that:

> liberal economists have always had another face, that of human capital, the importance of investing in health and education. We intend to give money for vouchers [individual vouchers] for health, day care and education, to invest in the training of children from 0 to 9 years old. The government has this emphasis: on the one hand, by the conservatives, on the family; on the other hand, the idea of massive investment in human capital. (Vilela, 2019)

Human capital has become a pervasive concern of public policy in education since the 1980s. Besides national governments, global institutions like the World Bank and the Organization for Economic Co-operation and Development often insist in measures and capabilities to track efficiency and the capacity of countries in generating and managing their human capital (Bakker et al., 2020). Basically, it emphasizes the productive capacity allowed by applied knowledge and the reproduction of labor force (Heydorn, 1972; Lin, 2001), that is, education is a matter of training and public educational systems must learn how to improve efficiency with management techniques, adaptation to the new learning environments of capital (distance learning, hybrid classes, etc.), and the privatization of collective responsibilities and wellbeing.

The concept of human capital, which comes from the economic agenda of the 1950s and the 1960s, has a diversified trajectory among the discussions of modernization attempts during the post-war order. In the works of Theodore Schultz, Jacob Mincer, Milton Friedman, Edward Fulton Denison, Sherwin Rosen, Mark Blaug, and Gary Becker, we can find foundational reflections on the need for the augmentation of productivity via knowledge as a cornerstone factor of production (Heckman, 2014). Schultz (1961, p. 3), in a discussion with the work of H. G. Johnson, Friedman and Horvat, synthesizes the main concerns of human capital, as he states that "individuals become capitalists not only via private property, but also through the incorporation of knowledge with economic purposes."

The discussion emphasizes the optimum decision based on marginal cost and marginal benefit, alongside the individual's responsibility and interest in investing in themselves, to improve their professional knowledge and personal skills and to foster human productivity (Chattopadhyay, 2012). The main axis of human capital research is *how capital relations can be part of human beings*, since people invest in themselves purchasing education, just like enterprises invest in business (Ierulli et al., 1995). Especially in Becker's version of the theory of human capital, we can track some key insights that shed light on the developments of privatization processes in education and, above all, a liberal diagnosis on the weakness of the public.

Becker applied neoclassical economic approaches to human behavior, pairing together education and business investment, taking individual choice and family (private realms of socialization) as primal stances for his theory. Education is an "investment decision," that is, it is part of a crisscross of rational choice in which private individuals associate in civil society with instrumental purposes and the increase of production (which echoes Adam Smith's classical theory of productivity) and valorization of earnings. In this sense, "a rational person would invest only if the expected rate of return were greater than the sum of the interest rate on riskless assets and the liquidity and risk premiums associated with the investment" (Becker, 1993, p. 91). On the one hand, this liberal assumption emphasizes the individuation processes of global capitalism (Morelock & Narita, 2021), stressing the role of the individual in financing and pursuing its skills. On the other hand, it leads to the valorization of "the quality of the work force through schooling," that is, the embodiment of capital relations in people (Becker, 1993, pp. 16–17). It is not only about how college education raises a person's income, but rather how educational systems and policies reinforce a privatist view of social production.

As a key factor of production, education trains *subjects*. Time and resources, for example, are not only to be allocated between market labor force activity and nonmarket consumption activity, but also as a subjective investment in human capital (Becker, 1993, p. 77). The calculus of education processes must always take into account the marginal costs of individual investments and, above all, how the distribution of wealth is reasonably approximated by a particular skewed distribution (Pareto distribution). Productivity depends not only on professional ability, but also on subjective motivation (Becker, 1993, p. 57). Human capital theory insists that the subject must work out on himself as an investment (Becker, 1993, p. 113), a subjective pressure that shaped the language of post-Fordist capitalism with the needs for individual "wellbeing" and proactive, engaged, resilient workers (Marazzi, 2002). On a subjective level, education rationalizes individual behavior with the "entrepreneurial capacity" and the benefits of competition in the job market (Becker, 1993, pp. 115–116). Human capital, thus, renders each individual a firm that reconciles human beings with all the objective (division of labor, class inequalities, etc.) and subjective constellations of capital.

Education is reduced to a matter of training. Under the need for practical skills and personal/emotional abilities committed to soften social relations in favor of the incorporation of market relations, education aimed at human capital acquisition reifies attempts at emancipation and feeds into an administered world managed by procedures and instrumental relations.

Becker is not simply arguing for the minimal presence of the state and the utopia of the free market. Instead, human capital theory seems to invert the factors: *how the state can be useful to optimize market conditions and how market efficiency can be integrated into state apparatuses.* Individuals only maximize their utility since their behavior is coordinated by markets (Becker, 1981, p. 10). The primeval nucleus of private socialization—the family—is the core of Becker's formulae. If "the optimal investment in family capital is more readily attained than is the optimal investment in public goods," (Becker, 1981, p. 184) public systems of education play only a compensatory role to redistribute resources for children in poor families (Becker, 1981, p. 191). The state and public policy are subsidiary processes in policymaking. This is the *reality* of the weakness of the public, which is to say, the state safeguards the general structure of society (law and very general conditions for the functioning of market), but is unable to maximize rational behavior (which depends on the individual), provide equilibrium to market relations and enhance efficiency provided by competition and capital. Policy design, in this sense, is conceived as a tool for the state to guarantee and integrate the proactivity of civil society and private rationale.

25.3 Marxism and the Critique of Human Capital

Human capital theory carries the typical neoliberal assumption of the decontextualized, rational actor. It emphasizes a presocialized individual, that is, as if it could be possible to abstract individual achievements and choices from social contexts and, above all, from the contradictions of capitalist society. On the one hand, it reinforces an ideology of individual merit, since the individualization of responsibilities can lead to the perception of achievements as outcomes of mere individual willpower, obscuring social asymmetries (Narita & Kato, 2020). Especially in Becker's formula, when inequalities are treated in terms of education, they only appear as problems that can be solved through better distribution of goods and school access, that is, it is a matter of improving the actualization of market rationality. On the other hand, human capital theory promotes a Robinsonade, as if individuals could be simply reified as isolated pieces pursuing their own rational interests, that is, human capital reinforces the ignorance of the social context of individual production. Instead, Marx's theory of individuation, as it is expressed in the *Grundrisse*, points to a materialist anthropological stance. The emphatic frame of "the individual" arose with the expansion of exchange systems (Marx, 1983, p. 95), according to the production of new needs and new forms of consumption. It is a dialectical problem: we became "individuals" at the same time as production became increasingly directed toward the social, in the form of broad systems of exchange.

The instrumental content of education in human capital theory points to how far rationalization and reification developed in capitalist society. One of the main features of capital is to unveil the social from its religious or mystical appearance. For Marx (1990, p. 124), it reveals the "pure economic form" of sociality, since individuals must face production as it is, which is to say, as valorization of capital and a mere relation of production without any ideal adorn. Culture and education are reduced to market rationality and the individual is deprived of autonomy, since its activity is reduced to the performance of a decontextualized rational actor seeking subjective resources for career and efficiency. Success in the market context comes in reified forms of accumulation—human capital, social status, financial assets. The marketized context, which is naturalized as a basic need for individual performance, becomes the primary delimiter of legitimated metrics, measuring quantifications of individual achievements as the evidence of the outcomes of education.

The narrowing of educational horizons to the building of employable skills actively catalyzes the reification of society, in Lukácsian terms. Lukács used the term "reification" in reference to a cultural tendency in capitalist society involving a mutual entanglement of commodification (in the Marxian sense) and rationalization (in the Weberian sense). In this way, the colonization of culture by the logic of exchange value includes colonization by forms of instrumentalism, quantification, and means-ends rationality. Reification dovetails capitalist rationalization with the prevalence of calculus of individual performance to better the reproduction of capital (Lukács, 1977, p. 262). As a form of rationalization of social behaviors, human capital individualizes the responsibility for production, rendering every abstract individual as a system of skills devoted to pursue self-interest, metrics, and profitability (Lukács, 1977, p. 266) via utility maximization. Self-investment in education, in this case, is an investment in the production process, as an attempt at training the competitive individual. The subjective investment in self-improvement removes the possibility of autonomy, since the reified individual kowtows to the heteronomous structure of market pressures.

Human capital theory reinforces a privatist view of the individual responsibilities for their own education. The individual makes their own path as an abstract unity detached from the state, and public compromises to support education. As a result, the weakness of the public erodes not only socialist agendas, but also the capacity of the state to plan and coordinate public policy for wellbeing. In Latin America, many private institutions, like Unibanco Institute, Ayrton Senna Institute, Lemann Foundation, Bradesco Foundation and Santander, are committed to better education via private investment and private management techniques in public schools. This process reinforces the weakness of the public, since those institutions occupy public structures and insert private/market logics into the state, and, above all, it implies a redefinition of public commitment with social policy. Capitalist modernizing moves are grounded in the re-engineering of learning environments with pro-profit technologies of infrastructure (digital campuses) and subjectivity (adaptability, cooperation, etc.), turning human capital into a cornerstone for the processes of accumulation in the global economy.

Any solution based only on the distribution of educational resources, as if valuable knowledge per se would soften inequalities and could be detached from the structure of capitalist society, stumbles when up against capitalist appropriation of education. Knowledge is embedded in the modernizing moves that make possible innovation and became a main asset of globalized societies (Amsden, 2003). As part of the Marxian general intellect, the "social knowledge" (Marx, 1983, p. 602) becomes a productive force since it is objectified (*vergegenständlichte*) in the making of commodities, that is, education remains a platform for human capital via the accumulation of a trained working force that reproduces society. Knowledge is not free; rather, it is applied to generate technology and innovation (Charminade et al., 2018), that is, to produce value. Especially in peripheral societies, knowledge is an input that is difficult to manufacture, since it implies systematic training and an effective network of school system. The state, in this case, may be the coordinator of public policy committed to the improvement of market development, turning national economies more competitive and making citizens an investment. Human capital, thus, favors the general administration of society as a government over people and things, reifying people in mere components for calculus and for the improvement of accumulation.

For a critique of human capital, it is not enough to improve the functioning of market, or argue that inequalities can be fought with policy committed to the terms where human capital works, that is, those set by the market. In other words, if human capital and market rationality are problematic, it is also important to point to the contradictory nature of welfare policy and the limits of the reformist politics (Pemberton, 1983). Marx (1987, p. 22) in his 1875 political program stated that it is not enough to distribute, but rather to restructure the *social* control of the means of production. Especially in education, if we conceive it as a basic factor for social welfare and development of human capabilities, the private appropriation of assets corrodes the very notion of the common good. Even the labor of teachers is affected by human capital investment, since their conditions are defined competitively through performance management, increased automation and quantification, at the level of the individual, the subject or discipline, the institution, and between national sectors (Hall, 2022).

The pervasive presence of market relations in educational sectors reinforces a sense of alienation, or, in other words, the experience of the atomized individual, with recourse only to their personal resources and competitive process for their welfare and life satisfaction, as the primary subject of society. The emphasis on individual achievement actively participates in the proliferation of individualist ideology, which stands against class consciousness and collective mobilization. In these terms, the framework of human capital serves the reproduction of capitalism. Yet not only is the theory of human capital blind to class cleavages, it also carries the typical neoliberal assumption of the decontextualized, rational actor. Skills and knowledge have different capital values depending on the demographics of the human who can develop and mobilize them. In education, they also have different values and meanings depending on the contexts within which they are to be employed. Within the academy, the production of knowledge has an ingrained conservative bias toward a particular narrow subset of Euro-American modes, traditions, and institutions of knowledge.

This centripetal pattern largely concerns the determination of which knowledge is considered legitimate, intertwined with whether the delivery of this knowledge conforms to the habitus of publishing and presentation. The world of journal publishing is dominated by hierarchies of legitimation, epitomized by the metric of importance ascribed to journals, the "impact factor." This works to reproduce the peripheral condition of science produced in poor countries (Beigel, 2014). To be granted a secure academic position and to maintain a respected academic standing, one needs to publish in the "top" journals of one's field—in other words the journals with the highest impact factors. Impact factors indicate how often an article published in the journal is typically cited by other publications within a specified period of time, e.g., 5 years. In other words, this metric stands for other metrics—numbers of citations. And of course, citations in other intra-disciplinary top journals are worth more than citations from lesser known or even extra-disciplinary journals. There are other relations that could be mentioned, but they all contribute to the same general scenario: a palpably hierarchal system of publication, where the more deeply one's writings and citations are entrenched, the more success one is likely to have in their academic career in terms of publication and occupation. This sort of inwardness and isomorphism intrinsically supports methodological conservatism in academia, even where normative values may point in a more cosmopolitan direction.

25.4 A Decolonial Critique of Human Capital

Criticisms of the Eurocentrism of academia are decades old. Yet, it is one thing to launch a scathing critique of Western academia using tools already honored within Western academia, sticking to safe established harbors while arguing the importance of treading new ground. It is another thing to simply exit the centripetal pull and tread on new ground oneself, to have one's own writings substantively shaped, transformed, or grounded by ideas from outside the safety of the already-sanctified status quo, which is enmeshed with centuries of Eurocentric myopia. As it happens, academic production, however good-intentioned the actors, will follow the academic marketplace. Even if the use-value of local knowledges of the periphery is honored, the logic of exchange value rules academic production. Until there is a larger "payoff"—in terms of career advancement—for actually stepping substantively outside of the already-established horizons of academic knowledge, instances of such actual transgressions will remain of the margins of academe. In this way the obsessive striving for self-valorization through amassing academic human capital dovetails with the coloniality of academic power/knowledge. And this is why, calls for the incorporation of "southern theory" so chronically fall short of actualization in the academic core. Good intentions and calling out ethnogeographical inequalities and exclusions is a meaningful step, but the neoliberal university is systemically unconcerned with good intentions and with doing anything beyond the minimum required to maintain a profitable public image in responding to inequalities and exclusions.

In Latin America, the notions of peripheral science, academic dependency, scientific imperialism, and coloniality of knowledge have been playing a major role in the decolonial debate (Alatas, 2003; Lander, 2000). The economic integration of global capital reproduces matrixes of power, embedded in knowledge and cultural reproduction of society, grounded in the territorial hierarchies of colonialism (Quijano, 2005). The competitive context of capitalism, which is embedded in the notion of human capital, reiterates asymmetrical conditions that are naturalized under the ideology of the need for individual merit in obtaining the optimal economic performance. In other words, the reproduction of the competitive rationality of market ignores how national societies are asymmetrically integrated into the global structure of capital, depending on the historical effects of coloniality, socioeconomic dependence, etc. If Marxism is important to analyze human capital through the lenses of the critique of political economy, it is also important to consider how the mantras of global market gain specific contours in peripheral societies (like Latin American countries) in light of the effects of the long history of exploitation and coloniality.

Some versions of Latin American decolonial theory are skeptical about Marxism (Ballestrin, 2013). Their criticisms of it are part of a broad effort at decentering the European claims for universality (Grosfoguel, 2009), since Marxism is seen as a continuation of the Western/Enlightened ideal of emancipation (Smith, 2022, pp. 56–57). Another way to conceive of this tense relationship between Marxism and decolonial theory is the seeking for the colonial difference of Latin America, which is to say, a kind of historical mark (colonialism) whose effects were not enough analyzed by Marx. But the theoretical relationship between decolonial critique and Marxism remains ambivalent (Ciccariello-Maher, 2017), since many inspirations for decolonial thinkers (like Carlos Mariátegui or Alvaro Garcia Linera) are grounded in Marxist traditions.

These issues are highlighted in the radical difference pointed to by Mignolo (2003) regarding the construction of a critical epistemology from the borders. This is useful for detaching analytical schemes from the dominance of mechanical explanations grounded in European models, but stumbles when up against a broader consideration on the importance of Marxian categories for the critique of capitalism. Marxism is not the sole critical project of modernity (decolonial thinkers and Boaventura Sousa Santos are right about this), but the broadening of critique cannot imply abandoning Marxism as if it were marked *in nuce* by the domination of European thought (Grüner, 2002). In light of the Marxist critique of human capital, decolonial perspectives can help illuminate not only how knowledge operates within socioeconomic cleavages, but also the effects of coloniality. This affects how schooling embeds territorial hierarchies and the dominance of epistemologies grounded in the asymmetrical integration of regions into the modern world-system. Instead of reifying Marxism and decolonial theory as two isolated poles, we propose a dialogue between these two traditions, because the critique of political economy of human capital cannot be detached from the contexts (especially in Latin America, marked by coloniality) where human capital has been implemented.

Since the late 1980s, market reforms in Latin America have been imposed by national governments (be it young democracies, like Argentina and Brazil, or the military dictatorship in Chile). This new integration of a peripheral area into the global economy, which succeeded the colonial expansion of modernity (sixteenth and eighteenth centuries) and the discourse of civilization (nineteenth and early twentieth centuries) (Narita, 2020), has been marked by a new division of labor based on the racial hierarchies and social inequalities that expanded the colonial forms of domination (Grosfoguel, 2009). The discourse of market efficiency not only reinforces the economic exploitation, but also subjects local knowledge and livelihood to a subaltern position in global capital.

Mignolo (2002, p. 67) is correct when he affirms that epistemology has historical roots, and the effort at decentering it from a linear narrative (that extends from ancient Greek to contemporary North Atlantic knowledge) is useful. In this sense, since the production of knowledge is rooted in places, the geopolitics of knowledge implies that global capital plays an important role in the definition of valuable knowledge, human capital investment (according to the needs of market structures), and the production of silences regarding national traditions in peripheral countries. The introduction of colonial difference is also important in that it reveals how knowledge can be subalternized by coloniality through the asymmetrical integration of peripheral countries into the modern world-system (Mignolo, 2002, p. 74), be it via the diaspora of brains, the precarious investment in public school systems, global oligopolies of education that capture national school systems or precarious research conditions (Ciocca & Delgado, 2017).

If Marx offers a materialist background against the decontextualized individual of human capital theories, the decolonial approach can offer a broader view of the global asymmetries of education. Human capital embeds the market into citizenship, equating the useful citizen with the economic optimum grounded in private performance, obfuscating how educational outputs are affected by colonial difference and the geopolitics of knowledge. In a competitive landscape, it takes for granted that the socialization of knowledge does not take place in a neutral arena where individuals compete in the same conditions. Individuals are crisscrossed by multiple asymmetries from class cleavages to the integration of national systems into global capitalism.

Against the privatist viewpoint reinforced by human capital, which has fed the weakness of the public, we argue that social asymmetries and coloniality can only be reversed with a strong public infrastructure that defines education as a common good. In this sense, public policy cannot be confined to the reproduction of state domination. Instead, it must be committed with an agenda for social development paving the way for autonomy and the recognition of social needs.

25.5 Public Policy and Social Development

Social development comprises a set of policies committed to improving social welfare, with public intervention regarding the basic needs of the population, such as minimum income, public health, education, etc. (Midgley, 2013). In this sense, public policy may serve projects of social justice in correcting the structural asymmetries of market-driven modernization, especially in peripheral countries (Hardiman & Midgley, 1982). In the early 2000s, in light of adverse social effects from two decades of neoliberal policies (Indart, 2019; Puiggrós, 1999; Cornia et al., 1987; Ghai, 1991), the debate moved towards the problem of providing capabilities and empowering communities for redistributive justice (Sen, 1999), emphasizing the role of public policy to counter social asymmetries. In this context, conditional cash transfer programs have been important innovations in Latin American social policy since the late 1990s, applying multidimensional approaches to implement inter-sectorial actions in education, nutrition, health and, employment (Cecchini & Atuesta, 2017) to cover populations historically excluded from social protection services. The Mexican "Progresa" (a public program devoted to education, health and food, initially conceived for rural areas, in 1997) (Cohen et al., 2006), the Colombian "Família en Acción" since 2002 (Attanasio et al., 2008), and the Brazilian "Bolsa Família" (Rego & Pinzani, 2014) are relevant examples of public policy designed for vulnerable groups, promoting income and education as platforms for social development.

Redistribution might be important in peripheral contexts, where policies deal with chronic levels of poverty and precarious social welfare. However, as Marx stated, any redistributive attempt is not enough to overcome the structural distress of capitalist society if policy cannot restructure the way capital is organized. Human capital is one of the main symptoms of the subsumption of education under capital and the restructuration of social relations cannot take for granted how education reproduces capital. From a decolonial perspective, this effort might be combined with the restructuration of social policy committed to the global hierarchies of the production of knowledge and the racial and social vulnerabilities of populations affected by coloniality. The critique of human capital can push forward the prospects for the emancipation of society from the subjective structures (materialized in education processes) that pressures individuals to lose autonomy in favor of the heteronomous market structures.

The importance of public policy beyond human capital is also relevant, above all, due to the chronic inequalities in Latin America. The privatist view of education embedded in human capital theory may also reinforce a perception that success or failure are primarily connected to individual achievements (Scalon & de Oliveira, 2020), instead of being part of a broader public responsibility regarding the wellbeing and autonomy of the population. Thus, besides an agenda that conceives education as a primary good for citizenship and human capabilities (CEPAL, 2022), the colonial matrixes of inequality based on race, with Afro descendants and indigenous populations (CEPAL, 2021a), implies political challenges with inclusion and social cohesion. Deprivation and the precarious access to cultural assets, like education, can be analyzed as an alienation of the individual from social ties, blocking subjects from developing their human capabilities and demanding social justice. It damages sociality and conforms the human with its needs (*Bedürfnisse*) in a false horizon of reconciliation confined to the pure reproduction of the needy life of animals (Marx, 1968, pp. 540–544), which becomes estranged from the cultural reproduction of society and the development of humanity.

The need for public policy and state action to correct the distortions of the market may also favor social cohesion and redistributive policy. Fraser's (1995) theory of redistribution and recognition is particularly relevant for this topic. The struggle for recognition has marked postsocialist conflicts with the emphasis on citizenship and inclusive, progressive agendas with a myriad of social agencies (LGBTQ movements, black movements, etc.). Cultural domination and identity became important factors for the perception of social justice, but the recognition of differences *always* takes place amidst socioeconomic inequalities. Fraser's articulation of recognition and redistribution as major strategies for public policy leads us to a critical framework for policy that emphasizes how social development may comprise educational assets not only for empowering local communities or improve market relations with a human face, but rather conceiving education as a matter for social justice.

On the one hand, the school system has been challenged with the problem of the mass inclusion of people historically excluded or silenced. In this case, socioeconomic inequalities overlap with identity issues, mixing asymmetries of power that lead public policy towards a multidimensional approach to counter deprivation. The defense of public schools to promote equity (Puiggrós, 1999) and the valorization of education as a common—a political principle that reinforces social management and conceives basic goods beyond private appropriation and state monopoly— imply the use of a social infrastructure (public budget, public facilities for schools, etc.) to integrate working classes and poor groups into the educational system.

According to research led by the Economic Commission for Latin America and the Caribbean in Argentina, Ecuador, Mexico, Honduras, Chile, Costa Rica, Venezuela and Uruguay, the crisis of the COVID-19 pandemics affected brutally the school trajectory of the poor youth, estimating that 3.1 million students can never go back to school (Seusan & Maradiegue, 2020; CEPAL, 2021b). In this case, more than changing learning environments and working to flexibilize school sites with hybrid formats, it is important to place redistribution at the center of the educational asymmetries. Another way of integration into school system can be based on the principle of recognition and the need for representation of racial and gender cleavages in curricula and school practices (Leonardo, 2014).

On the other hand, especially in Latin American, social movements and popular-oriented state policy may serve as a pressure for social justice and challenge the imbalances of social asymmetries (Narita & Kato, 2020). Beyond human capital and individual training for market skills, popular projects for education may reinforce popular agency and construct a sense of autonomy based on the recognition of the protagonism of local collectives. This topic is particularly relevant for the projects of popular education that combine social and epistemic forms of justice. In terms of social justice, we are referring to critical pedagogical commitment with vulnerable communities, fed by popular pedagogy. In terms of epistemic justice, we are referring to epistemological recognition of local knowledge and the critique of the colonial stigmas regarding intercultural education and knowledge, since local knowledges are frequently not treated as worthy of being included into school curricula (Jara Holliday & Narita, 2022; Mejía et al., 2017). The lessons from the radical left in power in Venezuela are also relevant in this context: the inclusion of poor students of the *barrios* into the public higher education system (Narita et al., 2022; Tarragoni, 2013) has promoted socialist policy by paving opportunities for the youth via redistributive policy, but the outcomes are prone to crises and remain ambiguous, because those attempts took place without a structural transformation of market relations.

If state apparatuses are crucial to reconstruct the notion of the public, it is also important to critically consider the role of the state for social development.

It is not enough to redistribute. Marxist analyses reinforce that the social control of common goods (in our case, education) needs restructuring. In this sense, we argue that a first step may be the implementation of policies that provide autonomy and a sense of social belonging for individuals. Especially in peripheral societies from Latin America, where the effects of coloniality are still strong (like decolonial theorists emphasize), this sense of recognition can empower subaltern groups. Public policy in education is not an end in itself, but rather a political technology that can help reconstruct the notion of the collective, common good. In this case, the combination of recognition and redistributive policy constitutes an important platform to design educational approaches and to counteract the distortions of market economies, moving beyond the prevalence of human capital and asymmetries of power.

Acknowledgments We would like to thank Rany C. Oliveira for the continual support and the editors for the critical engagement with this chapter.

Disclosure Statement None of the co-authors has any financial interest or benefit that has arisen from the direct applications of this research.

References

Alatas, S. (2003). Academic Dependency and the Global Division of Labour in the Social Sciences. *Current Sociology, 51*(6), 599–613.
Álvarez Aragon, V., Suazo Miranda, B., & Sverdlick, I. (2010). *El derecho a la educación vulnerado: la privatización de la educacón en Centroamérica*. United Nations Economic Commission for Latin America and the Caribbean.
Amsden, A. (2003). *The Rise of the Rest: Challenges to the West from Late-Industrializing Economies*. Oxford University Press.
Arretche, M. (1995). Emergência e desenvolvimento do welfare state: teorias explicativas. *Boletim Informativo e Bibliográfico de Ciências Sociais, 39*(2), 111–139.
Attanasio, Orazio; Fitzsimons, Emla; Gomez, Ana; Gutierrez, Martha; Meghir, Costas & Mesnard, Alice. (2008). *Child Education and Work Choices in the Presence of a Conditional Cash Transfer Programme in Rural Colombia*. IFS Working Paper (WP06/01). Institute for Fiscal Studies.
Bakker, B., Ghazanchyan, M., Ho, A., & Nanda, V. (2020, August 13). Lack of Human Capital Is Holding Back Latin America's Growth. *International Monetary Fund Blog*.
Balarin, M. (2016). La privatización por defecto y el surgimiento de las escuelas privadas de bajo costo en el Perú. *Revista de la Asociación de Sociología de la Educación, 9*(2), 181–196.
Ballestrin, L. (2013). América Latina e o giro decolonial. *Revista Brasileira de Ciência Política, 11*(2), 89–117.
Becker, G. S. (1981). *A Treatise on the Family*. Harvard University Press.
Becker, G. S. (1993). *Human Capital: A Theoretical and Empirical Analysis with Special Reference to Education*. University of Chicago Press.

Beigel, F. (2014). Publishing from the Periphery: Structural Heterogeneity and Segmented Circuits. The Evaluation of Scientific Publications for Tenure in Argentina's CONICET. *Current Sociology, 62*(5), 743–765.
Betancur, N. (2008). *Las reformas educativas de los años noventa en Argentina, Chile y Uruguay*. Banda Oriental.
Briggs, A. (1962). The Welfare State in Historical Perspective. *European Journal of Sociology, 2*(2), 221–258.
Castañeda, J. (1993). *Utopia Unarmed*. Vintage.
Cecchini, S., & Atuesta, B. (2017). *Conditional Cash Transfer Programmes in Latin America and the Caribbean*. Social Policy Series. United Nations.
CEPAL (Economic Commission for Latin American and the Caribbean). (2021a). *Afrodescendants and the Matrix of Social Inequality in Latin America*. United Nations.
CEPAL (Economic Commission for Latin American and the Caribbean). (2021b). *Los retos y oportunidades de la educación secundaria en América Latina y el Caribe durante y después de la pandemia*. United Nations.
CEPAL (Economic Commission for Latin American and the Caribbean). (2022). *Social Panorama of Latin America*. United Nations.
Charminade, C., Lundvall, B.-Å., & Haneef, S. (2018). *Advanced Introduction to National Innovation Systems*. Elgar Publishing.
Chattopadhyay, S. (2012). *Education and Economics: Disciplinary Evolution and Policy Discourse*. Oxford University Press.
Ciccariello-Maher, G. (2017). *Decolonizing Dialectics*. Duke University Press.
Ciocca, D., & Delgado, G. (2017). The Reality of Scientific Research in Latin America. *Cell Stress Chaperones, 22*(6), 847–852.
Clarke, T., & Pitelis, C. (1993). *The Political Economy of Privatization*. Routledge.
Cohen, E., Franco, R., & Villatoro, P. (2006). México: el Programa de Desarrollo Humano Oportunidades. In E. Cohen & R. Franco (Eds.), *Transferencias con corresponsabilidad: una mirada latinoamericana*. Latin American Faculty of Social Sciences.
Cornia, G., Jolly, R., & Stewart, F. (1987). *Adjustment with a Human Face*. Clarendon Press.
Esping-Andersen, G. (1990). *The Three Worlds of Welfare Capitalism*. Princeton University Press.
Feldfeber, M., Puiggrós, A., Robertson, S., & Duhalde, M. (2018). *La privatización educativa en Argentina*. CTERA.
Fraser, N. (1995). From Redistribution to Recognition. *New Left Review, 212*(1), 68–93.
Garcia, T. (2018). A gestão escolar no contexto da privatização na educação básica. *Revista de Política e Gestão Educacional, 22*(2), 30–41.
Ghai, D. (Ed.). (1991). *The IMF and the South: the Social Impact of Crisis and Adjustment*. Zed Books.
González López, J., & Parra Moreno, D. (2016). Privatización de la provisión educativa en Chile. *Educação e Sociedade, 37*(134), 102–126.
Grosfoguel, R. (2009). Para descolonizar os estudos de economia política e os estudos pós-coloniais. *Periferia, 1*(2), 41–91.
Grüner, E. (2002). *El fin de las pequeñas historias: de los estudios culturales al retorno (imposible) de lo trágico*. Paidos.
Gustavo Ortiz, I. L. (2021). Financiación de la educación en Colombia y lógicas de privatización en ciclo obligatorio. *Fineduca, 11*(2), 98–126.

Habermas, J. (1996). *Die Einbeziehung des Anderen: Studien zur politischen Theorie*. Suhrkamp.
Hall, R. (2022). Alienation and Education. In A. Maisuria (Ed.), *Encyclopaedia of Marxism and Education*. Brill.
Hardiman, M., & Midgley, J. (1982). *The Social Dimensions of Development*. John Wiley.
Heckman, J. (2014, May 10). Private Notes on Gary Becker. *Forschungsinstitut zur Zukunft der Arbeit*. Discussion Paper No. 8200.
Heydorn, H.-J. (1972). *Zu einer Neufassung des Bildungsbegriffs*. Suhrkamp.
Ierulli, K., Glaeser, E., & Tommasi, M. (1995). Introduction. In K. Ierulli & M. Tommasi (Eds.), *The New Economics of Human Behavior*. Cambridge University Press.
Indart, G. (2019). *Economic Reforms, Growth and Inequality in Latin America*. Routledge.
Jara Holliday, O., & Narita, F. Z. (2022). Extensión crítica y educación popular: aportes latinoamericanos desde la sistematización de experiencias. *Cadernos CIMEAC*, *12*(1), 6–15.
Kummer, V. (2019). Menos igualdad: la privatización de la educación. *Políticas Educativas*, *13*(1), 59–72.
Lander, E. (2000). *La colonialidad del saber: eurocentrismo y ciencias sociales*. CLACSO.
Leonardo, Z. (2014). Contracting Race: Writing, Racism, and Education. *Critical Studies in Education*, *56*(1), 86–98.
Lin, N. (2001). *Social Capital*. Cambridge University Press.
Lukács, G. (1977). *Geschichte und Klassenbewusstsein*. Luchterhand.
Marazzi, C. (2002). *Capitale e linguaggio: dalla new economy all'economia di guerra*. DeriveApprodi.
Marx, K. (1968). *Ökonomisch-phiosophische Manuskripte aus dem Jahre 1844*. MEW 40. Dietz.
Marx, K. (1983). *Grundrisse*. MEW 42. Dietz.
Marx, K. (1987). *Kritik des Gothaer Programms*. MEW 19. Dietz.
Marx, K. (1990). *Ökonomisches Manuskript 1861–1863 – Teil I*. MEW 43. Dietz.
Mejía, M. R., Narita, F. Z., & Kato, D. S. (2017). La globalización capitalista y el lugar epistémico de la educación popular en América Latina. *Cadernos CIMEAC*, *7*(2), 8–35.
Midgley, J. (2013). *Social Development: Theory and Practice*. Sage.
Mignolo, W. (2002). The Geopolitics of Knowledge and the Colonial Difference. *The South Atlantic Quarterly*, *101*(1), 57–96.
Mignolo, W. (2003). *Historias locales/disenos globales: colonialidad, conocimientos subalternos y pensamiento fronterizo*. Akal.
Morelock, J., & Narita, F. Z. (2021). *The Society of the Selfie: Social Media and the Crisis of Liberal Democracy*. University of Westminster Press.
Moschetti, M., Fontdevilla, C., & Verger, A. (2019). Políticas, procesos y trayectorias de privatización educativa en Latinoamérica. *Educação e Pesquisa*, *45*(2), e187870.
Narita, F. Z. (2020). *A experiência da aceleração: paisagem, infraestrutura e o imaginário da modernidade*. Postdoctoral Research Report (Federal University of São Carlos).
Narita, F. Z., Avlona, N.-R., & Ivancheva, M. (2022). Radical Higher Education Alternatives: Lessons from Socialist Pasts and Neoliberal Presents. *Journal of Contemporary Central and Eastern Europe*, *30*(1), 20–31.
Narita, F. Z., & Kato, D. S. (2020). Construção democrática e educação popular. *Cadernos CIMEAC*, *10*(3), 29–61.

O'Neil, P. M. (2009). Privatization. In R. Kitchin & N. Thrift (Eds.), *International Encyclopedia of Human Geography*. Elsevier.

Ortiz, I., Lozada, I., Gómez, B., & Urbano, M. (2021). *Lógicas de privatización y desigualdad en la educación colombiana*. Campaña Latinoamericana por el Derecho a la Educación.

Pemberton, A. (1983). Marxism and Social Policy: A Critique of the Contradictions of Welfare. *Journal of Social Policy, 12*(3), 289–307.

Puiggrós, A. (1999). *Neoliberalism and Education in the Americas*. Routledge.

Puiggrós, A., & Narita, F. Z. (2020). Da crise orgânica à educação popular. *Cadernos CIMEAC, 10*(1), 8–13.

Quijano, A. (2005). *Colonialidade do poder, eurocentrismo e América Latina*. Clacso.

Rego, W. L., & Pinzani, A. (2014). *Vozes do Bolsa Família*. UNESP Press.

Rosanvallon, P. (1981). *La crise de l'état providence*. Seuil.

Scalon, C., & de Oliveira, P. P. (2020). Inequality and Social Justice in Latin America. In X. Bada & L. Rivera-Sánchez (Eds.), *The Oxford Handbook of the Sociology of Latin America*. Oxford University Press.

Schultz, T. (1961). Investment in Human Capital. *The American Economic Review, 51*(1), 1–17.

Sen, A. (1999). *Development as Freedom*. Anchor.

Seusan, L., & Maradiegue, R. (2020). *Educación en pausa*. UNICEF.

Smith, M. N. (2022). The Limits of Postcolonial Critique of Marxism. In N.-G. Sabelo & M. Ndlovu (Eds.), *Marxism and Decolonization in the 21st Century*. Routledge.

Tarragoni, F. (2013). L'éducation populaire comme art du possible. *Tracés, 25*(2), 147–166.

Toro, J. B. (2005). *A construção do público: cidadania, democracia e participação*. Senac.

Verger, A., Moschetti, M., & Fontdevila, C. (2017). *La privatización educativa en América Latina*. Education International.

Vilela, R. (2019, February 2). Guedes: reforma da previdência e abertura de mercado são prioridades. *Agência Brasil*.

CHAPTER 26

Marxism, (Higher) Education, and the Commons

Krystian Szadkowski

26.1 Introduction

The common (and the commons) lay at the center of Karl Marx's interests from the beginning of his work (Basso, 2012, 2015). It is not surprising that together with the widely declared "return of the commons" (Vercellone, 2015; Vercellone & Giuliani, 2018), education researchers look into his works for insights and inspiration (De Lissovoy, 2011; Means, 2013, 2014; Lewis, 2012; Slater, 2014; Backer, 2017; Kamola & Meyerhoff, 2009; Roggero, 2010; Neary & Winn, 2012; Haiven, 2014, 2017; Ford, 2015, 2017; Moroz & Szwabowski, 2017; Pusey, 2017; Means et al., 2017; Szadkowski, 2019; Erdem, 2020; Szadkowski & Krzeski, 2022). Yet, the very connection of Marx and the common may seem counterintuitive for representatives of various Marxist currents. Some will instead connect the commons with Elinor Ostrom (1990); Hess & Ostrom, 2007), a Nobel Prize laureate and a mainstream economist who aimed at the humanization of capitalism rather than its revolutionary abolition. For others, especially Anglophone readers, commons sound familiar and refer simply to a historical form of governance to which references remained in their daily lives. Still others will associate the commons with free access to knowledge, i.e., the open access movement that aims at its democratization (Benkler, 2006; Peters, 2009). Once again, in this case, our intuition will suggest a stable element of the capitalist status quo rather than a projection

K. Szadkowski (✉)
Adam Mickiewicz University, Poznań, Poland
e-mail: krysszad@amu.edu.pl

of its revolutionary gravediggers. Each formulation of the aspects of the common is correct—however, neither articulates Marx's main interest.

Above all, because the author of *Das Kapital* was most interested in the abolition of capitalism rather than its reform, his interest lay in the radicalization of social relations rather than their co-optation. In other words, Marx was interested in the anti-capitalist character of the commons, their strength to sustain the alternative emerging in front of us and which can still be derived from the more archaic forms that preceded capitalism. Regardless of the contemporary use of the term, Marx had his specific idea of "the commons," which needs to be clarified and reconstructed before moving on to the main task facing this chapter. That is, to show how a Marxist perspective on the common can be used not only to understand and interpret the reality of capitalistically-structured education (and above all, higher education), but how we can change it.

In this chapter, I will limit myself to the sphere of higher education. This move assumes a bias, as still many countries of the Global South struggle with providing a mass access to higher education. Nevertheless, while even in the countries that reached universal access to higher education, it is a much smaller and small-scale system than general education, within its narrow confines, the general logic behind the Marxist commons project in education (including primary education) can be made clear enough. And the primary task of this chapter is to provide its reader with the conceptual and analytical tools for further research.

However, before we depart several classical Marxist works on the common and the commons in education need to be mentioned (Backer, 2017; De Lissovoy, 2011; Ford, 2015, 2017; Lewis, 2012; Means, 2013, 2014; Means et al., 2017; Slater, 2014), as they form a coherent stream of reflection. Most of the authors mentioned rely on the autonomist Marxist tradition, seeing the emergence of the importance of the common as connected with the development of cognitive capitalism and the growing importance of knowledge for capital accumulation and valorization. Moreover, while concrete empirical references to the sphere of the commons in education as a system are present, these works tend to focus on more abstract and ontological aspects of the common. In this, it is seen as: "a shared social condition" or "collectively shared production, experience, and activity" (De Lissovoy, 2011, p. 1121); "an infinite non-representational force" (Means, 2013, p. 50) of human potential in the sphere of language and general communicative capacities; or general "social ontology" (Means et al., 2017, p. 4).

While politically sharp and analytically insightful, these works rarely deal with the organizational and institutional aspects of the common. As this chapter aims to provide the reader with ideas for how we can address the common as an alternative mode of organization of our educational environment, I will stay with the references to higher education research only.

Conceptual Clarifications

Some clarifications are needed before we can further explore the realm of the commons in higher education. "The common" is a concept from the ontological order. The common always precedes the community; it forms the ontological ground on which the latter's expansion and prosperity can be understood. Thus, the common is the name of a fundamental, ontological aspect of reality, that of "relationness" of reality itself, a fundamental connection between all that exists, as all that exist exists in common. In this chapter, the common has been equated with "wealth" in the Marxian sense expressed in *Grundrisse*, as something positive and of fundamental nature for the expansion of any historical system of production.

The crucial role of the common in production relies on its dual status (Roggero, 2010). It is simultaneously a fundamental resource that makes any social formation productive, and also that which allows the transcendence of any limited social formation. The common offers the key to an understanding of any social system—in this case, the system of capital's domination of production in higher education—as finite and dependent. It offers a perspective that goes beyond capital, with its imposed limitations on social production. Moreover, the common is often considered an actual subject of emancipatory change—no matter whether it is addressed more as a political principle (Dardot & Laval, 2019) or as a productive characteristic of the living (Hardt & Negri, 2017).

In this context, "the commons" moves the discussion beyond abstractions and grounds it in concrete operations of communities. It allows for highlighting the actual manifestations of the common—the common in action. The commons are both historical and contemporary, preceding capitalism, inhabiting its margins but sometimes operating in the center of its interest, and sometimes transcending its rule. In the most general terms, "the commons imply a plurality of people (a community) sharing resources and governing them and their relations and (re)production processes through horizontal doing in common" (De Angelis, 2017, p. 10). With such a general definition one could expect to find commons, as practice and as a theory, in different areas of social life.

Therefore, we can identify at least three streams of interpretative traditions of the commons (Broumas, 2017). First, liberal theories of the commons, where they are approached as a way of governing resources in ways that are functional for both the state and the market, and which can compensate for their failures. Similarly, like in the current inspired predominantly by Ostrom's research (1990; Hess & Ostrom, 2007), liberal theorists of the commons identify a space in which they prosper alongside the regular operations of capitalism. Second, social democratic theories use references to the commons to propose a more humane vision of state-led, reformed capitalism, where they can offer a paradigm for the inclusion of social autonomy (Benkler, 2006; Peters, 2009). Finally, there are the revolutionary and Marxist theories, to which I refer in this chapter (e.g., Erdem, 2020; Neary & Winn, 2012; Roggero, 2011), that sees in the commons capital's actual gravediggers.

A final concept that needs to be clarified is "commoning," which accounts for social practice and the processual aspect of the common that makes the whole system expand and reproduce. As defined by Massimo de Angelis, commoning is "the form of social doing (social labor) occurring within the domain of the commons" (De Angelis, 2017, p. 121). Commoning is, therefore, a praxis that moves the common, and it forms a backbone of any actions aimed at transgressing the rule of capital.

Overview of the Chapter

This chapter tracks the Marxist reflection on the commons and highlights its potential for researching and changing higher education. This will involve a series of dialectical jumps. The chapter's next section focuses on positioning the Marxist perspective developed here. I will explain where we can trace Marx's references to the commons, as well as how I understand his perspective's political and theoretical consequences. The third section will refer to the various Marxist takes on the commons. The reader will be provided with a broader panorama of the problems researched within the Marxist approaches to the commons. In the fourth section, the focus will move to the diachronic and synchronic reading of the examples of existing higher education institutions and practices, which operate along the lines of the commons. Finally, I will discuss some potential lines of research on higher education through the commons and conclude the chapter.

26.2 WHAT MARX? WHAT MARXISM?

What kind of Marx are we talking about when we suggest that the common, rather than capital or value, is the main object of his interest? Marx's work can be read as a continuous effort to evidence the robust processes by which capital captures and molds a positive ontological force: life-living labor that transforms nature and gives substance to social relations. Capital is a pernicious form of mediation, a power that transposes the forces of labor into a detached representation of money or value. Thus, although Marx seeks to capture the movement of capital in its totality, his starting point is the transhistorical, but graspable concept of wealth, about which he writes in a well-known passage of *Grundrisse*:

> In fact, however, when the limited bourgeois form is stripped away, what is wealth other than the universality of human needs, capacities, pleasures, productive forces etc., created through universal exchange? The full development of human mastery over the forces of nature, those of so-called nature as well as of humanity's own nature? The absolute working out of his creative potentialities, with no presupposition other than the previous historic development, which makes this totality of development, i.e., the development of all human powers as such the

end in itself, not as measured on a predetermined yardstick? Where he does not produce himself in one specificity, but produces his totality? Strives not to remain something he has become, but is in the absolute movement of becoming? (Marx, 1973, p. 488)

Therefore, while capital is coagulation, solidity and death, the wealth (or the common) is the living, becoming, and moving flow. As John Holloway (2015) aptly pointed out, we can grasp the core of *Das Kapital* by looking at the category of wealth. For it is from wealth, not the commodity, that Marx starts in his first sentence of *Das Kapital*, laying the ontological platform for his project of the critique of political economy. He uses it frequently, consciously, and consistently in *Das Kapital* and his other economic works. This is because the transhistorical point of view, the point of view of wealth, represents for him the possibility of tracing history, that is, the history of the changing forms of wealth, in their transience.

However, the role of the common in Marx's work is not limited to the question of the ontological-political perspective that permeates his work. Already in his early article on the problem of theft of wood, Marx (1842) drew attention to the role of the commons in sustaining the autonomy of social reproduction, as well as the importance that its enclosures had for the newly-installed capitalist order (Linebaugh, 1976). In the *Economic and Philosophic Manuscripts of 1844*, on the other hand, he outlines the question of the common ontology of the human species being (Hardt, 2010)—which is the historically variable and dynamic result of the human activity of transforming themselves and the world around them.

This concept is developed further in the sixth *Thesis on Feuerbach*, taking the form of a concise but succinct definition of the essence of a human being as: an "ensemble of social relations," a dynamic and fluid nonessentialist essence (Balibar, 2017). Human, for Marx is a fundamentally communal being, a "social individual," suspended in a web of relations constantly woven in the course of his activity (Basso, 2012). From here, the work of the early Marx enables contemporary critiques of neoliberal individualism and its artificial creation—the atomized individual producer.

However, Marx was always interested not only in the conceptual basis of the common but also in how it reveals itself in the course of class struggles. From this grows his interest in the cooperative movement (Marx, 1864). Whatever their limitations, co-operatives, and associations—the various forms of cooperation outside the management of capital—are the practical and theoretical basis of a different political economy and have the historical task of bringing about the dissolution—the destruction—of the present capitalist system of production (Marx, 1864). Marx's observations about the positive aspects of the common, manifested in the growing cooperative movement, find their reverse in his analysis of the process of primitive accumulation on the pages of *Das Kapital*. Marx is unequivocal; transforming people into wage laborers requires the destruction of the basis for their autonomous social reproduction. This process is accomplished in the course of the expropriation of the commons, which underpins the constantly reproducing, "historical origins" of capital.

Liberation from the yoke of capital thus depends on the recovery of the power of the common. This kind of conclusion brought Marx late in his life to an interest in forms of primitive communism (Anderson, 2016; Basso, 2015; Musto, 2020). His ethnographic studies allowed him to abandon a linear understanding of capitalist development—leading "with iron necessity" through successive phases of violence and destruction of the commons—and the resulting concept of rupture. He gave emphatic expression to this in his draft letters to Vera Zasulich and in the preface to the Russian edition of *the Communist Manifesto*, written jointly with Engels. The historically-manifested elements of the common, such as rural communal landownership (*obshchina*) in Russia, can provide the beginnings of an alternative to capitalism and make it possible to skip "the stage" of destructive capitalist dispossession. Thus, the common pervades the whole of Marx's work and should also be a point of reference in thinking about alternatives in higher education.

Marxism, growing out of the above recognitions, is first and foremost a current that, when looking at contemporary capitalism, sees rather two disparate forces (capital and the common) joined by violence into a single totality (Hardt & Negri, 2009). It is a theory that sees the common preceding capital and becoming its nourishment, rather than the totality of capital splitting into two opposing camps, resulting from workers' class struggle. Thus, it is a Marxism that does not fetishize labor or workers, in their historically-defined, coagulated forms. Instead, it knows how to capture the common in its autonomy and to understand how it precedes capital and all forms of production based on it. Such an interpretation may sound like heresy for the followers of Moishe Postone or the proponents of the New Reading of Marx currently in vogue in Western Left circles. Nonetheless, it is not only possible to ground it in Marxist texts, but it is also politically, tactically, and organizationally useful. For instance, for the working classes of the global South and East, struggles based on the historical roots of the commons dared to establish viable alternatives to capitalism.

The Marxism from which the reflection that makes up this chapter grows is the tradition of György Lukács and Rosa Luxemburg, Antonio Negri and Michael Lebowitz, Harry Cleaver, Massimo De Angelis, and George Caffentzis and Silvia Federici. That is to say, all those who see Marxism as a constant source feeding the class struggles of the diverse subjects seeking liberation from the yoke of the blind coercion of capital. This Marxism can be called autonomist or operaist, but it is a Marxism that takes up the philosophical and historical components contained in Marx's work at face value. It does not shy away from engaging with ontological conceptions, emphasizing the question of antagonism, and rather than instructing struggling subjects, it seeks to learn from them, and as such serves as a weapon in their struggle against capital.

26.3 Marxism and the Common(s)

If the common lies at the heart of the Marxian project, then we find interest in it in the work of numerous Marxists. To organize the long discussions around the common within different streams of Marxism, we can distinguish five critical contexts for consideration.

Firstly, the commons are discussed in relation to the forms of socio-economic organization historically preceding the capitalist mode of production. In this context, authors highlight the centrality of the historical enclosures processes to establishing conditions that promote the spread of wage labor. In other words, every time free commoners were to transform themselves into laborer working under the baton of the capitalist, they had to be separated from the possibility of effective reproduction based on shared resources. Every time capital enters a new area and seeks to transform and subordinate this movement of mutuality, it is reproduced. As a result, the communal management of resources is destroyed, the commoners organizing this process are displaced, and their labor is spun into a system of capitalist production. For Rosa Luxemburg (2003), the commons represent the historical frontier of the development of capitalism, while the Midnight Notes collective (1990) pointed to their centrality in the successive stages of the development and transformation of capitalism. David Harvey (2003), rounding off this phenomenon in the context of the spatial expansion of capital, speaks of repeated accumulation by expropriation. In this context, Sandro Mezzadra (2011) rightly draws attention to the reactivity of capital, in its following and colonization of the constantly reproducing commons.

Secondly, some works highlight the ontological dimension of the common. Marx uses the common as the departure point for his critique, both in the introduction of the *Grundrisse* in 1857, and on the opening pages of *Das Kapital* in 1867. Here, he refers to commonality or wealth of relations as something that precedes the naturalized capitalist forms, like commodity or individual. Equally important are such ontological groundings for the critiques of the naturalized forms of social life under neoliberalism or cognitive capitalism. They allow for imagining forms of social organization beyond the capitalist subsumption process, allowing for more precise analytical contouring of domination itself. Thus, there are references to Marx's ontological concepts like wealth (Holloway, 2015; Szadkowski & Krzeski, 2019) or general intellect (Hall & Winn, 2017; Virno, 2004), in forming a point of departure for broader Marxist critiques of contemporaneity.

Thirdly, the commons may be seen as a resource that allows the reproduction of the working class, a class of autonomous producers, and one whose parallel existence with capital is crucial for its effective duration and expansion. Particularly in the context of new forms of production and accumulation, based more on knowledge, in its processing and creation, the availability of the commons constantly feeds the transformation of knowledge into a commodity. As a result, the possibility of selling it seems crucial. Massimo De Angelis (2013,

2017) suggested that faced with a general crisis of social stability, capital is turning to the commons. This happens either as a result of its contradictions or as a result of the resistance to its expansion, where the fundamental principles on which the stability of capitalist extended social reproduction operates are undermined. It is necessary to employ what he terms "the common fix," that is, a solution to the general problem of the crisis of social stability, based on the inclusion and instrumentalization of the commons. At the same time, this assumes their domestication and partial deactivation. In all the cases of co-optation, "commoning is turned into something for a purpose outside the commons themselves. The purpose is not to provide alternatives to capital, but to make a particular node of capital (…) more competitive" (De Angelis, 2013, p. 612).

Fourthly, Marxists refer to the commons to design the basis of an alternative to the capitalist system (Hudis, 2012). The commons constitute the logical matrix of relations in a world liberated from the power of capital. This picture does not seem utopian, since it assumes that the common both existed prior to capital, and capital paradoxically fosters its proliferation (although it feeds on it) (Roggero, 2010). It is also the common that can necessarily form the foundation of the horizontal and self-managing relations that will follow liberation from capital's rule.

Fifthly and finally, thinkers of a Marxist orientation also see the commons as a subjectivity (De Angelis, 2017; Hardt & Negri, 2017)—that is, an organizational formula for action and political-economic practice. The common, in this view, is an anti-capitalist subjectivity which, by extending itself and its activities and base, creates a permanent foundation for what is new and to come. Or in other words, the common forms the subjectivity from which growth and dominance of capital shrink, and a viable alternative is created (De Angelis, 2017).

26.4 Existing Examples of the Common-Led Practices in Higher Education

The commons surround us, especially in higher education, where they permeate almost every aspect of its daily functioning. Without them, neither learning nor research would be possible, and neither would many elements of the daily functioning of faculties and institutes, whole institutions or systems. One crucial task facing critical reflection on higher education is learning to recognize, support, and help them prosper. Usually, however, we notice commons when it is too late—when they are threatened by enclosures and destruction (Caffentzis & Federici, 2014; De Angelis, 2017). This is no different in the context of the university, where collective forms of governance begin to be appreciated when no trace of them is left. Notwithstanding, the commons offer a progressive agenda as well, and alternatives based on the commons are developing in different parts of the planet, both transforming spaces of universities and functioning outside of them.

We should look at the commons in higher education from at least two complementary perspectives: *diachronic*, looking at their development over time, in their disappearance and re-emergence in various areas of higher education; and *synchronic*, looking at the dynamics of the conflicts ongoing around higher education, and how they are manifested in educational organization forms and knowledge production based on the common.

Diachronic Perspective

The *diachronic* perspective allows us to bring to light the historical foundations of the commons, as well as how, in the course of successive struggles against the commodification of the public universities (taking place in parallel to their subsumption under capital), other elements of the commons were installed within them. The organizational form of academic institutions in Europe from their early beginnings resembled that of the commons (Gieysztor, 1992). Even today, when we share knowledge, gather for self-education in scholarly, grassroot organizations, or organize a conference together on a topic that is important to us, we are reproducing practices that are pervaded by the logic of the common. By coming together in university communities, we create the commons of knowledge, sharing and learning new practices through them.

Common Ontology of Higher Education

The commons are the starting point of existing practices performed by both students and academics. They constitute the everyday functioning of institutions at all their levels, their operational everydayness (Marginson, 2004; Roxå & Mårtensson, 2014), in the same sense in which Cook (2013, p. 59) wrote about already existing UK higher education institutions sharing many of their "preferences, assumptions and behaviors" with co-operatives. In this context, it is not even necessary to refer to radical and Marxist diagnoses. The somehow spontaneous form that the sharing of knowledge or education takes is the common, operating under a particular logic. For the reproduction or development of a particular resource, we interact within communities that themselves regulate the rules of conduct, as well as ways of access to those resources. David Harvie (2004) rightly pointed out that research, open-access learning materials, and also entire institutions can be treated as vast sets of the commons. It is this dimension that we often forget, and notice only once capital has already transformed practices in its own image for the purposes of self-valorization.

However, the everydayness of operating in relations resembling the commons in our university spaces are a historical legacy of academic practices shaped over centuries. We owe this legacy both to very ancient traditions (Gieysztor, 1992) and to new struggles being waged in higher education worldwide (Katsiaficas, 2018). One thing, then, is the form of student associations which, as in the UK, Belgium, or Poland, are responsible for organizing socially reproductive spaces at universities, running canteens or shops, or dormitories. Another is the formula, dating back to the Enlightenment, of scientific societies that animate research and scientific communication, publish journals and book series, or the libraries and scholarly publishing houses that are active in many universities and create knowledge commons (often with a global reach). Finally, there are elements of participatory governance in the public higher education sector, where in many countries (such as Denmark, Sweden, Poland, or the UK), the inclusion of student and doctoral student representatives emerged as result of specific student struggles for representation in these structures.

The Commons as a Legacy of Past Struggles
Although the logic of the common permeates all these forms, they have accumulated at different moments in the development of specific higher education systems, sometimes in situations of open confrontation, but sometimes through a less conflictual evolution. Not coincidentally, however, they all find themselves in actual, more or less open conflict with capital as it advances its domination over the sector. Student cooperatives are being pushed out of European campus spaces by private companies; open access projects run by libraries are under constant threat from shrinking public budgets; large oligopolies are successively buying up journals run by scientific societies; and, in successive reforms of public higher education sectors in Europe, managerial centralism is gradually displacing more participatory forms of governance. Being clear about how often these forms of academic activity are made objects of co-optation by capital or university managers (Kamola & Meyerhoff, 2009), we can also see in them the potential of the common, as it is being purged.

Finally, knowledge in its epistemic dimension is a constant element of the commons in which we live. The specific theories or lines of research that address the issues emerging from emancipatory protest movements also make up the global common, and this is created and reproduced by researchers worldwide. However, while social movements, from feminist, Black, LGBTQ+, and anti-colonial movements, through to grassroots and autonomist Marxists, feed research agendas and lead to establishing of entire fields of study in universities around the world, capital has mastered the cognitive pacification of these demands and ways of knowing. The "methodological university" of which Hall (2021) writes effectively grinds these currents in its mills of abstraction. Nonetheless, the impulses and radical perspectives, from which the knowledge that makes up Black studies or LGBTQ+ studies, Marxist studies or postcolonial critique, represent the potential contained within the common handed down to us by generations of radical scholars. We can use it to further struggles to liberate practices of knowledge production.

A diachronic perspective on the common in higher education, as it is subsumed under capital, allows us to see it in reality around us. It also allows us to understand its conflicting origins and to see the threats coming from the state and capital. The commons are neither given (they are won over) nor will they stay with us once and for all (enclosures constantly threaten them). The second, *synchronic* perspective highlights precisely this conflictual dynamic.

Synchronic Perspective

A *synchronic* perspective allows us to grasp the commons' parallel functioning within, against, and beyond the university subsumed under capital. It is not only fragments of our academic reality that are structured according to the logic of the common. Sometimes entire academic institutions adopt such logic and organize their activities according to it. A special case of the institutions of the common is co-operative universities, the most famous case being the Basque university run by the Mondragon co-operative (Winn, 2015; Wright et al., 2011). Primarily oriented towards vocational training, Mondragon not only integrates its employees into the university's ownership relationship by requiring a financial contribution upon employment, but pays a dividend based on the employee's share of ownership. This guarantees participation in a certain proportion of the institution's annual revenue and allows students to work in a network of co-operative enterprises, but it is also part of a broader movement to change economic relations in the region. Although the institution itself has been subjected to multifaceted critique over the years, this does not change the fact that it is one of the few, long-established co-operatives from the sphere of higher education (Winn, 2015).

Common Institutional Form
Discussing cooperative universities as "institutions *in potentia*," Joss Winn (2015) distinguished three pathways leading to the possible constitution of such institutions: conversion, dissolution, and creation. While conversion implies the transformation of entire institutes (e.g., public) into full-scale co-operatives and is a relatively rare phenomenon, dissolution involves the gradual decomposition of public institutions, strengthening the constituent, individual institutes, or departments through a cooperative form of governance. Finally, the third path consists of the creation of cooperative institutions from scratch and outside the existing system. Few projects follow the third path.

Nonetheless, the perspective of the commons is not so focused on the institutional form of the university itself, and this allows us to capture the more diverse forms in which autonomously-governing communities create and reproduce the knowledge and learning resources crucial to their functioning. Moreover, this perspective assumes that the commons already surround us, providing models for effective action. Part of our efforts should focus not so much on constituting them as on liberating them. Additionally, while all co-operatives (including co-operative universities) are based on the logic of the common, not all commons in higher education resemble co-operatives in their shape.

The difference between cooperative universities and common-pool, resource-based institutions can be seen in the case of the Ecuadorian Polytechnic run by the Salesians in Quito (Carrera & Solorzano, 2019). The transformation of the polytechnic into a common-pool, resource institution—created and reproduced by staff and students through a shared horizontal process—was a conscious decision and direction set by the university's leadership. The critical point, however, is that in no way can this kind of initiative be said to be anti-capitalist. Although distanced from the pathologies of competition and the market, and outside the direct influence of state authorities, the university does not take an antagonistic stance towards them. Existing examples, whether cooperative universities or entire institutions based on the commons, cannot withstand Marx's critique of the limitations of co-operatives (Marx, 1864).

Multiplicity of Common Struggles
The commons also develop in a more antagonistic dimension—against the capitalist university. They arise in a movement of protest against the restrictions imposed by the capital and the state on the development of living knowledge (Edu-factory Collective, 2009; Roggero, 2011; Dokuzović, 2016). On the one hand, the communities of protest themselves are using a form of the common to sustain the momentum of their actions. The last two decades in global higher education have been marked by a series of protests against the capitalist transformations of the higher education sector: the introduction or increase of tuition fees; the neoliberal restructuring of public universities; the spread of metrics or competitive logic within the system; and, issues of racial injustice or colonial legacies. In these protests, the question of the reproduction of the protest movement itself—the need to create institutions to sustain its persistence and development over time—becomes crucial.

In many cases, spontaneously created and established commons proved to be helpful. Whether it be the Croatian protest movement using the form of a democratic plenum to manage the protest (Bousquet & Drago, 2009), the Austrian occupations at the Fine Arts Academy (Dokuzović, 2016), the British series of university occupations during the tuition fee increase protests, the Californian wave of occupations, the South African #FeesMustFall protests (Cini, 2019), the long series of Chilean protests against public sector tuition fees (Fleet & Guzmán-Concha, 2017), or the Italian *Onda anomola* (Cini, 2016). Everywhere, the focus of the student and academic workers' movements was placed on the practices of the commons developed during the protests.

Also, the knowledge generated in their course, in terms of the postulates of the protesters, the causes of the protests and their effects, or the tactical reflections on the forms taken by the protests themselves, each contribute to the global, anti-capitalist common. This can and does benefit those fighting for higher education beyond the imperative of accumulation (Bousquet & Drago, 2009). On the other hand, as I mentioned above, ongoing protests have a feedback effect on the system, as in the case of the recent events in Chile that led to the transformations of the system in which tuition fees were abandoned (Fleet & Guzmán-Concha, 2017). All these actions make the public sector more common-based (Vercellone, 2015).

Higher Education Commons Beyond the University Walls

Another aspect of the protest commons is that protesting communities shift into institutions that function outside the official system. Examples vary in this area. On the one hand, in Western countries, autonomous learning institutions have developed as a result of the experience of protests against tuition fees, such as the Lincoln Social Science Centre (Neary & Winn, 2012) or the Really Open University (Pusey, 2017). Both institutions focused on the energies of specific protesting communities and transformed them into a longer-standing processes of self-education.

On the other hand, we can find transnational hubs dedicated to amplifying and multiplying the struggles in the university sector. An example of the institution of the common born out of protest is the transnational group Edu-factory, which, as Lina Dokuzović (2016, p. 52) writes, "began in 2006 as a transnational mailing list, discussion platform, and online archive, and was centered around university transformations, knowledge production, and the publication analysis and statements of protests, conflicts, and actions in institutions of knowledge production." The Edu-factory and the activists and researchers gathered around it assisted in mobilizing and organizing synergies between national protesters seeking to make struggles common and beyond—most notably on both sides of the Mediterranean. As a result, not only in Europe during the Occupy or Indignados periods, but also during the Arab Spring, this linked grassroots student organizations opposing the imposition of precarity.

Born out of this activity, the Knowledge Liberation Front, an ephemeral organization dating back to a transnational meeting of student movements in Paris in February 2011, continued this activity. It organized further meetings where activists from all over the world could pool their knowledge and experience as well as plan joint actions. Both Edu-factory and KLF acted as institutions of the common (Roggero, 2011) responsible for extending and strengthening, and communicating the struggles carried out in the global space of the capitalist university.

In countries with a tradition of strong authoritarian rule (Dönmez & Duman, 2021), autonomous, common-led learning organizations represent an opportunity to withdraw from violent relations imposed by the state. An important case in this context is the creation of the Solidarity Academy network in Turkey (Erdem, 2020; Erdem & Akın, 2019) in response to the mass dismissal (more than 5000 by 2017) of academics from higher education institutions as a result of the purges carried out after the failed coup of July 2016, and the state of emergency declared in its aftermath. The dismissed academics began to organize independent, grassroots, and nonhierarchical forms of self-governance with their academic activities (both education and knowledge creation) outside the system. Erdem and Akın (2019) call these "communities of commoning," autonomous institutions that are based on values of resistance, critical inquiry, democracy and social inclusion, and solidarity. In the course of their activities, the Academies of Solidarity, established in Koceli, Ankara,

Istanbul, and elsewhere, were primarily concerned with organizing academic life. They enabled students or PhD students to interact with dismissed academics in participatory learning, giving affective support to dismissed and often broken scholars, and working together to further political activism.

I attended a conference organized in Koceli in 2018, in which academics wanted to explore both the historical tradition of autonomous education in Turkey, closely linked to the labor movement and its institutions. They also wished to learn from examples of transnational struggles (such as the KLF and Edu-factory, in which I was also active in the past). However, by this time the network was already on the downward trend in its activism. This reminds us that the commons organized against capital and the state with its public university are fragile and unsustainable. The representatives of the collective stressed that, although in their first year of activity, they had managed to support the dismissed academics with funds collected from those who remained in the system, the following years of activity were marked by a struggle for existence and survival. In addition, the easily recognizable "secret agents" appearing at the sessions made it clear how difficult and dangerous the struggle of the commons was, against the authoritarian state.

Whilst some co-operatives, as well as institutions of the common growing out of protests, took root in institutional forms, some projects do not fit into this framework. Autonomous knowledge creation projects often have no ambition to submit to the regime of university certification and validation—they work to transcend rigid disciplinary boundaries and responding to the needs of social actors. On the one hand, we can point to SHURE University in Japan, an institution where students shape their own educational program (Li, 2017). In a system that is simultaneously extremely competitive, characterized by high tuition fees and a general aversion to the humanities and social sciences, SHURE gives students a free space in which they can develop their passions and manage the design of their study programs themselves. Finally, it is worth mentioning the Indian Lokavidya movement, the folk knowledge movement, a movement for the radical integration of everyday knowledge into the structures of emancipatory knowledge production (Dokuzović, 2016).

These common-led practices and organizations within, against and beyond higher education are a fundamental resource for thinking about the transgressing rule of capital in the sector. Their development is a task that demands transformative practices—in academic- or student-led movements—as well as research and further theoretical reflection.

26.5 Potential Lines for Further Research

What are the future directions for Marxist research on the commons in (higher) education? Capital is the forgetting of the common. Hence, research must constantly undertake the work of history, dealing with the past forms of practices in higher education based on the anti-capitalist commons. Anti-capitalist commons exhibit a transient nature, as demonstrated by the examples of institutions operating under these principles. They are often temporary, vanishing in front of our eyes. Consequently, we need to document those tiny bits of the common that emerged within, against, and beyond the capitalist subsumption of higher education under capital.

A second area for further research on the commons in education is the ontological-political reflection. We must enhance our understanding of the common as a separate mode of being, distinguishing it in its autonomy from the public and the private, the state and the market. While existing reflection touches upon this area, there is still much to be done. It is imperative to identify the commons in practice before it is too late, as capital often encloses them before we even realize their existence and scale. Ontological-political reflection on the common will aid in bringing it into sharper focus.

The third area for further research assumes a theoretical practice conducted from within the commons' movement. It deals with the internal logic of practices and generalizable elements of anti-capitalist commons. Here we can find a critique of the political economy of capitalistically-structured higher education, grounded in the production of the common. But also, a positive political economy of the common is a reflection that helps us to grasp the foundations of a possible project of expanded reproduction of higher education based on the common.

Within the framework of this future research, however, the most crucial element is the question of the antagonism into which these two distinct forms of organization of social relations enter: the common on the one hand; and capital on the other. For it is the understanding of the irreconcilable antagonism that is the key to the success of the commons in higher education. Indeed, future research should develop a political economy based on struggles, entering into relations—rather than mediating them—with revolutionary movements for sustainable change in the higher education sector. In doing so, it should not be forgotten that the common has its enemy not only in capital but in the corrupted form of the common. It is the instrumentalization of the common by the community of producers—the academic community—traversed by numerous hierarchies and using archaic methods of signaling value (prestige and recognition, as their "yardsticks") to divide the producers and consumers of knowledge worldwide.

26.6 Conclusion

In this chapter, I provided a specific interpretation of Marx's theory of the common and its potential application to the reflection and change of capitalist higher education. Indeed, the commons are not only an intrinsic part of a possible alternative to the prevailing relations in the sector (in all areas of its functioning) but are also an intrinsic resource that feeds its extended reproduction, as well as being a form of organization of the subjectivity that can bring about this change. In this way, it seems complicated to conceive of a Marxist theory in the field of higher education that would abstract from this dimension—a fundamental, positive expression of relations not dominated by the logic of capital accumulation.

However, the commons, and anti-capitalist commons in higher education especially, are not widespread. As I have shown in the section on existing practices and common-led actions, the ephemeral nature of anti-capitalist commons in higher education, alongside their impermanence and their temporality, makes it difficult to think in the near horizon about fundamental transformations. However, this does not mean that we should succumb to the impulses of discouragement. In particular, we should repel Marxist theories that make the diagnosis of the domination of capital and the absolutization of the form of value a justification for passivity, for the postponement of any effort to build an alternative. As Mario Tronti (2019) wrote, and his words echoed in numerous works by Italian Marxists, the end of capital emerges not where capital is weakest but where the working class is strongest. In the higher education sector, too, we see that those places that are organized stably, according to the logic of the common, respond to capitalist penetration in the most decisive way—demanding change, adaptation, and compromise on it. We must think that this is the case when we are dealing with a not yet radicalized potential of the commons. We must think both what and then when might there be a shift of vectors, and the consolidation of these practices into a full cycle of liberation struggles?

The common in higher education offers hope for changing current practices. In turn, its theory and practice provide a logic for not only deepening our understanding, seeing the potential of autonomous practices where narratives of individualization and competition obscure them, but also finding a point of support for possible change—for an organization focused on abolishing the status quo. Even though the narrative contained in this chapter may seem to privilege a marginal sector, the consideration of the commons across sectors allows us to unite the horizon of struggles. And these struggles have a common goal. This goal is to put an end to capital and its capture of our collective productive energy.

Acknowledgements I want to express deep gratitude to Richard Hall and Inny Accioly for their comments that helped me improve the chapter. Special thanks are due to Jakub Krzeski, who always supports me with his friendship, expertise, and critical dialogue. All standard caveats apply.

Disclosure Statement Author has no financial interest or benefit that has arisen from the direct applications of this research.

References

Anderson, K. B. (2016). *Marx at the Margins*. University of Chicago Press.
Backer, D. I. (2017). Educating the Commons Through Cooperatively-Run Schools. In A. Means, D. F. Ford, & G. B. Slater (Eds.), *Educational Commons in Theory and Practice: Global Pedagogy and Politics* (pp. 209–229). Springer.

Balibar, E. (2017). *The Philosophy of Marx*. Verso Books.
Basso, L. (2012). *Marx and Singularity: From the Early Writings to the Grundrisse*. Brill.
Basso, L. (2015). *Marx and the Common: From Capital to the Late Writings*. Brill.
Benkler, Y. (2006). *Freedom in the Commons: A Political Economy of Information*. Yale University Press.
Bousquet, M., & Drago, M. (2009). *The Occupation Cookbook: Or the Model of the Occupation of the Faculty of Humanities and Social Sciences in Zagreb*. Autonomedia.
Broumas, A. (2017). Social Democratic and Critical Theories of the Intellectual Commons: A Critical Analysis *tripleC, 15*(1), 100–126.
Caffentzis, G., & Federici, S. (2014). Commons Against and Beyond Capitalism'. *Community Development Journal, 49*(suppl_1), i92–i105.
Carrera, P., & Solorzano, F. (Eds.). (2019). *The University-Commune. The Centrality of Community Action in the Management Model and Practices of Universities*. ABYA YALA UPS.
Cini, L. (2016). Student Struggles and Power Relations in Contemporary Universities: The Cases of Italy and England. In R. Brooks (Ed.), *Student Politics and Protest* (pp. 49–64). Routledge.
Cini, L. (2019). Disrupting the Neoliberal University in South Africa: The# FeesMustFall Movement in 2015. *Current Sociology, 67*(7), 942–959.
Collective, M. N. (1990). The New Enclosures. *Midnight Notes, 10*, 1–9.
Cook, D. (2013). *Realising the Co-operative University. A Consultancy Report for the Co-operative College*. Retrieved March 21, 2023, from http://josswinn.org/wp-content/uploads/2013/12/realising-the-co-operative-university-for-dissemination.pdf
Dardot, P., & Laval, C. (2019). *Common: On Revolution in the 21st century*. Bloomsbury Publishing.
De Angelis, M. (2013). Does Capital Need a Commons Fix? *ephemera, 13*(3), 603–615.
De Angelis, M. (2017). *Omnia Sunt Communia. On the Commons and the Transformation to Postcapitalism*. Bloosmbury Academic.
De Lissovoy, N. (2011). Pedagogy in Common: Democratic Education in the Global Era. *Educational Philosophy and Theory, 43*(10), 1119–1134.
Dokuzović, L. (2016). *Struggles for Living Learning: Within Emergent Knowledge Economies and the Cognitivization of Capital and Movement*. Transversal Texts.
Dönmez, P. E., & Duman, A. (2021). Marketisation of Academia and Authoritarian Governments: The Cases of Hungary and Turkey in Critical Perspective. *Critical Sociology, 47*(7–8), 1127–1145.
Edu-factory Collective. (2009). *Toward a Global Autonomous University*. Autonomedia.
Erdem, E. (2020). Free Universities as Academic Commons. In J. K. Gibson-Graham & K. Dombroski (Eds.), *The Handbook of Diverse Economies* (pp. 316–322). Edward Elgar Publishing.
Erdem, E., & Akın, K. (2019). Emergent Repertoires of Resistance and Commoning in Higher Education: The Solidarity Academies Movement in Turkey. *South Atlantic Quarterly, 118*(1), 145–163.
Fleet, N., & Guzmán-Concha, C. (2017). Mass Higher Education and the 2011 Student Movement in Chile: Material and Ideological Implications. *Bulletin of Latin American Research, 36*(2), 160–176.
Ford, D. R. (2015). The Pneumatic Common: Learning in, with and from the Air. *Educational Philosophy and Theory, 47*(13–14), 1405–1418.

Ford, D. R. (2017). *Communist Study: Education for the Commons*. Rowman and Littlefield.

Gieysztor, A. (1992). Management and Resources. In H. de Ridder-Symoens (Ed.), *A History of the University in Europe, Volume 1* (pp. 108–143). Cambridge University Press.

Haiven, M. (2014). *Crises of Imagination, Crises of Power: Capitalism, Creativity and the Commons*. Bloomsbury Publishing.

Haiven, M. (2017). Commons as Actuality, Ethos, and Horizon'. In A. Means, D. F. Ford, & G. B. Slater (Eds.), *Educational Commons in Theory and Practice: Global Pedagogy and Politics* (pp. 23–37). Springer.

Hall, R. (2021). *The Hopeless University: Intellectual Work at the End of the End of History*. MayFly Books.

Hall, R., & Winn, J. (Eds.). (2017). *Mass Intellectuality and Democratic Leadership in Higher Education*. Bloomsbury Academic.

Hardt, M. (2010). The Common in Communism. *Rethinking Marxism*, 22(3), 346–356.

Hardt, M., & Negri, A. (2009). *Commonwealth*. Harvard University Press.

Hardt, M., & Negri, A. (2017). *Assembly*. Oxford University Press.

Harvey, D. (2003). *The New Imperialism*. Oxford University Press.

Harvie, D. (2004). Commons and Communities in the University: Some Notes and Some Examples. *The Commoner*, 8, 1–10.

Hess, C., & Ostrom, E. (Eds.). (2007). *Understanding Knowledge as Commons: From Theory to Practice*. MIT Press.

Holloway, J. (2015). Read Capital: The First Sentence: Or, Capital Starts with Wealth, Not with the Commodity. *Historical Materialism*, 23(3), 3–26.

Hudis, P. (2012). *Marx's Concept of the Alternative to Capitalism*. Brill.

Kamola, I., & Meyerhoff, E. (2009). Creating Commons: Divided Governance, Participatory Management, and Struggles Against Enclosure in the University. *Polygraph*, 21, 5–27.

Katsiaficas, G. (2018). *Global Imagination of 1968: Revolution and Counterrevolution*. PM Press.

Lewis, T. E. (2012). Exopedagogy: On Pirates, Shorelines, and the Educational Commonwealth. *Educational Philosophy and Theory*, 44(8), 845–861.

Li, Y. (2017). SHURE: A Democratic University in Tokyo. Alternative Education Resource Organization. Retrieved March 21, 2023, from http://www.education-revolution.org/store/shure-a-democratic-university-in-tokyo/

Linebaugh, P. (1976). Karl Marx, the Theft of Wood, and Working Class Composition: A Contribution to the Current Debate. *Crime and Social Justice*, 6, 5–16.

Luxemburg, R. (2003). *The Accumulation of Capital*. Routledge.

Marginson, S. (2004). A Revised Marxist Political Economy of National Education Markets. *Policy Futures in Education*, 1(1), 439–453.

Marx, K. (1842/1975). 'Proceedings of the Sixth Rhine Province Assembly. Third Article. Debates on the Law on Thefts of Wood'. In *Marx & Engels Collected Works Vol 01: Marx: 1835–1843* (pp. 224–265). Lawrence & Wishart.

Marx, K. (1864/1975). 'Inaugural Address of the Working Men's International Association'. In *Marx & Engels Collected Works Vol 20: Marx and Engels: 1864–1868* (pp. 5–13). Lawrence & Wishart.

Marx, K. (1973). *Grundrisse*. Penguin.

Means, A. (2013). Creativity and the Biopolitical Commons in Secondary and Higher Education. *Policy Futures in Education*, 11(1), 47–58.

Means, A. J. (2014). Educational Commons and the New Radical Democratic Imaginary. *Critical Studies in Education, 55*(2), 122–137.
Means, A. J., Ford, D. R., & Slater, G. B. (Eds.). (2017). *Educational Commons in Theory and Practice: Global Pedagogy and Politics*. Springer.
Mezzadra, S. (2011). The Topicality of Prehistory: A New Reading of Marx's Analysis of 'so-called primitive accumulation'. *Rethinking Marxism, 23*(3), 302–321.
Moroz, J., & Szwabowski, O. (2017). Solidarity, Dark Solidarity, the Commons and the University'. *Power and Education, 9*(2), 145–158.
Musto, M. (2020). *The Last Years of Karl Marx: An Intellectual Biography*. Stanford University Press.
Neary, M., & Winn, J. (2012). Open Education: Common(s), Commonism and the New Common Wealth. *ephemera, 12*(4), 406–422.
Ostrom, E. (1990). *Governing the Commons: The Evolution of Institutions for Collective Action*. Cambridge University Press.
Peters, M. A. (2009). Open Education and the Open Science Economy. *Yearbook of the National Society for the Study of Education, 108*(2), 203–225.
Pusey, A. (2017). Towards a University of the Common: Reimagining the University in Order to Abolish It with the Really Open University. *Open Library of Humanities, 3*(1), 1–27.
Roggero, G. (2010). Five Theses on the Common. *Rethinking Marxism, 22*(3), 357–373.
Roggero, G. (2011). *The Production of Living Knowledge*. Temple University Press.
Roxå, T., & Mårtensson, K. (2014). Higher Education Commons – A Framework for Comparison of Midlevel Units in Higher Education Organizations. *European Journal of Higher Education, 4*(4), 303–316.
Slater, G. B. (2014). Constituting Common Subjects: Toward an Education Against Enclosure. *Educational Studies, 50*(6), 537–553.
Szadkowski, K. (2019). The Common in Higher Education: A Conceptual Approach. *Higher Education, 78*(2), 241–255.
Szadkowski, K., & Krzeski, J. (2019). In, Against, and Beyond: A Marxist Critique for Higher Education in Crisis'. *Social Epistemology, 33*(6), 463–476.
Szadkowski, K., & Krzeski, J. (2022). Conceptualizing Capitalist Transformations of Universities: Marx's Relevance for Higher Education Research. *Critique, 50*(1), 185–203.
Tronti, M. (2019). *Workers and Capital*. Verso Books.
Vercellone, C. (2015). From the Crisis to the 'Welfare of the Common' as a New Mode of Production'. *Theory, Culture and Society, 32*(7-8), 85–99.
Vercellone, C., & Giuliani, A. (2018). Common and Commons in the Contradictory Dynamics Between Knowledge-Based Economy and Cognitive Capitalism. In A. Fumagalli et al. (Eds.), *Cognitive Capitalism, Welfare and Labour: The Commonfare Hypothesis* (pp. 132–172). Routledge.
Virno, P. (2004). *A Grammar of the Multitude*. Semiotexte.
Winn, J. (2015). The Co-operative University: Labour, Property and Pedagogy. *Power and Education, 7*(1), 39–55.
Wright, S., Greenwood, D., & Boden, R. (2011). Report on a Field Visit to Mondragón University: A Cooperative Experience/Experiment. *Learning and Teaching, 4*(3), 38–56.

CHAPTER 27

Marx, Critique, and Abolition: Higher Education as Infrastructure

Abigail Boggs, Eli Meyerhoff, Nick Mitchell, and Zach Schwartz-Weinstein

27.1 Introduction

What is the relevance of Marx to the study of higher education? In this chapter, we attempt to find one resource in abolitionist invocations of Marx and the Marxist tradition. Our consideration of the latter emphasizes the centrality of *accumulation* to understanding the university as an historical object and does so by reading the university as an infrastructure for capitalism. We take up the term *infrastructure* as it describes material systems constructed, often under the auspices of state and capitalist planning and regulation, for the purposes of organizing the movement of people, ideas, and other entities over time and

---

A. Boggs
Wesleyan University, Middletown, CT, USA
e-mail: aboggs@wesleyan.edu

E. Meyerhoff (✉)
Duke University, Durham, NC, USA
e-mail: eli.meyerhoff@duke.edu

N. Mitchell
University of California, Santa Cruz, CA, USA
e-mail: nmitchel@ucsc.edu

Z. Schwartz-Weinstein
Bard Prison Initiative, Annandale-on-Hudson, NY, USA

© The Editor(s) (if applicable) and The Author(s), under exclusive license to Springer Nature Switzerland AG 2023
R. Hall et al. (eds.), *The Palgrave International Handbook of Marxism and Education*, Marxism and Education,
https://doi.org/10.1007/978-3-031-37252-0_27

space. Infrastructure, in the sense and scale at which we invoke it, forms a major part of the social machinery of domination and exploitation.

But it shouldn't be understood in this sense only. As we will suggest, to pay attention to the university as infrastructure also offers a lens onto emergent and oppositional modes of social reproduction. University infrastructure might also provide organizational ballast for the radical transformation of life-making systems. This approach, we contend, might offer a novel angle from which to read Marx and the Marxist tradition, because, within it, Marx appears simultaneously as a central theorist *and* as an effect of the university as an accumulation infrastructure. As we suggest, one way of contextualizing Marx as we know him is as a *product* of the accumulation infrastructure of the Prussian university system, which had by the 1830s gained international distinction as an institution capable of producing scientific achievement by emphasizing research on modern social problems.[1]

For an approach to the contemporary university attentive to its infrastructural functions for capitalism, we start by exploring Marx's own relationship to the university, to nineteenth-century disciplinary formation, and to critique as institutional infrastructure. Next, we pick up on W. E. B. Du Bois's combination of the Marxist and Black radical, abolitionist traditions. As we have argued in our prior work, taking seriously the insights and politics of these lines of thought enables an abolitionist approach to the study of higher education through an historical periodization of the university that highlights how the university transforms along with its changing interrelations with capitalism, especially its accumulative functions, as it is inherently imbricated with and productive of the logics of embodied difference upon which accumulation relies.[2] In the third section, we briefly demonstrate this approach by turning to two key periods in the history of US higher education: the post-emancipation US university that helped transform indigenous land into capital, and the post-World War II Cold War university that absorbed the surplus population of returning soldiers so as to avoid social disruptions. In the fourth section, we present a mode of theory for describing these historical transformations that is conducive to abolitionist movements: going beyond a critique-based mode of theory, we promote an affirmative mode of theory that highlights world-making movements alternative to capitalism. Using this mode of theory, we describe higher education as infrastructure for racial-colonial capitalism, an approach that unsettles the normal taken-for-grantedness of these institutions and opens our imaginations to alternative infrastructures for making other possible worlds. In the final section, we discuss the potential uses of the university for alternative world-making movements—for 'red and Black' abolitionism—that seek to end the racial-colonial capitalist regime of accumulation while also challenging the hegemonic role of higher education.

27.2 Marx, Critique, and the University

'[E]veryone,' wrote Karl Marx to Arnold Ruge in 1843, 'will have to admit to himself that he has no exact idea what the future ought to be' (1975, p. 142). The everyone in question included, most notably, those professional philosophers who aspired to comment on the political world. As the rightward shift in

Prussian rule met with increasingly revolutionary responses, its internationally celebrated university system straddled a series of contradictions that found their way, in complex form, at both the center and periphery of Marxist thinking. For the Prussian state, the university was a key piece of infrastructure, an institutional technology imagined to provide the material and conceptual grounds upon which social order operates and through which the future could be shaped (Larkin, 2013, p. 329). The university was also, as Marx's observation suggests, subject to the uncertainties of any form through which people, resources, and ideas move, frustrating such efforts to predetermine what is to come.

Before Marx*ism* emerged in its revolutionary aspirations as a critique of political economy, the young Marx developed his critical program in conflict and in collaboration with philosophy and philosophers. The choice of philosophy as an object of criticism reflected more than the simple fact that it was Marx's discipline of training. Philosophy, rather, played a pivotal role in the institutional structure of Prussian higher education. As Paul Reitter and Chad Wellmon (2021, p. 166) have written, philosophy in the early nineteenth century 'became more autonomous and professionalized,' emerging in the 1830s as a central discipline in university reforms that privileged the organization of knowledge into distinct disciplines.

Philosophy, in this context, signified something more significant than one discipline among others. Philosophy, rather, served as a regulative project for the university itself, the embodiment of the new institutional norm of *Wissenschaft*, which promised to unify a university system that increasing disciplinary differentiation threatened to fragment. Reitter and Wellmon suggest that philosophy's straddling the particular and general was exemplified by the new 'doctor of philosophy' degree, which could distinguish an individual trained in any field. To become an expert in a discipline was in this way to be regulated in some way by the faculty and idea of philosophy. Awarded to men of achievement in various disciplines, the emergence of the Ph.D. bespoke a faith in philosophy as a discourse for communication *between* fields of specialization as much as within them: chemists, historians, geologists, and literary scholars operated, at their highest level, as philosophers.[3] As the German Idealists imagined it, philosophy could provide a unifying foundation for knowledge (Reitter & Wellmon, 2021, p. 29).

In practice, *Wissenschaft* in the Prussian university system emerged as a site for the formal and informal development of the modern laboratory system. Enterprising intellectuals navigated its sanctions and prohibitions and formed what would today be touted as public–private partnerships that combined the use of university research capacity with the construction of independent institutes for research in chemistry, medicine, and manufacturing. Justus von Liebig, an internationally renowned chemist, developed the field of organic chemistry while establishing some of the most influential frameworks for chemical fertilizers.

The development and expansion of capitalism relied persistently on technological development in agriculture to generate surpluses. As European crop yields declined in the early nineteenth century, anxious narratives about the 'worn-out' nature of the soil took hold. German soil science, helmed by Liebig, offered the prospect that in the absence of surpluses of land—new soil—the fecundity of European soil could be restored by way of the application of expert knowledge derived from scientific research (Brock, 2002; Foster & Magdoff, 1998). Just as the Prussian university would present itself as the answer to an accumulation crisis, the imitation of the German model as a way to reform the US university would offer the same by mid-century, when the prospect of the abolition of slavery presented itself to US statesmen. By the 1860s, as Nathan Sorber (2011) emphasizes, a significant cohort of bourgeois university reformers had studied botany, geology, and chemistry abroad in Germany. These men organized widely, building state agricultural societies and lobbying for the creation of agricultural colleges.

In this idealized role for philosophy, critique was fundamental. Critique, understood here less as a practice than as institutional infrastructure, a prescribed mode of engagement and relation, was developed as a means of deploying self-consciousness toward the end of self-regulation. Constructed in this way, critique emerged for the practitioners of modern disciplinarity as the practice of philosophy outside of philosophy proper, organized toward the end of choreographing knowledge for the production of an organic, integrated, whole. Left Hegelianism, however, added an additional wrinkle to this understanding of critique. Having been rejected by the rightward drift of Prussian state authority in the 1830s, Left Hegelians trained in philosophy, like Marx himself, were increasingly dispelled from academic institutions. By the mid-1840s, and following the Prussian regime's backlash against left Hegelianism, Marx largely abandoned his prior plans for an academic career (Sperber, 2013, pp. 53–80). But we would argue that Marx never fully abandoned a certain belief in education and the university's institutional forms—particularly critique.

Even as Marx sought to free the university's institutional forms from their role in the reproduction of bourgeois society, he was unable to free himself from the idealization of criticism itself. Indeed, though Marx and Engels are at pains to distance themselves from the fetishized 'critical criticism' of the other Young Hegelians (1998, p. 53), it was Marx himself who had just a few years prior valorized criticism as the vanguard of a radical publication project. In a letter to Arnold Ruge, Marx wrote, 'I am referring to ruthless criticism of all that exists, ruthless both in the sense of not being afraid of the results it arrives at and in the sense of being just as little afraid of conflict with the powers that be' (1975 p. 142).

Marx and Engels's critique of capitalist society in *The German Ideology* mirrors the university's disciplinary critique, if toward markedly different ends. In a capitalist society, 'each man has a particular, exclusive sphere of activity, which is forced upon him and from which he cannot escape. He is a hunter, a fisherman, a shepherd, or a critical critic, and must remain so if he does not want to lose his means of livelihood' (1998 p. 53). Communist society will free man from this division: 'each can become accomplished in any branch he wishes, society regulates the general production and thus makes it possible for me to do one thing today and another tomorrow, to hunt in the morning, fish in the afternoon, rear cattle in the evening, criticize after dinner.'[4] Criticism, no longer an elite specialization cloistered in the university, has in this speculative scenario, become one form of labor among others.

We know that Marx's revolutionary idiom was deeply shaped by the contradictions of life in Prussian society, thanks largely to the voluminous historical, theoretical, and biographical writing that takes up this question. Less available, however, is a way of accounting for the larger institutional infrastructure that made Marx possible. To pursue the latter question, we must attend to the history of the university itself. One useful first move, in step with the larger aim of this volume, would be to reverse the order of questioning. Alongside asking how we might use Marx better to understand the university, we might also ask how the university *already* lives—as a resource, as a problem, as an infrastructure—in Marx and Marxism.

In his oft-cited 1798 book *The Conflict of the Faculties*, Kant famously outlines the systemic architecture of the university (1992). There, as Wellmon (2016, p. 145) describes it, Kant had 'explicitly made the case that the university was the only technology capable of sustaining the continuity of philosophy, and thus scientific thought, as a practice.' Kant provides a systemic architecture through which universities are a kind of infrastructure for the state, but one that needs to enjoy relative autonomy from the state while simultaneously receiving its financial support. The infrastructural functions of the university were to accumulate funding from the state and turn this funding into means of living for intellectuals, and thereby into the means of knowledge production. Knowledge production benefits the state precisely as a function of this autonomy because university intellectuals are free to produce truth rather than to produce knowledge in the form and content demanded by the state. The promise, ultimately, is one of the reproduction of state power *over time*.

This promise could not be sustained amid a regime of increasing disciplinary differentiation. This university infrastructure became one feature in a larger process characterized by the accumulation of intellectuals. Absent a 'productive' means for their incorporation, therefore, one of the byproducts of this university infrastructure was the 'overproduction' of intellectuals—some employed by it and others produced by the vanguardist iteration of philosophy that organized it. One way of reading the emergence, for instance, of the Young Hegelians, and of the proliferation of radical publications in the 1840s, is as an outcome of a larger crisis of overaccumulation—one leading, in part, to the revolutions of 1848. The idea of critique that these intellectuals developed was an outcome of the university as an accumulation infrastructure. Marx was in this accumulation infrastructure (and of it), but he was perhaps so *of it* that he was not capable of theorizing it as such—even when he was no longer *in* it—because its institutional frameworks so substantially shaped his own trajectory as an intellectual.

What, after all, is Marx without critique? Marx, of course, ruthlessly lampooned Stirner and other 'critical critics' in chapters later collected as *The German Ideology*. Still, little in the history of Marxist thought seems to treat as significant Marx's relationship to critique, the idea and practice at the heart of nineteenth-century German university reform. This is significant for reasons that include but extend beyond our ability to account for the revolutionary thinker whose famous work was subtitled *A Critique of Political Economy*. Since those German university reforms have had an outsized influence on the organization of modern universities themselves, we think that Marx's formation in them has implications that resonate more broadly. These implications call for attention to the undertheorized nature of education—and particularly higher education—in Marx, even as Marx's oeuvre itself aspired to offer a revolutionary contribution to proletarian education.

Marx's formation in higher education infrastructure needs more attention, if for no other reason than its impact on Marxist thinking on education more broadly.[5] Those who continue, like Marx, to see education as an essential site of revolutionary struggle have a stake in this conversation. Inasmuch as, like Marx, we are formed by (and in spite of) an education system we might like to topple, this effort to read Marx better constitutes an effort to better read the larger historical context in which we ourselves have been produced. Marx and Engels, in a famous document calling for the abolition of private property, did not call for the same with education. In the *Communist Manifesto* (1975a, p. 502), their injunction, as education went, was not one to abolish but rather to 'rescue.' The Communists, they write, seek to save education 'from the influence of the ruling class.' Thus, education itself somehow remains largely beyond critique in much of Marx's work, invisible, mostly, as a space of potential and terrain of struggle, save for the famous exemplary schoolteacher whose conditions of employment are interchangeable with a sausage factory for the purposes of determining the productivity of his labor (Marx, 1992, p. 644).

Radicals today find themselves in a similar position to Marx. We want to destroy the capitalist infrastructure of the university but we also want to use the resources concentrated in it. We often use critique as a way to disavow our implication in this infrastructure (seeing ourselves as 'not of it'), while simultaneously using the university's claim to power. Indeed, many of us are the products of these institutions and spend our time and sustain our lives through the labor of teaching and research routed through them. We move through and attempt to both use and abuse the university infrastructure while frequently thinking ourselves as autonomous from the university and the various structures of state and capital with which it is entangled. As a possible antidote to such disavowal, we suggest that talking about the university in terms of 'infrastructure' offers a theoretical tactic for navigating a more materialist and ambivalent relationship to the university.[6] In the next section, we examine W. E. B. Du Bois's ambivalent relations to the university with his combination of the Marxist and Black radical, abolitionist traditions.

27.3 Abolition and Accumulation

To invoke Marx's name in relation to abolitionism first evokes his advocacy, with Engels, for the abolition of private property, the family, class distinctions, individuality, nations, and bourgeois conceptions of the past (Marx & Engels, 1975a). These calls for the abolition of 'the existing social and political order of things,' do not prescribe a 'ready-made system' of 'actually existing communism' that other socialists have promoted under a 'dogmatic banner,' but rather suggest that 'we must try to help the dogmatists to clarify their propositions for themselves' (Marx, 1975). For the purposes of our thinking about the history, politics, and theory of higher education in the United States, however, it is generative to consider Marx's work in relation to another moment and form of abolitionist praxis: the formal abolition of the slave economy upon which the US social order was formed. In this section, we first discuss the links and differences between Marx and Du Bois on abolitionism, the Reconstruction period, and higher education. Next, we describe how attending to what Du Bois theorized as abolitionism's dual-sided character—its world-ending and world-making dimensions—is necessary for both resisting and creating alternatives to racial capitalism's violent processes of accumulation.

Marx and Du Bois on Abolition, Reconstruction, and Universities

Marx's writing has been critiqued for its lack of sustained engagement with the question of race and racialization as central logics of the capitalist mode of production. In *Marx at the Margins*, Kevin Anderson (2010) sets out to amend this perception. He draws his readers to consider an 1846 letter Marx wrote to Pavel V. Annenkov. There, Marx makes explicit his recognition that racial slavery was, 'an economic category of paramount importance' and indeed the 'necessary condition for large-scale machine industry.'[7] Writing for *Die Presse* in 1861, the opening year of the US Civil War, Marx warned that '[t]he war of the Southern Confederacy is thus not a war of defense, but a war of conquest for the extension and perpetuation of slavery' (Marx in Marx & Engels, 2010, p. 44). Aligning with radical abolitionists, Anderson contends that Marx saw in the possibility of a Southern victory the threat of 'a new form of capitalism, openly structured upon racial and ethnic lines' (2010, p. 90). In other words, Marx lays bare the crucial role of enslaved labor as the foundation of the accumulative process of the global capitalist economy.

In Anderson's reassessment of Marx's writing during the Civil War, he builds on the work of W. E. B. Du Bois, whose 1935 book, *Black Reconstruction in America*, was 'grounded in Marx's Civil War writings' (2010, p. 80). Du Bois analyzes the post-Civil War period of Reconstruction: on the one hand, the white labor movement's failure to adequately support the Black freedom struggle foreclosed the revolutionary potential of Reconstruction, while on the other hand, this period gave birth to fleeting moments of 'abolition democracy' through shared struggles across racial lines (Anderson, 2010, p. 81; Du

Bois, 1969 [1935]). Du Bois grounded the unfinished movement for abolition—to end the afterlives of slavery—in an interweaving of the Black radical tradition with the work of Marxists and other movement-embedded intellectuals. Du Bois situated Marx in relation to the abolition of slavery in the US and as in solidarity with radical abolitionists.

Both Marx and Du Bois saw the stakes of the Civil War as about the future development of capitalism. While Marx did not write on US universities in relation to post-Civil War capitalism, Du Bois forcefully indicted university-based intellectuals for framing the history of the Civil War, abolition, and Reconstruction in ways that undercut their revolutionary potential. In his chapter of *Black Reconstruction* titled 'The Propaganda of History,' he writes that '[t]he real frontal attack on Reconstruction, as interpreted by the leaders of national thought in the 1870s and for some time thereafter, came from the universities and particularly from Columbia and Johns Hopkins' (1969 [1935], p. 718). The attacks often came from the 'Southern teachers [who] have been welcomed to many Northern universities' as well as from Southern students who influenced Northern professors, while 'often Negro students have been systematically discouraged' from these universities, thereby giving rise to 'a nation-wide university attitude' of 'propaganda against the Negro' (p. 719).

These university-based scholars' studies of Reconstruction share a set of understandings: 'first, endless sympathy with the white south; second, ridicule, contempt or silence for the Negro; and third, a judicial attitude towards the North, which concludes that the North under great misapprehension did a grievous wrong, but eventually saw its mistake and retreated' (ibid). While highlighting white people's perspectives, these studies ignored the views of 'the emancipated slave himself,' thereby perpetuating racist histories that Du Bois sought to counteract by writing an abolitionist history that centered Black people's perspectives (p. 721). Notably, the year before Du Bois published *Black Reconstruction*, he returned to Atlanta University, which he had left in 1910 to serve as director of research for the NAACP. And it was from there that he articulated his argument for 'abolition democracy.'

Dual-Sided Abolitionism Against Violent Accumulation in Capitalist Institutions

Abolitionist frameworks in the contemporary US continue what Du Bois saw as the simultaneously destructive and creative dimensions of abolitionism— ending slavery and building 'abolition democracy'—with abolitionist projects that, for example, call for eliminating prisons and police while meeting people's needs for prevention and repair of harm with transformative justice practices.[8] For instance, Angela Davis sees abolition democracy as enabling 'the creation of an array of social institutions that would begin to solve the social problems that set people on the track to prison, thereby helping to render prison obsolete' (2005, p. 96).

Another way to articulate these dual dimensions of abolitionism is in terms of simultaneous 'world-ending and world-making,' with Robyn Maynard stating: 'Given that racial and ecological violence are interwoven and inextricable from one another, more now than ever, Black and Indigenous communities—who are globally positioned as "first to die" within the climate crisis—are also on the front lines of world-making practices that threaten to overthrow the current (death-making) order of things' (Maynard & Simpson, 2022, pp. 26–27). In bringing the commitments, histories, and practices of this form of abolitionism to bear on the study of the university as infrastructure, we turn to the crucial insights of prison abolition.

Prison abolition work has been predicated on a materialist analysis that recognizes the place of 'rational violence' for the accumulative project of capital. In Marx and the Marxist tradition, accumulation offers a key concept in linking the processes whereby capital is produced and valorized with the historical development of capitalism.[9] What is specific about the capitalist 'mode of accumulation' in contrast with other modes is that in capitalism, 'land, labor, wealth and goods are commodified and strongly exposed to the forces of price-setting markets and accumulation occurs primarily through the production of commodities using commodified labor' (Chase-Dunn & Hall, 1997, p. 30). Competition in capitalism compels capitalists to reinvest the surplus value that they extract from the exploitation of labor, that is, to constantly accumulate surplus value by transforming it into further capital.

In short, to pay attention to accumulation offers an approach keyed to the practice of confronting capitalism and its apologists with its own historical conditions of possibility. Rich traditions of anticolonial critique and histories of slavery have insisted that the violence and expropriation that made capitalism possible are not external features of it. Rather, these are internal features of its logic.[10] Accumulation is therefore the manifest condition of an entire range of often overlapping forces and arrangements—war, patriarchy, colonial violence, displacement, enslavement, enclosure, and even education. These forces, often held at an analytic remove from the 'purely' economic, created the differential distributions, of life, land, death, debt, power, wealth, and self, that were necessary for capitalist production to emerge, and to reproduce itself, over time.

Education tends to be romanticized as an institution untainted by capitalism. Yet, when we examine the history of emergence of education's key elements, including a vertical imaginary of ascending levels, a pedagogy of shame and esteem that becomes institutionalized with grades, and binary figures of value and waste (the educated vs. uneducated, graduates vs. dropouts, etc.), we see how these have served as disciplinary techniques to shape individuals for participation in capitalist governance (e.g., with dispositions of obedience, acceptance of hierarchies, competition, valorizing hard work, and desires for capital and property accumulation) (Meyerhoff, 2019). Education has functioned as a precondition for capitalist relations, as a form of 'primitive accumulation,' in the sense of creating new relations of separation between individualized producers and the means of production. Education is a particular, historically contingent 'mode of study' that emerged in co-constitution with the capitalist world-making project, in opposition to alternative modes of study in association with alternative world-making projects.

As institutions of 'higher education,' colleges and universities are often granted an exceptional status even as they are co-constitutive with the broader education system and participate in its functions. They are thoroughly bound up with K-12 schools in processes of disciplining young people to take on' dispositions needed in capitalism and of hierarchically differentiating the value of their labor (e.g., by serving as the societally valued 'higher' levels toward which young people are supposed to ascend, up the vertically arranged grade levels of preK-12 schools, with tracking along relatively valued and devalued trajectories, such as college-bound vs. vocational, while masking the political character of these processes with ideologies of meritocracy, development, equality of opportunity, social mobility, adulthood as mature independence, etc.).

In combination with such cross-systemic functions for the capitalist system, higher education institutions have also performed their own particular, historically shifting functions in processes of accumulation, circulation, and the production of new forms of knowledge that fuel capitalist and state expansion. A guiding feature of an abolitionist approach to the study of colleges and universities in the United States is an understanding of how higher education institutions function as sites for both the accumulation and circulation of land, lives, resources, and relationships under specific conditions of capitalism. To understand the work of the university as such entails seeing universities as complex terrains of world-making (and world-ending), with tension-riddled infrastructures, rather than reducing them to the representative spaces of the classroom, quad, or laboratory.

Consider specifically some of the important functions shared from the perspective of institutional accumulation, between universities and prisons, which partly animate our framing here. We are inspired here by Ruth Wilson Gilmore's account, in *Golden Gulag* (2007), of the four surpluses—finance capital, land, labor, and state capacity—that converged in the process of California's massive project of prison expansion in the 1980s. While Gilmore does not use this term, one way of viewing the form this convergence takes is to understand prisons as infrastructures of institutional accumulation. Though these kinds of comparisons between universities and prisons are always risky, they can be illuminating and surprising as well. As Mattie Armstrong-Price (2015) has shown, prisons inherited from the university a genealogy in the deployment of state technologies of debt-financed construction. The perspective offered by the standpoint of institutional accumulation can thus offer a way not simply of comparing—in the sense of rendering equivalent—universities and prisons but rather of grasping how both institutions extend and enable the stratification of wageless life, in the sense that Michael Denning (2010) has used the term.

From the perspective of capital, in the abstract, prisons and universities both offer highly scalable state-guaranteed investment opportunities for low-interest, low-risk bonds that stabilize other, riskier investment opportunities. Both universities and prisons are capable of effectively disappearing surplus populations from the labor force and thereby disappearing capitalism's structural generation of unemployment. Both universities and prisons are capable of taking surplus lands out of agricultural production and repurposing them as large-scale social investments. This perspective also allows us to forego some of the ideological sheen that the university arrogates to itself as a function of its own historical privilege.

By taking up this more capacious understanding of accumulation, the abolitionist university studies we propose can also attend to the tensions and ambivalences of accumulative infrastructures. Other kinds of accumulative practices exist and operate alongside, within, and against the accumulative function of capitalism in the service of alternative world-making projects. These forms of accumulation might include the accumulation of debt (financial and otherwise), of suspect and subjugated knowledges, of untoward relationships. For Harney and Moten (2013, p. 61), for instance, the accumulation of 'bad debt,' the debt that cannot or simply will not ever be paid, is the very condition of possibility, the very principle upon which a fugitive public can form. That is, if, as they write, 'credit is a means of privatization' then debt is 'a means of socialization,' it is social and mutual. Abolitionist movements can both resist capitalist accumulation and engage in alternative forms of accumulation, or abolitionist infrastructures, with alternative modes of study for world-making projects alternative to capitalism.

Where We Start the Story of the University Matters

Too often, studies of US higher education rely on nostalgia for an era in the mid-twentieth century to conjure the imagined goodness of an expansive and expanding public university system flush with federal and state support.[11] Here, the university exists as a redistributive institution through which the masses can acquire upward social mobility. Almost invariably, however, this story neglects the ways this expansion was underwritten by militarized funding priorities, nationalist agendas, and an incorporative project of counterinsurgency. This model serves not only to emplot narratives of decline from the mid-twentieth century to the neoliberal present; it also enables universities to narrate the relation between the past and present as a tale of progress. Such narratives provide active cover for institutional complicity in imperialism, coloniality, and dispossession.

By attending to dispossession, displacement, and accumulation as constitutive and contested processes of university making and remaking, abolitionist university studies takes as part of its task to trouble the will to epistemic exculpation, to refuse the university's constant and obliviating self-absolution. Toward these ends, we need critique, certainly, but we need also to be unsettled by critique's privileged place in the institutional epistemology of the university, in which the status it enjoys as a good in itself is enshrined by the same logic deployed by the university's public relations wing. Abolitionist university studies collaborates with movements that seek to dismantle universities' fixedness within the afterlives of slavery and ongoing forms of 'accumulation by dispossession' in order to invigorate a new epistemic approach to social possibilities today (Harvey, 2004; Melamed, 2015).

An abolitionist approach requires rethinking how we historicize US higher education. Where we start our history of the university matters. To invoke the language of abolitionism is to position this project in relationship to and in continuity with the abolitionist movement of the nineteenth century, which worked not only to abolish slavery but also to establish an abolition democracy. The nineteenth century story of the university allows us to get to the question of what the university is in a way that starting the story in the twentieth century may turn us away from. Recent scholarship on the university enables just such a shift, revealing the US academy's roots in white-supremacist, settler-colonial capitalism, and insisting that contemporary work on the present circumstances and future possibilities of the university must grapple with these foundations.[12] To varying degrees and ends, such work documents the vast extent to which the colleges and universities often romanticized as the most prestigious in the US and Europe were materially dependent upon the dispossession and exploitation of Black and Native American peoples' labor and land, while concomitantly authorizing the very knowledge formations through which such actions were rationalized.

But this work is not uniformly abolitionist. Many recent efforts by a number of well-resourced and elite universities to acknowledge their historical complicities (and in some cases active involvement) in slavery and the slave trade have taken the form of public relations campaigns. Partly because they are able to take for granted the progress story put into play by the Golden Era university narrative—in which the university's social function is presumed to be ameliorative—these efforts are able to presume a university past that is radically discontinuous with the university present. Through reports, public statements, special task forces on university history, and the renaming of buildings, the knowledge form itself is thus called upon to do the work of redress. Brand management, today's university officials understand, involves 'owning' one's institutional history.

An abolitionist approach is attuned to the political stakes of periodization. Different periodizations of the history of higher education can have various functions for movements: they can cut off continuities that might become apparent otherwise, push away events that are embarrassing or less savory, and obscure or highlight possibilities of resistance and alternatives. Consider, for example, how these functions have emerged in the debates around periodization between the anti-racist 1619 Project and the right-wing reaction of the 1776 Report, which argue, respectively, for rooting the foundations of the US nation-state in the enslavement of African people or in the American War of Independence (Hannah-Jones, 2021; Arnn et al., 2021). Ultimately, periodizations are about what's important: they shape what we consider we need to talk about together and they can enliven or shut down debates about what constitutes the present.

27.4 Historicizing US Higher Education—An Abolitionist Lens

An account of universities' relationship to capital accumulation therefore requires careful periodization. Two moments in particular take on outsized importance, particularly in the context of US universities—the emergence of the post-emancipation university (1862–1890), and the postwar moment of rapid expansion (1944–1969), which was precipitated by the Servicemen's Readjustment Act of 1944 (colloquially known as the G.I. Bill) and the onset of the Cold War.

We use the term 'the post-emancipation university' here, as opposed to 'post-slavery' in our earlier work (Boggs et al., 2019). We do so to emphasize the distinction between the narrow form of freedom actually achieved by the emancipation proclamation and thirteenth, fourteenth, and fifteenth amendments to the US constitution, and wider visions of freedom. By the latter, we mean to gesture towards W.E.B. DuBois's understanding of 'abolition-democracy' as the social movement of the 'dark proletariat' to emancipate itself and therefore its labor, and, in so doing, to free 'that basic majority of workers who are yellow, brown, and black' (Du Bois, 1969, p. 16).

The 1862 Morrill Land Grant Act (named for Vermont Senator Justin Morrill) stands as a pivotal element of an emergent postwar acceleration of settler colonialism and primitive accumulation.[13] US imperial expansion west of its initial borders and colleges and universities' involvement in, enablement of, and profiting from that expansion both predate the Morill Act, but it was the Morill Act that systematized the network of state universities financed through ongoing expropriation of indigenous land (Lee et al., 2020). Cornell University, in Ithaca, New York, was the largest single beneficiary of the first Morrill Act, awarded nearly a million acres of indigenous land in what are now the states of Wisconsin, Michigan, Minnesota, California, Kansas, and Colorado, among others. The land bequeathed to colleges and universities by the Morrill Land Grant Act was not simply, then, used to build campuses upon, but instead mostly to build endowments—it was sold to speculators and developers, mined and deforested, and ultimately turned into railroads, subdivisions, neighborhoods, and WalMart parking lots. In crafting a free-labor future built upon white supremacist expropriation of the west for and by white settlement, the post-emancipation university demonstrates a comfortable accommodation of anti-black sentiment and anti-slavery ideology, much as the white workerist language around 'wage slavery' did during the same period (Roediger, 1991).

If, as Manu Karuka (2019) shows, the allocation of Western Land was already, by 1862, a strategy for securing for industrial capitalists the infrastructural basis for building massive railroad projects, then the land grant might be understood as a technology of imperial consolidation. It was a means of courting and crafting public–private investment in securing national infrastructure by way of the displacement and elimination of Native peoples. Indeed, the Morrill Act was the fraternal twin of the Homestead Act, which similarly allotted indigenous land to white 'homesteaders' for private settlement. Viewed through the prism of the Morrill Act, then, the 'post' in post-emancipation university signifies, as we have written elsewhere, 'not a simple chronological "after," and not the ideological "after" of slavery that consists in a transparent liberal freedom.' Instead, the 'post' of 'post-emancipation' constitutes a settler-colonial project to valorize and exploit free white labor, using the knowledge form to recoup lost extractive capacities (Boggs et al., 2019). If universities had played a direct role in settler colonial projects since the seventeenth or eighteenth century—Wilder (2013, p.44) notes, for example, that the College of William and Mary operated as a colonial garrison and as a prison camp for Tuscarora hostages—the Morrill Act formalized and systematized universities' conscription into the accumulation project of the post-emancipation state.

Railroads, in particular, were 'a core part of the infrastructure of 19th-century liberal imperialism, amplifying the development of the era's other key industries, including telegraph, steel, lumber, coal, and steamships.' Each of these industries, Manu Karuka (2022) writes, 'rapidly consolidated into monopoly form, carving up the planet while seeking new arenas for growth.' Karuka reads Du Bois, in 'The Souls of White Folk,' as arguing that 'competition among these monopolies catalyzed the "Great War."' Du Bois, Karuka argues

> connected the violently legal enforcement of racial segregation on trains to the voracious consumption of racialized labor and the unrelenting extraction of resources from the darker world, for the enrichment of coteries of investors based in the major cities of Europe and North America. Competition among these cohorts, he argued, carried the violence they visited on their colonies into Europe itself.

The Land Grant, an important technology of enclosure and allotment, marks the complicity, at the very least, of the US university in this trans-imperial circuit of violence.

A new regime of accumulation was inaugurated in 1862 in which the land-grant university played a critical role in capital accumulation. Through enclosure and allotment of indigenous lands, World War II and its aftermath initiated universities as central to the new regime of accumulation that characterized the early decades of the so-called American century. Even after universities ceased their temporary wartime function as garrisons and training grounds for soldiers, they remained important *accessories* of the emergent military-industrial complex. This was not only through ROTC programs which transformed students into officers, but, perhaps more importantly, through their role as incubators and laboratories for military-applied technosciences, and through absorbing the surplus labor of returning combatants. The servicemen's readjustment act, colloquially the G.I. Bill, poured federal appropriations into tuition benefits to channel the surplus population of returning veterans into universities, where decommissioned military personnel could be easily reabsorbed.

Writing in the first issue of *Zerowork*, the Marxist philosopher George Caffentzis (1975) argued that in the university 'two forms of unwaged labor for capital' were appropriated. These were, respectively, 'the development of new "forces of production" through scientific research, and what Marx called "the power of knowledge objectified"' and 'the reproduction of labor power and so reproduction of the hierarchy of labor powers of different qualities (selection, division and stratification)' (p. 129). Caffentzis explains that following the recession cycles of the 1950s, in which federal funding for higher education had stagnated relative to the previous decade, the Kennedy administration (1961–1963) increased higher education spending in an effort to use the university to stimulate growth and mitigate unemployment by restructuring the labor market around human capital. Stratifying the working class through grading and sorting, the university would be in the business of 'collect[ing], divid[ing], and select[ing].' Yet, instead of 'conquering' class struggle, Caffentzis explains, the human capital strategy transferred it onto campuses. Rather than simply being managed and funneled for the purposes of capital and the state, students used the structure of the university to organize (pp. 130–132). In response, administrators and politicians sought to use austerity as a form of labor discipline against wageless student labor (pp. 136–141).

27.5 Education as Infrastructure for Racial-Colonial Capitalism

The above historical fragments are just a taste of an abolitionist, Marxist history of US higher education. An abolitionist history that centers accumulation can supplement the dominant Marxist approaches to understanding the university—those focused on ideology and social reproduction—with an infrastructural understanding. A key Marxist theorist of education as ideology is Louis Althusser, as argued in his essay, 'Ideology and Ideological State Apparatuses' (1971). This distinguishes 'repressive state apparatuses,' including the police, prisons, and military, that function by violence, from 'ideological state apparatuses,' including churches, family, media, law, and education, that transmit the state's norms, shape obedient subjects, and reproduce capitalist relations.

Here, another useful tradition of Marxist theories in education relates to social reproduction, with key earlier works including Bowles and Gintis (1976), Willis (1977), and Bourdieu and Passeron (1977).[14] The basic argument of this school of social reproduction theorists was that educational institutions, contrary to their professed ideals of promoting equality, performed the opposite by reproducing and reinforcing the inequalities and hierarchies of the dominant capitalist order in a given country (Collins, 2009).

We are indebted to both of these modes of thinking about the university. Ideology-based frameworks emphasize the ways that university education, structure, and organization provide the material foundation for the naturalization of capitalist social relations. In form as in content, such frameworks suggest that educational institutions think themselves through *us*. In this way, they displace thought and consciousness from a sovereign or self-determined figure to a complicated effect and negotiation with the arrangement of the world. Social reproduction-focused approaches, by contrast, shift the focus from the question of how capitalism naturalizes and rationalizes itself at the level of ideas. Their aim is to account more holistically for how capitalism continues itself over time—from today's working day to tomorrow's as much as from one generation to the next.

Our intervention emerges from one location that the ideological and social reproduction frameworks approach but do not fully account for: the way that an essential feature that defines higher education in its historicity is its *accumulative*, not simply the educative, function. Accumulation, in this regard, is a prior condition of education: it makes the latter possible *at scale*, and the scaling up of education is driven by the convergence and (re)articulation of different accumulation projects. The reconceptualization of higher education along these lines leads us toward an approach that we see as a generative supplement to the ideological and social reproduction frameworks: namely, what we might provisionally call the *infrastructural* approach to higher education.

The infrastructural approach to education and accumulation might unfold around a cluster of different perspectives, outlined very briefly here:

- **Land**: Absent land, no infrastructure is possible. Therefore, attention to the continued accumulation processes that form the land base of university operations and architecture offers a crucial perspective (Sorber, 2018). Because this accumulation is dependent on extinguishing other (i.e., indigenous) claims to the land, displacement is a key feature of this process (Lee et al., 2020; Urbanski, 2022);
- **Capital**: University infrastructures facilitate the accumulation and flow of different forms of capital. University building and expansion at the public level is often conducted through public campaigns that leverage confidence in state solvency to issue low-interest bonds. In many locations, universities are the foundation of local real estate markets, where they operate as both massive investor in real estate investment trusts and as landlord (Chua et al., 2023);
- **Population:** On the scale of the nation-state, the multi-year absorptive function of schools, colleges, and universities to prevent crises of surplus populations (e.g., with the G.I. Bill, absorbing veterans returning from World War II), maintains what Marx (1992) called a 'reserve army';
- **Labor:** University infrastructure enhances states' absorptive capacities for labor. Because labor force calculations exclude students (as workers or as unemployed), and because university education is an overwhelming prerequisite for employment, the tens of millions enrolled in universities supply a labor force that either pays to work or works for no wages (Caffentzis,

1975). Because universities link private concerns with flows of public resources and legitimacy, capital can rely on them, at little or no cost, for reproducing a set of skills, knowledges, and habits that it requires. Universities additionally employ a considerable and deeply segregated labor force and operate as a significant agency in the overall social architecture of exploitation (Kelley, 1996);

- **Knowledge:** With the reconfiguration of the racial-capitalist mode of production from slavery to the post-emancipation era, capital needs new sciences for guiding and legitimating the means of accumulation, extraction, and hierarchization as they expand and transform in reaction to shifting social, political, environmental, and economic conditions. These include sciences of agriculture, mining, population, statistics, race, sex, eugenics, childhood, among others (Wilder, 2013; Sorber, 2011; Foster & Magdoff, 1998; Marcus, 1985).

One of our reasons for turning to an infrastructural approach is that it can help overcome the limits of the ideological and social reproduction frameworks with their critique-based mode of theory. Their focus on critique makes them ignore the alternative modes of life—alternative to the racial-colonial capitalist world—that people are enacting all the time. Further, this neglect limits their ability to see how changes in the capitalist system are often reactions to these alternatives as they create threats to its dominance. Critique can become its own mode of organizing. Thereby, it can be accumulated, absorbed, and contained in the university. Thus, a mode of theory based on critique is insufficient for an abolitionist approach to universities. Instead, an abolitionist perspective calls for going beyond critique to an affirmative mode of theory—one that affirms the practices of world-making movements alternative to capitalism. This mode of theory supports abolitionism's dual-sided character, in the sense of being both world-ending and world-making.

Our inspiration for thinking about different 'modes of theory' is from Nick Montgomery and carla bergman's Joyful Militancy (2017). They contrast a critique-and-direction based mode of theory with an 'affirmative mode of theory,' which is 'a kind of theory that participates in struggle and the growth of shared power rather than directing it or evaluating it from the outside,' and it highlights how 'people are always enacting alternatives to the dominant order of things, however small, and there are always new connections and potentials to explore' (pp. 27–28). They draw their 'affirmative mode of theory' from a wide variety of radical movement-grounded intellectuals, including anarchists and autonomist Marxists. The autonomist Marxist feminist, Silvia Federici (2004), practices this kind of affirmative theory with her highlighting of rebellious women's feminist commons and networks of care that enact alternatives to the capitalist, patriarchal family. The anti-colonial Marxist, Glen Coulthard (Yellowknives Dene), theorizes the 'grounded normativity' of indigenous peoples' reciprocal relationships with the land that ground the ethical frameworks of their world-making projects that are alternative and resistant to settler-colonial capitalism (2014, p. 60). Further sources for affirmative modes of theory in Marxist traditions include the autonomist Marxists' use of 'general intellect' and 'mass intellectuality,' which Hall and Winn (2017, p. 3) describe as a way to call 'attention to the proliferation of alternative educational practices,' which are 'rooted in the desire and potential for reclaiming the knowledge, skills, practices and techniques that form the general intellect.'

Another such source is Stuart Hall's use of Antonio Gramsci, which Jack Halberstam (2011 p. 16) describes as 'low theory': 'Hall says, Gramsci practiced a genuinely 'open' Marxism … Open here means questioning, open to unpredictable outcomes, not fixed on a telos, unsure, adaptable, shifting, flexible, and adjustable.' Halberstam presents (p. 18) a 'great example of low theory' in Peter Linebaugh and Marcus Rediker's The Many-Headed Hydra: Sailors, Slaves, Commoners, and the Hidden History of the Revolutionary Atlantic (2000), which 'traces what they call "the struggles for alternative ways of life" that accompanied and opposed the rise of capitalism in the early seventeenth century.'

From the abolitionist, Black radical tradition, we also find examples of affirmative, low modes of theory, which variously overlap and have tensions with Marxism. W.E.B. Du Bois (1969) highlighted the perspectives of Black people's 'bottom up' struggles, such as in his theorizing of the 'general strike of the enslaved' that was crucial for the Union victory in the Civil War. Likewise, his theorization of 'abolition democracy' affirmed the revolutionary political agency of Black people during the Reconstruction period. The radical Black geographer, Clyde Woods (1998, p. 29), theorized the 'blues epistemology' of African-American, working-class intellectual traditions and social organizations that emerged from their struggles against the plantation regime.

A key theorist of the Black radical tradition, Cedric Robinson, in *Black Marxism* (2000), according to Joshua Myers (2023, p. 174), gives a critique of 'the Marxist conceit that Black people were merely cargo, a laboring class of junior partners in a still-to-come revolution,' to instead give a history of Black resistance that shows 'how a tradition of Black folk who struggled against capitalist modernity devised its own practices of revolution, as well as how it existed alongside other traditions.' The contemporary abolitionist and critical disability studies scholar, Liat Ben-Moshe (2020, p. 126), theorizes both 'abolitionist epistemology and dis-epistemology,' in which the latter involves 'letting go of attachment to certain ways of knowing,' including 'forms of knowledge that rely on certainty,' 'prescriptive and professional expertise,' and 'specific demands for futurity.'

By combining an affirmative mode of theory with infrastructural analysis, we see the latter as a form of 'abolitionist dis-epistemology.' Infrastructure normally 'recedes into the background for those who are not busy building or repairing or analyzing it' (Hetherington, 2019, p. 6). Conversely, infrastructural analysis is 'the performance of a figure-ground reversal, what Bowker (1994) called "infrastructural inversion," which brings the background to the foreground.' Infrastructural analysis involves destabilizing and letting go of attachments to one's knowledge of what is normally foregrounded and backgrounded, letting go of a desire for the comfortable certainty of the taken-for-granted background structures, bringing them to the foreground, problematizing their previously assumed 'infra-ness,' and treating them as controversial matters that need critical analysis through tracing their connections with other entities. Discussing something as infrastructure is, what Larkin (2013, p. 330) calls, a 'categorical act,' or 'a moment of tearing into those heterogenous networks to define which aspect of which network is to be discussed and which parts will be ignored.' As a tactic for an affirmative mode of theory, infrastructural analysis articulates new, open-ended questions that call for tracing new connections and raising controversies about them. Any infrastructural analysis frames questions in a necessarily selective way, and if the analyst is reflective about this selectivity, the analysis 'comprises a cultural analytic that highlights the epistemological and political commitments involved in selecting what one sees as infrastructural (and thus causal) and what one leaves out.'

An infrastructural analysis foregrounds and treats as controversial the educational institutions that are normally treated as taken-for-granted background structures. To take a view of schools, colleges, and universities as *infrastructure* is to make a conceptual flip of how we normally view them—that is, as being the foregrounded institutions that are supported by other systems, which are seen as background infrastructure (e.g., roads, water and wastewater treatment, stormwater, electricity, communication, governmental administration, corporations, etc.). Through this 'infrastructural inversion,' we grapple with the many tensions involved in thinking of education in infrastructural terms.

On this view, we can ask how re-situating education institutions as infrastructural, and thinking of their interrelations with other infrastructures, can shift our epistemological and political commitments in ways more useful for understanding and engaging with abolitionist struggles in our current conjuncture.[15] Particularly, this kind of infrastructural analysis is useful for affirming the agency of actors who are normally excluded from or marginalized in social movement activities, including children and those who are framed as child-like in normative discourses. According to Toby Rollo (2022, p. 160), childhood is 'a modality of being in which certain forms of human agency—the child's unmediated, exploratory, and experimental ways of engaging with the world—are most prominent and privileged,' and these forms of agency continue into adulthood, while combining with representational, linguistic, and logical forms of agency. Their agency is treated as not-yet-fully human, partly because it is seen as in formation through their development in education institutions. Marxist approaches tend to be 'almost entirely unconcerned or unaware of childhood emancipatory agency,' as they 'include the young only as child laborers who must be liberated (usually so they can attend school …) or as passive objects of adult labor (e.g., collective childcare).'[16]

By devaluing children's agency, Marxists also implicitly devalue the agency of those people who are treated as child-like in normative discourses, including

Black people and indigenous people (who have been demeaned in white-supremacist, colonial discourses as 'child races'), as well as women and disabled people (Rollo, 2018). Marx's critique-and-direct mode of theory elevates adults' representational agency while devaluing children's non-representational, enactive agency. By contrast, an affirmative, low mode of theory could resonate with and involve children (and other childized people), affirming their agency as co-participants in shared struggles, and most importantly, to support the alternative world-making movements that they are already enacting.

27.6 Conclusion: Infrastructures of Abolition, Liberation, and Decolonization

With an affirmative mode of theory, an infrastructural framing offers abolitionists a better way to talk about their dual-sided approach of simultaneous world-ending and world-making: attending to infrastructures both of the racial-capitalist world and alternative worlds. For thinking about abolitionist infrastructures, Ruth Wilson Gilmore speaks of the 'infrastructure of feeling' that constitutes 'the Black Radical Tradition' as 'a constantly evolving accumulation of structures of feeling whose individual and collective narrative arcs persistently tend toward freedom' (2017, pp. 237–8).

Reflecting on the George Floyd uprising in Minneapolis, Charmaine Chua theorizes the 'local efforts to build an abolitionist infrastructure' of 'care and repair' by 'mutual aid organizers [who] sought to engage Minneapolis residents in intentional, affirmative, and often fractious efforts to organize forms of collective care and provisioning' (2020, p. 129). In the wake of disasters of hurricanes and floods in the Caribbean that ruined the capitalist, statist infrastructure, Leniqueca A. Welcome highlights 'the liberatory infrastructures being crafted from crisis by the Caribbean populations most vulnerable to disasters,' with their 'abolitionist praxis' both dismantling the dominant order and building 'the political infrastructure necessary for achieving freedom for all' (2020, pp. 98–99). Combined with abolitionist praxis within and against the capitalist educational infrastructures, we can also organize *outside* them for building alternative studying practices and counter-institutions that are bound up with radical organizing. These might reflect upon the history of the people's schools and labor schools that were organized by the Communist Party in the 1940s–1950s (Hines, 2022).

Considering such abolitionist infrastructures of mutual aid, solidarity, and grounded relationships with the land, we can ask how studying can happen in and through these infrastructures in ways alternative to the educational infrastructures of capitalism. How should abolitionist organizers relate with the dominant educational infrastructures—grappling with the tensions of organizing within, against, and beyond them? How can they try to dismantle the educational infrastructures, transform them, escape from them, and/or steal resources from them for use in abolitionist movements? How can they engage in such studying and organizing in ways that avoid absorption, co-optation, and pacification? Drawing from geographer Kai Bosworth (2022), we ask: what is the 'ratio' between, on the one hand, the technical alienation that we experience as cogs in the machine of the dominant infrastructures and, on the other hand, our political-affective organizing of infrastructures that expand our collective capacities for making alternative worlds? How does the education infrastructure's individualizing affects (of shame, honor, and anxiety) separate us from our collective capacities and limit our ability to understand the causes of our reduced capacities? Conversely, how can alternative modes of studying in abolitionist infrastructures build our capacities for collective analysis and action?

Disclosure Statement None of the authors has any financial interest or benefit that has arisen from the direct applications of this research.

Notes

1. This distinction was developed partly out of a systemic architecture famously outlined by Kant in his oft-cited 1798 essay *The Conflict of the Faculties*. There, as Wellmon (2016, p. 145) describes it, Kant had 'explicitly made the case that the university was the only technology capable of sustaining the continuity of philosophy, and thus scientific thought, as a practice.'
2. For a longer consideration of these arguments, see Boggs et al. (2019).
3. To specify: 'men' here does not signify a general term for humanity in general. German universities did not admit women until well into the twentieth century.
4. One can of course only criticize after dinner if there is already dinner on the table, thus pointing to one of the persistent criticisms by Marxist feminists of Marx's failure to rigorously account for the labor of social reproduction in his theory of capitalism or his speculations about communist society.
5. Marx's third thesis on Feuerbach, for instance, uses the problem of education as a framework for understanding the problem of revolutionary praxis as a whole (Marx, 1969).
6. On ambivalence and infrastructure, see Berlant (2016).
7. Cited in Anderson (2010, p. 83). Marx in Marx and Engels (1975b, p. 168).
8. Some key texts on contemporary abolitionism include: Critical Resistance (2008), Davis (2003), Gilmore (2022), Kaba (2021), Kaba and Ritchie (2022), Purnell (2021).
9. This sentence and much of the following paragraphs in this section are reproduced from our earlier essay, Boggs et al. (2019).
10. See, inter alia, Coulthard (2014), Du Bois (1969 [1935]), Federici (2004), Harvey (2004), Luxemburg (2013 [1913]), Melamed (2015), Robinson (2000 [1983]).
11. Attention to accumulation helps us get to the import for a history of the university present that diverges from the dominant approach of Critical University Studies, the decade-or-so-old para-disciplinary formation which has eked out a meaningful institutional footprint and intellectual impact. Some key texts in Critical University Studies include: Williams (2012), Readings (1996), Slaughter

and Leslie (1997), Noble (2001), Ohmann (2003), Washburn (2005), Berry (2005), Bousquet (2008), Donoghue (2008), Newfield (2008), Massé and Hogan (2010), Mettler (2014), Newfield (2016).
12. Recent scholarship includes: Wilder (2013), Lee et al. (2020), Harris et al. (2019), Paperson (2017, Stein (2022), Fuentes and White (2016), Williams et al. (2021), Rothman and Mendoza (2021). Also, see the Universities Studying Slavery consortium's website at https://slavery.virginia.edu/universities-studying-slavery/
13. The Yellowknives Dene political theorist Glen Sean Coulthard defines settler colonialism as a form of 'structured dispossession,' a 'particular form of domination; that is, it is a relationship where power—in this case, interrelated discursive and nondiscursive facets of economic, gendered, racial, and state power—has been structured into a relatively secure or sedimented set of hierarchical social relations that continue to facilitate the dispossession of Indigenous peoples of their lands and self-determining authority.'# For Coulthard, the dispossessions of the various settler-colonial projects—his immediate referent is Canada—are fundamentally the dispossessions described by Marx in the section on 'so-called primitive accumulation,' which concludes the first volume of *Capital*. If, for Marx, dispossession and enclosure are violent processes central to the expropriation of the worker and thus the creation of a proletariat with no ability to sustain itself beyond the ability to sell its own labor-power for a wage, in the context of settler colonialism, Coulthard argues, dispossession must be taken seriously in its own right, rather than as a mere prelude to subsequent proletarianization (Coulthard, 2014, pp. 6–7,9–15).
14. Our critique of social reproductionists here applies to this earlier work and not to the more recent, more nuanced theories of social reproduction that have been developed by Marxist feminists (such as Ferguson, 2017).
15. We are not the first to theorize 'education as infrastructure.' One precedent is in Alex Posecznick's book (2017), which is based on his ethnography of a small regional university. Another is a recent dissertation by Sarah D'Adamo (2022) who, like us, takes an infrastructural and abolitionist approach to university studies, as she 'reads the global projects of [US and Canadian] higher education systems as an infrastructure that conditions learning and credentialing as forms of anti-social, settler national and managerial self-development,' and she 'argues that the double binds produced by university globalism in these settings present a pedagogical occasion for abolitionist study in our time of planetary crises' (dissertation abstract).
16. Rollo (2016, pp. 248–9). On Marx's neglect of the importance of play for children, in favor of labor and education as essential for human development, see Small (1982).

References

Althusser, L. (1971). Ideology and Ideological State Apparatuses (Notes Towards an Investigation). In *Lenin and Philosophy and Other Chapters*. Monthly Review Press.

Anderson, K. (2010). *Marx at the Margins: On Nationalism, Ethnicity, and Non-Western Societies*. University of Chicago Press.

Armstrong-Price, M. (2015). Securitization, Risk Management, and the New University. *Reclaim UC*. Retrieved March 14, 2023, from https://reclaimuc.blogspot.com/2015/01/securitization-risk-management-and-new.html

Arnn, L. P., Swain, C. M., & Spalding, M. (Eds.). (2021). *The 1776 Report*. Encounter Books.

Ben-Moshe, L. (2020). *Decarcerating Disability: Deinstitutionaliztion and Prison Abolition*. University of Minnesota Press.

Berlant, L. (2016). The Commons: Infrastructures for Troubling Times. *Environment and Planning D: Society and Space, 34*, 393–419. https://doi.org/10.1177/0263775816645989

Berry, J. (2005). *Reclaiming the Ivory Tower: Organizing Adjuncts to Change Higher Education*. Monthly Review Press.

Boggs, A., Meyerhoff, E., Mitchell, N., & Schwartz-Weinstein, Z. (2019). Abolitionist University Studies: an Invitation. *Abolition: A Journal of Insurgent Politics*. Retrieved March 14, 2023, from https://abolitionjournal.org/abolitionist-university-studies-an-invitation/

Bosworth, K. (2022). What is "Affective Infrastructure"? *Dialogues in Human Geography, 13*(1), 1–19. https://doi.org/10.1177/20438206221107025

Bourdieu, P., & Passeron, J. (1977). *Reproduction in Education, Society, and Culture*. Sage.

Bousquet, M. (2008). *How the University Works*. New York University Press.

Bowker, G. (1994). Information Mythology and Infrastructure. In L. Bud-Frierman (Ed.), *Information Acumen: The Understanding and Use of Knowledge in Modern Business* (pp. 231–247). Taylor and Francis.

Bowles, S., & Gintis, H. (1976). *Schooling in Capitalist America: Educational Reform and the Contradictions of Economic Life*. Basic Books.

Brock, W. (2002). *Justus von Liebig: The Chemical Gatekeeper*. Cambridge University Press.

Caffentzis, G. (1975). Throwing Away the Ladder: The Universities in the Crisis. *Zerowork, 1*, 128–142.

Chase-Dunn, C., & Hall, T. (1997). *Rise and Demise: Comparing World-Systems*. Routledge.

Chua, C. (2020). Abolition is a Constant Struggle: Five Lessons from Minneapolis. *Theory & Event, 23*(4), 127–147. Retrieved March 14, 2023, from https://www.muse.jhu.edu/article/775394

Chua, C., Fields, D., & Stein, D. (2023). When the Public University Is the Corporate Landlord. *LPE Project*. Retrieved March 14, 2023, from https://lpeproject.org/blog/when-the-public-university-is-the-corporate-landlord/

Collins, J. (2009). Social Reproduction in Classrooms and Schools. *Annual Review of Anthropology, 38*, 33–48. https://doi.org/10.1146/annurev.anthro.37.081407.085242

Coulthard, G. (2014). *Red Skin, White Masks: Rejecting the Colonial Politics of Recognition*. University of Minnesota Press.

Critical Resistance. (2008). *Abolition Now! Ten Years of Strategy and Struggle Against the Prison Industrial Complex*. AK Press.

D'Adamo, S. (2022). *Globalism for Undergraduates: Pedagogies and Technologies of Global Education in the US and Canada*. PhD Dissertation. McMaster University. Retrieved March 14, 2023, from https://macsphere.mcmaster.ca/handle/11375/28179

Davis, A. Y. (2003). *Are Prisons Obsolete?* Seven Stories Press.
Davis, A. Y. (2005). *Abolition Democracy.* Seven Stories Press.
Denning, M. (2010). Wageless Life. *New Left Review, 66*, 79–97. Retrieved March 14, 2023, from https://newleftreview.org/issues/II66/articles/michael-denning-wageless-life
Donoghue, F. (2008). *The Last Professors: The Corporate University and the Fate of the Humanities.* Fordham University Press.
Du Bois, W. E. B. (1969 [1935]). *Black Reconstruction in America: An Chapter Toward a History of the Part Which Black Folk Played in the Attempt to Reconstruct Democracy in America, 1860–1880.* Atheneum.
Federici, S. (2004). *Caliban and the Witch: Women, the Body, and Primitive Accumulation.* Autonomedia.
Ferguson, S. (2017). Children, Childhood and Capitalism: A Social Reproduction Perspective. In T. Bhattacharya (Ed.), *Social Reproduction Theory: Remapping Class, Recentering Oppression* (pp. 112–130). Pluto Press.
Foster, J. B., & Magdoff, F. (1998). Liebig, Marx, and the Depletion of Soil Fertility: Relevance for Today's Agriculture. *Monthly Review, 50*(3), 32–45.
Fuentes, M. J., & White, D. G. (2016). *Scarlet and Black, Volume 1: Slavery and Dispossession in Rutgers History.* Rutgers University Press.
Gilmore, R. W. (2007). *Golden Gulag: Prisons, Surplus, Crisis, and Opposition In Globalizing California.* University of California Press.
Gilmore, R. W. (2017). Abolition Geography and the Problem of Innocence. In G. T. Johnson & A. Lubin (Eds.), *Futures of Black Radicalism* (pp. 225–240). Verso Books.
Gilmore, R. W. (2022). *Abolition Geography: Chapters Toward Liberation.* Verso.
Halberstam, J. (2011). *The Queer Art of Failure.* Duke University Press.
Hall, R., & Winn, J. (2017). Mass Intellectuality and Democratic Leadership in Higher Education. In R. Hall & J. Winn (Eds.), *Mass Intellectuality and Democratic Leadership in Higher Education* (pp. 1–15). Bloomsbury.
Hannah-Jones, N. (Ed.). (2021). *The 1619 Project: A New Origin Story.* One World.
Harney, S., & Moten, F. (2013). *The Undercommons: Fugitive Planning & Black Study.* Minor Compositions.
Harris, L. M., Campbell, J. T., & Brophy, A. L. (Eds.). (2019). *Slavery and the University: Histories and Legacies.* University of Georgia Press.
Harvey, D. (2004). The 'New' Imperialism: Accumulation by Dispossession. *Socialist Register, 40*, 63–87. Retrieved March 14, 2023, from https://socialistregister.com/index.php/srv/article/view/5811/2707
Hetherington, K. (2019). *Infrastructure, Environment, and Life in The Anthropocene.* Duke University Press.
Hines, A. (2022). *Outside Literary Studies: Black Criticism and The University.* University of Chicago.
Kaba, M. (2021). *We Do This 'Til We Free Us: Abolitionist Organizing and Transformative Justice.* Haymarket Books.
Kaba, M., & Ritchie, A. (2022). *No More Police: A Case for Abolition.* The New Press.
Kant, I. (1992). *The Conflict of the Faculties* (M. J. Gregor, Trans.). University of Nebraska Press.
Karuka, M. (2019). *Empire's Tracks: Indigenous Nations, Chinese Workers, and the Transcontinental Railroad.* University of California Press.

Karuka, M. (2022). Riding with Du Bois. *Public Books*. Retrieved March 14, 2023, from https://www.publicbooks.org/racial-divisions-railroads-infrastructure/

Kelley, R. D. G. (1996). The Proletariat Goes to College. *Social Text, 49, The Yale Strike Dossier*, 37–42.

Larkin, B. (2013). The Politics and Poetics of Infrastructure. *Annual Review of Anthropology*, 42, 327–343. https://doi.org/10.1146/annurev-anthro-092412-155522

Lee, R., Ahtone, T., Pearce, M., Goodluck, K., McGhee, G., Leff, C., Lanpher, K., & Salinas, T. (2020). Land-Grab Universities: A High Country News Investigation. *High Country News*. Retrieved March 14, 2023, from https://landgrabu.org

Linebaugh, P., & Rediker, M. (2000). *The Many-Headed Hydra: Sailors, Slaves, Commoners, and the Hidden History of the Revolutionary Atlantic*. Beacon Press.

Luxemburg, R. (2013 [1913]). *The Accumulation of Capital* (A. Schwartzschild, Trans.). Routledge.

Marcus, A. (1985). *Agricultural Science and the Quest for Legitimacy: Farmers, Agricultural Colleges, and Experiment Stations, 1870–1890*. Iowa State University Press.

Marx, K. (1969). Theses on Feuerbach. *Marx/Engels Selected Works, Volume One* (W. Lough, Trans.) (pp. 13–15). Progress Publishers.

Marx, K. (1975). Letters from the Deutsch-Französische Jahrbücher. *Karl Marx and Friedrich Engels: Collected Works, Volume 3, Marx and Engels 1843–1844* (C. Dutt, Trans.). International Publishers.

Marx, K. (1992). *Capital, Volume One* (B. Fowkes, Trans.). Penguin.

Marx. K., & Engels, F. (1975a). The manifesto of the Communist Party. *Collected Works of Karl Marx and Friedrich Engels, 1845–48, Volume 6*, 477–519. International Publishers.

Marx, K., & Engels, F. (1975b). *Collected works of Karl Marx and Friedrich Engels, 1845–48, Volume 6*. International Publishers.

Marx, K., & Engels, F. (1998). *The German Ideology*. Prometheus Books.

Marx, K., & Engels, F. (2010). *Marx and Engels collected works, 1861–64, Volume 19*. Lawrence & Wishart.

Massé, M., & Hogan, K. (2010). *Over Ten Million Served: Gendered Service in Language and Literature Workplaces*. State University of New York, NY Press.

Maynard, R., & Simpson, L. B. (2022). *Rehearsals for Living*. Haymarket Books.

Melamed, J. (2015). Racial Capitalism. *Critical Ethnic Studies*, 1(1), 76–85. https://doi.org/10.5749/jcritethnstud.1.1.0076

Mettler, S. (2014). *Degrees of Inequality: How the Politics of Higher Education Sabotaged the American Dream*. Basic Books.

Meyerhoff, E. (2019). *Beyond Education: Radical Studying for Another World*. University of Minnesota Press.

Montgomery, N., & Bergman, C. (2017). *Joyful Militancy: Building Thriving Resistance in Toxic Times*. AK Press.

Myers, J. (2023). *Of Black Study*. Pluto Press.

Newfield, C. (2008). *Unmaking the Public University: The Forty-Year Assault on The Middle Class*. Harvard University Press.

Newfield, C. (2016). *The Great Mistake: How We Wrecked Public Universities and How We Can Fix Them*. Johns Hopkins University Press.

Noble, D. (2001). *Digital Diploma Mills: The Automation of Higher Education*. Monthly Review Press.

Ohmann, R. (2003). *Politics of Knowledge: The Commercialization of The University, The Professions, and Print Culture*. Wesleyan University Press.

Paperson, L. (2017). *A Third University is Possible*. University of Minnesota Press.

Posecznick, A. (2017). *Selling Hope and College: Merit, Markets, and Recruitment in an Unranked School*. Cornell University Press.

Purnell, D. (2021). *Becoming Abolitionists: Police, Protests, and the Pursuit Of Freedom*. Astra House.

Readings, B. (1996). *The University in Ruins*. Harvard University Press.

Reitter, P., & Wellmon, C. (2021). *Permanent crisis: The Humanities in a Disenchanted Age*. University of Chicago Press.

Robinson, C. (2000 [1983]). *Black Marxism: The Making of the Black Radical Tradition*. University of North Carolina Press.

Roediger, D. (1991). *The Wages of Whiteness: Race and The Making of The American Working Class*. Verso.

Rollo, T. (2016). Democracy, Agency, and Radical Children's Geographies. In R. J. White, S. Springer, & M. L. de Souza (Eds.), *The Practice of Freedom: Anarchism, Geography, and the Spirit of Revolt* (Vol. 3, pp. 233–253). Rowman & Littlefield.

Rollo, T. (2018). The Color of Childhood: The Role of the Child/Human Binary in the Production of Anti-Black Racism. *Journal of Black Studies, 49*(4), 307–329. https://doi.org/10.1177/0021934718760769

Rollo, T. (2022). Childing the World. In C. J. Bergman (Ed.), *Trust Kids: Stories on Youth Autonomy and Confronting Adult Supremacy*. AK Press.

Rothman, A., & Mendoza, E. B. (Eds.). (2021). *Facing Georgetown's History: A Reader on Slavery, Memory, and Reconciliation*. Georgetown University Press.

Slaughter, S., & Leslie, L. (1997). *Academic Capitalism: Politics, Policies, and the Entrepreneurial University*. Johns Hopkins University Press.

Small, R. (1982). Work, Play and School in Marx's Views on Education. *The Journal of Educational Thought, 16*(3), 161–173.

Sorber, N. (2011). *Farmers, Scientists, and Officers of Industry: The Formation and Reformation of Land-Grant Colleges in the Northeastern United States, 1862–1906*. Ph.D. Dissertation. Pennsylvania State University. Retrieved March 14, 2023, from https://eric.ed.gov/?id=ED540338

Sorber, N. (2018). *Land Grant Colleges and Popular Revolt: The Origins of the Morrill Act And the Reform of Higher Education*. Cornell University Press.

Sperber, J. (2013). *Karl Marx: A Nineteenth Century Life*. Liveright.

Stein, S. (2022). *Unsettling the University: Confronting the Colonial Foundations of US Higher Education*. Johns Hopkins University Press.

Urbanski, C. (2022). *Spiritual Conquest: Desecration and Settler Colonial Extraction on Sacred and Stolen Lands*. Ph.D. Dissertation. University of California, Santa Cruz. Retrieved March 14, 2023, from https://escholarship.org/uc/item/4c65w7kg

Washburn, J. (2005). *University, Inc.: The Corporate Corruption of Higher Education*. Basic Books.

Welcome, L.A. (2020). The Infrastructures of Liberation at the End of the World: A Reflection on Disaster in the Caribbean. *Small Axe, 24*(2), 96–109. Retrieved March 14, 2023, from https://muse.jhu.edu/article/762559

Wellmon, C. (2016). *Organizing Enlightenment: Information Overload and the Invention of the Modern Research University*. Johns Hopkins.

Wilder, C. S. (2013). *Ebony and Ivy: Race, Slavery, and the Troubled History of America's Universities*. Bloomsbury Press.

Williams, B. C., Squire, D. D., & Tuitt, F. A. (2021). *Plantation Politics and Campus Rebellions*. State University of New York, NY Press.

Williams, J. J. (2012). Deconstructing Academe: The Birth of Critical University Studies, *The Chronicle of Higher Education*. Retrieved March 14, 2023, from https://www.chronicle.com/article/deconstructing-academe/

Willis, P. (1977). *Learning to Labor: How Working Class Kids Get Working Class Jobs*. Columbia University Press.

Woods, C. (1998). *Development Arrested: The Blues and Plantation Power In The Mississippi Delta*. Verso.

CHAPTER 28

Toward a Decolonial Marxism: Considering the Dialectics and Analectics in the Counter-Geographies of Women of the Global South

Lilia D. Monzó and Nidžara Pečenković

28.1 Introduction

It is important for Marxist scholars and activists to engage with Marx's works in light of today's concrete struggles. For us, this means recognizing the brilliance of his philosophy of revolution, and, especially, the humanism he developed that acknowledges our agency as makers of history (Marx, 1961; Dunayevskaya, 2000). However, this also recognizes that Marx was writing at a particular historical time and from a particular vantage point. Much work has been developed since that draws on Marx's philosophy but also challenges it. Engaging this work, especially when it is written from the perspective of the Global South, which in some ways derives from the vantage point of the peoples that Marx claimed to be the revolutionary Subject, is critical. Paulo Freire (2005, p. 44) reiterated this argument more succinctly when he stated that 'the great humanistic and historical task of the oppressed [is] to liberate themselves and their oppressors as well.'

L. D. Monzó (✉)
Chapman University, Orange, CA, USA
e-mail: monzo@chapman.edu

N. Pečenković
Santiago Canyon College, Orange, CA, USA
e-mail: pecenkovic@chapman.edu

© The Editor(s) (if applicable) and The Author(s), under exclusive license to Springer Nature Switzerland AG 2023
R. Hall et al. (eds.), *The Palgrave International Handbook of Marxism and Education*, Marxism and Education,
https://doi.org/10.1007/978-3-031-37252-0_28

One of the most important aspects of Marx's philosophy of revolution is the dialectic, based on Hegel's model of development toward freedom, as the resolution of contradictions (Hegel, 1977). This philosophy is based on the struggle for negation as necessary to the development of a new humanism. An important movement coming from the Global South, in particular from Latin America and the decolonial school of thought whose ideas are rooted in Duselian philosophy, is that breaking down is not necessary for building up (Alcoff, 2019). Dussel engages Marxist thought but argues for an analectic of liberation—a process of building up, bringing together what has been learned throughout history for the purpose of liberation (Dussel, 2019). Here, development challenges the assumption that the illusion of binaries is at the heart of relations of domination and instead argues for a perspective of development that centers on learning and building knowledge as we develop. This is a process of letting go of that which is oppressive and adopting more progressive and humanizing values and practices as we move through the world as historical beings.

Marx, as a journalist, concerned himself with following the movement of the people (Dunayevskaya, 1991). In this process, we saw him develop new ideas and reverse earlier ones; in particular, the Eurocentrism of his youth began to dissipate as he grew in knowledge about the Non-western world.[1] His ideas can be traced to the specific struggles that he witnessed happening in the world at the time, which he often had to investigate as a journalist. He came to an understanding, which we fully support, that it is the people whose knowledge of their particular circumstances must be heard and understood to develop a revolution from the ground up (Monzó, 2021). Marx argued that the intellectuals are too far removed from the social conditions of the oppressed and instead often seek to do *for* the oppressed, revealing an elitism that Dunayevskaya (1991) argued is dangerous in its potential to turn revolutionary efforts into their very opposites.

In this chapter, we question and examine the histories of the dialectic and analectic to understand the extent to which they derive from the struggles of their day. We question whether only one universal form of development is observed in today's concrete struggles and in particular one that has been highly influenced by the women of the Global South, specifically the Zapatistas, to understand the ways in which the analectic and/or the dialectic can be discerned. We also discuss what these concepts mean for education.

28.2 The Dialectic—Development as the Resolution of Contradictions

Marx's philosophy of revolution is grounded on the dialectic, which gave rise to the perception of history as a possibility and the human Subject as a protagonist. Marx's dialectic, often referred to as dialectical materialism, can be traced back conceptually to Hegel, whose thought was influenced by and went beyond Kant's 'transcendental dialectic' and his 'antinomies of pure reason.' Kant (1998) was concerned with articulating a philosophy that allowed for *a priori* judgements that went beyond both analytical reasoning and empirical science; that is, universal regulatory categories of thought which held commonsense beliefs and moral groundings, including the belief in God, freedom, and immortality. Kant believed that although we were not born with any innate knowledge, we were born with categories of thought that interacted with our external world in ways that affect experience. Specifically, Kant argued that space and time were 'pure forms of intuition' that allowed us to make sense of the world spatially and temporally and that, therefore, we could only come to know objects in the world through these sensibilities. This was his answer to the antinomies that he believed troubled metaphysics. That is, he believed that for every argument there was a counterposing argument—a thesis and an antithesis—that seemed naturally plausible. According to Kant, the only way to resolve these contradictions was to accept the transcendental ideal—that objects can never be known *in themselves*; rather, they can be known only in relation to experience, as they appear to us—as *objects for us* (Kant, 1998).

Hegel argued that Kant's treatment of the categories as regulative forms that gave objects content through sensuous perception had left them empty and set out in *Logics* to show these categories as having content of their own. Hegel's treatment of the categories opened them up to go beyond guiding our understanding of sensual experience to also 'disclose by themselves—the purely intelligible structure of the world' (Houlgate, 2015, p. 24). The content of 'categories of thought,' in Hegel's development, consists in the complex unities of opposing determinations (Houlgate, 2015). Furthermore, Hegel rejected the view that all we could come to know was the appearance of things, for then, surely, experience itself would also be only appearance. According to Houlgate (2015), Hegel perceives that Kant reduces knowledge of the world to appearance because he treats the two most important components of his philosophy—sensible intuition and the categories—as subjective. Because the categories are treated as subjective, they turn all objects we perceive as *objects for us*.

Hegel rejected Kant's purely subjective knowledge. He argued that if the thing is the object of knowledge then to know the thing always *differently than as it is* is to know nothing. In *Logics*, Hegel completely disavows that our thoughts, because the source is the Subject, are only our thoughts and rejects the strict separation of object and subject. For Hegel, the 'categories of quantity, causality, and so on, disclose the quantity and causality in being itself, and so in that sense belong to being as much as they do to thought' (Houlgate, 2015, p. 30). Furthermore, if reasoning is contradictory, then the object of thought must also be contradictory. Hegel argued that in understanding the object through these *a priori* categories, we are also drawing on the object *in itself*. He noted that the unity of subject and object allows for negation, which gives us the *thing in itself*. The object is the negative of the categories' determinate thought. Furthermore, Hegel was able to perceive the positive that could result from the antinomies through their unity.

Hegel (1977) sets out to demonstrate how these contradictions were resolved in history and moved development forward, potentially toward the ultimate objective of our species being—the realization of freedom. Examining the history of science and philosophy, Hegel posits principles of identity that reveal the necessary contradictions between subject and object; A is A but A is also not A. Through the unity of these opposites, it can be recognized that these are actually aspects of a broader idea, an abstraction of particular diverse qualities, which together form a universal.

Specifically, Hegel (1977) elaborated a path to human development that involved the movement from consciousness (a direct apprehension of the world as it appears to be, or the knowing of the world) to self-consciousness (the recognition of our consciousness as a human abstraction—an object that turns on us as alienated reality) to the Absolute Idea, which '*alone is being, imperishable life, self-knowing truth, and is all truth* (which is affirmed in the annulment of the alienated object)' (p. 735). Hegel describes this process as the negation of the negation, or absolute negation—a process that ultimately resolves the contradiction, unifies, and presents a new and creative step forward (Anderson, 2020).

Although Hegel developed his ideas in response to the enlightenment, he did not reject science but rather developed a more dialectical view of object and subject. Some thinkers of the enlightenment era posited a science that severed the human being from their relation to nature and spirit (the Divine) and constructed an objective rationality that was tied to observable material reality in a way that denied subjectivity as mere superstition or mystical illusion. Yet for Hegel, science and rationality were not diametrically opposed but interconnected with nature and spirit. According to Cyril Smith (2002), for Hegel, science was the work tasked to humanity to complete God's purpose. Although he emphasized achieving freedom in consciousness, Hegel was highly influenced by the French Revolution and the process of industrialization that took place during his lifetime and, thus, recognized the objective reality of human subjectivity. Indeed, it was Hegel who first recognized that the 'rabble' created through capitalist industrialization would increase the subjective alienation of labor (Dunayevskaya, 1991; Ruda, 2011).

Marx took Hegel's dialectic further. Also influenced by the French Revolution and carefully following the Paris Commune, Marx came to realize that objective conditions were influenced by but also influenced subjectivity. As such, human beings could no longer be perceived as mere captives of history. It was Marx who recognized our agency and grounded us to the Earth as Subjects who *move* within it—active agents, made of body and mind, moving through history. Here, Marx recognizes that consciousness alone cannot liberate humanity. Material conditions are as much an element of development and transformation as is the Mind (Marx, 1961).

Marx appreciated and appropriated the Hegelian dialectic—the notion that development was pushed forward through the resolution of contradictions. These contradictions could be found in the underlying foundations of most of our constructed concepts or ideas—a positive and a negative position in constant tension, whose resolution allows us to move forward as a species. Yet Marx argued that Hegel's approach was faulty, his dialectic perceives a 'false positivism' that results from the self-affirmation that is achieved when we recognize the object as an alienated object of our own production. As Marx (ibid, p. 161) notes, this constitutes a process by which 'reason is at home in unreason as unreason.' This process of confirmation of self in his alienated consciousness re-establishes the alienated essence as an aspect of self-consciousness.

> In Hegel, therefore, the negation of the negation is not the confirmation of the true essence, effective precisely through negation of the pseudo-essence. With him the negation of the negations is the confirmation of the pseudo-essence, or of the self-estranged essence in its denial; or it is the denial of this pseudo-essence as an objective being dwelling outside man and independent of him, and its transformation into the subject. (ibid, p. 161)

For Marx (ibid, p. 161) 'true knowledge and life' is 'self-affirmation in contradiction with the abstracted object and self-alienation.' This negation of the negation transforms the human being into a Subject who has come to recognize their alienated character and 'supersedes' the pseudo-essence of our humanity—the abstracted object and our alienated character.

In addition, Marx critiqued Hegel for treating the subject of the dialectic as thought alone. Hegel's expression of freedom appears as consciousness freed from the shackles of a 'natural,' or naive, consciousness. Development exists as moments of true consciousness or thought that 'regards itself as free only when it is conscious of being at variance with what is generally recognized, and of setting itself up as something original' (Hegel, 1820, para. 6). Marx (1961) argued that, for Hegel, the truth of our humanity is 'hidden under sensuous disguises' (p. 162).

> ... for only *mind* is the *true* essence of man and the true form of mind is thinking mind, the logical, speculative mind. ... The *humanness* of nature and of the nature begotten by history—the humanness of man's products—appears in the form that they are *products* of abstract mind and as such, therefore, phases of mind—*thought entities*. (ibid, 150)

Some Marxists have argued that Marx turned Hegel 'right side up' and conjured up a historical materialism made up of the base and superstructure in which class relations were foundational to other forms of oppression (Fischer, 1996). However, these were distortions that led Marx to famously proclaim, 'I am not a Marxist.' This crude materialism that has been attributed to Marx neglects his dialectical approach and the human agency that he so famously recognized in his call to workers to 'unite!'

An important contribution that Marx makes to the Hegelian dialectic was to articulate the materiality within it. For Marx, dialectics was about the complexity of inter-relationships—materiality and consciousness were each an aspect of the other. Attempting to determine whether material conditions lead to thought processes or whether thought processes spur material conditions is a futile process—both are interrelated. However, that does not necessarily suggest that he gave a greater or more foundational role to the materiality of class relations than he did to the ideologies that both developed and supported them.

A Marxist-humanist interpretation has argued that Marx was much more dialectical in his analysis of capitalism than this interpretation suggests as he recognized the material and the ideational as presumed opposites that must be unified in the Revolutionary Subject. Lilia, first author, has articulated this elsewhere:

> [I]n *Capital*, Ch. 7, Marx writes of "free conscious activity" as the hallmark of being human, something that the worker under capitalism is denied. Freedom must be sought dialectically—in body and mind, objectively and subjectively—and that the process of becoming free on both these planes must be recognized as one process—a unity of presumed opposites (like idealism and materialism)—wherein our consciousness is liberated in the process of developing freedom from material constraints. (Monzó, 2019a, p. 21)

Through this process of simultaneously considering the Subject in their material conditions and upholding the quest for universality, that which transcends the particularities of the very individuals trapped in their material reality, Marx frames the proletariat as the Subject of the revolution, a revolution whose fundamental objective is class struggle.

The first negation is not only a conscious recognition that what we produce in thought and essence are abstractions of our human action, but the real struggle is against this alienation and the articulation of these products as embodiments of our own creative labor. The second negation comes when we recognize that we cannot challenge alienated labor within the existing system—that by definition, the system within which we live demands alienated labor and therefore must be dismantled to develop a new way forward or as Dunayevskaya (1991) often phrased it, 'a new humanism.' Yet, even here, the socialism that would engender this new humanism was not an end game, but rather what Marx perceived as the next stage of development.

Rather than attempting to invent something out of nothing, development is an ongoing process wherein the next step is always already present in its initial stages—a pre-existence, if you will, that is birthed through absolute negativity. Marx clearly recognized this potentiality in the many political and economic struggles of his time, struggles that have changed in character and focus but that ultimately remain unresolved. This is witnessed in how the second negation, the striking down of the white, supremacist capitalist patriarchy, has remained beyond our grasp. Yet, it is clear that there are many people at work attempting to challenge the world system—the possibilities in embryonic form can be found all around us as different groups attempt to create new social relations based on socialist-humanist principles (Monzó, 2019b).

Marx's dialectic recognizes that as human beings we are both body (material reality) and mind (consciousness). Here, Marx moved away from ideologies that dismember the body from the mind (often attributed to Descartes). Marx's dialectic was grounded in the body but did not fail to equally recognize the ideologies that allow such atrocities to take place. This dialectic of material and ideational reality speaks to teaching and learning as processes that are each an aspect of the other and involve the whole persons. As such, teaching and learning become reciprocal processes that must take into account the material realities of students and teachers, their cultural ways of being, their beliefs, values, and interests, and the spiritual and psychological aspects of their being. In the North American context, for example, critical scholars have increasingly discussed the importance of teaching and 'caring' for the whole child (Noddings, 2002). It has been noted that this is especially important for BIPOC (Black, Indigenous, and other People of Color) students in the Global North who are often marginalized in Eurocentric schools whose teaching force is predominantly white and female (Love, 2019). Similar patterns are likely to appear in the Global South where Indigenous communities have also been relegated to the margins in public schools (Cruz-Saco & Cummings, 2018).

While this is only one aspect of the dialectic, we can begin to see how absolute negation works. Treating the teaching and learning processes as reciprocal, recognizing historically oppressed students as human beings, with knowledge, cultures, and languages that are in-and-of themselves valuable but even more so given their histories of oppression and the insight and impetus that these experiences bring to revolutionary efforts is the first negation. Here, negation becomes an affirmation of the oppressed and a challenge to white supremacist, sexist, heteronormative, and other forms of relations of domination that are based on false notions of human hierarchies. The second negation would require that we bring down the systems that demand that we continue to engage through such relations of domination. Capitalism, white supremacy, patriarchy, and heteronormativity hold each other up and are founded on relations of domination. It will require an alternative to the existing racial capitalist patriarchy to rid us of the structures that continue to perpetuate relations of domination.

An important critique of Marx, brought to bear by the decolonial school, following in particular the work of Dussel, is the conflict character of the dialectic wherein development is always a function of tearing down in order to build up (Alcoff, 2019). Dussel proposes analectics, challenging the dialectic as a perceived, western universal, and instead incorporating a subjective geopolitical grounding, rooted in the Global South and Indigenous epistemologies, which articulates a process of development that progressively builds from generation to generation (Dussel, 2019).

28.3 Dussel and Analectics

Enrique Dussel was born and initially educated in Argentina. Continuing his studies and eventually receiving a doctorate in Europe, and heavily influenced by the work of Emmanuel Levinas, he laid the groundwork for a decolonial school of thought that centers around subjectivity. He positioned the western canons of Hegel and Marx, and in particular, the dialectic, as rooted in a view of the world and development that perceives from the position of domination—even though their work attempts to create a philosophy for liberation (Alcoff, 2019; Dussel, 2019). Dussel argues that our social and geopolitical positionings in the world and in relation to the positioning of others provide a particular vantage point and make other vantage points at best invisible to us and at worst constructed to omit perspectives that may challenge the positions that serve to benefit those in power. Dussel's philosophy of liberation centers the Indigenous Subject of the Americas, whose ways of being and knowing have been articulated by the white man as 'uncivilized, animalistic, emotional and subhuman.' Dussel points out, echoing Adorno, that it is in the negative—what is lacking from our consciousness and in particular from the western canons that has insights to the ways we understand the world, development, and the possibilities of a liberated humanity (Dussel, 2019).

Dussel's philosophy is not one that attempts to replace the western canons. Decolonial scholars argue that we need a philosophy that acknowledges important previous works, even where Eurocentric, but that also recognizes their limitations and moves beyond them to capture what has historically been ignored or dismissed (Mignolo, 2009). His critique of the dialectic stems from a conviction that conflict theories of development are rooted in the historical conditions of genocide and domination that the white man developed and perpetrated against predominantly his Other (here we use a purposeful gender specificity).

Dussel challenges the notion that the search for freedom is our human vocation and instead argues that 'material life'—improving the living conditions of humanity—is the driving force of our human action. In Dussel's view, the destructive aspect of the dialectic has been used to justify atrocities against entire peoples, with the excuse that this is a necessary part of creating something better. However, it must be noted that massacres and other atrocities precede Hegel's writing (Carpenter, 2015). Still, Dussel's argument that freedom cannot be achieved through destruction is certainly worthy of consideration. For Dussel, it is life preservation or 'the protection of material life that will ensure the creative capacity of the species' (Alcoff, 2019, p. 19). He argued that a focus on freedom actually diminishes freedom (Dussel, 2019). Certainly, the 'freedom' adopted by capitalism is a false narrative that produces the pauperization of much of the Global South through market competition and social and political domination. For Dussel, it is in discovering what is missing from historical development, what was left out, either materially as well as ideologically, in the process of development and in our understandings of this history, that will result in a reconstruction—one that is 'life giving.'

Focusing on education as an important contributing context and aspect of liberation, Dussel argues for a *pedagogics* of liberation rather than a pedagogy of liberation (Dussel, 2019). In pedagogics, Dussel centers the face-to-face relationships that are fostered in the learning encounter and which must take place in contexts of caring. Rather than focusing on equalizing relations of power as may be perceived in Freire's dialectical approach, Dussel argues that differences in status and power between the teacher and the student, or the parent and child, are natural, but that teaching and learning become life-affirming activities when these are perceived as aspects of caring relationships. These cross-generational encounters, Dussel argues, are to be found at all levels of society—within the family, community, and at a global scale in international relations.

In Dussel's view (2019), major philosophers of education focus on presumed universal ideals that have been aligned to Eurocentric views. Centering his argument on the work of Rousseau's *Emile*, Dussel points out that Rousseau articulates the teacher as the person who can impart this universal ideal, and positioned the parent, in contrast, as rooted in a particularity that does not allow for further development. From this perspective, the teacher is the anti-parent in opposition to the parent, and from a dialectical perspective must eject that parent within, in order for the student's development to be future-bound. Dussel critiques this universalizing approach that has been used to justify the erasure of community experiences and argues that this universalism is colonizing. Recognition of the colonizing experiences of particular communities and other forms of oppression are, according to Dussel, important aspects of the development of the next generation—since development is not abstract but rooted in real-life experiences.

Here, Dussel focuses on the particularity from which the universal ideal can be articulated. Pedagogics requires a non-ideal approach; cross-generational caring relationships require a recognition of the specific context of oppression that particular students face. Furthermore, Dussel (2019) argues that teachers must construct an 'exteriority' to the system, meaning thinking critically from a perspective outside that which has been developed within the system. In education, this means constructing an exteriority to the curriculum that has developed within institutions of domination and which merely reproduce structures of oppression in the service of racial capitalism. This exteriority involves both observation of the actual social conditions and relations, and then an analysis of these conditions (Alcoff, 2019).

Another related and equally important aspect of analectics is that it does not require annulment or ejection of a presumed opposite in order for something new to develop or to transcend what was. Dussel argues that the child is always an Other of the parent, for they are always and necessarily an amalgam of two other beings and therefore never a replica of the previous generation. Rather, the child transcends the parents to whom it is always and necessarily an Other. Thus, the next generation is always already transcendent without the need for the destructive element found within the dialectic.

In the colonial context in which Dussel frames his work, the analectic reasoning involves recognizing the child's creative capacity and their thinking as rooted in, but also transcendent of, their particular cultures. They do not come into the classroom as an empty vessel, nor do they come in with backward ideas that must face the violence of erasure. Rather, drawing on Freire, Dussel argues that it is in this cross-generational relation of caring 'dialogue,' that the teacher and child meet as 'epistemic Subjects' and construct an exteriority that reaches beyond what is intelligible or even imaginable within the dominant sphere of thought and practice (Dussel, 2019).

28.4 An Intersectional Marxism

There is no doubt that Dussel makes important contributions to Marxist thought. However, Dussel draws on some misconceptions of Marx's philosophy and the dialectic, which if understood with greater nuance, would bring Dussel's work into greater alliance with Marx. Moreover, it would do so especially with Marxist-humanism, which has recently begun to articulate an intersectional Marxism (Anderson et al., 2021).

First, Dussel is correct to point out that western philosophers, including many Marxists, have often failed to recognize the racial dimension of capitalist social relations. However, it must be noted that Marx in *Capital vol. I* articulated that a 'so-called' primitive accumulation was rooted in colonial relations and intimated with his phrasing that colonialism and imperialism would be an ongoing and necessary aspect of capitalism (Anderson, 2010). Furthermore, a thorough reading of Marx's body of work reveals important growth on his part in regard to his early Eurocentrism (Anderson, 2010). By the late 1850s, Marx has begun to recognize English colonizers as the actual barbarians rather than Indigenous peoples and has adopted more anticolonial attitudes; in his *Ethnological Notebooks*, Marx began seeking knowledge about more equitable relations in the history of the family, as documented among Indigenous communities (Anderson, 2010).

Furthermore, Marx writes of the women of the Paris Commune as agentic and courageous, and recognizes that equality of gender is a measure of the extent to which we have become human (Brown, 2013). Beyond this, Marx articulated that imperialism and colonization did not merely provide the primitive accumulation that jump-started capitalism but were necessary, ongoing processes for the maintenance of capitalism (Marx, 1977). In addition, Marx challenged the interpretation of so-called Marxists who universalized his theories to make determinations of the development of capitalism in other nations and at other times in society. In the foreword of the French translation of Capital, the version that he explicitly demanded be made the version from which all future translations would follow, Marx clarified that his was an analysis of capitalism based on the way that it had developed in England. Unfortunately, his wishes were not honored and many societies have argued that a centralized system of capitalism is necessary for the development of socialism (Anderson, 2010).

However, it is clear that this was not Marx's intent. Indeed Marx, as a journalist, was all about observing what was happening on the ground, in particular struggles and developing theory that stemmed from the experiences and philosophies of the revolutionary Subjects. Marx argued that philosophers were far too removed from the realities of the working class and unlikely to take the necessary risks or to know the movement that could be made (Monzó, 2021). In this too, Marx and Dussel coincide, arguing that it is the oppressed whose 'force and reason' are necessary for revolution.

Hegel's conception of the dialectic has also been taken as universal. However, Findlay (1977) argues that Hegel also articulated that his dialectic was contingent on time and space and cultures. According to Finalay, Hegel developed his *Phenomenology* based on history, but he did not contend that the future would not bring a different process of development, that his approach was not a universalizing philosophy. It can be argued, therefore, that the dialectic is not necessarily the only process of development nor even the only one indicated within his own cultural context. The notion that development need not be based on destruction, but that it develops naturally as the ongoing process of the birthing of the new generation, which necessarily transcends the previous generation, is certainly intriguing and provides a hopefulness for liberation efforts. Crucial here is the idea that we do not need to resort to war to end the monster of capitalism and that the new generation has the potential to develop something new without the need to destroy the previous. Yet, Dussel falls into the same trap that much postcolonial theory falls into, in that it offers a new philosophy—the analectic, a philosophy that affirms without negation, all the while *negating* the dialectic (Hill et al., 2002). Thus, Dussel engages an analectic that does exactly what it contends not to do, by drawing on negation to bring itself forward.

We would like to argue that we need not decide on one process of development, which inherently presumes the universalization that Dussel argues is colonizing, and which we agree to be so. Examining current processes of development, as Marx did in examining the current social movements of his time, we find that both of these processes of development can co-exist, although one process may seem to be more prevalent under certain social conditions than the other. Indeed, just as we find socialism within capitalism, we can perceive that a particular movement has developed more through one approach than another, or that a particular social movement has drawn on both approaches at different times in order to create liberatory progress.

Marx was well aware that the exploited class brings insights and creative capacity, as well as impetus and force that cannot be garnered through the intellectual and their existence. Their life opportunities reflect privileges that grant them the status of the *petit bourgeoisie*, and they are unlikely to know deeply enough the experiences of exploitation that come from actually being the exploited class. This false consciousness extends itself to the fields of education and academic research wherein the intellectual approaches the Subject in a similar colonizing manner with a focus on the extraction of knowledge and conquering the exploited Subject rather than disrupting the history of hegemonic practices. It is the daily experiences that afford exploited communities insights about exploitation, empathy and solidarity, and the ability to take the risk necessary for revolutionary transformation. Marx recognized these as a creative philosophy that went beyond what the intellectual could develop through their books as armchair philosophers.

In this same vein, it is unfair to suggest that the dialectic is responsible for developing the anti-parent among teachers in educational contexts. While we would agree that this is typical of western education, particularly in the teaching of non-dominant groups, we would argue that the dialectic can just as well be utilized, and, we would argue, is necessary toward ejecting this anti-parent among teachers and educators. A mere building up of positive perspectives of or opportunities for oppressed communities within a broader society that is entrenched with significant material disparities and deficit perspectives is very unlikely to lead us toward freedom. Indeed, there is a long history of attempting to add educational reforms to support greater educational achievement for marginalized students and yet education along with all other institutions continues to be deeply entrenched in racism, sexism, and class inequalities (Payne, 2008).

For Marx, the revolutionary Subject was the proletariat. While he did recognize the significant oppression of Black peoples and Women, and the impact of racism and other antagonisms on capitalism, he did not articulate these key aspects of the proletariat. Dussel's focus on the colonial contexts makes colonized peoples an important revolutionary Subject whose creative capacity exists in their transcendence from previous generations, inheriting aspects of their cultures but creatively transforming them. This creative capacity can be triggered through the pedagogical analectic, wherein an exteriority is created which reaches 'beyond what is imaginable' within the current system.

Marxist-humanism, although not Dusselian given its foundational roots in the dialectic, is developing an intersectional Marxism that recognizes that capitalism is a racialized and misogynist system that cannot be abstractly separated or universalized from those on whose backs it developed and triumphed into a global system (Monzó, 2020). Currently being developed within the contexts of the United States, this intersectional Marxism recognizes the importance of observing and learning from and *with* the revolutionary Subject and reconceptualizing the revolutionary Subject to align with the various identities that the proletariat and other oppressed communities are taking up today. The concept of intersectionality, initially developed by Kimberly Crenshaw (2017), refers to the various intersectional identities held by most people and to the fact that these intersections often lead to different material conditions. Although

Crenshaw's work has often been used to depict mere subjectivities divorced from class relations, we understand that these identities have developed within a system of racial and patriarchal capitalist relations. An intersectional Marxism is useful because it acknowledges that multiple structures of oppression are co-constituted and that the elimination of any one of these structures will require the elimination of all. For example, some of the success of the Black Lives Matter (BLM) movement can be attributed to the movement's ability to recognize that Black people are predominantly working class but also Black women, Black members of the LGBTQIA+ communities as well as members of other communities. Importantly, these intersecting identities and the oppressions they embody coincide with Grosfoguel's (2009) coloniality of power matrix discussed above.

Although not previously articulated through this terminology, an important contribution of Marxist humanism has been the recognition of Black masses as the vanguard of the revolution, and in particular Black women. In the US context, Black peoples have been the leaders of revolutionary movements, whose relation to other international movements can be seen as crucial to the goal of liberation (Dunayevskaya, 2003). However, it is also important to see that communities of color in the US are continuously being pitted against each other, and that this oppression-Olympics is another form of division, which serves the status quo and is reflective of Eurocentric and capitalist assumptions of competition and false binaries. Here, Marxist humanists can learn to recognize the creative capacity of all oppressed communities, finding areas of shared experiences and shared interests around which coalitions can be developed. It is in this way that we, as a society, but especially teachers, movement organizers, and other cultural workers, can support the development of more Revolutionary Subjects, and together build a liberatory society that reaches beyond that which is currently imaginable.

While this sounds contradictory to the Marxist notion that the future is held within the present, we do not understand Dussel's notion of transcendence to mean the creation of something completely new. The cross-generational and historical aspect of analectics recognize that transcendence comes from building upon what has come before. In the case of the colonial context, this means building upon the epistemologies, cultures, and experiences of colonized peoples. How this transcendence can develop without any initial conflict is what is difficult to imagine, given that a focus on history remains a critical aspect of both the dialectic and the analectic. Below, we examine the case of the Zapatistas; in particular, we consider its development as a movement and aspects that can be perceived as dialectical and/or analectical.

28.5 The Zapatistas: A Case Example

An important contribution of the Decolonial school has been to articulate that the 'enunciator' is a thinking Subject whose voice reflects particular world views, knowledges, and ways of knowing that are rooted in experiences tied to particular geo-political locations. As opposed to notions of objective truth that are presumed to float outside the individual, language, voice, thought, and actions must always be understood as stemming from individuals who are grounding in sociohistorical experiences that are also geo-politically based. According to Grosfoguel (2009), the knowledge and experiences of the colonized peoples of the Americas have been shaped by their experiences of the 'coloniality of power' (Quijano & Ennis, 2000), an entangled power matrix that includes (1) a particular capitalist formation that gives power and control to those who own the means of production and other economic resources, (2) an international division of labor that privileges the Global North over the Global South, (3) an inter-state system of political and military organizations that favor those in power, (3) a global racial/ethnic hierarchy that privileges white peoples, (4) a global gender hierarchy and patriarchy formations that privileges men, (5) a sexual hierarchy that marginalizes LGBTQIA+ communities, (6) a spiritual hierarchy that privileges Christians, (7) an epistemic hierarchy that privileges Western epistemes, (8) and linguistic hierarchy that privileges European languages (Grosfoguel, 2009). Presumably, given the hyper-exploitation of Indigenous women under this articulation of power, those of us concerned with transforming social relations would seek to privilege their particular world views and insights. Yet we find still within this framework, as in Marxism, that the male location of enunciation remains dominant, with few articulations of these theories among women of the Global South. Our goal here is to examine these processes of development within the counter, geo-political locations of Zapatista women.

The Zapatistas are the Indigenous peoples of Chiapas, Mexico, who form the *Ejército Zapatista de Liberación Nacional* (EZLN). On January 1, 1994, the Zapatistas rose up in arms against the Mexican government to claim the right to exist as autonomous stewards of the lands in which they lived. Spurred on by centuries of exploitation at the hands of capital, and declaring '*Ya Basta!*' the Zapatistas initiated their revolution on the same day in which NAFTA (North American Free Trade Agreement) was signed, which would have made foreign investments even more lucrative, at the cost of Indigenous peoples lands and livelihoods. In the face of significant international support for the rights of the Zapatistas, the Mexican government retreated and has since accepted their autonomy, although it has never officially recognized it. For over 25 years, the Zapatistas have run their internal politics, developing a direct democracy with socialist principles. They control a large part of Chiapas, and as of 2018 held 55 municipalities and supported over 300,000 people. They have their own schools and hospitals and have raised their own teachers and doctors (Vidal, 2018).

The Zapatistas have had a strong female presence in all areas of Zapatista life, including as political leaders, insurgents, doctors, and teachers. Although Zapatista women faced initial resistance, the Zapatistas passed the Women's Revolutionary Law, granting women equal rights, safety and dignity in Rebel territory, even before the 1994 uprisings, which facilitated women's active participation in large numbers. Hilary Klein (2015) documents that women's participation in the movement shed light on the systemic injustice and abuse women often endured in the home and in society. Working together through the democratic councils gave the women a sense of strength as well as practical tools to demand women's rights, outlaw sexual and physical assault, and normalize women having greater choice regarding marital status and reproduction, and in turn this positively impacted their material lives as well as increased their consciousness, confidence, and agency. It is well recognized that Zapatista women have had a strong hand in influencing the movement's direction toward a community-focused, democratic organizing and governance structure (Nail, 2013).

Although the major spokesperson, Subcomandante Marcos, is a non-Indigenous man, he has made clear from the onset that the Zapatistas are led by the Indigenous people who make their voices heard through democratic councils. According to Nail (2013), the Zapatistas have led the movement toward *horizontalidad*, which is an approach to 'leading together' that functions as an alternative to the party system. The political party system is one based on competition, fraught with conflict, and ultimately demands losers and winners. In contrast, horizontalism among the Zapatistas involves caracoles, or administrative centers, that represent three levels of autonomous government: the community, the municipality, and the Council of Good Government. The first two are based on grassroots assemblies. The last takes elected representatives from the prior ones but on a rotational basis, in order to have large participation. Assemblies work democratically through open discussions where the goal is for everyone to have a voice and to be heard. The goal is to reach consensus and establish relationships. This 'affective politics' is non-hierarchical, anti-authoritarian, and without leaders (Sitrin, 2006).

From this synopsis, it is evident that the Zapatista movement has developed in some ways dialectically and in other ways analectically. Because the Zapatista Movement grew out of conflict, initially raising arms against the Mexican government in 1994 to fight for autonomy and freedom, it can be said that the Zapatistas emerged triumphant out of negation, reflecting a view of development that is dialectical, or as the resolution of contradictions. Though the group is not militant any longer and the war between it and the Mexican government is considered frozen, guns continue to be part of protecting the perimeter of the group's territory. Although there has been some resolution to the contradiction, this is ultimately only a very limited resolution, one that involves constant vigilance and readiness to fight off the negative that emerges from the positive. Nonetheless, it can be said that new forms of governance and values have emerged out of this, albeit, limited resolution.

For example, if, as Marx argued, freedom must be achieved in both mind and body to achieve our full human potential, the two-pronged move toward a more liberated life for the Zapatista women is dialectical, in its political and consciousness raising effects, on one hand, and the more material social and economic changes, on the other. Though strong female presence is a necessary aspect of what establishes the movement as more egalitarian, equal, and community-centered, the initial resistance among some men frames this important aspect of the movement as emerging from a negation of contradictions.

At different times, however, the Zapatista movement has also developed through an analectic approach in order to create liberatory progress. The EZLN's Women's Revolutionary Law suggests that a breaking down is not always necessary for building up and moving toward a new humanism, painting the movement in Dusselian analectic light. Dussel argues that improving material conditions of humanity is the driving force behind our human action; in that sense, that which is life-giving is evident in the EZLN's Women's Revolutionary Law as a reflection of a cross-generational and historically rooted reconstruction.

Similarly, both the dialectic and analectic seem to be at play in Zapatista governance. The dialectic is reflected in the challenge to the western hierarchical notion of leadership that carries with it corruption and divisiveness, the Zapatistas' resolution of this contradiction emerged as a new answer to ways of organizing, one that prioritized grassroots organizing, collective input, democracy, and equality. While it can be said that the development of horizontalism is the result of negation, we can also recognize the analectic, a building up that emerges beyond the initial negation, and that is based on the acknowledgement of historical conditions and the Subjectivities these develop. It is also the result of the growth that emerges from cross-generational, Freirean dialogue that seeks to discover what is lacking in the current, white supremacist, capitalist patriarchy, alongside what the Other can develop 'beyond what is currently imaginable.'

The actual development of Zapatista governance involves the recognition of Indigenous values for well-being, life affirmation, and stewardship of the Earth. The 'schooling' that the Zapatistas have developed also affirms this analectic, wherein the child is honored with the space and time to bring forth their Otherness in a context of cross-generational caring and shared responsibilities. Zapatista students learn both modern curricula of literacy, math, and science but also engage in productive community work as part of their schooling experience that develops their sense of social responsibility to their communities. Therefore, Spanish is not taught as a replacement for Indigenous languages and math as preparation for the job market in a capitalist society; rather than as coercive methods of molding students and teachers into obedient and unquestioning citizen-consumers, under Zapatista teaching philosophy, these more traditional subjects are viewed as useful tools toward self-preservation in the larger world (Subcomandante Marcos, 2022). Unlike that of the state-sanctioned schools, the Zapatista philosophy of education comes from below, best captured by the Zapatista adage *Preguntando Caminamos* which demonstrates the way participatory democracy generates the Zapatista curriculum. This horizontal approach to education that centralizes the histories and needs of the people through geopolitically contextualized subjects such as organic agroforestry, food sovereignty, and medicinal herbs, as well as regional

Indigenous languages are in themselves acts of decolonization (Gahman, 2016). In its centering of the Indigenous Subject of the Americas, Dussel's notion of the analectic might seem a better fit in describing the Zapatistas movement, but there is no denying that they exist as an autonomous region as a result of conflict and resolution andcontinue to exist as a result of the armed guards that protect them from government encroachment.

28.6 Calling for a Decolonial Marxism

The case of the Zapatistas reflects both dialectical and analectical reasoning. That is, the movement has developed both out of conflicts and their resolutions and out of building up from the diverse epistemologies of the Indigenous women who make up a significant 'force and Reason' (Dunayevskaya, 1991; Monzó, 2019a) of the Zapatista movement. That is, Zapatista women have developed diverse epistemologies—knowledge and ways of understanding the world that are informed by a long history of oppression and exploitation, including their histories of genocide, rape, removal, sexism, and other aspects of colonization. Given that women have been crucial to the Zapatista movement, their epistemological diversity can be recognized in the ways in which the Zapatista movement has developed and evolved.

Following the Dusselian argument that the geopolitical location of the enunciator is critical to our understanding, we disclose that we have come into this analysis with our understandings grounded in our particular histories, experiences, and focused readings. Lilia, first author, identifies as a woman of color and of the Global South, having been born in Cuba but raised working-class in the US, and also as a Marixst-humanist, with a strong conviction that capitalism has always been grounded in white supremacist patriarchy. Nidžara, second author, was born in Bosnia and Herzegovina and immigrated to the US as a refugee, and, as a doctoral student, is interested in engaging with intersectional Marxism as a framework to develop a pedagogy of anti-capitalism, of challenging white supremacist patriarchy as well as other systems of oppression, but also one of co-constructing a more humanizing future.

From these locations, we see the hopefulness that can be found within the analectic and recognize that the analectic speaks to honoring the critical insights that come from our experiences of coloniality; it both acknowledges our histories of oppression as distinct but also our epistemologies rooted in these experiences. Dusselian philosophy centers coloniality, which has long been ignored in much of western thought, even among Marxists. Even though Marx recognized the significant and continuous role of colonialism and imperialism in the development and maintenance of capitalism (Marx, 1977) and he turned to learn from Indigenous communities only in his later years (Marx, 1974), this work has not been taken seriously or studied carefully. Here, it is also crucial to recognize the important theoretical argument that liberation cannot be borne out of negation (i.e., destruction). Yet recognition of the importance of this statement is not necessarily agreement.

The concrete example of Zapatista development, at least in our view, lends greater credence to the dialectic. While we can recognize the analectic at work—the building of ideas and processes—these seem to always come after the negation that has allowed for the analectic to flourish. Furthermore, neither Hegel nor Marx ever indicated that there was any one-to-one correspondence between negation and transcendence. Thus, the development of something new that results from the resolution of contradictions is not necessarily an immediate result but can certainly be conceived of as a progressive building of something 'beyond what is currently imaginable.' Indeed, in the *Critique of the Gotha Program*, Marx (2023) explicitly distinguishes between a higher and lower phase of communism, recognizing that communism would be developed over time, with the more humanistic aspects—for example, 'from each according to their ability, to each according to their needs'—to be developed at a higher phase of communism. It is important to note that Marx did not mark these phases as distinct historical periods (Hudis, 2023). The differentiation that some scholars have made between socialism and communism are not reflected in the *Critique of the Gotha Program* wherein Marx writes only of communism. Peter Hudis notes that this is because he used the terms interchangeably (p. 12). It is clear then that Marx understood that a socialist revolution would not immediately result in full equality and eliminate alienation but that these would be increasingly viable aspects as people began to develop a new humanism, with a greater value for social responsibility and began to recognize that the benefits to society were also of benefit to the individual.

Here, we can recognize that what Dussel refers to as the analectic, the building up from diverse perspectives, is certainly evident within Marx's philosophy of revolution, but that it is an aspect of the dialectic. From a Marxist-humanist perspective racial-colonial, patriarchal capitalism *does* need to be struck down, but this does not preclude the building up of ideas and processes prior to and after a new socialist administration of the people has been secured. Indeed, as Marx and Freire have argued, it is the insights of the oppressed that are most likely to lead us to revolution and to establishing a path to freedom. It is interesting to note that while the Dusselian analectic challenges negation, it does so by negating the dialectic, which is reminiscent of the same circular argumentation that has challenged much of the field of postmodernism (Hill et al., 2002). It is also important to note that the intersectional Marxism that we have discussed has developed out of the work of scholars in multiple traditions, including Marxism, Critical Pedagogy, Critical Race Theory, Decolonial Theory, and Feminist Theories, in an attempt to build a theory that reflects and draws upon the interests and concerns of historically marginalized groups.

We do, however, appreciate the Dusselian centering of Indigeneity, intersectionality, and coloniality, and therefore, call for a decolonizing Marxism that builds on the intersectional Marxism that Marxist-humanists have begun to articulate. A decolonial Marxism moves the intersectional argument further by focusing on the colonial experience and the globalized aspect of the racial and gender divisions of labor. It further pushes Marxists to contend with the practice of decolonizing, which embeds an aspect of action toward addressing colonial relations that is certainly Marxist-humanist but that has rarely been treated in the Marxist literature. We would be remiss if we did not point out that de(colonizing) embeds an aspect of negation.

For education, a decolonial Marxism, suggests that we must examine the role that education plays in maintaining a racial-colonial capitalist patriarchy but also we must recognize the agency of teachers, students, and historically colonized communities. Unlike how they are often presented, these are engaged communities, many of whom have a long history of struggle, with significant insights toward what they perceive as important to their communities in the moment but also in the long struggle toward an alternative to capitalism. The active verb in decolonizing refocuses our attention to challenging relations of domination, not only within the broader structures but in our everyday interactions in schools, in our organization, and in broader society. It also challenges Marxist-humanists to recognize and remember that we do not just hold multiple identities, but that many of us have a history of colonization that we do not forget and that must be addressed.

Acknowledgements We are very grateful to Peter Hudis for his thoughtful review of our work and his excellent feedback. None of the authors has any financial interest or benefit that has arisen from the direct applications of this research.

Disclosure Statement Neither of the authors has any financial interest or benefit that has arisen from the direct applications of this research.

Note

1. In the spirit of the radical-left tradition of disrupting relations of domination in text by capitalizing references to historically oppressed groups, we capitalize references to Non-western communities, Communities of Color, and the Global South while lowercasing references to the dominant group.

References

Alcoff, L. M. (2019). Foreword. In E. Dussel, *Pedagogics of Liberation: A Latin American Philosophy of Education* (D. I. Backer & C. Diego, Trans.) (pp. 11–30). Punctum Books.

Anderson, K. (2010). *Marx at the Margins: On Nationalism, Ethnicity, and Non-Western Societies*. University of Chicago Press.

Anderson, K. (2020). *Dialectics of Revolution: Hegel, Marxism, and Its Critics through a Lens of Race, Class, Gender, and Colonialism*. Daraja Press.

Anderson, K., Durkin, K., & Brown, H. (Eds.). (2021). *Raya Dunayevskaya's Intersectional Marxism: Race, Gender, and the Dialectics of Liberation*. Springer.

Brown, H. (2013). *Marx on Gender and the Family: A Critical Study*. Haymarket Books.

Carpenter, J. (2015). Archeologists Uncover a Neolithic Massacre in Early Europe. *Science*. Retrieved April 28, 2023, from https://www.science.org/content/article/archaeologists-uncover-neolithic-massacre-early-europe

Crenshaw, K. (2017). *On Intersectionality: Essential Writings*. The New Press.

Cruz-Saco, M. A., & Cummings, J. T. (2018). Indigenous Communities and Social Inclusion in Latin America. Prepared for the United Nations Expert Group Meeting on Families and Inclusive Societies. New York Headquarters. Retrieved April 28, 2023, from https://www.un.org/development/desa/family/wp-content/uploads/sites/23/2018/05/2-1.pdf

Dunayevskaya, R. (1991). *Rosa Luxemburg, Women's Liberation, and Marx's Philosophy of Revolution* (2nd ed.). University of Illinois Press.

Dunayevskaya, R. (2000). *Marxism and Freedom: From 1776 Until Today*. Humanity Books.

Dunayevskaya, R. (2003). *American Civilization on Trial: Black Masses as Vanguard*. News and Letters Committees.

Dussel, E. (2019). *Pedagogics of Liberation: A Latin American Philosophy of Education* (D. I. Backer & C. Diego, Trans.). Punctum Books.

Findlay, J. N. (1977). Foreword. In G. W. F. Hegel, *Phenomenology of Spirit* (A. V. Miller, Trans.) (pp. v–xxx). Oxford University Press.

Fischer, E. (1996). *How to Read Karl Marx*. Monthly Review Press.

Freire, P. (2005). *Pedagogy of the Oppressed* (30th anniversary ed.). Continuum.

Gahman, L. (2016). Zapatismo versus the Neoliberal University: Towards a Pedagogy Against Oblivion. In S. Springer, M. Lopes de Souza, & R. J. White (Eds.), *The Radicalization of Pedagogy* (pp. 73–100). Rowman & Littlefield.

Grosfoguel, R. (2009). A Decolonial Approach to Political Economy: Transmodernity, Border Thinking and Global Coloniality. *Kult 6—Special Issue Epistemologies of Transformation: The Latin American Decolonial Option and Its Ramifications*. Department of Culture and Identity: 10–38. Retrieved April 28, 2023, from http://www.postkolonial.dk/artikler/kult_6/GROSFOGUEL.pdf

Hegel, G. W. F. (1820). Philosophy of Right (A. V. Miller, Trans.). Marxists.org. Retrieved April 28, 2023, from https://www.marxists.org/reference/archive/hegel/works/pr/preface.htm

Hegel, G. W. F. (1977). *Phenomenology of Spirit* (A. V. Miller, Trans.) (pp. v–xxx). Oxford University Press.

Hill, D., McLaren, P., Cole, M., & Rikowski, G. (Eds.). (2002). *Marxism Against Postmodernism in Educational Theory*. Lexington Books.

Houlgate, S. (2015). Hegel's Critique of Kant. *Proceedings of the Aristotelian Society Supplementary, 89*, 21–41.

Hudis, P. (2023). Introduction. In K. Marx, *Critique of the Gotha Program* (K. B. Anderson & K. Ludenhoff, Trans.). PM Press.

Kant, I. (1998). *Critique of Pure Reason* (P. Guyer & A. W. Wood, Eds. and Trans.). Cambridge University Press.

Klein, H. (2015). *Compañeras: Zapatista Women's Stories*. Seven Stories Press.

Love, B. (2019). *We Want to Do More Than Survive: Abolitionist Teaching and the Pursuit of Educational Freedom*. Beacon Press.

Marcos, S. (2022). *Zapatista Stories for Dreaming An-Other World* (Lightning Collective, Trans.). PM Press.

Marx, K. (1961). *Economic and Philosophic Manuscripts of 1844* (M. Milligan, Trans.). Foreign Language Publishing House.

Marx, K. (1974). *Ethnological Notebooks of Karl Marx*. Marxists.org. Retrieved April 28, 2023, from https://www.marxists.org/archive/marx/works/1881/ethnographical-notebooks/notebooks.pdf

Marx, K. (1977). *Capital, Volume 1: A Critique of Political Economy* (B. Fowkes, Trans.). Vintage Books.

Marx, K. (2023). *Critique of the Gotha Program* (K. B. Anderson & K. Ludenhoff, Trans.). PM Press.

Mignolo, W. (2009). Epistemic Disobedience, Independent Thought and Decolonial Freedom. *Theory, Culture & Society, 26*(7–8), 159–181.

Monzó, L. D. (2019a). *A Revolutionary Subject: Pedagogy of Women of Color and Indigeneity*. Peter Lang.

Monzó, L. D. (2019b, November). Humanism in the Crevices of Violence. *3rd Critical Pedagogy Conference*, Guangzhao, China, November 16.

Monzó, L. D. (2020). Colonialism, Migration, Pandemic: The Immutable Evidence that Capitalism is Racist and Misogynist. *Monthly Review, 72*(3). Retrieved April 28, 2023, from https://monthlyreview.org/2020/07/01/colonialism-migration-pandemic/

Monzó, L. D. (2021). The Dialectic in *Marxism and Freedom* for Today: The Unity of Theory and Practice and the Movement of Today's Concrete Struggles. In K. Anderson, K. Durkin, & H. Brown (Eds.), *Raya Dunayevskaya's Intersectional Marxism: Race, Gender, and the Dialectics of Liberation* (pp. 141–168). Springer.

Nail, T. (2013). Zapatismo and the Global Origins of Occupy. *Journal for Cultural and Religious Studies, 12*(3), 20–38.

Noddings, N. (2002). *Educating Moral People: A Caring Alternative to Character Education*. Teachers College Press.

Payne, C. (2008). *So Much Reform, So Little Change*. Harvard Education Press.

Quijano, A., & Ennis, M. (2000). Coloniality, Eurocentricism and Latin America. *Nepantla: Views from South, 1*(3), 533–580.

Ruda, F. (2011). *Hegel's Rabble: An Investigation into Hegel's Philosophy of Right*. Continuum.

Sitrin, M. (Ed.). (2006). *Horizontalism: Voices of Popular Power in Argentina*. AK Press.

Smith, C. (2002). Marx, Hegel, the Enlightenment and Magic. *The Commoner, 3*, 1–6. https://thecommoner.org/wp-content/uploads/2019/11/Marx-Smith-Hegel-Enlightenment-Magic-Cyril-Smith.pdf

Vidal, J. (2018). Mexico's Zapatista Rebels: 24 Years On and Defiant in Mountain Strongholds'. *The Guardian*. Retrieved April 28, 2023, from https://www.theguardian.com/global-development/2018/feb/17/mexico-zapatistas-rebels-24-years-mountain-strongholds/

CHAPTER 29

The (Im)possibilities of Revolutionary Pedagogical-Political Kinship (M)otherwise: The Gifts of (Autonomous) Marxist Feminisms and Decolonial/Abolitionist Communitarian Feminisms to Pedagogical-Political Projects of Collective Liberation

Sara C. Motta

29.1 INTRODUCTION

This piece emerges out of the connections, disconnections, resonances, and dissonances between heritages of Marxist feminisms (De La Costa and James, 1975; Federici, 2004; Mason-Deese, 2020; Motta, 2013; Motta et al., 2023) and decolonial/indigenist feminism (Anzaldúa, 1987, 2002, 2015; Lugones, 2010; Motta, 2018, 2023a, 2023b; Simpson, 2016, 2017), and their (non) relationships and/or sometimes begrudged and sometimes loving kinship with (Southern) heterodox Marxisms (Gramsci, 1971; Cardoso, 1972; Holloway, 2002; Mignolo, 2002; Tischler, 2014; Ndlovu-Gatsheni & Ndlovu, 2022). These are not abstract (feminist) theoretical constructions about and for, codifying and naming the analysis of categories from a critical distance, but co-creation with/as critical intimacy (see Motta, 2016 for the conceptualization of critical intimacy). Rather, my (t)racing, and attempt at bringing-to-text

---

S. C. Motta (✉)
Politics, NBS, University of Newcastle, Mulubimba-Newcastle, NSW, Australia
e-mail: sara.c.motta@newcastle.edu.au

© The Editor(s) (if applicable) and The Author(s), under exclusive license to Springer Nature Switzerland AG 2023
R. Hall et al. (eds.), *The Palgrave International Handbook of Marxism and Education*, Marxism and Education,
https://doi.org/10.1007/978-3-031-37252-0_29

these lineages together, captures some of the complexities of *mestizaje*[1] (non) belonging, and the collective threads of sense-making of my/our in-relation, complex Black/Indigenist/abolitionist feminist revolutionary praxis/medicine-making in the South. This embodies the yearning, and embraces the desires, for pluridiverse meeting-places that epistemologically-politically-pedagogically take seriously the feminized and racialized Southern body, and/as flesh for a revolutionary praxis for our times(Motta, 2018, 2023a, 2023b).

Marxist feminism and decolonial/indigenist feminists are deeply pedagogical *both* in *and* as their epistemological-political project of (decolonial), post-patriarchal, revolutionary transformation. Both have complex (non) relationalities with traditions of (Southern) heterodox Marxism, either as their devalued underside as in (Autonomous) Marxist feminisms (De La Costa and James, 1975; Federici, 2004; Ni Una Menos, 2018) or in their direct disavowal as in Decolonial and Indigenist communitarian feminisms (Ciccariello-Maher, 2017; Motta, 2017a, 2018; Wilderson, 2003). However, both these feminist, pedagogical-epistemological traditions gift practices and rationalities, languages and embodiments/enfleshment, which can feminize/make feminist and also decolonize both the revolutionary subject and the onto-epistemologies of much Marxist praxis. They foreground pluridiverse pedagogical-political projects of liberation (Motta, 2014, 2017a, 2018; Motta et al., 2020, 2023).

This tentative dialogue between these feminist revolutionary/abolitionist lineages foregrounding both their pedagogical nature but also their (non) relationship with (Southern) Marxisms is no accident of abstraction or mode of trendy radicality. It is an attempt to bring to text and thought lineages of which I (in-relation and as collective) attempt to navigate in the struggle of co-creating popular revolutionary (decolonizing) feminist praxis. Our praxis refuses to (re)produce the devaluations of feminist Marxism often found in Eurocentric Marxist (Southern) praxis, or the disavowal by Eurocentric revolutionary traditions of Indigenist/decolonizing feminist thought and practise. I (w)rite as storyteller, in myth and materiality, imminently shamanically pedagogizing (Anzaldúa, 1987; Keating, 2012; Motta, 2018; Otto, 2017) the text, so that it might reach you, the reader, in your own revolutionary pedagogical praxis and being-knowing in/as the world/word.

First, I weave a mapping of elements of the epistemological-pedagogical praxis of Marxist feminisms centered around the axis of care, social reproduction, and communing, as these are embodied politically in revolutionary women (educators) in and around Fortaleza, Brazil. I then move to the decolonial/feminist revolutionary praxis as medicine-making in the tricultural movements in and around Cali, Colombia, and in relation to the threads of the flesh, the sacred and medicinal pedagogical-epistemologies. For both, I end with reflections on how their epistemological-pedagogical praxis suggests alternative axes of knowledge/revolutionary languages of the political, other subjects of revolutionary praxis and centers other medicinal and care-based practices of knowledge-making as world-making (beyond and against the event).

I then return to the lands that hold me and my children, the unceeded lands of the Awabakal and Worimi, where fresh and salt waters meet in the mangroves/*manglares*, and tenderly explore the emergence of *mestizaje* intercultural decolonizing/Indigenist feminist/feminized medicine-making as sovereignty, making reparative practise in relation to the plant kin of lemon balm and the mangroves, and the struggle for First Nations' sovereignty. I end here with a reflection on how the ongoing disavowal and denial and/or devaluation of such pedagogical-political-epistemological practices leave the revolutionary subject empty of spirit and revolutionary praxis parched, which can lead to complicity in (re)producing the violent codifications and containments of hetero-patriarchal capitalist-coloniality.

I relate and dialogue to these lineages of embodied and enfleshed struggle from the axis of the South. The South here does not merely refer to geographical positioning but to a (non)relationship to power, both political and (onto)epistemological, and the presence of emergent feminist (decolonial) revolutionary praxis as it is being trailblazed in the South.

29.2 Politicizing Pedagogically Social Reproduction and (Feminist) Revolutionary Subjects/ivities

These stories, as epistemological-pedgogical medicine-making and re-worlding, were told, witnessed, and kneaded into the bread of our liberations during dialogues with comadres, mothers, and grandermother militants and educators, in and around Fortaleza, Ceará, Brazil, in 2016–2017.

We are driving to work at the State University of Ceará with Claudiana Alencar, activist, poet, popular educator and critical decolonial/feminist linguistics scholar. She is co-founder of Viva a Palavra: an activist-scholar collective that works with racialised women and gender diverse poets from the periphery of Fortaleza with the objective of strengthening their cultural grammar as onto-epistemological projects of reoccupation in the face of systemic violations and denial of their knowing-being. We have left the children and dog with a female friend of a family friend, and are talking of the exhaustion and of being mothers in this struggle for popular education, decolonial languages of freedom making and collective liberation. Claudiana talks of her fears of not being able to keep up, of being too tired and of letting others down, of being told that she is failing by the administration. We talk of how this individualising logic just reproduces us as the problem, places blame upon our shoulders. I talk of how in the movements in Inglaterra one of our biggest struggles has been to have care recognised as a site of a value creation, of struggle and oppression and of political knowledge making. I talk of the project of interviewing and sharing the stories of militant mothers and grandmothers to bring to our thought and to our struggles a política da maternidade/politics of motherhood in which we do not have to self-sacrifice in the name of liberation. We vision that project as a project in which we are imbricated, and we continue to dialogue for the coming years. Claudiana supports me to run story circles and individual narrative interviews with mother and grandmother militants over the coming months.

Sandra is one of these women, irmã, companheira and comadre. I remember when we first met her. I was in Brazil as single mestiza mother with two daughters, one 10 and one just over one. We'd been staying in one of the favelas in Rio and arrived on the thread of connection made between us by our dear hermana revolutionary feminist Jewish popular educator and thinker Joyce Canaan. Now gone but not forgotten. We arrived to Fortaleza. I'd run out of money and J had itchy round patches on her skin. Straight away, they took us to a doctor and she was diagnosed with a serious skin infection. If we'd left it longer it could have been fatal. I remember how Sandra and her family let her run around without her nappy on as she learnt to use the potty, weeing every now and then on the wooden floor of their small yet vibrant apartment in central Fortaleza. Sandra is one of the founders of the Workers Party in Fortaleza, a popular educator, professor, president of the teachers' union, has a decades-long relation with the MST and with the radical pedagogical project of the movement Educação do Campo as pat of her cofounding and ongoing coordinating role in the Laboratoio de Estudios de Edcuacoa do Campo (LECAMPO), and as an activist researcher with women in the Ze Maria do Tome MST settlement. She is one of the founders of the Masters program in Popular Education and Social Change at the State University of Ceará which brings together militants and popular educators from community and social movements to explore action research that is in responsible relation with their community and creates knowledge with that community as part of their honours thesis research. An axis of her praxis is with women of the movimeinto sem terra and in particular the women's collective of Mãos que Criam.

From the Zé Maria do Tomé settlement, Sandra describes how the women from Mãos que Criam have been at the forefront of bringing visibility to women's wisdoms and experiences of the violences of agribusiness and its toll on the health and wellbeing of mothers and children. Their struggles on the frontline when the settlement is threatened by government and militarised interventions, and in nurturing alternative social economies have placed them at the nexus of collective meaning making to expose the inherent connections between capitalism and patriarchy. This has involved working to bring visibility to the gendered divisions of labour in social reproduction and to the ways in which women can co-organise other forms of family farming that collectivise the labours of food social (re)production and caring labours of kin in relation. They have played a key role in remembering ancestral knowledges that are fundamental to the co-construction of social economies based in agroecological models in which relationships of care between community and land are centered, and in which devalued methods of cultivation, seed protection and restoration, and care of land are revalued. This praxis embodies the emergence of the MST revolutionary female peasant as a central figure in the struggle for food sovereignty and land redistribution.

We had gone in Sandra and Ernandi's car to a workshop as part of educação do campo in the settlement of Zé Maria do Tomé and the car had broken down. I needed to get back to Fortaleza in time for the evening to get my baby son from childcare and so myself and Lourdes Vicente, organiser, leader at both regional and national levels of the women's section and education sections of the MST, and comadre decide to take the bus. As opposed to a sit-down interview, we dialogue on the bus on our journey home as we become stuck in the rush hour traffic entering Fortaleza from Limeiro do

Norte and other regions. She talks to me about her own journey into the extended family of the MST and how the settlement of Zé Maria do Tomé is a homeplace for her, to be safe and held and to take respite from the struggle. She describes how this is a form of family and kin that is beyond biological family. She speaks of the hidden histories of women MST militants and leaders, of the women's stories untold, of the practices of mistica[2] that are below the surface of the publicly seen and often politically valued, of the painting of the body with mud from mãe Terra in the light of the full moon, and the wisdoms and strengths, the reconnections and other forms of revolutionary politics and political subject that emerge when we begin our telling of stories to be told from this place and praxis of re-membering.

I share these stories and immanent, prefigurative, philosophy of liberation, pedagogical moments to foreground a revolutionary feminist politics of care and communing. This politics is itself deeply pedagogical, if we understand the pedagogical to be the processes through which we come to learn/unlearn/relearn new forms of social relationships, subjectivities, and practices of world-making, alongside the politics of knowledge that underpin these (Motta & Cole, 2013, 2014). They expand, refuse, and rupture narrow codifications of Marxist thought and pedagogical practice, which reify: first, the masculinist, proletarian subject as the key subject of revolutionary agency; second, cognitive (abstract) theory making (in which the local is only ever particular and identarian) as the font of revolutionary thought; and third, the event as the core moment of revolutionary transformation. (Motta, 2014, 2017a, 2018).

The pedagogical here is *both* the formal pedagogical processes of constructing new-ancient social economies, *and* practices of feminizing and collectivizing social reproduction (Mason-Deese, 2020), in particular, food production and care for land/mãe Terra, childcare, and kinship. These criss-cross the conditions of emergence of *Mãos que Criam* and the women/feminised revolutionary figure of the MST (da Catarina, 2017; de Carvalho et al., 2020; de Carvalho & Motta, 2018). It is embodied in the pedagogical reflectivity embedded *both* in the tending to this praxis of feminized, social, and political economic change, *and* individual and in-common emergence of revolutionary forms of feminized peasant subjectivity (de Carvalho et al., 2020; de Carvalho & Motta, 2018; Goncalves et al., 2020; Imperial, 2019; Desmarais, 2003; Motta et al., 2023; Tarlau, 2019a, 2019b). It is embodied in the remembering together of ancestral knowledges of planting, in the extended care to the children and elders in their settlement, and in valorizing the epistemological wisdoms of women militants' stories, of *both* oppression and exclusion *and* strength and survival.

The pedagogical is here also in the informal, militant sociabilities that are co-constructed in the everyday intimacies of the struggles to appear as political-intellectual subjects at all (Motta & Esteves, 2014; Motta & Gonzalez, 2023). They are in the naming and re-narrating of the (mis)representations that attempt to make us as feminized racialized subjects, to blame for our structural exhaustion. These attempt to make us self-blame for the spaces, institutions, and temporal productivist logics, premised upon our exhaustion and untimely, messy, presence/absence (Motta & Allen, 2022; Motta & Bermudez, 2019; Motta & Gonzalez, 2023). They are the ways in which we embody other forms of care and/or sense-making. They are how our critical reflexivity is of and in the body, and is enabled and articulated through deep listening (Ungunmerr, 2017), vulnerability as openness to disruption (Ettinger, 2009; Motta, 2018), the creation in the cracks of (im)possibility of fugitive time (Vázquez, 2012; Motta & Bermudez, 2019; Holloway, 2002; Tishler, 2019) and relation, making other stories to be told that must, if they are to emerge at all, embody mutual recognition (Fanon, 1961; Motta & Gonzalez, 2022).

They are in the (in)visible practices of rituals in the light of the moon, with the earth, our mother, across our bodies, and the cries of (in)justice and medicine-making kinship, with which we plant and tend to the seeds of new political-pedagogical possibilities of becoming revolutionary women. They are in the telling of the hidden histories that weave threads of insurgent, feminized presence within the revolutionary movement of the MST (de Carvalho et al., 2020; de Carvalho & Motta, 2018; Goncalves et al., 2020; Imperial, 2019; Desmarais, 2003; Motta et al., 2023). They are in a politics of maternity/motherhood, not reducible or confined to the maternal body but to forms of collective kinship making, in which homecoming is part of sovereignty taking and creating across generation, gender, and hetero-patriarchal containments of possessive individualism and family (Motta, 2023a, 2023b). They are in the relationships of unlearning and re-membering with the cycles and energies of the Mãe *Terra*, and of our own bodies, through the stages of life and our cycles of transformation. They are in the remembering of our comadres and sisters in life as in their passing, beckoning to their absent presence. Here, the ancestors become fonts of wisdom and strength (Vázquez, 2012), of a rootedness (m)otherwise not constrained by the violent borders of nation-states and their imperial map-making pedagogies of cruelty (Segato, 2015), and as dispossession (Motta, 2023a, 2023b).

All of these revolutionary feminist/feminized, pedagogical-political praxis are embedded in a politics of knowledge, or epistemological project that takes seriously: first, the stories and knowledges *both* of the feminized Southern body, *and* of the languages that emerge in order to speak these stories, otherwise untold and relegated to silence; and second, refuse the amnesia of a biopolitical political economy project of anti-life of capitalist coloniality. They bring to the political-epistemological center, social reproduction and the sphere of the private, and the everyday intimacies of our lives and bodies (Federici, 2004; Mason-Deese, 2016, 2020), (as feminized Southern subject and earth/ancestors) as sites of value-making and violent super-exploitation, but also as sites from which another politics of care and revolutionary communing is emergent (Arruzza et al., 2019; Cavallero & Gago, 2021; Federici, 2018; Gago, 2020). They there therefore in irreverent and often rebellious sisterhood to traditions of popular pedagogy, and/as revolutionary Marxist praxis, which often commit epistemicide and relegate the knowledges of the body (as feminized, Southern subject and the body as land/ancestors), the sphere of social reproduction, and the intimacies of everyday life, to mere spheres of culture, of specificity, or the conservative dogma of folklore (see Motta, 2014, 2017a, 2017b, 2017c, for a critique of this in relation to Open Marxism, Neo-Gramscinism, Autonomous Marxism of Hardt and Negri, Zizek, and broader traditions of critical social theory respectively).

29.3 Refusing Blanqueamiento: Decolonizing Feminist/Feminized Ceremonial Enfleshment of Collective Liberation

The stories that follow as epistemological-pedgogical medicine-making, and re-worlding as enfleshment (m)otherwise, were told, witnessed, co-weaved during dialogues with comadres in Cali, Colombia 2017–2018, and then virtually between Cali, Colombia, and Mulubimba-Newcastle, in so-called Australia between 2020 and 2022. We conceptualized them as research/prefigurative ceremonies, bringing to text and enfleshment the role of feminist/feminized spirituality in our political-pedagogical praxis of communal and decolonizing feminist politics.

> *Norma, Elizabeth and I sit around a small white table with a locally weaved cloth from the Nasa Indigenous peoples, Valle de Cauca with representations of the four elementals and of our collective lineages laid out with geographical connection around the table. Elizabet holds a Sahumeiro, or smoking ceremony to cleanse and open the energies for our sacred dialogue of knowledges and experiences. We then invoke Bachué the goddess-mother of the Muisca nation of the Eastern Cordillera that marks the spine of Colombia, who populated the world with peoples and then taught them/us how to feed them(our)selves with potato, cubio and maize. She then withdrew with her lover to the sacred Lake Iguaque where they lie intertwined as sacred snakes. From here on the nights of the dark moon she reminds women of their right to watch the stars, to sentipensar and share the secrets of the night, to make kin with the snakes and the earth, to leave aside any fear of the dark Mother.*
>
> > *Con madre Tierra, con mi tacto/piel/manos-pies, mis percepciones, caminando, sembrando y cosechando;*
> > *con madre Agua, con mis ojos/vista, mis aguas internas, mis emociones siempre sintiendo y limpiando;*
> > *con el Aire/viento, mis oídos-escucha/empatía, enlazando e hilando el sentipensamiento propio y colectivo;*
> > *con el abuelo Fuego/gusto, boca-palabra/alimento, en constante alquimia, transmutando-transformando;*
> > *con el Corazón/nariz/olfato, mi intuición, sensibilidades, vínculos- conexión/ alteridad con la inmanencia y el cosmos.*
>
> *We introduce ourselves as daughters of mothers, grandmothers, great mothers some of whom survived keeping us alive:*

Norma Lucia Bermudez Gomez and Elizabeth Figueroa Miranda, live, love, resist and nurture a (m)other feminist and decolonial politics in Cali, Colombia. Elizabeth is a mestiza as an ethical-political choice (Anzaldua, 1987) that allows her to recognise her privileges and oppressions, and her Afro maternal roots and lineages. She is daughter of Olga Cecilia, granddaughter of Evengelina, great-granddaughter of Petronila and great-great-granddaughter of Policapra, Black peasant women from the Valle de Cauca, Colombia. She is a healer, mother, witch, popular educator who seeks decolonising which weaves the spiritual, ancestral, cultural and pedagogical to unlearn the dominant construction of being a woman and to bring decolonising love to all elements of her life and struggles. Norma is an activist for women's rights, a communitarian feminist participating in networks, collectives and movements that center the defence of life and a politics of life against the capitalist, colonial and patriarchal system. She has explored multiple languages—of the academic, the popular, art-activism (artivismo)—in her journey of resistance/re-existencia. Sara Catherine Motta a subject who lives across borders as an Indigenous-Mestiza of Colombian-Muisca, Eastern European Jewish and Celtic descent who currently lives, loves, resists, mothers and cultivates a (m)other feminist decolonial politics in the unceded lands of the Worimi and Awabakal, where fresh and salt waters meet, in so called Southeast Australia. She is mother, survivor of state and intimate violences, poet, political theorist, popular educator, and bare-breasted philosopher who has co-created numerous projects of decolonising and feminist healing and community wellbeing spanning the last three decades, against and beyond the carceral logics and (ir)rationalities of the current system.

This is the first in numerous research/prefigurative ceremonies—that we continue to hold over the coming years—bringing to text and enfleshment the role of feminist/feminised spirituality in our political-pedagogical praxis. We begin at another beginning situating ourselves against and beyond the processes of blanqueamiento or whitening that we have experienced in our complex relationalities and (non)belongings to and with the territory now known as Colombia and the formation of this 'great' Mestizo capitalist-colonial nation-state. How this has involved a forced forgetting of our Indigenous and/or Afro descendent lineages and knowledges but that in our feminist/feminised spirituality in relation we are re-membering these wisdoms and onto-epistemological possibilities of re-worlding our feminist and revolutionary decolonising practise. We talk of how traditions of institutionalised White feminisms have reproduced the banishing of (our) spirit and the divine in their renditions of political subject and strategy and that this is not only a banishment of racialized and feminised bodies but also an epistemological banishment of the very grounds of possibility for understanding what an Indigenist/decolonising/Black communitarian feminist revolutionary ceremonial praxis might include and center pedagogically and politically. We share how our experiences of left revolutionary Marxian inspired politics also left us bereft and excluded the knowledges that come from the exteriority of the modern White/Mestizo proletarian hetero-patriarchal masculinised subject of revolution. How instead we were/are faced with derision and devaluation denied as epistemological feminised and racialised bodies enfleshing revolutionary theory and critique. How our pregnant bodies were seen as burdens, our babies which we have fought for were seen as distractions, how the knowledges of our ceremonial rememberings were mis-recognised as folkloric and conservative and/or a block on the possibilities of political and social change.

We end this session with a call again to the great mother in Bachué, to remember a politics of the (m)other but not the sacrificial or disembodied Black/Indigenous mother who has been targeted by capitalist-coloniality, not a mother who carries the burdens and the labours of care and healing on her own, ending up exhausted, depleted and full of las emociones tristes. No, we commit to visioning and enfleshing through our ceremonial epistemological-pedagogical practices a politics of the transliberatory (M)other which nurtures the body-land and body-flesh as our bodies in relation, which is alive and re-awakens the five senses and their power of attentiveness, vision, deep listening and deep feeling. This is a re-turn to a (M)other who is full and whole without closure, plural and becoming, honouring of the seasons and cycles of life, and her life in common, and of herself as lover, enchantress, witch, a weaver of worlds as word in and through the erotic.

This is where we ended our research as ceremony for that moment. Here is where we continue to weave such a politics of the (M)other as I (w)rite.

This is our research as ceremony and pedagogical-epistemological medicine-making, which in process and in journey are the imminent emergence of decolonial feminist revolutionary feminized political subjects in relation (Bermúdez, 2013; Bermúdez and Tamayo, 2017; Motta & Bermudez, 2019; Motta et al., 2020, 2024). We are always already-plural, in relation with deep and spiral time and insurgent temporalities, with place as plural, against and beyond the violent containments of empire and the nation-state (north and south, east and west), and land's sorrowful rendition to commodity. Enfleshments of time are deeply relational and beyond many Marxian renditions of temporality, which are anthropomorphic (see for these critiques for example, Motta & Bermudez, 2019; Salleh, 2020), and/or focus on moments of rupture or the event as reifications of revolutionary potential (for these critiques, see for example, Holloway, 2002; Motta, 2018; Tischler, 2008, 2014). They move us into relationality with more-than-human and non-human kin, and to the presence of deep time of the ancestors and present futurity of future generations (Kimmerer, 2021; Simpson, 2017; Vázquez, 2009). We pedagogically travel and dance with our own plural and complex lineages beyond their banishment and negation inherent to many renditions of the White (revolutionary) subject, whose existence is premised upon anti-Blackness and the disavowal of Indigenous sovereignties (Ciccariello-Maher, 2017; Motta, 2014, 2017a, 2018; Wilderson, 2003).

Our pedagogical-epistemological medicine-making stories of coming into being (m)otherwise emerge from our inhabitation of the co-constitutive underside of hetero-patriarchal modernity/coloniality. They emerge from the (re)production of us in the plural, and in relation to this non-being and exteriority, as flesh of the racialized and feminized, less-than-human, captive subjects, in the intimacies of capitalist-colonial frontier of reason, right, law, governance and knowing-being itself (Motta, 2021, 2022, 2023a, 2023b; Spillers, 1997; Weheliye, 2014). In (t)racing of the "hieroglyphics of the flesh"[3] (Spillers, 1997), first, as anti-Blackness and the disavowal of Indigenous lifeworlds and sovereignties, second, and/as attempted destruction of the racialized (M)other through *blanqueamiento*, third, as onto-epistemological project of anti-life in nation-state/governance formation and (re)production, fourth, in White colonial/modern (liberal) feminisms (see for articulation of these onto-epistemological violations for example, hooks, 1981, 1990; Mohanty, 1984; Motta, 2023a, 2023b; Robinson-Moreton, 2020; Lorde, 1984, 1990) and fifth, in revolutionary Leftist/Marxist institutionalized politics/histories of political codification (see, for example, how this articulates itself in the pedagogical projects of radical education in Mexico, Colombia and Chile, in Motta et al., 2020), we help to bring to text the markings of the violating onto-epistemological intimacies of the frontier, in the interstices of our everyday subjectification as/to flesh (Hartman, 2008; Motta, 2023b; Stoler, 2010). In this, we develop pedagogical and prefigurative medicine-making and/as healing, liberatory praxis that foregrounds how "white modernity is bathed in the blood of its victims" (Saleh-Hanna, 2015), and is thus bathed in our blood.

Our pedagogical-epistemological, medicine-making, however, moves beyond this exposure, and speaking of the violences of containment and captivity, towards an affirmative presence of exteriority of the flesh. Here, we commit to epistemological-pedagogical praxis in-relation, to speak in the flesh to all of us that escape (Motta, 2018). Here, we enflesh in text as relationality, word, and being-knowing as metaphor, myth, onto-epistemological materiality, the re-membering of the plural-sided, survivance, and dark wisdoms (Hill Collins, 1991) of the impurity of our racialized and feminized blood(lines).

This is not an affirmative exteriority which reifies or idealizes a fixed, ahistorical, identitarian essence of Black, Indigenous, and colonized life and lifeworlds, or of the plural life nurturing possibilities of a politics of the (M)other (Morrison, 1987, p. 123). Rather, it is a political-epistemological ground of decolonizing revolutionary, feminist/ized exteriority wrought from the flesh, as the experience of living plurally in, and collectively politicizing pedagogically the entanglements of the intimacies of modern/colonial frontier, and its imminent beyondness (Anzaldúa, 1987, 2009, 2015; Lugones, 1992, 2010).

We thus take seriously the affirmative exteriority conceptualized in Enrique Dussel's (1985) later work, in his quest to find the possibility and sites of enunciation of (a) revolutionary subject(s) beyond the moment of negation in dialectical and revolutionary thought /praxis (Ciccariello-Maher, 2017, pp. 110–118), and thus rupturing the constraints and constitutive exclusion of modern/colonial, critical, Marxist social theory and/as political practise (Ciccariello-Maher, 2017; Motta, 2018; Wilderson, 2003). As Dussel (1985, p. 173) explains:

It is not only the denial of the denial of the system on the basis of the affirmation of the totality {ie dialectical negation of the negation}. It is the overcoming of the totality but not merely as the actuality of what is present in the system as potential. It is the overcoming of totality on the basis of internal transcendentality or exteriority, that which has never been within. To affirm exteriority is to realise what is impossible for the system... It is to realise the *new*, that which is unforeseeable from the perspective of the totality, that which emerged from an unconditioned, revolutionary and innovative freedom.

It is thus from this affirmative exteriority of the feminized and racialized flesh that we can think, (t)race, and (w)rite into knowing-being an epistemological-pedagogical medicinal politics of the sacred and the possibilities of a transpolitics of the (M)other. Here, we breathe into knowing-being a pluridiverse meeting place between revolutionary thought, Black and Indigenous feminisms and decoloniality. Here, the Black and Indigenous mother and her knowledges, life-making praxis, and philosophies of the sacred move from their relegation to social and epistemological abyssal anti-life to the center of the (im)possibilities of enfleshing revolutionary praxis and/as pedagogies of the sacred as the profane, and the profane as the enfleshment of the sacred.

29.4 Ample *Mestizaje* Hearts

I-in relation move to the placedness of the unceded lands of the Worimi and Awabakal peoples, Mulubimba-Newcastle, in so called Australia, understanding place as more than physical boundary or commodified object, but rather *senti-pensando* place as ancestral, emotional, energetic, moving into the shadow places of the unseen, (in)visibilized places in which we survive and attempt to flourish in responsible relation. I do this to enflesh in text the *mestizaje*, decolonial, feminist, revolutionary pedagogical praxis of which I (w)rite and (t)race beyond the borders, boundaries, and codifications of the modern/colonial nation-state, and to honour my placedness that is plural, weaved across, between, and as multiple territories of the South. I weave threads of (re)connection across the South to inter-cultural, inter-class, inter-generational collective kinship making in, against, and beyond the urban/colonial city and its pinnacle of knowing subjectivity in the modern/colonial university, and its pedagogical project of cruelty and/as dispossession.

We drop more deeply into the terrains of affirmative exteriority of the fleshed sovereignty struggles as healing epistemological-pedagogical medicine-making that stands as and in kinship with the struggle for Indigenous sovereignty in these lands (Moreton-Robinson, 2000, 2015; Watego, 2022). We move to the plant ancestors as they (t)race the scars and refuse the ongoing violent markings of the settler-colonial-capitalist project, premised as it is on Indigenous disavowal and the nexus of private property, hetero-patriarchal family, and possessive individualism (Kimmerer, 2021; Midnight, 2023; Motta, 2023a, 2023b; TallBear, 2018, 2020). The plant kin offer us fonts of knowledge and care, of wisdoms and rememberings that move us to joyfully resist and undo Empire, as it attempts to pierce our ample *mestizaje* hearts (Anzaldúa, 1987).

The stories which follow as epistemological-pedgogical medicine-making and re-worlding as enfleshment (m)otherwise, were told, witnessed, co-weaved during dialogues and plant circles with comadres and kin in Mulubimba-Newcastle, in so-called Australia, from 2021. We are conceptualizing them as a thread in the weave of co-weaving the ecologies of intimacy (Simpson, 2017) and infrastructures of care, out of which our survivor-led, intersectional feminized sanctuary homeplace, and radical education meeting-place, is emergent (Motta, 2023b).

Its oh so simple, in that it is oh so flowing and smooth. We sit in circle with fresh lemon balm leaves. Place some in a vase of water in the hope that they might root and then be planted into the collective medicinal garden below. We boil water and place the rest to sit for 20 minutes as we reconnect and call to presence the day our plant circle is held in relation to the lineages of one of us. It is between day 8 and 9 of the counting of the Omer, we are between Chesed she'b'Gevurah (heart expansion with strong holding) and Gevurah she'b'Gevurah (strong holding with strong holding). I sing the Omer Daily Blessing. We sit for a while dropping into the energies and learnings of those words and blessings.

There are books and files with notes from years of learning from wisdom keepers of the sacred plant teachers. We look for Lemon Balm and hir properties. We remember that they are called Melissa also for in some books of wisdoms there is no mention of lemon balm. We explore hir languages through the emotional, physicalal properties, spiritual connections and dependent on need/ailment/condition.

We share what we 'know' already and connect in more deeply by pouring a tea for us each. We touch the cup and bring it up to our noses to smell in the resonance, and gently place a drop on the tip of our tongues, savouring the delicate and calming lemon taste. We then gently drink some of hir brew. Ingesting in this way is more than drinking a cup of tea, it is a form of communing with the plant kin hirself, and of inviting in reverence the somatic and energetic wisdoms to flow into presence.

They have felt and seen these lands for eons and their energy of ease and peace, of playfulness and knowing innocence, allow for co-regulation of our bodies often already disassociated for the (un)belonging we must walk in the intimacies of the everyday frontiers of the modern/colonial city, state and university. We meander without destination sharing stories of lemon balm and grandmother healing hands in Caracas of the 1970s, forgotten for so long as something to be dropped in the pursuit of success, now re-embraced for that which connects and points the way and the vision for an other worlding. For an other world making in this time when the violences of Professionalism and the Academy, of border regimes and passport offices, of courts and state interventions have been felt and fought for too long that now it is time for rest and retreat as possibility otherwise not as defeat and (self)denial.

We meander further to Lviv and Krakow as we read a section from the Ashkenazi Jewish Herbal Medicines book, and even though Melissa is not present in this text, we meander further into the new-ancient cartography in this Materia Medica from other territories where we find both recognisable and new plant kin. There are recountings of the stories of maternal grandfathers and resistance fights, of suicides as an act of resistance and dignity, of death in Aushwitz-Burkenau, of living in the shadow of the holocaust and the ways this criss-cross our bodies and families like the barbed wire of the borders erected by Empire then and now, everyday in the intercises of the modern-colonial violent present, and the split into fragments of our lineages and possibility of belonging and collective liberation. Of how we find ourselves here right now, so many of us from stories of displacement, dispossession, and desire and survivance, and with threads not to be forgotten or elided of invasion and colonisation. Of how listening to all our grandmothers' stories and finding reconciliation and responsible relating may we well offer threads towards tiqqun, of piecing back together without devaluing our brokenness into shards of scattered glass.

What is this I hear the revolutionary leaders say. Perhaps they might laugh at us for our talking in tongues to lemon balm kin. For the way we allow things to wander as a prefigurative, Indigenist-abolitionist, feminist pedagogy of walking, as we sit still in circle and move through the tender layers of place and place-in-relation as kin through deep time and future generations (Motta, 2011). We are here moving against and beyond the revolutionary political as moment of rupture (Motta, 2018). We are tired of this move and (self)containment. We are moving together in plural cyclical ways (Aunty Shaa Smith et. al. (2020)). We are (re)learning to come back into our bodies as flesh and as feminized and racialized queer bodies in the plural. We are dropping into the place of the body-flesh-territory-land, in which the barbed wire edges can no longer tear at our skin and beyond a reading/(w)riting of us within the borders, however, "liberatory" of a hieroglyphics of the flesh. We are moving, tentatively and tenderly like the pot plants on the kitchen ledge in the sun, that sometimes die and sometimes live to be planted downstairs, in a sun that might be too strong or not present enough, towards something in which we are not merely surviving, but are enfleshing/embodying together in deep relation across time and space an other decolonizing abolitionist feminist sovereignty-making as life-making in the plural. There are no guarantees here. This is not a pedagogical-political onto-epistemological project of mastery, of monologue, of certainty. But this is where we have arrived. This is where we sit talking and taking off the burdens we have carried for so long to hold up the world, a world premised upon our social, spirit, and epistemological death (Gonzalez et al., 2023).

I end with the offering of this story below as epistemological-pedgogical medicine-making and sovereignty-making in relation, told, witnessed, co-weaved with my sis-hermana Aunty Theresa Dargin, traditional custodian, Onebygamba, Worimi lands, cultural healer and lead language teacher. These stories were shared from 2022 to the present, as part of our Nurungil project of cultural revitalization and healing well-being, for Indigenous and non-Indigenous youth and community.

We laugh a lot, Theresa and me. Similar in age, both racialized women, both the center of our families, she an elder of these lands, me an impure curandera across territories. She tells me of her longing to re-learning Gathang language of how her pop was fluent but if they spoke language in the street or at school that the kids might be taken away, stolen by the state. She shares with me the cards with the words in English and the wor(l)ds in Gathang. And the drawings of her older daughter. And how my elder daughter might paint with her. To help them survive the ongoing and ancestral traumas. They both struggle a lot. We laugh a lot, so much at the Institutions and their ridiculous f***ing logics. We rage too, cry sometimes, when these logics reproduce the missionary manager in the lives of Theresa and her kin, when they see her as always-already suspect, when financial and institutional systems already always see us as potential thieves.

There are always these magic encounters, with an environmental collectives as Theresa is out walking on the mangrove/manglares, listening and watching for the mud crabs and the pelicans. They meet, one is one of my students too, we agree to clear up the mangroves and support the ecologies of intimacy and survivance to thrive again. We search for old maps and knowledge holders to share how they were. Theresa remembers as a child how the crabs were so much bigger. The plague of bats and bat poo was not there. Last clean-up we found 60 used syringes- the remnants of the disease of this ongoing violence of the colonial-settler city. We need to re-present to the Institution to receive the funds that are rightly hers and the community so that they might be able to fund the cultural and language work of remembering with the young ones so that they too might survive and thrive, be the leaders in relation of the future. We do this naming/re-presenting to the Institution with meaning and with irreverence at the same time.

Nurungil-spirited/re-turn of spirit is the word as worlding that we choose to re-present our kinship in the making, our worldmaking motherwise and our pedagogical-epistemological medicine-making as sovereignty making, reparations and healing for Indigenous youth and community (indigenous and non-Indigenous) on these lands.

> Nurungil
> Nurungil
> I think if I repeat it in text that You might listen, and I/we don't mean just listen, we mean epistemologically-politically-pedagogically listen.
> Nurungil
> Nurungil.

29.5 Feminizing/Feminist and Decolonizing Abolitionist Pedagogical-Political Revolution/ary Subjects (M)otherwise

In this piece, emergent from over three decades of critical intimacy, I have desired and had the responsibility to bring together the pedagogical-political-conceptual-(onto)-epistemological gifts of lineages of autonomous Marxist feminisms and decolonial/abolitionist communitarian feminisms both of the South, in terms of what they bring to a pedagogical-political project of revolutionary transformation and collective liberation. I have foregrounded through story and/as conceptual-pedagogical reflection how both are deeply pedaogical-epistemological, and both live/re-exist often as either the devalued underside or disavowed and erased other within many projects and theoretical-political renditions of Marxism.

In the lineges of the former, I-in-relation foreground the place of care, the body, the everyday community and homeplace, and the concept of social reproduction as key in expanding politicization and conceptualization of the capital-relation. This accordingly expands: *both* the site of class struggle to the private/home, and the subject of revolutionary transformation to the feminized homeworker and women revolutionary subject. It foregrounds practices through which we might collectivize social reproduction in care (for land and each other), kinship, food production towards agroecological political economies; *and* the place-based knowledges of the feminized (and racialized) peasant/proletarian body, embraced pedagogically as epistemologically priveledged essence of this expansion and political-pedagogical deepening/feminizing of Marxian (pedagogical) praxis and practices of revolutionary change.

In the lineages of the latter I-in-relation enflesh a third set of categories, concepts and onto-epistemological-pedagogical threads emergent from the constitutive underside of hetero-patriarchal, capitalist-coloniality, and birthed from the plurally sided flesh of the racialized and feminized Indigenous, Afro, and colonized (non)subjects of modernity/coloniality. These expand beyond the containments of humanness, reason, and subjectivity of the modern/colonial and many Marxian codifications of revolutionary thought and practice, beckoning and enfleshing other epistemological grounds of political-pedagogical becoming. These include the flesh, more-than human ancestral and non-human kin, multiple temporalities of deep time and future-present, and plural enfleshments of reason, which are pedagogically kneaded into the bread, roses, and territories of our pluridiverse communitarian projects of collective healing liberations. They center a politics of Indigenous sovereignties and reparations and refuse the anti-Blackness and Indigenous disavowal often re-produced in the institutional practises and theoretical conceptualizations of Marxism lineages of revolutionary (pedagogical) praxis. They/we thus call to account and responsibility these lineages and hold out an invitation as part of our pedagogical-political weaving of gift relationalities and world-making, to come walk with us, sit with us, and listen deeply and (onto)epistemologically in the mangrove swamps/*manglares* of healing-sovereignties and enfleshing revolutionary futurities (m)otherwise.

Notes

1. *Mestizaje* here has its lineages in the use of the term mestiza consciousness in Gloria Anzaldúa's great contribution *Borderlands/La Frontera: The New Mestiza* (1987) and in further pieces such as 'La Prieta' (2009). I use *mestizaje* (Motta, 2018, 2023a) as a play and usuprtion of the term mestizo/a, which was a key part of nation-state building in the southern lands of Abya Yala which attempted to whiten or create a process of blanqueamiento of these territories to disawoval indigenous sovereignties and deny afro-slave descendents' presense. This project of anti-Blackness and/as Indigenneities has been central to the foundation and (re)production of capitalist modernity-coloniality. However, some strands of decolonial and indigenist feminisms take back such terms to suggest a politics that ruptures, refuses, and contests the violent bordering practices that seek to reduce racialized and feminized subjects and communities to (non)knowing being, and instead point towards pluridiverse lifeworlds and practices of re-worlding.
2. Mística, is at once a public, expressive dramatic performance and, drawing on Christian mysticism, a way of making contact with a transcendent reality. Mística draws on Christian theology generally, and specifically on the practices of the Christian base communities associated with liberation theology which were key in the emergence of the MST. It fortifies activists with the high commitment needed to engage in land occupations and the creation of farming communities through which the MST pursues its central goal of agrarian reform and an alternative emancipatory pedagogical-political project. It is a regular practice of the MST. It is intended to promote a sense of identity as a separate group and commitment to the group's purposes. The term mística refers not just to the performance, however, but to the whole world view that underlies it, drawing on traditions of Christian mysticism to affirm unity with a transcendent reality. Mística is sacramental in that its manifest physical reality is taken to represent the deeper meaning. It is impossible to separate the enactment of mística from the engagement with transcendence. Through participating in or observing mística, people express their ideals and believe that they come closer to attaining them (see Hammond, 2014 for further analysis and conceptualization).
3. The *hieroglyphics of the flesh* is not just the violence committed against the Black body, like the "chokecherry tree" on Sethe's back in Toni Morrison's *Beloved* (1987), but the flesh itself as a marker for racial violence no matter the institution [or form] whether scientific, social, political, educational or economic (Spillers, 1997). As she continues, "I would make a distinction in this case between 'body' and 'flesh' and impose that distinction as the central one between captive and liberated subject-positions. In that sense, before the 'body' there is the 'flesh,' that zero degree of social conceptualization that does not escape concealment under the brush of discourse, or the reflexes of iconography" (Spillers, 1997, p. 67).

REFERENCES

Anzaldúa, G. (1987). *Borderlands/La Frontera: The New Mestiza*. Aunt Lute Books.
Anzaldúa, G. (2002). Now Let us Shift… the Path of Conocimiento… Inner Works, Public Acts. In G. Anzaldua & A. L. Keating (Eds.), *This Bridge We Call Home* (pp. 540–578). Routledge.
Anzaldúa, G. (2009). La Prieta. In A. L. Keating (Ed.), *The Gloria Anzaldúa Reader* (pp. 38–51). Duke University Press.
Anzaldúa, G. (2015). Let us be the Healing of the Wound: The Coyolxauhqui Imperative—la sombra y el sueno. In A. L. Keating (Ed.), *Light in the Dark/ Luz en lo Oscuro* (pp. 120–122). Duke University Press.
Arruzza, C., Bhattacharya, T., & Fraser, N. (2019). *Feminism for the 99%: A Manifesto*. Verso Books.
Aunty Shaa Smith, Neeyan S., Wright. S., Hodge, P., & Daley, L. (2020). Yandaarra is Living Protocol, *Social & Cultural Geography*, 21(7), 940–961. https://doi.org/10.1080/14649365.2018.1508740
Bermúdez, N. L. (2013). Cali's Women in Collective Crossing for Three Worlds: Popular Education, Feminisms and Nonviolence for the Expansion of the Present, Memory and for Nurturing Life. In S. C. Motta & M. Cole (Eds.), *Education and Social Change in Latin America* (pp. 239–259). Palgrave Macmillan.
Bermúdez, N. L., & Tamayo, J. (2017). *Liderazgos Sutiles: Histórias de re-evoluciones cotidianas de mujeres populares en la Comuna 18 de Cali, Colombia*. Casa Chontaduro.
Cardoso, F. H. (1972). *Dependency and Development in Latin America*. University of California Press.
Cavallero, L., & Gago, V. (2021). *A Feminist Reading of Debt* (L. Mason-Deese, Trans.). Pluto Press.
Ciccariello-Maher, G. (2017). *Decolonising Dialectics*. Duke University Press.
Collins, P. H. (1991). *Black Feminist Thought: Knowledge, Consciousness, and the Politics of Empowerment*. Routledge.
Da Catarina, S. M. (2017). 'Um feminism que brota da terra' Movimiento dos Trabahadores Rurais sem Terra, 12 August. Retrieved May 11, 2023, from https://mst.org.br/2017/08/12/um-feminismo-que-brota-da-terra/
De La Costa, M., & James, S. (1975). *The Power of Women and the Subversion of Community*. Falling Wall Press.
de Carvalho, S. M. G., da Silva, M. N., & Barbosa, L. P. (2020). Enfrentamentos e Aprendizados: a Insurgéncia Feminina no Acampamento Zé Maria do Tomé, Chapada do Apodi-CE [Confrontations and Lessons: The Feminine Insurgency in the Zé Maria do Tomé Encampment, Chapada do Apodj- CE]. *Revista Dialogo Educacional*, 20(67), 1808–1836. https://doi.org/10.7213/1981-416X.20.067.DS14
de Carvalho, S. M. G., & Motta, S. C. (2018). Educacao do Campo Movimentos Sociais e Feminismo: Resisténcias e Aprendizados em Contexto Neoliberal. In S. M. G. de Carvalho, J. E. Mendes, & M. D. M. Segundo (Eds.), *Politica Educacional, Docéncia e Movimentos Sociais no Context y Neoliberal* (pp. 195–206). Universidade Estadual do Ceará.
Desmarais, A. A. (2003). The Via Campesina: Peasant Women at the Frontiers of Food Sovereignty. *Canadian Women's Studies*, 23(1), 140–145.
Dussel, E. (1985). *Philosophy of Liberation*. Orbis Books.
Ettinger, B. L. (2009). Fragilization and Resistance' and 'Neighborhood and Shechina'. *Studies in the Maternal*, 1(2), 1–31. https://doi.org/10.16995/sim.141

Fanon, F. (1961). *Black Skin White Masks* (R. Philcox, Trans.). Grove Press.
Federici, S. (2004). *Caliban and the Witch: Women, the Body and Primitive Accumulation.* Autonomedia.
Federici, S. (2018). *Re-enchanging the World: Feminism and a Politics of the Commons.* PM Press.
Gago, V. (2020). *Feminist International: How to Change Everything* (L. Mason-Deese, Trans.). Verso.
Gramsci, A. (1971). *Selections from the prison notebooks.* London: Lawrence and Wishart.
Gonzalez, Y., Motta, S. C., & Seppälä, T. (2023, forthcoming). Decolonising Feminist Solidarities. In S. Katila, E. Bell, & S. Meriläinen (Eds.), *Handbook of Feminist Methodology in Management and Organization Studies.* Edward Elgar Publishing.
Hammond, J. L. (2014). Mística, Meaning and Popular Education in the Brazilian Landless Workers Movement. *Interface: A Journal for and About Social Movements,* 6(1), 372–391.
Hartman, S. (2008). *Lose Your Mother: A Journey Along the Atlantic Slave Route.* Palgrave Macmillan.
Holloway, J. (2002). *Change the World without Taking Power.* Pluto Press.
hooks, b. (1981). *Ain't I Woman: Black Women and Feminism.* South End Press.
hooks, b. (1990). *Yearning: Race, Gender, and Cultural Politics.* South End Press.
Imperial, M. (2019). New Materialist Feminist Ecological Practices: La Via Campesina and Activist Environmental Work. *Social Sciences,* 8(8), 235. https://doi.org/10.3390/socsci8080235
Lorde, A. (1984). Age, Race, Class, and Sex: Women Redefining Difference. In A. Lorde (Ed.), *Sister Outsider* (pp. 124–144). Crossing Press.
Lorde, A. (1990). *Need: A Chorale for Black Women's Voices.* Kitchen Table, Women of Colour Press.
Lugones, M. (1992). On Borderlands/La Frontera: An Interpretive Essay. *Hypatia,* 7, 31–37. https://doi.org/10.1111/j.1527-2001.1992.tb00715.x
Lugones, M. (2010). Toward a Decolonial Feminism. *Hypatia,* 25(4), 742–759. Retrieved May 11, 2023, from https://www.jstor.org/stable/40928654
Keating, A. (2012). Speculative Realism, Visionary Pragmatism, and Poet-Shamanic Aesthetics in Gloria Anzaldúa—and Beyond. *Women's Studies Quarterly,* 40(3/4), 51–69. http://www.jstor.org/stable/23333473
Kimmerer, R. W. (2021). *Braiding Sweetgrass.* Milkweed Editions.
Mason-Deese, L. (2016). Unemployed Workers' Movements and the Territory of Social Reproduction. *Journal of Resistance Studies,* 2(2), 65–99. Retrieved May 11, 2023, from https://resistance-journal.org/wp-content/uploads/2021/04/Volume-2-Number-2-Liz-MD.pdf
Mason-Deese, L. (2020). New Forms of Feminized Resistances and their Role in the (Re)creation of Emancipatory Political Subjectivities in Latin America. In S. A. Hamed Hosseini, James Goodman, Sara C. Motta, & Barry K. Gills (Eds.) *The Routeldge Handbook of Transformative Global Studies.* Routledge.
Midnight, D. (2023). *The Persistent Desire.* https://dorimidnight.com/writing/lecha-dodi-for-a-sabbath-butch/
Mignolo, W. D. (2002). The Geopolitics of Knowledge and the Colonial Difference. *South Atlantic Quarterly,* 101(1), 57–96.
Mohanty, C. T. (1984). Under Western Eyes: Feminist Scholarship and Colonial Discourses. *Boundary,* 2(12/13), 333–358. Retrieved May 11, 2023, from https://www.jstor.org/stable/302821

Moreton-Robinson, A. (2000). *Talkin Up to the White Woman: Indigenous Women and Feminism*. University of Queensland Press.

Moreton-Robinson, A. (2015). *The White Possessive: Property, Power, and Indigenous Sovereignty* (Indigenous Americas). University of Minnesota Press.

Motta, S. C. (2011). Notes towards Prefigurative Epistemologies. In S. C. Motta & A. G. Nilsen (Eds.), *Social Movements in the Global South* (pp. 178–199). Palgrave Macmillan.

Motta, S. C. (2013). "We Are the Ones We Have Been Waiting For": The Feminization of Resistance in Venezuela. *Latin American Perspectives*, 40(4), 35–54. https://doi.org/10.1177/0094582X13485706

Motta, S. C. (2014). 21st Century Emancipation: The Pedagogical Practices of Social Movements. *Interface: A Journal for and About Social Movements*, 6, 1–24

Motta, S. C. (2016). Decolonising Critique: From Prophetic Negation to Affirmative Prefiguration. In A. C. Dinerstein (Ed.), *An Other Politics in the Social Sciences: Women Theorising without Parachutes* (pp. 33–48). Routledge.

Motta, S. C. (2017a). Latin America as Political Science's Other. *Social Identities*, 23(1), 701–717. https://doi.org/10.1080/13504630.2017.1291093

Motta, S. C. (2017b). Emancipation in Latin America: On the Pedagogical Turn. *Bulletin of Latin American Research*, 36, 5–20. https://doi.org/10.1111/blar.12526

Motta, S. C. (2017c). Mass Intellectuality from the Margins. In R. Hall & J. Winn (Eds.), *Mass Intellectuality and Democratic Leadership in Higher Education* (pp. 185–197). Bloomsbury Academic.

Motta, S. C. (2018). *Liminal Subjects: Weaving (Our) Liberation*. Rowman & Littlefield.

Motta, S. C. (2021). Decolonsiing Our Feminist/Ized Revolutions: Enfleshed Praxis from Southwest Colombia. *Latin American Perspectives*, 48(4), 124–142. https://doi.org/10.1177/0094582X211020748

Motta, S. C. (2022). Decolonising (Critical) Social Theory: Enfleshing Post-Covid Futurities. *Thesis Eleven*, 170, 58–77. https://doi.org/10.1177/07255136221104265

Motta, S. C. (2023a). Weaving Enfleshed Citizenship (M)otherwise. In L. Šimić & E. Underwood-Lee (Eds.), *Mothering Performance: Maternal Action* (pp. 185–203). Routledge.

Motta, S. C. (2023b). The Epistemological Intimacies of the Urban Frontier: Mangrove Swamps, Possessive (Non)belonging and Kinship (M)otherwise. *Globalizations*, 19(3), 208–224. https://doi.org/10.1080/14747731.2023.2177433

Motta, S. C., & Cole, M. (Eds.). (2013). *Educatin and Social Change in Latin America*. Palgrave Macmillan

Motta, S. C., & Cole, M. (2014). *Constructing 21st Century Socialism: The role of Radical Education*. Palgrave Macmillan.

Motta, S. C., & Esteves, A. M. (2014). Reinventing Emancipation in the 21st Century: The Pedagogical Practices of Social Movements. *Interface: A Journal for and About Social Movements*, 6, 1–24. Retrieved May 11, 2023, from https://www.interface-journal.net/wordpress/wp-content/uploads/2014/06/Interface-6-1-Editorial.pdf

Motta, S. C., & Bermudez, N. L. (2019). Enfleshing Temporal Insurgencies and Decolonial Times. *Globalizations*, 16, 424–440. https://doi.org/10.1080/14747731.2018.1558822

Motta, S. C., & Allen, M. K. (2022). Decolonising Critique in, Against and Beyond the Business School. *Ephemera: Theory and Politics in Organization, 22*(3), 21–51. Retrieved May 11, 2023, from https://ephemerajournal.org/sites/default/files/2022-12/22.3%20Motta%20Allen.pdf

Motta, S. C., & Gonzalez, Y. (2022). Popular Sovereignty and (Non)recognition in Venezuela: On the Coming into Political Being of 'el *Pueblo*'. In M. Oswald (Ed.), *The Palgrave Handbook of Populism*. Palgrave Macmillan. https://doi.org/10.1007/978-3-030-80803-7_18

Motta, S. C., & Gonzalez, Y. T. (2023). Yes we speak, si temenos voz; Refusing epistemological terra nullilus. In Special Issue S. C. Motta, & Y. Gonzalez-Torres (Eds.), 'Refusing epistemological Terra Nullius' *Journal of Critical Southern Studies*. https://jcss.demontfortuniversitypress.org/.../4/issue/0

Motta, S. C., de Carvalho, S. M. G., de Alencar, C. N., & da Silva, M. N. (2023). 11: Feminised and Decolonising Reoccupations, Re-existencias and Escrevivências: Learning from Women's Movement Collectives in Northeast Brazil. In C. Eschle & A. Bartlett (Eds.), *Feminism and Protest Camps: Entanglements, Critiques and Re-Imaginings* (pp. 195–214). Bristol University Press.

Motta, S. C., Bermudez Gomez, N. I., & Miranda, E. N. (2024). An Erotic and Poetic Political Subjectivity of the Sacred (En)Flesh(ed). *Globalizations*, Special Issue, Decolonising and Feminising Citizenship.

Motta, S. C., Bermudez Gomez, N. L., Valenzuela Fuentes, K., & Dixon, E. S. (2020). Student Movements in Latin America: Decolonizing and Feminizing Education and/as Life. In *Oxford Encyclopedia of Politics*. Oxford University Press. Retrieved May 11, 2023, from https://oxfordre.com/politics/display/10.1093/acrefore/9780190228637.001.0001/acrefore-9780190228637-e-1721;jsessionid=B82328C06497B5736AEA9FB4BE099EA9

Morrison, T. (1987) Beloved. Plume Contemporary Fiction.

Ndlovu-Gatsheni, S. J., & Ndlovu, M. (2022). *Marxism and Decolonization in the 21st Century Living Theories and True Ideas*. London: Routledge.

Ni Una Menos. (2018). *Amistad Política + Intelligencia Colectiva: Documentos/Manifiestos 2015/2018*. Ni Una Menos.

Otto, M. (2017). Poet-Shamanic Aesthetics in the Work of Gloria Anzaldúa and Wilson Harris: A Critique of Postcolonial Reason. *The CLR James Journal, 23*(1/2), 135–156. Retrieved May 11, 2023, from https://www.jstor.org/stable/26752150

Robinson-Moreton. (2020). *Talkin up the White Woman: Indigenous Women and Feminism*. University of Minnesota Press.

Saleh-Hanna, V. (2015). Black Feminist Hauntology Rememory the Ghosts of Abolition?. *Champ Pénal/Penal Field, XII*, 1–34.

Salleh, A. (2020). A Materialist Ecofeminist Reading of the Green Economy: Or, Yes Karl, the Ecological Footprint is Sex-Gendered. In S. A. Hosseini Faradonbeh, J. Goodman, S. C. Motta, & B. K. Gills (Eds.), *The Routledge Handbook of Transformative Global Studies* (pp. 247–258). Routledge.

Segato, R. L. (2015). *Contra-pedagogias de la crueldad*. Prometeo Libros.

Simpson, A. (2016). The State is a Man: Theresa Spence, Loretta Saunders and the Gender of Settler Sovereignty. *Theory and Event, 19*(4). Retrieved May 11, 2023, from muse.jhu.edu/article/633280

Simpson, L. B. (2017). *As We Have Always Done: Indigenous Freedom through Radical Resistance*. University of Minnesota Press.

Spillers, H. (1997). Mama's Baby, Papa's Maybe: An American Grammar Book. *Diacritics: A Review of Contemporary Criticism, 17.*

Stoler, A. L. (2010). *Carnal Knowledge and Imperial Power: Race and the Intimate in Colonial Rule.* University of California Press.

TallBear, K. (2018). Making Love and Relations beyond Settler Sex and Family. In A. Clarke & D. Haraway (Eds.), *Making Kin Not Population* (pp. 145–164). Prickly Paradigm Press.

TallBear, K. (2020). On Revising Kinship and Sexual Abundance. *for the wild,* 187. Retrieved May 11, 2023, from https://forthewild.world/listen/kim-tallbear-on-revivingkinship-and-sexual-abundance-157

Tarlau, R. (2019a). From a Language to a Theory of Resistance: Critical Pedagogy, the Limits of "Framing," and Social Change. *Educational Theory, 64,* 369–392. https://doi.org/10.1111/edth.12067

Tarlau, R. (2019b). *Occupying Schools, Occupying Land: How the Landless Workers' Movement Transformed Brazilian Education.* Oxford Academic.

Tischler, S. (2008). The Crisis of the Classical Canon of the *Class Form* and Social Movements in Latin America. In W. Bonefeld (Ed.), *Subverting the Present, Imagining the Future: Insurrection, Movement and Commons* (pp. 161–178). Autonomedia.

Tischler, S. (2014). Detotalization and Subject: On Zapatismo and Critical Theory. *South Atlantic Quarterly, 113*(2), 327–338. https://doi.org/10.1215/00382876-2643648

Ungunmerr, M.-R. (2017). To be Listened to in Her Teaching: Dadirri: Inner Deep Listening and Quiet Still Awareness. *EarthSong Journal: Perspectives in Ecology, Spirituality and Education, 3*(4), 14–15. https://doi.org/10.3316/informit.732386012034745

Vázquez, R. (2012). Towards a Decolonial Critique of Modernity Buen Viivir, Relationality and the Task of Listening. In *Capital, Poverty, Development.* Wissenschaftsverlag Mainz.

Vázquez, R. (2009). Modernity Coloniality and Visibility: The Politics of Time. *Sociological Research Online, 14*(4), 109–115. https://doi.org/10.5153/sro.1990

Vázquez, R. (2012). Towards a Decolonial Critique of Modernity: Buen Vivir, Relationality and the Task of Listening. In R. Fornet-Betancourt (Ed.), *Capital, Poverty, Development. Denktraditionen im Dialog: Studien zur Befreiung und Interkulturalität* (Vol. 33, pp. 241–252). Wissenschaftsverlag Mainz. Retrieved May 11, 2023, from https://www.prismaweb.org/nl/wp-content/uploads/2017/07/Towards-a-decolonial-critique-of-modernity-Buen-vivir-relationality-and-the-task-of-listening%E2%94%82Rolando-V%C3%A1zquez%E2%94%822012.pdf

Watego, C. (2022). *Another Day in the Colony.* University of Queensland Press.

Weheliye, A. G. (2014). *Habeas Viscus: Racializing Assemblages, Biopolitics, and Black Feminist Theories of the Human.* Duke University Press.

Wilderson III, F. (2003). Gramsci's Black Marx: Whither the Slave in Civil Society?, *Social Identities, 9*(2), 225–240. https://doi.org/10.1080/1350463032000101579

CHAPTER 30

Marxism in an Activist Key: Educational Implications of an Activist-Transformative Philosophy

Anna Stetsenko

30.1 Introduction

One of the urgent tasks in education today is to critically and radically challenge and change—in fact, to completely overturn—the dominant foundational conception of education in light of deep sociopolitical, economic, and environmental crises currently underway in "our world on fire" (Moraga, 1983). This situation requires novel and daring modes of thinking and acting, including in theorizing education, all while moving beyond the unsustainable status quo, which is in fact killing us—that is, killing both people and the planet itself, as is becoming increasingly clear (see e.g., Case & Deaton, 2021).

This foundational conception of education in need of a radical overturn consists of many interrelated aspects and layers such as a theory of the self/subjectivity and agency, mind and knowledge, teaching and learning, society and culture, and of history, ethics, and morality. In this chapter, I focus on the topic of agency as applied to the notion of "learner," which is the centerpiece of the whole education system. Indeed, the notion of a learner relates to education systems and practices like their microcosm, absorbing and refracting all other assumptions about education. This is similar, to use Vygotsky's metaphor, to how "the word is a microcosm of consciousness, related to

A. Stetsenko (✉)
The Graduate Center, The City University of New York, NY, USA
e-mail: astetsenko@gc.cuny.edu

© The Editor(s) (if applicable) and The Author(s), under exclusive license to Springer Nature Switzerland AG 2023
R. Hall et al. (eds.), *The Palgrave International Handbook of Marxism and Education*, Marxism and Education,
https://doi.org/10.1007/978-3-031-37252-0_30

consciousness like a living cell is related to an organism, like an atom is related to the cosmos" (1987, p. 285). The currently dominant notion of a learner is not the only culprit creating problems in education, which is currently in a state of crisis and disintegration, just like capitalism itself. Yet its role should not be underestimated. Being tacitly imposed (often via brutal top-down reforms) on education communities, both teachers and students, this notion is a powerful tool of neoliberal capitalist regimes with their ideologies of acquiescence with, and adaptation to, the *status quo* and its imposed normativity of reproducing "what is."

The dominant conception of education, overall, prioritizes a top-down, unidirectional transmission of knowledge to learners who are supposed to absorb and process this knowledge, each as a solitary "achiever" in individualized pursuits of academic success and other personal gains. Relatedly, learners are posited to be *passive recipients* of education, rendered essentially powerless, agentless and voiceless, as they are literally *subjected* to what is *happening to them* in classrooms and beyond. Learners have practically no say in the process of education as they, essentially, *do not matter*—being "given" knowledge, information, and so on. Accordingly, their minds and identities are seen as in need of being molded through education, especially with the goal to fit in with the world as "it is." Moreover, this is done with a clear agenda of assimilating (aka "socializing") learners into pre-established social structures—all supposed to be stable and indomitable, destined to continue in line with long-standing rules and norms guiding them, in no need of radical changes. Importantly, this dominant conception is inherently political and de facto oppressive since it operates as an instrument of producing the workforce for a supposedly immutable capitalist society, ignoring all of its flaws of exploitation, inequality, subordination, top-down control, individualism, cut-throat competition, alienation, and rigid hierarchies, including along the axes of class, race, and dis/ability.

My argument in this chapter is that Marxism—on a condition that it itself is radicalized and pushed to critical conclusions as an activist-transformative philosophy (as proposed in this chapter)—is a vital conceptual resource that is indispensable for challenging and changing the very core of how we theorize education, including the concept of a learner. An important dimension of radicalizing Marxism, I suggest, is coupling it with other theories of resistance, especially those developed by scholars of color and those from the Global South. I discuss, first, how Marxism offers a number of useful conceptual tools yet also can be pushed forward in some of its core tenets such as ontology and epistemology, including its notion of reality (based on my works on *transformative activist stance*, or TAS, see e.g., Stetsenko, 2017a). Second, I outline how a concept of learner can be reconceived from a radicalized Marxist perspective, with critical implications for other aspects of education (although not all are addressed due to space limitations). In particular, I suggest that in place of seeing learners as passive and agentless, Marxism lays grounds for positing them as active contributors to the "world-historical activity" (Marx & Engels,

1845–1846/1978, p. 163), or struggle, of making and remaking the world, which is in the process of ceaseless historical transformations. That is, I argue for seeing learners as *agentive actors (or active agents) of a continual world-and-history-making.*

Overall, I demonstrate how, in radicalizing Marxism, a solid philosophical foundation can be elaborated for a dramatic change in perspectives on education that overturns its currently dominant core. This change is premised on the notion of *collective transformative praxis* in which *every person matters* and which is driven by "what is not yet," as per radical imagination and critical commitment to creating a better future. The radical implication of this position is that people (as learners, too!) do not, and never can, passively dwell in reality, nor deal with and know reality "as is," because—most radically, in a conceptual step beyond Marx—*nothing simply "is."* Instead (as I elaborate based on TAS), we inevitably participate in and, more critically, contribute to the continuous making of the world via our own being-knowing-doing in a *mutual spiral of co-realizing-the-world-and-ourselves.*

Therefore, for education, it is critical for learners not so much to grasp how things are in the "here and now," since—to put it plainly and straightforwardly—this is an impossible and futile task. Rather, the critical task for education is to support, promote, advance, scaffold, and furnish spaces and ways for learners to expand their abilities (which are in place from the get-go) of joining in with transformative struggles (or collective projects) currently underway, always already taking place in the world, including—importantly!—as these implicate projects of our own becoming. That is, the task of education is to facilitate learners' joining with, and finding their own unique place and role within, *ongoing struggles of synchronically co-realizing the-world-and-ourselves.*

One important caveat is that Marxism is not a rigid canon. Instead, it offers useful conceptual tools albeit as they themselves need further developments and upgrades, exactly in the spirit of this philosophy itself—which is all about historicity and continuous transformations without bounds. What I present in this chapter is my critical take (necessarily selective and partial) on Marxism, with some modifications, changes of focus, and expansions—conducted as a dialogue with Marxism in its various incarnations. This method (see Stetsenko, 2015, 2016, 2020a, 2022) aims to avoid the pitfalls of following historical legacies by the "letter," thus risking an "antiquarian killing" of authors such as Marx (Bloch, 1986, p. 1361). In this vein (centrally for this chapter and my other works on TAS), I foreground the learners' agency—itself reliant on the novel transformative-activist concept of reality—much more than is typical for most versions of Marxism and Marx's own works. Importantly, I endeavor to coordinate Marxism with other related perspectives such as, especially, in the rich tradition of the intersecting scholarship of resistance by scholars of color and those from the Global South, which shares a great deal in common with Marxism (see Stetsenko, 2023, in press).

I see the task of radically changing the notion of "learner" along the lines of prioritizing agency to be part of larger efforts to shift away from eurocentric and neoliberal models (Stetsenko, 2022, 2023, in press) marked, as they are, with the ethos of adaptation, conformity, and political acquiescence. The alternative I outline aligns with the very gist of Marxism (even if not following it by the letter)—namely, its ethos of "revolutionising the existing world, of practically attacking and changing existing things" (Marx & Engels, 1845–1846/1978, p. 169). This alternative also aligns with perspectives of "trans-modernity" (Dussel, 1995) that move beyond both modernity and postmodernity, instead constructing an alternative invigorated by the *ethos of resistance*. This ethos elevates the voices of "the oppressed other," as highlighted by Paulo Freire, Frantz Fanon, Enrique Dussel, Audre Lorde, James Baldwin, and Gloria Anzaldúa, among others.

30.2 Problematizing and Radicalizing the Notion of Reality in Marxism

Marxism, typically, is associated with the economic theory of capitalism and the materialist theory of history, summarized by Marx in his premise that "the mode of production of material life conditions the general process of social, political and intellectual life" (Marx, 1859, np). However, his economic and historical works, arguably, were subordinate to, or at least tightly intertwined with, his overall *ethical-political* system of thought pertaining to humanity's struggles, possibilities, and aspirations, as a systematic theory of social reality premised (though only implicitly, in large part) on a future-oriented stance and commitment. This stance, ethical-political and conceptual at once (which is the hallmark of Marxism in need of explication), is about charting prospects for developing a just and humane society without exploitation, hegemony, alienation, and hierarchy. This ethical-political philosophy includes conjectures about human nature and development, directly relevant to education, premised on a broad worldview, ethical principles, and original onto-epistemology. Indeed, Marx can be seen to be "a great *philosopher*-economist" (Dussel, quoted in Burton & Osorio, 2011) and, in my view, quite critically, a great *activist* philosopher-economist.

The central idea developed by Marx, in ethical-political cum philosophical terms, is that the core of "humanness" coincides with, and consists of, the process of people materially and collectively producing conditions and means of their existence. In this process, according to Marx, human beings *create themselves*, contra dominant views (at the times of Marx and still today!) about some reified human nature that is somehow pregiven as a fixed and unchanging "essence." In this approach, the answers about humanity, including its history and development, can be found in human activity—or social practice of labor (aka *praxis*). This is a process of an active interchange with the world through which people bring into existence (create, produce) both themselves and their world. In Marx's words, "In creating an objective world by his [*sic*] practical activity, in working-up inorganic nature, human being proves himself a conscious species being" (Marx, 1844/1978a, p. 76). That is (as needs to be emphasized), labor does not stand merely for instrumentally producing materials and goods. Instead, it stands for processes that create all forms and expressions of human existence, individually and collectively—humans together engaging and acting in and on the world through changing conditions and circumstances of their lives.

One possible interpretation of these core Marxist ideas is that human praxis constitutes the process in which, out of which, and through which material production co-emerges and co-evolves with all aspects and forms of human subjectivity and interactivity (see Stetsenko, 2005, 2017a). This conjecture implies that *human praxis is what exists*, as the "fabric" of the world/reality itself and that, therefore, the reality/world is not separate from human beings and not "out there" as some neutral, human-less objectivity. My suggestion has been to see that this radical reading of Marx, in moving beyond Marx, breaks the spell of (a) identifying human existence with the principles of adaptation to the world in its *status quo*, in its "givenness" and stability in the present and (b) bracketing off human agency and subjectivity from reality, as if they were some mysterious, other-worldly phenomena. Note that this interpretation goes against "canonical" and most popular readings of Marx. Indeed, it is commonly assumed that Marx conceived of reality as objectively existing outside of, and separately from, social practice, history, and human subjectivity. Accordingly, traditional interpretations of Marx portray knowledge as reflecting independent, objective reality. Indeed, "in education, orthodox Marxism is known for its commitment to objectivism" (Leonardo, 2009, p. 45).

However, it can be argued that Marx did offer preliminary steps to move beyond understanding the world/reality in such an objectivist (disenchanted) way. This is actually clear already from one of the most famous of Marx's passages, from *The Theses on Feuerbach*, which is, strangely, overlooked in its core meaning. Namely, as Marx writes, "The chief defect of all hitherto existing materialism … is that the thing, reality, sensuousness, is conceived only in the form of the *object or of contemplation*, but not as *human sensuous activity, practice*, not subjectively" (1845/1978, p. 143, emphasis in original). Note how Marx states, apparently controversially, that it is not conceiving reality *subjectively* that is the main defect of existing philosophies! As suggested in my works (e.g., Stetsenko, 2014, 2017a, 2019a), Marx can be seen to move in the direction (though not without internal contradictions) of superseding the narrow notions of objectivity versus subjectivity, instead suggesting that reality is a *subjective*, sensuous human activity, or practice, while, importantly, *not* implying that reality is thus somehow non-objective (my term *s/objectivity* captures this dialectical merger of subjectivity and objectivity, see Stetsenko, 2014, 2017a, 2023).

Indeed, Marx also explicitly questions the notions of reality "out there," as some pristine nature, in writing that "the nature that preceded human history … is nature which today no longer exists anywhere" (Marx & Engels, 1845–1846/1978, p. 171). The whole world as it now exists, writes Marx, "is an unceasing sensuous labor and creation" (ibid.). In this emphasis, nature is understood as a human-made realm, that is, in its dynamic, historically evolving entanglements, and even a fusion, with human practices, rather than as an ahistorical and timeless "given."

This interpretation, though on the margins of existing Marxist approaches, is consonant with Gramsci's (1971, p. 446) notion that praxis signifies a "unitary process of reality"—a "dialectical mediation between man and nature." In this position, nature is exactly not "a beyond" of the practical-historical reality, nor something alien to humanity (cf. Haug, 2001). Recent works by Marxist-feminist scholars also reimagine the social (albeit not reality as a whole) as a historically subjective human practice, connecting such practice to human experience and social relations (e.g., Allman, 2007; Bannerji, 2005). These authors stress that Marx's emphasis on material relations does not entail economic determinism because these relations are *historical* and, thus, include mutual determination of subjectivity and material production. This is in affinity with a position explicated within the cultural-historical activity theory (e.g., Stetsenko, 2005) reformulating its premises toward a more dialectical focus on material practice, social relations (and attendant forms of intersubjectivity), and phenomena of human subjectivity and agency as all co-arising and co-evolving together.

30.3 Expanding Marx: Understanding Reality as a Lived Struggle

The central ontological and epistemological status of social praxis—taking it to be *what exists*—as well as the profound implications of this position for practically all aspects of theorizing human development and education, needs to be more fully explored and taken to its quite radical conclusions. In works on TAS (e.g., Stetsenko, 2008, 2017a, 2020b, 2020c, 2020d, 2020e, 2023, in press) my effort is to explicate and expand Marx's philosophical worldview, starting with the core premise that reality is composed of communal praxis that is stretching through history, across generations, de facto uniting all human beings in "an inescapable network of mutuality, tied in a single garment of destiny" (to use Martin Luther King Jr.'s, 1965, expression). In these works, I elaborate the following core points: *the transformative* and *forward-directed* nature of social praxis, taken as the foundational reality both ontologically and epistemologically; the centrality of the world constantly changing and evolving beyond the present as grounding all forms of human being-knowing-doing; social praxis superseding the objectivity-versus-subjectivity dichotomy, instead implying that material reality is imbued with human interactivity and subjectivity, as a unified ethico-ontoepistemology; *the nexus of the world-and-self-co-realization* as one process; transcending the separation between individual and social dimensions of praxis through the notion that *each person* matters in the overall world-historical dynamics via unique contributions to it.

One of the central deliberations in my works, as relates to education, is the need to elevate *human agency* within an expanded Marxist worldview. To do so, human praxis needs to be understood to transcend not only the objectivity–subjectivity and individuality–sociality dichotomies but also the very separation of human beings from the world (e.g., Stetsenko, 2012, 2013a, 2013b, 2019b, 2020b, 2020c, 2020d, 2023). The alternative is to posit people and the world as being mutually enfolded, or blended and meshed together, in the process of them co-evolving, co-arising, and co-realizing each other. The core process, in expanding upon Marx's notion of reality, is that of a *seamless oneness*, as *duo in uno*—the dynamic flow of ceaseless back-and-forth transactions and exchanges between people and the world in the process of their mutual and synchronous co-realization. The emphasis is neither on the "objective" world that is somehow neutral and purged of human dimensions and presence, nor on any features and characteristics of individuals taken as separate, autonomous, and self-sufficient "entities." Instead, the emphasis is on *the dialectical nexus* in which these two poles are brought into one unified and *dynamically changing realm* with its own historicity and a fluid, forever emerging, and permanently fluctuating becoming. It is this dynamic, ongoing, and uninterrupted circuit of continuous transactions between human beings and the world—as one dynamic and unified (albeit not homogenous) processual realm—that is posited in TAS to be at the core of human reality and all forms of human being-knowing-doing including in education. That is, the "external" world, on one hand, and human development in all of its incarnations, on the other, appear as co-arising, co-evolving—and, even more radically, *co-realizing, each other*, since they do not pre-exist each other—all through fluid, bidirectional, conjoint, and continuous enactments in and by transformative practices.

Furthermore, in this activist-transformative (or TAS) approach, the world is understood to be a shifting and continuously evolving terrain of social practices that are constantly reenacted by people acting together in performing their *individually unique and authentically authorial*, or answerable, yet *always also* deeply and profoundly social, deeds. Each person joining in with this collective terrain, right from birth, is the core foundation for human development and personal becoming. That is, reality is reconceived as that which is being constantly transformed and brought forth by *people themselves*—and not as solo individuals acting alone, but as *actors* of social, communal practices. Importantly, as such actors, people are not only fully immersed in collaborative practices but, more critically, co-constituted by *their own active/agentive contributions* to them. In other words, what is brought to the fore is *the nexus* of people changing the world and being changed in this very process. These are but two poles of one and the same, perpetual and recursive, mutual co-realizing and bringing forth of people and the world, in and as the process of a simultaneous *self-and-world/history-co-realization*.

In the next conceptual step, the TAS approach posits human development to be grounded in purposeful and answerable—or, *agentive* and *activist*—contributions to the dynamic and ever-emerging world-in-the-making. These contributions constitute shared communal practices which are, therefore, imbued by visions of, stands on, and commitments to, particular sought-after futures, always ethico-politically non-neutral. People come to be themselves and come to know their world and themselves (and also learn about these) *in the process and as the process* of changing their world (while changing together with it), in the midst of this process and as one of its facets, rather than outside of, or merely in some sort of a connection with, it. In this dialectically recursive and dynamically co-constitutive approach, people can be said to co-realize themselves and the whole fullness of their being-knowing-doing in the agentive enactment of changes that bring forth the world, and simultaneously their own lives, including their selves and minds.

This ethico-ontoepistemologically primary realm (Stetsenko, 2013a, 2013b, 2020e, 2023) can be understood as the "lived world," but not in the sense of people merely being situated or dwelling in it as it exists in its *status quo*. Instead, this realm is better designated as a "lived struggle"—an arena of human historical quests and pursuits, enacted as collective projects and efforts at becoming fraught with contradictions and conflicts—infused with values, interests, struggles, power differentials, and intentionality including goals, visions, desires, and commitments to the future. This position aligns with Marx's passionate statement at the very start of the *Communist Manifesto*:

> The history of all hitherto existing society is *the history of class struggles* ... oppressor and oppressed, stood in constant opposition to one another, carried on an uninterrupted, now hidden, now open fight, a fight that each time ended, either in a revolutionary re-constitution of society at large, or in the common ruin of the contending classes. (Marx & Engels, 1848/1978, pp. 473–474)

In this radical formulation, Marx strongly resonates with the scholarship of resistance which, not incidentally, has also prioritized theories stemming from struggles:

> US peoples of color have long acted, spoken, intellectualized, lived out what Cherríe Moraga calls a 'theory in the flesh,' a theory that allows survival and more, that allows practitioners to live with faith, hope, and moral vision in spite of all else. (Sandoval, 2000, 6.7)

Marx's emphasis on praxis, too, can be interpreted as prioritizing a "theory in the flesh" that comes out of struggles for justice and liberation and is premised on ethical-political visions and commitments. It is this linkage of theoretical work to the struggles on the ground, with a conviction that things should be different, that unites the resistance scholarship with Marxism. This is reflected in Marx insisting on "identifying our criticism with real struggles ... We develop new principles to the world out of its own principles" (Marx, 1844/1978b, p. 14). In further elaborating this view, my suggestion has been to understand people's relations to the world as primarily *con/fronting* it in active work and effort at becoming via simultaneously co-realizing-oneself-and-the-world, while coming face-to-face also with ourselves because we simultaneously are co-created in and through such con/frontations. Notably, at the core of both Marxism and the resistance scholarship is the standpoint of the oppressed—resulting in theories being created from *bottom up*, as a manifesto for the oppressed, exploited, and dispossessed, as tools of their struggles. It is in inspiration by the voices of the oppressed that the struggle for a better world, against all odds—as an incarnation of human praxis, its de facto mode of existence in the present historical context—can be seen to be ethically and onto-epistemologically primary in contrast to what is traditionally taken as an objective/neutral world. In this expansion upon Marx, in alliance with the scholarship of resistance (for more details, see Stetsenko, 2017a, 2023, in press), my suggestion is to understand reality to be *an arena of human struggle and activist striving*, and therefore, as inherently infused with agency—while not ceasing to be material and practical/productive at the same time.

30.4 The Radical Ungivenness of the World: Educational Implications

Marxism opens ways to see reality/world as constantly and irreversibly moving, permanently in the process of becoming and changing, where nothing is ever stable nor exempt from radical transformations. This can be understood to suggest that change is more real than any, ostensibly more permanent and tangible, "things," any established structures, regimes, and institutions. That is, in radicalizing Marx, reality itself can be posited to be, at bottom and through-and-through, a dynamic, fluid, perpetually on the move, ever-unfolding and changing process that is always in-the-making by people who are also making themselves in this very same process. Importantly, this is an immanent field of forces in perpetual imbalance, creating the present filled with tensions and conflicts, struggles and strivings, and hence tending towards, and even existing in a state of, unfolding crises and radical ruptures. In this TAS perspective, it can be further stated that, because the present/*status quo* cannot be presumed to endure, the forward-looking stance and a commitment to sociopolitical and ethical projects of social transformation—in view of a *sought-after future that people posit for themselves*—is a necessary, immanent dimension of all forms of being-knowing-doing including learning (on implications for education, see e.g., Stetsenko, 2010, 2014, 2017a, 2017b, 2019c; Vianna & Stetsenko, 2011, 2014, 2019).

This *activist-transformative* take on reality (as part of TAS), suggested herein in the spirit of Marx, is strongly supported by a sociopolitical/economic rationale. Indeed, as applied to our current historical epoch, the present regime of capitalism is mutating and moving in the direction of disintegration and, therefore, a necessary, unavoidable transition to another social order—to be achieved through social revolution (as already diagnosed by Marx). Indeed, as

Marx (Marx & Engels, 1882) stated in the Preface to *The Communist Manifesto*, this core work "had, as its object, the proclamation of the inevitable impending dissolution of modern bourgeois property." I would add to this that it is this conviction about the impending dissolution of capitalism, as the core determination of reality, that needs to be taken centrally in theorizing human being-knowing-doing including in education. It is the fidelity in the impending collapse of capitalism—and not as an article of blind faith but a firm conviction based in sober (albeit not dispassionate) explorations into capitalism's contradictions and failings—that grounds the need to commit to sociopolitical projects of working out new forms of society and humane relations, including in education. In the spirit of Marx, this is about the need to work on providing conditions to transition to a society (a communist one, per Marx) that will realize ethical demands for freedom, social justice, and equality.

This *activist-transformative*, or TAS, approach has many radical implications for education. Most critically, in expanding upon Marx, it uncompromisingly rejects understanding humans—including as learners—to be recipients of outside stimuli and merely *products* of culture and society, who only adapt to the world in its *status quo* (as is typically assumed in mainstream approaches across the board, in philosophy, psychology, education, etc.). Indeed, traditional models of education (and broader, of dominant ways of thinking) are marked by the ethos of adaptation, conformity, and political quietism and acquiescence. In these models, the world is understood to be fixed, stable, and immutable, with people expected to merely adjust to, rather than change, it. Accordingly, research supposedly needs to record, catalogue, and document "what is," objectively and dispassionately, while excluding political motivations and struggles. Most critically for education, people and their agency are believed to not matter, especially in terms of large-scale structural changes. Thus, the dominant models take the world in its *status quo* for granted and, therefore, expect learners to get to know it "as is"—since it is assumed to be fixed and immutable, extending into the future unchanged, supposedly impervious to changes and unaffected by learners' agency.

The alternative view that I have been advancing is to understand humans as active co-creators of the world and themselves, who *agentively contribute to co-realizing the-world-in-the-making*. Moreover and critically, the TAS approach suggests that people come into being by developing their agency as an ability to matter, precisely through and as such contributions. Note that this is about simultaneously reformulating both the world (reality) and human being-knowing-doing, together with the very terms of their relationship.

Perhaps most critically, in a significant upgrade of Marxism, the TAS approach suggests that there is no world/reality "out there," which people can simply dwell in, experience, know, and learn about, somehow objectively and dispassionately—all without personal engagement in terms of caring, struggling, and striving. Instead, the "givenness" of reality is understood to be superseded through the ever-changing dynamics of human praxis made up of transformative acts carried out by people in pursuit of their goals and commitments—all as parts of communal struggles for a better world. In this light, there is no aspect of being-knowing-doing, including in the process of learning, that can be carried out from nowhere, in a vacuum, that is, from 'the hubris of the zero point' (Castro-Gómez, 2007) and, I would add, from *the hubris of a zero commitment to a particular future.*

Therefore, in an activist-transformative (TAS) approach, learning is not about getting to know how the world *is*—because nothing simply "is," that is, nothing is set in stone, out there to be grasped/understood/learned about in its ostensible constancy and putative "givenness." Nothing exists outside and independently of our agentive con/frontations with, and contributions to, a collective social praxis incarnated in struggles, such as those for social justice and a better world. This is because we, both together and one at a time, are continuously (with no interruption at any point) and *always-already* transforming "what is" (the world) and, *therefore*, also ourselves into something new and different, in a bi-directional and perpetually evolving spiral of a mutual co-becoming/co-realization.

One element of this view can be illustrated with Pirandello's (1921/2004) poetic metaphor: "A fact is like a sack which won't stand up when it is empty. In order that it may stand up, one has to put into it the reason and sentiment which have caused it to exist." This is a great way to express the notion that all knowledge ("facts," etc.) is produced in—and only exists as—part of the social fabric of human communal endeavors (praxis) and individual mattering that is constitutive of these endeavors. All knowledge needs to be understood in its often-hidden roots in, and as stemming from, these endeavors and struggles and also, importantly, as embodying these in the present (as is widely acknowledged, for example, in Vygotsky's tradition; see e.g., Stetsenko, 2010, 2017a). Yet critically important to add, in my view, is that in order for knowledge "to stand up"—that is, to be meaningful and mattering within the reality of human struggles—every learner also has to put into it *one's own* reason and sentiment/commitment. In other words, for knowledge and learning to be meaningful, they have to be imbued with learners' own feelings, positions, stances, and commitments to changing the world in view of their own sought-after futures. It is only in this case that knowledge gains relevance and significance—thus becoming alive and meaningful, rather than random and mechanical "information" to be "processed," of questionable, actually less than zero, validity and relevance.

Given the activist-transformative take on reality (as suggested in TAS), to engage in meaningful learning, it is of prime importance for learners to con/front reality and grasp its struggles, as these are unfolding at a given historical moment. The challenge is for learners to take a stance on one or the other side in these struggles, positioning themselves vis-à-vis these struggles through, most critically, committing to a particular sought-after future. Note that doing so cannot be avoided since we all are always already and inevitably immersed and implicated in these struggles anyway (in various ways, with differential responsibility and accountability). Education, thus, is about making it possible for learners to establish and advance *their* interests, positions, desires, and passions (all of which they already have, even as very young children—which needs to be honored by educators), as these are refracted in an ability to take a stance and commit to particular life projects embedded in communal struggles. This is grounded in understanding human existence/life itself as an indivisible and seamless, unitary (non-composite) process of humans engaging and co-realizing the world—in the totality of their lives. This process cannot be broken into disconnected parts such as learning, on the one hand, and being/becoming a certain sort of a person, on the other. Instead, all of these endeavors and acts need to be seen as *one seamless flow*, where various facets and moments mutually interpenetrate, co-realize each other, and are represented in each other, as not reducible to a chain of discrete episodes or disconnected levels and dimensions (Stetsenko, 2017a).

Thus, to learn anything is possible *only* from within one own's life agenda, from a position *and* a forward-directed stance and, moreover, in a process and *as* a process of changing the world, all while contributing to the always politically non-neutral *collective projects* of world-changing and history-making. Learning is not about acquiring or processing information but instead about advancing one's own life project of becoming an active community member, with a mission of contributing to this community's struggles. This indicates the radical need to go beyond situations one confronts and the very "*is-ness*" of the present. To paraphrase Marx, in expanding on his key message, *the goal of education is not to interpret the world but to change it*. This includes being able to envision the future—as an act of political imagination—and commit to realizing this future via activist deeds of being-knowing-doing (if even in only small ways).

Learning is possible only within and as part of learners' personal, yet never a-social, projects of becoming, through the lens of "what's in it for them," what is the significance and relevance of knowledge—and of learning about it—within their own becoming. Emphatically, this is *not* about individualized learning since this is not about learners as isolated individuals in pursuit of some self-serving goals. Instead, this is about *collectividual* learning (Stetsenko, 2013b), where learners are understood to be community members who *come into being* via *mattering in the struggles of their communities*. Knowledge must become part of learners' own meaningful, activist life projects, specifically as community members—that is, be drawn into the only reality of their own world- and history-making, in light of sought-after futures they commit to. This is the necessary condition for any humanely significant, alive, and *vital* learning that, therefore, can never be removed from communal struggles and, thus, can never be neutral, "objective" or apolitical.

By extension and quite critically, what is *not yet* can be actually rendered more real than anything in the present, in the immediate "here and now." This expansion is consistent with what marks Marxism as a unique ethical/political-cum-philosophical (or activist-transformative) system of thought, namely, its *fidelity to an event that has not yet happened* (c.f. Thompson, 2016). Moreover,

I understand this as a fidelity to not being stuck in the oppressive present and instead, to commit ourselves to moving beyond this present in a struggle for a future that will bring freedom, social justice, and equality for all. In such a move, the future can be said to exist now, being always-already-in-the-making (see e.g., Stetsenko, 2017a).

The TAS approach can be illustrated with a research project carried out by Eduardo Vianna (in collaboration with this chapter's author as an academic advisor), together with and for the benefit of residents in a group home for adolescent boys (see Vianna, 2009; Vianna & Stetsenko, 2011, 2014, 2019). As described by Vianna, the institutional context, at the project's start, was marked by outright oppression and a self-perpetuating, vicious cycle of control and resistance, all under horrific structural pressures of the US foster care system with its racism, poverty, and class inequality. Although Vianna was initially hired to address the dire situation by individually working with youth, his work drastically expanded into a collaborative project to radically transform the institution into a more livable context and an alternative learning site. The project took great effort and even sacrifice from the lead investigator, Eduardo Vianna, who assumed a position of solidarity with residents (at first, against much resistance from staff and administration). Through several years of work, Vianna was able to gradually gain the residents' trust to then together work on changing the institution (including via organizing learning workshops and other collaborative projects for residents).

The core feature of this project was that youth were provided with space and tools, including conceptual knowledge, for them to develop and implement their own activist, transformative agendas while exercising agency in their community. Critically for the current chapter, the process of learning (first within workshops organized by Vianna, then expanding to school learning) gradually turned into a meaningful activity as part of the youth's activism coterminous with their identity development. The boys' initial view of learning as another form of control, tightly linked to white privilege, gradually gave way to them seeing how knowledge could be drawn for critique and resistance. Insofar as learning enabled the boys to see the possibility for change and the practical value of what they used to view as useless, "abstract" knowledge, learning turned into a tool of their activist agency and their projects of becoming (with many dramatic changes ensuing—from better living conditions, to boys developing solidarity among themselves, along with diverse interests and plans for the future, as well as them gaining staff and school teachers' respect and investment in them). Thus, this TAS-based research project was a catalyst of a synergistic, simultaneous transformation within one and the same process of participants changing their community practices and themselves—while drawing on knowledge and learning that became, in the process, deeply meaningful as a vital tool of activism.

30.5 Concluding Remarks: Drawing Links and Addressing the Next Steps

In activist-transformative (or TAS) approach, "what is" is in a constant flux, forever and continuously changing and becoming via individually unique contributions by each and every learner, each and every one of us. That is, we ourselves—including as learners (and we are all learners, no doubt, throughout life)—are not separate from the world's continuous changing/becoming since we all are directly entangled with, and moreover, immediately implicated in, its co-realizing as co-authors and co-creators. Learning, then, is directly and inevitably but a dimension of this process of the self-and-world-co-realizing. This approach elevates the future beyond the past and present—not as a utopian dreaming but as a *call to action*, to bringing future into existence here and now via our own actions and deeds.

And indeed, many critical and sociocultural perspectives on education converge on the importance of critique and imagination for education. For example, what is often highlighted is that learners need to be compelled "to go beyond the situations one confronts and refuse reality as given in the name of a reality to be produced" (Greene, 1973, p. 7), in summoning up "the possible, the what is not and yet might be" (Greene, 1987, p. 14). However, from an expanded, activist-transformative Marxist perspective, I suggest that instead of summoning up the possible, it is important to insist on the need to summon up the sought-after—*no matter whether it is deemed possible or not*. This is in line with the Marxist resistance movements (even more than Marxist philosophies per se, which often lag behind realities on the ground) insisting on *achieving the impossible* (as in the slogan "be realistic, demand the impossible"). This is also in line with the gist of the resistance scholarship, more broadly. Indeed, Baldwin (1963/2008, p. 203, emphasis added) insisted on no less than the need to "go for broke," in his seminal talk to teachers:

> We are in a revolutionary situation, no matter how unpopular that word has become in this country. The society in which we live is desperately menaced ... from within. So any citizen of this country who figures himself as responsible—and particularly those of you who deal with the minds and hearts of young people—must be prepared to 'go for broke.' ... The obligation of anyone who thinks of himself as responsible is to examine society and try to change it and to fight it—*at no matter what risk*. This is the only hope society has. This is the only way societies change.

This position is not about any future-oriented agendas being normatively defined, imposed by others, especially the powerful, or just taken for granted as established and invincible. Instead, these agendas need to be defined by learners themselves, as per their own commitments and convictions, based on their own explorations into the world and its ongoing struggles—as all of this can be facilitated by teachers. This is again in sync with Baldwin's striking message: Addressing the Black child, he said that the world belongs to this child, who does not "have to be bound by the expediencies of any ... given policy, any given time—that he has the right and the necessity to examine everything," with the whole world depending on each child.

Another expansion on existing critical approaches is the following. Freire's (1998, p. 93) words, "My practice demands of me a definition about where I stand," could be usefully expanded by saying that all of our being-knowing-doing, including *all acts of learning*—demand of us a definition of where we stand and where we want to go next. The act of taking a stand and staking a claim—a position on sociopolitical struggles of the day, including as these are refracted in seemingly mundane situations that we all deal with on a daily basis—constitutes the core formative dimension of learning that can meet the challenges of today, where the stakes are extraordinarily high given unfolding crises and turmoil. At stake is figuring out what ought to be, coterminous with the process of a continuing self-definition/realization of who we are and where we speak from (cf. Dussel, 2011), and which direction to go, in a forward-looking activist stance.

There are no universal, timeless answers as to what the core struggles of today are. These answers need to be co-constructed in the process of learners taking up reality, facing up to its challenges, in and as a con/frontation with the world and themselves, from a distinctive place and historical time, with a unique commitment to a sought-after future. The contours of this struggle today are tied, in my view, to overcoming the "cosmology of capitalism ... built upon alienations and separations embedded within a world view of individualism, maximization of material gain and processes of subjectification" (Motta & Esteves, 2014, p. 1). The scholars of resistance have further insisted that the tasks of today have to do with "the yearning of the oppressed for freedom and justice, and their struggle to recover their lost humanity" (Freire, 1970/2005, p. 44) and, hence, the need for a political struggle for "a new humanity" (Fanon, 1961/2004, p. 2; cf. Leonardo & Porter, 2010).

This struggle includes overcoming mindless profit-seeking, ruthless exploitation of people and natural resources, and exuberant consumption, all at the core of capitalism that is destroying the planet and its inhabitants. This also includes overturning worn-out conceptions of education that posit learners as passive and agentless, thus harming the prospects for a better future for these learners and the whole world. My understanding is that it is in joining with, and contributing to, such core struggles of today that the opportunities for a *radical-transformative agency* (Stetsenko, 2019a, 2020c, 2023) and, relatedly, for a meaningful and *vital* (as opposed to lifeless) learning are opened up.

Martin Luther King Jr. (1967) has prophetically distilled the essence of the historical moment of his time—and, importantly, this moment is still here with us today, more than a half-century later:

> We are now faced with the fact that tomorrow is today. We are confronted with the fierce urgency of now. In this unfolding conundrum of life and history, there is such a thing as being too late. ... Now let us begin. Now let us rededicate ourselves to the long and bitter – but beautiful – struggle for a new world.

These words are truly in the spirit of Marx and all those many activists, in education and beyond, who today risk their lives to protest and resist, all over the world, the deadly capitalist regime that is killing us, especially people who are marginalized and oppressed. It is these activists who bravely reject the dominance of the present and the shackles of "*is-ness*" that prevent a much-needed movement beyond capitalism, including in education.

Acknowledgements The author expresses gratitude to the volume editors for a productive collaboration in preparing this chapter for publication.

Disclosure Statement The author has no financial interest or benefit that has arisen from the direct applications of this research.

References

Allman, P. (2007). *On Marx: An Introduction to the Revolutionary Pedagogy of Karl Marx*. Sense.

Baldwin, J. (1963/2008). A Talk to Teachers. In M. Cochran-Smith, S. Feiman-Nemser, D. J. McIntyre, & K. E. Demers (Eds.), *Handbook of Research on Teacher Education* (pp. 203–207). Routledge.

Bannerji, H. (2005). Building from Marx: Reflections on Class and Race. *Social Justice, 32*(4), 144–160.

Bloch, E. (1986). *The Principle of Hope*. Blackwell.

Burton, M., & Osorio, J. M. F. (2011). Introducing Dussel: The Philosophy of Liberation and a Really Social Psychology. *PINS (Psychology in Society), 41*, 20–39. Retrieved April 24, 2023, from http://www.scielo.org.za/scielo.php?script=sci_arttext&pid=S1015-60462011000100003

Case, A., & Deaton, A. (2021). *Deaths of Despair and the Future of Capitalism*. Princeton University.

Castro-Gómez, S. (2007). The Missing Chapter of Empire: Postmodern Re-organization of Coloniality and Post-Fordist Capitalism. *Cultural Studies, 21*(2/3), 428–448. https://doi.org/10.1080/09502380601162639

Dussel, E. (1995). *The Invention of the Americas: Eclipse of 'The Other' and the Myth of Modernity*. Continuum.

Dussel, E. (2011). From Critical Theory to the Philosophy of Liberation: Some Themes for Dialogue. *Transmodernity, 1*(2), 16–43. Retrieved April 24, 2023, from https://escholarship.org/uc/item/59m869d2

Fanon, F. (1961/2004). *The Wretched of the Earth*. Grove.

Freire, P. (1970/2005). *Pedagogy of the Oppressed*. Continuum.

Freire, P. (1998). *Pedagogy of Freedom. Ethics, Democracy, and Civic Courage*. Rowan and Littlefield.

Gramsci, A. (1971). *Selections from the Prison Notebooks* (Selected and Trans. Q. Hoare & G. N. Smith). Lawrence and Wishart.

Greene, M. (1973). *Teacher as Stranger: Educational Philosophy for the Modern Age*. Wadsworth.

Greene, M. (1987). Creating, Experiencing, Sense Making: Art Worlds in Schools. *Journal of Aesthetic Education, 21*(4), 11–23.

Haug, W. F. (2001). From Marx to Gramsci—From Gramsci to Marx. Historical Materialism and the Philosophy of Praxis. *Rethinking Marxism, 13*(1), 69–82.

King, M. L., Jr. (1965). Commencement Address to Oberlin College in June 1965 (Oberlin, Ohio). Retrieved April 24, 2023, from https://www2.oberlin.edu/external/EOG/BlackHistoryMonth/MLK/CommAddress.html

King, M. L., Jr. (1967). *Beyond Vietnam: A Time to Break Silence*. Speech Delivered on April 4, 1967. Retrieved April 24, 2023, from https://wilpfus.org/sites/default/files/docs/5-MLK-Beyond-Vietnam-speech-in-sections.pdf

Leonardo, Z. (2009). *Race, Whiteness, and Education*. Routledge.

Leonardo, Z., & Porter, R. K. (2010). Pedagogy of Fear: Toward a Fanonian Theory of 'safety' in Race Dialogue. *Race Ethnicity and Education, 13*, 139–157. https://doi.org/10.1080/13613324.2010.482898

Marx, K. (1844/1978a). Economic and Philosophical Manuscripts. In R. C. Tucker (Ed.), *Marx/Engels Reader* (pp. 66–125). Norton.

Marx, K. (1844/1978b). For a Ruthless Criticism of Everything Existing. In R. C. Tucker (Ed.), *Marx/Engels Reader* (pp. 12–15). Norton.

Marx, K. (1845/1978). Theses on Feuerbach. In R. C. Tucker (Ed.), *Marx/Engels Reader* (2nd ed., pp. 143–145). Norton.

Marx, K. (1859). A Contribution to a Critique of Political Economy. *Marxists Internet Archive*. Retrieved April 24, 2023, from https://www.marxists.org/archive/marx/works/download/Marx_Contribution_to_the_Critique_of_Political_Economy.pdf

Marx, K., & Engels, F. (1845–1846/1978). The German Ideology. In R. C. Tucker (Ed.), *Marx/Engels Reader* (pp. 146–200). Norton.

Marx, K., & Engels, F. (1848/1978). Manifesto of the Communist Party. In R. C. Tucker (Ed.), *Marx/Engels Reader* (pp. 473–500). Norton.

Marx, K., & Engels, F. (1882). Preface to *The Manifesto of the Communist Party*. Marxists Internet Archive. Retrieved April 24, 2023, from https://www.marxists.org/archive/marx/works/download/pdf/Manifesto.pdf

Moraga, C. (1983). Refugees of a World on Fire. Foreword. In C. Moraga & G. Anzaldua (Eds.), *This Bridge Called My Back: Writings by Radical Women of Color* (pp. 1–5). Women of Color Press.

Motta, S. C., & Esteves, A. M. (2014). Reinventing Emancipation in the 21st Century: The Pedagogical Practices of Social Movements. *Interface: A Journal for and About Social Movements, 6*(1), 1–24. Retrieved April 24, 2023, from https://www.interfacejournal.net/wordpress/wp-content/uploads/2014/06/Interface-6-1-Editorial.pdf

Pirandello, L. (1921/2004). *Six Characters in Search of an Author*. Methuen.

Sandoval, C. (2000). *Methodology of the Oppressed*. University of Minnesota.

Stetsenko, A. (2005). Activity as Object-Related: Resolving the Dichotomy of Individual and Collective Types of Activity. *Mind, Culture, and Activity, 12*(1), 70–88. https://doi.org/10.1207/s15327884mca1201_6

Stetsenko, A. (2008). From Relational Ontology to Transformative Activist Stance: Expanding Vygotsky's (CHAT) Project. *Cultural Studies of Science Education, 3*, 465–485. https://doi.org/10.1007/s11422-008-9111-3

Stetsenko, A. (2010). Teaching-Learning and Development as Activist Projects of Historical Becoming: Expanding Vygotsky's Approach to Pedagogy. *Pedagogies: An International Journal, 5*(1), 6–16. https://doi.org/10.1080/15544800903406266

Stetsenko, A. (2012). Personhood: An Activist Project of Historical Becoming through Collaborative Pursuits of Social Transformation. *New Ideas in Psychology, 30*, 144–153. https://doi.org/10.1016/j.newideapsych.2009.11.008

Stetsenko, A. (2013a). The Challenge of Individuality in Cultural-Historical Activity Theory: 'Collectividual' Dialectics from a Transformative Activist Stance. *Outlines-Critical Practice Studies, 14*(2), 7–28. https://doi.org/10.7146/ocps.v14i2.9791

Stetsenko, A. (2013b). Theorizing Personhood for the World in Transition and Change: Reflections from a Transformative Activist Stance. In J. Martin & M. H. Bickhard (Eds.), *The Psychology of Personhood: Philosophical, Historical, Social-Developmental, and Narrative Perspectives* (pp. 181–203). Cambridge University Press.

Stetsenko, A. (2014). Transformative Activist Stance for Education: Inventing the Future in Moving beyond the Status Quo. In T. Corcoran (Ed.), *Psychology in Education: Critical Theory-Practice* (pp. 181–198). Sense Publishers.

Stetsenko, A. (2015). Theory for and as Social Practice of Realizing the Future: Implications from a Transformative Activist Stance. In J. Martin, J. Sugarman, and K. Slaney (Eds.), *The Wiley Handbook of Theoretical and Philosophical Psychology: Methods, Approaches, and New Directions for Social Sciences* (pp. 102–116). Wiley.

Stetsenko, A. (2016). Vygotsky's Theory of Method and Philosophy of Practice: Implications for Trans/formative Methodology. *Revista Psicologia em Estudo, 39*, 32–41. https://doi.org/10.15448/1981-2582.2016.s.24385

Stetsenko, A. (2017a). *The Transformative Mind: Expanding Vygotsky's Approach to Development and Education*. Cambridge University.

Stetsenko, A. (2017b). Science Education and Transformative Activist Stance: Activism as a Quest for Becoming via Authentic-Authorial Contribution to Communal Practices. In L. Bryan & K. Tobin (Eds.), *13 Questions: Reframing Education's Conversation: Science* (pp. 33–47). Peter Lang.

Stetsenko, A. (2019a). Hope, Political Imagination, and Agency in Marx and Beyond: Explicating the Transformative Worldview and Ethico-ontoepistemology. *Educational Philosophy and Theory, 7*, 726–737. https://doi.org/10.1080/00131857.2019.1654373

Stetsenko, A. (2019b). Radical-Transformative Agency: Continuities and Contrasts with Relational Agency and Implications for Education. *Frontiers in Education, 17*. https://doi.org/10.3389/feduc.2019.00148

Stetsenko, A. (2019c). Creativity as Dissent and Resistance: Transformative Approach Premised on Social Justice Agenda. In I. Lebuda & V. Glaveanu (Eds.), *The Palgrave Handbook of Social Creativity* (pp. 431–446). Springer.

Stetsenko, A. (2020a). Transformative-Activist Approach to the History of Psychology: Taking Up History from a Philosophy of Resistance and Social Justice Stance. In W. Pickren (Ed.), *The Oxford Research Encyclopedia, Psychology*. Oxford University Press. Online Publication: Retrieved April 24, 2023, from https://oxfordre.com/psychology/view/10.1093/acrefore/9780190236557.001.0001/acrefore-9780190236557-e-466

Stetsenko, A. (2020b). Critical Challenges in Cultural-Historical Activity Theory: The Urgency of Agency. *Cultural-Historical Psychology, 16*(2), 5–18. https://doi.org/10.17759/chp.2020160202

Stetsenko, A. (2020c). Radical-Transformative Agency: Developing a Transformative Activist Stance on a Marxist-Vygotskyan Foundation. In A. Tanzi Neto, F. Liberali, & M. Dafermos (Eds.), *Revisiting Vygotsky for Social Change* (pp. 31–62). Peter Lang.

Stetsenko, A. (2020d). Personhood through the Lens of Radical-Transformative Agency. In J. Sugarman & J. Martin (Eds.), *A Humanities Approach to the Psychology of Personhood* (pp. 65–83). Routledge.

Stetsenko, A. (2020e). Research and Activist Projects of Resistance: The Ethical-Political Foundations for a Transformative Ethico-Ontoepistemology. *Learning, Culture and Social Interaction, 26*. Retrieved April 23, 2023, from. https://doi.org/10.1016/j.lcsi.2018.04.002

Stetsenko, A. (2022). Radicalizing Theory and Vygotsky: Addressing the Topic of Crisis through Activist-Transformative Methodology. *Human Arenas*. https://doi.org/10.1007/s42087-022-00299-2

Stetsenko, A. (2023). The Tasks of Reality and Reality as the Task: Connecting Cultural-Historical Activity Theory with the Radical Scholarship of Resistance. In N. Hopwood & A. Sannino (Eds.), *Agency and Transformation: Motives, Mediation and Motion* (pp. 56–83). Cambridge University Press.

Stetsenko, A. (in press). Reclaiming the Tools of the Past for Today's Struggles: Radicalizing Vygotsky, via Marx, in Dialogue with Audre Lorde. In A. Levant et al. (Eds.), *Handbook on Activity Theory*. ibidem/Columbia University Press.

Thompson, P. (2016). Ernst Bloch and the Spirituality of Utopia. *Rethinking Marxism, 28*, 438–452. https://doi.org/10.1080/08935696.2016.1243417

Vianna, E. (2009). *Collaborative Transformations in Foster Care: Teaching-Learning as a Developmental Tool in a Residential Program*. Verlag Dr. Müller.

Vianna, E., & Stetsenko, A. (2011). Connecting Learning and Identity Development through a Transformative Activist Stance: Application in Adolescent Development in a Child Welfare Program. *Human Development, 54*, 313–338. https://doi.org/10.1159/000331484

Vianna, E., & Stetsenko, A. (2014). Research with a Transformative Activist Agenda: Creating the Future through Education for Social Change. In J. Vadeboncoeur (Ed.), *Learning in and Across Contexts: Reimagining Education. National Society for the Studies of Education Yearbook, 113*(2), 575–602. Teachers College Press.

Vianna, E., & Stetsenko, A. (2019). Turning Resistance into Passion for Knowledge with the Tools of Agency: Teaching-Learning about Theories of Evolution for Social Justice among Foster Youth. *Perspectiva, 38*(4), 864–886. https://doi.org/10.5007/2175-795X.2019.e61082

Vygotsky, L. S. (1987). *The Collected Works of L. S. Vygotsky. Volume 1: Problems of General Psychology* (R. W. Rieber & A. S. Carton, Eds.). Plenum.

CHAPTER 31

Series Editor's Afterword: Weaving Other Worlds with, Against, and Beyond Marx

Richard Hall

The chapters in this collection reverberate in relation to Aimé Césaire's (1956/1969, p. 39) invocation: 'I must begin//Begin what?//The only thing in the world that is worth beginning: //The End of the World, no less.' In this, they are a gift, precisely because they demonstrate the breadth and depth of struggle and refusal against the materiality of capital. They are a gift, precisely because they reverberate with the potential for (re)imagining the world otherwise. They are a gift, precisely because they center humanity and humane values of courage, faith, dignity, justice, and hope.

The critiques and examples that erupt through this Handbook exemplify how, in the struggle of humanity to exist inside capital's war against life-beyond-value, we might work collectively, generously, and generatively for an emancipatory politics. This is a fundamental realization, because, as Chuǎng (n.d.) noted,

> [w]ithin the material community of capital, there can be no true hermit kingdom. All is encircled by capitalist accumulation—the red dust of living death—and all who attempt to flee are returned to it, in the end. Future communist prospects, then, will find no hope in reclusion. The only emancipatory politics is one that grows within and against the red dust of the material community of capital.

R. Hall (✉)
De Montfort University, Leicester, UK
e-mail: rhall1@dmu.ac.uk

There can be no possibility or potentiality in isolation. There can be no hope in cleaving ourselves off from human and non-human life, precisely because the red dust of living death clings to our skin. It clings as a reminder of our inability to escape the systemic reproduction of cycles of alienation, fed by our labor (paid or unpaid), inside an existence framed by global emergencies. In this reality, significant numbers of the privileged minority, who might once have had access to white privilege or the resources of whiteness, are also proletarianized and lacking meaningful representation. Thus, we are reminded that there is no way out but through, and this demands sitting with and learning from communities-in-struggle.

Sitting with and learning from open-out the possibility for weaving our own lived experiences with those of others, offering 'the absolute working-out of [our] creative potentialities', beyond the separations and one-sided specificity imposed by capitalist social relations (Marx, 1857/1993, p. 488). Such one-sided specificity, which fetishizes surplus (as value, labor, time, money), is the reduction of human and non-human life to 'universal objectification as total alienation' and is the 'sacrifice of the human end-in-itself to an entirely external end' (ibid.). Weaving and re-weaving our own being, doing and knowing, requires a deep process of listening, shaping a pedagogy from below. It works for a new, humane beginning and end for life, situated in-community, through which many-sided, human potentiality emerges (Marx & Engels, 1846/1998).

Such weaving, as a pedagogical project that begins from humans and their communities, including non-human animals, reminds us of bell hooks' (1994, p. 13) focus on teaching as a 'sacred' project, grounded in 'the practice of freedom'. Her practice cautions us against learning and teaching as things to be objectively, algorithmically or cybernetically, managed and finessed. Rather, as a process, it is woven through the souls of students and teachers, and in symbiosis with 'the necessary conditions where learning can most deeply and intimately begin' (ibid.). This process opens out a horizon for individuals to reimagine themselves, beyond the idealizations of professor, researcher, teacher, librarian, administrator, student. Such normalized idealizations attempt to concretize people, 'to remain something [s/he/they] has become', as one-sided, rather than living 'in the absolute movement of becoming' (Marx, 1857/1993, p. 488).

Throughout his work, Karl Marx emphasized human being in-community, as the absolute movement of becoming. His work creates a space inside which we might think through issues of freedom and dignity, need and necessity, sociability and association, totality and community, and the structures, cultures, and practices that condition them, historically and materially. This conditioning offers us a way of thinking about the metabolism that operates within cycles and circuits of production and consumption (of value and sociability) and the ways in which humans relate to non-human animals. Marx (1894/1991, p. 959) stresses that freedom can only emerge from socialized humans working in association, such that they might govern the human metabolism with nature in a rational way, bringing it under their collective control, instead of being dominated by it as a blind power; accomplishing it with the least expenditure of energy and in conditions most worthy and appropriate for their human nature.

It is worth re-emphasizing that the domination of all life by the blind power of capital and its desire for-value does not create conditions that are worthy and appropriate for human and non-human nature. Instead, it breeds competition and domination, alienation and estrangement, exploitation and expropriation, and extraction. Moreover, as countless, courageous individuals and communities have recounted, this inhumanity makes-as-other, demonizes, makes invisible or voiceless, and eradicates people and non-human animals, differentially. As The Combahee River Collective (1982, p. 13) remind us, in our work we must be

actively committed to struggling against racial, sexual, heterosexual, and class oppression and see as our particular task the development of integrated analysis and practice based upon the fact that the major systems of oppression are interlocking. The synthesis of these oppressions creates the conditions of our lives. As Black women we see Black feminism as the logical political movement to combat the manifold and simultaneous oppressions that all women of color face.

Thus, there is the necessity for a deep analysis of current conditions and revolutionary intentions.

Although we are in a sensual agreement with Marx's theory as it applies to the very specific economic relationships he analyzed, we know that this analysis must be extended further in order for us to understand our specific economic situation as Black women. (ibid., p. 16)

This echoes through other Indigenous, intersectional, intercommunal, and intergenerational struggles, which deliberately de-center white, male, cis-privileges, and stress how individuals bearing such privileges cannot make the revolution (Marcos, 2002). Moreover, they cannot be responsible for weaving the revolution either, precisely because trust cannot emerge from within a society framed by whiteness. In a society whose tapestry is whiteness and coloniality, the revolution must refuse, unpick, and re-weave, as a way of overcoming the 'ontological cleavages—between human beings and their innermost capacities' (endnotes, 2013). To undo is to destroy and to reconnect—by divesting from the whiteness and coloniality of capital, we open up potential access to many-sided human capacities. This points toward the 'dignified human existence, which is a common desire we share', emphasized by Achille Mbembe (2017, p. 182). It is his realization that reparation of 'the humanity stolen from those who have historically been subjected to processes of abstraction and objectification' must be 'based on the idea that each person is a repository of a portion of intrinsic humanity. This irreducible share belongs to each of us' (ibid., pp. 182, 183).

The chapters in this collection highlight these ontological cleavages, as capital's need for-value reproduces life as a death spiral. Crucially, they offer us multiple access points to new horizons for realizing human capacities. This reminds us that Marx (1843, p. 144) was clear from a very early stage that vanguardism and the idea of the Party/revolutionary leader would fail, in the face of the multiplicity of human desires:

> We shall not say, Abandon your struggles, they are mere folly; let us provide you with the true campaign-slogans. Instead we shall simply show the world why it is struggling, and consciousness of this is a thing it will acquire whether it wishes or not.

The beauty of the stories told here lies in our being shown why the world is struggling. They remind us of Subcomandante Insurgente Marcos (2002, p. 34) emphasizing 'the hope of converting rebellion and dignity into freedom and dignity'. Marcos (ibid. 2002, pp. 32–3) bases this on the reality that

> [n]ot everyone who hears the voices of hopelessness and conformity are carried away by hopelessness. There are millions of people who continue without hearing the voices of the powerful and the indifferent. ... They don't hear a voice that comes from above; they hear the voice that is carried to them by the wind from below, a voice that is born in the indigenous heart of the mountains. ... They also say the wind and the rain and the sun are now saying something different: but with so much poverty, the time has come to harvest rebellion instead of death.

From multiple perspectives, geographies, ways of living, being, and doing, these stories emphasize the need not to be carried away by hopelessness, and instead to foreground dignity as 'that motherland that has no borders and that we often forget' (ibid., p. 269).

Thus, this collection highlights how our capitalist, educational institutions—with their internal structures, cultures, and practices; their commodification of time and outcome; their objectification and othering of relationships; and their instantiation of alleged methodological rigor as-truth—plot a miserable course, which sacrifices life. The richness of the engagement by these authors with Marx helps us to ground Mario Tronti's (2019, pp. 9, 204) statements that 'there is no revolutionary *movement* without revolutionary *theory*' and that the dialectical relation between lived, concrete, experience and a theory of abstraction offers 'an alternative way of counter posing a subaltern history of the exploited, for the purposes of struggle'.

In the process of counter-posing, the Handbook reminds us of the possibilities for struggle through theoretical-practical engagement with Marx and Marxist analyses. Here, our analyses of historical materialism demonstrate entanglements between idealism, materialism, and storytelling (Hall, Chap. 2), and flow into a deep analysis of how value as a web of social forms is *both* shaped by human labor-power *and* might be ruptured by human activity, re-purposed in-struggle (Rikowski, Chap. 3). This web of social forms rests on the exploitation of labor-power that breeds alienation across national contexts (Poutanen, Chap. 4). While estrangement, alienation, and ill-being increasingly describe the human impacts of educational activity, concrete analyses enable such descriptions to offer the potential for disalienation.

However, increasingly, there is a need to place an engagement with historical materialism as a science from below, and its entanglements with value and alienation, in dialogue with explorations of ontological and epistemological cleavages. In this way, the explanatory power of these abstract categories might become emancipatory, through an ongoing engagement with expanding forms of feminist, anti-racist, anti-colonialist, and anti-imperialist knowledge (Carpenter and Mojab, Chap. 5). In rethinking and challenging the co-constitution of social relations through race, gender, and class, this gives us concrete, historical examples that offer lines of reconnection with our onto-epistemological assumptions.

Here, the Handbook challenges us to think through these assumptions, in relation, not only to the co-constitution of social relations but also to the historical process of scientific, technological, and cultural production of social groups, in particular framed by labor and working-class education (Ramos, Chap. 6). While we take examples from Brazil, in relation to the theme of polytechnic education, the Handbook offers further examples and possibilities from within dependent, capitalist states, in order to understand the relationship between education and social (re)production. Thus, it is possible to explore the contingencies of liberation theology (Martínez Andrade and Allan Coelho, Chap. 7), in relation to the ways in which popular education might refuse the domination of life by the fatal dynamics of capitalism.

This process of looking beyond academia in the global North, in order to uncover the educational work of Marxists in revolutionary organizations, is a deep, pedagogical process and is also analyzed in relation to adult education (Holst, Chap. 8). Looking beyond also emerges from examinations of the commodification, measurement, and insistence on commensurability that exists within the University, and which is reproduced as a trap, sapping the intellectual life force from academic labor (Krzeski, Chap. 9). In looking beyond academia in the global North, either through counter-projects outside or through refusals inside, we are also gifted the potentiality that exists for struggle within the classroom, defined *both* as formal and institutional, *and* as informal or alternative (Das, Chap. 10).

Yet, the inhuman, totalizing realities of capital's web of social forms, operating through educational structures, cultures, and practices, remind us to be attentive to the ways in which educational work is subsumed and commodified. The Handbook evidences this further by reading our thinking through: first, competitive, project-based funding and science communication (Arboledas-Lérida, Chap. 11); second, the imposition of standardized, high-stakes testing, and the control of educational time, as socially necessary labor time (Au, Chap. 12); and, third, the use of schools and schooling for the reproduction of capitalism's dominant ideology, norms, and attitudes (Ruuska, Chap. 13).

These Marxist modes and characteristics of analysis in education are rooted in and spring from a deep, categorical understanding of what it is to be inside a toxic system of social reproduction that attempts to enforce homogeneity, while catalyzing a range of global emergencies as its waste products. They set up a rich engagement against this reality and the ways in which it is experienced differentially through a set of analyses of emerging currents in Marxism and education. These begin by relating Marx to specific, geographical contexts: first, transnational policy reforms in Mozambique, pivoting around markets, productivity, and human capital (Accioly, Chap. 14); second, the material history of workers' education in Chile and its relationship with European Marxism (Rueda, Chap. 15); third, the specificities, within Brazil as a dependent state, of commodification and financialization in education, with lessons for how to de-mercantilize world education (Leher and Balbinotti Costa, Chap. 16); and, fourth, critical, environmental education in Latin America, with a focus upon reimagining ontological cleavages, through a process of social struggle that resists capital's society-nature metabolism (Augusto Costa and Loureiro, Chap. 17).

Such a deep analysis of how we might re-purpose Marx's explanatory categories in a range of geographical contexts flows through into a set of chapters that weave together a desire to rupture those contexts intersectionally, intercommunally, and intergenerationally. Thus, thinking about the socio-economic and class-based specificities of South Asia, we might come to enrich our thinking around Green Marxism and the potential for decolonizing education through alternative pedagogic practices (Dey, Chap. 18). This decolonial framing also enables us to think about issues in relation to Indigenous epistemologies and cultures in the United States and to show how we all must reckon with the invisible war enacted by whiteness, for-value (Orie, Chap. 19). However, it is also possible to think about a framing, in relation to Marx's earlier work, which seeks to queer our normative models of education and to advance a queer Marxism that is attuned to the specificities of historical socialism (Popa, Chap. 20).

It is central that these analyses of emerging currents highlight spaces and times for struggle: first, in relation to the unique potential of teachers and teaching unions, guided by historical and material, social movement practices, in helping us envision the schools we want and deserve (Weiner, Chap. 21); and, second, through contemporary student movements and mobilizations as integral to anti-capitalist, class struggle against alienated labor (Cini and Ríos-Jara, Chap. 22). This, then, sets us up for an unfolding engagement with the potential for moving beyond such alienating social relationships, in order to ask whether it is possible to define other ways of becoming in the world, beyond the value-form.

The Handbook begins to address this question with a focus upon need and a critique of the idea of the needing subject/needed object, in relation to capital's historical mode of production. Instead, we move toward a new ontology that is human and non-violent (Lazarus, Chap. 23). Such a new ontology represented in relation to human needs might then be woven with an analysis of modes of mediation, the production of new relations of production, and the decolonial concept of analectics to question (social) reproduction in struggle (Backer, Chap. 24). This opens out a terrain for us to consider state and public policy, against which needs and reproduction might be situated, with a focus upon redistribution, emancipation, and dignity (Narita and Morelock, Chap. 25).

Redistribution, emancipation, and dignity, in relation to both resources and identity, lie at the heart of our historical reconsideration of the Commons and the potential for Commoning as an alternative form of being, doing, and knowing the world (Szadkowski, Chap. 26). Here, we might regard Commoning as a way of becoming-beyond education, which destabilizes our educational institutions, as infrastructure for racial-colonial capitalism. In this way, as a process that might be woven into our everyday practices, it might become an abolitionist approach that not only unsettles the taken-for-grantedness of these institutions but also opens our imaginations to infrastructures for alternative world-making movements (Boggs, Meyerhoff, Mitchell, and Schwartz-Weinstein, Chap. 27).

In doing this work, much of the Handbook's direction of travel refuses to center settler-colonial and racial-patriarchal realities in education as anything other than degenerative of human flourishing. It is, therefore, important to note that the final three chapters amplify voices and analyses, in relation to the entanglements of education and pedagogy with Marx, through: first, decoloniality and counter-geographies of women of the global South, in order to crack the toxic idea that there is no alternative to a universal conception of development (Monzó and Pečenković, Chap. 28); second, the potential for revolutionary transformation and collective liberation that erupt, as a gift, from an abolitionist, onto-epistemology, which itself weaves kinship, care, and knowing the world (m)otherwise into our consciousness (Motta, Chap. 29); and, third, the potential for taking an activist-transformative philosophy into our spaces, times, and relationships, in order to generate collective transformative praxis (Stetsenko, Chap. 30).

Collectively, then, this work reminds us that the hegemonic ways of being, doing, and knowing the world cannot provide guidance for new horizons of possibility. Our pathological and competitive identities, governed and regulated against capitalist schooling and reproduced methodologically for-value, have to be hospiced as they pass away and composted as waste (Andreotti, 2021). In hospicing and composting, the Handbook offers us examples of experiments in-community, which move us beyond concerns over fetishized, educational, commodity production and exchange, divisions of labor, private property, and markets. They offer us the potential to think about ways of knowing, rather than subsuming and commodifying knowledge, in-line with the desire to commodify the world at large. This is the possible liberation of what Marx (1857/1993) referred to as the general intellect, as a form of *mass intellectuality*, or as a set of *mass intellectualities*. The process of liberation is a mode of praxis, or a movement of becoming, filled with promise for new lines of flight, away from value.

New lines shape new horizons, which might re-engage humans with the historical and material conditions inside which they reproduce the world. The Handbook highlights the necessity of this re-engagement, beginning from a thick dialogue grounded in lived experiences of exploitation, expropriation, and extraction, requiring a politics of representation, as well as of redistribution (Fraser, 2013). Taken collectively, its voices ask us to recognize the pedagogic possibilities embedded within our composting of individual and collective anger, grief, and trauma, catalyzed by our differential experiences of capitalist reality. This is an educational process that explicitly refuses the social web of the commodity and the value-form, and instead centers the dignity of relationality (French et al., 2020; Tuck, 2018).

Thus, the Handbook's contributors offer us a challenge to think inside, against, and beyond Marxist traditions. They offer us conceptual, psychological, and social maps for how we might weave our concrete histories and ways of knowing the world with people, place, philosophy, values, communities, axiologies, and cosmologies, in order to generate 'relational accountability' (Wilson, 2008, p. 77). This pushes us to remember and reconsider Marx's (ethnographic) work in light of the thinking of numerous intellectuals, teachers, elders, and activists who have sought to synthesize and distill, weave and unwind, compost and mulch our rich, differential experiences of capitalism (Krader, 1974). In relating these experiences to global emergencies, this work pushes us to remember how to use storytelling to connect, precisely because in sitting with those stories:

> All that is solid melts into air, all that is holy is profaned, and [humans are] at last compelled to face with sober senses [their] real condition of life and [their] relations with [their] kind. (Marx & Engels, 1848/2002, p. 13)

Deconstructing the dialectical links between materialism, idealism, and storytelling, in relation to Marx, might help us to grapple with Tuck's (2018) question: '[H]ow shall we live?'. Mindful of Marx's (1852) argument that social revolutions 'cannot take [their] poetry from the past but only from the future', it is crucial that our dialogues with historical materialism center storytelling. This points us toward a poetry of positive transcendence of capitalist social relations, and the ability to tell out communism, beyond the sublation of private property, to become:

> the real *appropriation* of the *human* essence by and for [hu]man[s]; communism therefore as the complete return of [the hu]man to [themselves] as a *social* (i.e., human) being—a return accomplished consciously and embracing the entire wealth of previous development. This communism, as fully developed naturalism, equals humanism, and as fully developed humanism equals naturalism; it is the *genuine* resolution of the conflict between man and nature and between man and

man—the true resolution of the strife between existence and essence, between objectification and self-confirmation, between freedom and necessity, between the individual and the species. Communism is the riddle of history solved, and it knows itself to be this solution. (Marx, 1844, *emphasis* in original)

Here, we are reminded that this communism emerges from practical and historical activity, which we might see as '*a process of learning hope*' (Dinerstein, 2015, p. 16, *emphasis* in original), as an anatomy of resistance that pushes beyond *being-emancipatory* toward *becoming-decolonizing*. In communizing, humans might negate the commodification and alienation imposed by capitalist time, abolish settler-colonial and racial-patriarchal identification, and transcend one-sided identity.

Abolition, negation, and transcendence are fundamental to this process of communizing. Marx and Engels (1846/1998), p. 57) called communism 'the real movement which abolishes the present state of things'. This is a collective movement, which is 'not possible without the community … [which gives] each individual the means of cultivating [their] gifts in all directions' (ibid., p. 77). Moreover, it demands the abolition of mediations like private property and the division of labor in order that humans 'can turn [productive forces] into free manifestations of their lives' (ibid., p. 438). This is the potential that emerges imminently from the transcendence of a society predicated upon 'the enslaving subordination of the individual', in which humans 'are regarded *only as workers* and nothing more is seen in them, everything else being ignored' (Marx, 1875, *emphasis* in original).

This is the final lesson that I take, in reflecting upon the gift of sitting with these 30 chapters. They offer a consensus that our ontological, epistemological, and methodological horizons must push against the law of value. Yet they also unfold myriad ways of analyzing with Marx how we might move through intellectual work in society, such that a new form of becoming accepts and shapes the individual as a many-sided being (in dialogue with other, many-sided beings). At the heart of the matter then is our ability in-common to tell stories of dignity and mutuality that generate the courage and faith to enable:

> the narrow horizon of bourgeois right be crossed in its entirety and society inscribe on its banners: From each according to [their] ability, to each according to [their] needs! (ibid.)

Or, as Marcos (2002, p. 49) urges us to remember: 'Everything for everyone. Until this is true, there will be nothing for us.'

References

Andreotti, V. (2021). *Hospicing Modernity: Facing Humanity's Wrongs and the Implications for Social Activism*. North Atlantic Books.

Césaire, A. (1956/1969). *Return to My Native Land*. Archipelago Books.

Chuăng. (n.d.). Red Dust: The Transition to Capitalism in China. *Chuăng, 2*. Retrieved May 17, 2023, from http://chuangcn.org/journal/two/red-dust/

Dinerstein, A. (2015). *The Politics of Autonomy in Latin America: The Art of Organising Hope in the Twenty First Century*. Palgrave.

The Combahee River Collective. (1982). A Black Feminist Statement. In G. T. Hull, P. Bell Scott, & B. Smith (Eds.), *All the Women Are White, All the Blacks Are Men, But Some of Us Are Brave: Black Women's Studies* (pp. 13–22). The Feminist Press.

endnotes. (2013). Spontaneity, Mediation, Rupture. *endnotes, 3*. Retrieved May 18, 2023, from https://endnotes.org.uk/issues/3/en/endnotes-spontaneity-mediation-rupture

Fraser, N. (2013). *Fortunes of Feminism: From State-Managed Capitalism to Neoliberal Crisis*. Verso.

French, K. B., Sanchez, A., & Ullom, E. (2020). Composting Settler Colonial Distortions: Cultivating Critical Land-Based Family History. *Genealogy, 4*(3). Retrieved May 18, 2023, from https://www.mdpi.com/2313-5778/4/3/84/htm

hooks, b. (1994). *Teaching to Transgress: Education as the Practice of Freedom*. Routledge.

Krader, L. (1974). *The Ethnographical Notebooks of Karl Marx (Studies of Morgan, Phear, Maine, Lubbock)* (Trans. and Ed., with an Introduction by L. Krader). Van Gorcum & Co.

Marx, K. (1843). Letter to Arnold Ruge, September 1843. *Marxists Internet Archive*. Retrieved May 18, 2023, from https://www.marxists.org/archive/marx/works/1843/letters/43_09-alt.htm

Marx, K. (1844). Economic and Philosophical Manuscripts. *Marxists Internet Archive*. Retrieved May 18, 2023, from https://www.marxists.org/archive/marx/works/1844/manuscripts/comm.htm

Marx, K. (1852). The Eighteenth Brumaire of Louis Bonaparte. *Marxists Internet Archive*. Retrieved May 18, 2023, from https://www.marxists.org/archive/marx/works/1852/18th-brumaire/ch01.htm

Marx, K. (1857/1993). *Grundrisse: Outline of the Critique of Political Economy*. Penguin.

Marx, K. (1875). Critique of the Gotha Programme. *Marxists Internet Archive*. Retrieved May 18, 2023, from https://www.marxists.org/archive/marx/works/1875/gotha/

Marx, K. (1894/1991). *Capital, Volume 3: A Critique of Political Economy*. Penguin.

Marx, K., & Engels, F. (1846/1998). *The German Ideology: Including Theses on Feuerbach and Introduction to the Critique of Political Economy*. Prometheus.

Marx, K., & Engels, F. (1848/2002). *The Communist Manifesto*. Penguin.

Mbembe, A. (2017). *Critique of Black Reason* (L. Dubois, Trans.). Duke University Press.

Subcomandante Insurgente Marcos. (2002). *Our Word Is Our Weapon: Selected Writings* (J. P. de León, Ed.). Seven Stories Press.

Tronti, M. (2019). *Workers and Capital*. Verso Books.

Tuck, E. (2018). *I Do Not Want to Haunt You but I Will: Indigenous Feminist Theorizing on Reluctant Theories of Change*. University of Alberta.

Wilson, S. (2008). *Research as Ceremony: Indigenous Research Methods*. Fernwood Publishing.

Index[1]

NUMBERS AND SYMBOLS
#FeesMustFall, 500

A
Abolition
  abolitionism, 515–517, 520
  abolitionist university studies, 519
  prison abolition, 517
Abstraction, 8, 15, 17, 20, 28, 29, 33, 35, 40, 48, 49, 64–65n2, 76, 96, 97, 106, 107, 137, 202, 216n4, 223–237, 267, 273, 344, 359, 456, 457, 491, 498, 540, 542, 560, 603, 604
Abundance, 288, 319, 366, 446–447
Abya Yala, 38, 327, 331n2, 574n1
Academic capitalism, 71–85, 255
Academic labour, 163–178, 203, 208–215
Acceleration, 11, 86n10, 164, 421, 521
Accumulation
  of capital, 247, 264, 269, 271, 323, 324
  by dispossession, 324, 520
  primitive, 323–325, 493, 517, 521, 530n13, 546
Adolescents, 383, 387, 388, 390, 593
Adorno, Theodor W., 7, 28, 31, 34, 39, 76, 86n4, 544

Africa, 21, 270, 273–276, 278, 300, 402, 421
  Sub-Saharan, 21, 274
Alberta Teachers Association (ATA), 402
Alienation, 17, 20, 21, 71–85, 114, 116, 118, 124, 137, 165, 184, 197n1, 197n2, 320, 348, 358, 366–373, 375, 383–386, 405, 436–439, 443, 447, 448, 478, 482, 529, 540, 542, 554, 582, 584, 595, 602, 603, 605, 609
Allende, Salvador, 295
Althusser, Louis, 21, 76, 183, 187, 196, 243–256, 417–419, 455–457, 459, 460, 523
Analectics, 453, 464–468, 537–555, 607
Anti-ecological, 335, 336, 342
Anti-parent, 545, 548
Appropriation, 79, 82, 84, 85, 86n10, 111, 118, 178, 265, 269, 271, 277, 319, 321–323, 385, 391, 414, 458, 472, 477, 478, 483, 522, 608
Argentina, 281–284, 288, 295, 323, 472, 480, 483, 544
Art, 119, 121, 124, 125, 193, 250, 333, 381–393, 407, 465
Assimilation, 132, 356–357, 366, 371

---

[1] Note: Page numbers followed by 'n' refer to notes.

Audit
  audit culture, 78
  auditing, 78
Aufhebung, 16, 27
Austerity, 136, 301–303, 313, 413, 421, 523
Automation, 154, 478
Autonomy, 5, 8, 11, 35, 72, 79, 80, 82, 83, 94, 123, 124, 178, 213, 250, 266, 305, 308, 401, 440, 457, 460, 476, 477, 481–484, 491, 493, 494, 503, 513, 551

B
Babbage, Charles, 269–271
Benchmarking, 164, 168, 171, 173
Bibliometric indicators, 170
Biology, 188, 361, 362
Black, 32, 35, 39, 101, 103–105, 191, 225, 229, 365, 398, 399, 441, 510, 514–517, 521, 526, 528, 548, 549, 560, 566, 568, 569, 574n3, 603
Black and Brown youth, 356, 359, 366, 367, 372
Black Lives Matter (BLM), 18, 104, 405, 549
Blackness, 35, 104, 567, 568
Black Radical Tradition, 516, 526, 528
Bloch, Ernst, 137, 583
Bologna process, 78, 170, 255
Bonefeld, Werner, 7, 49, 50, 52, 53, 64n2
Bourdieu, Pierre, 245, 254, 455, 523
Bourgeois revolution, 286, 300
Bowles, Samuel, 80, 165, 208, 236, 244, 245, 252, 523
Brazil, 20, 111, 112, 124–126, 275, 277, 299–314, 315n5, 322, 323, 472, 480, 560–562, 605, 606
British Columbia Teachers Federation (BCTF), 402
Bullying, 383, 388–392, 394n16

C
Caffentzis, George, 422, 494, 496, 523, 525
Capital accumulation, 204, 213
Capitalist relations of production, 202, 203, 207, 208, 214
Capitalocene, 8, 20, 336–338
Capital (the book)/*Das Kapital* (the book), 14, 28, 29, 47, 49, 52, 56, 60, 61, 66n9, 76, 86n3, 132–134, 136, 137, 166, 229, 247, 266, 267, 281, 285, 300, 334, 376, 377n2, 398, 414, 435, 453, 454, 490, 493, 495, 530n13, 542, 546
Caring, 5, 83, 86n12, 243, 345, 346, 402, 543, 545, 546, 552, 562, 590
Carnoy, Martin, 244, 252, 453, 458–461, 467
Central economies, 270–272, 277
Charter schools, 227, 228, 401, 472
Chicago Teachers Union (CTU), 407
Chile, 20, 132, 149, 206, 281–296, 300, 421, 472, 480, 483, 500, 568, 606
Citizenship, 286, 471, 473, 481, 482
Civilizing mission, 361
Civil society, 30, 97, 121, 152, 154, 286, 301, 437, 438, 472, 474
Class
  class-neutral, 196
  relation, 49, 51, 102, 103, 106, 107, 185, 186, 188, 191, 194, 197, 248, 335, 398, 473, 541, 549
  ruling, 76, 139, 185, 186, 188, 189, 195, 273, 311, 348, 397, 401, 403, 425, 437, 459, 464, 466, 467, 514
  struggle, 20, 50, 51, 83, 98, 102, 107, 108, 119, 125, 137, 141, 151, 165, 166, 183–197, 253, 268, 300, 301, 303, 304, 314, 413, 414, 417–419, 424, 426, 435, 453, 455, 456, 459, 461, 467, 468, 493, 494, 523, 542, 573, 588, 606
Classroom, 8–11, 16, 20, 26, 30, 31, 33, 36, 184–197, 229, 230, 232, 233, 236, 237, 250, 333, 337, 345–347, 351, 397, 398, 406, 407, 408n1, 437, 441, 448, 460, 467, 518, 546, 582, 605
Cleaver, Harry, 47, 49, 166, 184, 197n1, 255, 494
Cognitive capitalism, 172, 424, 490, 495
Colonialism, 77, 94, 100, 139, 148, 149, 334, 339, 341, 351n1, 361, 362, 368–370, 373, 440, 479, 480, 521, 530n13, 546, 553

Coloniality, 33, 35, 136, 142, 320, 329, 330, 473, 479–482, 484, 519, 549, 550, 553, 554, 564, 567, 573, 603
of power, 136, 549, 550
Commensuration, 168, 172, 176
Commodification, 202, 203, 205–208, 210, 214
of education, 301, 303–310, 312, 313, 330, 447, 606
Commodity fetishism, 72, 76, 86n3, 141, 231–233, 359, 365, 366, 372
Commodity-form, 9, 42, 47, 209, 211, 214, 267
Commodity production, 206, 209–211
Commoning, 177, 492, 496, 501, 607
Common sense, 10, 83, 263, 303, 304, 307, 459, 607
Common, the, 15, 155, 157, 173–175, 178, 228, 478, 489–504, 588, 603
Communism, 9, 10, 22, 75, 154, 156, 157, 166, 173, 189, 295, 343, 383–385, 433, 436, 439, 494, 515, 554, 608, 609
Communist
education, 149, 300, 514
movement, 154
Party schools, 149, 528
Communist Labor Party (USA), 153
Communist Manifesto (the book), 12, 26, 116, 281, 283, 292, 494, 514, 588, 590
Communist Party of Chile (CPCh)/ Partido Comunista de Chile (PCCh), 287, 292, 295
Community, 3, 6, 12, 13, 15, 17, 21, 28, 30, 35, 37, 38, 56, 74, 78–81, 83, 84, 93, 100, 104, 105, 130, 139, 150, 153, 164, 176–178, 192, 203, 205, 209–212, 215, 216–217n7, 227, 230, 235, 237, 248, 283, 286, 302, 315n5, 323, 328–330, 333, 337–343, 345–351, 351n3, 352n8, 356, 363, 366–368, 370–372, 374, 399, 407, 431, 441, 444–449, 460, 463, 465, 466, 481, 483, 491, 497, 499–501, 503, 517, 543, 545, 546, 548–553, 555, 555n1, 562, 566, 571–573, 574n1, 574n2, 582, 592, 593, 601–603, 607–609

Competition, 205, 206, 212, 213, 215
competitionalization, 53–56
competitiveness, 73, 77–79, 85, 134, 319
Consciousness, 4, 9, 19, 28, 34–39, 61, 96–99, 102, 106–108, 114, 117, 119, 122, 140, 150–152, 155, 197n7, 233, 243, 268, 269, 289, 303, 304, 331n1, 334, 339, 340, 371, 385, 386, 391, 405, 432, 433, 436, 438–444, 447–449, 455, 457, 478, 524, 540–544, 548, 551, 574n1, 581, 582, 604, 607
Constitutional assembly of salaried workers and intellectuals, 295
Contradictions, 5, 9, 14–17, 27, 28, 30–36, 38, 40–42, 61, 62, 93, 94, 102, 108, 111, 112, 114, 116–118, 121, 122, 124–126, 139, 142n1, 151, 153, 192, 194, 252, 266, 268, 272, 276, 277, 302, 327, 336, 337, 361, 384, 405, 418, 422, 458–461, 463, 464, 467, 473, 475, 496, 511, 513, 538–544, 552, 585, 588, 590
resolution of, 538–544, 551, 552, 554
Co-operatives, 9, 15, 42, 63, 82, 175, 178, 287, 289–291, 334, 407, 493, 497–500, 502
cooperative university, 175, 499, 500
Crisis, 8, 26, 50, 56, 94, 103, 120, 153, 156, 245, 246, 265, 302, 304–306, 309, 310, 320, 326, 333, 348, 387, 389, 413, 418, 421, 425, 444, 483, 496, 512, 513, 517, 528, 581, 582, 595
financial, 305, 413
Critical environmental education, 18, 317–331
Critique, 3, 4, 6, 7, 10, 14, 18, 20–22, 25, 26, 29, 31–37, 39, 41, 52, 71, 72, 76, 82, 83, 86n10, 93, 95–98, 101, 104, 105, 118, 130–137, 141, 163–178, 183, 190, 191, 194, 235, 253–255, 263–278, 314, 366, 376, 381–386, 388, 392, 393, 397, 403, 408, 416–419, 421–422, 433, 439, 443, 446, 450n3, 453, 455, 457, 463, 473, 475–483, 493, 495, 498–500, 503, 509–529, 543–545, 565, 567, 593, 594, 601, 606

614   INDEX

Critique of the Gotha Program (the book), 15, 116, 273, 285, 554
Cultural heteronomy, 300
Curriculum, 9, 16, 27, 29, 31, 53, 62, 100, 104, 125, 194, 196, 228, 229, 233, 236, 256, 275, 306, 343, 350, 351, 357, 369, 371–373, 383, 386, 397, 398, 400, 401, 407, 459, 545, 552

D
Davis, Angela, 16, 516
De-capitalization, 307, 333–351, 351n1
Decolonial, 21, 83, 135, 138, 368–377, 438, 449, 453, 464, 467, 468, 473, 479–482, 484, 537–555, 559–573, 606, 607
Decoloniality, 21, 148, 569, 607
Decolonization, 5, 194, 300, 333–351, 368, 369, 371, 373, 466, 528–529, 553
Deficit model, 360
Dehumanization, 15, 29, 42, 139, 364, 372, 374
Democracy, 81, 85, 123, 193, 202, 248, 290, 321, 404, 405, 415, 417, 441, 459–461, 473, 480, 501, 515, 516, 520, 550, 552
Democratic Party, 287, 289, 292, 293, 398
Dependent capitalism, 112, 299–314, 317, 320, 323, 329
Deprofessionalization, 80, 401, 402
Devaluation, 356, 359, 360, 367, 560, 561, 566
Developed economies, 172, 277, 511
Development, 4, 6, 8, 11, 13–16, 18, 19, 21, 28–30, 33, 39, 49, 53, 55, 57–63, 64n2, 66n14, 78, 79, 94, 95, 99, 102, 107, 114, 116, 119–122, 126, 135, 136, 139, 150, 152, 153, 165–167, 170, 193, 209, 210, 214, 255, 265, 266, 268–271, 274, 275, 283, 291, 300, 303, 307, 314, 319, 325–327, 331, 334, 335, 338–344, 350, 351, 360, 362, 363, 383–386, 389, 391, 392, 398, 405, 416, 419, 431, 437, 438, 440, 444–447, 460, 471–484, 490, 492, 494, 495, 497, 498, 500, 502, 511, 516–518, 522, 523, 527, 530n16, 538–547, 549–554, 583, 584, 586, 587, 593, 603, 607, 608
Dialectical materialism, 7, 8, 20, 21, 27–30, 37–42, 438, 538
Dialectics, 17, 20, 27–32, 35, 36, 40–42, 95, 96, 105, 107, 108, 133, 150, 151, 216n1, 237, 339, 389, 406, 434, 457, 464, 466, 537–555
 negative, 31, 35, 42
Disalienation, 73, 75, 82, 84, 85, 605
Du Bois, W.E.B., 510, 514–516, 521, 522, 526
Dunayevskaya, Raya, 28, 31, 32, 34, 41, 537, 538, 540, 542, 549
Dussel, Enrique, 6, 7, 130–132, 317, 323, 325, 326, 330, 453, 458, 464–468, 468n2, 538, 543–549, 552–554, 568, 584, 595

E
Ecocentric pedagogies, 333–351
Eco-curricular, 351
Economic and Philosophic Manuscripts of 1844 (the book), 52, 73, 75, 86n3, 134, 358, 493
Economic growth, 135, 136, 202, 203, 247, 269, 271–275, 314n2, 319, 426
Education policy, 51, 62, 63, 74, 77, 78, 84, 85, 227–229, 234, 249, 255, 272, 274, 275
Emancipation, 34–35, 74, 104, 118, 122, 132, 152, 155–157, 197, 283, 284, 287, 295, 374, 382, 392, 414, 473, 475, 480, 482, 521, 607
Enlightenment, 9, 196, 286, 300, 387, 393, 419, 432, 497, 540
Environment, 19, 25, 38, 73, 79, 81, 134–136, 165, 184, 188, 193, 309–310, 322, 323, 327, 329, 334, 335, 337–351, 352n9, 363, 370, 372, 388–391, 472, 474, 477, 483, 490
Epistemic erasure, 369, 370

Epistemology, 20, 37, 38, 41, 96–98, 103, 106, 138, 361, 362, 368, 370, 373, 382, 448–449, 464, 480, 519, 526, 543, 549, 553, 582, 606
Equal rights, 366, 550
Essence, 11, 12, 14, 15, 17, 25, 26, 30–33, 37, 40–42, 75, 94, 99, 102, 105, 107, 108, 113, 230, 236, 267, 268, 273, 327, 371, 386, 391, 438, 445, 493, 541, 542, 568, 573, 584, 595, 608, 609
Ethnographic Notebooks (the book), 15, 38
European Commission (EC), 204
European Union (EU), 20, 78, 86n9, 170, 204, 246, 255
Evaluation, 77, 133, 164, 170–172, 175, 217n7, 227, 228, 301, 307, 308, 312, 359, 361, 363, 365, 366, 371, 373, 389, 403
Evaluative state, 169, 170
Excellence, 8, 40, 42, 62, 78, 168–170, 414
Existence, 7, 9–11, 13, 14, 17, 25–27, 30, 31, 36, 38–40, 42, 47–50, 54, 55, 59, 66n9, 75, 99, 111–113, 118, 120–122, 124, 125, 136, 157, 202, 209, 216n1, 232, 253, 265, 267, 276, 286, 287, 291, 315n5, 317, 319, 328, 338, 349, 359, 385, 406, 426, 433, 438, 439, 457, 495, 502, 503, 547, 567, 584, 585, 589, 592, 594, 602, 603, 609
Exploitation, 8, 14, 15, 17, 20, 25, 29, 38, 63, 72, 81, 82, 99, 108, 116, 124, 131, 134, 136, 138, 141, 167, 186, 196, 210, 232, 251, 264–266, 269, 272, 276, 278, 282, 285, 286, 290, 294, 300, 305, 312, 318, 319, 321, 323, 325, 327, 329, 330, 334, 337, 348, 360, 362, 364, 366, 374, 381, 383, 414, 416, 418, 419, 424, 426, 427, 431, 436, 456, 479, 480, 510, 517, 520, 525, 548, 550, 553, 582, 584, 595, 603, 608
  of labor power, 13, 81, 265, 276, 319, 414, 418, 419, 424, 605
Extractivism, 322–326
  logic of, 322–326

F
Factory model of schooling, 358, 363
Fanon, Frantz, 138, 139, 339, 440, 564, 584, 595
Fascism, 304
Federación Obrera de Chile (FOCH), 291, 293
Federici, Silvia, 31, 81, 83, 106, 455, 494, 496, 525, 559, 560, 564
Feminism
  autonomous Marxist feminism, 559–573
  feminist theory, 83, 86n12, 94, 554
Film, 63, 243, 244, 256, 383, 387–392
Finland, 20, 72, 81, 83, 85
Fordism, 425
Formal subsumption, 203, 205, 208–210, 212–215
Fourth Congress of the Communist International 1922, 295
Framework Programme for Research and Innovation, 204
Freedom, 12, 32, 39, 57, 104, 107, 108, 121, 122, 130, 183, 195, 197n1, 276, 308, 318, 322, 417, 419, 437, 440, 441, 444, 445, 515, 521, 522, 528, 538–542, 544, 548, 551, 554, 561, 569, 590, 593, 595, 602, 604, 609
Freedom Road Socialist Organization (USA), 155
Freire, Paulo, 5, 108, 130, 137–141, 142n1, 148, 150, 245, 304, 318, 448, 537, 545, 546, 554, 584, 595
Fromm, Erich, 76, 86n5, 138, 139, 432, 450n3
Funding
  agencies, 204–207, 209–215, 216n4
  competitive project-based, 201–215
  grant, 205, 207
  institutional, 205–207
  performance-based, 78

G
Gender
  genderification, 383, 391, 392
Geography, 18, 188, 191, 325, 345, 604

German Ideology (the book), 12, 30, 52, 98, 106, 244, 432, 433, 512, 514
G.I. Bill, 521, 522, 524
Gintis, Herbert, 236, 244, 245, 252, 523
Global educational reforms, 263–278
Globalization, 135, 136, 255, 271, 326, 329, 459
Global protests, 414, 421, 425, 500
Governance, 16, 18, 36, 78, 79, 169, 365, 416, 420, 465, 489, 496, 498, 499, 517, 551, 552, 568
Gramsci, Antonio, 112, 120–126, 137, 150, 183, 191, 192, 247–249, 254, 255, 256n5, 272, 300, 303, 304, 458, 459, 526, 559, 586
Grant funding, 205, 207
Green Marxism, 20, 21, 333–351, 606
Grosfoguel, Ramon, 479, 480, 549, 550
Grundrisse (the book), 13, 61, 64n2, 74, 76, 81–83, 102, 166, 167, 216n4, 398, 403, 423, 434, 435, 462, 476, 491, 492, 495
Guevara, Ernesto "Che," 150

H

Habermas, Jürgen, 417–419, 442, 450n5, 471
Hall, Stuart, 165, 526
Hardt, Michael, 50, 163, 423, 425, 491, 493, 494, 496, 565
Harvey, David, 71, 74–76, 81, 82, 86n10, 136, 155, 176, 245, 246, 265, 324, 325, 420, 425, 454, 495, 520
Hegel, G.W.F., 13, 28, 34, 40, 41, 73, 432, 465, 538–541, 544, 547, 554
Hegelians
 left, 461, 512
 young, 512, 513
Hegemony, 112, 120, 125, 151, 247, 249, 252, 254–256, 272, 301–304, 313, 323, 325, 330, 356, 359, 364, 365, 369, 372, 376, 437, 458, 460, 466, 467, 584
Heterogeneity, 171, 177, 178
Higher education (HE), 4, 8, 20, 28, 52, 56–60, 66n9, 71, 72, 74, 77, 78, 84, 85, 125, 163, 170, 207, 214, 253, 255, 272–278, 304, 308–310, 315n5, 337, 338, 397, 402, 413, 437, 472, 483, 489–504, 509–529, 530n15
Historical materialism, 20, 27, 76, 95–97, 111–114, 186, 264, 276, 381, 390, 432, 440, 456, 541, 604, 605, 608
Holloway, John, 5–7, 49–52, 59, 62, 63, 65n3, 166, 167, 493, 495, 559, 564, 567
Homogenization, 172, 176
Horizontalism, 551, 552
Housework, 83
Human capital
 strategy, 523
 theory, 264, 271, 275, 473, 475–477, 481, 482
Humanism, 20, 120, 123, 124, 458, 537, 538, 542, 549, 552, 554, 608

I

Idealism, 4, 13, 20, 29–31, 37, 38, 98, 456, 542, 604, 608
Identity, 5–7, 15, 19, 28, 31–35, 37–39, 42, 81, 83, 85, 103–107, 185, 190, 191, 195, 233, 342, 344, 358, 362, 382, 383, 389, 405, 415, 426, 445, 482, 483, 540, 548, 549, 555, 574n2, 582, 593, 607, 609
Ideology, 4, 96, 98, 102, 103, 108, 130, 136, 141, 186, 187, 197, 244, 245, 249–254, 256n3, 265, 268, 284, 292, 301–303, 307, 319, 327, 335, 344, 347, 359, 360, 362, 365, 370, 371, 373, 374, 376, 393n1, 405, 417, 418, 420, 456–458, 460, 473, 475, 478, 479, 518, 521, 523, 542, 543, 582, 606
Immaterial labor, 172
Imperialism, 94, 101, 149, 192, 246, 282, 300, 304, 305, 323, 416, 418, 459, 479, 519, 522, 546, 553
Inclusion, 101, 104, 107, 334, 471, 482, 483, 491, 496, 498, 501
Independent working-class education, 148
Indian boarding schools, 356, 369, 370

Indigenous
  communities, 15, 192, 329, 335, 338–340, 342, 352n8, 517, 543, 546, 553
  futurity, 369–371
  knowledge, 344, 346
  lens, 368
  people, 94, 191, 330, 356, 361–363, 366, 368–375, 525, 528, 530n13, 546, 550, 551, 565
  teachers, 373
Inequality, 4, 83, 93, 131, 177, 178, 183, 186, 192, 196, 232, 244–246, 251, 252, 255, 256, 285–287, 319–322, 325, 326, 361–363, 367, 398, 400, 403, 405, 407, 431, 464, 472, 475–477, 479, 480, 482, 483, 523, 548, 582, 593
Informal workers, 155
Infrastructure, 5, 11–15, 20, 126, 171, 176, 247, 305, 337, 416, 418, 471, 477, 481, 483, 509–529, 530n15, 570, 607
Institution, 3–5, 10, 14–16, 32, 33, 41, 49–57, 60–63, 65n3, 71, 73, 77–79, 81–85, 95, 100–102, 104, 105, 118, 134, 168, 170, 171, 175, 176, 187, 196, 203, 205–207, 209, 211–215, 217n7, 217n12, 230, 245–250, 253, 254, 273, 275, 295, 300, 302, 306–309, 315n5, 323, 325, 335–342, 346–351, 351n4, 358, 360, 367, 368, 372, 397, 413, 415–417, 419, 420, 425, 426, 431, 438, 441, 446, 455, 456, 460, 461, 464, 466, 467, 471–473, 477, 478, 492, 496, 497, 499–503, 510, 512, 514, 516–519, 523, 524, 527, 545, 548, 563, 572, 574n3, 589, 593, 604, 607
  institutionalization, 50
International agencies, 270, 273, 274
International division of labor, 204, 264, 271, 272, 276, 277, 550
International standards, 400
Intersectionality, 19, 103, 149, 548, 554
Investment funds, 301, 305–307, 311, 313–314

J
Justice, 18, 142n2, 285, 391, 404–406, 481, 483, 516, 588, 595, 601
  social, 19, 138, 157, 398, 402–404, 406, 408, 471, 481–483, 590, 591, 593

K
Kant, Immanuel, 513, 529n1, 539
Knowledge
  knowledge-based economy, 78, 170, 426
  production, 11, 12, 38, 165, 168, 169, 172, 175–178, 202, 205, 208, 209, 211–215, 268, 334, 337, 338, 340, 343–347, 350, 373, 406, 422, 424, 425, 497, 498, 501, 502, 513
Knowledge Liberation Front, 501
Kosík, Karel, 138, 268

L
Labor
  abstract labor, 20, 47–49, 54, 55, 64n2
  labor-time, 32, 48, 54, 84, 265, 606
  labor-time (socially necessary), 11, 20, 48, 49, 53–55, 166, 172, 212, 217n11, 223–237, 606
  of love, 8, 81, 84
  surplus, 8, 185, 209, 210, 216n3, 319, 360, 522, 602
  theory of value, 156, 414
  two-fold nature of, 48
  wageless, 523
Labor-power
  maintenance of, 61
  reproduction of, 61, 62, 265, 523
  social production of, 55, 60–62, 65n3
Land, 5, 38, 39, 86n10, 131, 185, 192, 264, 272, 276, 305, 324, 329, 330, 331n2, 336–338, 340, 352n8, 356, 363, 364, 368–371, 375, 510, 512, 517–522, 524, 525, 528, 530n13, 550, 561–563, 565, 566, 569–573, 574n1, 574n2

618 INDEX

Language, 37, 39, 94, 99, 100, 104, 105, 119, 121, 125, 188, 234, 264, 302, 331n2, 361, 366, 383, 384, 390, 397, 407, 444, 445, 467, 475, 490, 520, 521, 543, 550, 552, 553, 560, 561, 564, 571, 572
Latin America, 20, 129, 133–135, 141, 142, 148, 155, 270, 275, 278, 283, 317–331, 472, 473, 477, 479, 480, 482, 484, 606
Law of value, 166, 172, 173, 609
League of Revolutionaries for a New America (LRNA), 153–156
League of Revolutionary Black Workers (USA), 153
Lean production, 399
Learning, 8, 10, 11, 13, 14, 16, 26, 30, 60, 66n9, 82, 93–108, 121–124, 142n1, 147, 150, 157, 184, 196, 223, 229–231, 233–237, 269, 273, 302, 303, 305, 306, 309–311, 313, 335, 337, 339–351, 359, 363–367, 370, 373, 376, 397, 398, 400–402, 404, 405, 431, 464, 472, 474, 477, 483, 496, 497, 499, 501, 502, 530n15, 538, 543, 545, 548, 570, 581, 589, 591–595, 602
Lefebvre, Henri, 453, 458, 461–464, 467, 468n1
Lenin, Vladimir I., 27, 28, 32–34, 36, 40, 41, 112, 118, 120, 121, 125, 126, 184, 186, 189, 289, 304, 305, 308, 439, 459
LGBTQ+, 498
Liberalization, 270, 271
Liberation, 4, 6, 10, 11, 15, 17, 20, 21, 29, 35, 129–142, 274, 320, 330, 440, 446, 464, 465, 467, 494, 496, 504, 528–529, 538, 544, 545, 549, 553, 559–573, 587, 588, 605, 607, 608
Lincoln Social Science Centre, 501
Linebaugh, Peter, 493, 526
Luxemburg, Rosa, 28, 138, 139, 289, 494, 495

M
Managerialism, 77, 401, 420, 421
Mancomunales, 287, 288
Mandel, Ernest, 77, 419, 426
Marcuse, Herbert, 16, 17, 40, 418, 419, 426, 432, 439, 440, 450n3
Mariátegui, José Carlos, 137, 141, 294, 480
Market, 3, 8, 13, 15, 30, 41, 53, 54, 57–58, 77, 79, 80, 106, 126, 130, 134–136, 141, 155, 164, 172, 174, 185, 186, 188, 193, 206, 207, 209, 210, 228, 231, 246, 248, 250, 263, 271–277, 302, 305, 307–314, 323, 328, 335, 337, 345, 401, 403, 419–421, 423, 424, 459, 461, 471–484, 491, 500, 503, 517, 523, 524, 544, 552, 606, 607
Marketization, 18, 53, 57–58, 63, 66n9, 79, 174, 420, 421, 437
Maslow, Abraham, 432, 443, 448
Mass intellectuality, 19, 82, 84, 85, 526, 607–608
Measurement, 20, 78, 163, 164, 167, 168, 173, 224, 230, 232–234, 236, 363, 605
Mediation, 12, 13, 15, 41, 50, 118, 119, 122, 141, 171, 174, 176, 178, 265, 267, 326, 453, 458–461, 467, 492, 586, 607, 609
Merit pay, 400
Method, 4, 6, 11, 18, 34, 36–41, 74, 95, 97, 98, 116, 123, 124, 130, 138, 139, 141, 142, 166, 188, 225, 251, 264–269, 272, 276, 277, 303, 330, 335–337, 356, 361, 370, 371, 375, 387, 393, 406, 449, 456, 459, 463, 503, 552, 562, 583
Metrics, 78, 80, 164, 165, 171–175, 228, 397, 476, 478
Metrification, 208
Military-industrial complex, 522
Money, 26, 49–53, 56–59, 62, 63, 64n1, 64–65n2, 66n9, 74, 133, 154, 157, 184, 186, 205, 207, 211–215, 217n8, 217n9, 227, 229, 230, 265, 266, 305, 309, 357, 390, 404, 437, 454, 462, 473, 492, 562, 602
Monopoly, 74, 124, 250, 264, 270, 271, 277, 314n2, 325, 483, 522
Morrill Act, 521, 522
Mozambique, 5, 20, 264, 274, 275, 277, 606

N

Nation, 94, 95, 99, 106, 125, 170, 204, 230, 246, 248, 254, 266, 269, 339, 356, 364, 370, 372, 415, 463, 515, 516, 546, 564–566, 569

Nature, 8, 14, 16, 26, 28, 30, 32, 35, 39, 41, 48, 50, 52, 53, 62, 64n1, 86n10, 101, 102, 113, 117, 119, 121, 122, 124, 125, 136, 149–153, 155–157, 167, 173, 174, 177, 184, 190, 194, 210, 214, 246, 253, 265–267, 277, 282, 285–287, 304, 308, 311, 317, 318, 320–323, 326, 328–331, 331n1, 333, 334, 336, 339, 340, 342–349, 351, 351n3, 361, 370, 371, 382, 385, 386, 399, 433, 434, 436, 438, 441, 459, 463, 477, 491, 492, 502, 504, 512, 514, 540, 541, 560, 584–586, 603, 608

Needs, 3, 29, 64n1, 81, 96, 112, 135, 151, 164, 184, 204, 236, 268, 291, 311, 317, 339, 360, 381, 400, 427, 431–449, 457, 471, 490, 513, 581, 602, 604–607, 609

Negation, 6, 7, 13, 15, 16, 28, 264, 318, 319, 328, 463, 538–543, 547, 551–555, 567–569, 609

Negri, Antonio, 163, 166, 172, 423, 425, 491, 494, 496, 565

Neoliberalism, 103–105, 112, 125, 141, 148, 170, 191, 254, 295, 397–408, 420, 423, 425, 426, 495

New Reading of Marx, 494

New social movements, 149

Nondualism, 448, 449

Non-identity, 7, 28, 31–35, 38, 39

Nonviolent Communication (NVC), 433, 443–449

O

Objectification, 20, 29, 42, 74, 79, 231, 318, 322, 331n1, 359, 361, 363, 364, 367, 368, 386, 433, 434, 436, 442, 602–604, 609

Objective conditions of production, 208, 209, 211, 215

Onda anomola, 500

On the Jewish Question (the book), 285

Ontology, 38, 96–99, 102, 103, 106–108, 169, 432–435, 441, 447, 448, 465, 493, 497–498, 582, 607

Organization for Economic Cooperation and Development (OECD), 78, 170, 205–207, 247, 255, 300, 402

Othering, 106, 362, 604

P

Participatory action research, 141, 152

Partido Obrero Socialista (POS), 282, 284, 285, 287, 289, 291, 292, 295

Party of Liberation and Socialism (USA), 155

Patriarchy, 20, 94, 102, 107, 108, 405, 517, 543, 550, 552, 553, 555, 562

Peasants, 123, 129, 141, 193, 273, 324, 325, 329, 336, 337, 340, 418, 562, 563, 566, 573

Pedagogy, 9, 19, 20, 107, 112, 123, 138, 142, 148–155, 229, 233, 256, 301, 303, 304, 307, 311, 321–322, 327, 333–351, 370, 382–387, 390, 392, 431–449, 456, 483, 517, 553, 564, 569, 571, 602, 607

Performance pay, 400

Periodization, 510, 520, 521

Peripheral economies, 270–272, 277

Platformization, 402

Political economy, 8, 10, 12, 13, 18, 34, 39, 40, 73, 75–78, 82, 96, 134, 156, 165, 166, 168, 172–175, 178, 186, 202, 247, 263–278, 303, 314, 384, 387, 392, 393n1, 432, 436, 438, 468n1, 472, 479, 480, 493, 503, 511, 564, 573

Popular education, 137–141, 148, 284, 483, 561, 562, 605

Population, 13, 14, 136, 216n2, 216n4, 224–226, 266, 267, 270, 272–275, 286, 319, 323–325, 328–330, 360, 366, 416, 424–426, 459, 481, 482, 510, 519, 522, 524, 525, 528

Positive psychology, 432, 443, 448

Postcolonial theory, 83, 547

Poulantzas, Nicos, 248, 249, 254, 255, 256n5

Praxis, 7, 21, 29, 78, 83, 85, 96, 98, 99, 102, 107, 108, 113, 126, 129, 130, 139, 141, 150–152, 300, 304, 318, 371, 373, 375, 376, 400, 433, 441–443, 445, 448–449, 457, 492, 515, 528, 529n5, 560–566, 568, 569, 573, 583–591, 607, 608
Precarity, 71, 78–81, 156, 157, 501
Precarization, 319
  of labor relations, 319
Preservation, 250, 286, 326, 454–455, 462, 467, 544
Private property, 3, 8, 12–14, 17, 41, 73–75, 114, 122, 186, 187, 193, 194, 246, 264, 265, 276, 277, 285, 287, 290, 324, 328, 383–386, 474, 514, 515, 569, 607–609
Privatization, 74, 125, 130, 263, 273, 306, 324, 328, 338, 399, 401, 402, 420, 472–474, 519
Productivity, 32, 49, 54, 55, 71, 80, 81, 121, 164, 168, 209, 216n3, 246, 264, 269, 271, 274, 275, 277, 338, 474, 475, 514, 606
Profit, 26, 37, 55, 56, 64n1, 114, 141, 156, 163, 177, 186, 187, 217n8, 246, 251, 270–272, 277, 304, 306, 307, 309, 312, 329, 337, 358, 360, 366, 397, 401, 403–407, 423
  rate of, 156, 157
Projectification, 207
Proletarianization, 80, 401–404, 530n13
Proletariat, 10, 27, 34, 134, 152, 155, 157, 289, 291, 292, 300, 325, 344, 349, 358, 359, 382, 418, 433, 438, 521, 530n13, 542, 548
Protest, 59, 66n13, 81, 236, 296, 333, 413–419, 421–426, 498, 500–502, 596
Public good, the, 71, 73, 74, 77, 79, 80, 85, 272, 308, 309, 472, 475
Public policy, 20, 21, 103, 471–484, 607
Purchasing power, 212

Q
Queer
  Marxism, 20, 381–393, 606
  pedagogy, 383, 384, 386–387
  theory, 381–383, 386, 387, 390, 392, 393n1, 394n13
  thrival, 383, 391, 392

R
Race, 5, 9, 19, 34, 77, 93–108, 148, 149, 151, 185, 193, 195, 226, 234, 272, 273, 276, 329, 356, 358, 362, 370, 376, 382, 441, 482, 515–516, 525, 528, 582, 605
Racial
  capitalism, 359–362, 515, 545
  disproportionality, 356
  racial-colonial, 510, 523–528, 554, 555, 607
  racial-patriarchal, 9, 31, 42, 607, 609
Racialization, 99, 515
Rankings
  school rankings, 229, 301, 356
  university rankings, 78, 164, 170
Real subsumption, 209, 210
Recognition, 7, 14, 19, 40, 53, 101, 104, 248, 275, 286, 310, 321, 427, 446, 448, 449, 466, 481–484, 494, 503, 515, 540, 542, 545, 549, 552, 553, 564
Red International of Labor Unions (RILU), 291
Redistribution, 20, 41, 373, 415, 471–484, 562, 607, 608
Reform, 20, 51, 77–79, 81, 82, 84, 101, 105, 108, 123, 125, 154, 155, 185, 223, 227, 228, 237, 248, 254, 263, 264, 270, 272, 273, 275–277, 300, 302, 312, 313, 330, 370, 398–401, 416, 421, 472, 480, 490, 498, 511, 512, 514, 548, 574n2, 582, 606
Reification, 7, 29, 76, 96, 97, 103, 107, 359, 365, 372, 376, 476, 567
Relations
  capitalist, 52, 165, 172–174, 186, 202, 203, 207, 208, 214, 248, 454, 517, 523, 549, 602
  constitutive, 99, 102
  of production, 10, 12, 52, 116, 122, 124, 165, 175, 190, 202–205, 207–209, 214, 244, 247, 248,

250, 254, 371, 372, 398, 423, 453, 462–464, 467, 468n1, 607
social, 4, 6, 7, 9, 11–13, 15, 16, 26, 27, 29, 30, 32, 37–39, 41, 42, 49, 50, 52, 53, 59, 72–77, 80, 81, 84, 93–96, 98–108, 113, 119, 122, 124, 131, 136, 164, 165, 169, 175, 177, 178, 187, 193, 205, 209, 231, 232, 235, 248, 263, 265, 266, 268, 276, 319, 321, 327, 331, 338, 363, 366, 371, 372, 375, 386, 398, 399, 405, 406, 421, 456, 457, 462–464, 475, 482, 490, 492, 493, 503, 524, 530n13, 543, 546, 586, 602, 605, 608
Reproduction
of capital, 64n2, 265, 301, 304, 325, 476
social, 4, 8, 13, 17, 19–21, 30, 31, 34, 61, 64n2, 103, 245, 247, 252, 370, 453–456, 458, 460–462, 464, 467, 493, 496, 510, 523–525, 529n4, 530n14, 560, 563–565, 573
Revolution, 5, 10, 26, 27, 29, 82, 96, 102, 107–108, 121, 151, 155, 209, 254, 276, 286, 292, 299, 300, 312, 325, 334, 336, 384, 394n10, 416, 417, 419, 432, 433, 438, 441, 442, 463, 513, 526, 537, 538, 542, 547, 549, 550, 554, 566, 572–573, 603
social, 19, 154, 295, 589, 608
Revolutionary, 4, 5, 9, 10, 13, 14, 20, 27, 29–31, 34, 40, 41, 96, 98, 107, 138, 141, 147, 148, 150–157, 184, 186, 196, 217n8, 282, 284, 287–288, 292–294, 304, 400, 407, 413–419, 423, 426, 427, 438, 439, 489–491, 503, 511, 513–516, 526, 529n5, 538, 543, 548, 549, 559–573, 588, 594, 603–605, 607
organization, 147, 148, 153, 154, 605
subject, 42, 419, 448, 537, 542, 547–549, 560–565, 568, 573
Ricardo, David, 13, 265
Rousseau, Jean-Jacques, 432, 440, 545
Ruge, Arnold, 510, 512

S
Sartre, Jean Paul, 432
Scarcity, 11, 71, 319, 407, 408, 446–447
School, 4, 26, 47, 94, 115, 124–126, 135, 149, 184, 224, 243, 272, 284, 300, 337, 344–348, 355, 368–374, 384, 398, 418, 431, 455, 472, 518, 538, 572, 593, 606
schooling time, 266, 269, 277
Science, 4, 12, 13, 38, 39, 49, 50, 52, 76, 80, 85, 108, 114–116, 119–121, 123–126, 130, 136, 138, 154, 163, 164, 166, 168–176, 178, 192–193, 226, 227, 235, 254, 267, 271, 302, 318, 326, 328, 337, 342, 345, 351n4, 361, 374, 449, 478, 479, 502, 512, 525, 539, 540, 552, 605
communication, 201–215, 605
Self-actualization, 11, 17, 32, 84, 447
Self-consciousness, 13, 17, 28, 303, 512, 540, 541
Self-education, 13, 15, 17, 18, 36, 184, 197, 497, 501
Self-realization, 73, 74
Settler
-colonialism, 20, 365, 368–370, 373, 521, 530n13
futurity, 370, 371, 376
settler-colonial, 9, 31, 42, 356, 359, 362, 364–366, 368–372, 375, 376, 520, 522, 526, 530n13
Sexuality, 5, 19, 94, 95, 99, 100, 106, 148, 151, 362, 381, 382
Skills, 13, 25, 27, 32, 48, 49, 53–55, 60, 119, 120, 123, 217n11, 235, 251, 252, 269–277, 313, 346, 348, 357, 401–403, 459, 474–476, 478, 483, 525, 526
Smith, Adam, 114, 228, 265, 269, 474
Social individual, 9, 17, 166–169, 175, 178, 493
Socialism, 27, 126, 153, 157, 282, 283, 285–287, 289–291, 304, 371, 382–384, 393, 416, 419, 435, 459, 542, 547, 554, 606
Socialist
education, 384
party, 289–292
revolution, 299, 554

Socialist Party of Argentina (PSA), 283, 288
Socially-necessary labor time, 212
Social movements
  learning, 148, 157
  new, 149
  old, 148
Social relations of production, 205, 209
Sociometabolism of capital, 320
Species-being, 13, 14, 32, 75, 286, 368, 371, 438, 449, 493, 540, 585
Standardization, 163, 164, 167, 172, 401
Standardized testing, 223–227, 230–233, 236, 237
State, 6, 37, 49, 71, 116, 136, 149, 169, 185, 206, 227, 246, 248–249, 263, 294, 300, 320, 341, 357, 382, 397, 415, 439, 459, 471–484, 491, 509, 564, 582, 605–607, 609
State apparatuses
  ideological, 187, 243–256, 455, 523
  repressive, 250, 254, 523
STEM, 190
Stirner, Max, 514
Structuralism, 245, 252–255, 455–458, 467
Student
  movements, 20, 21, 300, 413–427, 501, 606
  politics, 195, 414, 427
Subcomandante Marcos, 551, 552
Subsumption
  formal, 38, 201–215, 216n5
  real, 209, 210, 212
Surplus labor, 209, 210, 216n3
Surplus population, 13, 366, 377n2, 510, 519, 522, 524
Surplus value, 208, 210, 216n3

T
Taylorism, 269
Teachers
  labor activism, 397–408
  unions, 398, 400–402, 404, 562, 606
  work, 397–408
Technology, 16, 32, 39, 49, 53, 54, 78, 80, 104, 119, 121, 133, 153–157, 226, 230, 247, 266, 270, 272, 275, 277, 300, 305, 313, 318, 320, 323, 324, 326, 337, 341, 342, 345, 373, 386, 397, 399, 401–404, 407, 415, 459, 477, 484, 511, 513, 518, 521, 522, 529n1
Territory, 120, 173, 323, 327–329, 550, 551, 566, 569, 571–573, 574n1
Theory, 10, 33, 61, 76, 94, 113, 130, 132–137, 147, 165, 185, 208, 245, 264, 285, 303, 321, 334, 358, 381, 400, 414, 432, 453, 473, 491, 510, 544, 563, 581, 603, 604
Time, 3, 34, 48, 80, 93, 125, 164, 185, 202, 223–237, 249, 265, 291, 312, 318, 336, 360, 384, 402, 422, 433, 462, 474, 497, 509, 537, 562, 595, 602, 604, 606, 607, 609
  collapsing of, 372
Totality, 10, 30, 36, 59, 103, 106, 117–119, 151, 152, 157, 167, 191, 194, 267, 268, 272, 273, 277, 302, 314, 318–320, 330, 334, 436–438, 447, 455, 462, 465, 466, 492–494, 569, 592, 602
Trade unions, 185, 281, 287, 288
Training, 53, 55, 60, 100, 101, 115, 118, 119, 125, 126, 133, 157, 194, 226, 269, 270, 274, 275, 284, 294, 302, 303, 305, 306, 310, 312, 341–343, 346, 347, 372, 472, 473, 475–477, 483, 499, 511, 522
Transcendence, 27, 28, 132, 433, 491, 548, 549, 554, 574n2, 608, 609
Trauma, 104, 105, 362, 368, 393n1, 572, 608
Truth, 9, 29, 34, 35, 38–40, 187, 226, 228, 268, 328, 431, 440, 457, 513, 540, 541, 550, 604

U
Underdevelopment, 135, 251, 270
Unification Congress of the (Argentinean) Workers' General Union, 288
Unions/union action, 111, 115, 116, 118, 129, 150, 185, 186, 250, 281, 287–292, 314, 398–408, 417, 562

United Kingdom (UK), 52, 56–59, 62, 65n4, 66n13, 72, 78, 79, 81, 83, 85, 149, 194, 202, 206, 217n12, 415, 421, 497, 498

Universal, 9, 17, 19, 25, 27–29, 32–40, 42, 79, 81, 85, 100, 102, 107, 116, 151, 165, 167, 211, 217n9, 300, 320, 328, 383, 385, 433, 434, 440–444, 447, 490, 492, 538–540, 543, 545, 547, 595, 602, 607

University, 4–8, 10, 11, 14, 33, 35, 36, 38, 39, 42, 49, 55–59, 65n4, 72, 74, 77–85, 86n8, 86n9, 86n10, 100–102, 104, 123, 124, 163–178, 183, 184, 188, 189, 191, 194, 196, 197, 201–203, 206, 207, 210, 211, 215, 246, 247, 253, 255, 275, 300, 308, 309, 313, 336, 338, 346, 352n8, 402, 413, 415–425, 431, 438, 455, 463, 479, 496–502, 509–525, 527, 529n1, 529n3, 529n11, 530n15, 569, 570, 605

Uruguay, 284, 295, 472, 483

U.S. Agency for International Development (USAID), 273

V

Valorization, 3, 5, 14, 20, 39, 94, 133, 168, 178, 328, 414, 420, 423, 424, 426, 472, 474, 476, 483, 490

Value
 exchange-value, 49, 57, 66n9, 133, 166, 209, 213, 214, 229, 230, 264, 324, 325, 358, 359, 363, 366, 372, 384, 435, 437, 476, 479

 surplus-value, 8, 26, 47, 51, 52, 55, 59, 60, 62, 64n1, 80, 84, 141, 156, 184–188, 208, 210, 216n3, 265, 285, 300, 304, 305, 319, 324, 360, 370, 423, 435, 436, 454, 468n1, 517

 use-value, 48, 60, 114, 133, 166, 185, 212, 229, 324, 325, 414, 435, 479

Vatican II Council, 129

W

Wealth, 11, 16, 27, 78, 112, 116, 166, 167, 173, 174, 177, 178, 185, 188, 192, 211, 213, 217n9, 245, 246, 263–266, 268–270, 275, 276, 278, 319, 323, 343, 373, 386, 392, 414–416, 418, 434, 437, 447, 475, 491–493, 495, 517, 608
 socialization of, 269, 276

Weber, Max, 137, 233

Welfare state, 72, 79, 83–84, 302, 422, 471

Working-class
 press, 284, 292–294
 women's education, 149

World Bank, 247, 255, 273–275, 300, 325, 397, 473
 World Development Reports, 397, 403

Z

Zapatista women, 550, 551, 553

Zapatistas, 538, 549–554